Business
Environment

The Business Environment

themes and issues

Edited by
Paul Wetherly and **Dorron Otter**

OXFORD
UNIVERSITY PRESS

OXFORD
UNIVERSITY PRESS

Great Clarendon Street, Oxford OX2 6DP

Oxford University Press is a department of the University of Oxford.
It furthers the University's objective of excellence in research, scholarship,
and education by publishing worldwide in

Oxford New York

Auckland Cape Town Dar es Salaam Hong Kong Karachi
Kuala Lumpur Madrid Melbourne Mexico City Nairobi
New Delhi Shanghai Taipei Toronto

With offices in

Argentina Austria Brazil Chile Czech Republic France Greece
Guatemala Hungary Italy Japan Poland Portugal Singapore
South Korea Switzerland Thailand Turkey Ukraine Vietnam

Oxford is a registered trade mark of Oxford University Press
in the UK and in certain other countries

Published in the United States
by Oxford University Press Inc., New York

First published 2008

British Library Cataloguing in Publication Data

Data available

Library of Congress Cataloging in Publication Data

The business environment : themes and issues / edited by Paul Wetherly and Dorron Otter.
     p.   cm.
   Includes bibliographical references and index.
   ISBN-13: 978–0–19–920305–5
   1. Business.   2. Industries—Social aspects.   I. Wetherly, Paul.   II. Otter, Dorron.
HF1008.B86 2008
650—dc22
                                                          2007032933

Typeset by Graphicraft Limited, Hong Kong by 9.8/12pt Minion
Printed in Italy on acid-free paper by L.E.G.O. S.p.A.

ISBN 978–0–19–920305–5

10 9 8 7 6 5 4 3

To my wonderful girls, Laura and Rebecca (PW)

To Ingrid, Søren, Freddie and Ferdy as well as Mum, Dad and Ley (DO)

Brief contents

Detailed contents

14   Entrepreneurship and enterprise   386
Alison Price and Martyn Robertson

15   Business and sustainable development   416
Eamonn Judge

16   Conclusion: themes and issues—looking
ahead   445
Dorron Otter and Paul Wetherly

List of cases

About the authors

Photograph by Kiran Mehta

Paul Wetherly (right) studied economics and public policy for his first degree before obtaining an MA in political sociology and a PhD in political theory. Paul has worked in higher education as a teacher, researcher, and manager for more than twenty years. Currently Reader in Politics in the School of Social Sciences at Leeds Metropolitan University, he previously worked in the business faculty of the university where he was responsible for leading a large Business Environment module. Paul's other publications involve a range of articles and books on British politics, the state, and political theory.

Dorron Otter (left) is Head of the School of Applied Global Ethics at Leeds Metropolitan University. Having studied Politics, Philosophy and Economics at Oxford University, he worked in fields as diverse as youth and community work, retailing, tourism, and insurance. In 1984, he undertook a PGCE and spent five years teaching Economics and Business at Queen Mary's Sixth Form College in Basingstoke. During this time he served as an A level examiner in Economics. He completed his Masters in Development at the University of Leeds whilst working in Further Education. He was the first British Petroleum Fellow in Economic Awareness at the University of Durham and then was appointed to Leeds Metropolitan University where he became Head of the School of Economics and HRM. He has extensive experience of developing new approaches to learning and teaching in introductory economics and business modules and has led wider curriculum developments in these and other areas. He has worked closely with Paul in developing the Business Environment module taught at Leeds Business School. While he has wider research interests in the political economy of global development and responsibilities as an academic manager, he retains his passion and commitment to teaching issues relating to the business environment.

Contributors

David Amos is a law lecturer and solicitor. He qualified as a solicitor in 1993. He continued in practice until 1999 when he became a senior lecturer at Leeds Metropolitan University where he was in charge of the part-time Legal Practice Course (LPC). He moved to Manchester Metropolitan University in March 1995 where he is a Principal Lecturer and the Course Director for the LPC. He is currently a member of the Solicitors Regulation Authority's Working Party on the Written Standards for the LPC.

Dave Chesley is a Senior Lecturer in Human Resource Management at Leeds Metropolitan University. He is the Course Leader of both the Postgraduate Certificate and Postgraduate

Diploma in Management, which is a programme for strategic-level management on a part-time basis. He teaches across a range of HR and Organizational Behavioural programmes at undergraduate, postgraduate, and post-experience level. Dave gained his undergraduate degree from Middlesex Polytechnic and an MA in Industrial Relations from the University of Warwick in 1992. He is a Corporate Member of the Chartered Institute of Personnel and Development. His research interests are focused on work–life balance and employee retention.

Roger Henderson is Reader in International Finance and Deputy Director of the European Regional Business and Economic Development Unit (ERBEDU) in the Faculty of Business & Law at Leeds Metropolitan University. His principal teaching and research interests are in the fields of corporate finance and European business and regeneration studies. He is the author of numerous publications including a textbook on European Finance.

Eamonn Judge is Professor of Economics and Spatial Policy in the Faculty of Business and Law, Leeds Metropolitan University, and Visiting Professor, Polish Open University, Warsaw. His principal teaching and research interests are in the field of transport, environment, and business /development, particularly in relation to the UK and Poland.

Stratis Koutsoukos is Senior Research Fellow at ERBEDU. His principal areas of research and consultancy are European Regional Policy, economic regeneration, and European enlargement. He teaches European Business Strategies on the Jean Monnet funded module of the Leeds MBA.

Chris Mulhearn is Reader in Economics at Liverpool John Moores University. His work has appeared in a range of journals including: *World Economy, Journal of Economic Perspectives, World Economics*, and *Industrial Relations Journal*. His most recent book (with Howard Vane) is *The Nobel Memorial Laureates in Economics: An Introduction to their Careers and Main Published Works* (Edward Elgar, 2005). At present, with Howard Vane, he is writing a book on the euro to be published by Edward Elgar in 2008.

Alison Price is Director of the HEFCE funded Centre for Excellence in Teaching and Learning, the 'Institute for Enterprise'. Alison has many years of experience teaching enterprise and supporting curriculum development which has been enhanced by US experiences gained from an MIT entrepreneurial programme at Sloan Management School. Alison has published in the fields of strategic management, corporate social responsibility, and small business development. Her most recent research and consultancy have included projects for National Council for Graduate Entrepreneurship, Higher Education Academy/ DFES, and the Small Business Service.

Martyn Robertson is Director of Graduate Enterprise at Leeds Metropolitan University. He works closely with regional, national, and international partners to embed creativity, innovation, and enterprise within and across the university. He is a government specialist advisor on supporting new businesses and has a lead role in the Centre for Graduate Entrepreneurship in Yorkshire. He has held directorships in research, publishing, property, communications, and design companies and worked at board level for PriceWaterhouseCoopers and the RMC Group.

Rev. Simon Robinson is Professor of Applied and Professional Ethics, Leeds Metropolitan University, Associate Director, Applied Ethics Centre of Excellence, and Visiting Fellow in Theology, University of Leeds. Ongoing research interests include: religious ethics and care, professional ethics, ethics in higher education, spirituality and professional practice, corporate social responsibility, and ethics in a global perspective. Simon has written a number of books on social responsibility, ethics, and business, as well as on the teaching and practice of professional ethics.

Richard Rooke is a Senior Lecturer in Social and Policy Studies at London South Bank University. He is the Course Director of a multilingual Postgraduate Master in European Policy Studies collaborating with EMLV, LDV, Paris, France and FHWR, Berlin, Germany. His principal research interests include media policy, governance, and policy development at UK and EU levels. He has undertaken consultancy work for the Home Office on public service management issues. He is authoring a book on European media policy for Pearson Education to be published shortly. For over 10 years he was a practicing officer in local government.

Stephen Taylor is a Senior Lecturer in Human Resource Management at the Manchester Metropolitan University Business School and a national examiner for the Chartered Institute of Personnel and Development (CIPD). He previously taught at Manchester Business School and worked in a variety of HR management roles in the hotel industry and in the NHS. He is the author/co-author of several books including *People Resourcing*, *Employment Law: An Introduction'* (with Astra Emir), *The Employee Retention Handbook*, and four editions of *Human Resource Management* (with Derek Torrington and Laura Hall). A new book by Stephen entitled *Contemporary Issues in HR* will be published in 2008. He regularly represents parties in employment tribunals.

Howard R. Vane is Professor of Economics at Liverpool John Moores University. His main research interests lie in the area of macroeconomics and his work in this field has been published in many different languages. He has co-authored/edited fifteen books and has had articles published in a wide range of journals including: *American Economist*, *Journal of Economic Perspectives*, *Journal of Macroeconomics*, *World Economics*, and *World Economy*. His most recent books include: (with Brian Snowdon) *Modern Macroeconomics: Its Origins, Development and Current State* (Edward Elgar, 2005); and (with Chris Mulhearn) *The Nobel Memorial Laureates in Economics: An Introduction to Their Careers and Main Published Works* (Edward Elgar, 2005). He is currently writing a book on the euro with Chris Mulhearn, which will be published by Edward Elgar in 2008.

About the book

This book is designed primarily for students taking their first undergraduate module in the Business Environment or similar introductory modules on a range of related business degree, foundation degree or vocational programmes. The book will also be a useful resource for more advanced studies. The editors both have considerable experience of teaching Business Environment, and the approach of this book is based on this experience and the comments of successive generations of students. In addition to the editors' own chapters in the book, a team of contributing authors has been brought together to write specialist chapters based on their own areas of expertise.

All of the chapters are written in an accessible and engaging style and follow a standard layout with common pedagogical features. A key feature of the approach taken throughout the book is to introduce students to debates and controversies surrounding the role of business in modern society, and to help them to think critically. In this way it is the intention of the book to provoke lively discussion and debate.

Themes and issues

There are two parts to the book: Part One introduces the core political-legal, economic, social-cultural and technological environments of business, and their interrelationships. Part Two however goes beyond these topics and invites students to analyse a range of contemporary issues in the business environment such as globalization, corporate social responsibility, sustainable development and work–life balance. These issues have been selected due to their prominence in discussions within business and the wider society, and their importance in shaping the future of business.

The book utilizes an innovative thematic approach to provide a consistent framework for analysis of business and the business environment. The eight themes are intended to help the reader to organize their own thinking about business. Each chapter begins with an overview of how these themes relate to the particular chapter and the themes are then signposted by the use of markers in the margin, as shown here:

Diversity	Diversity of business
	Business is a diverse category

Internal/ external	Internal/external
	The environment is both inside and outside organizations

Complexity	Complexity of the environment
	The external environment is multi-dimensional or complex

Spatial levels	Variety of spatial levels From the local to the global
Dynamic	Dynamic environment The environment of business does not stand still
Interaction	Interaction between business and the environment There is interaction between business organizations and their environments
Stakeholders	Stakeholders Individuals and groups that are affected by business decisions
Values	Values Business decisions involve ethical questions

The themes are introduced fully at the start of Chapter 1.

Format and pedagogical features

Each chapter follows a consistent format, providing a wide-range of pedagogical features including 'Stop & Think' exercises, mini-cases, highlighted key terms, review and discussion questions, and assignments. These features, combined with this innovative structure and analytical approach to the subject matter, will encourage students to fully engage with the issues raised and develop their interest in critical debate.

Real-world cases

The book is packed with examples, mini-cases, and end-of-chapter case studies looking at UK, European and international business, illustrating each topic in real-life contexts. Careful attention has been paid to select cases and examples to which the intended student audience will be able to relate. Examples include the Nintendo Wii, Blackberry, Nike, eBay, Nokia, easyJet and Toyota.

How to use this book

Learning objectives

Each chapter opens with a bulleted outline of the main concepts and ideas. These serve as helpful signposts to what you can expect to learn from each chapter.

Learning objectives

When you have completed this chapter you will be able to:

- Explain what is meant by 'work–life balance'
- Identify developments in the business environment which are dri agenda and its increased prominence
- Describe the government's response and its objectives
- Set out the major policies and practices developed by employers to better combine working with domestic life
- Examine the dimensions of the 'pensions crisis', and analyse it as

Themes

Diversity	Diversity of business
	The macroeconomic environment is of crucial signi izations in the public and voluntary sectors. The economy will pose threats and opportunities for bus ample, a **recession**, a period of sustained prosperity different kinds of questions that business must try t
Complexity	Complexity of the environment
	Economies are complex things—they are the produ taken everyday by businesses, governments and ind is an attempt to render this complexity more manag

Themes

The key themes, introduced in Chapter 1 and running through the book, are described at the beginning of each chapter. This description shows how each set of themes is relevant to the topic being covered. Markers in the margin throughout the text indicate where one or more of the themes are illustrated, helping put them into context.

Mini-cases

The book is packed with real-life examples to show how organizations have reacted to, or have shaped, the business environment in which they operate.

Mini-Case 3.3 **The real computer games batt**

The competitive battle for the attention (to the consternation of parents!) of computer games players is intense and is primarily fought through technology (and marketing). Sony, Microsoft and Nintendo are the combatants and their weapons are their respective marketing machines and their products: Sony's Playstation 3, Microsoft's Xbox 360 and Nintendo's Game Boy turned Wii.

Sony became the market leader by targeting the teenage and young adult market but Microsoft is keen to catch up and Nintendo is trying to develop a product that will appeal across the age ranges.

The cost of the technology is very high and yet it is not the

cost price but th sumers to buy the other Internet se which interests T platform there is disks that will re and in a direct ec Beta-max there is to adopt the one

It is a high risk will be the compa

Stop & Think

These are short questions and examples which give you the opportunity to 'pause for thought' and relate the topic to your own experience.

> at the company's expense. Action can also be taken at common law if there has been [...]
> the minority of shareholders.
>
> **⮑ Stop and Think**
> So far in this section we have looked at the different types of business organizations and the la[...]
> surrounding them. Imagine you were starting up a new business with a group of friends which [...]
> involved making high quality chocolates.
> Which form of business organization would you adopt?
> Explain the reasons for your decision.
> Would your answer differ, if at all, if you were merely seeking to open a small shop with your sp[...]
> sell such chocolates?
> In answering these questions you can, if you wish, refer back to your answer to the question po[...]
> about Cadbury Schweppes.
>
> **What is the company for?**
> Having considered the company's structure we need now to consider the purpose of a[...]

Glossary

> [...] the same
> [...] over the other
> [...]s using the
> [...]ed that where
> [...]pecialize in the
> [...] increasing
> [...]at each
> [...] of all goods
> [...]e).
>
> **best value** a term used both legally and managerially to quantify and qualify the 'best value' services available to the public from service providers: this was building on previous recommendations in relation to **value for money** (see below).
>
> **biodiversity** the totality of species and life forms on earth.
>
> **birth rate** the number of births per 1,000 of the population.
>
> **bureaucracy** the paid (normally) civil servants or officials

Key terms

Key terms are highlighted in blue where they first appear. They are also defined in the glossary at the end of the book.

Case study

A longer case study at the end of each chapter provides an opportunity to apply what you have learnt and analyse a real-life example.

> **Case study: 'UK plc'**
>
> This case study identifies some key aspects of contemporary Britain using the PEST framework.
>
> **Political**
> - Democratic system of government in which the people as a whole exercise political power through the right to vote for members of parliament (MPs) to represent their interests
> - Two-party system in which just two main political parties—Labour and Conservative—have dominated elections and government office for the last hundred years
> - Civil Society Organizations (CSOs) or 'pressure groups' represent specific groups or causes within the political process, e.g. Greenpeace. Pressure groups also target businesses directly to try to get them to alter their behaviour, e.g. to reduce carbon emissions
> - Business is a key political actor with distinctive interests, exercising a degree of power and influence arguably unrivalled by any other group
> - One of the basic issues in political debate concerns the purpose of politics and government, especially in relation to the operation of private sector business and the market system. Left–Right politics can be characterized in terms of a 'state versus the market' debate
>
> countries in terms of [...]
> The average annual ra[...]
> was 2.6% between 19[...]
> - The UK has undergone[...]
> industrialization' invo[...]
> manufacturing within[...]
> of the service sector. [...]
> for 72.7% of UK outpu[...]
> manufacturing accoun[...]
> 1993) (Office for Nati[...]
> - Large firms (with 250 [...]
> economy, accounting [...]
> in 2003. The largest fi[...]
> multinational corpora[...]
> in more than one cour[...]
> However the vast majo[...]
> sized enterprises (SM[...]
> less than 0.2% of ente[...]
> from 4 million)
> - The UK is one of the w[...]
> exports of goods and [...]
> Through trade and oth[...]
> increasingly integrate[...]

Review and discussion questions

Questions have been included at the end of every chapter to test your grasp of the key concepts and provide you with an opportunity for discussion.

Review and discussion questions

1   Explain the meanings of the terms 'society' and 'culture', and show why business has to pay attention to the social-cultural environment.

2   What are the implications of population ageing for business? You should think about different types of business, and distinguish opportunities and threats.

3   Is immigration g You should identi stakeholders.

4   Is fairness or soci be concerned abo efficiency and pro

Assignments

1   *Skills*: You are thinking about becoming an entrepreneur but need to understand whether you have the skills to start up a business on your own, or whether you should create a team with broader skills. Undertake a self-analysis of your current skills and either devise a personal development plan to gain the additional skills you might need to start a new venture, or indicate the skills you need in additional team member(s).

3   *Understanding entr interview, or choos use the Internet to

What type of entrep What sector do they How many business What stage of grow How have their valu

Assignments

These assignments are designed to test what you have learnt in the chapter and extend your understanding through more practical exercises and tasks.

Further reading and online resources

An annotated list of recommended reading on each subject will help guide you through the literature and key websites provide online hubs of information for writing essays or researching projects.

Further reading

Blair, A. and Hitchcock, D. (2001) *Environment and Business* (London: Routledge). Provides a useful contextualization of environmental issues into business, and will allow many aspects of this chapter to be explored in greater depth.

Hutchinson, A. and Hutchinson, F. (1997) *Environmental Business Management: Sustainable Development in the New Millennium* (London: McGraw-Hill). A good text on the practical implementation of environmental strategies in business organizations.

Ison, S., Peake, S. an *and Policies* (Londo background to many issues discussed in t

Starkey, R. and Welfo *Reader in Business* Earthscan). A collec at the real involvem development, but al

Online resources

Test your understanding of this chapter with online questions and answers, explore the subject further through web exercises, and use the weblinks to provide a quick resource for further research. Go to the Online Resource Centre at www.oxfordtextbooks.co.uk/orc/wetherly_otter/

The following suggestions are a tiny proportion of even the most useful sites. Generally, surf with care, and consider whether promoters of a site have an axe to grind.

Government departm www.defra.gov.uk: D and Rural Affairs) pro more.

www.dft.gov.uk: The material on environm the company travel pl

www.parliament.uk/

How to use the Online Resource Centre

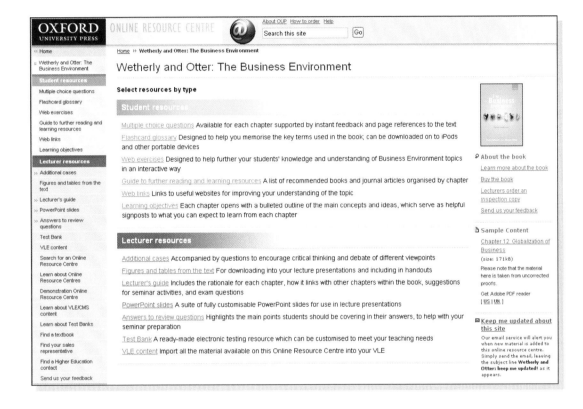

FOR LECTURERS

PowerPoint lecture slides

A suite of PowerPoint slides has been designed by the authors for use in your lecture presentations which highlight the main points from each chapter. These can be easily customized to match your own lecture style.

Test bank

For each chapter a set of twenty online questions has been devised by the authors in multiple choice, multiple response, true/false, and essay formats. The Test Bank is fully automated for quick and convenient use online: automated grading allows you to assess your students' progress via your university's Virtual Learning Environment and instant feedback shows your students what they need to work on for revision purposes.

Answers to review questions

Suggested answers to the end-of-chapter review questions in the book succinctly highlight the main points students should be covering in their answers to help with your seminar preparation.

Lecturer's guide

Finding stimulating ways of reinforcing students' understanding of the Business Environment can be difficult. A helpful chapter-by-chapter lecturer's guide has been provided by the authors to assist instructors in their teaching of Business Environment modules. This includes the rationale for each chapter, how it links with other chapters within the book, suggestions for seminar activities, and exam questions.

A bank of additional cases

Lecturers often tell us that the best way to communicate ideas to their students is through case examples, and the more the better! So in addition to the many case examples included in the text, a further collection of relevant and engaging case studies is available for your use in group tutorial work and assignments. These cases have been carefully chosen to appeal to students, cover a broad range of businesses and organizations, and span the local to the global business world. Each is accompanied by questions to encourage critical thinking and debate of different viewpoints, thus improving your students' analytical skills.

Web exercises

The internet can be a powerful research tool and is a popular medium for today's students. These ready-made online activities are designed to help further your students' knowledge and understanding of Business Environment topics in an interactive way. For each chapter, the student is asked to find out information and answer questions based on weblinks to relevant articles and information websites.

Figures and tables from the text

All figures and tables from the text have been provided in high resolution format to download to your lecture presentations and including in handouts.

FOR STUDENTS

Multiple choice questions

Ten online multiple choice questions for each chapter provide a quick and easy way to test your understanding during revision. These self-marking questions give you instant feedback and provide page references to the textbook to help you focus on areas which need further study.

Flashcards

Learning the jargon associated with the range of topics in the Business Environment can be a challenge, so these online flashcards have been designed to help you memorize the key terms used in the book. Click through the randomized definitions and see if you can identify which key term they are describing. You can even download them to your iPod for revision on the move!

www.oxfordtextbooks.co.uk/orc/wetherly_otter/

Acknowledgements

There are many people we would like to thank for their help during the production of this book, not least our families for their patience in dealing with the opportunity costs of our spending the time necessary to complete the book!

We are indebted to all of the Oxford editorial team for their terrific support throughout, especially Angela Adams (Commissioning Editor) for encouraging us to develop the idea for the book, and Helen Adams (Development Editor) for her ability to keep all of us on track with a smile and yet steady sense of purpose. We would also like to thank Helen Tyas (Production Editor), Claire Dickinson and Charlotte Dobbs (Design Team), and Fiona Goodall (Web Editor).

There are many of our colleagues who have contributed to this book in ways it is not always easy to quantify but we are immensely grateful to all the authors who have contributed their time and expertise to write chapters for the book. We are conscious that, at times, we have not been able to give them the speedy response to their queries that their efforts have merited. We are also grateful to Ian Belshaw for writing the additional case studies and web exercises on the Online Resource Centre.

Over the years spent teaching at Leeds Met we have been grateful for the comments and reflections of our students who have taken the Business Environment module and we hope that we have learned from them to produce a book which meets the needs of the intended audience of future students.

Finally, we have been grateful for the extensive comments from the many reviewers who have helped shape our approach to the book. We hope that you may be able to see your contributions within its pages. These include, but are not limited to:

- Peter Campkin, University of Northampton
- David Golby, Staffordshire University
- David Laughton, Sheffield Hallam University
- Kate Lennon, Glasgow Caledonian University
- Lindsey Muir, Liverpool John Moores University
- Nick Perdikis, University of Wales, Aberystwyth
- Aarti Rughoo and Alison Wylde, London Metropolitan University
- Alice Szwelnik, Oxford Brookes University
- Bob Turner, Cardiff University

The authors and publisher are grateful to the following for permission to reproduce copyright materials:

Table 5.4 Occupational class in Great Britain, 1911–91 (%) reproduced from Gallie, D. (2000) p. 288, table 8.4, 'The labour force', in Halsey, A. H. (ed.) *Twentieth Century British Social Trends*, Palgrave Macmillan; Figure 6.1 UK real GDP 1948–2005, £bn, 2003 prices, reproduced from the Office of National Statistics; Figure 6.2 UK real GDP 1986–2008, Figure 6.3 UK employment and unemployment rates, Figure 6.5 UK inflation and Figure 6.13 Volatility in UK inflation and real GDP growth, all reproduced from HM Treasury under the terms of the

Click-Use Licence; 'Bank of England—what it's for', Figure 6.14 Current CPI inflation projection, and news release 'Bank of England raises bank rate by 0.25 percentage points to 5.0%' all reproduced with permission from the Bank of England, www.bankofengland.co.uk; Figure 9.1 Intra- and extra-EU trade, and Figure 9.2 Europe's declining share of global output, both reproduced from OECD, Crown copyright 2005, Global Europe: full-employment Europe; Figure 9.4 EU budget expenditure 2005 © European Communities 2005, General Budget of the European Union for the Financial Year 2005; Table 9.4 Overview of the new financial framework 2007–2013 reproduced from the Communication from the Commission to the Council and the European Parliament: Building our Common Future—Policy Challenges and Budgetary Means of the Enlarged Union 2007–2013, European Commission; Figure 9.5 Regional policy support, reproduced from the European Commission © EuroGeographics Association for the administrative boundaries; Figure 10.1 Equilibrium model, reprinted from T. R. Dye, *Understanding Public Policy* (11th rev. edition), 2004, based on diagram Figure 2.2 The Group Model, with permission from Elsevier; Figure 10.2 Model of TME 2003/4 reproduced from P. Cullinane (ed.), *United Kingdom National Accounts: The Blue Book*, National Statistics, 2005 with permission from HM Treasury; Figure 10.3 Percentage of GDP spent on firefighting organizations, Figure 10.4 Population comparisons for fire deaths, and Figure 10.5 Comparative: is there a relation between spend and fire deaths? all created from data taken from *World Fire Statistics*, Information Bulletin of the World Fire Statistics, 22, October 2006; Figure 12.1 Non-oil commodity terms of trade 1977–1997 from Michael P. Todaro & Stephen C. Smith, *Economic Development* 9 edn, Pearson Education Ltd, © 2005, Addison Wesley; Original Washington Consensus (p. 341) and Augmented Washington Consensus (p. 345) both reprinted from the *Handbook of Economic Growth*, Vol. 1, Part 1, D. Rodrik, Chapter 14 Growth Strategies, © 2005, with permission from Elsevier; Table 15.1 How global indicators of relevance to the environment have been changing reproduced with permission from Charles Kibert, University of Florida 2006; Figure 15.1 The composition of global greenhouse gas emissions in 2000, Figure 15.2 Global growth of CO_2 emissions, 1900–2000, and Figure 15.4 The main contributors to GHG emission all reproduced with permission from the World Resources Institute (www.wri.org); Figure 15.3 Variations of the Earth's Surface Temperature: Year 1000 to Year 2100 reproduced with permission from the Intergovernmental Panel on Climate Change (IPCC); Figure 15.5 Location of main university facilities in Leeds reproduced with permission from Leeds Metropolitan University.

Crown copyright is reproduced under Class Licence Number C2006010631 with the permission of OPSI and the Queen's Printer for Scotland.

Every effort has been made to trace and contact copyright holders but this has not been possible in every case. If notified, the publisher will undertake to rectify any errors or omissions at the earliest opportunity.

Introduction: 'business' and its 'environment'

Paul Wetherly and Dorron Otter

Contents

01

Learning objectives

When you have completed this chapter you will able to:

- Recognize different uses of the term **business**, and understand the different forms of business in terms of, for example, private, public and not-for-profit organizations
- Describe the complexity of the **external environment** in which business operates and explain the idea of **environmental uniqueness**
- Understand the nature of the 'internal' environment of business
- Understand how businesses must respond to changing environmental factors in order to operate successfully, but also how they seek to influence the environment
- Use analysis tools such as PEST or SWOT to examine the business environment
- Understand the approach to the business environment of this book and how to use it in your studies

The approach of this book— themes and issues

Eight key themes that will help you to understand and analyse the business environment run through this book. You will encounter these themes in this introduction and in each of the subsequent chapters as you examine a range of issues in the business environment. The themes will be signposted by the use of markers in the margin:

Diversity of business: business is a diverse category

Internal/external: the environment is both inside and outside organizations

Complexity of the environment: the external environment is multi-dimensional or complex

Variety of spatial levels: from the local to the global

Dynamic environment: the environment of business does not stand still

Interaction between business and the environment: there is interaction between business organizations and their environments

Stakeholders: individuals and groups that are affected by business decisions

Values: business decisions involve ethical questions

The themes are ways of conceptualizing business and the environment in which it operates. You will master these themes increasingly as you work through the book, but it is useful to begin with a brief introduction to each one.

Diversity

- Business is a diverse category. It does not refer only to private sector, profit-making companies. Public and voluntary sector organizations may also be regarded as businesses. The boundaries between these sectors are contested and shift over time, for example as a result of the policy of privatization initiated by Conservative governments in the UK in the 1980s. Within the dominant private sector, businesses vary in a number of ways, such as legal structure, industry, size and market power, and geographical reach. This diversity also means that, although there are common elements in the business environment, each business operates in an environment that is, to some extent, unique.

- This book mainly deals with the external environment, the surrounding conditions and processes in the world outside the organization. However it is useful to think of the environment as also having an internal dimension. This is because a business organization is not really a single, unified entity but is internally differentiated. In other words, it is a complex system. Managers within business, to be effective, have to deal with this internal environment as well as the external one. In addition, the ability of an organization to operate successfully within its external environment depends, in large part, on the effectiveness of internal systems and procedures. The internal environment has to be managed and adapted to the demands and opportunities of the external environment.

  Internal/ external

- We might think of the external environment primarily in terms of economic conditions and trends, to do with the behaviour of competitors and customers. The economy is, of course, of major importance. However, a moment's thought makes it clear that the external environment in which business operates is more complex and needs to be analysed also in terms of its political-legal, social-cultural, and technological aspects. These aspects are interrelated, as we can see if we think of the role that political decisions made in government have in shaping the economic environment. We will also see that many issues facing business have economic, social, political and technological aspects.

  Complexity

- Spatial level refers to the geographical or territorial unit of analysis that we use to conceptualize the business environment. As citizens we live within the territory of a nation-state, such as the UK, and we tend to think of our identities at least partly in terms of nationality. Similarly the business environment tends to be discussed primarily at national level. For example, in the media we come across references to British business, the British economy, British society and the British government. However sometimes it is more appropriate to think of business and its environment at a more local level, perhaps in terms of an urban area or region. On the other hand it has become increasingly important to think of business and the environment on a much larger spatial level, such as European or global. There is much debate about the nature, extent and implications of globalization. Globalization refers, roughly, to the tendency of business and other economic, social and political processes and relationships to move across or beyond the borders of nation-states. One of the most important manifestations of this is the growth of multinational businesses.

  Spatial levels

- We live in a fast-changing world, especially in the advanced or rich societies such as in western Europe. We have come to expect that the society in which we live and the way we live our lives will change over time, even within fairly short periods. This can be seen most clearly in relation to technological innovation and its impact in all areas of our lives. Equally, the environment of business is dynamic. Because of this businesses have to respond and adapt to changes in their environment, and deal with uncertainty about the future. But, at the same time, business organizations are powerful agents of change. This can be seen very clearly from the example of technological innovation which is driven largely by business. Indeed the dynamism of western societies is deeply rooted in basic features of their market economies—competition and the profit motive. This is often discussed in terms of entrepreneurial behaviour, which involves risk-taking and innovation, rather than relying on tried and tested approaches. Competitive markets place emphasis on innovation as the means of keeping up or getting ahead.

  Dynamic

- There is two-way interaction between business organizations and their environment. Businesses influence and are influenced by their environments. Business organizations are not passive but seek to shape environmental factors to their own advantage. For example, business is an important actor in the political arena.

  Interaction

- Business decisions have to be made in a context of multiple stakeholder interests and demands. A stakeholder is any individual or group that is affected by, and thus has a stake in, business decisions. More than before business has to work to retain public trust.

  Stakeholders

- There are competing perspectives and values concerning the nature and purpose of business in society—relating to its power, responsibilities, performance and ethics. These are not just

  Values

debates that take place in universities on degree courses, but are part of everyday political discussion and dialogue in which business must engage.

What is business?

This is a book about the 'business environment'. The purpose of this introduction is to help you to get to grips with what the business environment is, why it is important to study and understand it, and the particular approach taken in this book. In simple terms, the importance of studying the business environment is that all businesses operate in a changing and, in some ways, unique environment that is the source of both threats and opportunities. Business decisions are concerned with operating successfully in this environment by countering threats and exploiting opportunities. For example, businesses may have to respond to changing market conditions affecting the demand for their products, the behaviour of competitors, or changes in government policy. We begin by looking more closely at the meaning of the two words in the title: 'business' and 'environment'. What do we mean by business, and how might we think about the environment in which it operates?

Business and the problem of scarcity

One way to think about the meaning of business is in terms of what economists call the basic economic problem that, it can be argued, confronts all societies, rich and poor. This is a problem of scarcity, which means that there is 'not enough to go round'. (This problem will be discussed in more detail in Chapter 2.) We are all used to the problem of scarcity in our daily lives as individuals or households, in not having enough money to do (or buy) all that we would like to and therefore having to make choices between alternative activities or forms of spending. The same problem faces society as a whole. In each case the problem is one of limited resources against the large, and even open-ended, set of wants, needs and goals that make demands on those resources. Scarcity creates the problem of how to allocate available resources of all kinds between competing wants which can't all be satisfied at once. Business is a way of dealing with this problem.

Business can be defined in terms of the activity of production—the transformation of various inputs (or 'factors of production') into diverse outputs in the form of goods and services to meet particular wants or needs of people in society. This involves a series of activities and chain of relationships between a number of organizations, from the initial procurement or acquisition of the factors of production (raw materials, labour, machinery) to the supply of the finished good or service to a consumer, buyer or user.

> Business is a mechanism for deciding the allocation of the resources available to society between various possible uses (or competing wants), the methods of production and the distribution of the output, in a situation of scarcity where not all wants can be satisfied.

We can add to this that businesses produce outputs for consumers (customers, users or clients) and in response to their requirements, wants or needs. For example a professional football club playing for an audience is a business whereas an amateur club, involved in the same activity, is not. Thus the relationship with consumers is an intrinsic aspect of business. This does not mean that the consumers have to be paying customers like those who go to watch Liverpool FC at Anfield, for they could be users of a public service for which there is no charge. The important point is that businesses always produce goods and services for consumers of one kind or another, and that the success of the business is always bound up to some degree with consumers' requirements and expectations.

We commonly think of businesses in terms of companies, firms or enterprises in the private sector of the economy. This is a good place to start since the private sector dominates the economic and business life of societies like the UK. However, as we will see, business also takes place outside of the private sector.

Diversity

The private sector of business

The private sector is made up of business organizations that are owned and controlled as forms of private property. The largest businesses take the form of public limited companies (PLCs) which are owned by their shareholders. These shareholders can be private individuals, although a majority of shares is owned by financial institutions such as pension funds and insurance companies. Private sector businesses can take other legal forms, such as sole traders, partnerships and private limited companies (see Chapter 13). Private ownership is the thread connecting all these types. However, the private sector is characterized by further specific features:

- production of goods and services for sale
- the profit motive
- competition.

Private sector businesses produce goods and services for sale to customers in a context of competition with other firms in the market and with the prime purpose of making a profit. We will examine in more detail how markets operate in Chapter 2, but here we can see in a fairly simple way how private business in a market system is a specific way of 'solving' the basic economic problem.

Firms interact with households in a way that is depicted in Figure 1.1. Households act both as consumers and as suppliers of labour or employees. Firms purchase the inputs needed for production from households (here we assume for simplicity that labour is the only 'factor of production') and supply goods and services to them. The profit motive means that private businesses produce only those goods and services that households are willing and able to buy at prices that generate a profit for the business. Profit is the difference between the total costs incurred by the business in the production process and the total revenue generated by sales of the products.

The profit motive makes businesses highly responsive to consumer demand or customer-focused. They want to be customer-focused, since this is the best way to make a profit. But they also have to be, for if they produce goods or services that people do not want or at unattractive prices they will not stay in business very long. Competition means that businesses cannot easily get away with products that consumers are not satisfied with, since they can 'shop around'. Thus both profit and competition keep businesses customer-focused.

The level of consumption that households enjoy depends on their ability to pay, and this is determined by their income in the form of earnings from employment. This, in turn, depends on the prices that the skills and knowledge that household members possess command in the labour market (wages and salaries). A higher standard of living can be obtained through the possession of skills that are in short supply and hence command a premium in the labour market (see Chapter 5). Thus the composition of output and its distribution are 'solved' by the interaction of firms and households through the distribution of earnings from employment and the preferences of consumers in households with different income levels. Looked at in another way, businesses act as mediators between households who supply labour for production and share out the resulting goods and services.

Figure 1.1 The interaction between firms and households—the circular flow of income.

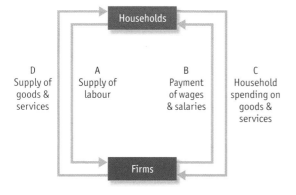

Notes: Households supply labour to firms (A) in return for payments of wages and salaries (B) (In this simple model labour is assumed to be the only input or 'factor of production').
Household income, derived from wages and salaries, finances spending on goods and services (C).
Firms produce and supply goods and services to meet demand from households (D).

There is another dimension to add—deciding the methods of production. Profit provides a motive, and competition a pressure, for continual improvements in efficiency. This is because greater efficiency means lower costs of production and cheaper products. It is rational for profit-seeking firms to strive to improve efficiency to keep up with or get ahead of their rivals. Firms that fall behind in the efficiency race end up pricing themselves out of the market. It is this continual pressure to increase efficiency that is built in to the market through profit and competition that drives the process of economic growth and rising living standards.

> **⊃ Stop and Think**
> Can you explain how profit and competition in the private sector of business 'solve' the components of the basic economic problem?
> Can you identify any shortcomings in this solution?

This is a very simple model of how private business operates in the market to 'solve' the economic problem. However, we will see in Chapter 2 and in subsequent chapters that things are more complicated and more controversial than is suggested here. There are strong disagreements about the advantages and disadvantages of the private sector model of business. These disagreements are an important element of the business environment. Let's try a taste of controversy.

The logic of the profit motive suggests that it doesn't really matter to business who the consumers are or what their wants are so long as a profit can be made. The customer is always right! This seems to be a good thing since businesses ought to treat everyone in the same way, and the market provides for a vast array of tastes. Yet, in practice, not everyone is treated in the same way and there are continuing problems of discrimination on grounds of race or sex in business (see Chapter 5). Of course this is not a problem that is specific to business, and it could be argued that business tends to reflect the values of the wider society of which it is part. Are there relatively few women in management positions because of discriminatory attitudes within business, or because of sexism within the wider society?

The idea that markets produce whatever customers want looks rather different when we consider the effort that goes into persuasive advertising. Businesses may be able to get away with producing goods and services that are of poor quality or even harmful. For example, food manufacturers and supermarkets have come in for criticism for producing and marketing unhealthy products, high in salt, fat and sugar, contributing to the obesity 'epidemic' (see Chapter 4). Gerald Ratner was forced to step down as chief executive of Ratners jewellery business in 1992 having described one of its products as 'total crap'. Although it is possible that this remark was meant as a joke, it seems to illustrate the point that private sector companies are not averse to selling products of dubious quality as long as they are profitable. Is it fair to criticize businesses for selling unhealthy foods or jewellery that isn't very good, or is it a reasonable defence to say that it is up to consumers what they buy? Are consumers really able to make these decisions for themselves, or are they manipulated by sophisticated marketing techniques?

> **⊃ Stop and Think**
> Do you agree that the logic of the profit motive goes against discrimination?
> Is the customer always right?

The private sector—on closer inspection

On closer inspection, common characteristics of the private sector of business—private ownership, competition and profit—are not as straightforward as they first appear.

Diversity

Free market vs. regulation?

Firms exist as legal entities, which means that they are defined by law, but the private ownership label covers businesses with different types of legal status. These include sole traders, partnerships, limited companies and cooperatives. The basic idea of private business is that firms are free to manage their own affairs and use their own resources as they choose. In this way private ownership of business may be likened to other forms of private property where the whole point of owning our own property is to use it as we please and for our own benefit or self-interest. In business terms this means that businesses should be managed in the interests of their owners, and this means making a profit. It might be added to this that businesses are best able to judge for themselves how to manage their affairs efficiently, and that by being left to do this there is benefit for the wider public through the resulting innovation and economic growth. However, in reality there is no such thing as a free market in the sense of businesses being left entirely free to make decisions for themselves. In all market systems the law is used extensively to regulate various aspects of business decisions and behaviour. As we will see in Chapter 4 the law is made and enforced by government and so constitutes a key element of the political environment of business.

One of the prime reasons for using the law to regulate business is recognition that a free market would have undesirable consequences for certain groups in society. Consumers and employees would be at a disadvantage in their dealings with business without various protections afforded by law. In other words, although business pursuing its self-interest produces substantial public benefit such as greater prosperity, there are many ways in which business self-interest and the public interest clash. For example, the Minimum Wage Act, requiring all businesses in the UK to pay a minimum wage, ensures that profit-seeking businesses facing competitive pressures do not harm vulnerable groups of employees by forcing wages down below a decent level. This means that although we refer to private ownership of business, decisions about managing those businesses are never purely private ones since they involve certain restrictions and obligations defined by law.

Of course, there are different views about how far the law should be used to regulate business, and the role of law varies both between different societies and between different governments within each market system. Chapter 13 will examine the difficulty of balancing the authority of the law with the freedom of business.

Values

Mini-Case 1.1   Guiding the 'hidden hand'—the minimum wage

The idea of the 'hidden hand' is a metaphor for the way the market system, though based on millions of independent decisions and not subject to overall plan or control by any actual hand, does not degenerate into chaos but operates in a highly coordinated way. It is as if a hidden hand is guiding it.

Adam Smith pointed out in the 18th century that even though businesses may be concerned only with their self-interest (profit) they would be guided, by and large, to serve the public good. This

seems like a paradox—promoting the common good by acting selfishly. Smith's insight was that it would only be by serving the needs of others (customers) that businesses would be able to make a profit. When businesses throughout the economy act in this way the result is that the supply of goods and services matches consumer demand.

The hidden hand of the market operates through the price mechanism. The price adjusts until balance is achieved between supply and demand. For example if supply exceeds demand the price will tend to fall, and vice versa.

However, the hidden hand can produce outcomes that are not socially desirable. In a market system profit-seeking businesses respond to ability to pay—it is not their purpose to act like charities. The problem is that the price determined by the hidden hand might be one that not everyone can afford to pay because of differences in levels of household income. Perhaps it doesn't matter that not everyone can afford a BMW, but it is more serious if some people cannot afford healthcare when they need it.

In labour markets price is the wage or salary that people receive for the jobs they perform. In this case the problem is that for some low paid occupations this price might not be sufficient to enable people to have a decent standard of life.

One solution to this problem is to use the law to guide the hidden hand through price controls. The Labour government introduced a National Minimum Wage (NMW) in 1999. The Department for Trade and Industry explains the rationale of the NMW as follows:

> The national minimum wage is an important cornerstone of government strategy aimed at providing employees with decent minimum standards and fairness in the workplace.

It applies to nearly all workers and sets hourly rates below which pay must not be allowed to fall. It helps business by ensuring companies will be able to compete on the basis of quality of the goods and services they provide and not on low prices based predominantly on low rates of pay.

www.dti.gov.uk/employment/pay/national-minimum-wage/index.html/

Since 1999 the NMW has been increased at a faster rate than average earnings, thus improving the position of low paid workers. As the NMW has increased it has embraced a larger share of the workforce, rising from 1 million in 1999 to 2 million in 2006. In October 2006 the NMW for adult workers was increased to £5.35 per hour.

The point of the NMW is that low paid workers are better off as a result of the visible hand of government than they would have been if wages were left entirely to be determined by the hidden hand of the market.

? How does the NMW affect the private ownership of business?

? If you were an employer, would you support the NMW?

Since 1999 the National Minimum Wage has been increased at a faster rate than average earnings thus improving the position of low paid workers.

© istockphoto.com/Silvia Jansen

Competition vs. market power?

So private ownership turns out not to be a straightforward idea. The same can be said of competition and profit. Competition is a key aspect of the environment in which businesses in a market system operate, and we will look at it more closely in Chapters 2 and 14. It is competition that keeps businesses responsive to consumers since they have the option of going elsewhere if they are not satisfied. However it seems clear that firms do not all face the same amount of competitive pressure and that some firms exercise more market power than others. If consumers really are 'sovereign' this suggests that firms have to respond to their preferences and have little or no power in the market themselves.

Yet firms are often felt to be powerful entities, particularly in the case of 'big business'. In recent years there has been much public debate about the power and impact of vast global businesses in the form of multinational corporations (MNCs) that operate in several different countries (Chapter 12).

Values

Spatial levels

It seems clear that firms have more power when they face no or few competitors and less power when they face a large number of rivals. When there are many firms in a market competitive pressure is increased and consumers can more easily shop around. In economic analysis these issues are examined in terms of distinctive market structures—principally monopoly, oligopoly and perfect competition. The prediction of economic theory is that market structure influences a firm's conduct or behaviour and performance so it is an important element of the business environment.

Profit vs. social responsibility?

The performance of business is conventionally measured in terms of profitability, because profit is seen as the prime motive of business in the private sector. However the notion of business 'success' is not quite so straightforward. This is because businesses may themselves have other non-profit objectives and because, in any case, other groups in society increasingly demand or expect business performance and success to be measured by criteria other than just profit. In the modern world businesses have come increasingly under pressure to legitimize their activities and role in society with reference to a wider range of social benefits. This is sometimes referred to as maintaining the 'licence to operate'. As we will see in Chapter 7, business has to engage in public dialogue in matters of business ethics and respond to the concerns and demands of a range of stakeholder groups.

Values

Stakeholders

This area of debate is often expressed in terms of 'corporate social responsibility'. A crucial question, discussed in Chapter 15, concerns the threat of climate change and the responsibility of business to demonstrate an ethic of care towards the natural environment.

The private sector of business has certain common characteristics—private ownership, competition and profit—that are important for an understanding of its decisions and behaviour and how it 'solves' the basic economic problem. However we have seen that the private sector is highly diverse, and the principal aspects of this diversity are summarized below:

- type of good or service produced (the industry in which the firm is located)
- legal status of the firm (e.g. sole trader, partnership, limited company)
- legal regulation of business (the variable use of law to place restrictions and obligations on private business)
- size (e.g. measured in terms of number of employees or sales revenue)
- geographical reach (i.e. the geographical spread of the firm's activities within and between countries)
- degree of competitive pressure (market structure)
- objectives (profit and corporate social responsibility)

Diversity

> **↪ *Stop and Think***
>
> Do you think that the sole purpose of business is or should be to make as much profit as possible?
>
> If your answer is 'no', would you think differently if you were a shareholder?
>
> If your answer is 'yes', do you think that the pursuit of profit leads business to serve the public interest or common good?

Other sectors of business— the public sector and the third sector

There is a good reason why people tend to think first of private sector firms when asked to think of an example of business, and this is that the private sector is the dominant element within the UK and other capitalist or market economies. In other words, most of the goods and services that we consume on a daily basis are purchased from private sector businesses, and most employees work in the private sector.

Diversity

Another reason is that the term 'business' is often associated specifically with the profit motive. Yet this is a narrow conception of business. If we think in terms of our broad definition—transforming inputs into outputs of goods and services to meet the needs and wants of consumers—it is clear that other types of organization are also involved in business. These are not-for-profit organizations operating in both:

- the public sector, and
- the 'third' sector of voluntary organizations.

Dynamic

Although these organizations make up a relatively small part of the business or economic life of the country, they are involved in the production of some key services, such as healthcare and education services. It is also important to note that the boundaries between these sectors are not fixed but can, and do, shift, largely as a result of political decisions. For example, in the recent past in the UK, mainly under Conservative governments in the 1980s and '90s, a programme of privatization transferred businesses that had operated for many years as parts of the public sector—such as British Telecommunications, British Gas and British Rail—into the private sector.

The point is that the public and third sectors also provide mechanisms for 'solving' the basic economic problem, and societies have to choose how to balance these different sectors of business. Therefore, in addition to the private sector, we should also think of business in terms of not-for-profit organizations operating in the public sector and the voluntary (or 'third') sector. Within these sectors business organizations are also diverse when considered, for example, in terms of the type of output they produce, their legal status and size.

Differences between the private and public sectors

Public and private sector organizations differ in important respects.

- *Revenue*. Public sector organizations like schools and NHS hospitals are largely financed through taxation rather than sales revenue generated by customers paying a price in a market.

Supermarkets are an example of an oligopoly.

© Brigitte Bott/Robert Harding World Imagery/Corbis

- *Accountability*. Private sector organizations are accountable to customers and shareholders. If they are not responsive to their customers they risk losing business to their more customer-focused competitors, and public limited companies (PLCs) are legally required to safeguard the interests of their shareholders. Public sector organizations do not have shareholders. Some of them do have users who may be thought of (and think of themselves as) customers (such as students), and they are expected to be more responsive to them than perhaps they were in the past. But some parts of the public sector deal with people who do not choose to be users of the service and are therefore not customers in this sense, for example the prison service. In general, political rather than market-based forms of accountability are more important in the public sector, meaning accountability to politicians or public officials (civil servants or local government officers).

- *Competition*. Finally, a characteristic of the private sector is that consumers can 'shop around' because firms operate in competitive markets. It is this that keeps businesses customer-focused and is the basis of consumer sovereignty. Of course, the amount of competition and consumer choice varies between markets and an important question concerns the operation of markets dominated by a small number of large businesses, known as oligopolies (e.g. supermarkets). Some public sector organizations also face competition in 'internal markets' where 'customers' have some ability to exercise choice (i.e. to 'shop around') between alternative service providers such as schools, universities or hospitals. However in general such choices are constrained and these organizations operate in less volatile, if not captive, markets.

Mini-Case 1.2 Is a school a business?

Values

Some people might describe a school as a business on the basis that it provides a service—it is 'in the business' of providing education for children. A school might well have a business plan, and we might expect the headteacher and governors to run the school in a 'business-like' way. The children, or their parents, might be referred to (and might think of themselves) as customers, just as they might be customers of McDonalds. In Britain, under the Labour government's policy of establishing 'City Academies', it became possible for individuals from the world of business to invest their own money in a school and play a leading role in its management and in determining its ethos.

These all look like good reasons for thinking of schools as businesses. Yet other people would reject the idea that a school can be thought of as a business, and prefer instead a term like public service. They might think that a business is primarily concerned with making money, whereas a school has other values and objectives such as ensuring that all children have the same opportunities regardless of their parents' income, and the chance to realize their potential.

This example illustrates the dispute over where the boundaries of business lie, but also shows that important issues can be at stake in what seems like a quibble over mere words. For the debate about whether a school should be thought of as a business is really a dispute about the purpose of schools and the ways they are managed. Those who reject the term business believe that making a school more 'business-like' threatens its public service mission or ethos, whereas those who think of schools as businesses will see this in positive terms of improving the efficiency of management and the performance of the school as measured by academic performance.

The dispute also illustrates, in a more general way, the debate about the role and purpose of business in society and whether, as in this case, there are certain areas of life that should be kept separate from business or business should be allowed to extend its role without limit. It shows, in other words, that the role of business in modern society remains controversial. What do you think?

Is a school a business?
© Photo by Christopher Furlong/Getty Images

❷ Do you think of yourself as a customer of your university? How does this differ, if at all, from the 'traditional' idea of a student?

❷ Do you have the same expectations and the same idea of your rights in relation to the university as you do in relation to a high-street business?

❷ Do you think it would be a good thing for universities to be run more on business lines? Would there be any disadvantages?

A simple model of business in its environment—transforming inputs into outputs

Business organizations are systems that interact with the external environment in which they operate. Business, in its broad sense, is the activity of transforming inputs into outputs or, in other words, the activity of producing goods and services to meet the wants and needs of consumers. The inputs come from, and the outputs are sent into, the environment. To be successful, businesses have to produce outputs that meet the expectations of consumers, and to do this they have to be able to acquire the necessary inputs at the right time, price, quantity and quality. Thus businesses have to understand the 'surrounding conditions and circumstances' at both the input and output ends of their operations. And in between they have to manage the process of transformation of inputs into outputs (production) within the organization (the internal environment). This understanding of business interacting with its environment through three stages of activity is shown in Figure 1.2.

Interaction

There are two other ways of picturing this transformation process:

- as part of a longer chain
- as a cycle.

The longer chain is the supply chain of which the individual business is normally only one link. The supply chain is the whole series of organizations, relationships and processes that link the consumer or end-user of the final or finished product back to the original raw materials which have been converted or transformed into that product. Thus in Figure 1.2 the inputs might not be raw materials but semi-manufactured products or components, and the outputs might not be final products for end-users but parts that enter into the next stage of the production process carried out by another firm.

The transformation process may be thought of as a cycle because for each organization the supply of outputs to consumers is not really the end of the process but leads back to the procurement of inputs to start the cycle again, as illustrated in Figure 1.3. Thus revenue earned from the supply of outputs is 'ploughed back' into the business to procure further inputs in order to carry on production of further outputs, and so on. In the private sector the profit motive means that firms aim to earn more from total sales revenue than was laid out as costs of production. Earning profit allows firms to

- expand the scale of production and grow the business

and/or

- pay out part of the profits to the owners of the business (e.g. payment of dividends to shareholders).

There is clearly a potential tension or trade-off between these two purposes or functions of profit, and between short-term and long-term objectives. Shareholders may expect short-term profits, but managers may wish to invest profits back into the business to secure long-term competitiveness and growth.

In the private sector inputs and outputs generally involve market relationships of exchange—buying

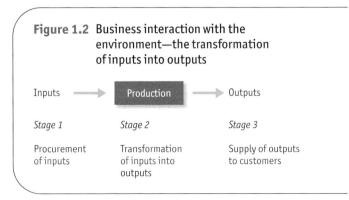

Figure 1.2 Business interaction with the environment—the transformation of inputs into outputs

Inputs	→	Production	→	Outputs
Stage 1		*Stage 2*		*Stage 3*
Procurement of inputs		Transformation of inputs into outputs		Supply of outputs to customers

Figure 1.3 The transformation process as a cycle

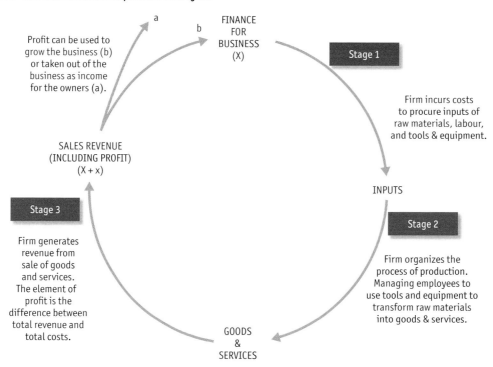

Notes: Profit (x) is what is left from total sales revenue after the total costs incurred by the business have been replaced (X). There is a tension or trade-off between two functions or purposes of profit: it may be taken out of the business as income for the owners (a) or used as retained earnings to grow the business (b).

and selling—but public sector organizations produce services, such as health and education, which are supplied to end-users free of charge (or mainly so). However, the inputs used by public sector organizations, such as drugs and medical equipment in the health service, generally have to be purchased in a market. The private sector does not operate entirely as depicted by the simple model, for businesses rely on some crucial inputs provided by government. For example the skills and knowledge of employees are developed largely through the state education system.

Understanding the environment of business in this way mainly involves understanding the market conditions that the firm faces in relation to procurement of inputs and sale of outputs, particularly how competitive these markets are. We can say that as buyers of inputs firms benefit (as do buyers generally) from competitive market conditions (though there can be a downside if, for example, your current supplier goes out of business), while as sellers of outputs competitive markets are sources of threat (though a competitive or contestable market may be an opportunity if, for example, the firm is a new entrant). Porter's well-known five forces model identifies five sources of competitive pressures (Porter, 1980).

Porter's 'five forces' model

- *Current competitors*

The most immediate and obvious threat comes from rivals in the market producing or selling the same product and trying to attract the same customers. In general markets are considered to be more competitive the greater the number of firms operating in them because it is easier for consumers to 'shop around'. However even when a small number of firms dominate a market, as with the major supermarkets, competition between them may be intense. As well as current competitors firms have to be aware of:

- *the possibility of new entrants into the market*

Entry may come from new start-ups or from existing businesses pursuing diversification strategies. Through diversification supermarkets have entered other markets such as for books and CDs, making it harder for existing businesses to survive. Entry may be deterred by barriers such as the ability of established firms to use advertising and branding to build up customer loyalty. Competition exists in a less direct form through.

- *the availability of substitute products*

A substitute is a different product which provides the same service or function, such as different modes of transport. Finally, firms have to deal with suppliers and customers at each end of the transformation process, in procuring inputs for the production process and selling their products. But these relationships of exchange also involve a dimension of power. Thus firms have to deal with

- *the power of buyers*, and
- *the power of sellers*

It is clear that a business will benefit if market conditions are reversed in relation to inputs and outputs so that there is buyer power in the former and seller power in the latter. For example, supermarkets are often accused of 'squeezing' their suppliers by demanding price reductions and more stringent quality criteria. In this case farmers, as sellers, have little power and supermarkets, as buyers, have much power. In effect, it can be argued, supermarkets are able to compete by offering low prices to their customers at the expense of farmers' livelihoods.

Conceptualizing the environment of business

Just as the term 'business' in reality refers not to a single type of organization but to a diverse range, so the environment of business is similarly diverse. Different types of business organization operate in different environmental settings or contexts.

Spatial level—local to global

The environment is usually thought of as the world 'out there', the external context, comprised of the wider social, cultural, economic, political, legal, technological and other systems in which businesses operate. In the context of debates about 'globalization' we may think of this external environment in terms of 'the world' in the sense that businesses may be affected by, and in turn influence, events on a global scale. This is particularly true in the case of companies that have a global reach or span of operations, especially multinational corporations (MNCs) that undertake production in more than one country.

Spatial levels

However, we can think of the environment in terms of different levels of analysis ranging from the small scale and local environment at one end of a spectrum through to global systems and events at the other. We might think of small and medium-sized enterprises (SMEs) as operating in a more localized environment, such as within the local economy of a town or city, and giant corporations operating in a more national or global environment. However, even small businesses may be affected by events at a national or global level because of the way they are often linked in with supply chains spanning several countries. For example, they may depend on imported raw materials or components. At the other end of the spectrum even the largest companies also have to deal with local issues and concerns. Indeed the term 'glocalization' has been coined to draw attention to the need for global businesses to remain sensitive to the peculiarities of the local contexts in which they operate.

External and internal environments

Internal/ external

Although the environment of business mainly suggests the external world 'out there', it also has a critical internal dimension concerned with relations and processes within the organization. We have already seen that the transformation of inputs into outputs involves the stage of production within the organization. But we can get further with the idea of an internal environment if we think of the organization not as a single unified entity but more as an internally differentiated system made up of different parts or 'sub-systems'.

For example, firms typically are made up of specialized sub-systems or departments dealing with particular aspects or functions of the business—such as production, marketing, finance, human resources (HR) and research. This may be seen as a division of labour within the organization which allows it to draw on the highly specialized knowledge of employees in these distinct functional areas. The other side of this differentiation is, of course, the need to ensure coordination so that individuals and departments are working together effectively to achieve the organization's goals. That is a key task of managers at the senior level of the organization.

Now we can see that a director of human resources, for example, has to operate within an internal environment, dealing with issues such as training and development of the existing workforce and, in the process, having to manage relationships with other departments. These are the 'surrounding conditions' in which the director of human resources has to operate. For example, faced with scarcity the organization has to deploy its available resources carefully to achieve its objectives. It has to make decisions about the allocation of these resources between different possible uses, weighing up how each might contribute to its success. In this situation the director of human resources might have to win the case for more investment in the 'human capital' of the organization in the form of staff development against competing claims on those resources from other departments.

Consideration of the internal environment raises the issue of the internal 'politics' of organizations (or 'office politics'). This is because we can see that businesses are arenas in which different views are put forward about the allocation of resources and questions of business strategy more generally. In other words there is scope for disagreement about the best way forward for the organization and this means that it has to be able to manage and resolve these disagreements in a positive way that contributes to the success of the business. This process of resolving disagreements is at the heart of what politics is about, and we will return to this question in Chapter 4.

The internal and external dimensions of the business environment are closely related since many business decisions cross over this boundary—they have internal and external aspects. For example, product innovation may involve not only internally managed research and development activity but also collaboration with external partners. Businesses have to ensure recruitment of the right people from the external labour market, but they also have to manage the internal labour market within the organization to deploy human resources effectively.

Interaction

It is also important to note that the character of internal processes may influence the speed and effectiveness with which organizations respond to external opportunities or threats. Indeed the internal environment may be shaped by the way the organization responds to its external environment.

Immediate and general environments

The 'immediate' environment involves those aspects which may require day-to-day or regular decisions and actions (e.g. relations with suppliers), while the 'general' environment is concerned with more distant or remote, but nevertheless consequential, issues (e.g. macroeconomic trends). On the whole, the general environment concerns events and systems that operate on a large scale and form a backdrop to day-to-day business decisions. The general environment also contains issues and events which are more beyond the capacity of individual organizations to influence or control. For example, the rate of growth of the economy, the level of unemployment and rate of inflation, and central bank (Bank of England) decisions on interest rates all form important elements of the general environment or backdrop of business decisions in the UK. These are macroeconomic phenomena and decisions (operating at the level of the economy as a whole), affecting all businesses in the economy, and over which no individual business has much (if any) influence or control. On the other hand the decision by a particular components manufacturer to raise its prices is part of the immediate environment only directly affecting other businesses which it supplies. This will affect day-to-day decisions by those businesses (e.g. to switch suppliers) and they may have some ability to influence the price change through negotiation.

Environmental uniqueness

The idea of 'environmental uniqueness' tells us that each business organization operates within an environment that is, to some extent, unique to it, and no two organizations operate in exactly the same environment. This idea warns against over-generalization in analysing the business environment. It reminds us that for environmental analysis to be useful to an organization it must be sensitive to the particular aspects of the environment that affect it and to which it must respond.

But we shouldn't take this idea too far—at its extreme it would suggest that a business environment textbook is required for every business organization in the economy! The absurdity of that idea shows us that generalization—meaning to make a statement with general application, about how things are in general terms, or that is intended to be true in most cases—is a necessary and useful approach in business and management. There are, in other words, general aspects of the environment that affect most businesses, so a firm should find environmental analysis useful that deals both with the general and the particular.

Interaction between business and the environment— responding, influencing and choosing

Responsiveness

In order to operate successfully businesses must be able to respond effectively to factors in their environment that affect them. The environment may be seen as presenting a range of threats and opportunities. A successful business will be one that is able to deal effectively with threats and take advantage of opportunities or, at least, is able to do so as well as or better than its competitors.

Interaction

Influence

However, success may also depend on the ability of business to influence the environment in which it operates to its own advantage. Advertising is a clear example of business activity that is intended to influence the environment. Shifts in consumer preferences and spending patterns may pose threats or opportunities to which businesses must respond. Such shifts may occur for a variety of reasons, such as

- changes in values and lifestyles in society
- greater affluence resulting from economic growth, and
- changes in the age structure of the population.

Some of these shifts result from large-scale social changes over which business has little or no influence, and which constitute aspects of the general environment. For example, the ageing of the population has implications for the pattern of consumer spending as older people have wants and needs that differ from those of younger people.

However, businesses do not simply respond to shifts in preferences and spending patterns among consumers but are active in seeking to influence these shifts to their own advantage. Through advertising and branding strategies businesses may be able to create new tastes and fashions in society to which they then apparently respond. Ageing is a good example of this. As people get older their wants and needs change, but the lifestyles of older people today have also changed compared to previous generations. Older people now want to have a more active lifestyle than in the past. This is in part due to higher incomes and improved health, but we can also see how business may play a powerful role in influencing these changing lifestyles as they develop and promote new types of goods and services, such as in the field of leisure and tourism.

This example of interaction between business and the environment—responding to and seeking to influence consumer preferences—has implications for how we understand the working of a market system. The idea of 'consumer sovereignty' expresses the idea that consumers are ultimately in charge of the economic system because it is their preferences which drive business decisions about what to produce.

Values

On the other hand the power of advertising leads us to question how far consumers really are in charge. The purpose of advertising is, after all, not merely to inform but to persuade. How far do we as consumers make decisions for ourselves, and how far are our decisions influenced by sophisticated advertising methods?

> ⊃ *Stop and Think*
> You make choices about the music you listen to and the clothes you wear. We all like to think of ourselves as making our own decisions. But what factors in your environment have influenced your choices? How far has business shaped your lifestyle choices?

Choice of environment

Beyond responding to or influencing the environment, businesses may be able to choose a favourable environment in which to operate. For example, businesses may be able to shift the geographical basis of their operations—moving into more favourable environments and away from unfavourable ones. When businesses expand into new markets, for example exporting to new countries, they are searching for favourable geographical areas in which to sell their products. The phenomenon of international trade is driven by the geographical expansion of business searching for opportunities for sales in new markets overseas. Whether these new markets will provide favourable trading environments will depend on factors such as culture, consumer tastes and income levels within the society. Thus as countries develop they may offer favourable environments for companies from Europe to increase their sales as consumers' incomes increase and, crucially, as 'western' lifestyles spread. An example of this is the way western tobacco companies have been seeking to increase sales of cigarettes in developing countries. These countries offer favourable environments as more people can afford to smoke and, to some extent, desire to emulate affluent western lifestyles. (Again, these lifestyle associations of cigarettes are promoted by the companies in their advertising.) At the same time the trading environment in western societies has become less favourable due to increased awareness of the health hazards of smoking among consumers and moves to limit smoking by governments, as in the UK.

Businesses can also choose the environment in which they operate by deciding the location of their production activities. In searching for favourable environments in which to carry on production firms are said to seek locational advantage. This applies to the establishment of new businesses or new offices or factories on the part of existing firms, but it can also involve transferring operations from one location to another. Locational advantage may derive from factors such as:

- the availability of skilled labour
- the cost of labour
- a favourable tax or regulatory environment
- the proximity of suppliers or consumers
- the quality of infrastructure such as transport.

The type of business that we most associate with this capacity to seek locational advantage, and particularly to transfer production between locations, is the multinational corporation (MNC). These are companies that control production facilities in more than one country. Although not all MNCs are large, MNCs include the largest businesses in the world, and the largest of them are bigger (measured by sales revenue) than all except the biggest countries (measured by GDP). These companies are often truly global in the sense that the production facilities they control are spread throughout the world, and they are the originators of readily identifiable 'global brands'. It

Mini-Case 1.3 Dyson: champion of British manufacturing?

James Dyson has been regarded as a champion of British manufacturing because of the success of his company manufacturing vacuum cleaners in Malmesbury, Wiltshire and because of his public statements supporting the need to retain manufacturing in the UK.

However in 2002 Dyson announced his decision to shift production to Malaysia with the loss of 800 jobs at the company's Wiltshire plant. The company had opened its first plant in Malaysia in 2000. The reason for the shift of production out of the UK were indicated by Dyson as follows:

> By moving to the Far East where many suppliers are based and where production is more cost effective, we would be able to continue to grow, invest heavily in new technologies and launch more products faster. ('Dyson to shift manufacturing operations to Asia', *Guardian*, 5 February 2002)

Labour costs in Malaysia were reported to be around one-third of those in the UK. Other factors influencing the decision were planning restrictions at the UK plant and the high value of the pound.

In 2003 Dyson announced plans to shift production of washing machines to Malaysia. The Malmesbury site would cease to function as a manufacturing facility.

However the company retained research and development activity at Malmesbury and announced that it was recruiting more employees at the site in high value-added and high-paid positions.

The decision to shift manufacturing to Malaysia and retain R&D in the UK shows the ability of Dyson to choose favourable environments for these activities. Malaysia offers advantages for low skill manufacturing operations particularly due to much lower labour costs than the UK. The UK offers advantages for R&D and design operations because of the availability of highly skilled workers with relevant scientific qualifications.

These decisions were taken by Dyson on commercial grounds. This case shows the vulnerability of UK manufacturing jobs in the face of low wage competition overseas. For critics it also shows the lack of commitment of a successful British company to its country of origin. Thus Dyson was accused by some of betraying British manufacturing.

❷ In moving production to Asia do you think that Dyson did the 'right thing'?

is sometimes argued that these companies are increasingly 'footloose' in the pursuit of their global business strategies. This means that they have no particular attachment to any country in which they operate but will shift production in search of favourable environments for their business.

> **⟳ Stop and Think**
> Can you think of other examples of how business is able to respond to, influence or choose its external environment?

The nature of the internal environment

The internal environment concerns all those activities and relationships within the organization that are involved in the transformation of inputs into outputs. The internal activities and relationships add value to the inputs. A successful business has to manage the internal environment effectively as well as interact with the external environment. Of course, the internal environment is not sealed off from the external one, rather there is an interface or relationship between the two.

Interaction

Businesses are, in other words, open systems that interact with their environments, not closed systems. Some 'internal' activities involve relationships with external people and organizations, most obviously suppliers and customers. For example, in a retail business and other services the interface with the external environment in the guise of customers is the core activity of the business. Therefore, managing the internal environment is, in part, concerned with managing this relationship or interface. Further, the internal environment may need to be adapted to suit the particular characteristics of the external environment if the business is to be successful. This means that there might not be just one way of organizing and managing the internal environment, but a variety of possible ways, depending on what works best in the particular situation of the firm. For example, if the external environment is characterized by rapid change or volatility it may be important to ensure flexibility of staffing or tasks within the business. On the other hand in a stable and predictable environment a more rigid, bureaucratic and rule-based approach might work well. Just as the external environment of each business is, in some degree, unique, the same can be said of the internal environment.

Analysing the internal environment involves looking at businesses as particular types of organizations. An organization can be defined as a group of people that comes together for the purpose of achieving a specific goal or objective, and which involves a series of activities and relationships undertaken within a framework of some kind of rules or procedures. The essential purpose of management, as an indispensable function of the organization, is to facilitate and ensure that clear organizational objectives are formulated and achieved.

What is an organization?

- objectives
- people/relationships
- tasks/functions
- technologies
- rules

We have already seen that the objectives of business may not be straightforward, but for our purpose here they can be stated quite simply, as follows:

- to produce certain types of output of goods and/or services
- to meet the wants and needs of customers
- to realize a profit (in the private sector).

Profit is the ultimate objective—the decision about the product mix and the aim to satisfy consumers are really means to this end.

The internal environment, in contrast to the external one, is much more within the control of the organization—so much so that we can think of the internal environment in terms of **organizational design**. Design involves the deliberate shaping of the **organization structure** and culture so that it supports effectively the achievement of organizational goals, rather than getting in the way of these goals. It involves the idea of managerial choice. Designing and implementing organization structure can take up a great deal of management time and energy, and there are always transitional costs in implementing change in the organization. For example, change can be experienced as demotivating when it involves changes to people's responsibilities. Existing working patterns and relationships may be discontinued and new ones need time to 'bed down'. It is probably true that there is no such thing as the perfect organization structure—every structure has its problems as well as its advantages. However, there is no doubt that organization structure can be an important factor in the success of a business.

Types of organization structure

There is a large literature on organization structure. Here we will only indicate some of the principal types. We can think of organization structure in terms of two key issues or problems that all organizations have to solve:

- the problem of division of labour—all organizations have to decide how to divide up the various tasks or functions that must be undertaken in transforming inputs into outputs
- the problem of management—all organizations have to decide how to arrange lines of authority and accountability.

Each of these problems involves an intrinsic tension or dilemma:

- the dilemma of the division of labour is between the fragmentation of tasks/functions and their effective coordination
- the dilemma of management is between the centralization and decentralization of authority and decision-making.

Functional structure

We referred earlier to the idea of an organization as a system interacting with its environment. This leads on to looking at the internal environment in terms of sub-systems or parts that make up the whole. In other words, organizations are internally differentiated. Typically, the design of business organizations involves a **functional structure** in which the sub-systems are specialized departments or units dealing with specialist tasks or functions that contribute to the transformation process. Classically these functions include production, finance, personnel (or human resources), marketing, sales, and research and development. The chief advantage of this structure is efficiency, and this derives from the fact that staff in each department or section specialize in specific tasks in which they may have expert knowledge, often based on academic and/or professional qualifications. It also means that there is a clear career path for staff within each department.

Figure 1.4 Functional structure

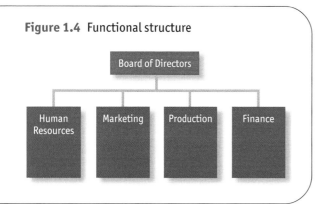

The chief disadvantage is the problem of coordinating the work of these various departments and making sure that they are all contributing effectively to organization goals. There is a risk that departments become parochial or inward-looking, or that rivalries between departments can hinder organizational effectiveness.

Matrix structure

A functional structure involves a vertical principle of organization design, with each department seen as a column usually with its own internal hierarchical levels of management and decision-making, as shown in Figure 1.4. A matrix structure introduces a horizontal principle cutting across the vertical departmental columns, often on the basis of project teams involving staff from many or all departments, as shown in Figure 1.5. This means that individuals operate within a two-way flow of authority and responsibility—vertically within their department and, at the same time, horizontally within the project team.

The chief advantage of a matrix structure is the focus it provides on projects or programmes and the ability to bring together relevant functional expertise. This ensures more of an external focus and can combat the parochialism of departments. The chief disadvantage is the confusion that can be created over 'who's in charge?' Individuals can feel pulled in two directions and unsure of who they are accountable to. Departmental managers and team leaders can feel unsure about the scope of their authority.

Figure 1.5 Matrix structure—University Faculty of Business

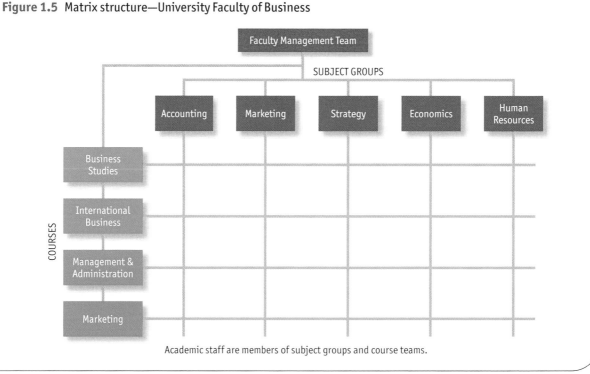

Academic staff are members of subject groups and course teams.

Divisions and operational units

The functional and matrix structures may operate across the whole organization. This may be best suited to single-product firms. On the other hand, there may be benefit in dividing up the organization into operational units on the basis of distinct products or services. Divisional structures are best suited to large companies with diverse product portfolios. In a divisional structure each division operates as a semi-independent business run as a separate profit centre, but within the parameters of the overall corporate strategy determined by the company's headquarters, as depicted in Figure 1.6. Within each division there may be a functional or matrix structure, although some functions, such as research and development, may be undertaken centrally. The chief advantage of a divisional structure is that it overcomes the limitations of centralized coordination and control of a large and diverse business. It allows each division to respond to its own market conditions. However there can be tensions between the semi-independence of divisions and the formulation and implementation of a corporate strategy for the company as a whole. The allocation of the central overhead costs to each division can be a source of conflict.

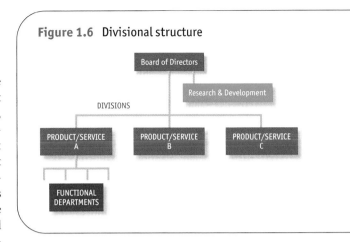

Figure 1.6   Divisional structure

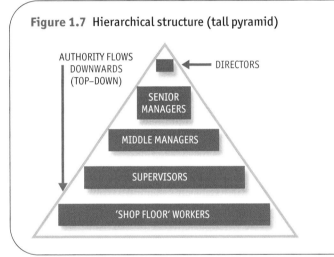

Figure 1.7   Hierarchical structure (tall pyramid)

Hierarchical structure

Business organizations are typically hierarchical, which means that authority is concentrated at the top of the organization and flows downwards. This usually involves a number of layers of authority. Those at the bottom of the hierarchy may have little or no authority and control—their role is to carry out instructions from above. This type of structure can be represented as a pyramid, as shown in Figure 1.7, with authority concentrated at the pinnacle. In a bureaucratic structure positions of authority are allocated on the basis of expertise. The chief benefit of the hierarchical structure is that the few at the top of the company are experts and best able to make decisions about corporate policies and strategy. It can also be argued that decision-making is more streamlined and decisions are authoritative. A major disadvantage is that hierarchies are not very good at drawing on the knowledge that exists in the lower layers of the organization, and that those at the bottom may not feel a strong sense of commitment to the organization. Having many layers of management within the hierarchy is also very costly for the business. These problems may be alleviated by moving to a flatter structure.

Delayering—flat structure

Businesses are never flat structures, but they may become flatter by reducing the number of layers or levels of management. In this way they become less-steep pyramids. The motivation for delayering may be to strip out managerial costs from the business to enhance competitiveness.

There may also be a desire to streamline decision-making further and bring senior management closer to those at the bottom of the hierarchy. This may improve employee motivation and commitment. An obvious drawback of a flatter structure can be an excessive workload on managers—there is a danger that the organization really needs those layers of management that are being removed.

> **⊃ Stop and Think**
> It is sometimes said that there is no perfect organization structure. Do you agree?

Environmental analysis

Dynamic

As we have seen, businesses have to understand the 'surrounding conditions and circumstances' in which they operate in order to be successful. Environmental analysis is needed because the environment does not the stay the same—it is dynamic. If the environment were static it would be possible to plan for the future on the basis of what was done in the past—to carry on in the same way. But because the environment is dynamic, businesses must operate under a general assumption that the future will be different from the past. Therefore it is necessary to know how it will change in order to respond to or influence this change in a way that will allow the organization to achieve its goals. Of course, remembering the point about environmental uniqueness, some firms operate in a more volatile environment than others, and there are some periods of relative environmental stability and others of greater dynamism. However the general point about change still stands, and business success depends on dealing with change effectively.

Uncertainty and 'bounded rationality'

Businesses can never have complete knowledge of how the environment will change. There are always limitations on knowledge, and therefore businesses must operate in a somewhat uncertain environment. Although businesses may strive to act rationally in monitoring the environment and responding to change in the most effective way, their rationality is always 'bounded' by limited knowledge. It is sometimes said that by the time firms have monitored environmental change, analysed their findings and formulated a response it is too late to do anything. If this were true then environmental analysis would be a waste of time. Certainly businesses have to make judgements about the resources and energy they invest in environmental analysis in terms of likely benefits of the exercise. However, we return to the point that some level of understanding of the environment is essential to business. The question then is not so much whether but how. In this section we will outline briefly some of the more familiar methods.

PEST (and its variants)

Complexity

Thinking about the external environment in terms of inputs and outputs is useful but not sufficient. It focuses attention on relationships with sellers or suppliers, competitors, and buyers or consumers. But there are other important types of organizations, processes and relationships in the external environment. The external environment is not just made up of markets but also includes political, legal, social, cultural, technological and other factors and influences. It is, in other words, multi-faceted and complex.

PEST is a simple framework for environmental analysis that distinguishes four categories or areas:

- political
- economic

- social
- technological.

Variations on this basic type are set out below. In each case the order of the factors is not intended to indicate their relative importance but rather to produce a memorable acronym.

- PEST (Political, Economic, Social, Technological)
- SLEPT (Social, Legal, Economic, Political, Technological)
- PESTLE (Political, Economic, Social, Technological, Legal, Ethical)
- STEEPLE (Social, Technological, Economic, Educational, Political, Legal, Environmental)
- SPECTACLES (Social, Political, Economic, Cultural, Technological, Aesthetic, Customers, Legal, Environmental, Sectoral)

    (Sutherland and Canwell, 2004: 113–14; Cartwright, 2001)

The purpose of the more elaborate frameworks is to allow a more comprehensive coverage of environmental factors, but this may be at the expense of becoming rather unwieldy.

SWOT (strengths, weaknesses, opportunities, threats)

SWOT analysis combines internal and external analyses—the strengths and weaknesses of the organization coupled with the opportunities and threats in the external environment. The capacity of a business to take advantage of opportunities and resist threats will depend on its internal strengths and weaknesses. An opportunity only really exists if an organization has the necessary skills or resources. Thus an opportunity is not simply a feature of the external environment. Like PEST, SWOT is a simple framework, but its sophistication depends on the quality of the analysis under each heading.

Strengths	Weaknesses
Opportunities	Threats

Alternative scenarios

A scenario is an imagined sequence of future events. It might be highly speculative or based on forms of expert knowledge or data. The idea of alternative scenarios is that there are different possible futures to imagine and be prepared for. These alternatives might be assessed in terms of whether they are more or less likely, but the point is that being aware of less likely outcomes allows for the preparation of contingency plans—just in case. It is also common to think in terms of 'best case' and 'worst case' scenarios.

Trend extrapolation

Extrapolation involves using known variables and data as a guide to unknown ones, or to estimate data beyond the existing range. Trend extrapolation involves using the past as a guide to the future by projecting established trends. For example, if sales of a product have been growing at a steady annual rate and over a reasonably long period we might feel confident in projecting that sales growth in years to come. The basic problem is that we cannot assume that 'everything else stays the same'. There might be wider factors that explain the growth of sales in the past and these factors might alter.

Expert opinion

Expert opinion involves just what it says: relying on expert sources of opinion to provide understanding of the environment and guide the company's thinking. Often these will be experts outside the company, such as consultancy firms. These firms, or other experts, may have knowledge that it is difficult to sustain within the company. The Delphi method draws on the opinions of a range of experts with each one offering advice independently. There will be a round of consultations with questions being refined at each stage with the aim of arriving at a measure of convergence or consensus among the expert opinions.

Stakeholder analysis

Stakeholders

A stakeholder is any individual, group or organization that is affected by and therefore has an interest in the decisions and behaviour of the business. This might not be a direct effect as some stakeholders have public interest motivations. For example, an environmental pressure group has an interest in a business on account of the perceived harm its actions cause to the environment rather than the direct effect on the group's members. Other stakeholders have a direct interest because of the benefits or harm of the firm's actions to them. All the internal members of a business are stakeholders, including employees, directors and shareholders. External stakeholders include customers, suppliers, competitors, politicians and policy-makers, and the community or general public.

Values

As well as being affected by a business stakeholders may seek to influence business decisions in their own interests. There is a debate about how far businesses ought to be accountable to a wide range of stakeholders, and a stakeholder model of business may be contrasted with the traditional view of the firm as primarily or solely concerned with profit. Firms may themselves have different views about the desirability of stakeholder engagement. In terms of environmental analysis, businesses need to have an understanding of:

- who their stakeholders are
- the nature and level of their interest in the business
- their power to exert influence.

A stakeholder map is shown in Figure 1.8.
    For each of the internal and external stakeholders shown:

a) identify the nature of their interests (e.g. the interests of students might include high quality teaching)

b) consider whether there are any conflicts between the interests of different stakeholders (e.g. do students and academics have the same interests?)

c) consider in what way and to what extent each stakeholder exercises power or influence (e.g. do you have any influence over university decisions? Should you have?)

> ⮎ *Stop and Think*
> Can you explain what is meant by each of the four terms that constitute the PEST framework: political, economic, social, technological?

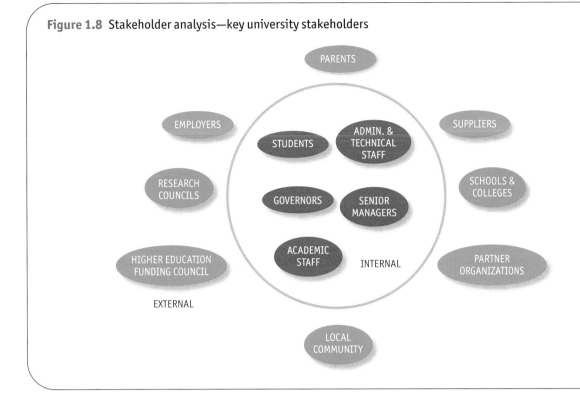

Figure 1.8 Stakeholder analysis—key university stakeholders

◈ *Summary*

- Business can be defined broadly as the transformation of inputs (or factors of production) into diverse outputs (goods and services) to meet the needs and wants of consumers. Business is a mechanism for deciding the allocation of the scarce resources available to society between various possible uses (or competing wants) in a situation of scarcity where not all wants can be satisfied

- In a narrow sense business is often used to refer to the private sector and the key characteristics of private ownership, competition and profit. The broad meaning of business includes organizations in the public and third sectors

- Market or capitalist economic systems, such as the UK, are dominated by the private sector. However, the boundary between the private, public and third sectors is not fixed. The private sector is very diverse

- The environment of business does not consist just of the world 'out there', or the external environment, but also has an internal dimension. The external environment can be thought of in terms of the immediate environment and the general environment

- Businesses can be understood as open systems interacting with their environments. Each business operates within an environment that is, to some extent, unique

- The external environment is complex or multi-faceted, dynamic, and must be analysed in terms of a variety of spatial levels or scales, from the local to the global

- The internal environment of business can be understood in terms of the design of organization structure so that it supports effectively the achievement of organization goals. There is a range of types of organization structure. Each has its advantages and disadvantages—none is perfect

- It is important for business to engage in monitoring and analysis of the environment. A variety of techniques is available. However, business can never have complete knowledge of the environment or how it will change

Case study: 'UK plc'

This case study identifies some key aspects of contemporary Britain using the PEST framework.

Political

- Democratic system of government in which the people as a whole exercise political power through the right to vote for members of parliament (MPs) to represent their interests
- Two-party system in which just two main political parties—Labour and Conservative—have dominated elections and government office for the last hundred years
- Civil Society Organizations (CSOs) or 'pressure groups' represent specific groups or causes within the political process, e.g. Greenpeace. Pressure groups also target businesses directly to try to get them to alter their behaviour, e.g. to reduce carbon emissions
- Business is a key political actor with distinctive interests, exercising a degree of power and influence arguably unrivalled by any other group
- One of the basic issues in political debate concerns the purpose of politics and government, especially in relation to the operation of private sector business and the market system. Left–Right politics can be characterized in terms of a 'state versus the market' debate
- Government plays an important role in economic and social life, for example making and enforcing laws, providing a range of public services and managing the economy. Public spending (spending by government) accounted for 41.1% of GDP (or the value of total economic output) in 2003/4
- The EU has become, in defined areas of competence, the supreme source of law and political authority. The UK also participates in a range of inter-governmental organizations (IGOs) and operates within a framework of international decisions and laws created by treaty, such as the Kyoto protocol on climate change

Economic

- Capitalist economic system in which business activity is organized primarily by private sector profit-seeking businesses producing goods and services for sale in a competitive environment
- Most people earn their living from the wages or salaries they receive as employees, and most employees work in the private sector. In spring 2004 29.7 million people were economically active in the UK, of which 28.3 million were in employment and 1.4 million were unemployed
- The UK is one of the richest developed countries in the world. In 2002 the UK was ranked sixth out of the EU

countries in terms of GDP per head (i.e. income per person). The average annual rate of growth of the UK economy (GDP) was 2.6% between 1950 and 2004

- The UK has undergone a long-term process of 'de-industrialization' involving a decline in the importance of manufacturing within the economy, coupled with expansion of the service sector. In 2003 the service sector accounted for 72.7% of UK output (up from 66.9% in 1993), while manufacturing accounted for 15.7% (down from 21% in 1993) (Office for National Statistics, *UK 2005*, p. 351)
- Large firms (with 250 or more employees) dominate the economy, accounting for 42% of private sector employment in 2003. The largest firms operating in the UK are multinational corporations (MNCs) with production facilities in more than one country, many of which are foreign-owned. However the vast majority of firms are small and medium-sized enterprises (SMEs). In 2003 large firms accounted for less than 0.2% of enterprises in the UK (approximately 6,000 from 4 million)
- The UK is one of the world's leading trading nations. In 2003 exports of goods and services accounted for 25% of GDP. Through trade and other linkages the UK has become increasingly integrated in the EU economy. The UK is also affected by processes of economic globalization, involving the stretching of economic relationships, such as trade and investment, across national borders

Social

- The UK has a growing population. In 2004 the total UK population reached 59.8 million, and is forecast to reach 67 million by 2031
- There has been a long-term upward trend of average life expectancy. Coupled with a declining birth rate, this has resulted in ageing of the population
- In recent years net inward migration has been the main contributor to population growth
- As a result of immigration since the 1950s Britain has become a multi-ethnic and multicultural society. In 2001 people from other than a White British ethnic background made up 11.8% of the population of Great Britain.
- British culture is diverse and fluid, due to immigration and other processes of social and economic change. However Britain can be seen as marked by certain characteristic 'western' values and attitudes such as individualism, consumerism and secularism
- Linked with its economic development, Britain is overwhelmingly an urban society

- The economic participation rate of females has increased and narrowed the gap with men. In spring 2005 70% of working-age women were in employment (compared to 79% for working-age men), up from 56% in 1971. However there remains a marked pattern of occupational segregation between males and females, and women are lower paid and more likely to work part-time than men

- The occupational order constitutes the basis for important class divisions in British society, e.g. between the best- and worst-paid occupations

- There are disparities in income levels and other social and economic measures of well-being between the UK regions, reflecting different rates and levels of economic development or decline. These disparities are sometimes referred to as constituting a North–South divide

Technological

- Britain's economic wealth and position as one of the world's richest economies can be attributed in large part to its level of technological advancement. Technological progress drives the process of economic growth through improvements in productivity, or output per worker

- Technology is a key determinant of competitiveness, at the level of firms, industries and nations. Technology is at the heart of price competitiveness gained through productivity improvement, but also boosts competitiveness through quality enhancement and product innovation

- Technological change is a disruptive force in business, destroying old skills, occupations and industries and creating new ones. The characteristic experience of modern life as subject to continual and speeded-up change is attributable largely to technological innovation

- The 20th-century 'Fordist' model of economic development was based on assembly line technology and mass production of standardized commodities, exemplified by the car industry and pioneered by the Ford motor company. This type of technological system has increasingly given way to a 'post-Fordist' model utilizing information and communication technologies (ICT) to enable flexible specialization

- Technological change has ushered in what some have referred to as a 'knowledge economy' in which the skills and knowledge of the workforce are seen as the most important assets of business and the nation. Hence education, life-long learning and upskilling are seen as key to the ability of the UK economy to respond to new global competitive challenges

- Technological change—especially in the fields of transport and communication—is at the heart of the process of globalization affecting all aspects of modern life. Globalization isn't a phenomenon just affecting economic and business life through trade, production and financial flows but also affects social, cultural and political life

- Growth of the world economy since the 19th century has been driven by the use of oil and other fossil fuels as energy sources. A switch to alternative sources of energy is now being compelled by the depletion of fossils fuels and concern over energy security, and by the damaging environmental impact of carbon emissions in the form of global warming

❷ Can you think of any other aspects of modern Britain under any of the PEST headings that have not been included above?

❷ In what ways do the aspects of modern Britain listed above impact upon business decisions and behaviour?

Review and discussion questions

1   Explain the nature of the 'basic economic problem' facing society, and show how business activity provides a solution to this problem

2   Describe and give examples of the elements that make up the external environment of business, and explain the idea of 'environmental uniqueness'

3   Give examples of the ways in which the external environment affects business decisions and behaviour, and the ways in which businesses may influence their environments

4   What is meant by the internal environment of business? Assess the advantages and disadvantages of the main types of organization structure

Assignments

1   You are asked to give a brief presentation to the director of a small business on whether to undertake some form of environmental analysis. Summarize the main points that you would make in the form of six 'bullet points'

2   Use the Internet to identify four recent newspaper reports that relate to factors in the external business environment under the PEST headings. Use a PEST grid to show the sources of the reports and to provide a brief bullet-pointed summary of each.

Further reading

Sutherland and Canwell (2004) provides a very useful source for understanding key concepts in business.

Online resources

Test your understanding of this chapter with online questions and answers, explore the subject further through web exercises, and use the weblinks to provide a quick resource for further research. Go to the Online Resource Centre at

www.oxfordtextbooks.co.uk/orc/ wetherly_otter/

www.intute.ac.uk/socialsciences/
Intute: social sciences is a gateway to resources on the web for education and research in the social sciences, including business and management.

References

Cartwright, R. (2001) *Mastering the Business Environment* (Basingstoke: Palgrave Macmillan).

Porter, M. (1980) *Competitive Strategy* (London: Free Press).

Sutherland, J. and Canwell, D. (2004) *Key Concepts in Business Practice* (Basingstoke: Palgrave Macmillan).

Environments

PART ONE

The economic
environment
Dorron Otter

Contents

02

Learning objectives

When you have completed this chapter you will be able to:

- Explore the nature of the economic environment in which business operates
- Examine the extent to which market forces shape and are shaped by business behaviour
- Apply a simple model to analyse how markets work
- Understand the nature of the competing perspectives about the market system and the need for government intervention

Themes

Diversity	**Diversity of business** Despite the variety of business types, economic techniques have been developed that allow us to look at the implications of the economic environment in general whilst also allowing us to focus in on the economic forces that shape individual business behaviour.
Internal/ external	**Internal/external** The internal strategic response of a business is very much dependent on the nature of the external environment in which it operates and in particular to the nature of the market in which it operates.
Complexity	**Complexity of the environment** Critics of economists accuse them of living in 'ivory towers' divorced from reality. However, reality is messy and the only way of making sense of this complexity is to find a vantage point remote from the seeming chaos. This enables the 'big picture' or a macro view to be assessed as well as being able to zoom in on particular areas and put these under a microscope view. These two approaches to looking at economic activity are called **macroeconomics** and **microeconomics**.
Spatial levels	**Variety of spatial levels** The economic environment is felt across all spatial levels. As consumers, workers and owners of resources we are all individual actors in the economic drama. We live in households and the local community and work and study in businesses which involve production processes drawn from the local through to the global. The nature of economic change means that change that occurs in one part of the world can intimately affect people in another.
Dynamic	**Dynamic environment** Change and uncertainty are at the heart of the economic environment and economics explicitly deals with these. What all economic commentators would like to do and what is expected of them is to devise economic crystal balls in order to predict the likely economic future.

Interaction	Interaction between business and the environment

A major issue in economics is the extent to which businesses use resources efficiently in furthering their own objectives and the affect that this then has on the external environment.

Stakeholders	Stakeholders

There is a potential conflict between the goals of the firm and the efficiency with which it uses resources. Which interests should business serve? Those of the owners of the business or the wider stakeholders affected by its activity?

Values	Values

Economics is centrally concerned with values; in the sense of the prices and costs of goods and services, values in the sense of 'value for money' and values in the sense of who benefits from the use of the resources. Just as with beauty, value is in the eye of the beholder and there may be differences in the value that different stakeholders place on the activity of the business.

> **⮎ Stop and Think**
> A manager may decide to cut costs by laying off some workers to improve the value of the company. How will the workers who lose their jobs see the value of this?

Introduction

There is one central debate concerning the nature of the economic environment in which business activity can flourish. Should businesses be left to be free to pursue their own private objectives or to what extent should governments intervene to ensure that business goals serve the interests of the wider society? This chapter outlines the contribution that economics makes in developing the efficiency criteria by which we can assess the impact of business and investigates the relative advantages and disadvantages of the economic systems that could be adopted to set the economic environment. In capitalist countries the preferred means of conducting business behaviour is through the market system and we will explore what this means and will also develop the market model that allows business behaviour in individual markets to be analysed. However, as we will see there are many cases where markets fail to achieve efficient outcomes and so governments need to intervene. We explore the general case for this leaving it to Chapter 6 to explore the way in which modern economies are managed. We will also see that in the modern world the economic environment is not confined within the borders of one country but involves economic links between countries and regions. These links will be explored at the European level in Chapter 9 and at the global level in Chapter 12.

Describing the economic environment

Economics is the study of how human beings seek to use resources to satisfy the whole range of their needs, wants and desires. In order to satisfy these we need resources. The economic environment is the source of these and we can group resources together into four categories.

Labour

Labour is that proportion of the population engaged in production. This will include anyone who produces anything, newspaper girls and boys through to the chief executive of a multinational company. Work such as caring for children or other dependents, housework or voluntary work can also take place without being paid work. This does not mean there is no value in it. For any business it is not just the quantity of the available labour supply that is important but its quality. The major influence on this is the extent to which education and training can improve labour productivity.

Land

This refers to all 'natural resources' and can be everything on the ground, underground, the sea, under the sea, the air, anything in the air, the sun, wind, etc. As we shall see in Chapter 15 there is increasing attention paid to the realization that many of these resources are 'non-renewable' and that the pursuit of short-term material prosperity is now becoming 'unsustainable'.

Capital

These are resources in the form of machinery, tools and factories. Capital goods are required to produce the final goods/services that people want. A major issue here is the extent to which technology can lead to big gains in production from investment in capital.

Enterprise

For many the entrepreneur is the key person without whom production would not take place. It is s/he who mobilizes resources to produce goods and services and we can view enterprise as the decision making process. Great attention is now paid on how to create a 'climate for enterprise' or an entrepreneurial environment or culture and this is explored in Chapter 14.

Developing the economic problem

Chapter 1 showed that at any moment in time there will be a limit to how many resources are available. There are 'resource constraints'.

Commodities

Anything that satisfies a need, desire or want is defined as a commodity. To produce commodities, resources are combined in the production process. The economy can be likened to the restaurant business. The capital is the physical restaurant and kitchen and the equipment that goes with this. Labour and raw materials are combined as if in a giant food mixer. The chefs are the entrepreneurs who make the decisions about how to produce the infinite menus that people may want and out of the kitchen come the meals requested.

But there are problems. Not everyone can get a seat. Some will go hungry. Many of the diners would like to request more expensive items but cannot afford them. In reality we are all aware of the problem facing the economy, society and each one of us. We would like more commodities to be produced for us. You would like more books, more DVDs, heating, food and indeed even time to do everything you want to do.

We live in a world of scarcity and in the words of one of the Rolling Stones' most famous songs, 'You can't always get what you want'. It appears that the demand for resources is insatiable. Even if we are fortunate to live in relatively prosperous national economic environments we still would like more. The media in most countries is dominated by stories of the seemingly limitless desires of the rich and famous and there seems to be no end to their spending and yet even they do not appear to be perfectly happy. If those with so much still have never ending needs and desires what about the rest of those whose command over resources is not so great and the vast mass of humanity who live in the developing world able to consume resources of no more than $1 a day? The economic environment is a hard one in that we are presented with a single inescapable fact that whilst there are limitless needs and wants from those of us that demand resources, the supply of these resources is limited.

The problem then is not simply that it appears that resources are constrained. If that was all then perhaps we could live with that. The more serious problem is that resources are limited in relation to people's needs/wants/desires.

At least then it appears that there can be certainty in economics. If scarcity is the 'fundamental fact of life' then it is more than likely that there will be a host of subsidiary facts of life that can be taught to people so that they can understand the nature of the economic environment in which they live. This is the heart of the economic problem and the starting point of all economic analysis. Economics does no more than study in detail the problems caused by this problem of scarcity.

Figure 2.1 develops the economic problem as outlined in Chapter 1. It is business that converts the resources into commodities but businesses have their own goals. To what extent does business behaviour bring about economic efficiency?

Let us first examine what economists would define as economic efficiency. This single inescapable fact entails three subsidiary problems and hard choices need to be made.

1. Allocation problem

If there are insufficient resources to satisfy every need/want then somehow decisions have to be made as to what to produce. In the box in Figure 2.1 are the limited resources. Outside in the vortex of economic space lie the infinite needs and wants which, just like the real universe, keep on

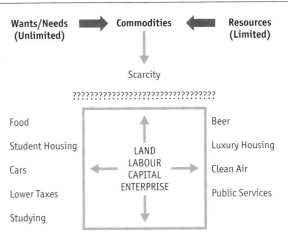

Figure 2.1 The business in its economic environment

For every choice there is an opportunity cost and the economy has to decide three things:

Allocation decision—what to produce (and not to produce)? Will the economy produce the 'right' things and minimize opportunity costs?

Production decision—how to produce? Will the goods be produced so as to produce maximum quality with minimum resource use? Will productivity be maximized so that average costs are minimized but output per unit of resource is maximized?

Distribution decision—who to give it to? Will the goods be distributed in a 'fair' way, i.e. maximizing **equity**?

Will economic decisions be efficient?

expanding. How can the resource-poor economy decide which voices to listen to out of the never ending demands which we put upon it?

> **⊃ Stop and Think: One simple business decision?**
>
> Let us simplify this rather mind-boggling picture. Picture a certain amount of labourers, raw materials, production decision makers and machinery which together cost £1m. You can decide what you want these resources to do for the next six months. Here are three ideas for you to consider:
>
> 1 These resources could be used to modernize private student houses with grants of up to £5,000 per house. Potentially 200 houses could be improved
>
> 2 A new state of the art lecture theatre complex could be built for £1m
>
> 3 Four luxury 5 bed-roomed detached houses in an affluent suburb of the city could be built at a cost of £250,000 each.

Whichever decision you make costs £1 million but it is the owners of the resources and the users of whatever is built that will benefit from this. There are however other real costs in your decision without corresponding benefits. Let's say option 3 is chosen. The real cost to the economy is not £1m but the lost opportunities of options 1 and 2. Once 3 is chosen then the chance of employing these resources to build 1 and 2 in the next six months is lost forever. Now of course we are unreasonable if we say that the real cost of the four houses is option 1 and 2 because you couldn't do both these. Instead we define this cost, this **opportunity cost**, as the cost of the next most desired alternative. There are opportunities that have been lost as a result of deciding that resources should be used in a particular way.

Business students need to be aware of the significance of opportunity cost. Students of today will be the decision makers of tomorrow. Decisions mean selecting between alternatives. When any decision is being made about resource use the full range of options has to be considered. Business managers have to live with the reality that any decision they make has costs in terms of the opportunities that have been lost as a result of this decision.

So how can we judge if allocative decisions are taken correctly?

If people are prepared to pay over and above the costs of having the commodity produced including a reasonable profit margin for the entrepreneur then we could argue that more of the commodity should be produced. However, if people are not prepared to pay a price which covers all of the costs then it could be argued that less should be produced.

The economy gets it right when the production of the commodity continues so that the price of the last or marginal unit we pay covers its costs of production sufficient to give the entrepreneur a satisfactory or normal level of profit. Economists refer to this cost as the marginal cost and if prices equate to this marginal cost of producing the commodity we can argue that businesses are allocating resources efficiently or in other words giving consumers value for money.

Any decision will be the right one if the marginal benefit of implementing it is greater than its marginal cost. We might reasonably expect that businesses operate in an economic environment which encourages them to give value for money to their customers. However, especially for privately owned businesses will this be how they act? Businesses will produce commodities so that they can make profits but will this be in such as way as to give consumers 'value for money'?

2. The production problem

How does the economy organize the production of the chosen commodity? Given that resources are scarce businesses should produce the maximum output of the highest quality for the minimum resource use or input. This is referred to as **productive efficiency**. If resource costs are minimized so must be the opportunity costs.

Any firm is being productively efficient if it produces a level of output at which the cost of all units, the average cost, is minimized. We need to carefully examine the ideal economic environment that would lead to such productive efficiency.

3. The distribution problem

When the economy has decided what to produce, and how, it must decide who gets it.

Values

This means that we ought to have a clear set of criteria for judging distributive efficiency or what can be variously described as equity, fairness or justice. In reality such judgements are all too often coloured by our value judgements. As we shall see very often there can appear to be a conflict between efficiency in allocation and production and people's views as to appropriate distributive justice.

This then makes any judgement of the role of business in the wider economic environment very complex, as if we are to judge business efficiency in its wider context we must relate this to these three aspects of efficiency. For private sector firms it is likely that it is only productive efficiency that will be uppermost in their mind and even here they may be more concerned to raise prices than cut costs. In the pursuit of profit it may well be that there is a conflict between how the business views its efficient operation and how society judges it. 'People before profit' is a cry often heard from critics of business with popular campaigns against the perceived irresponsible behaviour of businesses. Chapter 7 explores this in more detail.

Complexity

The economic problem then is easily defined but incredibly complex to solve. Every day millions of economic decisions have to be made regarding allocation, production and distribution. Given the vastness of this problem and the millions of competing claims for resource use and resource consumption as well as the variety of methods of producing commodities, it is not surprising that many people will not be satisfied with how these decisions are made.

Efficiency

For a business to be judged to be efficient in its impact we need to measure it in relation to the three parts of the economic problem.

Allocative efficiency: is it producing so that consumers are getting value for money? They are paying just the right amount of money to cover all the costs of the business whilst allowing the business to make a reasonable profit.

Productive efficiency: the level of output is such that the average cost of each item produced is minimized.

Distributive efficiency: the output is distributed in a 'fair' or equitable way.

Three important concepts

Opportunity cost and economic efficiency are two key concepts when exploring the economic environment of business.

We have also referred to the concept of marginality. In the economic environment, decisions about what to produce, how and for whom are constantly made. Any decision to be taken is by definition something to be decided next. We can only be sure that this is the best decision if we can prove that it is better than any other decision that could have been made.

Businesses are always operating at the margin. As we shall see they always have to react to changes in market conditions. The question is what is the best decision to make next and here we always must consider if the marginal benefit of doing this outweighs the marginal cost compared to the alternatives.

It might well be that in the past certain activities have meant that the production of commodities has been on the basis that benefits have outweighed costs but there can come a point where increases in production increase costs (e.g. if it expands above the capacity constraints available) and then costs rise above benefits. In this case it may well be that the business could make a big difference to its profits by a small reduction in its output.

Mini-Case 2.1 Marginal benefits vs. marginal costs

Consider the problem of road traffic congestion. The problem is not that people drive cars but that at certain times there is too much traffic and the traffic slows to a standstill. If we can marginally reduce the number of cars on the road then traffic flow eases and many of the problems of congestion are eased. Chapter 15 shows how more fully.

Consider the drinking of alcohol and other so called 'economic bads'. Medical advice is not against drinking but against drinking too much. Many people will have experienced the inefficiency of having exceeded their margins the morning after the night before. If people simply cut back on drinking, smoking, eating too much salt, fatty foods, etc., and did a bit more exercise then they would dramatically improve the quality of their lives. In business, marginal changes can have maximum results!

1 If you decide not to go to your next business class what decision have you made about the marginal benefit of not going compared to the marginal benefit that you might gain if you did? What is then the marginal cost of not attending this seminar?

2 How could your tutor persuade you not to skip further classes?

3 In general terms if a business decides to opt for decision A as opposed to decision B what must it have assumed to be the relative marginal benefit and marginal costs of A as opposed to B?

Road traffic congestion: marginal changes can achieve maximum results.

© istockphoto.com

Perspectives on the economic environment

Values

The central objective of this section is to analyse the ways in which economic decisions could be taken. The answer is complicated for two reasons:

1 The private goals of a business and its shareholders may conflict with the three-fold definition of efficiency outlined above.

2 What is the best environment which will cause business to operate efficiently?

Consider Figure 2.2: What do you see? Some of you will see a picture of a young woman, some an old one. Some of you will see both. Some of you will wonder why these images have been included. The same pictures but four different responses and for those of you that see the young woman you will not be able to immediately understand why people are seeing an old woman and vice versa. For those of you that see both you will smile knowingly and for those of you who can't see the point you will wonder what this has to do with the economic environment! The same factual information is presented and yet we have four different perspectives!

Economics begins with scarcity. All economists agree. But what do they agree on? What do they mean by scarcity?

> ### ➲ Stop and Think
>
> Consider the following statements:
>
> *Definition 1*
> - We will never satisfy all our wants and needs because they are infinite and resources are finite.
>
> *Definition 2*
> - We can improve standards of living through economic growth by using resources more efficiently.
>
> *Definition 3*
> - Inequality means that resources are used to satisfy the needs of the rich at the expense of the poor.
>
> *Definition 4*
> - Resources are finite. Economic growth must be sustainable and not exploitative.
>
> ❷ With which of these statements do you most agree?

Figure 2.2 Young/old woman

This famous figure was published in 1915 in *Puck*, an American humour magazine, and is credited to British cartoonist W. E. Hill. It is likely though that he in turn adapted this from an image that was popularly used on trading cards in the 18th and 19th centuries.

Source: Hill, W. E. 'My wife and my mother-in-law'. *Puck*, 10 (11) Nov. 1915.

There are competing views as to the ideal way of creating an economic environment that will allow businesses to operate efficiently and these views can be derived from the differing views of scarcity above. We can broadly distinguish four main schools of economic thought:

- a free-market or neoclassical view
- an interventionist or structuralist view
- a radical or Marxist view
- a Green or environmentalist view.

The end-of-chapter case study tracks these perspectives as applied to one important business: that of providing food, and Chapter 4 relates these perspectives to the political differences between 'left' and 'right'.

The economic environment has changed throughout history and accompanying such changes has been the development of these competing perspectives as to the 'ideal' economic environment in which business can prosper and grow.

Adam Smith was introduced in Chapter 1 and is widely regarded as the first person to rigorously explore the impact of the economic environment on business. Smith's central concern was to explain why British business was growing so rapidly in the 18th century. For Smith the answer lay in a fundamental change in the political and economic environment. This change saw the decline of the feudal system of agricultural production where the aristocracy and nobility controlled the land and labour forces and where the power of the central government stifled individual enterprise and severely limited the development of free markets. What emerged in the 18th century was a capitalist system where initially individual capitalist farmers exploited market opportunities to earn vast fortunes which they invested in industrial production thus giving rise to the industrial revolution.

Interaction

The section below summarizes the operation and advantages of a capitalist economic environment based on the market system and the price mechanism and relates this to the concept of efficiency.

The price mechanism

Allocative efficiency

The entrepreneur takes a risk by putting a product on the market and is motivated by the desire to further his/her own self-interest by earning a profit and this is the incentive for taking the risk.

Consumers have the ultimate power over the use of resources because they signal their desire as to what should be produced by their willingness to pay the price. If they do not want the product the price will quickly fall and the commodity will not be produced. If demand is high then prices will rise and more resources will be used by the entrepreneur to produce that commodity. In this way resources are allocated in accordance with consumers' preferences. They signal these by casting their economic votes in favour of the commodities they want simply by buying them. Economists refer to this as consumer sovereignty. People are rational and seek to maximize their satisfaction from their purchases.

Productive efficiency

Neither under/overproduction persists because price will either rise or fall in response so matching supply and demand. **Competition** and the profit motive combine to ensure that producers have the incentive to produce what consumers want and to produce quality and at lowest cost. Competition ensures that costs are always held low and that we get innovation and economic growth with profits being reinvested. Consumers are guaranteed choice and variety.

If the entrepreneur continues to make profits above a normal level then new entrepreneurs will come into the market so increasing supply and lowering price. This competition will also ensure that firms try to steal the competitive edge by innovation.

Distributive efficiency

Distribution of commodities is strictly on the basis of ability to pay. In order to improve this people now have an incentive to work hard and develop skills needed in the labour market or indeed become risk takers themselves. Potentially the rewards for risk taking can be very high but of course many businesses can fail. For most people income comes from labour and so if you want more from the market you have to secure a rewarding job. Owners of land and capital will seek to deploy these resources to get the best return.

The circle is complete. In order to better yourself you have the incentive to engage yourself in activities in turn dictated by the needs of commodity markets. The highest rewards are where demand is strongest and where businesses and resource owners are able to gain a competitive advantage.

All of this is achieved without any conscious intervention by an external agency. The market system is a brilliant coordinating device bringing together the millions of consumers with producers. Price is the invisible hand of the market mechanism.

Neoclassical economics

This is the classical perspective on the nature of capitalism. The keys to economic efficiency lie in quantifying the rules that underpin the effective functioning of the price mechanism. If prices are free to find their own level, then the correct signals will be sent to the economy ensuring an efficient allocation, production and distribution of commodities. The next major development in the formation of this perspective was the use of marginal analysis to identify the relationships which were thought to be the necessary pre-conditions to achieve efficiency. These ideas were developed in the early 20th century and formed the bedrock on which most textbook economic theory is founded. Students of economics are introduced to the market model where the influences on demand and supply can be studied and where general market models can then be applied to individual markets and predictions made.

It is clear from the above that a vital role is played by the external environment. It is the environment of a free market system that provides the bedrock for businesses to grow and prosper. However, what happens if the free market does not operate in such a free manner? Smith himself was very conscious that an obstacle to such an efficient operation would be if monopoly power were to exist and prevent competition. He was also aware that private businesses might not be prepared to take long term investment decisions even though they would yield public benefits for future generations. In many such projects the initial investment spending could be large. This outlay would not be paid back for many years into the future and so governments would need to undertake these.

Interaction

The case for government intervention

For a whole range of markets it is clear that the 'invisible hand' as outlined by Adam Smith will be sufficient to bring about economic efficiency, and for many businesses it should be markets alone that determine the external economic environment, and their role is to be left free to determine their strategic response to the market environment.

Interventionists or structuralists argue that for markets to work there needs to be institutions (or structures) that ensure that obstacles that may distort these markets do not occur. Governments need to intervene to ensure that competition is safeguarded and this will require a robust legal and regulatory system. They also see a wide range of circumstances in which markets might not serve the interest either of business or the wider stakeholders affected by businesses. Many of these were indeed explicitly recognized by Smith and comprise what we refer to today as **market failure**.

Interaction

The section below summarizes the areas in which markets can fail.

Disadvantages of the market system

Allocation

Merit Goods: there are goods that you might argue all people should have irrespective of their income. While we may disagree as to exactly what goes on this list we could say that there is a consensus in the modern world that all people should have shelter, heating, clean water, adequate nutrition, law and order, education and health. If we leave such things to the market many people may be priced out of the markets for these goods and so it is argued that the state should ensure that everyone has some basic access to these.

Public Goods: some goods cannot be supplied via markets because it is impossible to provide one person with them without excluding others, e.g. street lighting, defence, fire services. Here if people were allowed to opt out of paying then they would still benefit from those who did pay and it would be unfair if this was so or indeed may endanger anyone wanting to pay.

Externalities: market prices reflect the individual cost to the business and the benefit gained from the product. However, many economic activities have social benefits above the benefit to the user, e.g. in the case of health and education, the benefits of a healthy and educated population benefit society as a whole as healthy and educated people are more productive as workers and demand less spending by the state. On the other hand many activities have social costs beyond the user, e.g. cigarettes, cars or the producer. Of increased concern is the environmental impact of climate change brought on by our consumption and production behaviour. Without government intervention such costs/benefits would not be accounted for.

Production

- Many markets are dominated by monopolies. There will be a real possibility of exploitation of the consumer, suppliers and employees and a wasteful use or environmentally damaging use of resources as firms seek to minimize direct costs.
- Often such monopoly power is attained by using unfair anti-competitive practices but sometimes there are industries in which the most efficient scale of organization would be to just have one company, i.e. a **natural monopoly**. Can these be safely left to private firms?
- Competition can sometimes be highly damaging, e.g. if it leads to diminishing safety standards, and this is referred to as **destructive competition**.
- Markets can be very unstable and create uncertainty. Individual markets have a tendency to be unstable, e.g. agriculture and the economy as a whole can go through severe ups and downs.
- Provision of some projects requires huge outlays of capital that a private firm could not hope to recoup. The channel tunnel is a recent example of such a project as is the debate about how best to provide nuclear power stations. The capital costs and the provision for the needed decommissioning costs of these are so huge that people are sceptical that private businesses can afford these.
- Markets have a short term future and want to 'get rich quick'. Economic decisions sometimes require longer planning.

Distribution

Market systems lead to great inequalities of income and wealth. These inequalities may not reflect the rewards earned by people in their productive capacity but may reflect self-perpetuating social inequalities and barriers. One reason may be the persistence of inheritance and the class system or the power of certain groups over others.

Furthermore inequality distorts the whole basis of the economic system. The economic problem becomes circular with the demands of the rich determining what should be produced. A free market system will then reinforce inequality and make it difficult for the less advantaged to either get what they need or make their way in society.

Competing critiques—the need to acknowledge the modern nature of capitalism

Interventionists or structuralists argue that given these structural weaknesses in many areas of market activity there is need for government intervention in the running of the economy. Such approaches are many and varied, but attempt to devise a system that recognizes the inequalities created by the expansion of capitalism, the problems of operating the market in that context and the inherent instability of the market itself. Socialists and Marxists focus on the political and economic inequality and argue that all this can only be lessened within a framework of extensive common ownership or greater controls on business and the owners and managers of them. Within these traditions emphasis is placed on the degree to which businesses can exploit both consumers and employees.

In the late 19th and early 20th century it was clear that many industries were becoming dominated by powerful monopoly interests. Further, such a tendency was becoming intensified as the market economies of the west internationalized and under the protection of colonialization. This spotlighted not only internal differences in economic power but international economic power relationships too, with fears that people in the colonies were being exploited. Within the heartland of Europe economic rivalry between countries had its counterpart in political tensions that caused Europe to lead the world into two catastrophic wars.

During the 1920s and 1930s the capitalist world appeared to enter a terminal crisis. The depth of the interwar recession and the disruption of world trade were severe. This at a time when the Soviet Union was experiencing impressive rates of economic growth and using an economic system that sought to replace the market with extensive government control. Mini-Case 2.2 outlines how this economic system tried to operate and the problems that subsequently occurred.

The experience of western capitalism in the early 20th century convinced many that while they might not agree with the Marxist analysis of the problems of capitalism and while they didn't feel that substantial rejection of the market as happened in the USSR in 1917 was the answer, nevertheless capitalism could not simply be 'left to the market'.

The growth of the labour movement to try and have a say in the running of state power coupled with a certain amount of middle-class angst about the condition of the working class built up the pressures to change the way economies were run. The vast ranks of the poor, the dispossessed, the unemployed, the sick or other disadvantaged could not compete in the market and there were increasing calls for the intervention of the state to correct these deficiencies. At the supranational level it was argued that the countries of Europe needed to cooperate in such a way as to ensure that competition led to mutual advantage and at the global level it was recognized that if capitalism was to continue then there would need to be intervention at this level as well.

Spatial levels

The most famous economist of this time was J. M. Keynes. Keynes argued that there is no automatic tendency for market systems to produce short term full employment. What was needed was a concerted attempt by government to manage the economy in such a way as to achieve these goals. There was also a realization that the increased internationalization of economic activity required a system of regulation for international trade. What has been called the Keynesian Welfare Consensus dominated the economic environment in the western world from 1945 until the mid 1970s when a series of short term crises coupled with deeper seated long term problems led to a resurgence of the belief from the neoclassical perspective that the pendulum against the free market had swung too far and that the role of the state had to be 'rolled back'. We will explore this in more detail in Chapter 6.

The battleground for the competing perspectives is fought over this central issue of the degree and manner in which governments should intervene in the running of an economy. What is clear

Mini-Case 2.2 Command economies

In centrally planned or command economies the state decided the three parts of the economic problem. In the soviet system priority was given to industrialization as the best way of achieving economic growth and food production to feed the new urban populations. In order to achieve its goals the state 'collectivized' agriculture by banning the private ownership of farms and taking them into public ownership and took direct control of industrialization through central planning.

In order to administer the system a huge planning bureaucracy developed to set production targets for every industry and factory. The targets were set by agencies at a national, regional and local level. This involved developing sophisticated input/output analysis to ensure that factories got the resources needed and in the necessary quantities.

Distribution priorities were decided by the state. The overall priority was industrial goods at the expense of consumer items

The main reason so many GDR citizens came streaming through the Berlin Wall in 1991 was not to find 'freedom' but to find the freedom to shop till they dropped.
© Getty Images

and it was seen as vital that basic consumer goods should take priority over 'luxuries'. Within this system there was little room for prices. Factories were paid according to whether they hit their pre-agreed targets and consumer prices were largely irrelevant. The price of basic consumer items was very low. This meant that workers often built up large savings. In a market system this would find its way into luxury consumption. In the soviet style economies the role of the market was limited and distorted. In the former German Democratic Republic formed in the eastern part of Germany after the end of the Second World War, plenty of people had the money to buy the much sought after 'Trabbie' (Trabant motor car) but they had to wait on average ten years to acquire one. In such situations black market activity flourished.

Such systems can have enormous benefits especially if the goals of the planners coincide with the wishes of the people. In Britain, the Second World War saw one of the purest forms of planning ever seen. The state controlled all aspects of economic and even social life to boost war production and people had to put up with rationing and shortages. In the former soviet style economies, income was much more equally distributed and priority was given to basic necessities. Education and health and child care were safeguarded and public transport systems, the arts and sport were all heavily supported by subsidy. One should not underestimate the degree to which the people of these countries did feel that their systems scored over 'the west'.

However, it should be easy for you to deduce the problems that such systems experienced by referring back to the advantages of the market system.

There was a dearth of choice of goods for consumers. The main reason so many GDR citizens came streaming through the Berlin Wall in 1991 was not to find 'freedom' but to find the freedom to shop till they dropped. Not only was there simply not the sheer choice available but the quality of many goods was poor. In production, planning mistakes were inevitable and the lack of a profit motive meant that often more effort was put into achieving the target (or pretending that it had been achieved) than in ensuring high quality with low costs. Lack of prices meant that no one was accountable for costs and so often outdated methods of production were used. Managers often pressed for softer targets and often disguised the real capacity potential of their enterprises to have an easy life.

In terms of distribution the low standard of living meant that workers did not have the incentive to work and the lack of profits, rent and interest meant that innovation and invention were difficult to achieve. The lack of unemployment and the lack of bankruptcy meant that workers and managers alike had no pressure to work harder. In the end the problems of this type of planning overcame the system and following the attempt to reform the soviet system from within by Gorbachev in the 1980s the soviet economic and political system collapsed, ushering in the era of the transition to capitalism in many of the former command economies.

❷ How might the lack of a profit motive affect the motivation of business managers?

❷ What are the advantages and disadvantages of having an economic system that tries to produce greater equality?

is that in capitalist economic systems there is a large role across a range of microeconomic and macroeconomic policy areas. In terms of microeconomic management governments seek to intervene directly and indirectly in markets in a large number of ways. Most clearly many governments take a direct role in the provision of key public services such as health, education and welfare although the influence of the neoclassical perspective has been seen in the wave of **privatizations** that have occurred in many countries, most notably in the UK, and the recent attempts to fund public projects through public/private partnerships. A visit to the websites of any national government will give you an overview of the sheer range of government economic activities (for the UK government see www.hm-treasury.gov.uk).

Despite these differences in approach and notwithstanding that the process of economic growth has not been stable, the long term trend since the middle of the of the 20th century has been for rising prosperity in the more developed countries of the world. However, with this there has been growing concern expressed about the unsustainability of rapid economic growth and a call for a reassessment of prevailing economic models. This green view of economics has rapidly grown so that now throughout the political spectrum and increasingly within business itself there is a call for the need to place sustainable development at the heart of debates about the nature of the economic environment, and we will explore this in Chapter 15.

Markets and how they operate

It is vital for businesses to be able to understand the nature of the market for their products so that they can use this information to their commercial advantage. Microeconomics is fundamentally concerned with developing techniques to understand the operation on individual markets. To build a picture of the individual characteristics of each one would be a nigh on impossible task but the good news is that by using a technique called **equilibrium analysis** we only need build a model surrounding one commodity and see how that market operates and then using the same techniques applied to that market we can apply this to other markets to see how they behave.

Complexity

Dynamic

Spatial levels

Let us examine the operation of the market model by applying this to one commodity alone: the market for one brand of jeans.

Demand and supply

In a market there are consumers who demand the product and suppliers who would like to supply it. The first two questions then are:

- What influences a consumer's decision to demand the product (the determinants of demand)?
- What influences a producer to supply the product (the determinants of supply)?

What are the most likely influences on you if you considered buying a pair of jeans?

Obviously the price of the jeans is the key one but so would be your spending power or **disposable income**, fashion tastes and comfort, the prices and attributes of other types of jeans or trousers in general (or substitute commodities), the cost of going out to socialize (and other such **complementary** activities) and your general confidence in the future and expectations of the future course of prices.

What about the motives of the producer of the jeans? Well for the private business its primary aim is to make a profit and so its willingness to supply will depend on the price level it can get for each pair sold. However, this is not the only influence on supply. The business could supply other types of jeans or different types of product entirely. Profits depend on the costs of the resources that go into production and costs often depend on the state of existing technology. The business may not be a private one and may have other goals other than simply profit maximization and this will affect its production decision. Government policies can also affect business decisions.

We can formalize these guesses in the form of demand and supply functions. These simply encompass all of the possible influences that might affect consumers' decisions to buy a particular commodity or a producer's decision as to whether to supply. Obviously the influences that affect demand and supply will vary from commodity to commodity, person to person, business to business and time period to time period. Nevertheless, it is possible to derive a general model that can apply in varying degrees to all commodities.

There is one important influence or variable that is common to both producers and consumers and this is the price of the product itself. At the very least we can say that this price is a key influence or variable on both supply and demand. Study a general demand function below. This is *not* a mathematical statement but a shorthand summary of influences on demand.

The demand function

Da = f (Pa ⋮ Ps . . . Pc . . . Yd . . . T . . . SF . . . EPs)

where:

Da	the demand for commodity a
f	is a function of, depends on
Pa	the price of commodity a
Ps	the price of substitutes for commodity a
Pc	the price of complements for commodity a
Yd	disposable income
T	tastes
SF	sociological factors: age composition of population, culture
EPs	expectations about future prices, incomes

If we are to understand what will affect the demand for a commodity, we have a problem. There are many things. The approach taken in economics is to imagine that we could isolate each factor in turn and then have a best guess as to how demand would be affected if it were to change and then test if this is the case through empirical research. Just as with demand we can draw up a list of possible influences on supply as below.

The supply function

Sa = f (Pa ⋮ . . . Pbcd . . . Pr . . . Tech . . . Goals . . . GP)

Sa	the supply of commodity a
f	depends on, is a function of
Pa	the price of the commodity itself
Pbcd	the prices of other goods that the firm produces
Pr	price of resources, inputs, costs (labour, denim)
Tech	technology
Goals	goals of the firm
GP	government policy

Complexity

In the real world economic events are constantly changing and so are the variables in both the demand and supply functions. On one level then to try and understand market behaviour in such a complex and ever changing world is impossible and there could be a tendency to give up on the task. However, economic theory tries to develop a technique to make sense of this complex external world by using equilibrium analysis.

Using equilibrium analysis, we can try and at least start somewhere by isolating each factor in turn and seeing how demand and supply in turn would be affected if it were to change. Just as with weather forecasting, economists try to predict market changes. It is important for analysis to be able to ask questions about how economic factors might be related, by assuming that we can isolate the factors and freeze all other things that might affect the relationship. In this way, having established the relationship in isolation, we can then alter other things one at a time to see how our original analysis would be affected. In this way a picture can be built up of the market and how it is likely to react to predicted changes. However, as with weather forecasting the strength of the forecast depends on correctly identifying the likely changes. Provided that these occur in the predicted way then the forecast will be correct. Contrary to popular prejudice most weather forecasts are mostly correct as the meteorological offices have become very sophisticated in terms of gathering information and using their computer models. Forecasts can go wrong. This may not be because the models built were wrong but that an unexpected change occurred. If only that could have been predicted then the forecast would be right.

This is the same in economics and in many ways it is worse since the economic environment is so complex. We can do our best to try and look at all the influences on a market but all too often the unexpected happens and blows our forecast off course. Businesses have to deal with this uncertainty caused by the economic environment.

Let us start with the price of the commodity itself. How would a change in this affect both the demand and supply?

Demand and price

So how will a change in price affect the demand for a commodity? You could, in theory, ask every potential consumer how many pairs of the jeans they might buy in a given time period. In reality it would be impossible, and even if it were possible, in the time you had gathered in all your responses, so many other things would have changed that you could not be sure that all consumers were responding to the same set of constant other factors.

So economists don't do this. They assume that they could ask all consumers at the same time and that as they ask all consumers, all other influences on the demand for the jeans will stay the same, i.e. everything to the right of the dotted line is constant. So we ask our question. Armed with our hypothetical clipboard, we go out into the shopping precinct they call life and say:

> Excuse me Madam/Sir (and don't try running away and/or crossing over the road, because I am an economist and I have assumed you won't), imagine this brand of jeans were selling at the following prices, assuming that nothing else were to change, how many would you buy if the price were £20, £25, etc., etc. in the next few weeks?

Easy, isn't it! Then add up all the responses and you have the market demand curve. Well Table 2.1 saves you the bother and you can imagine that the research has been done for you.

We could illustrate this data diagrammatically. Since we are seeking to look at the effect on demand of a change in price we plot demand on the horizontal axis and price on the vertical one. What does this table or *demand schedule* show us? Simply that if, other things being equal, prices are low, then the demand for jeans will be high and that if prices are high the demand for jeans will be low. Now, of course the figures are hypothetical, but wouldn't this at the very least be a good hunch as to what would happen? Economists do often have to proceed like this. They want to investigate economic behaviour. They make a guess what would be most likely to happen, then make assumptions to isolate the dependent variables and then theorize what might happen. If possible they can then test this theory. You could do so if you want. Take a sample of people entering all jeans shops and ask them the question above. While your figures would be mere estimates, you would come up with the same trend. If people say they will buy a certain amount at a relatively high price they will say that they are going to buy more when prices are lower. They would be odd indeed if they rushed out and bought less if prices were to be less, assuming that all the other influences on demand were the same.

Demand curves

The information in the demand schedule overleaf can be plotted on a graph. Figure 2.3 shows this. The demand curve is downward sloping from left to right.

Table 2.1 The demand schedule

Price (£ per pair)	Demand (000s per month)
20	80
25	70
30	60
35	50
40	40
45	30
50	20
55	10

Figure 2.3 The demand curve

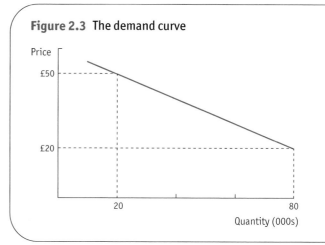

If the original price were £50 the demand would be 20,000 per month. If the price fell to £20 then demand would *increase from 20,000 to 80,000*.

Supply and price

Just as with demand it is likely that a significant variable will be the price that the firm can get for its jeans. Other things being equal, and here an important other is the firm's costs, if price rises, this will mean two things:

- the reason that price is rising is because demand is rising
- rising prices should mean rising profits if more are produced.

The hypothesis is that supply will rise when price rises. On the other hand what if price falls? Here you need to be cautious. A common response is to believe that a business might here try to increase sales to protect revenue.

However, consider this. The reason that price is falling is because consumers are deserting the product. Falling prices mean that profit margins are squeezed. Increasing supply would only make the situation worse! Let us assume that you have done the other half of your market research. You ask the producer what they would supply at the following prices *other things remaining the same*, and the information is displayed in Table 2.2.

Plotting the information below will give Figure 2.4.

Table 2.2 The supply schedule

Price (£)	Supply (000s of pairs per month)
20	0
25	10
30	20
35	30
40	40
45	50
50	60
55	70

Figure 2.4 The supply curve

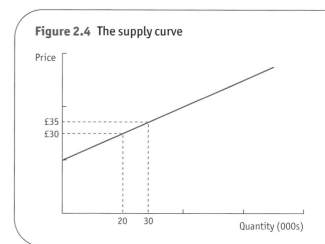

Table 2.3 Equilibrium in the market

Price (£ per pair)	Demand (000s per month)	Supply (000s per month)
20	80	0
25	70	10
30	60	20
35	50	30
40	40	40
45	30	50
50	20	60
55	10	70

Figure 2.5 The equilibrium position

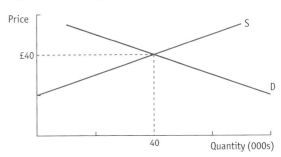

We are now in a position to put the two halves of the market together and analyse market movements. Demand and supply analysis is a very powerful economic technique for making sense of economic changes. Let us return to the original demand and supply schedules. Table 2.3 above combines the demand and supply functions.

We have plotted the separate halves of the market. Now let us put them together as in Figure 2.5.

Remember, the demand curve shows us what consumers will buy at various prices per month. It shows us their preferences, not what they actually buy.

The supply curve shows how many producers will produce per month at various prices. It doesn't tell us what they actually produce.

How then do the suppliers know what to do to match consumer preferences? In reality, they do not have the information as displayed above. They never ring us up at home to ask us what we are going to do! In order to understand how the invisible hand of Adam Smith works the formal framework of demand and supply was developed in the late 19th century. Imagine that the following happens.

Surplus in the market

The producers take a risk and initially decide to produce 60,000 pairs of jeans. In order for them to maximize their profits they want a price of £50 so this is what they charge. However, at that price how many will consumers buy per month? At a price of £50 consumers want 20,000. In Figure 2.6 overleaf we can see that there is a surplus of 40,000 being offered for sale every month.

Producers don't need to ask consumers what is going on. The surplus is immediately registered. To get rid of this surplus retailers will have to lower prices and will be unwilling to give the same price as before to the manufacturers. Thus the price begins to fall on the market. This signals to producers to produce less. If prices fall profits are squeezed and so firms cut back on production. They are hardly going to increase production given the fact that consumers are saying they will not buy so much. Producing such quantities will probably entail high costs per unit. If prices are falling producers will have to reduce output to cut costs.

Now of course the producers will not immediately produce the right amount next time. Even if they cut production to 50,000 and charge a price of £45 they still are faced with a surplus production relative to the demand if prices are £45. As long as there is a surplus, pressures will lead to falling prices. As prices fall suppliers progressively cut back on production and consumers will

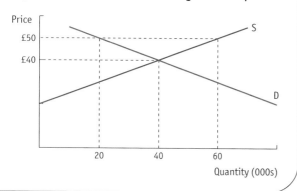

Figure 2.6 Market forces—dealing with a surplus

be prepared to start buying more per month. Eventually, in theory prices will fall to £40. At £40 consumers are willing and able to purchase 40,000 and producers are willing to supply 40,000 as long as they get £40. In this position both consumers and producers are happy. Economists say the market is in equilibrium.

> ### ➲ *Stop and Think*
> Before reading on try and answer the following:
>
> ❓ What would happen if producers initially produced too little, e.g. say they initially produce only 20,000 at a price of £30?
>
> ❓ What would be the imbalance in the market?
>
> ❓ What effect do you think this would have on price?
>
> ❓ How would this affect suppliers and why?
>
> ❓ How will the market rectify this imbalance?

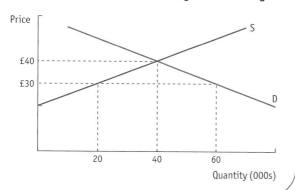

Figure 2.7 Market forces—dealing with a shortage

Shortages in the market

If producers initially produced 20,000, they would expect a price of £30. At this price the goods vanish from the shops like magic. Consumers would be willing to buy 60,000 at that price. See Figure 2.7. Retailers are desperate for new stocks and will be able to raise prices. Rising prices signal to producers to produce more. They will be prepared to incur the higher costs involved because of the higher prices.

Any shortages of goods will result in prices rising and this process will continue till the decisions of producers are in accord with the wishes of consumers, i.e. at the equilibrium point.

Anlaysing market changes: the significance of equilibrium

Internal/ external

Remember that while this theoretical adjustment process is taking place step by step we are assuming that all other things remain constant for both demand and supply. Given the original demand and supply preferences of the market, as long as nothing changes to alter this then equilibrium will be reached. This is a theoretical possibility. The market will have cleared.

In the real world, markets never reach this cosy equilibrium as things are always changing. It is akin to the artist trying to paint the beautifully still millpond. Unfortunately, fish keep jumping and little children keep lobbing in bricks. The artist knows that if only he waits long enough the millpond will be still, but it never quite gets there. The artist gives up and then paints from his imagination and no one is the wiser.

Economists do the same. By assuming that a particular market is in equilibrium, we can then use this possibility to predict the likely effect of dropping bricks into the market. This enables us to predict the effect of any change in market conditions. In the real world it is difficult to unravel the effects of one change in isolation, as lots of things are changing. Equilibrium analysis allows us to do this. Use of this technique can provide you with an invaluable aid to making decisions. All too often decisions are made on the basis of insufficient attention to the many factors that could affect the outcome of the decision. Equilibrium analysis can help you avoid this.

Equilibrium analysis explained

Demand and supply curves show what happens to demand and supply if price changes. Whenever a market is in equilibrium, the only reason for the price to change is if something changes to alter either the demand or supply curves. If this happens then one or other of the curves will shift and we will move towards a new equilibrium. The demand and supply functions show us all the possible causes of these shifts. Using the concept of equilibrium enables you to isolate any possible market change and predict what its effect would be if it alone were to change. It is a powerful tool if used correctly.

Proceeding like this, one change at a time, enables us to analyse the effect of individual changes and then build up a more complex picture of the possible combined effects of these changes. The information below is important as it takes you through the steps that you need to follow to apply equilibrium analysis correctly. Follow these and you have at your finger tips a most powerful marketing tool!

Equilibrium analysis—guidelines for use

Imagine that you want to predict the effect of a change in any market, anywhere, any time.

- Assume that market is initially in equilibrium.
- Introduce the change. The key thing to decide is if it is a change on the demand side or the supply side.
- If it is a change in one of the determinants of demand then the demand curve will shift and we move along the supply curve.
- Will it increase (and shift the demand curve outwards) or decrease (and shift it inwards)?
- If it is a change in one of the determinants of supply then the supply curve will shift and we move along the demand curve.
- Will it increase (and shift upwards) or decrease (and shift downwards)?
- What will now happen to the price and how will the market readjust?
- Compare the new equilibrium to the old. What has been the effect of the change? Will this change now reverberate and effect other markets?

The use of equilibrium analysis can enable you to investigate the likely changes in the external economic environment on any business. One example is illustrated in Mini-Case 2.3.

Understanding the basis of how markets operate is very useful in being able to explain business behaviour and forms the bedrock for many approaches to business strategy.

Interaction

Complexity

Mini-Case 2.3 Levi's

At the beginning of the 1980s Levi's were suffering from a drop in the sales of jeans as people switched to other forms of trousers such as tight black lycra leggings for women and chinos for men. Initially Levi's reacted by trying to diversify into other products such as shirts and shoes but in these markets they faced tough competition. Faced by falling prices for their jeans they sought to change the tastes of consumers by reinventing or reinvigorating the brand. They relaunched the original jean label and really reinforced the then dormant name of Levi 501s. In 1985 in a television advert broadcast in the UK, model Nick Kamen stripped down to his white boxer shorts in a launderette to the tune of Marvin Gaye's 'I Heard it Through the Grapevine'. This is estim-ated to have increased sales of Levi 501s by 800% as well as inadvertently launching a preference for British men to wear boxer shorts as their chosen underwear! (*partial source*: www.aber.ac.uk/media/Modules/MC30820/launderette.html)

1 Using equilibrium analysis shows how the downward shift in the demand curve for Levi jeans as a result of the initial shift in tastes affected the price and sales of Levi jeans.

2 Using the new equilibrium as your starting point now shows how the success of the advertising campaign was able to reverse this shift. What has happened to price and sales now?

When Levi's used model Nick Kamen in his boxer shorts to advertise their jeans, sales of Levi 501s are said to have increased by 800%.

© Image courtesy of The Advertising Archives

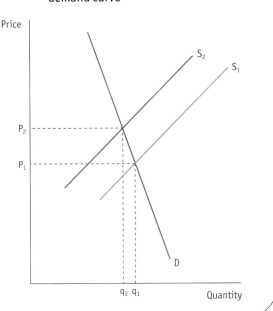

Figure 2.8 Shift in supply with a relatively inelastic demand curve

Figure 2.9 Shift in supply with a relatively elastic demand curve

Market power

So far we have developed a model that will enable us to predict with confidence the effect of any individual change in any market on the price and output of the firm in question.

However, what we cannot yet say is whether the change is a significant one for the business. When measuring the extent of these changes we must define 'lot' or 'little' to get a sense of proportion. Thus when measuring the extent of the changes in the market we use percentages. Price elasticity (see price elasticity of demand) is the measure we use to assess the extent of market changes.

Going back to our market model, if there is a given shift in the supply curve the impact of this on price and output will depend on the slope of the demand curve. Study the small shift in supply in Figures 2.8 and 2.9, both drawn to the same scale.

In Figure 2.8 as a result of the shift in supply from S_1 to S_2 there is a relatively large rise in price but a relatively small fall in demand. The same shift in Figure 2.9 produces the same change in direction of price and quantity but here there is relatively small rise in price and a relatively large fall in demand.

> **➲ Stop and Think**
> If you were a manager of a company in these markets which market would you prefer to be operating in if, for example, there was a rise in costs?

The reason for the different outcomes of the same market change in the above is because there is a different elasticity of demand in each case. Elasticity of demand measures the responsiveness of demand to changes in price. Does demand stretch by a relatively large amount or a little?

To calculate the price elasticity of demand the following formula is used:

$$\frac{\text{Percentage change in the quantity demanded}}{\text{Percentage change in price}}$$

E.g. if price changes by 1% does demand change by more than 1%, less than 1%, or is there a 0% change? The possibilities are summarized below.

The three degrees of price elasticity of demand

If the percentage change in demand is greater than the percentage change in price, i.e. price elasticity of demand (Ped) is greater than 1 then we say that it is relatively elastic:

Ped $= > -1$

If the percentage change in demand is less than the percentage change in price, i.e. price elasticity of demand is less than 1 then we say that it is relatively inelastic:

Ped $= < -1$

If the percentage change in demand is the same as the percentage change in price, i.e. price elasticity of demand is 1 then we say that it is unitary elastic:

Ped $= -1$

NB: the sign is -1 because of the inverse relationship between price and demand. The revenue of a firm is calculated as follows:

Revenue = Price $\times$ units sold

Let us see why the elasticity of demand facing a product is very important and will have a great effect on determining the effect on revenue of changes in market conditions. Consider the following cases where the demand is *elastic*, e.g. -2.

Imagine that a market change results in price rising by 5% but demand falling by 10%. If one half of our revenue formula rises by 5% but the other falls by 10% then overall revenue will have fallen.

Imagine that a market change results in price falling by 5% but demand rising by 10%. If one half of our revenue formula falls by 5% but the other rises by 10% then overall revenue will have risen.

In both these cases the demand is elastic but when price rises revenue falls and when price falls revenue rises. Consider the following cases where the demand is *inelastic*, e.g. -0.2.

Imagine that the price rises by 5% but demand falls by 1%—in this case revenue will rise.

Imagine that price falls by 5% but demand rises by 1%—in this case revenue falls.

Of course if elasticity of demand was unitary then a small change in price would have no change on revenue. The effect of elasticity on revenue is summarized below:

price	elasticity	revenue
rises	elastic	falls
rises	inelastic	rises
falls	elastic	rises
falls	inelastic	falls

One of the main determinants on elasticity of demand is the number of substitutes available for the product or the degree of competition that the product faces. If a business is operating in a market in which there is little or no competition then the elasticity of demand will be highly inelastic. If, on the other hand there is a high degree of competition then the elasticity of demand will be relatively elastic. The degree of elasticity of demand is thus hugely important for businesses.

If markets are competitive, as is assumed by the neoclassical perspective, the behaviour of firms will be to try and cut prices and costs so as to increase revenue and profits. It is likely that this economic environment will encourage businesses to be allocatively and productively efficient. If the existing number of firms is too few and each one is making considerable profits then providing that there are no barriers to entry other firms will enter the market and drive down prices. If resource markets are competitive the same thing should happen with owners of resources receiving fair incomes and so equity should be achieved.

However, if markets are not competitive the reverse will happen. Businesses will seek to push prices up and restrict their outputs. In so doing they will earn more revenue and higher profits. They will not be so interested in cutting costs as they can simply raise prices. It is likely that profits will be excessive and so allocative and productive efficiency will not be attained even though the firm is highly profitable. There will be a clear conflict here between the goals of the firm and the wishes of the wider stakeholders. In resource markets owners of resources can exploit their monopoly power to raise their incomes leading to income inequality.

Therefore a major characteristic of the economic environment is the degree to which it is a competitive environment, and where it is not the government has to play a role in ensuring that business does not exploit its potential monopoly power.

Income elasticity of demand

While changes in prices can exert short term changes on the profits of businesses, long term effects can be felt depending on the way in which consumers in a market react to changes in incomes. In the long term incomes in developing countries tend to rise. Income elasticity of demand measures the sensitivity of demand to changes in income. If as income rises demand rises by a greater percentage then the income elasticity of demand is elastic. If it rises but by a lower percentage then the income elasticity of demand is inelastic.

Another influence on firms, apart from the nature of the competitive environment which they are in, is the nature of the product that they produce. We can distinguish between three main types of business activity:

- *Primary*: mining, fuel extraction, farming, forestry
- *Secondary*: manufacturing
- *Services*: retailing, marketing, finance, travel.

In general, as economies grow the proportion of income spent on primary goods tends to decrease and that spent on manufacturing and especially services tends to increase. This can make life difficult for primary producers unless they can find ways of increasing market power through restricting competition.

We are witnessing for the first time in history a significant change in where in the world people live. We are now seeing the proportion of people living in urban areas just increasing ahead of those in rural areas. For most of human history the majority of people have been agricultural workers. Rural producers face enormous structural problems in markets and are often the poorest members of society in the absence of government intervention. A major cause of their problems is to be found in the fact that both the price elasticity of demand and income elasticity of demand for agricultural products is very low.

Figure 2.8 above can be used to illustrate one aspect of this structural problem. Imagine that the market illustrated is the world market for cotton and the initial equilibrium is $P_2 q_2$ with the original demand and supply curves being S_2 and D. Now let us assume that as a result of more efficient production world cotton supply shifts to S_1. Whilst this should be a cause for celebration we can see that the effect of this increase in supply is to actually lower the income gained from cotton!

It was to solve this problem that agricultural policy in America and Europe has been designed to provide minimum prices for farmers (in Europe through the Common Agricultural Policy).

The income elasticity of demand for agricultural goods gets more inelastic over time. This means that farmers need help to diversify and in some cases to move out of agriculture altogether.

© Robert Holmes/Corbis

For many farmers in the developing world their governments lack the funds to undertake similar support policies.

In the longer term, as economic growth raises living standards, people spend proportionally less on agricultural goods and more on manufactures or service goods. The income elasticity of demand for agricultural goods gets more inelastic over time. This means that farmers need help to diversify and in some cases to move out of agriculture altogether. Again in the developed world such assistance is available for farmers but this is not the case in the poorer countries.

⟨⊙⟩ *Looking ahead*

It is better not to talk of capitalism as such but as a variety of capitalisms across the world linked together through trade and with various attempts to regulate this trading system both nationally and internationally. Nationally, capitalism differs from country to country with each system trying to manage the mix between market and state in its own way. In Scandinavia a highly successful system of capitalism developed with extensive state provision of welfare services. In Germany a particular Christian/social democratic consensus developed a social market economy which is arguably still the most successful in Europe. The USA, which is often seen as the prime example of free enterprise, has an enormous government deficit and the government is active in the running of the economy and society.

Since the 1960s the fastest growing economies in the world have been the Asian Tigers in the Far East. While neoclassical economists paint these countries as paragons of free market virtue nothing is as simple as that. China, the fastest growing economy of all, operates a fast growing market system but within a system where the government still exerts great control. All of these countries are developing by having a particular mix of state and market control. Often policies suitable for one country simply do not fit the particular cultural, historical, social or political features of another. The economic environment of the 21st century continues to be shaped by the shifting attempts to try to balance the need to allow businesses to grow and pursue their interests in a free market environment supported by governments at the national, regional and global levels and regulated by them when it is clear that there is the danger of the abuse of market power.

Summary

- The economic environment is created by the existence of scarcity. The study of business from an economic standpoint is the study of the role that businesses play in efficiently resolving the economic problems of allocation, production and distribution

- There are a range of competing perspectives as to the best type of economic system to encourage businesses to be economically efficient

- There is an increasing focus on the role that business plays in sustainable resource use

- Markets play a significant role in setting the economic environment of business in modern economies and all economies are involved in trying to better develop these market systems

- It is clear that markets can often fail both at the microeconomic and macroeconomic levels and so any examination of the economic environment must involve a close examination of the role of the government in correcting these problems

 Case study: the food business

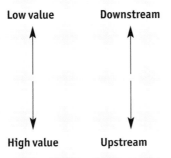

Low value	Downstream
Farming	
Distribution	
Food processing	
Brand development	
Marketing	
Distribution	
Selling	
High value	Upstream

We explored four possible meanings of scarcity in the chapter (see page 41). Let us consider how such statements can be interpreted by focusing on that most precious of all commodities, food supply. This is all too often in shortage in many parts of the world and yet in the affluent world a major preoccupation is eating too much food or too much 'bad' food. While the proportion of people working in agriculture is declining, food production and retailing is still the world's biggest business sector. We can distinguish between the 'downstream' business of agriculture where farmers struggle to maintain an income and the 'upstream' where the food manufacturers add value to their products by processing and constantly seeking to establish strong brands through ever more sophisticated marketing and product development. This modern form of food production is often referred to as 'agribusiness'.

Agribusiness involves a food chain whereby the food producers or farmers are often in fierce competition. This coupled with a low income elasticity of demand for food means that prices for food are low and as food production increases farm incomes decreases. On the other hand upstream food is processed and branded by a relatively few food companies. These companies

spend much money in developing new types of food products which are then vigorously marketed. These products are then sold and the structure of the food retailing industry is dominated by a few very large supermarket chains.

Look back at definition 1 of scarcity. This is very pessimistic. A sort of pack up and go home approach to economics. So many people can be heard saying this sort of thing. 'It's no use. Whatever they do it never gets better.' It's that perception of economics that perhaps has resulted in a popular perception of economics as being the 'dismal science'. This view is often expressed in relation to the re-occurrence of food shortages, especially in the developing world.

This is often embodied in the term 'Malthusian Pessimism'. Writing in the 19th century, Malthus argued that no matter what happened food production would always lag behind population growth. Famine was inevitable. To attribute this pessimism to Malthus would be unfair as he was not so abjectly pessimistic, nevertheless such views are represented today. Climatic failure, population growth, and war disrupting production are seen by some as the explanation for hunger in the Third World.

Definition 2 is much more hopeful, representing the belief of the modern age of the essential progress of human beings. We may have to toil but we can make our lives easier. The primary focus then is on allocative and productive efficiency. While it is true that resources are limited we can do our best to maximize the use of them to satisfy as many needs and wants as we can. In many parts of the world huge increases in food production have been made possible with technology and better use of agricultural markets.

Such views are embodied in both the free market and interventionist perspectives. For the former the best way to achieve efficiency is through private enterprise and free market forces. For the latter there is a role for the state in ensuring a measure of equity in the process of economic growth as well as in ensuring success in production. In the developed world farming is very much conducted through farmers selling into markets but these markets are heavily protected by governments with support for prices and subsidies. Furthermore, consumers need to be protected from exploitation by ensuring that there is rigorous food safety and that firms do not exploit their power over consumers by misleading advertising or selling of products that are not healthy even though they are profitable. Chapter 4 explores this in relation to the rising problem of obesity in many countries.

Definition 3 tends to develop this much further. The primary focus is on the issue of distribution as well as the power of the food industry. It may well be that there is not enough for everyone but the immediate problem is that out of what there is the rich in society take at the expense of the poor. Food processing companies and supermarkets are able to exploit both ends of the production chain by underpaying the food producers and overcharging the food consumers. They are able to do this because of the large amounts of market power that they have been able to acquire. Any notion of economic efficiency must concern itself with equity. Free Trade may not be Fair Trade.

In relation to food such a perspective would highlight not the lack of food but the sheer potential of economies to produce sufficient food. That there is scarcity is not a natural shortage but a shortage generated by political and social forces that are fundamental to the nature of capitalist society. Poor people go hungry because rich people's purchasing power diverts resources and production in such a way as to produce over-consumption for the few and under-consumption for the many. This view could be seen to represent a Marxist standpoint.

Definition 4 reflects a perspective which is of growing importance today. Environmentalists remind us of the possible limits to exploitation of the earth's resources. They put forward the prospect of our having to limit our needs to match our resources unless we can truly develop a sustainable development system. Often food sources are over exploited to provide short term profits. Cash crops in the developing world are produced to feed the ever more demanding tastes of consumers in the developing world. Intensive methods of farming involving large amounts of pesticides and fertilizers and increasingly GM technology, produce spectacular food surpluses and yet have created huge environmental costs and may even have exacerbated food problems and environmental degradation in the developing world.

❷ Why do agricultural producers in the developing world suffer from the tendency for prices of their output to fall?

❷ What is the difference between the competition faced by food producers and that faced by the food processing companies and supermarkets?

❷ Many products sold in supermarkets now carry a 'Fair-Trade' label. What does this signify?

❷ What are the major structural forces that shape the markets for the production, distribution and selling of food?

❷ In which areas of these markets would it be appropriate for governments to intervene?

Review and discussion questions

1   What is meant by the economic problem and its three constituent parts?

2   In July 2005 world attention was focused on the 'Make Poverty History' and Live 8 campaigns.

  'Every single day, 30,000 children are dying as a result of extreme poverty. This year, 2005, we finally have the resources, knowledge and opportunity to end this shameful situation.' (see www.makepovertyhistory.org)

  Which definition of scarcity as outlined in the section above would supporters of such campaigns feel best explain the continuance of poverty in the developing world?

3   The managing director of a prominent cosmetics firm is worried about possible rises in costs and would like to raise prices by 5% on three brands in particular: lip gloss, eye shadow and foundation. The firm's sales manager is worried about the effect on this on sales revenue and so commissions his marketing department to do some research on elasticities of demand.

The best estimates come in as follows:

lip gloss	−0.2
eye shadow	−1.0
foundation cream	−1.5

What would your advice be as to whether the price should be raised on all three goods?

4   One of the features of the UK economy in recent years has been the tendency for the market in owner occupied

housing to be 'overheated', i.e. for house prices to be constantly rising.

a) With the aid of a demand and supply diagram use equilibrium analysis to explain why this might be the case.

b) There are calls for the government to relax planning restrictions and allow a rapid increase in the supply of new houses. Use equilibrium analysis to show the effect on house prices of this increase in supply.

c) Why might there be opposition to such a house building programme?

d) In what other ways might the government intervene in the housing market to try to ease the pressure on house prices?

5 a) Identify the opportunity costs of the resources that will be used to enable you to study this chapter.

b) What are the benefits of studying this chapter?

c) Who should pay for giving you the opportunity of studying this chapter?

6 Find out the wholesale prices of a metric tonne of potatoes (see www.fwi.co.uk). Now find out how much a standard small packet of potato crisps costs in your local supermarket. Calculate the price of a metric tonne of potato crisps! Can you explain the relative prices of the potatoes compared to the crisps?

Assignments

1 Compile a market report into the recent trend of prices of gas. Using equilibrium analysis explain why these trends have been occurring.

2 What are the economic arguments for and against the charging of fees for students of Higher Education?

3 What are the economic advantages and disadvantages of the increase in the amount of food sold through supermarkets compared to smaller food shops?

Further reading

Sloman, J. (2004) *The Economic Environment of Business* (Harlow: Pearson). This text is a concise introduction to the economic principles that underpin business activity.

Mulhearn, C., Vane, H., and Eden, J. (2001) *Economics for Business* (Basingstoke: Palgrave). Another clear and accessible introductory economics text which explicitly relates economics to the business context and is written by the authors of Chapter 6.

Heilbronner, R. and Milberg, W. (2001) *The Making of Economic Society* (Harlow: Pearson). A very good explanation of the development of and perspectives applied to modern economic systems.

Online resources

Test your understanding of this chapter with online questions and answers, explore the subject further through web exercises, and use the weblinks to provide a quick resource for further research. Go to the Online Resource Centre at

www.oxfordtextbooks.co.uk/orc/ wetherly_otter/

www.economicsnetwork.ac.uk:
Managed by the economics network of the Higher Education Academy this site contains many useful resources and links.

www.hm-treasury.gov.uk:
This site is the main site for the UK government treasury.

www.bized.ac.uk:
An invaluable website for business studies and economics students run by the Institute for Learning and Research Technology.

www.vts/intute.ac.uk/he/tutorial/economist:
Contains links to a whole host of sources of economics information.

The technological environment

Dorron Otter

Contents

03

Learning objectives

When you have completed this chapter you will able to:

● Understand the meaning of technology and its impact on business

● Analyse the nature of the external environment that is needed to create the conditions for technology to promote national competitive advantage

● Explore the role of technology in creating individual business competitive advantage

● Debate the ethical dimensions of the impact of technology

Themes

Diversity	**Diversity of business**
	Technological improvements are possible across the value chain of any business.
Internal/ external	**Internal/external**
	This chapter explores both the internal and external environments that are conducive to the development and implementation of technological improvement.
Complexity	**Complexity of the environment**
	There is a range of conditions that need to be created in the external environment so that the political, economic and social environment can support technological change.
Spatial levels	**Variety of spatial levels**
	The external technological environment can be shaped by local, regional, national and global characteristics and technology affects all levels of a business's value chain. Globalization is rapidly combining with the new technologies to transform the external business environment.
Dynamic	**Dynamic environment**
	We live in a world where technological change is rapid and no business can afford to stand still in the face of this change.
Interaction	**Interaction between business and the environment**
	Technological improvement depends on the way in which the external environment supports change and the ways in which entrepreneurs seek to implement the technology. This involves appropriate organizational changes to take advantage of the new technology
Stakeholders	**Stakeholders**
	Whilst technological change is driven by the need to improve competitive advantage its impacts range across the wide range of stakeholder interests.
Values	**Values**
	Technology alters the business environment by providing new opportunities. However, while we are all fascinated by its potential there are fears that there may also be harmful consequences.

Introduction: what is technology?

Technological innovation could be said to define us as a species. Even *Homo habilus*, a very early species of our genus *Homo* (approx. 2 million years ago), is known as the 'handy man' for its dexterity with basic tools. We ourselves are *Homo sapiens*. Our technical skills lie not so much in simple manual tasks but in our application of knowledge. The greatest changes in the technological environment have come about as a result of the rapid development in the knowledge economy.

In the modern world it would be easy to see the role and future of technology as lying in the new technologies such as information technology, bio-technology and the emerging nano-technology all of which are discussed later in the chapter. The impact of these technologies is rapidly transforming the ways in which businesses operate, but the approach taken in this chapter is to focus on the debates about the creation of the right environment in which technology can develop, and the ethical debates about its impact. Furthermore, whilst technology can indeed be highly technical it does not have to be so. Technology can be 'low-tech' or 'high-tech' and the impact of the technologies lies not so much in the precise nature of the technology itself but in how it is used and the conditions that determine how it is used.

Diversity

Values

So what is technology? The simplest definition is to see it as being the application of knowledge to production. Often technology is associated with the works of the great inventors of history. Technological breakthroughs can occur as new products are invented and transform our lives (invention). However, technological advances also are fuelled by the process of innovation which improves or enhances original inventions (product innovation) or develops production processes (process innovation) that enable these to be more marketable and/or more profitable to produce.

From the outset it needs to be emphasized that technology itself cannot do anything. It is how this technology is used that is important and that fundamentally depends on the wider social, political, cultural and economic environment and the way in which people within business seek to exploit its commercial potential. The precise role of technology then will differ depending on the nature of this external environment.

Interaction

Many of the world-changing technologies were not originally intended to have the outcomes that they did. A key role is played, not by the original inventor or innovator but by the business or individual entrepreneur recognizing the potential for increased profits by developing the idea or innovation.

The World Wide Web is a good example of this. The Web has allowed the Internet to take off. The basis for this explosion was developed out of the scientific work at the CERN particle lab which is aiming to discover the building blocks of matter. This involves cooperation of scientists across the globe and in 1989, Tim Berners-Lee, a scientist at CERN, invented the World Wide Web as a means of enabling better communication between these science communities. The Web brings together the developing technologies of personal computers, their ability to be networked and the new language of hypertext to produce an instant global information system (for more information see www.info.cern.ch).

Use of the Internet depends on being able to bring users together but of course it is the way in which businesses and users have sought to use the Internet that has opened up opportunities for its commercial exploitation. Dot.com businesses have directly benefited from the Internet but all businesses have in some way sought to gain advantage from the new technology.

> ⤷ *Stop and Think*
> Which technological developments most affect you and in what way?

Mini-Case 3.1 Supermarkets—a personal journey through techno-time!

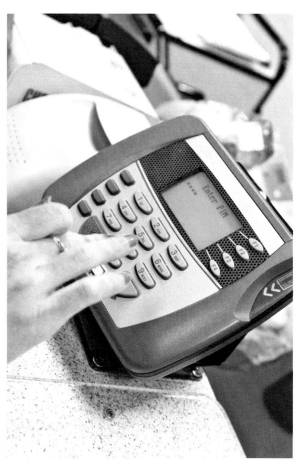

New technologies such as bar coding and electronic point of sale have turned shopping into a more efficient process—but what are the disadvantages?

© istockphoto.com/Sean Locke

Technological change is at the heart of the revolution in the way we shop. As a young boy in the 1960s I remember the walk along my local high street. On the corner was the Post Office where I would go to spend my 'Saturday sixpence' ($2\frac{1}{2}$ pence in today's money!). Next door was the sweet shop with the goods displayed in glass counters or in the stacked large glass bottles behind Mrs Edwards, the old lady who owned the shop. Along the road were the following: the hardware or Chandler's shop, the butcher, the baker (but no candlestick maker!), the chemist, the fish and chip shop, the fruit and vegetable shop, an off-licence, a flower shop,

the newsagent, three small banks and the grocer. This last small shop was full of wooden tubs of produce and the servers used a movable ladder to propel themselves up and along the shelves of drawers to obtain the produce that you pointed out. These would then be weighted and packed in brown paper bags for the (mostly female shoppers) to put into their shopping bags or to place in the trays under very large perambulators (or prams) which were left outside the shops. On the other side of the not so busy main road were two petrol stations. Shopping was a daily occurrence for most families as many households did not have refrigerators and in any case shopping was a way of socializing with shop-keepers and shoppers alike all of whom knew each other's names.

All those shops have now gone to be replaced by estate agents, saunas, coffee shops and restaurants. The petrol stations have now gone, the site of one remaining empty, but the subject of a contested planning application for a McDonalds and the other is now a car park for the only real shop in town: Sainsbury's. There are relatively few pedestrians along the high street now and cer-tainly no prams outside shops! The main road is now a constant stream of noisy traffic.

Supermarkets have transformed not only the high street where I was born but the whole face of many localities and this has been made possible by the rapidly changing technology at all parts of the food production chain. Agriculture is now a highly technical activity with the application of scientific techniques, pesticides and fertilizer and machinery. Food distribution has been trans-formed by road transport and international transportation changes mean that food can be conveyed across the globe. The nature of the food we eat has been altered beyond all recognition with food processing and food technology driving a reduction in food costs and new product development seeking ever more fan-ciful ways of producing products to tempt us. Supermarkets enable vast economies of scale to be produced and the new tech-nologies in-store such as bar coding and electronic point of sales has seemingly turned the whole process of shopping into a more efficient process. However, it is not all good news with many com-mentators voicing concern over this supermarket revolution.

❷ What are the benefits of supermarket shopping? Think about this in relation to food suppliers, distributors, consumers, workers and shareholders?

❷ What are the possible disadvantages of supermarket shopping? Think about this in relation to food suppliers, consumers, the government, the environment and the nature of community life?

How does technology foster business growth and development?

Technology is a process that enables businesses to boost production through better use of resources. We have seen that business operates in a world where at any moment in time resources are scarce. Business is the activity that converts inputs into outputs for use. Technology can enable business to utilize resources more efficiently and expand outputs at a greater rate than they increase use of inputs. Productivity is the term that is used to measure the rate of conversion of inputs into outputs. If a business is able to increase its output by a greater percentage for any given level of input of resources we can say that productivity is increasing. This will also mean that the costs of production will be falling.

Productivity is often expressed in relation to the size of the labour force employed and can be calculated as being:

Total ouput/total amount of labour

This would give us a figure for total output per worker. If productivity increases then this would mean that output per worker is growing and business is being more efficient. Crucially this will mean that costs of output are falling.

Figure 3.1 illustrates the impact of technological change on the economic growth of a country. Imagine that a country with a fixed amount of resources can produce either industrial or agricultural goods. The country can either employ all of its resources in industry (and produce no agricultural output), or all in agriculture (and produce no industrial goods). Or it can choose to deploy varying combinations of resources in each sector and thus produce different combinations of agricultural and industrial goods. A **production possibility frontier** can be drawn which shows all the possible combinations. In Figure 3.1, providing that the country fully uses all its resources efficiently, it can choose any combination of goods along the line PP, e.g. either x amount of industrial goods and y amount of agricultural goods or c amount of industrial goods and d amount of agricultural goods.

This illustrates many of the important concepts that we outlined in Chapter 2. In the short run, all economies have a resource constraint. The basic economic problem is one of scarcity. This means that choices need to be made about how to allocate these resources. If the economy above wants to produce more industrial goods then it must shift resources from agriculture to industry and the opportunity cost of the increase in industrial goods is the cost of having reduced agricultural goods.

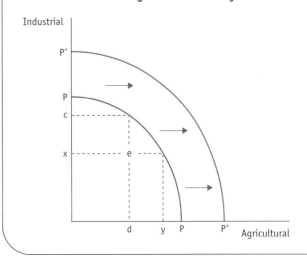

Figure 3.1 Impact of technological change on the economic growth of a country

In Figure 3.1, if a country has a fixed amount of resources so that it can choose any combination along PP then any combination such as xy or cd are possible. In Chapter 2 we explored the idea of productive efficiency. If all resources are used to maximize the output produced, the country can attain combinations of goods that lie on the frontier. If, for example, this economy was only operating at a point such as e which is inside the production possibility frontier then we can see that the country is not using its resources efficiently. If resources are being used efficiently then the country could choose any combination along PP.

However, what if there were to be technological improvements in both the agricultural and industrial sectors so that a greater output could be produced with the same levels of resources? This would then mean that the production possibilities for the country would increase and the production possibility frontier would expand to P'P'. Increases in productivity mean that the country can now produce increased amounts of both types of good and consumption levels and living standards can increase. Technological progress is a major cause of economic growth.

The increase in productivity does not have to occur in both sectors for economic growth. Study Figure 3.2. In Figure 3.2 there have been technological improvements in the industrial sector which now allows the country to either combine a greater amount of industrial goods with each level of agricultural goods or to allocate more resources from the industrial sector into the agricultural one and so boost output there. Of course if there were to be technological advances in agriculture then the result could be as shown in Figure 3.3. In Figure 3.3, as a result of the improvement in agricultural technology more agricultural goods can be combined with any given level of industrial goods or resources can now be reallocated out of agriculture to increase the output of industrial goods without reducing agricultural output.

The production possibility frontier helps us to gain an understanding of the impact of technology on economic growth. It can also help us to focus on another aspect of the benefits of technology and that is its effect on the costs of production. Consider the production possibility frontier in Figure 3.4. Imagine that we initially start on the production possibility frontier with no industrial output and quantity A

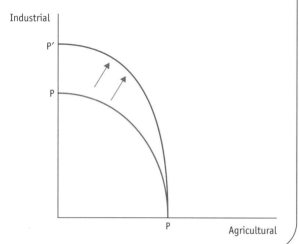

Figure 3.2 Technological improvement in the industrial goods sector

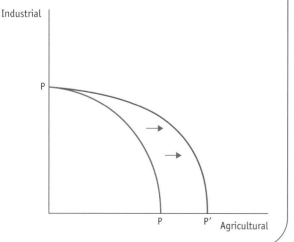

Figure 3.3 Technological improvement in the agricultural goods sector

of agricultural goods. All resources would then be used to produce agricultural goods.

Let us say that this country decides to shift some of its resources into industry and chooses point B. It is clear that, while the country now has to give up some agricultural output Ab, it has gained a much bigger proportion in terms of industrial output (0d). It can be seen that the opportunity cost of the increased industrial output is relatively small in terms of agricultural goods foregone, so why has that happened? Before we go on let us see what happens as we continue to transfer resources out of agriculture into industry. Let us move from B to C.

Now it is true that there is a gain in industrial output of de but this has been matched by an almost equal reduction in agricultural goods. If we continue from C to I we see now that we gain a smaller proportion of industrial output but lose a bigger proportion of agricultural goods.

In reality part of the explanation lies in the fact that it is unlikely that all resources are equally efficient at producing agricultural and industrial goods. However, this also shows the possibility that as more and more resources are put into one production activity they progressively become less efficient and this is referred to as the law of diminishing marginal returns.

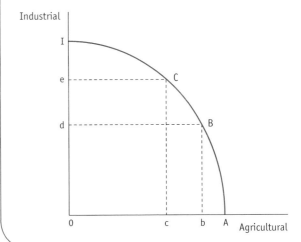

Figure 3.4 Increasing opportunity costs

> **➲ Stop and Think**
> In business how is it possible for 'many hands to make light work' when 'too many cooks spoil the broth'?

Imagine you are a restaurant owner with a fixed size of kitchen. In order to speed up the cooking and serving of meals there is an optimum number of staff that you will need so that tasks can be shared out. As a result of the popularity of your restaurant you need to speed up the cooking and service. In the short run though, you are limited by the capacity of the restaurant and the kitchen. You try to resolve this by hiring more staff but you notice that the extra number of customers you are able to serve does not rise in proportion to the additional staff costs. The Head Chef is complaining that s/he cannot possibly produce the extra meals given the amount of cooking rings and ovens and when you come into the kitchen you see people getting in each other's way and waiting staff hanging around and complaining that diners are getting restless waiting for food. Quite clearly productivity is declining.

The reason for this is that you have a capacity constraint which means that even if you increase the supply of labour the additional output that arises per extra worker is falling. This is not the fault of the additional workers hired but simply that the existing size of the restaurant and kitchen is too small.

You have two choices: either expand capacity or try to reorganize your resources in a better way by improving technology. This is why technology is so pivotal to the growth of a business.

The next two sections will explore the conditions which, both at the level of the individual business and at the national and global level, are likely to promote the best technological environment that will improve our quality of life. Too often in debates about technology it is easy to become fascinated by the technologies themselves without considering how the conditions occurred to encourage technological breakthroughs and developments.

Technology and national competitive advantage

Complexity

Internal/
external

At the national level, what are the conditions that need to occur in the external environment that can best help business to promote technological improvements and to develop their internal strategic response?

For Adam Smith it was the development of widespread markets that allowed the conditions for the rapid improvements in productivity that led to the rapid advance of capitalism. The greatest source of technological advance lay not in the sophisticated application of science or complex new technologies. It was the expansion of markets that propelled businesses to reorganize production to meet these new market opportunities. The crucial change in production techniques was in developing production processes that utilized the division of labour and specialization. Taking the example of an industrial product, a 'pin' (or nail) in the *Wealth of Nations*, Smith showed how huge gains in productivity could be obtained by a simple change in the organization of the production process to allow a greater division of labour. Smith demonstrated how specialization or the splitting of production into separate tasks allowed great gains in productivity of 'pins' to be gained.

It is a combination of internal and external factors that enables economic growth to occur through technological change. Clearly it was the opportunity created by the possibility of increasing markets that encouraged the business to explore the best technological means of exploiting these new opportunities. Changing the process and the scale of production allows increases in productivity through either the division of labour and specialization and/or the chance to exploit economies of scale which means that decreases in cost can be achieved. An important element in propelling the technological change is the response of the business and so we need to look at the entrepreneurial activity within the business. How do such entrepreneurs behave and what are the conditions that are most likely to exploit technology?

Of course this does not mean that there is no room for the development of technologically advanced machines and processes but that technology can have an enormous impact even with relatively simple changes to the productive processes. It is useful here to reflect on the way in which the industrial revolution both was spurred on and in turn gave rise to the rapid advance of technology.

The industrial revolution started not with new products but with new processes to produce existing ones. Before an industrial revolution is possible it is important that there are increases in the productivity of agriculture so that food supplies can increase. These are necessary so that people can be 'freed' from the land to work in factories. In England it has been estimated that it took 1,000 years for agricultural production to boost food yields from 0.5 tonnes per hectare to 2 tonnes, but in the 18th century it took only 40 years to raise this to 6 tonnes.

These changes came about not as the result of the application of capital intensive techniques or scientific changes. For centuries landowners primarily earned their wealth not from taking a direct interest in their land, but by simply collecting rents from impoverished farmers who worked their land. These farmers aimed to produce food for their own needs. In order to minimize the risk of climate and pests and to ensure some sort of variety of food, they would seek to produce a range of produce. Any surplus could either be stored or sold at market to provide the occasional 'luxury'. Under this system there was little incentive for farmers to produce surpluses as they knew that all that would happen is that landlords would raise the rents.

Capitalism and the increase in markets changed this system of agriculture. Now the landlords saw that they could make more money by directly selling produce themselves in the marketplace. They sought to specialize in the use of their land and sell the products on the market. Farmers were now either forced to specialize in the production of certain marketable foods or products or were evicted from the land to allow an increase in the scale of the production by combining farms and benefiting from economies of scale.

One of the first marketable products identified was wool. Vast tracts of land were given over to sheep rearing and the wool was then transformed into woven cloth through the process of spinning and weaving. Initially this was achieved through small scale 'cottage' industries where wool was largely spun at home by 'spinsters' and then woven into cloth in small scale weaving factories. However, in the 18th century industrialists began to develop the large scale modern factory systems powered initially by water and then steam. In these modern factory systems a clear division of labour took place with the introduction of new and vastly more productive machinery such as Hargreave's 'Spinning Jenny', the water frame developed by Richard Arkwright, often regarded as the person who first developed the modern factory system, and then the combination of these two processes in the form of Crompton's 'mule'. However, these innovations in themselves were not scientifically complex but made use of simple ideas and mechanical devices and yet with spectacular results in terms of output.

However, it was cotton that was the first major industrial product. The British had first learned about the possibility of manufacturing cotton by discovering the quality of Indian textiles. The Empire now ensured cheap and plentiful supplies of cotton especially from America where slavery ensured that cotton was cheap. Techniques developed to produce woollen cloth more cheaply were now used to spur the development of cotton.

The Industrial Revolution ushered in an era of immense technological change and rapid gains in productivity that transformed the living standards of people in the developed world but the benefits of this rapid economic growth were not uniformly spread across the world. Technological advance also allows the creation of competitive advantage and this has created a technological gap in the world. Whilst technology does not have to be 'high-tech' once productivity gains begin to occur, a virtuous cycle of reinforcing growth can occur.

The countries of Europe, North America and Australasia were able, through rapid industrialization to bring about big improvements in the social welfare of their people in the fields of health and education and poverty reduction. Not only did increases in productivity increase standards of living, in turn they led to the development of new industries and associated processes. The most influential change was that brought to production as a result of the developments in the motor car industry with the mass production techniques pioneered by Henry Ford being transferred to the production of a wide array of other goods. Some commentators indeed refer to this external business environment as being one of **Fordism** which it is argued pre-dated the Second World War but found its greatest expression in providing the technological backdrop for the rapid economic growth in the developed world in the post Second World War period. Human development is also in turn an important influence on technological development. Higher levels of education mean that people have the skills and are able to develop the knowledge to promote new products and processes. Higher Education can produce the skilled personnel to pioneer new developments but a general increase in educational skills allows people at all levels in organizations to adapt to change and master new techniques.

The history of the 20th century could be seen as the rapid development of a technological business environment in the developed world that with ever increasing speed rapidly brought about steady increases in economic growth rates. Most studies of economic growth show that it is technology that is the biggest single cause of this growth. For some commentators the challenge for less developed countries is to analyse how the developed countries harnessed technology in this way and to follow their lead. For others this is an elusive quest as it is difficult for other countries to try to copy this experience not least because of the sheer competitive strength that the developed countries now have. We shall explore these global dimensions to technological development in Chapter 11.

In the 21st century there is the hope that the nature of the new technologies means that the prospects for technological catch up are much brighter and this is something we will look at later on in this chapter. For now it is worth looking at what lessons if any we can learn from the way in which some countries have successfully been able to develop an external environment that is conducive to technological development and we will then explore the issues surrounding the individual strategic response of firms to this.

Spatial levels

↪ *Stop and Think*
What were the main social, economic and political changes that created the climate for entrepreneurial activity and the rapid development of technology?

Perspectives on creating a national environment to promote technology

Complexity

Dynamic

Chapter 2 outlined the broad competing views as to the best way of organizing economic activity. The same broad views can be distinguished when it comes to analysing the causes of economic growth and the precise role that technology plays.

We have seen that for Adam Smith the origins and causes of economic growth lay in the development of a market economic system and that the main agents of economic growth were the owners of capital or, what we would call today, the entrepreneurs. In their pursuit for profit and driven by the need to compete, businesses would constantly seek to develop new products and cut costs. This could be seen a neoclassical view of the impact of technological change. However, as we have seen, Smith was well aware of the wider structural factors that would be needed to support the market. It took changes in the political and social structure to allow the expansion of trade and a robust legal system to provide the rules to both protect the rights of businesses as well as the wider society from the possible exploitation by business.

> In Smith's analysis then, it is the accumulation of physical capital, technological progress, specialisation of labour and free trade that are the sources of expanding wealth. Economic growth will continue as long as capital is accumulated and new technology is introduced. Both competition and free trade contributed to making this process cumulative. (Cypher and Dietz, 2004: 107)

It is these wider institutional and structural ingredients in the external business environment that structuralist critics highlight when seeking to analyse the role of business in promoting growth.

There exists a mountain of research on the causes of economic growth. After the Second World War and in response to the economic recession that occurred in the developed world between the wars, and the relative state of backwardness of many developing countries, much attention focused on the role of government in actively encouraging growth. In the Keynesian framework, if the government could act to boost demand at the macro-level this would encourage firms to invest in the capacity needed. To secure the money needed to invest people would need to be encouraged to save so that funds would be available through the financial system for businesses to invest. If firms were unable or unwilling to invest, say for example because they were uncertain about the future, then governments should borrow and raise the level of capital spending directly. There was an implicit belief that capital growth would lead to growth. Despite initial successes in both the developed and developing world growth rates slowed markedly in the 1970s and many countries found that government borrowing had spiralled out of control, so the search was on for other explanations.

Perhaps one of the most influential theories of growth has been as a result of the work of Solow. It was Solow in 1956, who first argued that whilst a focus on capital growth and savings were important in order for growth not to slow, it was technological improvement that was important. Economists seek to measure the extent of increases in productivity through the use of total factor productivity. This is seen as being the residual increase in total output having allowed for the increase in the inputs of labour and capital. For Solow, technology is the explanation for this additional growth but technology itself occurs independently of the growth process. If technology then is the key, what causes this?

The latest addition to the growth literature is endogenous or New Growth theory. In this view, technology occurs as a result of economic growth itself. As growth occurs virtuous and self reinforcing cycles are created. Also of importance is the openness to trade between countries with technology flowing across frontiers as well as across businesses within one country. In this view technology will itself allow increases in productivity and decreases in costs. A vital role is played by human capital, i.e. the ability of people to learn and improve. As people learn they constantly improve on ideas and techniques and the returns to human capital can be increasing. This means that even if we accept that eventually returns from capital decrease, the increasing returns from human capital mean that overall growth rates can be maintained. In fact there can be constant returns to increases in capital investment. Thus the causes of economic growth can be seen as being the following:

Trade openness + diffusion of technology through education

Globally it is not necessary for all countries to be world leaders in technological improvement. All that is needed is for a few countries to be technological leaders with other countries being technological followers able to adapt and learn from the former. However, a major stumbling block to this would be if the owners of the human capital that had resulted in the new products or processes did not have the ability to benefit from their intellectual labour. It is important to have clearly defined property rights to protect the technological leaders from having their ideas stolen.

Increasingly attention is paid to the immense potential in the new technologies for exponential growth. In the 1960s, Gordon Moore, a co-founder of Intel, referred to the observed doubling of the number of transistors on an integrated circuit every two years (now referred to as Moore's law). This rapid increase in computing power has also been extended to other areas of ICT. Gilder's law now predicts a doubling of communications power every six months with huge advances in fibre-optic networks and the explosion of band width. Personal computers with a memory of 100 GB are now in many homes and people can carry hand held computers with 20 GB capacity (and yet it was only in 1993 that they were first introduced).

Optimists now argue that with globalization and the rapid advances made in new technologies, the digital and other divides that separate the developed from the developing world should decrease. In the words of Thomas Friedman, one of the most ardent believers in the ability of new technologies to transform the world, 'the world is flat' (Friedman, 2005) in the sense that the gap between rich and poor nations can potentially be closed.

One of the foremost business strategists is Michael Porter. Porter sees the creation of national competitive advantage as a diamond with four pole points. For Porter there is nothing natural about why some nations are more competitive than others. The key ingredient to establishing national competitiveness is the ability to constantly increase productivity and the main way in which this is done is through creating the environment in which technological improvement occurs (Porter, 1998).

Spatial levels

1 It is important to look at the forces that encourage firm rivalry. It is market structures that promote competition and that lead to increases in productivity and innovation.

2 Firms need to be able to respond to consumer demands.

Porter here seems to be supporting the neoclassical view that the key to success is simply free and fair competition but it is the following two pole points in Porter's diamond that really focuses on the role of technology and the conditions for the creation of an innovative technological environment.

3 A key ingredient in national (and therefore individual firm) success is how the related support industries are located in relation to the firm. Every business product is located at a particular point in the production chain. Chapter 2 showed that for any firm there is an upstream towards the point of sale and a downstream towards the sources of raw material supply. For Porter, if these linkages are close in spatial terms then this facilitates an exchange of ideas and information across the activities and creates the possibility of developing more productive technologies. This may entail the creation of business clusters so that creative

energies can be released. These clusters comprise geographical concentrations of interconnected companies supported by specialist suppliers of goods and services and institutions such as universities, standards agencies, and trade associations in relevant fields. Whilst individual businesses within the cluster are competing, collectively the cluster provides the ability for mutual support and cooperation.

4 In this way then it can be seen that the factor conditions are created and are not inherited. Governments have a vital role in creating such clusters.

It is the ability of countries to raise productivity that is the key to their competitive advantage and technology is a major driver. Let us now turn our attention to the conditions that need to take place at the level of the firm if technological progress is to occur.

Technology and business competitive advantage

Spatial levels

As well as looking at the conditions needed for national competitive advantage, Porter in *Competitive Advantage—Creating and Sustaining Superior Performance* emphasizes the importance of technology in creating the competitive environment at the level of the individual firm (Porter, 1985). He also emphasizes the danger of seeing technology as a goal in itself. Technology is not an end in itself but is best understood as a means to improving competitive performance and boosting profitability. All too often it is easy to assume that any technological change is good and further that the more costly and sophisticated the investment in technology the better this will be. However, as we have seen technological change does not have to be so costly and complicated. Using the concept of the **value chain**, Porter shows how every activity of a business in combining inputs into outputs has the potential to use technology to alter the production process and add value. In practice a firm is a collection of different technologies that can be applied, enhanced or implemented across all the different activities of the business.

A value chain can be seen as consisting of the following technologies:

horizontal functions or support services of a business in terms of its basic infrastructure (finance, planning, information systems, office technology), human resources (training and development), technology development and purchasing departments.

vertical or primary business operations in terms of inbound logistics (transport, handling, storage, information systems), production operations (process, materials, machines, packaging, design and testing) outbound logistics, marketing and sales and finally service.

All these activities together comprise the value chain and each operation involves the use of technology to combine inputs into outputs so there is the opportunity for technological improvement across the range of activities to improve the profit margins of the business. One technology that occurs across the range of activities is that of information and/or communications technology and this is indeed highlighted by Porter. For many commentators the recent huge and long lasting increases in economic growth have been fuelled by the rapid improvements in these new technologies.

It is clear also that individual businesses are intimately linked to technological changes in other businesses and in other industries. If competitors gain a technological advantage a business needs to respond or lose out. Changes in the technology of suppliers may impact on the business and if there are technological advances in related support industries then a business needs to adapt. Furthermore, a technical change in one part of the activities of a business might well call for changes in other technologies elsewhere.

Mini-Case 3.2 easyJet and the Internet

It was to be the Internet revolution that really enabled easyJet to take off.

© easyJet airline company ltd.

Low cost air travel can have many business models. The first low cost carriers tended to use old planes which they either leased or bought to operate on routes with little direct competition. easyJet broke with this. Helped by changes in the competitive environment as a result of legislation to allow competition on routes, easyJet used brand new planes which it bought to operate on competitive routes. In order to be competitive and pay for the considerable fixed costs of the aircraft and for the landing slots provided by the airports used, easyJet explicitly recognized the need to go for economies of scale by using their planes as much as possible and by filling each plane to reduce the average cost of each passenger. It engaged in ruthless cost cutting for all other operations such as not using the services of travel agents or catering services for in-flight meals, i.e. a no-frills service.

Originally, it was envisaged that people would book flights over the phone, however, it was to be the Internet revolution that really enabled easyJet to take off.

❷ How has the Internet enabled low cost air operators to be successful?

Technological change can improve the competitiveness of the firm if it either reduces costs or if it allows a business to differentiate its products or services from that of its rivals. We have seen already the complexity of cause and effect in relation to technology and other factors. Changes in the external market can create the possibility of untapped economies of scale that in turn call for a technological response to boosting production.

Technology cannot be ignored by business and it can either boost a firm's individual position or improve the profitability of the industry in which it operates. Conversely it can lead to a business declining as its competitors develop a technological advantage or technological change boosts alternative industries.

It is important for a business to adopt a technology strategy that enables it to respond to external changes as well as one which allows it to develop a consistent approach in relation to its goals.

Mini-Case 3.3 The real computer games battle?

The competitive battle for the attention (to the consternation of parents!) of computer games players is intense and is primarily fought through technology (and marketing). Sony, Microsoft and Nintendo are the combatants and their weapons are their respective marketing machines and their products: Sony's Playstation 3, Microsoft's Xbox 360 and Nintendo's Game Boy turned Wii.

Sony became the market leader by targeting the teenage and young adult market but Microsoft is keen to catch up and Nintendo is trying to develop a product that will appeal across the age ranges.

The cost of the technology is very high and yet it is not the technology that the consumers want but the quality of the games, software and range of Internet uses which the consoles can support. Sony is gambling on its new Playstation 3 with its powerful 'Cell' processor which it claims operates at 35 times the speed of Playstation 2 as well as using the Blu-Ray disc format for its discs. The cost of the technology means that each console sells at below

cost price but the real potential profits lie in persuading consumers to buy the games over the long term as well as accessing other Internet services and software products. It is this aspect which interests Toshiba. As well as this battle over the console platform there is another long term battle over the format of the disks that will replace DVDs. Toshiba is developing the HD DVD and in a direct echo of the earlier battle between VHS video and Beta-max there is a clear struggle to persuade the buying public to adopt the one technology over the other.

It is a high risk strategy in the short run but in the long run it will be the company that develops the best technology that translates into high quality games that will win.

❓ Is the competitive battle one to improve the technology or to gain competitive advantage?

❓ Are there any potential disadvantages in this competitive struggle over technology?

Playing on the Nintendo Wii. The cost of the technology means that each console sells at below cost price but the real potential profits lie in persuading consumers to buy the games.

© AFP/Getty Images

A major decision businesses need to make is whether to try and be technology leaders or technology followers. In general terms this requires a balance of risks.

If it is likely that a business would be able to maintain the technological advantage over time then there is an incentive for firms to innovate and/or develop new products. This can be the case where firms are able to assert their intellectual property rights through patents or where the cost of the research and development is so high as to deter competitors. As we shall see, some firms may try to simply outspend their rivals and then hope that the market appeal of such products is such as to allow costs to be more than recouped without the prospect of an alternative using cheaper technology. The rapid pace of technology though means that this might be a possibility.

Moving first can mean that a business is able to establish a reputation that survives even when alternative competitors enter the market. Being first can mean that a business can develop a strong lead and help it establish a position that it can set industry standards or develop favourable channels of distribution. Conversely, there is a huge risk in going first. Considerable sums of money can be expended and there is the risk that someone else can learn from your mistakes and develop a leaner and fitter product. Vast sums of money have been poured into developing the new generation of 3G phones including billons of pounds to obtain the operating licences but there is considerable doubt that these technologies will have market appeal and already phone companies are trying to develop simpler phones.

The technology debate

Take the following world changing products from the world of traditional industry, the energy sources on which the technology is based and the nature of the process or product breakthrough:

Product	Energy source	Process/breakthrough
Wool/cotton	Water/steam/coal	Factory system and Spinning Jenny, etc.
Trains (replacing canal barges)	Coal	Steam engine
Light in homes and work places	Electricity from coal/nuclear power	Light bulb and electricity generation and supply
Cars/lorries	Oil	Internal combustion engine, mass production techniques and new road-building techniques
Mass air travel and shipping	Oil	Jet engine, containerization

Values

Stakeholders

All of these products have transformed our world and brought about huge advantages. The evolution of the factory system brought about the rise of the industrial world and in turn the rates of growth which enabled living standards to increase. Electricity has literally brought light into the darkness and further fuelled industrial growth. Transport costs have fallen dramatically and with this the expansion of markets both nationally and now globally. However, each technological change has had its fierce critics with people fearful of the impact and being labelled 'techno-phobes'.

Technology is not always seen as being welcome. Not only can many technologies be used in a way to promote interests of certain groups at the expense of others but it is part and parcel of many technologies that there are costs and benefits.

Mini-Case 3.4 shows the fear that many people have about the effects of technology. The fears of the Luddites find echoes in modern day criticism of the effect that the new technologies of communication have on the ability of businesses to outsource their call centres or production to areas of the globe where costs are cheaper. It also shows that the effects of technology cannot be seen in isolation from other forces in the external environment. In the 19th century while there were many voices who argued for a halt to industrialization and wanted to conserve traditional society (the origins of today's Conservative Party), there were others who saw that if the free

Mini-Case 3.4　The Luddites: techno-phobes or techno victims?

The term 'Luddite' has come to mean anyone who is opposed to technology. The Luddite movement had its biggest influence in the early 19th century and was concentrated in the North Midlands and particularly in Lancashire and West Yorkshire. It was here that the factory system based on wool and cotton was expanding most rapidly and the new technology of weaving and spinning was propelling this. The Luddites were mostly traditional workers in the textile industry who were suffering from the lower prices of wool and cotton that were made possible by the introduction of the new stocking frames and from the prospect of being made unemployed as capital replaced labour. Their response was to break into factories at night and attempt to smash the new machines. Ultimately their cause was defeated with the British Government passing legislation to punish such acts either with the death penalty or through deportation to Australia. However, there were people who had sympathies with the Luddites, most famously the Romantic poet Lord Byron who spoke out passionately in their defence. For such people the changes to social conditions brought about by industrialization were horrific and indeed the response of the Luddites to the changes in their status from skilled artisans to poor unskilled labourers, or even worse the unemployed was a cause to champion. For the historian E. P. Thompson, the Luddites were not primarily opposed to technological progress but to the effects of the expansion of market forces in reducing wages and increasing the gap between rich and poor. This was happening against the backdrop to the Napoleonic Wars where food shortages were forcing up the price of food and where British landlords insisted on high tariffs against imported food so that they could benefit from the ability to charge high rents and take advantage of the food shortage. In this view it was not surprising that technological advances would be seen as being hostile as the benefits were not being fairly shared out.

❓ What were the main concerns of the Luddites?

❓ What were the criticisms of the social conditions brought about by industrialization?

market was operated in an environment where certain groups had monopoly power then technological development would be stalled. Economic liberals such as David Ricardo saw the answer in the active promotion of free trade and competition in the tradition of Smith. Ricardo was an active advocate of the repeal of the high import tariffs on food imports into Britain. For Ricardo the high food prices would mean workers would demand higher wages thus eating into the profits needed by businesses to develop technology. For Ricardo it was not the workers who presented a threat to business but the landlord classes who wanted to stand in the way of progress.

Industrialization

In the 19th Century it wasn't just Romantic poets who despaired of the new social conditions brought about by industrialization but also social reformers, novelists such as Charles Dickens and indeed some entrepreneurs themselves. Factory owners such as Joseph Rowntree, Titus Salt and William Lever tried to develop the new factory technologies but in an environment whereby the health and welfare of their workers were promoted through providing them with model villages. It was through his collaboration with Friedrich Engels that Karl Marx had a direct insight into the conditions of working people in 19th century Britain. To earn a living Engels worked in one of his father's factories in Manchester and was uncomfortable with the conditions that he found there. In his book *The Condition of the Working Class in England*, Engels paints as grim a picture of industrial life as Dickens does in his stories of Victorian poverty. Marx saw the process of industrialization as one which dehumanized people and made them slaves to their machines. Workers had become 'alienated' from themselves both in terms of their labour becoming subservient to the factory discipline and in terms of the products of their labour becoming the property of the factory owner and their receiving less than their fair share. In modern sociological analysis this idea of alienation is now commonplace and taken to refer to the problems that many people face in the modern commercial world where everything centres around money.

Debates about the role of technology are not confined to this area of philosophical and political debate. Many people since then have warned of the dangers of technology and the need to be careful as to assessing its effects and to always balance the costs and benefits. Most famously fierce debates have occurred in the fields of the application of science in the areas of security and health.

Military technology

A significant area of business activity is in the military field and technology spending is a huge part of this. The security of a nation both externally and internally are vital for the well being of its citizens but the ethics of the defence industry are hotly debated with the obvious danger that defence can be often used for attack. Research and development on the military absorbs the efforts of much of the scientific community and one line of argument concerns the opportunity costs of this work.

There is heated debate about the ethics of the effects of the use of armaments ranging from cluster bombs to mines and possible use of chemical warfare. However, the armaments industry provides employment and exports to producer countries. Indeed many of the by-products of military spending have had spin offs in commercial use.

Energy technologies

All of the technological breakthroughs in the list on page 77 rely on energy production and have enormous externalities not least in relation to global warming. The realization that our reliance on such energy sources has resulted in so much of the carbon that is responsible for global warming has given much support to those who have argued for alternative technology based on solar, water and wind power amongst others.

The great hope of 20th century technology in terms of energy production, the nuclear industry, has been attacked not only because of the environmental problems associated with the safety of nuclear plants and the problems of storage of waste but with the dangers that the technology can fall into the wrong hands and be used for terrorist outrages. Of course the nuclear industry is intimately tied to the armaments industry and it was a democratically elected government that chose to use this technology in war with the dropping of the atomic bombs on Hiroshima and Nagasaki. This prompted many of the scientists involved with this project to disown their work in developing nuclear technologies. The most famous of these was Joseph Rotblatt who was awarded the Nobel Peace Prize in 1995 and who died in 2005. He co-founded the Pugwash Conferences on Science and World Affairs together with the most famous scientist of all, Albert Einstein. In 1955 the Russell–Einstein manifesto was signed by many prominent academics of the day (Bertrand Russell being a respected philosopher) which ended with the following statement:

> There lies before us, if we choose, continual progress in happiness, knowledge, and wisdom. Shall we, instead, choose death, because we cannot forget our quarrels? We appeal as human beings to human beings: Remember your humanity, and forget the rest. If you can do so, the way lies open to a new Paradise; if you cannot, there lies before you the risk of universal death.
> (www.pugwash.org)

Of course the statement above is primarily concerned with the ethics of the technology of warfare; however, we have seen that across the range of technologies ethical implications must be considered. Einstein was keen to emphasize that technology in and of itself could not do anything but its impacts fundamentally depended on how human behaviour was shaped by the social, political and economic environment. Scientists working in Nazi Germany took a pride in their ability to develop the technology to kill millions of prisoners in concentration camps, but did not appear to consider the ethical implications of the use of that technology.

Values

New technologies

In our times there is a range of new technologies that have undoubtedly pushed the bounds of national and global production possibilities to new levels. Bio-technology, information and communications technology (all explained later in the chapter) and the prospect of nano-technology have or potentially will have an enormous impact on our lives but each technology brings with it potential costs. The task for business and governments both nationally and globally is to be aware of the balance between the potential benefits and costs. This entails the need to have robust systems of risk management. The costs of technology can be seen in four main categories:

- the cost to human welfare in general
- the damage to social organization and cohesion by giving certain groups more access to wealth and political power than others
- the cost to the environment
- the ability of businesses to use technology to establish monopoly control.

Consider the use of bio-technology. Bio-technology can manipulate the genetic material that makes up all organisms. It can be used to identify genes that cause defects in humans, animals or plants and potentially rectify these by developing transgenic technology. This technology could begin to cure previously incurable health related problems as well as reducing the costs of a wide range of treatments. It is also possible through cloning to eradicate genetic defects in humans and animals. Genetically modified (GM) plants hold out the prospect of reducing the vulnerability of many crops to pest or disease and thus raise food production. However, severe misgivings are held about such advances. The prospect of cloning causes grave concern about the psychological effects of possible future human clones as well as possible future health problems. Stem cell research holds out the prospect that people with genetic problems could have these corrected if tissue 'harvested' from embryos could be used for them. This provokes strong opposition from religious groups as well as some people with disabilities. GM technology is seen by many as being untested

Mini-Case 3.5 The Green Revolution

The Green Revolution was a term developed in the 1960s to refer to the introduction of new 'high yielding varieties' of food seeds. These HYVs were capable of raising food production but they did require changes in agricultural methods so as to allow more controlled irrigation and the use of petrochemical fertilizers.

> By the 1970s, these techniques had replaced the traditional farming practices of millions of Third World farmers. By the 1990s, almost 75 percent of Asian rice areas were sown with these new varieties. The same was true for almost half of the wheat planted in Africa and more than half of that in Latin America and Asia, and about 70 percent of the world's corn as well. Overall, it was estimated that 40 percent of all farmers in the Third World were using Green Revolution seeds, with the greatest use found in Asia, followed by Latin America. (www.foodfirst.org)

The debate about the Green Revolution still rages. Neoclassical writers point to the big increases in per capita food that was produced and the spread of markets made possible by the increase in food surpluses. They also refer to the ability of developing countries to attract developed world technical expertise and the increase in foreign capital investment in the farming sectors of these countries. However, other economists argue that introducing such technologies into countries where there were big income gaps between rich and poor and where land ownership was so unequal meant that the technology benefited the rich farmers and developed world interests whereas poor farmer incomes fell and indeed many agricultural workers were displaced from the land. Urban populations benefited from cheaper and more plentiful food but the poor in the rural districts found their incomes falling and therefore their ability to buy food being undermined. The same arguments now rage over the likely affects of this second Green Revolution of genetically modified technology.

❷ What were the advantages of the application of Green Revolution technology?

❷ Should countries be ready to now adopt genetically modified technology?

technology which not only may lead to future unseen health problems but may contaminate non GM crops. Other critics focus on the potential for the bio-technology firms such as Monsanto, Du-Pont and others to gain monopoly control of future food seeds to the detriment of farmers. Bio-piracy also raises the possibility of terrorists or 'rogue states' producing biological bombs and weapons of mass destruction.

This area relates to the political and legal environment discussed in Chapter 4. It also calls into question the role that we all have as consumers and citizens as well as the ethical behaviour of the people responsible for developing the technology. There is a general suspicion from the public about the work of scientists and a sceptical view that it is difficult for science to be objective, supported and funded as it is by businesses themselves. There is also a widespread belief that governments are not able to control the power of commercial interests and so objective risk assessment is impossible.

In this context the concept of the precautionary principle has been developed. The basis of this is that no new technology should be introduced if there is the risk that the costs will be too great even if there is not yet the scientific evidence to show that these costs might occur. This can, of course be defined in strong terms or weaker terms. E.g. the anti GM lobby would like there to be a total ban on GM technology in Britain convinced as they are that the science will show that it is dangerous. The UK government's view is to test the technology under controlled conditions and then come to a view. For the anti GM movement there is no such thing as a controlled test as wind pollination will mean that GM seeds will blow into surrounding fields and contaminate non GM fields and once in the food-chain will be uncontrolled.

> **Stop and Think**
>
> What are the benefits of adopting such a precautionary principle? What are the problems associated with this?
> Why might those in favour of urgent action to combat global climate change argue that the adoption of this earlier might have helped to reverse climate change?

Across the range of technologies then there is a balance of costs and benefits. Food technology is responsible for ensuring cheap food and a wide variety of foods but also raises the prospect of health concerns as a result of the use of pesticides and additives. The power of food businesses is seen as encouraging a change in eating habits that creates obesity amongst the population with calls for curbs on the advertising of unhealthy foods and campaigns for real food (see case study on obesity in Chapter 4) now joining earlier campaigns for products to be produced in traditional ways.

Information and communications technology is seen as ushering in a new paradigm of never ending growth as communication networks increase the spatial integration of business beyond geographical limits. The development of the World Wide Web as a means of navigating through the Internet and the explosion in the amount of computing power and corresponding software programmes to develop the potential uses of these new communication and information possibilities, have led to a massive increase in invention and innovations. This combination of the new information technologies and globalization has created the modern network age and this has had a huge impact on the way in which we now do business.

However, the spread of e-business brings in the possibility of Internet fraud and identity theft and the increased potential for sex offenders and pornographers to exploit the vulnerable. There is now widespread use of surveillance technology to protect civil liberties but these very technologies are seen by many civil liberties groups to actually undermine these. Potentially the new office technologies of e-mail and mobile phones should enable people to work more from home saving commuting which can cut the time spent travelling as well as reducing the environmental impact and office space costs. This should enable people to have a better work–life balance by being able to work more flexibly suiting their household responsibilities. However, there are fears that this instant communications world can mean that people feel or are regarded to be available on a '24:7' basis.

Mini-Case 3.6 Blackberry or Crackberry?

The Blackberry is a range of handheld wireless devices developed by a Canadian firm, that carries a range of Internet services but it is its free e-mail service that has attracted businesses to supply these to their employees. Introduced in 1999, primarily for the business user, they have now become a status item. The benefits of these are enormous and by visiting the company website you can see a number of business case studies showing how this instant communication between managers saves on data inputting and has increased the speed with which information can flow through businesses (see www.blackberry.com). Retail managers in outlets can quickly input sales figures which can be shared with marketing and production teams so that businesses can quickly respond to customer demands.

However, this ability to access e-mail at any time and no matter where the user is has led to reports about their addictive nature with users never being able to relax or feel 'off duty'. Hence the term 'Crackberry' after the highly addictive form of cocaine. It has even now begun to take on religious terminology with the secret glance downwards in meetings or even over the dinner table becoming known as the 'blackberry prayer'!

❓ What are the advantages and disadvantages of modern communication forms such as the instant messaging services of e-mail and mobile phones?

The most recent of the new technologies is nano-technology. This technology enables materials and machines to be created that operate at the nano-scale. This is approximately the size of a billionth of a metre. To put this into context each page of this book is about 100,000 nanometers in thickness. The uses of this technology are not yet at an advanced scale. However, it is envisaged that the technologies will be able to lead to advances in all of the following areas:

1 providing renewable clean energy
2 supplying clean water globally
3 improving health and longevity
4 healing and preserving the environment
5 making information technology available to all
6 enabling space development.
  (www.foresight.org)

A review of websites such as the one above (see also www.nano.gov, www.nanotech-now.com) shows the enormous potential. Already carbon 'nano-tubes' have been developed to produce light much more efficiently and their use in solar panels is seen as being able to dramatically cut the cost of solar power. There is the prospect that the technology will also help in a range of energy reducing activities. Nano-machines may well be able to be introduced into the body and perform micro operations not possible with existing medical technology. However, scenarios have been painted about how such technology once released may turn all matter into grey goo. Whilst this appears to be highly unrealistic the reality is that there is no clear evidence of exactly how such small particles might behave when set free into biological systems (see www.worldchanging.com. This website offers a balanced view on the costs and benefits of technology).

Indeed there are many people who question the real motivation for developing higher levels of technological development. We have seen how technology is important for enhancing competition but what happens if this then becomes a weapon for actually replacing competition by establishing and creating market dominance? This has been illustrated in the case study of the computer games above but for many commentators this is an inevitable consequence of capitalism with the primary aim of the development of the technology not being for the good of society but for the ability of one business to make more profit for itself. Marx was a fierce critic of the motivation for investment or what he referred to as 'accumulation'. For Marx it was an essential paradox of capitalism that businesses were forced to try to outwit the competition by constantly having to invest. This meant that all businesses were constantly forced to spend more and more on investment and yet face falling profits. Later Marxists argued that in fact what would happen is that the strongest would survive and capitalism would become dominated by large monopoly enterprises. In the 20th century an influential writer in this area was Joseph Schumpeter. He saw capitalism as being a process of 'creative destruction' by which he meant that indeed companies through innovation would be able to create monopoly positions but that they would face the prospect of other businesses developing alternative technologies which enabled them to provide new products or cut costs. Capitalism would be destructive in the sense that old companies, products and processes would indeed decline to be replaced by newly created and better ones. This idea is also discussed in Chapter 14.

For believers in free market capitalism all technology reduces costs and improves choice for consumers. Complex technologies involve high sums of money spent on research and development which in and of itself acts as a barrier to entry into an industry. The pharmaceutical industries are often accused of abusing their monopoly powers. However, developing new medicines can involve very expensive research and development costs which companies are keen to recoup and they need long periods to recoup this investment. One way of doing this is to protect themselves through intellectual property rights in the form of copyright or patents. If a dominant market position can be established then it can be very difficult for new entrants even where such new entrants develop less technologically expensive alternatives as the dominant company can seek to protect its position through aggressive marketing.

This raises difficult ethical questions which are explored in Chapter 7. Many people are critical of the power of 'Big Pharma' in that it is argued that they seek to exploit large monopoly profits by selling drugs which are heavily branded to cash-rich people in the developed world. This could be justified in this context as developed world health systems largely enable most people who need these drugs to acquire them (although not all people). In the case of global markets though there is a problem. In the developing world low incomes and poorly developed health systems mean people here do not have access to the drugs they need. These drugs could now be produced more cheaply and sold as generic drugs by local companies under licence but are prevented from doing this by the reluctance of the western pharmaceutical companies to 'give away' their intellectual property rights.

There is also evidence that often drugs are prescribed in cases where they are inappropriate or unnecessary and that the selling agents for the companies use highly unethical practices to persuade doctors, health authorities and patients that they do indeed need these expensive treatments.

The pharmaceutical industries are often accused of abusing their monopoly powers. However, developing new medicines can involve very expensive research and development costs.

© istockphoto.com/Millanovic

Appropriate technology

Diversity

Spatial levels

This chapter has sought to illustrate examples of technology that do not necessarily require massive amounts of investment and or scientific expertise and research. However, equally we have seen that in the competitive struggle between businesses in practice there can be this tendency to pursue ever more expensive and 'high-tech' solutions. Just as with the calls for the need for alternative technology to replace the polluting energy technologies that we have at the moment, there is a related debate that questions whether such high-tech solutions are universally necessary. It is clear that one possible motivation for high-tech solutions is to eventually establish dominant market positions in an industry. However, the infrastructure needed to support this level of research and development may be beyond many individual firms and indeed within certain countries, especially developing ones.

Here it is argued it is not necessary for developing countries to try and buy in the sophisticated technology of the developed world. What is needed is **appropriate technology** which is suitable for the external environment in which they are operating.

A revolutionary example of this was the development of the solar powered wind up radio. In villages without electricity or the money to buy batteries such a radio brings instant access to the outside world. Even where there is available appropriate technology such as basic tools to help farmers many people may not have the money to buy these. A major obstacle to development in agriculture in the developing world is credit. Modern banking systems are very sophisticated and heavily reliant on information technology and most developing countries simply do not have the infrastructure or educated banking personnel to develop this. The Grameen bank concept has meant that local communities are able to build their own credit facilities based on local mutual support using 'micro-credit' facilities and this in turn allows people access to basic but appropriate technology.

Indeed the fact that developing countries do not have the resources to engage in such high-tech activities can sometimes have advantages as firms or countries can simply wait until the technology has been developed and then adopt the technology when prices are low. In the developing world the mobile phone is transforming village life as farmers can begin to communicate with the cities far away and gain access to valuable market information such as prices that they hitherto were unaware of. This means that they can avoid the huge costs of developing fixed line telecommunication systems.

The use of computers is as yet very limited as these are still relatively expensive and even where people can gain access to the Internet the cost of software licences can be high. The development of refurbished lower spec computers using an alternative operating system called FLOSS (free (libre) open source system) that has been distributed for free are examples of this approach.

As always with technology there is room for optimism that the new technologies will enable people in the poorest parts of the world to improve their standards of living but as this chapter has shown it is important that the right external conditions are in place to enable the benefits of the technology to outweigh the costs.

◈ *Looking ahead*

The world of technology is often seen as the world of the future and as such it attracts a large amount of speculation as to what the future will hold. As always with future predictions opinion varies from wild optimism to dire pessimistic predictions.

From 1965 to 2003 in the UK the BBC used to produce, what is now seen as a classic TV programme, *Tomorrow's World* which

profiled developments in science and technology. In its hey-day the programme attracted audiences of over 10 million and its focus was invariably on optimistically predicting what it saw as future technological developments that would transform the world.

The world since 1965 has indeed changed as a result of technology and many of the technologies shown on this programme have indeed been world changing. However, the decision to axe the programme in 2003 can be seen as a symbol of a more cautious and sceptical attitude that the British viewing public has to technological change. Indeed this could be seen to be mirrored in the airing of two series of a programme called *Look Around You* in 2003 and 2005 which satirized programmes like *Tomorrow's World* in a way which showed the preposterous and often misguided nature of unquestioning optimism about the future of science and technology.

There is a tendency in looking ahead in terms of technology to focus on the exciting growth of the new technologies of information technology, bio-technology and nano-technology. The first two technologies have undoubtedly had a significant impact on the world of business and society but the debates as to how significant this impact is, and whether such impacts are good or bad, rage. In relation to IT, there is still a significant 'digital divide' in the world both between countries and between people in the same country. In relation to bio-technology there is the same hope that there was with the Green Revolution that world hunger might be eradicated but there are fears that such technology might simply widen the gap between rich and poor.

There is a large measure of public distrust and fear about science and technology and a clear message that public policy needs always to keep in mind the precautionary principle when it comes to developing the regulatory framework in which businesses operate. Perhaps the greatest challenge for businesses is to be able to show clearly how developing and using technology can indeed both improve profits as well as social well being and the task for the policy makers is to create an environment in which this possibility is maximized. Since we are now living in a global environment, this will increasingly involve cooperation between countries and legislation at the global level.

There is a current feeling that the potential of technology has not yet been realized and indeed has led to many of the problems facing us today. The UK government's Foresight programme is currently focusing on three aspects of modern life that it feels have deteriorated over time namely, mental well being, obesity and environmental sustainability. There is a general perception that, in the modern age, safeguards and action need to be taken in these three areas and that if technological changes in the past have contributed to these problems then science and technology should in turn be used to improve these.

◆ *Summary*

- Technology is often seen as being the use of complex developments in science and technology to improve business performance. While this may be the case in many technologies, in practice technology does not have to be inherently complex

- Successful use of technology improves the performance of business both in terms of performance and productivity. Whilst this can involve new inventions of products and processes more often than not it is technological innovation that is the key

- For technological change to be successful it is a combination of entrepreneurial endeavour and factors in the external environment that are important. This is vital for national competitive advantage. For businesses to be successful there are key strategies that need to be pursued at the national level and so public policy is important. Increasingly as business goes global these strategies also need to be coordinated at the supra-national level

- Technology is a major factor in shaping the forces that affect the competitive advantage of businesses. Businesses can choose to be leaders or followers and need to constantly review how technology impacts across the length of the value chain

- Technology is not value neutral. There are critics who see a conflict between the private desire of firms to make profits and the social impacts of technology and those that feel that a free market will ensure that firms can only indeed make profits if they satisfy social needs. Between these views lie those that argue that what is needed is a legislative framework which can protect society whilst encouraging businesses to be technologically inventive and innovative

- Technology can cause harm as well as good and it is important that we develop an ethical framework in which to analyse its effects. In practice there will be no easy answer to the question of its impact. To echo Schumpeter, technology leads to 'creative destruction'. Any change will have advantages and disadvantages and the task for the public policy is to create an environment which promotes technological change but one which also ensures that the costs do not outweigh the advantages. The use of the precautionary principle can help here but taken to its extreme can mean that no proposed technological change would be seen to be 'safe'

Case study: containerization

On 4 November 2006 the world's biggest container ship the *Emma Maersk* docked at Felixstowe on its maiden voyage having set out from Yentian port in China. Writing in the *Guardian* of 30/10/06, John Vidal reported that 'The British Christmas table would barely groan without the *Emma Maersk*'.

The size of the *Emma Maersk* is truly inspiring at a quarter of a mile long and 61 metres high but whilst the engineering of this ship is staggering (its diesel engine is the largest ever built) it is the simple technology of the containers that it is carrying that has done so much to transform the world in which we live. The *Emma Maersk* was carrying 11,000 of these of which 3,000 were to be unloaded at Felixstowe before she continued her journey to mainland Europe.

The container is simply a steel box in which goods can be placed to be transported. The simplicity of the container is that it can be carried on a multi-modal basis i.e. on a lorry, by rail by sea or air. They come in standard sizes and are measured in TEU or (twenty foot equivalent units). The most common size is a 40 foot container which would cost around $2,500 to buy. However, it has revolutionized the logistics of transporting goods to such an extent that to all intents and purposes it has reduced transport costs to an almost negligible level.

In essence the reason for this is simple. Economies of scale mean that by doubling the dimensions of a box you expand the storage capacity of this box many more times meaning that more goods can be placed into one container. Previously, the container loading and unloading goods for freight by sea was highly labour intensive and goods were in individual crates of different sizes and shapes that then had to be manually lifted and stowed in the holds of ships. Whilst the longshoremen involved in this were skilled at packing in the cases, the odd shapes meant that great care had to be paid to how the crates went in and not all available space could be used. There was the real risk that badly loaded cargo would shift when at sea and lead to breakages or even the capsizing of the vessel.

On unloading this cargo it had to be sorted and transferred onto vehicles for their final destination. Containerization did many things: Firstly it meant that there was the need for far fewer workers and it was much easier to stack containers. Secondly it meant that it was much easier to load and unload the containers. Each container is simply lifted onto a lorry and then off it goes. Having arrived at 18.08 on 4 November at Felixstowe, *the Emma Maersk* set sail out of the harbour at 5am on the 6 November having unloaded 3,000 containers. To give an idea of how many goods this involved the manifest revealed that just one container could carry: 334 cartons of cocktail shakers or 1.9 million Christmas decorations or 742 cartons of handbags or 2,120 boxes of books or 87,150 hair straighteners or 150 tonnes of New Zealand lamb!

The container then has truly revolutionized the world of transportation and since practically every good ever bought or sold has spent some time in a container it has had a huge impact on

The simple technology of containers has done much to transform the world in which we live.

© Olivier Lantzendörffer

all of us. Chapter 11 explores the growth of globalization and this chapter has shown how the network age has resulted from the combined growth of information technology and globalization. It is no coincidence that the *Emma Maersk*'s itinerary starts in China which is now the fastest growing exporter in the world.

The container ports of today are much more capital and technologically intensive compared to the docklands of old. However, the container itself is a simple idea. In his book, *The Box—How the Shipping Container Made the World Smaller and the World Economy Bigger*, Marc Levinson charts the conditions that led to its development and the huge impact the container has had on the world. In making shipping cheap the container also made it possible to have a world economy. This has had many impacts. This new world economy based on cheap transport costs most obviously had devastating effects on the traditional dock areas. In Liverpool and London the traditional life of the docklands was swept away causing huge structural problems in those areas with high unemployment and urban decay. As these ports declined new ports such as Felixstowe arose. However, the dramatic changes came in the developing world and especially in the newly industrializing countries of Southeast Asia. Here the fall in transport costs meant that these countries could engage in a fierce export drive to exploit the combination of technological advances and lower labour costs that were the basis of their industrialization. South Korea developed a very strong ship building industry centred around the new ships made possible by containerization. Not surprisingly the biggest container ports in the world are located in Southeast Asia.

Cheap transportation has revolutionized the supply chain for businesses. Firms no longer need to locate near to ports or locate different parts of the supply chain close together but can split it up and locate each production stage where costs are lowest. Firms could thus be truly international and in many ways are forced to go global. It is no longer possible for a firm to decide to simply locate production and supply locally as it is under constant pressure from competitor firms exploiting their global reach.

Such technological change has not been a universal benefit. The structural unemployment in the traditional ports created long term economic and social problems that are only now being overcome. While as consumers we benefit from the low costs and variety of goods, as workers the pressure of competition from low wage areas has created the demands for labour to be more 'flexible' which is a shorthand for reducing working conditions enjoyed by workers in the developed world in terms of hours and state benefits as well as actual wage levels and employment levels. On top of all this is the environmental cost of transporting these containers by sea and rail but especially by road and air.

Ironically, Levinson argues that it was to avoid road congestion that the first commercial venture into containerization was developed in the USA in the 1950s. While containers had been in limited use as one way of transporting goods by sea, it was the McLean Trucking corporation that really appreciated the revolutionary potential of containerization and that this, if used widely, would radically transform the whole transportation industry. McLean's first venture into containerization was to avoid the road congestion along the Eastern seaboard interstate highways. Trucks would deposit containers onto ships for these then to be sent by sea to destinations along the seaboard and then off loaded onto other trucks to be taken to the final destination. What McClean did was to see the potential in integrating shipping and road transportation and the huge economies of scale that could be derived from converting ships into container ships and the necessary changes that would need to be made to the trucks that would pull them and the way in which docks would operate in the future.

What is clear here is that it is not the invention of the container itself that led to the revolutionary changes in world shipping and freight transportation. It was down to an astute cost cutting entrepreneur who recognized that by using containers, the way in which transport could be organized would be completely different and would involve changes across the industry in terms of the way in which ports operated, the technology needed to operate these and the way in which transport companies would need to integrate their operations.

❷ What is containerization and how did the innovative use of containers transform the distribution of goods?

❷ What are the advantages of using containers to transport goods by sea, road and rail?

❷ What are the disadvantages of containerization?

❷ What role has containerization played in the development of a global economic system?

Review and discussion questions

1   How does technology potentially increase the production possibilities of a country?

2   What are the main conditions in the external national business environment that it is argued are necessary for technological change to increase economic growth?

3   How does technology affect the potential for a business to establish competitive advantage?

4   What are the main general disadvantages associated with technological change?

5   What are the different views as to whether technology is good or bad? Give some examples to illustrate your point of view.

Assignments

1   Research and then outline the main technological changes that have allowed supermarkets to become the dominant players in the grocery industry in the past fifty years. What have been the effects of these changes on the producers and other stakeholders during this time? On balance are supermarkets efficient?

2   Choose one from the following: information technology, bio-technology, nano-technology. What are the main future developments in the chosen area and what are the likely impacts of these on business?

3   How might the technological solutions being proposed to tackle global climate change impact on business behaviour?

Further reading

Levinson, M. (2006) *The Box—How the Shipping Container Made the World Smaller and the World Economy Bigger* (Oxford: Princeton University Press). This is an in depth study of how in the opinion of the author a low-tech development changed the world. He charts the combination of entrepreneurial drive and the external factors that enabled this drive to fundamentally change the internal organization of the logistics industry. This also reveals how the changes moved from a local environment to a national and global one.

Porter, M. E. (1985) *Competitive Advantage—Creating and Sustaining Superior Performance* (London: Collier Macmillan). Chapter 5 focuses on the role of technology in affecting the value chain of a company and the development of a technological strategy for a business.

Porter, M. E. (1998) *Competitive Advantage of Nations* (New York: Free Press). Chapter 1 gives a very succinct overview of Porter's belief that competitive advantage is created through the increases in productivity made possible by technological

change, and he outlines both the weaknesses in other theories used to explain competitiveness as well as broadly outlining his own diamond model. (This chapter is available online at: www.simonsays.com)

Young, W. (2004) *Sold Out—the True Cost of Supermarket Shopping* (London: Vision). This book looks at the rise of the supermarkets' dominance over the grocery trade and the technological changes within the industry. In so doing it highlights many of the concerns that are expressed about our modern technological world.

United Nations Development Programme (2001) *Human Development Report—Making New Technologies Work for Human Development* (available at http://hdr.undp.org). This report looks at the way in which new technologies have and are shaping living standards across the world. In so doing it focuses on the global disparities in technological development and the degree to which the poorer countries can gain technological advantages.

Online resources

Test your understanding of this chapter with online questions and answers, explore the subject further through web exercises, and use the weblinks to provide a quick resource for further research. Go to the Online Resource Centre at

www.oxfordtextbooks.co.uk/orc/ wetherly_otter/

www.worldchanging.com
This site is a discussion and news site to profile both the dangers and the possible benefits that technology can play in promoting human development.

www.foresight.gov.uk
Profiles the work of the UK government's Foresight programme which tries to coordinate science and technology projects.

www.bbc.co.uk
Up-to-date news about technological developments.

References

Cypher, J. M. and Dietz, J. (2004) *The Process of Economic Development* (London: Routledge).

Engels, F. (1989) *The Condition of the English Working Class*, edited by V. G. Kiernan (London: Penguin).

Friedman, T. (2005) *The World is Flat* (London: Penguin).

Levinson, M. (2006) *The Box—How the Shipping Container Made the World Smaller and the World Economy Bigger* (Oxford: Princeton University Press).

Porter, M. E. (1985) *Competitive Advantage—Creating and Sustaining Superior Performance* (London: Collier Macmillan).

Porter, M. E. (1998) *Competitive Advantage of Nations* (New York: Free Press).

United Nations Development Programme (2001) *Human Development Report—Making New Technologies Work for Human Development* (Oxford: Oxford University Press).

Smith, A. (1976) [1776] *An Inquiry into the Nature and Causes of the Wealth of Nations* (Chicago: University of Chicago Press).

Vidal, J. (2006) How world's biggest ship is delivering our Christmas—all the way from China, *Guardian*, 30 October, p. 13.

The political-legal environment

Paul Wetherly

Contents

04

Learning objectives

When you have completed this chapter you will be able to:

- Explain the nature of **politics** as concerned with making choices for society as a whole through law and public policy, including decisions and rules concerning the conduct of business
- Analyse the interdependence of business and government
- Identify key features of the UK political system as a **liberal democracy** based on the rule of law
- Analyse the different values and ideologies (e.g. left and right) involved in political disputes, and the implications of these views for the role of government in business decisions and behaviour, and the balance between the state and the market
- Examine the ideologies of the main political parties and their attitudes to business, including the character of **New Labour**

Themes

Diversity	**Diversity of business** Relationships between business and government are diverse.
Internal/ external	Internal/external The political environment impacts on the internal environment of business organizations. Politics may be seen as a feature of business organizations, e.g. in the form of office politics.
Complexity	Complexity of the environment Politics and government are key elements of the complex business environment.
Spatial levels	**Variety of spatial levels** Politics and governance operate on a number of levels or spatial scales—sub-national, national, and supra-national.
Dynamic	Dynamic environment The political environment is dynamic due to shifts in popular support, ideological adjustments, and changes of government. The role of the state in relation to the market has been characterized by periods of intervention and disengagement.
Interaction	**Interaction between business and the environment** Business and government are interdependent.
Stakeholders	Stakeholders The political process is characterized by a range of stakeholder groups with different values and interests.
Values	Values Political disagreement is driven by differences of values and interests. Politics concerns ideas of 'good government' and the 'good society'.

Introduction: what is politics? Why is politics necessary?

This chapter will examine the nature of politics, the relationship between politics and business, some key features of the UK political system, the main belief systems or ideologies, and the main political parties. We will see that politics is closely related to law, since politics is concerned with the making and enforcement of laws. However we will leave a detailed discussion of the legal framework and environment of business to Chapter 13.

Values

What is politics? For many people politics is about elections and voting, what goes on in parliament, 'spin', or politicians trying to 'climb the greasy pole' to the top. These may all be aspects of political behaviour, but they do not really tell us about the fundamental purpose of politics. Although a range of definitions of politics have been proposed, a good starting point is to define politics as an activity that is concerned with trying to shape the character of the society we live in and the direction it takes in accordance with the values or interests that people hold. In other words, politics can be defined in terms of competing views about the kind of society we want and the rules or laws which are necessary for us to live together in such a 'good society'.

For example, we have seen that all societies have to deal with the economic problem of how to allocate resources between competing uses or wants. In western societies the principal mechanism that has been developed to deal with this economic problem is the market system. Although dealing with scarcity seems to be essentially an economic problem it also has a crucial political dimension. This is because the market system does not arise spontaneously but depends on decisions made in society to create the necessary rules and institutions for markets to operate. For example, capitalism could not exist without the right to private property which depends on the law and politics.

Free market versus regulation

In fact politics in western societies has been dominated by the question of capitalism, pitching its advocates against those who favour a different kind of economic system altogether. Socialism and capitalism have been advocated as alternative versions of the 'good society'. Although arguments against capitalism and private enterprise are still part of political debate, political argument in the mainstream concerns what *kind* of capitalist system we want to live in. There are different versions or models of capitalism on offer. For example, we have to decide, as a society, how the relationship between employer and employee is going to work:

- Should this be on free market lines, as a voluntary exchange in which each party is left to make it up as they go along, making decisions on the basis of their own interests?
- Or should the law be used to set down certain rights and duties for each party?
- Should employers be allowed to hire employees on whatever criteria they choose?
- Or should the law prohibit them from discriminating on certain grounds, such as an applicant's race or ethnicity?

There is always likely to be disagreement on these issues. I might want to allow business to operate freely in the market, whereas you might want to see greater regulation of business by government. These different values might reflect our different positions and interests. I might be an employer wanting to make my own decisions about how I run my business in my own interests without interference; you might be an employee wanting regulation to afford you some protections in the workplace, such as against racial discrimination or unfair dismissal. But the difficulty is that we both have to live in the same society. We can't have both a 'free market' and 'regulation'

—we need a way of resolving these different opinions or values and making a decision. The decision might go one way or the other, or there might be a compromise in which each side gives up something in order to reach agreement, for example more regulation than the free market supporters would like but less than the regulators were after. Whatever the decision, it will remain up for debate, with the possibility of moving in a different direction in the future. The regulators may have to accept defeat today but will renew the fight tomorrow.

Here we see the fundamental purpose of politics—it is the activity of making (and preserving or revising) these decisions for society as a whole. The point is that the political decision cannot be ducked: not having race discrimination legislation is just as much a political choice as having it. (Chapter 13 looks further at balancing business freedom and the authority of the law.)

Constraints and opportunities

Political decisions may impose restrictions or constraints on our choices and behaviours, but they may also afford opportunities or resources that we would otherwise lack. Of course, in many cases a constraint for one person is an opportunity for another. In the example of race discrimination legislation it is the legal constraint on business that ensures the equal opportunity for all people to be considered for jobs on their merits regardless of whether they happen to be black or white.

Compliance

Of course, having rules in society is one thing, but it is also necessary to ensure compliance with the law. Compliance very often relies on individuals agreeing with the law or accepting its legitimacy. Most employers have no problem, in principle, with race discrimination legislation because they share the view, held widely in British society, that black and white people should enjoy equal opportunities. Here the law expresses the values of the society. However not everybody shares this view—racial discrimination has not disappeared from the workplace. Therefore the law has to be enforced. The capacity to make and enforce the rules under which we live is a unique form of power in society, exercised only by government or the state.

Narrow and broad conceptions of politics

Hence politics is often defined as the study of government. This view, of politics-as-government, focuses attention on the democratic procedures through which governments are elected, the rules and institutions involved in governing (the 'machinery of government'), and the decisions made and implemented by government. However a broader view of politics sees the focus on government as too narrow, as missing out some parts of the picture. For example, joining or supporting a political party is not the only way to influence government decisions. Individuals may join or support a 'civil society organization' (CSO) or 'pressure group' as a way of trying to get their beliefs and values taken seriously and acted on by government. For example, there is a range of environmental or 'green' pressure groups, such as Friends of the Earth, Greenpeace and the WWF that do not put up candidates for election but seek to influence the priorities and decisions of the political parties and government of the day (see Chapter 11).

Pressure groups can also try to bring about change by bypassing the formal political system altogether. For example environmental campaigns seek to influence business decisions directly using a variety of methods including research, public relations, engaging in dialogue with business, consumer activism and forms of direct action. They also, of course, seek to achieve environmental goals by advocating life-style changes among their supporters and the general public. Thus people can feel that they are part of a political movement by altering everyday behaviours in their private lives, such as recycling more rubbish, or using their cars less.

Recycling Bins

People can feel that they are part of a political movement by altering their everyday behaviours, such as recycling more rubbish.

© istockphoto.com/Frank van den Bergh

Internal/ external

Finally some people see politics as an intrinsic dimension of our personal lives and private sector organizations. For example, the long campaign for women to achieve equal opportunities with men in business through changes in the law, such as the Sex Discrimination Act (1975), has also involved a focus on domestic life. Who does the washing up and looks after the children can be seen as political questions because of the way the division of unpaid labour in the home affects the opportunities men and women enjoy in the world of business and paid employment. Politics is often seen as a feature of the workplace—as in the phrase 'office politics'—and this can be seen in relation to equal opportunities. The barriers to women's opportunities for advancement in business are not related just to discrimination as defined by the law or being 'chained to the kitchen sink' but to day-to-day assumptions and behaviours in the workplace that may, for example, create a sexist culture.

> **➲ Stop and Think**
> What is the meaning of the term 'politics'? Why is politics necessary in society? Are there any areas of life that politics should be kept out of? Is business one of these areas?

What has politics got to do with business?

One of the key questions in politics concerns its proper limits. In western societies freedom (or liberty) is a key political principle, and this involves the idea that people should be left, as far as possible, to get on with their own lives without interference from others or from government. This raises the difficult question of the appropriate balance between the capacity of government to make and enforce rules that govern our lives and our desire to live those lives as we please (see Chapter 13).

This question has a direct bearing on business. In a capitalist economy business activity is undertaken primarily by privately owned firms, through voluntary exchange in a market, involving the pursuit of self-interest (the profit motive). The basic idea of a market seems to be that individuals make decisions for themselves about how to use their own resources. So what could be the role, if any, for politics in a free market? Some say 'the government of business is no business of government', suggesting that businesses and individuals should be free to manage their own affairs.

Mini-Case 4.1 Obesity and the 'nanny state'

Increasing obesity is related to diet and exercise, but is the marketing of junk food to blame? Is there a responsibility for government to take action to tackle this problem?

© istockphoto.com/Lise Gagne

During the last few decades the rate of obesity has been rising in the UK to become a serious health problem. Particular concern has been expressed about the rate of childhood obesity and its implications for future health risks and life expectancy. Whereas in 1997 9.6% of children under 10 were obese, this had increased to 13.7% by 2003. Obesity rates are higher for 11–15 year-olds. In 2003, according to the Department of Health, there were 24.2 million obese or overweight people in the UK. It has been claimed that 'We are in danger of raising a generation of people who have a shorter life expectancy than their parents' (Waine, quoted in Carvel, 2006).

It is obvious that this problem is related to diet and exercise and the solution lies in healthier lifestyles. However the reasons why lifestyles have become less healthy over this period are disputed. Some say that individuals are responsible for these decisions, others point the finger at the food industry and the marketing of 'junk food', and others say that obesity is linked to poverty and low social status. Is there a responsibility for govern-ment to take action to tackle this problem? Or should we say that if people want to eat junk food and get fat that's up to them?

It might be argued that government should act because otherwise it, and therefore taxpayers, will have to pick up the cost of treating the diseases related to obesity through the NHS. Another argument is that government has a responsibility to care for the well-being of its citizens and sometimes knows better than they do what is good for them. In other words, the trouble with leaving people to live their lives as they please is that they some-times make poor decisions. For example government might see it as part of its responsibility to exhort us to eat five portions of fruit and vegetables each day. This conception of the respons-ibilities of government is sometimes characterized as the 'nanny state'. Usually this is intended as a pejorative phrase, but is a 'nanny state' really such a bad thing?

In the case of junk food the choices people make have to be seen in the context of the marketing effort of the food industry, especially in relation to children. Companies may say that they only sell products that people *want* to buy, but against that it can be argued that the companies *persuade* us to want them. In other words, in their relationship with business consumers may find it difficult to make good decisions. In part this may be because they rely on information presented by companies in a way that suits them, in the form of advertising and labelling. Perhaps we need 'nanny' to help us? For example:

- In 2006 the Food Standards Agency (FSA) introduced a non-compulsory 'traffic light' labelling system designed to alert consumers to foods high in salt, fat and sugar and help them to make healthier choices. Though adopted by some major supermarkets, three supermarkets and 21 food manufacturers formed a coalition to oppose it and launched their own alternative labelling scheme.

- In January 2007 Ofcom (Office of Communications), the media regulator, introduced a ban on television advertising of junk food (as defined by the FSA's labelling scheme) during programmes aimed at children under 16, or where children make up a high proportion of viewers. This ban has the force of law.

- ❷ Do you agree that 'if individuals want to eat junk food that's up to them, it's no business of government'? Or do you think the traffic light labelling system and the ban on junk food ads were justified?

- ❷ Do these measures go far enough to tackle the obesity crisis?

The state and the market

Values

In fact there is, speaking strictly, no such thing as a free market in the world today, and such an idea would be impossible to realize. This is because the operation of the market depends on certain forms of law and public policy (e.g. private property rights, law of contract, the regulation of money as a means of exchange, law and order). More generally, different views about the good society inevitably involve arguments about the purpose of business in society and how it should be managed. This is because business decisions have far-reaching consequences for society, shaping societal outcomes such as:

- the level, types and locations of employment
- the level and composition of output
- the types of jobs needed in the economy
- the environmental impacts of production.

Thus a key question in political debate is always going to be what balance or combination of the state and the market is necessary to achieve the public interest or common good of society. Is the common good best served by leaving economic decisions to the self interest of individuals and organizations in a market? Or does the common good require some forms of law and public policy to regulate or even replace market decisions? Notice that this is not an either–or question—the answer does not have to be either 'leave things to the market' or 'let government take charge of economic activity'. Instead, a range of answers is possible involving different combinations of the state and the market. As we will see, this question is at the heart of left–right and party political debate.

The interdependence of business and government

Interaction

Government involvement in economic life is a feature of all capitalist economies, though its precise nature and scope vary considerably between different societies. Politics and business are not separate but *interdependent*—in some ways business depends on government, and government in some ways depends on business. In all capitalist or market-based economies business is involved in a variety of *relationships* with government (Wilson, 2003: 1–8). Government:

- determines the legal framework within which business operates
- influences or determines the scope of market relationships and the balance or mix between the market and other sectors (public and voluntary/third)
- relates to private sector business as a major customer
- relates to private sector business as a provider of services and resources
- relates to private sector business as a tax collector
- manages the macroeconomic environment
- represents business interests in relation to foreign governments.

These relationships are all expressed in terms of what government does, but they can be turned around to make clear the interdependence between business and government. Thus:

- government consults business on law and public policy, and often relies on self-regulation
- the dynamism of private sector business tends to extend the scope of the market in relation to the other sectors
- business supplies goods and services to government
- business is a major user of services provided by the public sector
- business activity is a prime source of tax revenues
- private sector investment is the driving force behind economic growth and prosperity
- the strength of the domestic economy is a key ingredient of the influence of governments in world affairs.

Regulation

As we have seen, the basic task of government in all societies is to determine the rules within which people live, including rules governing business behaviour. Although business is often seen to be in favour of less regulation, the law plays an important role in creating markets and enabling them to operate. For example, although markets are based on voluntary agreements and exchanges, the law ensures the enforceability of these agreements or contracts. Where there may be little basis for trust between buyers and sellers the law gives each side the basis for confidence that the agreement will be honoured, and that redress can be sought if it is not. In modern capitalist economies the law affects all aspects of business activity:

- relations with employees (e.g. employee protection)
- relations with customers (e.g. consumer protection)
- competitive behaviours and relationships (e.g. competition policy)
- impacts on third parties and the environment (e.g. planning law).

Taxation

The development of modern government and the public sector has depended on the capacity to raise revenue through taxation. And decisions regarding taxation—how much to raise and who should pay it—have always been highly contentious. Although the necessity of taxation is generally recognized, it touches on key political arguments about individual freedom or liberty (expressed in terms of individuals being free to decide for themselves how to spend their own money) and fairness or equity (expressed in terms of what is a fair share of taxation in relation to what others pay, and in relation to services that are provided/value for money). A key question is what contribution to overall tax revenues should be made by business, particularly in the form of corporation tax and national insurance contributions.

Public services

Law or regulation and taxation are key elements of the government–business relationship, with business often being seen as favouring less of each. However the other relationships are also important. In the developed capitalist economies not all economic or business activity is left to private enterprise and the market. In mixed economies there is substantial public sector involvement in certain areas of business. Although public ownership of industry has been largely reversed, in the UK and elsewhere, through privatization, governments continue to have an important role in financing and providing a range of public services such as education, health and social care, and income support. In countries such as the UK citizens rely mainly on the welfare state rather than private sector businesses for provision of these services. We tend to think of welfare states primarily in terms of the benefits they bring to individuals, but it is important to recognize that business also has a stake in these services. That is because the efficiency and competitiveness of business depends on such favourable conditions as a healthy and educated workforce. When the then Prime Minister Tony Blair stated the priorities of the Labour government elected in 1997 to be 'education, education, education' he was putting this forward as an economic policy as much as a social policy, on the basis that education is the key to competitiveness in the global economy as well as the key to enhancing individuals' life chances. We can see how business has a stake in the education system from the frequent statements on this subject from business associations such as the Confederation of British Industry (CBI). Beyond what we conventionally think of as the welfare state, business has a stake in other areas of government activity that impact upon business performance, including grants, support for research and development, and the transport infrastructure.

Government as customer

Business has an important stake in these and other areas of government activity not only because businesses are direct or indirect users or beneficiaries but also because private business supplies goods and services to the public sector. Government is the principal customer for some firms and industries, such as pharmaceuticals, armaments and civil engineering, because government is the main or sole provider of health care, defence and physical infrastructure. Government could, in principle, own pharmaceutical or civil engineering businesses as part of the public sector but chooses to purchase these outputs from the private sector. As Wilson points out 'government is a customer, but a customer of a very special type, one that can be persuaded to buy a product not only through a combination of the usual commercial skills but also through political pressures' (2003: 1).

Managing the economy

As we will see in more detail in Chapter 6, government plays an important role in maintaining a favourable macroeconomic environment for business. During the period of Keynesian consensus managing the economy entailed a range of objectives including economic growth, high or 'full' employment, control of inflation, and a favourable balance of payments. More recently the shift to 'monetarism' and 'neoliberalism', inaugurated in the 1980s, involved a narrowing of these objectives, with emphasis on the fight against inflation. All businesses have a stake in government macroeconomic policy both because the goal, such as a low inflation climate, may be beneficial for business and the specific policy tools and decisions, such as decisions to raise or lower interest rates, have a direct impact on business. Although low inflation is generally good for business, higher interest rates which may be deemed necessary to realize this goal can be harmful, especially to certain sectors that rely upon borrowing such as construction and consumer durables.

The international dimension

International trade and foreign investment, associated with the phenomenon of globalization, mean that business operations (exchange and production) span national borders so that business–government relations are not confined to business's own national government. UK companies exporting to China or establishing production facilities there have to deal with the political institutions, rules and procedures of that country. In pursuing overseas expansion businesses may look to their own governments for assistance in, for example, negotiating market access and favourable trade rules. 'It is arguable that, in an era of increasing globalization, corporations need the assistance of their own home government more . . . in order to obtain favourable trading arrangements and protection of their property—including intellectual property—overseas' (Wilson, 2003: 5).

Spatial levels

These diverse relationships between business and government remind us that businesses never operate in a truly free market, but always in a political environment in which government decisions, to varying degrees, influence the threats and opportunities that business confronts. Second, these relationships are two-way, in the sense that they involve interdependence between business and government and that they have to be continuously negotiated and adjusted between the two sides. Government decisions on, say, employee protection laws always involve some level of consultation and discussion with business. It is inconceivable that any government in the UK would make a major decision affecting business without taking account of business opinion (though this does not necessarily mean business opinions will always be adhered to). In other words, there is a political dialogue between business and government about these relationships. Of course, business does not have exclusive access to government—many other stakeholders are affected by decisions in these areas and seek to influence government. Chapter 11 examines both the methods businesses and business associations use to participate in the political process and how effective these methods are.

Interaction

Stakeholders

> **➲ Stop and Think**
>
> For each type of relationship between business and government say whether you think this shows government as a friend of business, an enemy of business, or as acting in the public interest as a whole.
>
> Reflect on how easy or difficult it is to make these distinctions.

The UK political system

In this section some of the key features of the UK political system will be described and analysed. Here we focus on the narrow conception of politics-as-government. The political system comprises the range of institutions and personnel that are involved in making and enforcing rules for the society. In this section we will examine:

- the size and scope of the political system. This involves an overview of the growth of the state
- consider who rules and the rules governing rule-making. This involves an understanding of Britain as a democracy and some features of the constitution
- examine the conception of the UK as a self-governing nation-state. This requires us to consider the role of politics also at a supra-national level.

The modern state

The role of the state in modern societies is highly controversial. As we will see, it goes to the heart of left–right political debate. Do we want to grow the state, or shrink it? Very few people want to get rid of the state altogether, and very few people want the state to do everything. In mainstream political debate it is accepted that the state is necessary, but a key question is how big should it be? In particular, what is the best balance between the state and the market? (Another important question—how the state or public sector should be organized and managed—is examined in Chapter 10.)

For the moment we need to chart the size and scope of the state in modern Britain. What is the state? The term is often used interchangeably with 'the government'. However, when we refer to 'the government of the day' (for example, the Labour governments under Tony Blair from 1997) this refers to a group of elected politicians made up, principally, of the prime minister and the other members of the Cabinet. Government in this sense is also referred to as the executive, which means that it has responsibility for carrying out decisions and implementing public policies. For example, the chancellor of the exchequer, as a member of the Cabinet, has responsibility for managing the government's finances and carrying out government economic policy, in collaboration with Cabinet colleagues who share 'collective responsibility' for all aspects of government policy. The Cabinet is sometimes compared to the board of directors of a company.

In contrast with government, the state is comprised of the complex set of institutions that go to make up the public sector as a whole. The government–state distinction can be understood by thinking of the executive as one of three distinct branches or functions of the state. Before law and policy can be implemented (the task of the executive) there must be a process of law-making, and there needs to be a mechanism for adjudicating legal disputes when they arise. This gives rise to three branches of the state, defined by Heywood as follows:

- legislative branch (legislature)—'empowered to make law through the formal enactment of legislation' (Heywood, 2002: 425)
- executive branch (executive)—'responsible for implementing or carrying out law and policy' (Ibid., 423)
- judicial branch (judiciary)—'empowered to decide legal disputes and adjudicate on the meaning of the law' (Ibid., 425)

Typically there is institutional differentiation or separation within the state between these three branches, although this is sometimes far from perfect. In the UK the executive, in the shape of the prime minister and Cabinet, is comprised of members of parliament. Furthermore an important feature of the UK political system is executive dominance. This means that the executive (i.e. the government of the day) is normally able to dominate the legislature (parliament) because it is able to command a majority of MPs (members of parliament). Thus the government is effectively in charge of law-making as well as implementation.

However the state is made up of more than parliament (consisting, in the UK, of two 'Houses'—the Commons and the Lords), cabinet ministers and the court system. Cabinet ministers clearly do not implement law and policy single-handedly, but rely upon the assistance of junior ministers (who, like cabinet ministers, are usually also elected politicians, and are normally seen as members of the government in distinction to 'backbench' MPs) and civil servants. Senior civil servants who work closely with ministers are often seen as part of the executive. Beyond this, still quite restricted, grouping at the heart of political power, implementation of law and policy depends on a large number of public servants or officials carrying out the day-to-day tasks of delivering public services of various kinds. These include civil servants working in central government departments, local government officers and a wide range of professional, technical, clerical and other staff delivering health, education, policing and other services. Government, we can see, is a part of the wider state, but it is the part that is supposed to direct the whole.

> ⤷ *Stop and Think*
> Why is it important that there is separation between the three branches of the state?

Growth of the state

In this sense 'the state' refers to the entire public sector over which government presides. There is considerable variation between advanced capitalist societies in the size of the state, as measured in terms of public spending and employment. However to varying degrees all these societies have come to be characterized by the growth of 'big government', exemplified by the development of welfare states. The growth of the state was one of the key transformations of these societies during the 20th century, particularly in the decades following the Second World War. During this period, especially in European societies, a positive (broadly left-wing) attitude to the state dominated political debate—so much so that it is often characterized in terms of a Keynesian welfare consensus. From the 1970s on this consensus came to be questioned, particularly from a New Right perspective that was more sceptical of government as a force for good, and aimed to 'roll back' the state.

Dynamic

The 'caretaker' state

In essence the growth of the state reflected the acceptance by governments of a wider range of responsibilities in relation to social and economic problems within their societies. From being conceived essentially as a 'night watchman' primarily responsible for security and law-and-order, the state became a 'caretaker' responsible for looking after the welfare of its citizens through a range of public or collective services, and steering economic and social development. This included managing the performance of the macroeconomy, regulating business decisions and behaviour, and taking charge of important areas of business activity (public services and nationalized industries). The transition is described by Kay:

> The traditional functions of the state were to wage war, adjudicate disputes, and levy taxes to finance these functions. And government still does these things: but they are not now the principal things it does. Today we look to government to secure the provision of education and a transport infrastructure, to guarantee us medical treatment and security in old age, to organise the collection of rubbish and assure unfailing supplies of electricity. The main role of government today is in the provision of goods and services, rather than the exercise of authority. (Kay, 2004: 75)

> ➲ *Stop and Think*
> What is meant by a 'caretaker' state? Think of the ways in which the state affects your daily life.

Liberal democracy and the constitution

The state exercises a unique form of power—to make and enforce the rules under which we live. You don't choose to obey the law? The state can, through its police force, courts and prison system, apprehend and punish you. The state can appropriate a portion of your income through the tax system to use for its own purposes, whether or not you happen to agree with them. You choose not to pay your taxes? Again, the state can apprehend and punish you. Political power can be a force for good in society, or can be the cause of great harm. As Martin Luther King pointed out in relation to racial segregation in the

Table 4.1 UK government expenditure and revenue (2004/5)

	£ billion	%
Expenditure by function		
Social protection	138	28
Health	81	17
Education	63	13
Law & protective services	29	6
Defence	27	6
Debt interest	25	5
Other health & personal social services	22	5
Industry & agriculture	20	4
Housing & environment	17	3
Transport	16	3
Other	49	10
Total managed expenditure	**488**	**100**
Receipts		
Income tax	128	28
National insurance	78	17
VAT	73	16
Excise duties	40	9
Corporation tax	35	8
Council tax	20	4
Business rates	19	4
Other	62	14
Total receipts	**455**	**100**

Source: Office for National Statistics (ONS) (2004), *UK 2005*, p. 365, table 23.1.

American South, laws can be just or unjust. Taxes can be used to finance public services or to build palaces for dictators. Good or bad government is not just about politicians and rulers being evil and corrupt, but also a matter of incompetence. Governments can manage the economy effectively, providing favourable conditions for business to prosper, or their policies can do great damage to economic performance and business confidence. Thus we all have a stake in good government.

Rule by the people

To ensure good government it matters who our law-makers are and that they are not able to govern in an arbitrary manner. Among western capitalist societies some variant of liberal democracy has become the predominant framework governing who rules and the law-making process. The basic principle of democracy is simple to state: it is 'rule by the people' or **popular sovereignty**, meaning that political power is in the hands of the people as a whole and is exercised primarily through the right to vote. In essence democracy is supposed to ensure good government because the people choose their law-makers. If the current set of law-makers are doing a bad job—such as mismanaging the economy—democracy provides a peaceful and orderly mechanism for replacing them with a different set.

Democracy makes law-makers accountable to the people. The test of good government in a democracy is, then, public opinion—good government is whatever the people say it is. Of course, this does not mean that democratic politics always produces especially competent governments with high public approval ratings. On the contrary, opinion surveys often reveal low, or negative, approval ratings for politicians in the UK. It seems that people are in favour of the idea of democracy but sceptical or even cynical about the actual practice of democratic politics. Furthermore, it is in the nature of political disagreement that one person's idea of good government is different to another's. For example, democracy does not guarantee good government from a business perspective, since governments can be elected that are hostile to the private sector. In the past (though less so since the advent of New Labour) the prospect of a Labour government was unwelcome within much of the business community, either because the party was not regarded as competent in relation to economic policy or because its **ideology** was seen as antithetical to business interests. Because of disagreements over interests and values, democratic politics is difficult and often involves messy compromises rather than neat solutions to problems.

Democracy enshrines the ideal of political equality through the device of 'one person, one vote'. Each person has only one vote, and each person's vote has the same weight as that of any other. Democracy takes no account of status or income, or whether a person is male or female, black or white, etc. Whether you are an employer or an employee you just get one vote. Democracy is a device to ensure that governments act in the public interest. We can see that the democratic ideal involves the following principles:

- popular sovereignty (rule by the people)
- political equality (one person, one vote)
- common good (the purpose of government is to serve the public interest).

In order to realize these principles the basic features of a democracy include the following:

- all adults have the right to vote
- regular elections
- choice of candidates.

Having the right to vote is of little value unless elections are held at regular intervals and voters can choose between candidates offering alternative policies or programmes for government. In the UK a general election, to elect MPs to the House of Commons, has to be held every five years. Voters are able to choose from a list of candidates in each constituency or electoral area. Most candidates stand as representatives of political parties, and most voters choose between candidates on the basis of the party label rather than any qualities of the individual (about which most voters have little or no knowledge).

Peculiarities of the UK system

These three features are common to all democracies, but there is a lot of variation in the detail of how democratic systems work. In the UK political system these three democratic features have particular forms, and these have been debated in the context of concern over low voter turnout and the notion of a democratic crisis.

The right to vote: the electoral system used in the UK for elections to the House of Commons is often referred to as first past the post (FPTP). This involves single member constituencies in which, to be elected, a candidate simply has to receive more votes than any other candidate. The winning candidate does not need a majority of votes (i.e. more than half) and may be elected with quite a small share. Some people argue that it is undemocratic for an MP to be elected on the basis of a minority of the votes cast in his or her constituency. When all of the votes cast are aggregated at a national level the FPTP system creates an imbalance between the proportion of votes cast for each party and the proportion of seats won in the House of Commons. In fact it is normally the case that the party that is able to form the government on the basis of winning a majority of seats has a minority of votes (see Mini-Case study 4.2: The 2005 General Election).

Regular elections: the UK does not have a system of fixed term parliaments. The maximum period a government can remain in office is five years, after which parliament has to be dissolved and a general election called. It can be argued that this is too long for governments to be truly

Mini-Case 4.2 The 2005 general election

Voters leaving a polling station. At the 2005 General Election, many more voters abstained than voted for the winning party. Does low turnout matter?

© Getty Images

In a general election all seats in the House of Commons are contested. In the UK a general election has to be held every five years, though it is often called by the prime minister before the government has served a full term. For example the 2005 general election was held only four years after Labour had been re-elected in 2001. The 2005 results highlight some important issues about democracy in Britain.

Executive dominance. The 2005 election resulted in an historic third successive victory for Labour, with an overall majority of 64 seats. This was a reduced majority but sufficient to allow the government, most of the time, to get its bills passed into law without too much difficulty. This is because the government can generally rely on party loyalty and discipline among its own MPs to ensure that they will vote with the government. This 'executive

2005 General Election (UK results)

	Share of votes	Change 01–05	No. seats	Change 01–05	Share of seats
Labour	35.2	−5.5	355	−47	55
Conservative	32.4	+0.7	198	+33	31
Liberal Democrat	22.0	+3.8	62	+11	9
Other	10.4	+1.0	31	+3	5

Turnout 61.4%

Labour votes as share of eligible voters 21.6%

For every 56 Labour voters there were 100 non-voters.

Source: Data derived from Research Paper 05/33 available from the parliament website—www.parliament.uk

dominance' is good for the government, but it raises questions about the role and effectiveness of opposition parties and the House of Commons as a legislative assembly.

Low turnout. Turnout refers to the number of votes as a proportion of eligible voters. The turnout in 2005 was 61.4%. This was 2% above the 2001 figure, but that had been the lowest turnout since 1918. In other words the 'non-party of non-voters' was almost as large as the group of Labour and Conservative voters combined. Many more voters abstained than voted for the winning party. Does low turnout matter? Although there are many factors involved in abstentions, this degree of non-participation has been seen as a sign of political apathy and disengagement from the political process.

Non-proportional representation. Looking at the shares of seats suggests that Britain has a two party system. The two main parties—Labour and Conservative—between them account for 86% of seats. The third party—the Liberal Democrats—is a long way behind, suggesting that only Labour or Conservative have a realistic chance of winning an election. However looking at shares of the vote gives a different picture. The Liberal Democrat party is still in third place but it looks more like a three-horse race. What this shows is that the electoral system does not deliver seats in the same proportions as votes cast. The Liberal Democrats are losers in comparison with Labour and the Conservatives, gaining only 9% of seats in return for 22% of votes. But in 2005 the electoral system also favoured Labour relative to the Conservatives. The ratio of seats is 64:36 in Labour's favour, but this results from a ratio of votes in which Labour's advantage is much slimmer (52:48). Does this non-proportional representation matter? On grounds of fairness the answer seems to be yes. It can also be argued that the House of Commons would be more effective if a proportional system meant that no single party was able to dominate. On the other hand, supporters of the current system claim that one of its key benefits is precisely this tendency to produce stable governments with effective majorities rather than unstable coalitions.

❓ What light does the 2005 General Election result shed on what is 'wrong' with the UK electoral system?

accountable to the electors. In fact, governments rarely serve for the full five-year term, and this is usually because they call an earlier election at a time, say after four years, that they think will maximize their chances of re-election. For example, the government might try to call an election to coincide with a period when the economy is doing well in the hope of benefiting from a 'feel-good' factor. It can be argued that this is an undemocratic feature of the UK system since it shouldn't be up to governments to decide when they are to be held accountable to the people.

Choice of candidates: the right to stand for election is a basic democratic principle. Individuals can stand as independents, but in fact UK politics is dominated by political parties and independents rarely stand or win in parliamentary elections. It can be agued that one of the key benefits of political parties is that they rationalize the process of democratic choice. Voters are faced with a clear choice between a limited number of parties, each with a fairly distinctive set of values, image and programme. However there have been some criticisms of the party system.

Britain has what is often referred to as a two-party system dominated by the Labour and Conservative parties. It can be argued that in a two-party system there is not really much choice for voters. This feeling of a lack of choice is compounded by the argument that the two parties tend to converge towards the 'middle ground' creating a perception that it doesn't make much difference which one is in power. That perception may then contribute to low turnout. 'Two-party system' may seem an inaccurate description when you look at the share of the vote won by the other parties in recent elections, particularly the Liberal Democrats. However the term is valid in so far as only the two main parties have been able to form a government since early in the last century (the last Liberal Democrat (then Liberal) government was in 1906–14). Of course this two-party dominance points up the unfairness of the electoral system, since the Liberal Democrats have been the losers, obtaining a lower proportion of seats than votes cast.

The two main parties have been beneficiaries of the electoral system because the geographical concentrations of their electoral support have enabled a high rate of conversion of votes into seats. In the FPTP electoral system a majority of constituencies are 'safe seats', meaning that the incumbent has a large enough lead over the second-placed party to be almost certain to win. This seems to undermine the principle of choice of candidates—what choice is there if you live in a constituency where only one party has a realistic chance of winning? This also leads to the problem of 'wasted' votes, and may be a factor in low turnout.

> **➲ Stop and Think**
> What are the principal features of a democratic system of government?
> What makes democratic decision making difficult and 'messy'?

Laws about making laws

In modern democratic states government operates within a constitutional framework. A constitution can be seen as a set of rules intended to safeguard democracy and liberty, and ensure good government. Heywood (2002: 292) identifies the purposes of a constitution as to:

- establish the duties, powers and functions of the various institutions of government
- regulate the relationships between them
- define the relationship between the state and the individual.

Put simply, 'The constitution establishes "the laws about making laws" ' (Pierson, 1996: 18). The rule of law means that government, which has the power to make and enforce laws in society, is itself governed by law. Government actions must be lawful, not arbitrary. In this sense a constitution represents the highest form of law. If governments act beyond their lawful powers (*ultra vires*) they can be held to account through a legal process. This possibility requires the separation of the executive and judicial branches of the state, and the independence of the latter.

A constitution sets out the rights and freedoms that individuals enjoy, and so establishes the relationship between the state and the individual and, more specifically, limits to the authority of the state. In some states, such as the US, such rights are proclaimed in a constitutional document known as a Bill of Rights. In the UK individual rights have been created by Act of Parliament, in the Human Rights Act (1998). This Act incorporated into British law the European Convention on Human Rights. The rights of citizens may include a range of civil rights, such as freedom of speech and expression, association, assembly, movement and a right to privacy. The importance of a constitution for business is that business activity depends on certain rights, such as property rights, and business desires protection against arbitrary government interference.

Britain is usually described as having an 'unwritten' constitution. This sounds as though Britain doesn't really have a constitution at all, but in fact it means that the constitution is not codified in a single document but relies on secondary sources such as statute. In contrast the US has a written or codified constitution. A written constitution is harder to amend because a special constitutional procedure has to be gone through. For this reason it offers stronger protections to individuals. Britain's 'unwritten' constitution is easier to amend (e.g. by Act of Parliament) and thus more flexible, but arguably less effective for this reason.

Britain is traditionally defined as a **unitary state** in which power is concentrated at national level in Westminster in the form of parliamentary **sovereignty**. A unitary state may be contrasted with a federal system, such as the US, in which political power is shared out between the federal (national) government and the individual states. In the UK local government has no independent

powers—such powers can be established or abolished by central government through Act of Parliament. The doctrine of parliamentary sovereignty in principle means that parliament (or, more narrowly, the executive) is the supreme source of authority. From a business point of view, these features of the UK constitution clearly place a premium on relations with government at a national level.

Multi-level governance

The UK is conventionally described as a nation-state, which means that a nation occupying a specific territory governs itself (makes its own laws) through its own political institutions (i.e. its own state). The ability of a nation to govern itself is referred to as **national sovereignty**. A nation is a group of people or community that shares a national identity based on culture, way of life and language. For example British people may feel a sense of 'Britishness' based on our own culture and way of life that are different in some ways from those of other nations. Belief in national sovereignty arises from a desire to protect and sustain this particular way of life. For example it might be argued that Britain has its own way of doing things in relation to business and the role of government in economic life. The 'Anglo-Saxon' model of capitalism may be contrasted with the 'social model' found in other European states, the latter characterized by a stronger tradition of state intervention (Wilson, 2003). Belief in national sovereignty also arises from the idea that laws and policies need to be tailored to local circumstances. For example, by retaining its own currency Britain is able to determine its own interest rate policy in response to its own inflationary pressures. Of course, the pound is seen by some not just in technical terms of economic management but as a potent symbol of national identity.

Spatial levels

However the ideas of a nation-state and national sovereignty are poor guides to understanding the exercise of political power in the modern world. A better guide is the idea of **multi-level governance**, which points to the way political decisions are made at a variety of levels or spatial scales:

- sub-national, i.e. a level of political authority below or within the nation-state (e.g. local government)
- national, i.e. the nation-state
- supra-national, i.e. a level of political authority above the nation-state, of which the EU is the most important example.

In all democratic states, unitary and **federal**, the division of political power between national and sub-national (local and regional) tiers is an important question. The arguments in favour of local or regional government are that:

- rule from the centre may not be sufficiently sensitive to local circumstances
- communities at a local level may have their own sense of identity which local government can express
- local government brings political decision making closer to the people and affords opportunities for democratic participation
- sub-national government can act as a counter-weight to over-mighty national government.

A window seat in the MSP (Member of Scottish Parliament) offices of the Scottish Parliament buildings at Holyrood. An important element of New Labour's constitutional reform programme has been the creation of a Scottish Parliament and Welsh Assembly.

Adam Elder/Scottish Parliament © 2004 Scottish Parliamentary Corporate Body

For example New Labour established regional development agencies (RDAs) and promoted the idea of elected regional assemblies on the basis that there are strong regional communities and identities, and that regions constitute effective spatial scales for economic development policies (whereas local government is too small and national government too big).

An important element of New Labour's constitutional reform programme has been the creation of a Scottish Parliament and Welsh Assembly with limited legislative powers. Support for these measures of devolution, and the move towards devolved government in Northern Ireland, reflects the fact that the UK is not a nation-state in a straightforward sense but comprised of four nations each, to varying degrees, with its own sense of identity and desire for self-government.

From a business perspective, one of the disadvantages of local government can be the need to adjust to different rules and policies in different localities. On the other hand businesses can gain advantage from the ability to shop around and search for the location offering the most favourable conditions. For example, local authorities may compete to attract multinational companies by offering the most attractive inducements for investment.

The main arguments for centralized decision-making are that:

- some problems require national solutions
- resources can be mobilized more effectively (avoiding local duplication)
- centralization can ensure uniformity and equity of treatment.

Supra-national governance—the European Union

However in the modern world, with its globalizing tendencies, it may be argued that there is increasing need for supra-national governance, meaning the exercise of political authority above the nation-states involving the creation of inter-governmental organizations (IGOs). The most important example of supra-national governance is the European Union (EU). UK membership of the EU represents a substantial revision of parliamentary sovereignty, for EU law takes precedence over national law. In other words, EU law can be seen as the supreme law of the UK (and all other member states).

> The Community constitutes a new legal order for whose benefit the states have limited their sovereign rights, albeit within limited fields, and the subjects of which comprise not only the member states, but also their nationals. (Ruling of the European Court 1963, in Dearlove and Saunders, 2000: 717)

The 'limited fields' are those governed by EU treaty—in other areas member states retain their ability to make their own laws (their 'sovereign rights'). Some commentators see this legal order as involving a straightforward loss of sovereignty, but others see it as a pooling or sharing of sovereignty because the EU is a form of inter-governmentalism through which each member participates in developing laws by which all are bound (see Chapter 9).

Reluctant Europeans?

Stakeholders

Britain is often seen as a 'reluctant European', joining late (1973) and often resisting closer integration (e.g., not joining the single currency). British debate on EU membership has been marked by a strong strain of 'Euro-scepticism'. This scepticism has often reflected economic concerns—to maintain our own (felt to be superior) 'model of capitalism' and to fit economic policies to the requirements of the national economy. Yet the development of the EU has been driven largely by economic considerations, and Britain's entry reflected a desire to share the economic benefits. Chief among these are the gains in efficiency, competitiveness and growth that flow from the creation of a single market. By removing barriers to cross-border investment, trade and migration businesses can shift activities to the most advantageous locations and have unfettered access to a vastly expanded market, and competitive pressures will drive up efficiency. At the same time European integration creates the opportunity for harmonization of regulations and a 'level playing field' for business. Of course, such regulations can be business-friendly, but some commentators have also seen in the EU the opportunity for more effective regulation of business in order to afford stronger protections to other stakeholders such as employees and consumers (see Chapter 9).

Political values and ideologies

We have seen that politics is characterized by disagreement arising from differences of interests and values. More particularly, political debate can be understood in terms of competing ideologies, which can be defined as systems of political beliefs and values. All ideologies contain:

Values

- a vision of what the good society should look like (i.e. a vision of the kind of society that supporters of the ideology favour)
- an assessment of what needs to be changed or preserved in existing society
- a political programme or set of policies intended to bring about progress towards the good society.

Conservatism, Liberalism and Socialism are often seen as the three principal ideological traditions or frameworks. At a more general level, it is common to analyse politics in terms of the apparently simple duality of left versus right. The left–right framework seems to suggest that there are just two ideological positions, but it is usual to think of a spectrum of views ranging from left to right. This is reflected in references not only to the 'centre' but also more nuanced ideas of 'centre-left' or 'centre-right'. These terms are familiar in a British context, but can also be applied in other capitalist economies, giving political debate a familiar feel in, say, the various member states of the EU. In other words, although each country has its own distinctive political history and characteristics, knowledge of ideologies and parties in Britain can be fairly easily translated into other national contexts. This is reflected, for example, in the ability of the various national parties to work together in the European Parliament.

It is important to make sense of these terms so that we can understand what a left-wing or right-wing (or a socialist, liberal or conservative) view of business is. The left is associated with a socialist ideology, and in the British context Labour has traditionally been seen as the principal left-wing political party. The basic idea of 'New Labour' was to move the party away from a socialist outlook—for Tony Blair and Gordon Brown socialism was seen as the 'old Left', meaning old-fashioned, out of date and unpopular. But debate within Labour is still conducted primarily in terms of its positioning as a left-of-centre party.

Conversely the right is associated with a conservative ideology. Hence Thatcherism in the 1980s was sometimes referred to as the New Right, and David Cameron's attempt to transform the Conservative party involved trying to redefine what it means to be a right-of-centre political party. Liberalism may be seen as an 'in-between' ideology in the centre of the political spectrum and, reflecting this in the British context, the Liberal Democrats are often seen as a party of the centre. This way of looking at politics is a reasonable starting point, though we will see that there are some complications that we need to take into account.

Left versus right

The left–right debate goes to the heart of the issue of the role and purpose of business in the good society. Left and right are divided in their attitude to private business and the market economy. Those on the left may be described as 'market pessimists' whereas those on the right are 'market optimists' emphasizing, respectively, the failings and the advantages of private ownership of business, competition and the profit motive. Attitudes to government also divide left and right and may be seen as the other side of the same coin. (You will find it useful to refer back to the discussion of competing economic perspectives in Chapter 2.)

Market pessimists tend to look to government to step in to rectify the failings of markets, whereas market optimists want to restrict the role of government as far as possible and leave things

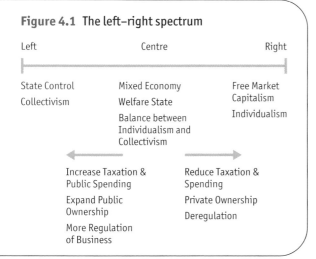

Figure 4.1 The left–right spectrum

to the 'free market'. Historically, therefore, the left has favoured 'big government', arguing for an increased share of national income to pass through government's hands in the form of taxation and public spending, and an extension of the reach of its interventions in economic life. Conversely the right has favoured reducing the tax 'burden' and deregulating economic life. Thus the market and government or the state seem to be counter-posed in the form market versus the state.

However it would be inaccurate to portray politics in countries such as Britain in stark 'market versus state' terms. This is because the ambition to replace capitalism altogether has always been a minority view on the left; most 'socialists' essentially favoured extensions of state control and intervention within what would remain a predominantly capitalist economy dominated by the private sector, coupled with the expansion of state welfare. This conception is sometimes referred to as the mixed economy, involving a mix of private and public sectors.

On the other hand, free market thinking has only been found on the fringes of the right; most right-wing thinkers accepted an important role for government in market economies. From this we can see that left–right political debate mainly concerns the balance between the market and the state. At times this debate has been dominated by the left, at others by the right; its main energies have been spent shifting this balance more towards the state or more towards the market. Thus if we think of left–right politics as a spectrum, political debate is mainly concerned with where society and the economy should be on that spectrum rather than moving to one extreme or the other (Figure 4.1).

Market pessimism versus market optimism

In a capitalist economy production is organized principally by private businesses and is driven by competition and profit. Profit is the main purpose of private sector business because without the prospect of profit individuals would not be willing to invest their resources in business. The profit motive provides an incentive for firms to ensure that they are responsive to consumer preferences and to strive for continuous improvements in efficiency. Competition also reinforces these behaviours as firms seek to keep up with (or ahead of) their rivals and stay in business. Profit is an incentive, competition is a discipline. Left and right tend to agree about this basic view of how a market works. But they disagree when it comes to weighing the advantages and disadvantages of the market (Table 4.2).

Why are those on the left market pessimists? What are the main disadvantages of the market from this viewpoint? Why are those on the right market optimists? What are the main advantages of the market from this viewpoint?

> ⟳ *Stop and Think*
> Consider the views of business from left and right. Which views do you find most persuasive? Why?
> (You will find it useful to review the discussion of economic perspectives in Chapter 2 in conjunction with this discussion of left and right)

Table 4.2 Left and right views of the market

	The disadvantages of private business and the market—a view from the left	The advantages of private business and the market—a view from the right
Customer focus	Markets are good at responding to consumer preferences and this is fine so long as you have money. But markets do not respond to the needs of those who cannot afford to pay. Profit comes before need.	Markets are good at responding to consumer preferences. They constitute a form of economic democracy in which consumers 'vote' for products every time they spend their money. This is the basis of consumer sovereignty.
Persuasive advertising	The idea of consumer sovereignty downplays the ability of business to influence consumer behaviour through persuasive advertising and branding. Business may persuade us to buy things that we don't really need or are bad for us (e.g. unhealthy food), cultivate a wasteful desire for novelty and the latest innovation or fashion, and promote a seemingly limitless appetite for increased consumption.	Advertising is a healthy feature of the market, acting as a channel of communication and information between firms and their customers. Advertising is an important form of free speech. Customers can decide for themselves which advertising messages they pay attention to.
Profit motive	The profit motive leads firms to engage in behaviours that are not socially responsible or beneficial. Such behaviours include corruption, environmental damage and mistreatment of employees.	The profit motive leads firms to engage in behaviours that are socially responsible or beneficial—using resources efficiently and responding to customer preferences. It is precisely because firms want to make profits that they serve others, their customers, effectively. In this way the market reconciles private self interest and the common good.
Employment relationship	Private ownership of business involves a conflict of interests in the workplace between employers and employees focused on the wage–effort bargain. This means that employers will strive for maximum effort from the workforce while 'keeping the lid' on wage costs, while employees will strive for higher wages and reduced intensity of work. Because of the way work is divided up and managed it becomes monotonous and meaningless for many, and denies opportunities for meaningful employee participation.	Employers and employees share a fundamental interest in the success of the business in which both parties are stakeholders. It is in the interest of both parties that the wage–effort bargain ensures that the business is able to remain competitive and profitable. Business success depends on a high-calibre management team exercising the right to manage.
Inequality	Market mechanisms tend to create inequality between the best and worst paid occupations, and a social divide between rich and poor.	There is nothing wrong with individuals using their own talents and efforts to become rich. Inequality is a desirable feature of markets because incentives are required to attract the best people into top jobs and to motivate performance. Efficiently run businesses benefit the whole of society because they power economic growth, thereby raising overall incomes and living standards, including those at the bottom.
Individualism	The market system encourages an individualist ethic in society focused on self-interest, and an attitude to social and business life as a competitive struggle or 'rat race'. Community and care for others tend to get squeezed out.	People are, by nature, individualistic and competitive and that is why human societies invented markets. In other words, markets are a reflection, rather than a cause, of these behaviours. Self-interest and competitiveness are generally positive because they drive economic progress.
Threat of closure	Competition may encourage performance but it also always leads to winners and losers. This is the source of chronic insecurity in a market system as firms face the risk of going out of business and employees face the risk of unemployment. The competitive process also leads to a small number of giant corporations becoming dominant in the markets in which they operate.	The threat of closure is a vital discipline in the market. It motivates performance and ensures that the best businesses survive. Dynamic markets provide opportunities for business start-ups and for employees who lose their jobs to find new work. Markets do need to be regulated to guard against the emergence of monopoly.
Business influence	Corporations exercise unrivalled influence over government which enables them to ensure that political decisions rarely go against business interests.	It is legitimate for business to have a political voice, and right that the needs of business should command government attention since the well-being of all members of society depends on a healthy economy.

Mini-Case 4.3   A left–right touchstone issue: taxation

Speech by George Osborne (Shadow Chancellor of the Exchequer) to the Conservative Party conference, 3 October 2006.

'I want lower taxes. Because lower taxes would help Britain to compete. I think we're crazy as a country to be raising our taxes when most of our competitors are cutting theirs. I look at Ireland and I see what lower business taxes can achieve. I believe that lower taxes extend the space of freedom in our society. I believe they help people to take greater social responsibility over their own lives, and the lives of others. And when it comes to spending over the economic cycle I want our economy to grow faster than our government. . . . We will share the proceeds of growth between the lower taxes this country needs and the increases in spending on public services every government should provide.'

In this speech Osborne refused to pledge the Conservative party to tax cuts because 'economic stability will always come first'. In other words tax cuts would only be introduced when they would not threaten economic stability. In the remarks quoted here Osborne also says that tax cuts will be balanced with increases in public spending, though public spending would fall as a share of national income. However the support for lower taxes is stated clearly, and Osborne presents the right-wing case.

1 The case for lower taxes is based on commitment to individual freedom—people should be free to decide for themselves how to spend their own money.

2 Lower taxes will boost competitiveness by reducing the burden on business.

3 Individuals should be more self-reliant and less dependent on the state. The state should do less; individuals, their families and communities should do more.

The traditional left-wing case for higher taxation rests on the following ideas:

1 Public spending financed by taxation often expands individual freedom by providing opportunities and resources that individuals might not be able to pay for in the market, e.g. health and education.

2 Public services often meet the needs of industry (e.g. for an educated workforce or efficient transport) and therefore increase competitiveness.

3 The tax system should be used to redistribute income from richer to poorer households in the name of a fairer society or **social justice**.

4 Spending on public services reflects a superior ethic of solidarity or community whereby we look after each other in society. We all pay taxes according to our income, and benefit (e.g. from healthcare) in time of need.

Note that in this debate left and right both accept the need for taxes—government is necessary and has to be paid for—but they contest the level of taxation and the size of government.

❷ Do you agree with George Osborne's arguments in favour of lower taxes?

❷ Would lower taxes be good for business?

Ideology and political parties

In democratic systems like the UK the chief organizations representing and expressing ideological views are the political parties. Parties compete in elections on the basis of rival programmes or manifestos that are supposed to have roots in the distinctive ideologies that each party represents. It could make a big difference to business whether a left-wing or right-wing party is elected. However the relationship between parties and ideologies is not straightforward, for the following reasons:

Internal party debate. Political parties are not usually ideologically 'pure' but contain within them ideological differences and disputes. This means that parties shift their positions according to the outcome of left–right struggles within them. The invention of 'New Labour' under Tony Blair and Gordon Brown in the 1990s may be seen as inaugurating a rightward shift of the party. Similarly David Cameron may be seen as taking the Conservative Party on a leftward course after his election as leader in 2005.

Popular support. Parties have to compete for votes and this means that they have to present ideas and policies that will command popular support. The dilemma for parties is that what they believe in and what the voters believe in might not be the same, so there may be a difficult trade-off between principle and popularity. As Chancellor of the Exchequer in the first Labour government elected in 1997 Gordon Brown moved away from commitments to increase taxation and spending because these were perceived as unpopular with voters.

Because of this electoral imperative political parties may behave somewhat like businesses in the market—adjusting their offer to consumer demand in order to stay in business, and running slick advertising campaigns. However parties are not supposed to be just like businesses, because we expect them to believe in the policies that they put forward whereas we don't generally expect this of businesses.

⮑ *Stop and Think*

Do you agree that all that matters to consumers is that businesses supply the goods and services that we want to purchase? Does it matter whether businesses have a genuine belief in or commitment to their products?

For example, if you want to buy locally grown apples because of your personal commitment to minimize 'food miles' does it matter to you whether or not the supermarket that sells them is genuinely committed to tackling climate change or is just responding to a new market niche?

If a political party puts forward policies that you favour (perhaps to abolish university tuition fees) does it matter whether the party really believes that this is the right thing to do or is just 'chasing votes'?

Circumstances. Political parties compete for votes by making commitments to certain policies and courses of action if they are elected into government. But the powers and capacities of government are limited, and the ability of governments to achieve their aims depends on the circumstances that they confront. Circumstances and unforeseen events might hold them back. For example, the ideological beliefs of Conservative politicians may incline them to promise tax cuts, but Cameron held back from this in part because adverse circumstances, such as a deficit in the public finances, might make it difficult to honour in government.

The main political parties

The Conservative party

The Conservative party is on the right of the political spectrum. It has long been seen as the main party of business, in the sense of representing business interests. As the name suggests the main ideological tradition on which the party draws is conservatism. However in the 1980s, during Mrs Thatcher's premiership, traditional conservative ideas were combined with a new emphasis on neoliberalism. It was this amalgam that came to be referred to as 'Thatcherism' or the 'New Right'. Although Thatcher was ousted as leader of the party and prime minister in 1990, Thatcherism continues to exert a strong

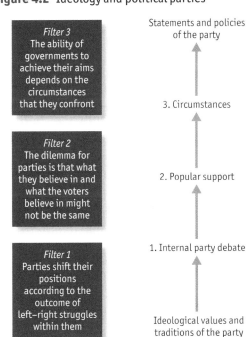

Figure 4.2 Ideology and political parties

Note: Ideological beliefs have to pass through three 'filters' before being translated into policies.

influence over debates about the direction of the party, and British politics more generally. The traditional conservative elements of the mix include:

- A 'conservative' attitude, meaning that conservatives generally wish to preserve existing institutions and traditions, and are sceptical of proposals for large-scale change. Sometimes conservatives are seen as backward-looking, wishing to return to society as it existed in the past.

- Support for private enterprise and the market, though this has not always been the case. In the nineteenth century conservatives were often critical of the individualistic and competitive market system for creating social division and breakdown. At this time conservatism was associated with an aristocratic class of landowners. In the twentieth century the party became strong supporters of capitalism and associated with the business class, especially the financial sector (the City).

- Belief in the inevitability and desirability of inequality. Conservatives are not troubled by some individuals being wealthy or by earnings differentials in the market. They generally believe that these reflect differences in ability and effort, and are important in providing incentives.

- Emphasis on the nation and the importance of social cohesion. Defence of 'national interests' finds expression in a strong vein of 'Euro-scepticism', because the EU is seen as taking away the ability of Britain to govern itself as an independent nation. 'One nation' conservatism has been reflected in a willingness to go along with social reform (the welfare state) as a means of binding the nation together. Maintaining social cohesion is also seen as requiring strong families and communities, and shared values and a sense of 'Britishness'.

- Strong families and communities are important in preventing crime and anti-social behaviour, but conservatives are also strong advocates of law and order, reflected in support for more policing and tougher prison sentences. This is the prime role for government within society.

The 'neoliberal' strain involved a revival of classical liberal ideas whose origins lay in the nineteenth century. The key value of liberalism is individual freedom or liberty. Liberals believe that individuals should be free to live as they choose; to use their own resources, talents and efforts to make the best of their lives according to their own lights. Individuals would naturally make different choices about how they live and this should be allowed, indeed celebrated, within a context of mutual tolerance and so long as individuals don't harm others. This commitment to liberty is connected with business because the market is seen as a system of voluntary exchange that allows individuals to make decisions for themselves about how they use their own resources. It was this 'market optimism' that Thatcherism embraced. Sometimes referred to as a belief in 'free markets', the main thrust of this approach was a critique of 'big government' which was seen as restricting the freedoms of individuals to live as they choose and of businesses to manage their own affairs and compete freely in the market. Hence the main thrust of Thatcherism was to 'roll back' the state. In adopting these ideas the Thatcherites were critical of previous Conservative governments in the period after the Second World War who were seen as having gone along with the growth of the state. The aim of Thatcherism was to turn this tide. Specific ideas and policies included:

- Privatization—the transfer of assets from the public sector to private ownership. The central thrust of this policy was the selling off of nationalized industries such as British Telecom (1984) and British Gas (1986), but it also included other measures such as the sale of council homes to their tenants. The principle objective was to increase efficiency as competition and the profit motive were seen as making private enterprise more efficient than public ownership. It was also felt desirable to widen share ownership within the general public.

- Tax reduction—cutting big government down to size would enable tax cuts. People would thus be able to keep a larger share of their own money and decide for themselves how to spend it (see Mini-Case 4.3).

- Reduction of public spending—the corollary of tax cuts. This would require reductions in spending on the welfare state. The Thatcherites developed a critique of state welfare as inefficient, producer-led (rather than customer-oriented) and creating a dependency culture (especially the benefits system). Individuals were encouraged to be more self-reliant and provision by the private sector was encouraged. However rather than pursue outright privatization of services market disciplines were introduced into the public sector through internal markets (e.g. in health and education).

- Deregulation—removing the burden of 'red tape' from the private sector. It was believed that the competitiveness of UK business was damaged not only by high taxation but by the cost of regulatory compliance.

- Right to manage—tackling excessive trade union power. It was believed that the power exercised by trade unions in the workplace had become a major barrier to competitiveness. For example, trade unions might demand unrealistic wage increases, resist new technologies, and disrupt business through strikes and other forms of industrial action. Thus the Thatcher governments sought to tip the balance of power back in favour of employers and restore the 'right to manage'.

Thus Thatcherism expressed right-wing market optimism in a strong form. Though not supporting a 'free market' in the strict sense, it was certainly an attempt to move the British economy and society more towards a pure capitalist model. Private enterprise, markets, competition and the profit motive were celebrated, and the public sector was denigrated.

The Labour party

The Labour party is generally seen as on the left of the political spectrum. It was founded at the start of the last century to represent the interests of trade unions and working people in parliament. For most of its existence the party has espoused a form of left-wing market pessimism and socialist ideology. This has meant that Labour has tended to be seen as hostile to, or at least not in touch with, business interests. However Labour has never been a thorough-going socialist party in the sense of seriously aiming or attempting to replace capitalism and private enterprise with an alternative economic system. Rather the party has aimed at reforming and managing capitalism so as to achieve some degree of state control over economic life and greater fairness and equality in society. Traditional or 'old Labour' ideas and policies included the following:

- Public ownership of key industries, creating a 'mixed economy' (i.e. with a mixture of public and private ownership). Public ownership would introduce an element of democratic control over economic life.

- Making the private sector serve the common good through an element of centralized planning of the economy and regulation. Macroeconomic policy would prioritize the maintenance of full employment, reflecting commitment to the notion of a right to work.

- Creating a legal framework to ensure that trade unions can bargain effectively with employers, and supporting trade union struggles for improved wages and working conditions. Supporting moves towards greater 'industrial democracy' and 'employee participation', giving employees a say in corporate decisions.

- Generously funded welfare state to ensure that all citizens have rights to health care, education, housing and other public services. For example the NHS is seen as expressing the anti-market principle of equal treatment for equal need (regardless of ability to pay).

- Using the tax system and public spending to redistribute income from rich to poor, eradicating poverty and reducing the degree of inequality generated by the market.

These ideas and policies have been supported by the party and adopted, with varying degrees of conviction, by previous Labour governments. They can be seen as a major influence on the character of consensus politics in the postwar period. However the emergence of New Labour in the 1990s represented a decisive reinvention of the party through which many of these ideas and policies were watered down or rejected (see Case Study).

The Liberal Democrats

The Liberal Democrats are usually seen as in the centre of the left–right spectrum, although the party tends to disavow left–right terminology. This may be because the party appears squeezed between the Labour party on the left and the Conservative party on the right and faces the tactical dilemma of how to position itself in relation to the two main parties. Should it be leaning towards the left and Labour as an anti-conservative party, or vice versa? In rejecting the left–right view of politics the party may be trying to escape from this dilemma. As the name of the party suggests, the main ideological tradition on which it draws is Liberalism. This would seem to suggest a close link with Thatcherism. However an obvious difference is that the Liberal Democrats do not draw on the tradition of conservative thought. Also, the Liberal Democrats have tended to emphasize other dimensions of individual liberty. Whereas Thatcherism emphasizes the economic dimension of liberty in terms of private property and the market, the Liberal Democrats highlight the importance of civil liberties, such as freedom of speech. The liberal tradition also contains a strand (sometimes known as New Liberalism or liberal reformism) that emphasizes that individuals cannot really be free to live as they choose if they are poor or badly educated. This leads to support for the welfare state rather than just leaving things to the market.

> ⮑ *Stop and Think—political 'cross-dressing'?* **(See case study p. 117)**
>
> 'Cross-dressing' refers to parties stealing each others' clothes (or policies and ideas) in order to win popular support. Such tactics have the effect of blurring the left–right distinction and party differences.
>
> ❷ Was Blair 'cross-dressing' when he drew on elements of Thatcherite conservatism to create New Labour?
>
> ❷ Did Cameron in turn steal some of Blair's clothes?
>
> ❷ Is cross-dressing a feature of a healthy political system, or a practice that puts people off politics?

◈ *Looking ahead*

The end of the Blair era and the succession of Gordon Brown as prime minister is unlikely to lead to a major shift in the Labour government's policy towards business and economic management. Despite continuing media discussion of disagreements between Blair and Brown it is important to recognize that both were 'architects' of New Labour.

A general election in the UK will be held within the next few years, most likely in 2009 or 2010. Although the outcome of the election is hard to predict, polls in 2006 and early 2007 showed a loss of support by Labour and some success for Cameron in reviving Conservative support. It is likely that a general election will involve both major parties trying to claim the 'centre ground' of politics.

Poll ratings in 2006/7 have led some commentators to predict that the outcome of the next general election may be a hung parliament in which no party has an overall majority. This could create a situation in which the Liberal Democrats hold the balance of power. If this happens it would make electoral reform (a key policy of the Liberal Democrats) more likely, and that would lead to a permanent shift in the balance between the political parties.

Despite the tendency towards convergence in the centre, political debate will continue to be expressed in left–right terms. For example, arguments over the levels of taxation and public spending, and the balance between the state and the market will continue to be central.

Politics at national and European levels will become more focused on tackling climate change. Policies developed to tackle this global problem will have a major impact on business, for example tighter restrictions on emissions of CO_2 from cars.

Globalization and the challenges posed by global problems will push governments more towards greater involvement with forms of supra-national governance, including the EU and at a global level. Climate change and Third World development are prime examples of such problems.

Summary

- Politics is concerned with decisions and choices that affect the whole society: determining the rules under which we live together and creating a 'good society'

- Society is characterized by diverse interests, opinions and values. Politics provides a mechanism for dealing with the disagreements and conflicts that arise. Politics can involve winners and losers, but it also enables the search for compromise through dialogue

- Politics is a key element of the business environment. There is interdependence between business and government. One of the key questions in political debate concerns the nature and responsibilities of business and the type of capitalist economy we want to live in. In other words business is politically controversial

- The UK political system is a liberal democracy based on the principle of rule by the people. The state exercises a unique form of power in society—to make and enforce rules.

- However rule is not the main function of modern states— they have become 'caretaker' states responsible for a range of public services and steering social and economic development

- Politics is not conducted just at a national level but is characterized by multi-level governance. The EU is the most important example of supra-national politics in the modern world

- Politics is characterized by debate between rival ideologies. The left–right spectrum is a useful framework for understanding political arguments relating to business

- The UK has a two-party system in the sense that Labour and the Conservatives have dominated government for the last century. Historically these parties have roots in the two major economic groups or interests in capitalist society— labour and business

 Case study: politics after Thatcherism—the rise of New Labour

After Tony Blair was elected as leader of the Labour party in 1994 he pushed forward, in collaboration with Gordon Brown and other key 'New Labour' figures, a process of transforming the party and its ideology. There were two main drivers of this process of transformation. On the one hand, the reformers or 'modernizers' argued that the left-wing or socialist policies advocated by the party in the past would no longer work in the modern world. Society had changed and the party would have to change with it if was to remain relevant. A key example of this change is globalization which, it was argued, requires a new approach to economic policy with an emphasis on competitiveness. With the emergence of a 'knowledge based economy' the key to competitiveness had become skills, thus giving prime importance to education and training. Second, modernization was seen as essential if the party was to reconnect with the voters. By 1994 the Labour party had lost four successive general elections to the

Conservatives, and it looked to some as though Labour might never win an election again. Making the party electable involved recognizing that many of the policies introduced by the Conservatives, particularly under Margaret Thatcher in the 1980s, had popular support and would therefore have to be accepted by Labour. By the same token, much of what the party had stood for in the past was no longer popular.

New Labour is an example of the way political parties have to reinvent or update themselves from time to time in response to environmental forces. Parties always have to adapt to processes of social and economic change, and must ensure that they do not become disconnected from voters. The party's ideology should provide firm anchorage in this updating, but ideologies are themselves somewhat flexible and parties can feel the need for ideological repositioning. Blair and Brown argued that New Labour remained committed to traditional left-wing values such as social

Prime Minister Gordon Brown and his wife Sarah arrive at 10 Downing Street for the first time as Premier in June 2007.

© Andrew Parsons/PA Wire

justice and concern for the poor and disadvantaged in society. But critics argued that New Labour, in its embrace of elements of Thatcherism, involved an ideological shift to the right. For this reason it was opposed throughout Blair's leadership by those in the party who saw it as a betrayal of Labour's true socialist principles.

New Labour is not, of course, the only example of politicians and parties reinventing themselves. Mrs Thatcher had also transformed her own party, the Conservatives, after being elected as leader in 1975 and as Prime Minister from 1979 to 1990. Like Blair, Thatcher defined her own political approach largely by rejecting the policies her party had supported in the period of consensus politics after the Second World War (i.e. after 1945). These policies were seen as an accommodation to left-wing ideas of 'big government'. The new approach, which aimed to 'roll back' the state was labelled the 'New Right', 'neoliberalism' or simply Thatcherism. Thatcherism is a clear example of ideologically driven change, even though she claimed that hers was the true conservatism. It was also put forward as a necessary response to Britain's economic difficulties.

From 'old Labour' to 'New Labour'

In the move to 'New Labour' the party:

- renounced its historic commitment to public ownership of industry
- stepped back from pledges to renationalize industries that had been privatized by the Conservatives
- moved away from the party's association with 'tax and spend' (i.e. a commitment to high public spending funded by high levels of taxation)
- declined to restore trade union rights that had been removed by the Conservatives, and distanced the party from the trade unions.

In other words, there was to be no going back to the days of 'big government' and, at the same time, the party adopted a much more 'market optimist' attitude to the benefits of the private sector and the market. Indeed the thrust of New Labour can be seen as making the party much more 'business-friendly'.

New Labour ideas and policies include:

- A new emphasis on boosting the competitiveness of British business. Whereas in the past Labour may have been perceived as championing social justice to the neglect of competitiveness, the New Labour approach emphasized that the two go hand-in-hand. The welfare state was to be reformed to make it more functional for wealth creation. For example, a new emphasis on 'welfare to work' was embodied in the programme of New Deals for the unemployed. The idea was to provide a package of support that would help individuals make the transition from welfare into work, rather than merely paying out cash benefits. This was described as a 'hand up' rather than a 'hand out'.
- Education and training were seen as providing the key to competitiveness in a new globalizing 'knowledge-based' economy. Higher levels of skill would allow the UK to meet the competitive challenge posed by the rise of China and India. This is reflected in the expansion of higher education. Education would thus be both a social policy—helping individuals to make the most of their talents—and an economic policy—helping business to compete. There would be emphasis on vocational skills and knowledge.
- Competitiveness also required a shift towards more flexible labour markets. Employees needed generic skills to help them adjust to shifts in the jobs market. Employers needed to be able to manage their workforces flexibly.
- Business confidence required macroeconomic stability. This was to be achieved through the adoption of strict fiscal rules and, perhaps more important, moving control over interest rates to an independent Bank of England.

Cameron's new brand of Conservatism

When David Cameron was elected as leader of the Conservative party in 2005 he found himself in a similar situation to Tony Blair in 1994. The Conservative party had lost three successive elections to New Labour and so Cameron faced the problem of making the party popular again. He began his own process of transformation with the aim of developing a new brand of Conservatism. This rebranding involved rejecting some aspects of the Conservatives' image and policies that were seen as unpopular, and accepting some elements of New Labour's approach. For example, the Conservatives committed themselves to New Labour's pledge to eradicate child poverty. In terms of economic policy, the party moved away from its identification with a policy of tax cuts at all costs and unqualified support for business. Tax cuts were to be introduced only when economic circumstances would allow, and the party would 'stand up to' as well as 'stand up for' business. Just as Blair was criticized by opponents on the left of the Labour party, Cameron faced opposition from his own internal critics on the right. Many commentators argued that the two main parties were seeking popular support by a strategy of occupying what is described as the 'middle ground' or 'centre' of British politics, moving away from their traditional left-wing (Labour) and right-wing (Conservative) identities.

❷ Summarize the principal differences between 'old' and 'New' Labour. Would you expect the business community to prefer 'new' or 'old'? Why?

Review and discussion questions

1 Explain the nature of politics, and consider whether it is possible or desirable to keep politics out of business.

2 With reference to the UK political system, explain what is meant by the term democracy.

3 What is an ideology? Consider your own ideological views and the reasons why you hold them.

4 Examine critically the main ideas of left and right in relation to business.

5 Examine the reasons for the emergence of New Labour, and consider how this approach differs from 'old Labour'.

Assignments

1 Find the 2005 General Election Manifestos of the following political parties on their websites. Produce a report on the key differences and similarities in their approaches to business.

- Labour
- Conservative
- Liberal Democrat

2 Identify key points for the Politics quadrant of a PEST analysis for one of the following firms or industries:

- Tesco
- airlines
- food industry.

Further reading

There are many good general introductions to politics. See, for example, Heywood (2002), Dearlove and Saunders (2000) or Jones et al. (2007).

For analysis of the 2005 UK general election see Geddes and Tonge (2005). Also go to the parliament website—www.parliament.uk

Heywood (2000) provides a brief discussion of the terms 'left' and 'right'. See also Jones et al. (2007) and, for a lengthier discussion, Giddens (1998). Dearlove and Saunders (2000) chapter 10 provides a discussion of the politics of Labour and the Conservatives, including New Labour. See Driver and Martell (2006) for a detailed analysis of New Labour.

Online resources

Test your understanding of this chapter with online questions and answers, explore the subject further through web exercises, and use the weblinks to provide a quick resource for further research. Go to the Online Resource Centre at

www.oxfordtextbooks.co.uk/orc/ wetherly_otter/

Intute is a gateway to a wide range of social science resources on the web, including politics. Here you can follow links to political parties, parliament and other useful websites. Go to www.intute.ac.uk/socialsciences/politics/

The BBC website is a useful source for reports on contemporary politics and current affairs. Go to http://news.bbc.co.uk

Parliament website—www.parliament.uk/

10 Downing Street—www.number-10.gov.uk/

Look on the political party websites for information on policies relating to the economy and business.

The Labour party—www.labour.org.uk/home

The Conservative party—www.conservative-party.org.uk/

The Liberal Democrats—www.libdems.org.uk/

References

Carvel, J. (2006) Child obesity has doubled in a decade, *Guardian*, 22 April.

Dearlove, J. and Saunders, P. (2000) *Introduction to British Politics* (Cambridge: Polity).

Driver, S. and Martell, L. (2006) *New Labour* (Cambridge: Polity).

Geddes, A. and Tonge, J. (2005) *Britain Decides—the UK General Election 2005* (Basingstoke: Palgrave).

Giddens, A. (1998) *The Third Way. The Renewal of Social Democracy* (Cambridge: Polity).

Heywood, A. (2000) *Key Concepts in Politics* (Basingstoke: Palgrave).

Heywood, A. (2002) *Politics* (Basingstoke: Palgrave).

Jones, B. et al. (2007) *Politics UK* (Harlow: Pearson).

Kay, J. (2004) The state and the market, *Political Quarterly*, July, Supplement 1, Vol. 75.

Office for National Statistics (2004) *UK 2005*.

Pierson, C. (1996) *The Modern State* (Abingdon: Routledge).

Wilson, G. K. (2003) *Business and Politics* (Basingstoke: Palgrave).

The social and cultural environment

Paul Wetherly

Contents

Learning objectives

When you have completed this chapter you will be able to:

- Explain the nature of the social and cultural environments, and their importance for business

- Analyse demographic trends and the implications of an ageing population for business

- Explain what is meant by the term multiculturalism and examine the impact of immigration on business and society

- Analyse class differences and patterns of inequality in Britain, and relate these issues to business responsibility

- Examine the causes and implications of the changing role of women in British society and business

Themes

Diversity	**Diversity of business**
	Certain industries have a profound impact in shaping the wider culture—the culture industries.
Internal/ external	**Internal/external**
	Culture is part of the internal environment of business—**organization culture**. Business reflects the wider culture, e.g. racism and sexism.
Complexity	**Complexity of the environment**
	This chapter demonstrates the complexity of the business environment by showing that it is not just economic but has important social and cultural dimensions. It also shows how the social and cultural are interrelated with other dimensions of the environment.
Spatial levels	**Variety of spatial levels**
	This chapter shows how social and cultural life cannot be understood only at a national level. For example, nations are multicultural and even multinational. Also changes in social and cultural life have to be seen in terms of the growing interconnectedness of societies as a result of globalization.
Dynamic	**Dynamic environment**
	This chapter identifies key social trends, showing how many aspects of social and cultural life are different today than in the past.
Interaction	**Interaction between business and the environment**
	Business not only has to respond to changes in social and economic life but also has a powerful influence in shaping these changes. E.g. through product innovation, the growth of 'cultural industries', and advertising.

Stakeholders

Stakeholders

Analysing the social environment also involves identifying a range of stakeholder groups with differing interests in relation to business, e.g. sections of the population defined by social class, gender, ethnicity, age.

Values

Values

Modern societies are pluralistic or 'cosmopolitan', characterized by diversity of lifestyles and values.

Introduction: what is the social and cultural environment?

In broad terms, the social-cultural environment includes everything that is not included in the economy or the political system. Economic life is organized primarily through a market in which individuals relate to one another as buyers and sellers and the purpose is production. In political life individuals relate to one another as citizens and the basic purpose is making collective decisions and rules. The economic and political systems together create the conditions—goods, services and rules—which we all need in order to live the kinds of lives that we choose. The social-cultural environment, then, consists of the whole range of behaviours and relationships in which individuals engage in their personal and private lives, including:

- the characteristics of the population (e.g. age, sex, race or ethnicity, class)
- values and attitudes
- lifestyles and relationships.

Culture is an attribute of groups, and this can mean society as a whole (e.g. national culture), groups within society (sub-cultures), or even groups of societies and nations (trans-national culture). For example, it is quite common to speak of 'western culture'. This term implies that there are certain values and ways of life that western societies might be said to share, such as:

Spatial levels

- Secularism—this refers to the increasing influence of rational and scientific thought, and the decline of religion as a framework of understanding and guide to behaviour.
- Consumerism or materialism—this refers to the view that achieving higher levels of consumption of goods and services leads to greater happiness. A good life means having more 'stuff'. This attitude lies behind the belief that economic growth is always a good thing.
- Individualism—this usually refers to the idea that individuals make their own life-style choices and are motivated primarily by self-interest. It can also involve the idea that individuals should strive to be self-reliant.

However these attitudes or values vary in strength between western societies (e.g. UK society is more secular than the United States), and they also have their own distinctive cultural traits. For example, 'Britishness' might be said to include (among other traits):

- an attitude of reserve (e.g. compared to American outspokenness)
- a sensitivity to class differences (as expressed by accent and manners)
- a sense of fair play.

A game of cricket on the village green—is this the meaning of 'Britishness'?

© istockphoto.com/
Lance Bellers

The very idea of Britishness is contested by some on the grounds that British society contains a diverse range of cultures. For example, Britain is often described as a 'multicultural' society, referring to the co-existence of different communities defined by their race, ethnicity or faith. Sub-cultures can also be related to class membership (e.g. working class culture) or age (e.g. youth culture). Youth culture is, of course, itself diverse, partly reflecting lifestyle choices in relation to clothing and music.

Dynamic

In analysing the social-cultural environment of business it is important to recognize that society and culture are not homogeneous or fixed. Rather they are diverse and fluid or dynamic. Social and cultural change is a hallmark of modern societies (more than in the past), symbolized by the widely recognised phenomenon of a **generation gap**. This refers to the way in which, due to social and cultural change, each generation tends to feel somewhat out of touch with (and even bewildered or shocked by) the attitudes and behaviours of the next. Business needs to stay in touch with social and cultural shifts.

> ➲ *Stop and Think*
>
> What do you see as the main aspects of the culture of your own society?
>
> Do you agree that the cultural traits listed above are characteristic of western / British society?
>
> Do you share all aspects of the culture of your society?
>
> Can you think of any aspects of the culture that relate to the role of business in society?

What has it got to do with business? Society, culture and business

As with other aspects of the environment, the relationship between business, culture and society involves a two-way interaction. Although we tend to think of business as operating according to a distinctive instrumental rationality of profit-and-loss and the 'bottom line' it is also influenced by the social-cultural setting in which it is embedded. At the same time business affects the wider culture and society profoundly. For example, a good deal of what we think of as making up the culture of modern society consists of the outputs of private sector businesses in what might be called the culture industries, such as popular music, films, literature, newspapers and magazines.

Interaction

These influences can be seen as either positive or negative. For example, aspects of the culture of a society might be seen as hindering or assisting business performance. Therefore governments might be interested in promoting cultural change as a way of boosting economic competitiveness. On the other hand business might be seen as having harmful or beneficial effects on the wider society or culture, and governments might want to influence or regulate business behaviour for this reason.

Examples of social-cultural impacts on business

Business is an activity undertaken by people whose values and attitudes are shaped by the culture and society of which they are a part. To some extent the roles we perform in business are quite discrete from other aspects of our lives and require that we adopt different behaviours and personas. However there is not, of course, a complete separation between 'work' and 'life'. We carry values and attitudes shaped by the wider culture and society into our roles as managers, employees and consumers.

- It can be argued that capitalist business owes its historical origins and development in part to non-economic factors. Max Weber argued that the 'spirit of capitalism', or ethos of capitalist business, with its emphasis on accumulating wealth, can be traced to religious belief—the 'Protestant ethic'. This religious belief encouraged the reinvestment of wealth in business rather than the pursuit of a life of luxury, thus fuelling economic growth and dynamism (Giddens, 2006: 103–4). A version of this theory persists today in the idea that economic success depends on the prevalence of a 'work ethic' in society which sees work as a morally desirable activity. We can perhaps see this reflected in the welfare-to-work initiatives of the Labour governments since 1997 with their emphasis on seeking and accepting employment as a moral responsibility.
- Some writers have argued that the UK's relatively poor long-term economic performance has been due in part to wider cultural factors such as an emphasis on the arts rather than science, engineering and technology and a weak entrepreneurial culture. The basic idea here is that societies that prize business and entrepreneurship are more likely to be economically successful. Since the 1980s both Conservative and Labour governments have attempted to make the wider culture and society of the UK more supportive of business. For example, the opportunity for members of the public to buy shares in privatized industries in the 1980s was intended, in part, to create a 'share-owning democracy'. Owning shares would, it was thought, give people a stake in business and foster a more positive attitude towards it. Other important areas of policy have included encouraging business start-ups (see Chapter 8) and a stronger emphasis on vocational education.

Values
- An important process of social change in western societies has been the declining influence of racist and sexist attitudes and behaviours, though these problems have not gone away. Equal opportunities legislation, such as the Sex Discrimination and Race Relations Acts in the UK in the 1970s, both reflected and promoted these shifting attitudes. These laws prohibit discrimination in the offer of employment on grounds of the sex or race of the applicants. The need for these laws reflects the way social attitudes permeate business. In other words, if sexist attitudes are prevalent in the wider society it is likely that they will also show up in the business arena. This influence is all the more striking since, on the face of it, discrimination is irrational in terms of the 'bottom line'. In other words, sexism is bad for business (see below 'A Woman's Role?').

Values
- In economics textbooks consumers are often portrayed (like businesses) as 'rational maximizers', meaning that they allocate their spending so as to maximize their personal self-interest. Yet this view seems to be at odds with the growth of 'ethical consumerism' (see Chapter 11). Here consumers are willing to trade-off their own interests against those of others by, for example, paying more for fair trade products to ensure a better deal for producers in 'Third World' countries. This is a prime example of consumer behaviour, and therefore the behaviour of business in response, being shaped by shifts in the values of the wider society—in this case towards a greater concern for Third World poverty. It can be argued that the increasing emphasis on corporate social responsibility also reflects the way in which business leaders have been influenced by shifting social attitudes and values (see Chapter 7).

Mini-Case 5.1 Should religion be kept out of business?

Britain is often described as a 'secular' society but also, confusingly, as a 'multi-faith' society. The first term refers to the claim that the influence of religion has dwindled in modern societies. Although the 2001 census showed that 77% of people in Great Britain have a religious (mostly Christian) faith, the secular description is based on the claim that for most this faith is very shallow, with only a tiny minority being actively religious (e.g. attending church regularly). The 'multi-faith' label refers to the co-existence within British society of many faith communities, largely as a result of immigration. After Christians, Muslims are the next largest religious group. To many of those who do have a deep religious faith it plays a very important part in their lives and they want to express this belief publicly. But how far should people be allowed to carry religious beliefs into business? Is it reasonable for businesses to ban expressions of religious belief (e.g. by wearing religious symbols) on the part of employees in the workplace? In 2006 British Airways learned that these can be very difficult issues to manage.

In October 2006 BA ruled that a check-in worker at Heathrow could not wear a small Christian cross on her necklace because it infringed the company's uniform policy. This was not a ban but a ruling that such symbols should be worn underneath the uniform, not on display. It seems that the BA policy was based on the view that the uniform is an important symbol of the company and that a religious symbol, or other form of jewellery, may detract from it. In other words the company wanted to retain control of how it presents itself, via the uniform of its employees,

to its customers. This was a small discreet cross, but what if an employee wanted to wear a large, ostentatious cross?

There are other possible grounds for banning the wearing of a cross or other religious symbol:

- In some circumstances there may be health and safety considerations

- There may be concern that wearing a religious symbol may cause offence to others (customers or colleagues) of a different faith or none. An employer may want to keep religious conflicts out of the workplace or avoid putting off customers.

If the policy was designed to protect the company's image and to attract customers, it seems to have back-fired on both counts. BA found itself involved in a high profile public controversy, facing:

- a threat of legal action by the employee
- criticism from the prime minister
- a call on Christians to boycott the business
- a threat by the Church of England to divest itself of BA shares.

In response the company was forced to announce a review of its uniform policy, and ultimately to scrap the rule.

❓ Was BA right to change its uniform policy?

➲ *Stop and Think*

Can you identify other ways in which business is influenced by the wider culture and society, either positively or negatively?

Examples of business impacts on culture and society

The terms on which we interact with business have a profound influence on our lives. Work is a central aspect of our lives and the vast majority of employees work in the private sector. We also depend very largely on the private sector to supply the goods and services we consume on a daily basis. It is not surprising, then, that business has major impacts on culture and society.

Interaction

- The culture industries make up a significant part of business activity, reflecting the shift from manufacturing to service industries in the wealthy economies (see below—the occupational order). Culture has become increasingly big business as a growing share of consumer expenditure is dedicated to 'lifestyle' purchases rather than material necessities. This can be seen in the growth of the wide range of businesses concerned with leisure and tourism. For example, cheap flights have enabled growing numbers to widen their cultural horizons through foreign travel (or, of course, just sit in the sun). More generally, affluent societies, the products of business growth, afford their members vastly increased lifestyle choices and opportunities. For example, the rapid development of information and computer technology has transformed the way we communicate with each other, consume cultural products such as music, and gain access to information. Cultural trends are driven powerfully by product innovations spurred by business's competitive pursuit of profit.

- On the other hand critics point to the negative impacts of business on culture and society. Apart from the serious environmental risks flowing from affluence, it can be argued that consumerism has got out of hand and become a recipe for unhappiness. This is because we have got caught up in a continual desire for more and the latest thing that can never be satisfied. Similarly some people argue that the pursuit of increasing affluence has lead us into an unhealthy imbalance between 'work' and 'life' in which long hours committed to work squeeze out other aspects of a good life such as family life. More generally it can be argued that the 'capitalist mentality' of self-interest and competition invades other areas of life, creating an individualistic society and undermining community.

➲ *Stop and Think*

Can you identify other ways in which the wider culture and society is influenced by business, either positively or negatively?

Organization culture

Culture is also part of the internal environment of business. As we have said, although business cannot be isolated from the wider culture it does to some extent constitute a discrete sphere of activity with distinctive roles, attitudes and behaviours. It follows from this that the culture of a business organization can be an important factor influencing its success or failure, and that shaping this culture is a key managerial task. Organization culture may even be seen as a managerial tool (though arguably not a precision instrument). The workplace may be seen as an arena in which competition between rival value systems is played out. For example, an 'us and them' culture characterized by a confrontational relationship between management and employees (fostered,

Internal/ external

Values

in some cases, by attitudes on both sides), may be contrasted with a culture emphasizing shared interests, partnership and teamwork (see below—**class structure**).

Demographic trends—an ageing population

In this section and the subsequent one we will focus on the following dimensions of the UK population and demographic change:

- population size
- population structure (by age, sex and ethnicity).

The UK population is growing. In 2006 it reached 60.2 million—its highest ever level. Growth since the early 1970s had been approximately 6%. Population projections into the future are difficult because we can't be sure what will happen to factors such as **birth rates**. However, growth is expected to continue up to the middle of this century, peaking at roughly 67 million (ONS, 2005: 8).

Population size is determined by the combined effects of

- natural change resulting from birth and **death rates** (i.e. the number of births/deaths per 1,000 of the population)
- net migration (i.e. the difference between inward and outward migration flows).

Until the late 1990s natural increase was the main source of population growth, but since then net in-migration (the excess of in-migration over out-migration) has been the principal factor. For example, in the year to mid-2005 migration contributed two-thirds of the UK population increase of 375,000 (see Table 5.1).

> ⮕ *Stop and Think*
> Take time to review the data on UK population change shown in Table 5.1 and make sure you can describe them in your own words.

Table 5.1 UK population change 2004/5 (thousands)

A. Population at the start of the period	59,834.3
B. Population at the end of the period	60,209.5
C. Total change (= B − A) (= D + E)	+375.1
D. Natural Change (= D1 − D2)	+126.8
D1. (Births)	(717.5)
D2. (Deaths)	(590.6)
E. Net migration and other changes	+248.3

Source: Office for National Statistics (2006b) (www.statistics.gov.uk).

An ageing population

The **age structure** of the population refers to the number and proportion of people within each age band (as shown in Figure 5.1 and Table 5.2), and reflects mainly changes in birth and death rates.

Figure 5.1 shows a 'snapshot' of the UK population structure, but Table 5.2 reveals trends and projections. The shape of Figure 5.1 reflects life expectancy (the height of the 'pyramid') the increase in the death rate with movement up the age bands (the narrowing of the pyramid) and past changes in the birth rate (the bulge in the middle of the pyramid reflects a rising birth rate from the late 1940s to the early 1960s and a falling birth rate in the late 1960s and early 1970s).

Figure 5.1 Population: by gender and age, mid-2005

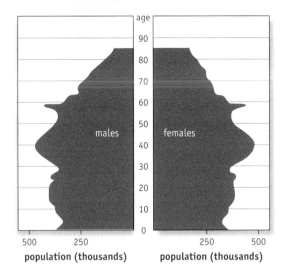

population (thousands)   population (thousands)

Source: ONS, 2006a.

Table 5.2 UK population by sex and age. Percentages and millions (totals)

	1971		2001		2021	
	Males	Females	Males	Females	Males	Females
75+	3	6	6	9	8	11
65–74	7	10	8	9	10	11
55–64	11	12	11	11	13	13
45–54	12	12	13	13	13	13
35–44	12	11	15	15	13	12
25–34	13	12	15	14	14	13
16–24	14	13	11	11	11	10
Under 16	27	24	21	19	18	17
All ages (millions) (= 100%)	27.2	28.8	28.8	30.2	31.4	32.4
All ages (M + F) (millions)	56.0		59.0		63.8	

Source: ONS, 2005, p. 9, table 1.2.

The UK has an **ageing population**, which means that there is a growing number and proportion of people at the top end of the age structure. This can be seen by comparing the age structure in 1971 with that projected for 2021 (Table 5.2). In 1971 10% of males were aged 65 and above, whereas this is expected to rise to 18% in 2021. For females the figures are 16% and 22% respectively, reflecting higher life expectancy than for males. The proportion of the total population aged 65 and over is projected to increase from 13% to 20% over this fifty year period. Ageing of the population means that the average age is rising. For example, the average age in the UK increased from 31.1 years to 38.8 between 1971 and 2005. This is due partly to a falling death rate as people live longer. Increased life expectancy shows up as a falling death rate because within each age band more people survive into the next. For example, a larger proportion of people in their seventies live on into their eighties, so the death rate among 70–79 year-olds declines. At the bottom end the ageing of the population is also an effect of a falling birth rate, since a fall in the number of young people also shifts the balance towards the top end, so the ratio of old to young increases and, with it, the average age. At 11.7 million in 2003 the number of children under 16 was 18% less than in 1971 (ONS, 2005: 8). As the table shows, this age group is projected to fall from 27% of males and 24% of females in 1971 to 18% and 17% respectively in 2021.

Implications of ageing for business

It is obvious that increased average life expectancy is a 'good thing' since we would all prefer to live a longer life. Yet the ageing of the population is often portrayed as presenting a challenge for the economy and society, even a crisis. It seems to be, at best, a mixed blessing. To understand this it helps to think about increased life expectancy in terms of 'work–life' balance or, more particularly, the balance between working life and 'non-work life'. (The issue of work–life balance is examined in more detail in Chapter 8.) All societies have to find ways of supporting the non-working population (or the periods in individuals' lives when they are not working) from the output produced by the working population. Increased life expectancy presents a challenge to society because it increases part of the non-working population, that is those in retirement. Is it possible, as people live longer, for society to support more years in retirement?

Increased longevity is not the only cause of increased non-work life, as we can see by looking at the typical or average male in OECD member states (the OECD is an organization of rich economies). Between 1960 and 1995 (roughly a single generation) average male life expectancy increased from 68 years to 76 years. But over the same period work life (the number of years spent in work) reduced from 50 to 38 (Guillemard, 2001). In other words the non-work life of the average male increased from 18 to 38 years, including childhood, education, unemployment (the period includes years of high unemployment in OECD states) and retirement. Over this period the working life became shorter at both ends, due to increased years spent in education and earlier exit from work. The typical man gained more than eleven years of retirement over this 35 year period.

The challenge for society can be seen by imagining a typical man saving a fixed proportion of annual earnings during his work life to provide an income during retirement. The rise in the ratio of retirement years to work years means that his retirement income will fall relative to his earnings from work. How can individuals, and society at large, avoid this undesirable consequence of living longer? The first report of the Pensions Commission (often referred to as the Turner Commission after its Chair Adair Turner) in 2004 proposed a mix of the following options:

- increased taxes and/or National Insurance contributions devoted to pensions
- higher savings for retirement
- later retirement.
  (Pensions Commission, 2004)

Stakeholders

Values

These adjustments (singly or in combination) are difficult to make. Many men have come to see retirement at 65 as a right, and people are reluctant to save more or pay higher taxes for their retirement. Governments are faced with having to make unpopular decisions. But there are also important issues for business as a stakeholder, particularly:

- the responsibilities of businesses to existing and new members of occupational pension schemes, balancing affordability for the business and adequate pension benefits for employees
- the extent to which increased taxation or NI contributions to finance state pensions should be borne by business
- the willingness of business to tackle age discrimination and afford opportunities for people to extend their working lives on a full- or part-time basis and retire later.

Business may be encouraged to adopt a more positive attitude to older workers by problems of labour shortage resulting from the declining birth rate. In other words, a decline in the number of people entering the labour market could be offset in part by increased participation at the other end, including later retirement. As we will see, immigration can also provide a solution to labour shortage, as it has in the past.

Changes in the age structure of the population affect business not only in terms of workforce participation but also through their impact on the pattern of consumer spending. In this regard what matters is not just the size of each age cohort but income level and tastes. In the 1950s and 1960s business responded to the new phenomena of 'youth culture' and a growing youth market resulting from the coming together of the postwar baby boom and affluence. As these same 'baby-boomers' reach retirement they are now contributing to the ageing population and the novel phenomenon of a growing market of older consumers. Old age and retirement has traditionally been a period of relative poverty but, while this is still true for many, in recent decades there has been increasing affluence among the elderly due, in part, to the growth of occupational pension schemes in the

Herbert Hamrol, 103 year-old survivor of the 1906 San Francisco earthquake, is still working. Business may be encouraged to adopt a more positive attitude to older workers by problems of labour shortage resulting from the declining birth rate.

© Getty Images

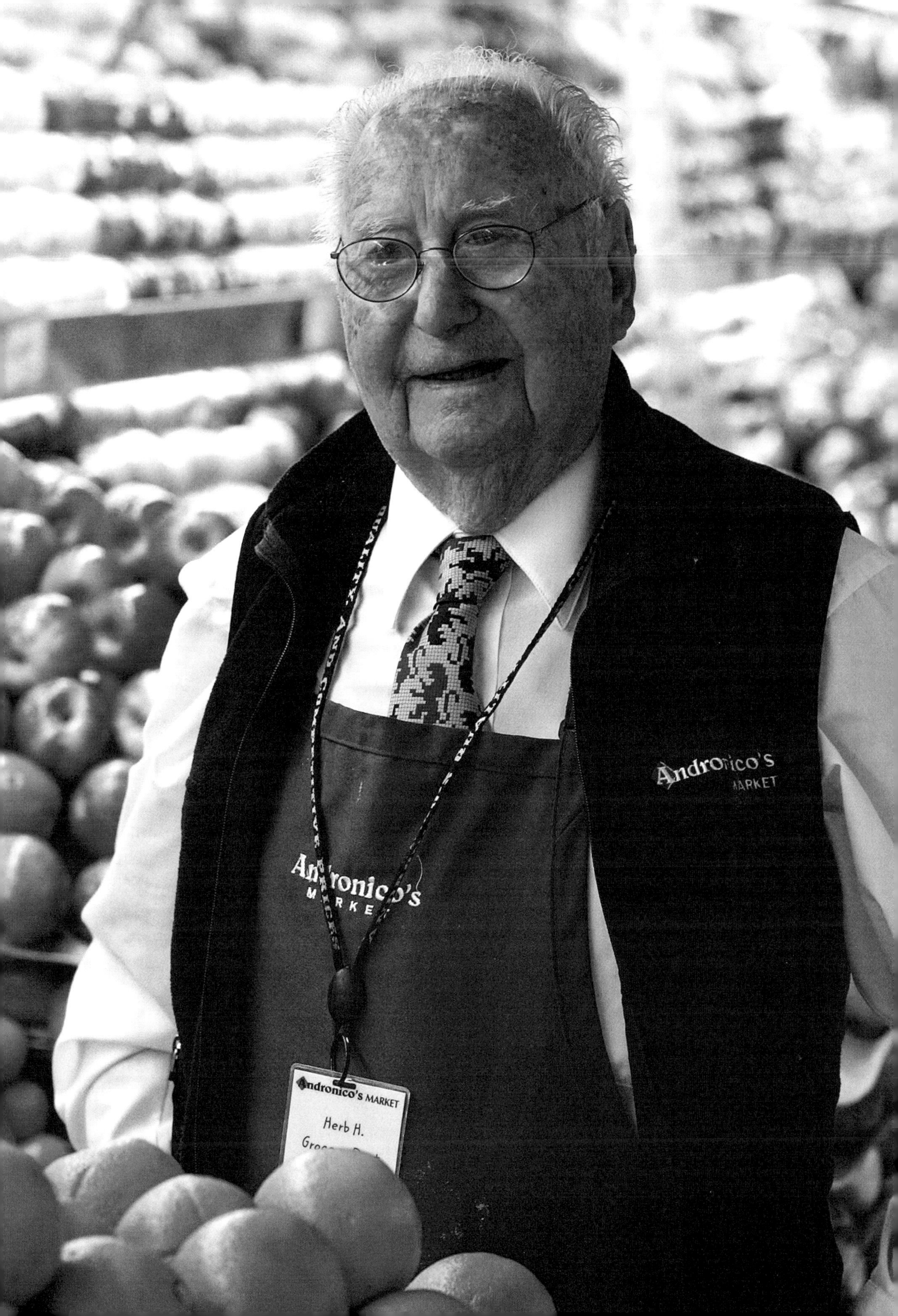
Andronico's MARKET
Herb H.

second half of the last century. Increased numbers and increased wealth has meant important new markets for business. The pattern of spending by the elderly has also shifted due to a change in the 'meaning' of old age as people want to maintain more active lifestyles than was typical of earlier generations. This is reflected, for example, in the growth of leisure and tourism marketed specifically for older people.

> **➲ Stop and Think**
>
> Why is an ageing population seen as a challenge for society as well as a good thing?

Immigration and multiculturalism

The pattern of immigration to the UK has created a multicultural or 'cosmopolitan' society, which is a society characterized by the co-existence of many cultures rather than a single homogeneous culture. This can be seen by looking at the composition of the population in terms of self-defined ethnic group (Table 5.3).

Although Britain has experienced immigration throughout its history, the creation of a multicultural society is largely the product of immigration in the period after the Second World War— from the Caribbean in the 1950s and 1960s, and from India, Pakistan and Bangladesh in the 1960s and 1970s. In the postwar boom years of full employment immigration was encouraged as a way of meeting labour shortages. In more recent decades the growth of the Black and Asian ethnic minority populations has largely been that of the second and third generations, that is of people who were born and have grown up here.

Spatial levels

Table 5.3 shows that non-white ethnic groups are diverse and together make up a small proportion of the population. The figures conceal the extent of diversity since it should not be assumed that members of a particular ethnic group share the same culture. For example, 'Asian or Asian British' is a culturally diverse group in terms of religion. A map of multicultural Britain shows that non-white ethnic minority communities are not evenly spread. Major cities, especially London, have higher proportions of ethnic minorities and are more cosmopolitan, meaning that their populations comprise a wide range of ethnic groups. It is predicted that Birmingham will become a majority-minority city by 2011, meaning that ethnic minorities will comprise a majority of its population. The prevalence of ethnic minorities in particular areas or wards within cities has been characterized controversially by some in terms of segregation and the creation of 'ghettos', making integration into the wider society more difficult to achieve (this view was expressed in 2006 by Trevor Phillips, chair of the Commission for Racial Equality, www.cre.gov.uk).

More recently the UK has experienced significant immigration from other EU states, particularly the ten 'accession countries' that joined the EU in 2004, such as Poland. In 2004–5 net in-migration was 235,000, resulting largely from entry of people from these countries. It is difficult to predict whether these flows will continue on a similar scale in the future, or

Table 5.3 Great Britain population by ethnic group

	Thousands	%
White (incl. White British, White Irish, other White)	52,481	91.9
Mixed	674	1.18
Asian or Asian British	2,329	4.07
Black or Black British	1,148	2.01
Chinese	243	0.43
Other ethnic groups	229	0.49
All non-white ethnic groups	4,623	8.1
All ethnic groups (total population)	57,104	100.0

Source: ONS, 2005, p. 11, table 1.5.

It is predicted that Birmingham will become a 'majority-minority' city by 2011, meaning that ethnic minorities will comprise a majority of its population.

© Gideon Mendel/Corbis

this will prove to be a short-lived effect of EU expansion. This will depend greatly on the success of economic development in Poland and the other accession states in increasing job opportunities and raising living standards. It seems likely that a large proportion of Polish and other immigrants will not settle in the UK but return to their home nations within a few years, effectively coming to the UK as temporary 'guest workers'. In 2006 the government announced that it would not permit unrestricted access to the UK labour market of nationals from the next accession countries in 2007 (Romania and Bulgaria). This decision was influenced by concerns about the capacity of the UK to absorb effectively a further significant flow of in-migrants.

Implications of immigration for business and society

The creation of a multicultural society through immigration has been, and remains, the subject of controversy. Racist attitudes towards non-white ethnic groups are less prevalent than in the 1960s and 1970s but have not gone away. Commitment to the principle of equal opportunity, established in law for over thirty years since the 1976 Race Relations Act, has become more widespread. However, ethnic minorities continue to experience various forms of disadvantage in modern British society and business. In recent years there has been renewed debate over whether the UK's 'experiment' in multiculturalism has been successful, and the costs and benefits of continued immigration are contested. The arguments are broadly cultural and economic in character.

- In cultural terms there is a division between those who emphasize the enrichment of British society as a result of immigration and those who see multiculturalism undermining social cohesion or as a threat to our 'traditional' culture and way of life. In the first view, interaction with people from other cultures enriches our lives because it introduces us to new ideas and experiences, such as new styles of cuisine or music. In the second view, multiculturalism can be seen as having emphasized difference at the expense of a shared sense of Britishness, encouraging separateness rather than social cohesion and integration. Some argue that multiculturalism brings with it the danger of ethnic tensions because, it is believed, people generally prefer to live among their 'own kind'.

- In economic terms, the benefits of immigration are seen in terms of augmenting the supply of labour and business start-ups. For example, immigration in the 1950s and 1960s was encouraged to meet labour shortages, particularly in relation to low-skilled and low-paid occupations. Immigrant communities have also created or sustained certain types of business such as, to give a familiar example, Indian restaurants. The downside of immigration in economic terms is seen in terms of pressure on public services (such as housing, schools and family doctors), and competition for jobs resulting in downward pressure on wages in some sectors. These economic effects can fuel culturally-based resentments.

> **⊃ Stop and Think**
>
> What is a multicultural society? What is meant by 'integration' of ethnic minorities? What difference does operating in a multicultural society make to business?

Mini-Case 5.2 Immigration from eastern Europe—good for business?

In May 2004 ten new member states joined the EU, taking its membership to twenty five. The ten accession states included eight former Communist east European states, among them Poland, the Czech Republic and Hungary. Because these states were poorer than the existing EU 15 it was anticipated that entry would lead to migration to the richer countries in search of employment. The wage differential between the UK and Poland would provide a strong incentive for Polish workers to migrate to the UK.

However it was very difficult to predict the likely magnitude of this flow. Of the EU 15 only Britain, Ireland and Sweden adopted an 'open door' policy allowing immediate access for east European migrants to their labour markets. The UK government predicted an annual immigration from east Europe of 5,000 to 13,000 workers. However this estimate has turned out to be inaccurate. In fact, by the end of June 2006 the government reported that 427,000 migrants had come to the UK and been registered for work. The larger number was an embarrassment for the government, but this does not necessarily mean that it was undesirable for the economy and society. There are different opinions on what would be a 'good' number of east European immigrants, and this depends in part on how different groups in society are affected.

Sir Digby Jones, former Director-General of the Confederation of British Industry, sees it this way:

'Like many Western countries, we in Britain have grown complacent. We have to get off our backsides and do the jobs that need doing.

You cannot blame migrants if they are prepared to come here and work for wages which, though they may seem low to us, are a lot higher than in their own country. They come here with the skills that we no longer seem to be able to provide our own workforce.' (Jones, 2006)

In this view immigrants are good for business and for the economy because they augment the labour supply. Specifically they:

- help to fill 'skill gaps' in the workforce (e.g. in the construction industry)
- accept low wage jobs that indigenous workers are reluctant to take or stick at (e.g. seasonal work in agriculture).

Jones also makes the point that these immigrants are not a 'burden' on the country. 'Instead through taxes they are contributing to our pensions.'

Although Jones emphasizes the problem of labour shortage, it can be argued that competition from migrant workers may be at the expense of British workers, tending to depress wages and reduce job opportunities. For example, a construction industry initiative to encourage immigration of Polish workers has been criticized because it is 'claimed that migrant labour reduces by half wages in the building sector' (Mathiason, 2006).

❷ Do you agree with Digby Jones? Would you agree if you were a trade union official representing workers in the construction industry?

Class structure

The meaning of class

The existence of different classes is often seen as an important feature of British society, and as an undesirable feature. What is seen as undesirable about a class system is that it involves a hierarchy: some people are in higher positions in society and some in lower positions. Some people are 'better off' (enjoy a higher standard of living) than others, or simply 'better' (enjoy a higher social status). Class may be a key source of social division and conflict, and a major barrier to individuals realizing their potential. However class is a controversial concept, and some people argue that class differences are natural and desirable. For example, class differences may be seen as reflecting differences between individuals in terms of talent and effort. Others claim that the importance of class has declined, or even that it is no longer useful to look at society in this way.

In British society people are familiar with the language of class, and most, if asked, could define their own class position. The most familiar terms are 'working', 'middle' and 'upper' class, though finer distinctions are often made such as 'lower-middle' and 'upper-middle'. But what do these terms mean? What criteria can we use to distinguish between, say, the working class and the middle class? How are class distinctions related to business?

It is common to see class distinctions in terms of aspects of behaviour such as: accent, manners and lifestyle. It can be argued that British people are highly sensitive to these behavioural markers of class, such as whether a person speaks with a 'posh' or 'common' accent. However these behavioural differences may be seen as outward expressions of more basic determinants of class, relating especially to economic factors such as income and economic role. Income seems to provide a straightforward way of defining class: on the whole the middle class is better off than the working class, and the upper class is at the top of the income scale. Income is correlated with behavioural differences to some extent, partly due to the obvious point that higher incomes afford more expensive lifestyles.

Income is closely related to economic position and role, because income is generated primarily by business activity and each person's share is determined by the role they play in business. There are two ways of relating class differences to the business system: the first sees the basic class distinction in capitalist economies as between employers and employees, and the second defines class position in terms of a person's occupation.

Stakeholders

Capitalism and class

Capitalism is based on private ownership of business, and the vast majority of people depend for their livelihood on the wage or salary they earn as employees through selling their labour or ability to work to an employer in the labour market. Some have seen this employer–employee relationship as a basic form of class division that is characteristic of capitalist economies. Employers make up a business class (capitalist class), while the very large group of employees constitute the working class. In this view the economic role that defines class position is ownership and control (or not) of business. This is also a distinction in terms of income: profit (business class) versus wage/salary (working class). The importance of this class division is that it may be seen as a perpetual source of tension and conflict because the interests of the two classes are opposed: the profit motive of the business class leads to pressure to hold down wage costs and increase effort and productivity, and members of the working class will resist this pressure. Thus industrial relations are inherently prone to conflict. Some difficulties with this view of class are:

- It can be argued that employers and employees, far from being in conflict, share a basic interest as stakeholders in the success of the business. Employees have a stake in competitiveness and profitability to ensure their own job security. These two views can be reconciled by arguing that employees' interests do tend to bring them into conflict with

Stakeholders

employers, but that this conflict is played out within limits imposed by the need to secure the survival of the business.

- Identifying the business class is not straightforward. In the modern economy private ownership of business means, to a large extent, ownership of shares by financial institutions such as insurance companies and pension funds. Indirectly this seems to mean that the millions of policy holders who, for example, contribute to pension schemes as employees have an ownership stake in business. In addition the people who run large corporations on a day-to-day basis are not shareholders but directors and senior managers who are, in effect, salaried employees of the business (though very highly paid ones). Finally, the world of 'big business' is far removed from those who own and manage small and medium-sized enterprises (SMEs) or work on their own account, so we might not think of the chief executives of, say, the few major building contractors as belonging in the same class as the proprietors of the numerous 'small-time' outfits in the SME sector. The business class today, then, seems to be comprised mainly of executives at the most senior levels within corporate hierarchies, together with wealthy individuals who continue to play a significant role in ownership of business, and spokespersons for business in organizations such as trade associations, employers' organizations and business think-tanks.

- Although earning a wage or salary is something that all employees share in common, to refer to them all as 'working class' seems to overlook differences between occupations in terms of skill, status and income. It can be argued that it makes more sense to see employees as constituting different classes—such as 'working' and 'middle'—according to occupation.

The occupational order

The occupational order provides a snapshot of the character of the economy at a particular time, a framework for identifying processes of change, and also provides a way of thinking about class. Occupation is the common currency of class—we tend to define a person's class in terms of the type of job they do. Social classes (or 'socio-economic' or 'occupational' classes) are identified by grouping occupations together in broad categories. Although there are a very large number of individual job titles, the logic of this approach is that broad groups of occupations are alike in some way and distinct from other groups.

Dynamic

The occupational order is dynamic. During the last century the UK has experienced a transformation of the occupational order, so that the types of jobs that people are engaged in today, the skills that they are required to exercise, and the distribution of people between those jobs, are very different from early in the 20th century. As we will see, these changes have been interpreted by some as involving a transformation of the class structure—a decline of the working class and expansion of the middle class.

Table 5.4 Occupational class in Great Britain, 1911–91 (%)

	1911	1931	1951	1971	1991
Higher professions	1.0	1.1	1.9	3.3	5.3
Lower professions	3.1	3.5	4.7	7.8	13.9
Employers & proprietors	6.7	6.7	5.0	4.2	3.3
Managers & administrators	3.4	3.7	5.5	6.8	15.1
Clerical workers	4.5	6.7	10.4	13.9	15.4
Foremen, supervisors	1.3	1.5	2.6	3.9	3.8
Sales	5.4	6.5	5.7	5.5	5.6
Manual workers	74.6	70.3	64.2	54.7	37.7
Skilled manual	30.6	26.7	24.9	21.6	14.4
Semi-skilled manual	34.4	28.8	27.2	20.6	17.6
Unskilled manual	9.6	14.8	12.0	12.5	5.7
Total in employment (000s)	18,347	21,029	22,514	25,021	24,746

Source: Gallie, 2000, p. 288, table 8.4.

Table 5.4 shows the changing occupational class structure during the last century. Here occupations are divided into eight broad categories or occupational classes, including employers and proprietors. The class of manual occupations is further divided into three sub-groups on the basis of level of skill. A major transformation was the decline by half in the share of manual (or 'blue collar') workers within the workforce, from approximately 3 in 4 in 1911 to 3 in 8 in 1991. You can see that this decline accelerated in the second half of the century. Early in the last century manual workers constituted the vast bulk of the workforce, but by its close had become a minority. At the same time there was expansion of all other (non-manual or 'white collar') occupations (except employers and proprietors). The shares of the professions, managers and administrators, and clerical workers have increased by factors of between 3.4 (clerical) and 5.3 (higher professions). The actual numbers, within an expanding workforce, have increased by larger factors. For example, the number of people employed in the higher professions increased by a factor of 7.14, from 184,000 to 1,314,000 (1911–91). 'In short, there was a change from an occupational structure heavily dominated by manual work to one where there was a fairly even division between three broad categories: professional/managerial work, intermediary occupations and manual work' (Gallie, 2000: 289). This occupational shift can also be understood in terms of:

- The shift of the industrial structure from *manufacturing* to *services*. The dominance of manual work in the first half of the century reflected the importance of manufacturing within the economy (although manual jobs are not confined to manufacturing). The declining share (and number) of manual workers in the second half mirrored the process of manufacturing decline. Conversely, the growing non-manual occupations were predominantly in (though not confined to) the expanding service sector.

The growth in call centres is a result of the transformation from a manufacturing industrial structure to a service-led one.

© Jagadeesh/Reuters/Corbis

Table 5.5 All in employment by socio-economic classification (NS-SEC) (%)

	2001 (Q2)	2006 (Q2)
1. Higher managerial & professional	13.2	14.5
2. Lower managerial & professional	26.4	28.7
3. Intermediate occupations	13.1	12.2
4. Small employers & own account workers	9.2	9.9
5. Lower supervisory & technical	11.3	10.3
6. Semi-routine occupations	15.4	14.2
7. Routine occupations	11.6	10.3
All in employment (000s)	27,636	28,856

Source: Office for National Statistics (no date) 'Table 19: All in employment by socio-economic classification (NS-SEC)'.

- The growth of non-manual jobs (particularly professional occupations) is explained partly by the growth of the welfare state in the period after the Second World War (post 1945).

- There is a *gendered* dimension to occupational change. The expansion of non-manual service occupations has been a major source of increased female participation in the workforce. This is particularly marked in the feminization of clerical occupations. In fact clerical occupations switched from being male-dominated at the start of the century to being female-dominated at its end. It is interesting to note that as clerical work has become more feminized there has been a decline of its relative pay and status. It can be argued that this reflects the under-valuation of 'women's work' in our society.

- In general the shift in the occupational structure is associated with a process of *upskilling* of the workforce, meaning a rise in the average level of skill required. Although this average conceals ups and downs, with some occupations experiencing deskilling, upskilling is the predominant trend. Gallie reports that in 1992 63% of all employees reported that the level of skill required to do their job had increased during the last five years.

- The transformation of the occupational order during the twentieth century has been interpreted as an overhaul of the *class structure* of British society, involving a decline of the working class and expansion of the middle class. This interpretation stems from a definition of the working class as comprising all those in manual occupations and the middle class as being made up of non-manual workers. In this view Britain's social structure has changed from one that was overwhelmingly working class to one in which the middle class predominates. (You may find it helpful to read the end-of-chapter Case Study at this point.)

Since 2001 official statistics have been published using the National Statistics Socio-economic Classification (NS-SEC), based on the Standard Occupational Classification 2000 (SOC 2000). This classification differs from that used in Table 5.4, particularly in not distinguishing manual and non-manual occupations. Table 5.5 shows the class structure for the period 2001–6 based on NS-SEC. The table shows continued expansion of managerial and professional occupations (classes 1 and 2), accounting for 43% of employment by 2006. At the same time there has been decline in the share (and number) of people employed in occupations at the bottom end (classes 5, 6 and 7). Routine occupations (class 7) now make up 10.3% of the total. This is consistent with the trend of upskilling observed in the last century.

Social mobility

How far does class position limit opportunities in life? In particular, what are the chances of children from working class backgrounds gaining entry to middle class occupations (i.e. movement up the scale, referred to as inter-generational upward social mobility)? In the last century there appeared to be a good deal of such upward mobility due to the expanding non-manual occupations recruiting employees from working class backgrounds (there was more room in the middle and at the top). However, the general picture is one in which social mobility is restricted and limited in range. In other words the chances of working-class children entering middle-class professions are not good.

Adding together the data on social mobility of men from a number of generations spanning much of the last century, Heath and Payne show that sons of working class fathers were likely to follow in their footsteps. For example 70% of sons whose fathers were semi-skilled or unskilled manual workers ('lower working class') either remained in the same class (38%) or moved up only into the 'higher working class', including skilled manual workers (32%). Only 18% made it into the 'higher and lower salariat' of professionals and managers (roughly equivalent to classes 1 and 2 in Table 5.5). Conversely, 69% of sons whose fathers were in the highest class (the higher salariat) themselves remained in that class (46%) or the lower salariat (23%) (Heath and Payne, 2000: 262–5). The odds of a child making it into the middle class as opposed to ending up in the working class are much better for a middle class child than one from the working class. The ratio of these odds across modern societies (i.e. not just in Britain) has been calculated to be 15:1 (Aldridge, 2004). These findings indicate that class background exercises a strong influence on life chances or opportunities in terms of the labour market.

Relevance of the class structure to business

- The changing class structure (whether understood in terms of ownership or the occupational order) is driven largely by the dynamic operation of the business system, influenced by state intervention. — *Dynamic*

- Class distinctions are closely bound up with the nature of the employment relationship and managerial strategies. 'Working class' occupations tend to be characterized by a 'labour contract' whereas 'middle class' occupations tend to be characterized by a 'service relationship'. The nature of the employment relationship involves managerial choice. This will be guided by efficiency considerations, but it also raises questions about how employees should be treated. — *Values* — *Internal/ external*

- The degree of social mobility has implications for competitiveness and economic performance. A low level of social mobility not only means that individuals from working class backgrounds may not have the opportunity to realize their talents but also suggests that business is missing out on a pool of untapped talent.

- Class is a useful concept for understanding attitudes to work and conflict in the employment relationship. Working class occupations and a labour contract type of employment relationship have been associated with conflictual 'us and them' attitudes and the development of trade unions to represent employees' interests in the workplace. — *Internal/ external*

- Class is a useful concept for understanding the behaviour of consumers because of the link between class, income and lifestyle. In this way class can be used as a way of analysing different market segments.

> ➲ *Stop and Think*
> What is the meaning of the term 'social class'? How would you define your own class position? What criteria do you use to define your own class position?

Inequality

The question of class is closely connected with the issue of inequality in society because of the link between class, occupation and income. As in relation to class, there are sharply divided opinions on the question of inequality: some see inequality as natural and desirable, while others see it as one of the most damaging social problems within modern societies (and as a problem between societies in terms of the gap between rich and poor nations). Most debate does not take the form — *Values* of inequality *versus* equality, but concerns the degree of inequality that is felt to be acceptable. Should we accept whatever pattern of income distribution the market throws up? Or should we seek to narrow the gap between rich and poor?

Equality of opportunity versus equality of outcome

An important distinction within this debate is between equality of *opportunity* and equality of outcome. Some argue that what matters is that people should have the same opportunities to get on in life and earn as much as they can, if that is what they want to do. As long as opportunities are equal it is fair enough, in this view, if some get ahead and others fall behind. Others argue that we should still be concerned about the outcome, to ensure that some don't get left too far behind or that some don't pull too far ahead. The first view is consistent with having laws to ensure equal opportunities through education and by prohibiting discrimination (e.g. the Sex Discrimination Act, Race Relations Act, Disability Discrimination Act). The second view suggests the need for government to do more than this, such as using the tax and benefit system to redistribute income.

The tax/benefit system

Complexity

In fact there are no advanced societies where the distribution of income is left just to the operation of a free market. In welfare states, such as the UK, the distribution of earnings is modified by government through the tax and benefit system. To varying degrees the effect is generally to reduce inequality through progressive income tax whereby higher earners pay a larger share of income in tax, and through benefits paid mainly to low income households. However the impact of the tax and benefit system is complex and subject to policy change. Indirect taxes can be regressive, meaning that the poor pay a larger share of their income in such taxes than the rich. This has been a reason for criticism of 'green' taxes such as petrol duty. In the 1980s, 'Thatcherism' overturned the postwar consensus by introducing changes to the tax and benefit systems that widened inequality, particularly by reducing the top rate of income tax. In contrast New Labour governments after 1997, though rejecting calls to raise the top rate of tax, introduced reforms (particularly tax credits) designed to raise substantially the incomes of the poorest households and reduce the incidence of poverty.

Public services

New Labour has also used the law to modify the distribution of earnings through the introduction of the minimum wage. Public services, such as education and healthcare, should also be seen as influencing inequality in society. People's living standards depend not just on their earnings but also on the value of these services. In welfare states, access to these services is removed from the market and ability to pay and provided as a right of citizenship. For example, the NHS was founded on the principle of equal treatment for equal need. All children have a right to education up to the age of sixteen. In this way the welfare state tends to have an equalizing effect, although there are some important qualifications to this statement. For example middle class parents tend to get more value from the education system because their children are more likely to attend the best state schools and more likely to go on to higher education. According to the Office for National Statistics (ONS) 'In 2002, 77 per cent of children in year 11 in England and Wales with parents in higher professional occupations gained five or more A* to C grade GCSEs. This was more than double the proportion for children with parents in routine occupations (32 per cent)' (ONS, 2004b).

The earnings distribution

Inequality in terms of earnings can be analysed by dividing the earnings distribution into ten bands each containing 10% of earners. A measure of the dispersal of earnings can be obtained by comparing the top and bottom bands or deciles. 'For 2005, at the bottom of the distribution, a tenth of full-time employees earned less than £235 per week, whereas at the other end of the scale a tenth earned more than £851 per week' (Dobbs, 2006: 45). This gives a ratio of 3.6:1. In other words the person at the 90th percentile in the distribution earned 3.6 times as much as the person at the 10th percentile (Dobbs, 2006).

This measure doesn't tell us about earnings above and below these cut-off points in the distribution, and nor does it show what occupations are involved. Another approach is to identify the highest and lowest paid occupations. Table 5.6 shows that in 2003 the highest paid occupation was directors and chief executives of major corporations, and the lowest paid was retail cashiers and check-out operators. The ratio of their average gross weekly pay was greater than 10:1, nearly three times the ratio between the 90th and 10th percentiles.

Table 5.6 Highest and lowest paid[1] occupations,[2] April 2003, Great Britain

Highest paid	
Directors and chief executives of major corporations	2,301
Medical practitioners	1,186
Financial managers and chartered secretaries	1,124
Lowest paid	
Bar staff	218
Launderers, dry cleaners and pressers	218
Retail cashiers and check-out operators	208

[1] Average gross weekly pay (£)
[2] Full time employees on adult rates
Source: ONS (2004), table 11.6, p. 148.

Executive pay

These figures are averages and so conceal differences within each occupation. It is interesting to look more closely, in particular, at trends in executive pay. A survey of executive pay of FTSE 100 companies in 2005 showed that average pay of chief executives was £2.4 million (including basic pay, bonuses and other rewards). Eight chief executives earned basic salaries of nearly £20,000 per week, over eight times the average pay of directors and chief executives shown in Table 5.6 (Finch and Treanor, 2006). Directors' pay rose by 28% in the year compared to 3.7% for average earnings. This widening gap between the pay of directors and the average is part of a longer trend. By 2006 FTSE chief executives earned 'at least 76 times the average pay of their staff, when in 1980 it was just 10 times' (Toynbee, 2006).

Analysis of earnings does not provide a complete picture of income inequality because it leaves out other sources of income. At the bottom of the scale it misses those who have no earnings and rely on income from benefits. Groups without earnings account for a majority of the poorest fifth of the population (Hills, 2004: 36). At the other end of the scale other forms of income such as from property inflate the incomes of the richest. Analysis of income provides an incomplete picture of inequality because it leaves wealth out of account. The distribution of wealth (or assets) is more unequal than that of income.

Household income

The limitations of data for earnings are overcome by analysing the distribution of disposable income of households to which individuals belong, that is total income from all sources after deducting tax and National Insurance contributions. Again, the distribution can be analysed by dividing all households into decile groups, as shown in Figure 5.2. The richest 10% of households accounted for 28% of total income, a greater share than the whole of the bottom half (Hills, 2004: 23). At the other end the poorest 10% of households account for 3% of total income. This gap between the richest and poorest households has widened considerably since 1979. In that year the

Figure 5.2 Shares of total disposable income: by decile group, 2002/03, Great Britain

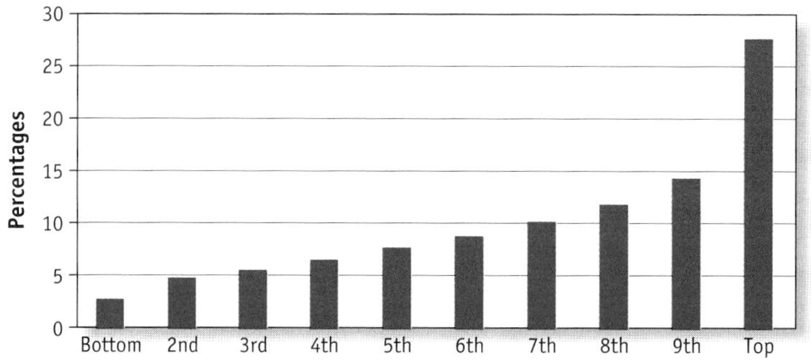

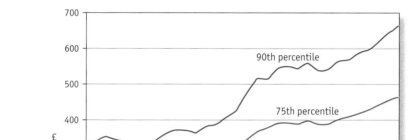

Source: ONS, 2005, p. 73, Fig. 5.14 (also provides explanation of how data are calculated).

Figure 5.3 Distribution of real disposable household income United Kingdom/Great Britain

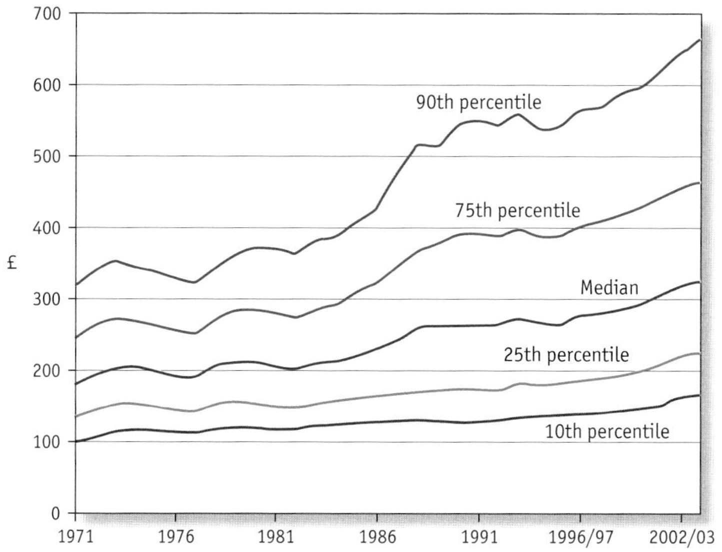

Source: ONS, 2005, p. 72, Fig. 5.1 (also provides explanation of how data are calculated).

shares of the richest and poorest decile groups were 21% and 4% respectively (Hills, 2004: 23). These shares understate the dispersal of income because they do not show the ratio between the lowest incomes and those at the very top, say the richest 1%. There is a wide spread of incomes within the richest 10% of households which stretches the overall distribution (Hills, 2004: 12).

The trend of increased inequality since 1979 is also depicted in Figure 5.3 which shows increased dispersal below and especially above the median. The median household income is that of the household halfway up the distribution—the level at which 50% of households are richer and 50% are poorer. Whereas in 1979 the ratio of household income at the 90th and 10th percentiles was 3:1, by 2002/3 it had increased to 4:1.

> ⮎ *Stop and Think*
>
> Do you think the gap between rich and poor is:
>
> **a)** too wide
>
> **b)** about right
>
> **c)** too narrow.
>
> How did you decide?

What has inequality got to do with business?

There are opposing views on whether (widening) inequality is a social problem and the extent to which business is responsible.

To judge whether income inequality is a social problem we need to consider its economic and social impacts. These impacts can be both positive and negative. As we have seen the main debate is about the degree of inequality that is acceptable. Most people agree, for example, that chief executives should be paid more than their employees in the business, but they are likely to disagree about whether the widening gap can be justified. The debate is often framed in terms of two key principles: efficiency and fairness (or social justice).

- Incentives

Inequality can be seen as good for efficiency on the basis that incentives are required to attract talent and motivate performance. In other words the very high rewards of chief executives are needed to attract the best people to perform these important jobs. Having the most talented people running our companies means that they are more likely to be efficient and successful. The high rewards available at the top will motivate others to perform to a high level in order to progress up the career ladder.

- The going rate

In effect the scarcity of talent bids up the price of chief executives and of other highly rewarded occupations. Medical practitioners, as we have seen, is one of the best-rewarded occupations and the same logic applies here: high earnings attract talented people into these jobs. Against the accusation that CEOs are 'fat cats' awarding themselves excessive pay, it can be argued that companies have to pay the 'going rate' in a competitive market. Just as football clubs have to pay huge sums in transfer payments and salaries to attract top players such as David Beckham, they also, like all other businesses, have to pay whatever is necessary to recruit the best manager. The alternative is to risk loss of competitiveness and the prospect of sliding down the league table.

The same argument applies at the other end of the scale. In other words, check-out operators are low paid because their wages are also determined by competition in the labour market. Only in this case there is no scarcity to bid up the price, rather a plentiful supply of workers able to do this job holds wages down. Again, companies have to pay the going rate since if one company pays more than its rivals it puts itself at a competitive disadvantage by increasing its costs.

- Trickle down

Does the market produce a fair distribution of earnings? For some people the gap between the top and bottom of the earnings distribution seems like an obvious case of unfairness. In fact this seems to be a view that is held widely: a large majority of the British population agrees that 'the gap between those with high incomes and those with low incomes is too large' (British Social Attitudes survey, quoted in Hills, 2004: 32). This suggests that there may be a trade-off between efficiency and fairness: if we want to promote efficiency through incentives this will involve inequalities in earnings that are perceived as unfair, but reducing such inequalities in the name of fairness may reduce incentives and so damage efficiency.

Against this, it can be argued that efficiency and fairness go hand-in-hand through what is sometimes referred to as the **trickle down** effect. The most important form of this argument says that we all benefit, in the end, from the high rewards of chief executives because we all benefit from successful businesses. For example employees of Marks & Spencer benefited from Stuart Rose's leadership of the company because he turned the business around and in the process made their jobs more secure and better rewarded. More generally, the argument is that the lowest paid may be better off than they would otherwise have been because the high pay awarded to chief executives generates improved performance of the economy and rising living standards.

- Social cohesion

However, even if that is true, many check-out operators and others towards the bottom end of the earnings distribution, though better-off than in the past, are still likely to feel a sense of unfairness. This is because people tend to care not only about their absolute level of earnings but also their position relative to others in the hierarchy. In this view inequality is a social problem because being at the bottom of the hierarchy, in a society that celebrates affluence and consumption, is associated with failure and low status. For example those who can afford luxury cars and other forms of 'conspicuous' consumption are sending out a signal that they are successful whereas an extension of this outlook suggests that those who use public transport must have failed in life. Critics of inequality say that it is difficult to sustain social cohesion—the sense that we are all members of a shared society—in the context of a division between rich and poor and a perception of unfairness.

- Morale

Values

This dimension of social cohesion has important implications for business in the sense that employees are encouraged to see themselves as working for the good of the team. This sense of team membership may be undermined by a feeling among employees that executives are taking more than their fair share out of the business and are motivated more by greed than the benefit of the team. Because this feeling may undermine morale and work performance it can be argued that a greater sense of fairness in business is a key ingredient of efficiency.

- Greed and social responsibility

Values

That's all very well but it's beside the point if, as was suggested above, companies effectively have no choice but to pay the going rate. Even if they want to be fairer the earnings of chief executives and check-out operators (and all occupations in between) are driven by competitive conditions in the market. However this view is open to question. It is obviously true that firms operating in competitive markets have to have regard for the going rate for various types of jobs. But this does not mean that firms have no discretion or choice in relation to pay, and therefore no responsibility for the earnings gap. For example, it can be argued that there is not really a highly competitive market driving up the earnings of scarce managerial talent. Rather, the growth of boardroom pay may reflect, at least in part, a shift in the culture of business in modern Britain in which, according to critics, greed has replaced the moral restraints that previously maintained a lower ratio of boardroom pay to workforce earnings. Critics also maintain that increases in boardroom pay are often not justified on the basis of excellent performance, but occur despite mediocre or poor performance. Inequality is a reflection of market forces, but it is also a question of corporate social responsibility.

> ⤴ *Stop and Think*
> Is there a trade-off between efficiency and fairness in business, or do the two go hand-in-hand?

A woman's place?

Values

Attitudes towards women and their place in society have shifted considerably in Britain and other western societies in recent decades—within the space of one lifetime. In the middle of the last century a widely held view could be summed up in the phrase 'A woman's place is in the home', referring to a division of labour (that may have been thought of as 'natural') in which men worked to earn a family wage while women stayed at home as mothers and 'housewives'. By the turn of the century this view had largely been replaced by support for the idea of equal opportunity—that women should have the same opportunities (and rights) to engage in paid employment as men. This shift is reflected in labour market statistics, showing increased economic activity among women. Whereas in 1975 half of mothers with dependent children (age 0–18 years) worked, in 2005 this had increased to 67%. For mothers of pre-school children (aged 0–4 years) the increase was from 28% to 55% (Equal Opportunities Commission, 2006).

Dynamic

More women are in paid employment than ever before (ONS, 2005). Women have narrowed the gap with men in terms of economic activity and employment rates. 'Since 1975 men's employment has declined from around nine out of ten to eight out of ten (79%) for men of working age (16–64). At the same time women's employment has increased from around six out of ten to seven out of ten for women of working age (16–59)' (Equal Opportunities Commission, 2006). The UK has among the highest employment rates of the EU 25 for both men and women (ONS, 2005). In 2002 women made up 44% of the economically active population, meaning there are nine economically active women for every eleven men (Women and Equality Unit). Yet this apparent evidence of a trend towards equalizing opportunities between men and women conceals some marked and persistent differences in male and female experiences of paid work. These differences can be analysed in terms of:

- the types of jobs that men and women do
- the distinction between traditional and flexible patterns of working
- the amount that men and women, on average, are paid.

Occupational segregation

Occupational segregation refers to the fact that men are far more likely than women to work in certain occupations, and women are more likely than men to be found in others. In other words there is a pattern of segregation in the labour market which means that some occupations are male-dominated and others are female-dominated. To some extent this pattern reflects cultural norms concerning 'women's work' and 'men's work'. Some of the female dominated occupations reflect the household tasks for which women have traditionally been primarily responsible (e.g. caring, cleaning and catering).

Table 5.7 shows the extent of 'horizontal' segregation. There are some occupations in which men and women are equally (or nearly equally) likely to be represented (professional, associate professional and technical, elementary), although closer inspection would reveal differences within these broad

Table 5.7 UK employment by sex and occupation, 2004 (per cent)

	Males	Females
Managers and senior officials	18	10
Professional	13	11
Associate prof. and technical	13	14
Administrative and secretarial	5	22
Skilled trades	19	2
Personal service	2	14
Sales and customer service	5	12
Process, plant and machine operatives	12	2
Elementary	12	12
All occupations	100	100

Source: ONS, 2005, p. 52, table 4.11.

categories. For example, within 'professionals', schoolteachers are predominantly women. There are three occupational groups in which women are more likely to work than men (administrative and secretarial, personal service, sales and customer service). The segregation is most marked in administrative and secretarial occupations: more than one in five women work in these occupations compared to one in twenty men.

Table 5.7 also shows a pattern of vertical segregation, in which women are less likely than men to be found in managerial positions. Nearly one in five men are managers and senior officials compared to one in ten women. This 'under-representation' of women is often referred to as the glass ceiling, meaning, that women face a barrier to their progression to the most senior positions in organizations. Vertical segregation is most pronounced at the very top: only 4% of executive directors of the UK's top one hundred companies are women (Fawcett Society).

Flexible work

Flexible work includes temporary and part-time work, and is often contrasted with 'traditional' full-time, 'permanent' (i.e. of indefinite duration) jobs. In the UK the share of part-time jobs has been increasing. Women are much more likely than men to work part-time. For example, of 6.4 million people working part-time in 2004 5.2 million (over 80%) were women (ONS, 2005). Women are more likely to work part-time when they have dependent children. In 2005 58% of working women with dependent children worked part-time, whereas the figure for working women with no dependent children was 33% (Equal Opportunities Commission, 2006). By contrast having dependent children makes it *less* likely that men work part-time. In 2005 just 4% of working fathers worked part-time, whereas the figure for working men with no dependent children was 12% (Equal Opportunities Commission, 2006).

Low pay

The gender pay gap has narrowed but remains substantial. Comparing full-time mean hourly earnings, in 1975 women's pay was nearly 30% less than men's and this gap had reduced to 17% in 2005. However, as we have seen, women are more likely than men to work part-time, and part-time work attracts lower pay than full-time work. Comparing women's part-time hourly earnings with men's hourly pay in full-time work, the gender pay gap in 2005 was 38% (Equal Opportunities Commission, 2006). The gender pay gap can be explained largely by occupational segregation: the occupational areas in which women are clustered are low paid compared to those occupations where women are under-represented. The 'pay gap' and 'opportunity gap' are closely related. This does not mean that the jobs women do are less skilled—it may be that these jobs are undervalued and the skills involved unfairly less rewarded than skills exercised in some jobs done by men (Women and Work Commission, 2006). Similarly, the part-time gap is explained by the types of jobs that are offered on a part-time basis being low paid, that is a lack of quality part-time jobs.

Comparing weekly or annual earnings shows a bigger gender pay gap because men, on average, work longer hours and are more likely to receive overtime pay and bonuses. Median gross annual earnings for full-time men in 2005/6 were £25,800, compared to £20,100 for full-time women (ONS, 2006). The Equal Opportunities Commission (EOC) has used ONS data to estimate a lifetime earnings gap of around £330,000 for the average woman working full-time compared to full-time men (EOC, 26 October 2006a).

Taking a broader view than pay, the income gap between men and women for all adults was 44% in 2003/4. In other words, the mean total weekly income of all women (aged 16 and over) was 44% less than for men, taking all sources of income into account. This income gap is highest for the retired, at 47%. This reflects distinctive aspects of women's working lives: they are more likely to be discontinuous or 'two-stage' due to women taking time out of the workforce to look after children, and women are more likely to work part-time.

Mini-Case 5.3 Can opportunities ever be equal?

The idea of equal opportunity is that men and women, on average, should have the same chances of, say, becoming the chief executive of a FTSE 100 company, or of pursuing careers in management at all levels. What individuals make of their lives should depend on their talents, choices and efforts, and not on artificial barriers such as sexual discrimination. We might expect that equal opportunities will lead to roughly equal representation of men and women in management, or at least that representation at this level will reflect the balance between males and females within the workforce. Should we expect 50% of managers to be women? If so, British business is clearly a long way short of the mark. However, this outcome should only be expected if men and women have, on average, the same talents and make the same choices. It can be argued that part of the 'under-representation' of women in management is a reflection of women having, as a group, different attitudes to work and careers than men. In particular, if a proportion of women choose home (i.e. being a stay-at-home mother looking after young children) over career then we would expect men, on average, to be more successful in their careers than women.

'Mummy, I *want* to be a housewife' (Hakim, 1996)

Hakim's research suggests that some women choose to prioritize 'home' over 'career', and that these choices go some way to explain occupational segregation and pay differences: 'sex differentials in employment experience . . . are . . . due to personal choice as much as to sex discrimination'. She claims that there is a polarization of the female population between 'career women' and 'home-centred women'.

This research suggests that we need to distinguish between support for the principle of equal opportunity and approval of working wives/mothers among women, and the personal choices of many women about their own lives.

However this argument is controversial, because, it can be argued, we need to consider the pressures and constraints that influence women's 'choices'. These choices might be explained by cultural norms concerning femininity, or by the refusal of men to take on a fair share of childcare and household chores.

❷ Do you agree that 50% of managers ought to be female?

❷ If not 50%, then what percentage would you settle for?

> ➲ *Stop and Think*
>
> What is meant by equality of opportunity?
>
> Have women achieved equality of opportunity with men?

Is business responsible?

The rationale for sex discrimination legislation is that women have faced discrimination in the workplace from some employers (and would, without the law, continue to do so). If there was no discrimination, the law would not be necessary. The law is intended to change behaviour, by confronting employers with the threat of sanctions if they continue to discriminate. More generally, the law can be seen as a public expression of the values of society and may lead to a change in behaviour through its educative effect.

Values

On the face of it discrimination appears to be an anomaly since it is not rational from a business point of view—the rational approach is to select the best person for the job, regardless of sex or other irrelevant characteristics. Discrimination might seem rational to employers if they believe that women will be less reliable or committed employees than men (e.g. on the grounds that they are likely to have a career break to have children).

Discrimination might also be explained by a desire to restrict female entry into a male dominated work environment and culture. For example, senior management has sometimes been likened to a 'clubby' male environment into which women are not welcome. 'Most leading companies are run by a self-perpetuating elite of middle class white men who recruit in their own image and find women—not to mention ethnic minorities—an exotic choice of colleague' (Hargreaves, 2006).

If this is true it suggests that business values and priorities (efficiency, competitiveness) have been distorted to some extent by the interests of men in retaining their relative advantages in the workplace.

Internal/ external

Prejudicial or discriminatory attitudes towards women in business might also reflect the prevalence of these attitudes in the wider society. In this way business reflects the culture of the society it inhabits—if sexism is rife in society it is no surprise to find it in business. As values change in the wider society—e.g. towards greater acceptance of equal opportunities and a woman's equal right to work—this will be reflected in business.

To the extent that employers have discriminated against women (and continue to do so) then they are indeed responsible in part for the 'under-representation' of women in management and other areas of business. Ensuring that women enjoy equal opportunities in business requires employers to be law-abiding and, more generally, to follow good practice, such as advocated by the Equal Opportunities Commission.

However it is important to recognize that there may be limits to the progress that even the best employers can make. For example employers can seek to recruit females in male dominated areas of business through **positive action** initiatives, but they can do very little if women do not apply for these positions. Employers cannot do very much to influence women's career aspirations and choices. These might reflect wider social and cultural factors that can act as influences or constraints, such as:

- dominant norms in society concerning 'masculine' and 'feminine' characteristics and behaviours, reflected in ideas about 'men's work' and 'women's work'. These ideas can be transmitted in the media, through advertising images, and in films and television programmes

- the different upbringing or 'socialization' of boys and girls in the family and the education system

- the unequal sharing of tasks in the household, with women still expected to take on primary responsibility for childcare and domestic chores and to fit paid work around these responsibilities.

Does it matter?

If men and women (or other groups, such as old and young, black and white) do not enjoy equal opportunities in business there are harmful consequences for individuals, organizations and society:

Values

- Opportunities being unequal matters on grounds of fairness—it is unfair if women are, on average, less likely to achieve some valued position in society (such as a managerial post) and the rewards that go with it just because of their sex (as opposed to their talents and choices).

- Business organizations lose out because they fail to recruit the best person for the job. They may also lose the particular contribution that women could make to the organization. For example it can be argued that women can bring specific skills and aptitudes to managerial roles (e.g. perhaps, being less confrontational and more team-oriented).

- Society loses out because a pool of talent that could be making a contribution to improved economic performance and growth is not being tapped. For example, research by the EOC in 2006 suggested that one in five of the more than two million women who stay at home to look after families and households would choose to work if they could do so flexibly. In other words the barrier to this group of women working is the lack of flexible working arrangements. These women miss out on opportunities, the firms miss the talents that they could bring, and society foregoes a potential boost to economic output of perhaps £20 billion per year (*Observer*, 8 October 2006).

◈ *Looking ahead*

As in the past, British society and culture will continue to change. Shifts in values and attitudes will continue to give prominence to issues such as equal opportunities, environmentalism and social responsibility, and trust.

Processes of globalization, including trade and migration, will continue to make British society more diverse and cosmopolitan.

Population growth will be driven mainly by immigration. Migrant labour from the new EU member states in eastern Europe will continue to be an important feature of the social and economic landscape.

Ageing of the population is a long-term trend that will continue to influence political and business agendas.

Britain is still learning how to operate successfully as a multicultural society. Sensitivities relating to different values and lifestyles, such as the wearing of religious symbols, will continue to pose challenges for politics and business.

The occupational order and class structure will continue to alter as a result of economic change. In particular, globalization will continue to make it difficult to sustain low skill jobs in manufacturing in the UK.

Income inequality has widened markedly in the UK since the 1970s. New Labour has set ambitious targets to reduce poverty but has not accepted that inequality should be tackled as a social problem. Determined political action to reduce inequality seems unlikely in the foreseeable future. However there will continue to be controversy over executive pay and business will have to respond to criticism on this issue.

The long-term shift towards greater equality between men and women in economic life will continue. Business will continue to face challenges and criticism, e.g. in relation to the so-called 'glass ceiling'. The wider equalities agenda (e.g. concerning age and disability) will continue to be pressed.

◈ *Summary*

- The social-cultural environment consists of the range of behaviours and relationships in which people engage in their personal and private lives

- The relationship between business, culture and society involves a two-way interaction. People carry values and attitudes shaped by the wider culture into business (e.g. sexist attitudes). At the same time business affects the wider culture and society profoundly (e.g. the culture industries)

- The UK population is increasing, and growth is expected to continue to the middle of the century. In recent years immigration, notably from eastern Europe, has been the principal driver of population increase

- The UK has an ageing population, an effect of the combination of falling death rates and falling birth rates

- Immigration to the UK, particularly during the last 50 years, has created a multicultural or **cosmopolitan society**

- Class is an important feature of British society. There are different ways of conceptualizing the class structure—a common approach is to define class in terms of occupation. Changes in the class structure are driven by economic change. In the 20th century the major transformation involved the decline of manual occupations. This experience has stimulated a debate about the decline of the working class

- Britain has experienced a widening of income inequality since the 1970s

- Women have entered the workforce in larger numbers and the idea of equal opportunity—that women should have the same rights and opportunities as men to engage in paid employment—has gained wide support. However sexist attitudes have not gone away, and there is still some way to go

Case study: decline of the working class?

The concept of class is of interest to social scientists, and relevant to business and management, because of the way class position exercises a strong influence over people's lives. The point of identifying different classes is that class position tends to involve experiences of life that are shared in common by members of that class, and therefore tend to distinguish them from other classes. In other words the lives of 'working-class' people are, in general, different to those of 'middle-class' people in important ways. These ways include:

- identity, values and beliefs
- lifestyle and behaviour
- life chances or opportunities.

Class is important but it is not, of course, the only influence. Sex and ethnicity, for example, also influence people's lives in these ways. And individuals are, to some extent, able to make choices about their lives regardless of their class, sex or ethnic backgrounds. For example, women can aspire to a successful career in traditionally male dominated areas of work, challenging 'masculine' and 'feminine' stereotypes and prejudice. Similarly a theme of much discussion of class is the aspiration of people from working class backgrounds to attain middle-class lifestyles.

For much of the last century, as we have seen, the occupational order was characterized by the preponderance of manual occupations. This gave rise to the conventional view of the working class, still influential today, as comprising all those employed in manual jobs (and their families). Of course such a large grouping was bound to be diverse in many ways rather than homogeneous. To take an obvious example, skilled manual workers enjoyed higher incomes and status than unskilled workers and were liable to feel a strong sense of separate identity based on craft. However the working class label was based on the view that there were strong elements of a shared experience of life, such as:

- A shared *experience of work* as being least advantageous in terms of pay, status, the exercise of control, working conditions, job security, and prospects for advancement
- Less favourable *life chances and opportunities* in terms of income, consumer expenditure and choice, housing, educational attainment, health and life expectancy, and risk of being a victim of crime (Figure 5.4)
- Shared aspects of *lifestyle and culture* such as leisure activities (e.g. music hall, the pub, working men's associations, football)

Figure 5.4 Life expectancy at birth: by social class and sex, 1997–99, England & Wales

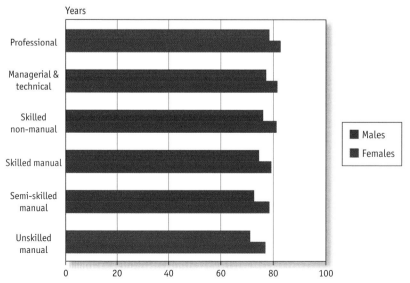

Source: Office for National Statistics, 2004a.
There is a strong relationship between life expectancy and social class—males born into the professional class can expect to live, on average, 7.4 more years than those born into the unskilled manual class.

- A sense of shared identity and *common economic and political interests*. This can be seen in 'us and them' attitudes to the employment relationship and the development of economic and political organizations to represent working class interests (especially trade unions and the Labour Party)

This view of the class structure seems to be less useful than in the past on account of changes in the occupational order and wider economic changes, particularly:

- the decline of manual occupations
- the perception that the occupational order has become more diverse and complex and that the manual/non-manual boundary has become blurred
- the increasing affluence of workers has weakened their sense of class identity and solidarity

It is certainly true that changes in the occupational order require a rethinking of what it means to be working class (or middle class) today. For example deindustrialization and the decline of manual occupations led to the demise of industries and occupations that were the backbone of the labour movement (the trade unions and Labour party) for much of the last century (e.g. docks, coal, steel, shipbuilding, engineering). This has also involved the breakup of geographical communities built up around these industries that sustained working class identity and culture. Growing affluence and the development of the welfare state may have weakened support for trade unions and the Labour party as organizations designed to secure improvements in living standards and life chances for working people. In other words it may be felt that these organizations are not needed to do this job as much as in the past. In this sense it can be argued that these organizations have been victims of their own successes. These changes can help us to understand the decline of trade union membership, the weakening of the link between class and voting behaviour in politics ('class dealignment') and the invention of 'New Labour' in the 1990s to try to broaden the appeal of the party beyond its traditional (and shrinking) working class constituency.

However some argue that what has happened is not so much the shrinking of the working class as its recomposition so that today it includes a range of non-manual occupations. In other

Deindustrialization led to the demise of the mining industry in the UK.
© Karen Kasmauski/Corbis

words, occupations that were in the past regarded as middle class might today be thought of as working class. Clerical occupations provide a prime example of this process: as they expanded in the last century they suffered a decline in status and relative income. Whereas clerical occupations used to be classed as skilled non-manual, today much clerical work is semi-routine. The pay of clerical work also tended to fall behind that of skilled manual occupations. The same point applies to some of the newer forms of non-manual service sector employment. For example, call centres are often referred to as modern-day factories.

The experience of work continues to be sharply differentiated between those at the top and bottom of the occupational structure. This can be seen from the principles that are used to distinguish classes in the National Statistics Socio-economic Classification (NS-SEC) shown in Table 5.5 (p. 138). Managerial and professional occupations (especially class 1) are characterized by a 'service relationship' in which employees enjoy not only higher salaries in return for a 'service' rendered to the employer but also

Values

a high level of discretion and control in their work based on trust, job security and opportunities for career advancement. At the other end of the scale class 7 (routine occupations) is characterized by a 'labour contract' in which a wage is paid on the basis of hours worked or level of output. In a labour contract employees perform routine tasks with little discretion, are subject to managerial authority rather than controlling their own work, have less job security and little opportunity for advancement. These features are typical to a lesser degree of occupations in classes 5 and 6. Thus the workforce tends towards a dichotomy between these two types of employment relationship, with intermediate forms characterizing class 3. This distinction seems to provide a logical basis for distinguishing between working and middle class occupations in today's workforce.

❷ What does the term 'working class' mean?

❷ Does Britain still have a working class?

❷ What is the relevance of class for business?

Review and discussion questions

1 Explain the meanings of the terms 'society' and 'culture', and show why business has to pay attention to the social-cultural environment.

2 What are the implications of population ageing for business? You should think about different types of business, and distinguish opportunities and threats.

3 Is immigration good for Britain's economy and society? You should identify the implications for different stakeholders.

4 Is fairness or social justice an issue that business should be concerned about? Or should it be concerned only with efficiency and profitability?

Assignments

1 Identify key points to complete the 'society' quadrant of a PEST analysis in relation to a specific business or industry.

2 Prepare a brief written or verbal presentation on what steps a business should take to be an equal opportunity

employer. You should refer to good practice guidance from the Equal Opportunities Commission and the Commission for Racial Equality.

Further reading

Social Trends, an annual report from the Office for National Statistics (ONS), provides an overview of social, economic and political aspects of life in Britain.

Giddens (2006) is a comprehensive sociology text which provides further information on the themes dealt with in this chapter.

Halsey (2000) provides analysis of key dimensions of social change in the UK in the last century.

Hills (2004) provides a detailed analysis of inequality in the UK.

Online resources

Test your understanding of this chapter with online questions and answers, explore the subject further through web exercises, and use the weblinks to provide a quick resource for further research. Go to the Online Resource Centre at

www.oxfordtextbooks.co.uk/orc/ wetherly_otter/

The ONS website provides a gateway to a wealth of data— www.statistics.gov.uk

For data on women and work go to: www.womenandequalityunit.gov.uk (Women & Equality Unit)

www.eoc.org.uk (Equal Opportunities Commission)

www.fawcettsociety.org.uk (Fawcett Society)

References

Aldridge, S. (2004) *Life Chances and Social Mobility: an Overview of the Evidence*, Cabinet Office: (www.cabinetoffice.gov.uk)

Dobbs, C. (2006) Patterns of pay: results of the Annual Survey of Hours and Earnings 1997–2005, Office for National Statistics: (www.statistics.gov.uk)

Equal Opportunities Commission (2006) *Facts about Women and Men in Great Britain 2006*, EOC.

Equal Opportunities Commission (2006a) 'Press Release—Pay gap translates into a loss of around £330,000 over a woman's working life', 26 October.

Finch, J. and Treanor, J. (2006) Britain's soaring boardroom pay revealed, *Guardian*, 2 October.

Gallie, D. (2000) The labour force, in Halsey, A. H. (ed.) *Twentieth Century British Social Trends* (Basingstoke: Palgrave).

Giddens, A. (2006) *Sociology* (Cambridge: Polity).

Guillemard, A-M. (2001) Work or retirement at career's end?, in Giddens, A. (ed.) *The Global Third Way Debate* (Cambridge: Polity).

Hakim, C. (1996) 'Mummy, I *want* to be a housewife', *Times Higher Education Supplement*, 14 June.

Halsey, A. H. (ed.) (2000) *Twentieth Century British Social Trends* (Cambridge: Palgrave).

Hargreaves, D. (2006) This self-perpetuating elite only recruit in their image, *Guardian*, 2 November.

Heath, A. and Payne, C. (2000) Social mobility, in Halsey, A. H. (ed.) *Twentieth Century British Social Trends* (Cambridge: Palgrave).

Hills, J. (2004) *Inequality and the State* (Oxford: Oxford University Press).

Jones, D. (2006) These industrious workers are filling the skills gap, *The Independent*, 22 August.

Mathiason, N. (2006) Fast track to UK for Polish builders, *Observer*, 8 October.

Office for National Statistics (no date) 'Table 19: All in employment by socio-economic classification (NS-SEC)' (www.statistics.gov.uk).

Office for National Statistics (2004) *UK 2005*.

Office for National Statistics (2004a) 'Health: Manual workers die earlier than others', 7 December (www.statistics.gov.uk).

Office for National Statistics (2004b) 'Education: Exam results differ by social status', 7 December (www.statistics.gov.uk).

Office for National Statistics (2005) *Social Trends 35*.

Office for National Statistics (2006) '2006 Annual Survey of Hours and Earnings' (www.statistics.gov.uk).

Office for National Statistics (2006a) 'Population Estimates: UK population grows to more than 60m', 24 August (www.statistics.gov.uk).

Office for National Statistics (2006b) 'Population Change: UK population increases by 375,000', 24 August (www.statistics.gov.uk).

The Pensions Commission (2004) *Pensions: Challenges and Choices. The First Report of the Pensions Commission* (www.pensionscommission.org.uk).

Toynbee, P. (2006) I was the hapless decoy duck for David Cameron, *Guardian*, 28 November.

The Women and Work Commission (2006) *Shaping a Fairer Future*, Women & Equality Unit (www.womenandequalityunit.gov.uk).

Issues

PART TWO

Keeping the economy stable

Chris Mulhearn and Howard R. Vane

Contents

06

Learning objectives

When you have completed this chapter you will be able to:

- Explain what is meant by the terms macroeconomics and macroeconomic policy
- Describe the three main objectives of macroeconomic policy and explain their importance
- Explain the importance of macroeconomic stability
- Explain the two sides of the stabilization policy debate
- Explain how the present UK macroeconomic policy framework has been informed by the continuing debate over stabilization policy

Themes

Diversity

Diversity of business

The macroeconomic environment is of crucial significance to firms and organizations in the public and voluntary sectors. The general condition of the economy will pose threats and opportunities for businesses of all kinds. For example, a **recession**, a period of sustained prosperity, or high **inflation** all raise different kinds of questions that business must try to answer.

Complexity

Complexity of the environment

Economies are complex things—they are the product of millions of decisions taken everyday by businesses, governments and individuals. Macroeconomics is an attempt to render this complexity more manageable.

Spatial levels

Variety of spatial levels

The macroeconomy is most easily understood at the level of the nation—as in the UK economy or the South African economy. However, it is important to understand that macroeconomics is underpinned by the microeconomics introduced in Chapter 2 and this often operates at the local and regional levels. At the same time, national economies interact and compete with each other and, accordingly, the present chapter also contains examples drawn from the international level.

Dynamic

Dynamic environment

This chapter will show that macroeconomic thinking is itself an evolving phenomenon. Macroeconomic priorities change over time and therefore so too do the policies that governments pursue at the macroeconomic level.

Interaction

Interaction between business and the environment

The chapter briefly explores the tension between **economic growth** and economic development and possibly irreparable damage to the environment.

Stakeholders

Stakeholders

Businesses, governments and individuals are all stakeholders in the performance of the macroeconomy. When this performance is poor or unstable, we are all potentially damaged.

Values

Values

As we have seen in Chapter 2 there are a range of perspectives as to the role of the government in the economy. This chapter explores this further in relation to the debate about government intervention at the macroeconomic level.

Introduction: the macroeconomy and macroeconomic policy

The business environment works at a number of levels. Business organizations need to attend to matters of critical detail—the price firms charge for a product relative to their competitors is an obvious example. Small errors here can have profound consequences. At the same time, firms need to be mindful of more general considerations that may affect their performance and—in consequence—prompt them to change their behaviour. Thus, the prospect of an economic downturn could make firms rethink their investment and output strategies. It would, for example, clearly be dangerous to merrily produce more and more goods at a time when general consumer demand is falling. While the general economic climate might not be a matter for everyday focus, it is something about which all firms need to retain awareness. The same is true for organizations in the public and voluntary sectors. Business planning, budgetary priorities and human resource strategies may look very different when resources are constrained by recession, as compared to an environment in which tax revenues are healthy and charitable giving is buoyant.

Interaction

In Chapter 2 we saw that it is convenient to think of the business environment as operating at two levels: the microeconomic and the macroeconomic.

Spatial levels

Microeconomics focuses on issues at the level of the individual—the individual consumer, the individual firm or public sector organization, the individual market and so on. Typical questions here ask:

- What motivates consumer decisions to buy or not buy goods and services in a market?
- What steps should a firm take to ensure profit maximization?
- What factors explain the presence of many or few firms or even one firm in a particular industry?

Microeconomic considerations—and the answers to these and other similar questions—were the focus of Chapter 2.

In the present chapter our interest is in macroeconomics. Macroeconomics is concerned with the behaviour and performance of the economy as a whole. Here, rather than looking at individual consumers, business organizations and markets, we focus simultaneously on all consumers, firms and organizations in all the markets that together compose a national economy such as the UK. What are the principal features of interest of the macroeconomy? To an extent, these are simply the aggregations of the things we find relevant at the microeconomic level. For example, the microeconomic matter of the output of goods and services of an individual firm, public sector organization or industry becomes, at the macro level, the output of all firms, organizations and industries. Similarly, an interest in the rate of change of the price of a particular product becomes an interpretation of the rate of change of all product prices taken together—something conceptualized as the macroeconomic phenomenon of inflation.

We saw in Chapter 2 examples of how government may choose to intervene at the microeconomic level to correct individual market failures, to ensure competition or to protect consumers or employees from exploitation. Governments can also intervene in the macroeconomy.

Macroeconomic policy is concerned with the attempts of policymakers to influence broad economic conditions in order to in turn improve the performance of the whole economy. All governments practice macroeconomic policymaking; however, the extent and form in which they do so are both controversial. There are continuing debates about whether governments actually need to do very much at the macroeconomic level and, indeed, about whether they are actually capable of engineering the positive economic outcomes they desire.

Before reviewing some of these debates we first need to establish what exactly it is that governments, business, workers and other economic agents actually want from the macroeconomy. Simply—what do we expect from an adequately-performing economic system; and, for that matter, what aspects of economic underperformance should cause us most concern? Fortunately, there is some degree of consensus here and we can in fact identify a number of macroeconomic policy objectives. Broadly, when these are *consistently* attained it is safe to say that we have a well-functioning business environment.

The objectives of macroeconomic policy

Complexity

It is possible to identify three main macroeconomic policy objectives. These are:

- a stable and satisfactory rate of economic growth
- a high and stable level of employment, and a consistently low level of unemployment
- a low and stable rate of inflation.

Before discussing each of these objectives in some detail it is worth noting a common theme across all three—the notion of macroeconomic stability. This is particularly important in a business environment context. It should be intuitively evident that increased uncertainty in the macroeconomy makes business, organizational and, indeed, personal decision-making a more difficult process. In the corporate world, decisions regarding output levels, recruitment, investment, diversification, acquisitions and so on, carry more risk when decision-makers have less reliable information about general economic prospects. It would, for example, be more questionable

Mini-Case 6.1 Macroeconomic stability and its relevance to students at university

We will see shortly that, for the past decade or so, the British economy has grown at a reasonably steady rate, especially when compared to its performance during the 1970s and 1980s. This is a positive thing for people—such as students—who will be seeking jobs in the near future. Were the economy to oscillate between boom and slump, the job prospects of new entrants to the labour market would be dimmed as employers—depressed by a climate of uncertainty—shelved recruitment plans. Student readers of this book will be aware that the decision to stay in education carries some notable opportunity costs. Students must contribute significantly to their education in terms of tuition fees,

living costs and earnings foregone while at university. Such costs are worth incurring when set against potentially higher earnings in the future. But in the presence of macroeconomic instability, self-investment on this scale may appear a riskier proposition than when the economy is growing steadily and producing new jobs. So, macroeconomic stability is good for students: it makes the future a little more certain and helps them make more informed and better choices.

❷ Why might macroeconomic stability be good for students at university?

for a firm to embark on a major investment project when the medium-term prospects for the economy are unclear than it would when, say, economic growth, growth in consumer demand and inflation are settled at satisfactory rates for the foreseeable future. The implication here is, of course, that uncertainty in the business environment tends to inhibit business activity—firms become hesitant about investment and expansion—and this in turn may provoke a vicious circle of deepening macroeconomic malaise. Overall then, while it is important to achieve macro-economic policy objectives *per se*, it is just as important that this happens in a general climate of macroeconomic stability.

A stable and satisfactory rate of economic growth

Economic growth, introduced in Chapter 1, is the most basic measure of a country's economic performance. It simply measures the percentage rate of increase, year-on-year, in the value of the output of goods and services of countries like the UK or Vietnam or Zambia, or indeed any other country. We use value or price because this reflects the estimate of worth people freely put on the goods and services they buy. The total value of all goods and services produced by an economy each year is known as its gross domestic product, or GDP.

Consider Table 6.1. This shows that in 2006, according to the International Monetary Fund, the UK's GDP growth rate was 2.7%. This means that in 2006 the UK produced 2.7% more goods and services than it did in 2005—more houses, cappuccinos, medical and educational services, music downloads, cinema attendances, and so on. Note that the UK's performance was actually bettered by both Vietnam and Zambia, where growth was respectively 7.8 and 6%. But this comparison is only half the story. Table 6.1 also shows that, in absolute terms, the UK's economy is much larger than that of either Vietnam or Zambia. In fact, expressed in US dollars (to make comparisons easy), the output of the UK in 2006, at $2,206 billion, was about 85 times that of Vietnam in value terms, and about 679 times that of Zambia. This means that although the UK is growing more slowly than either of the other two economies, because of its immense relative size this 'modest' growth translates each year into a lot more goods and services produced.

From the final column in Table 6.1 we can see that the value of the UK's additional overall output of goods and services in 2006 was $58 billion, while the additional outputs of Vietnam and Zambia were much smaller. These data provide an important clue as to why we are interested in economic growth. Simply, the maintenance of a satisfactory growth rate over a sustained period means that a country is generating the potential to significantly raise its standard of living. And this—ultimately—is what a society wants: to generate high material living standards for its inhabitants. The fact that living standards in western Europe are higher than those of Africa and Southeast Asia is a reflection of the long-term industrialization of Europe and the long-term growth associated with this process. At its 2006 growth rate it would take Vietnam 57 years to surpass the UK's present scale of output. Were Zambia able to continue to grow at 6% for the next hundred years, its economy would reach a little more than half the present size of the UK economy. In both cases these economies would be producing houses, medical services, education, and entertainment and all the rest in much greater quantities than their present size and sophistication allows. And, of course, given some qualifications, Vietnamese and Zambian living standards would therefore be much higher. Why is the UK so far ahead? One crucial factor among many

Table 6.1 GDP compared for selected countries, 2006

Country	Real GDP growth (per cent)	GDP in absolute terms (billions of US $, constant prices)	Increase in GDP in billions US $
UK	2.7	2,206	58
Vietnam	7.8	26	1.9
Zambia	6	3.25	0.19

Source: IMF and own calculations.

Vietnamese coffee beans—part of Vietnam's GDP. Vietnam is the world's second largest exporter of coffee.

© Reuters/Corbis

others is that the UK's modern growth period began around 1750—simply, the UK has been engaged in the industrialized growth process for much longer.

Although GDP is relatively straightforward to understand as the sum total of the value of goods and services an economy produces, there are two additional points to make about it at this stage. First, to avoid the problem of double counting, we refer here only to final or finished goods and services. Think about the physical components of the book you are reading: essentially paper, glue and ink. If we included the price of the book as a GDP item and also included the price paid by the publisher for each of the paper, glue and ink, we would be counting all these components twice—once on their own as raw materials and then again in the final good—the book itself. To avoid artificially inflating the GDP total in this way, we count only final goods and services.

Second, consider what would happen to GDP if most prices in the economy were rising rapidly. The market price of books would also be rising and so would their 'contribution' to GDP—we would end up with a bigger total; note this would be the case even if the output quantity of books in the economy remained the same. For this reason we are interested in real GDP. You will notice that in Table 6.1 the GDP figures are given 'at constant prices'. This means that the figures have been adjusted to strip out the effects of continually rising prices or, more correctly, inflation. Increases in real GDP tell us that output is definitely rising—we have more goods and services. Increases in GDP solely generated by higher prices for a given quantity of goods and services— what is known as money GDP—do not indicate that there has been any improvement in economic performance as we don't have more output.

> ➲ *Stop and Think*
>
> When you work are you interested in whether any increase in your earnings is a real or money increase? You should be able to see that money increases may not leave you better off and could even leave you worse off. Real increases always leave you better off. If prices on average are rising by 3% and your money wages also rise but only by 2%, your real wages—meaning what you can afford to buy—have fallen by 1%. You earn more money but you can't buy as much as you did before. On the other hand a real increase, above 3%, leaves you unambiguously better off. The lesson here is that it's not the amount of money we have that counts but the quantity of goods and services into which money can be turned.

Long-term growth

Before we discuss in more detail economic growth as an objective of macroeconomic policy, let us briefly review the growth performance of the UK economy. Figure 6.1 depicts the long-term growth in absolute GDP since 1948. One thing is immediately clear—over this long period the UK has indeed tended to produce more and more output, to the extent that we are now a trillion (a thousand billion) pound income economy, a milestone of prosperity reached in 2000. Is the broad upward trajectory of GDP a testament to the competence of macroeconomic policy as practised by governments over the past 60 years? Unfortunately, the answer to this question is no. In the longer term, capitalist economies tend to grow because of certain innate properties that have relatively little to do with the characteristically shorter-term time horizons of many governments. Long-term growth in these economies is predicated on rising productivity.

Chapter 3 introduced us to productivity which refers to the quantity of goods and services that people produce in a given time period. Referring back to our country comparisons, it appears that the UK is much more productive than either Vietnam or Zambia but to be more certain about this we need to know something about the populations of all three countries. The UK has 60.2 million people, Vietnam 82.2 million and Zambia 11.7. Thus, although Vietnam has more people than the UK we know from Table 6.1 that the UK produces far more goods and services, which suggests that UK citizens are indeed much more productive than their Vietnamese counterparts. Although Zambia's population is only about a fifth of the UK's, again from Table 6.1 we know that the UK is not five but actually more than 600 times more productive than Zambia. So what explains the UK's relatively high productivity?

There are four main factors determining a country's capacity to efficiently produce:

- its investment in physical capital
- its investment in human capital
- its application of new technologies
- its endowments in natural resources.

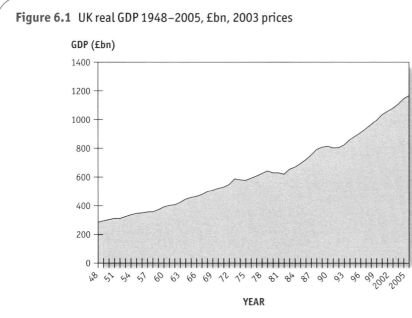

Figure 6.1 UK real GDP 1948–2005, £bn, 2003 prices

Source: National Statistics.

Physical capital is the tools and equipment used in factories, offices, shops, hospitals, schools, transport systems and so on. Physical capital makes the people who use it more productive. It follows that the more we invest in advanced machinery or computing systems or intelligently designed buildings, the more productive our economy becomes. Take the example of shipping as reviewed in the long Case Study in Chapter 3. Before containerization, sea transport involved the laborious loading and unloading of many small-capacity ships by very large numbers of dock workers. Now we have much more efficient large-capacity container ships which can be handled by just a few people. In terms of tons of cargo moved, the modern approach is much more efficient and the people doing the work are immensely more productive than their pre-containerization counterparts.

Human capital is the skills and knowledge accumulated by people that can be deployed in an economic setting. As you progress through the course you are presently studying you are investing in your own human capital. This is personally beneficial because, in the future, it will increase your earning potential. But would an employer be willing to pay you more money just because you are highly educated? Well, no; human capital increases the range of tasks of which we are all capable. So your future employers will pay you very well not because they like having qualified people around but because qualified people will be more productive than the less qualified.

The application of new technologies entails taking advances in human knowledge and using them in an economic setting. Perhaps the best modern example is the diffusion of computing technologies throughout very many aspects of economic life. Consider that this book has been written on a computer, deploying some of its authors' human capital (knowledge of software and keyboard skills) in a physical capital setting (the PC itself). The physical process of all kinds of writing is now much easier than it was in the typewriter age and, accordingly, the physical productivity of writers is now higher. Note that new technology is not precisely the same thing as physical or human capital. Presently, genetic engineering holds out the possibility that it may transform the productive potential of activities such as agriculture, animal farming and medicine. Only if the potential of this new technology is fulfilled will we then see investment in related forms of physical and human capital.

Finally, some countries enjoy prosperity and satisfactory rates of economic growth because they are able to produce particular goods or services in large quantities given their natural resource endowments. The obvious example here is oil, which has transformed the economic trajectories of many of the economies that possess it. In a similar manner, the possession of a good climate and attractive landscape enables countries to efficiently produce tourist services.

So the UK is a high-productivity economy in comparison to Vietnam and Zambia because it scores highly on most, in fact probably all, of the above characteristics. The UK is fortunate enough to be able to invest heavily in physical and human capital, it is a technologically sophisticated society and it also possesses a valuable natural resource in North Sea oil. It is this combination that explains the long-term pattern of growth depicted in Figure 6.1.

Short-term growth

Dynamic

> ⤴ *Stop and Think*
>
> **From long-term to short-term growth**
>
> Look again carefully for a moment at Figure 6.1. Notice that the GDP curve is not very smooth in places. When is it bumpiest? Answer: roughly between 1974 and 1993. During this period, the curve appears to both rise above its long-term trend and to fall below it. What's going on? The answer is that we are detecting here variations in short-term growth rates around the long-term trend. Now, while governments cannot really claim much credit for long-term growth, they can significantly influence the pattern of growth in the short term. Whether or not they should try to do this is a highly controversial matter in macroeconomics and one we explore in some detail below.

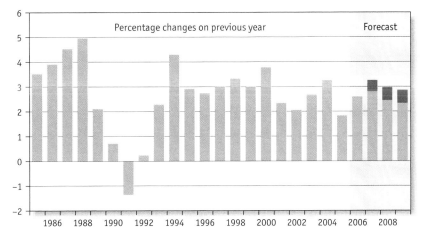

Figure 6.2 UK real GDP 1986–2008

Source: HM Treasury (reproduced under the terms of the Click-Use Licence).

Figure 6.2 depicts recent short-term UK GDP performance. The series consists of three distinct episodes. First in the mid-to-late 1980s, the economy experienced a run of four years of relatively high and sharply accelerating growth. Glance back at Figure 6.1; this above-trend run is evident there too. This period is followed by a very sharp contraction in growth—also plain in Figure 6.1—even to the extent that the rate becomes negative in 1991. This means that the UK entered a recession and actually produced fewer goods and services than it did in 1990—effectively, the economy shrank. Since 1993, however, there has been relatively steady growth which closely follows the trend in Figure 6.1. In fact, this latest period is the UK's most sustained run of economic growth since records began.

So, if an objective of macroeconomic policy is that economic growth should be stable and satisfactory, then this objective is currently being attained. But note from Figure 6.2 that GDP growth has hovered around 2.5 to 3% for more than a decade now. This is certainly stable but why exactly is it satisfactory? If Vietnam and Zambia can enjoy rates at 7.8 and 6%, why cannot the UK do the same? After all, if growth is the key to living standards, higher growth would mean still higher living standards for UK citizens. The point here is that the trend line in Figure 6.1 approximates potential GDP, that is: the real GDP associated with the full employment of all the economy's resources. In the late 1980s the UK expanded beyond this long-run potential; in other words it over-used its resources for a time but found this impossible to sustain.

The intensive use of an economy's resources raises another issue—the tension that exists between economic growth and damage to the environment. Growth may mean rising living standards but if it comes at the expense of severe climate change and the exhaustion of renewable resources such as forests and fish stocks then perhaps we need to rethink our growth priorities. It is already evident that governments and businesses are trying to address the sustainable growth agenda: governments through regulation and tax policy for example, and businesses through the adoption of 'greener' production techniques and operating principles. We will explore the issue of sustainable growth in Chapter 15.

Interaction

One last issue here—if the UK's potential GDP growth rate is somewhere a little below 3%, how do poorer countries often manage to sustain much higher and sometimes double-digit rates? The answer is that their relatively low levels of development mean they have both under-utilized resources and much greater scope for productivity improvements.

A high and stable level of employment, and a consistently low level of unemployment

There are strong connections between economic growth, employment and unemployment. When the economy grows consistently near potential GDP its resources—including labour—are close to being fully utilized; there is, in other words, near-full employment. Conversely, in periods of slow growth or outright recession resources are under-utilized and higher levels of unemployment emerge as a policy problem.

Before we consider the actual path of employment and unemployment in the UK, let us reflect on the structure of the UK's labour force. The UK government divides the working-age population into two main categories:

- the economically active = the employed + those unemployed people actively seeking work, and
- the economically inactive—those of working age, not seeking work and therefore excluded from the unemployment figures.

Members of this last group would include, for example, people engaged in care of their own children, early retirees and lottery winners who've walked away from their jobs.

We are now in a position to define the unemployment and employment rates. The unemployment rate is the proportion of the economically active population (i.e. those in employment or actively seeking work) that do not have jobs. The unemployment rate is calculated as follows:

unemployment rate = (number of unemployed / number economically active) × 100.

The employment rate is the proportion of the working-age population that is in employment. It is calculated as follows:

employment rate = (number of people employed / working-age population) × 100.

Figure 6.3, when read in conjunction with Figure 6.2, illustrates the dynamic relationship between economic growth and the labour market. Notice that the sharp deceleration of growth in the late

Figure 6.3 UK employment and unemployment rates

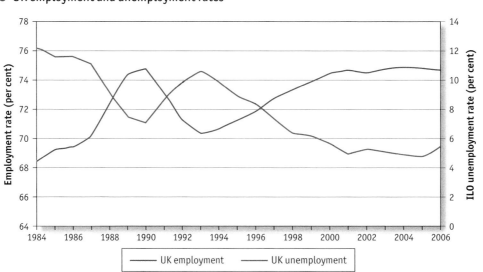

Source: HM Treasury (reproduced under the terms of the Click-Use Licence).

1980s and the recession of the early 1990s (depicted in Figure 6.2) is reflected in Figure 6.3 in the slowing of the fall in unemployment and then its reversal, to the point at which the unemployment rate creeps back over 10% in 1993. At the same time the employment rate, from a peak of just over 74% in 1990, falls to around 70% by 1993 as the recession bites and people leave jobs to become either unemployed or economically inactive and no longer seeking work.

Let us briefly consider why we desire high rates of employment and judge unemployment a problem. We know that economic growth is desirable as it is an effective means of securing rising living standards. The same reasoning applies in the case of employment. The greater the proportion of the economically active population that is able to secure employment, the greater the number of goods and services that can be produced and the better off the UK plc becomes.

The issue of unemployment is slightly more complex as here there are social as well as economic difficulties. We will deal with the economic difficulties first. Any introductory economics textbook tells us that economics studies the choices that all societies have to make in trying to match the scarce resources they possess to the limitless wants of their populations. No matter how materially wealthy it becomes, no society can escape difficult decisions about which wants to meet and which to leave unfulfilled. What is left understood here is that societies do try to use all the resources they have; waste is not really on anyone's agenda. Yet this is actually what unemployment amounts to—a waste of what is arguably a society's most precious resource: its economically active people. And it gets worse. It is a costless exercise to leave coal or oil reserves in the ground; nor do these reserves decay or disappear if we neglect them. The same cannot be said for labour. In a modern, civilized society unemployed people are supported through the tax and benefits system. Those in work pay tax and a proportion of this money is transferred to the unemployed—thus it actually costs society as a whole to waste resources in this way. Also lost are the direct taxes the unemployed themselves would have contributed were they in jobs (i.e. income tax and national insurance contributions), as well as lost indirect taxes (i.e. VAT) associated with a fall in expenditure by the unemployed. Moreover, the longer people are unemployed, the more likely it is that they will find their skills outdated, their human capital eroded, even to the point at which they may stop seeking work and become economically inactive.

The social difficulties that unemployment brings are of two kinds. First, those experienced by the unemployed themselves and their families. Despite the social security systems that exist in the advanced economies, unemployment is associated with low incomes and poverty. Lack of money leads to other problems: for example, unemployed people and their families tend to suffer poor health and lower than average levels of educational attainment. More generally, the effect of unemployment—especially if it is prolonged—is to economically disenfranchise sections of the population. Such social exclusion may carry a range of wider consequences: political and racial tensions and rising crime have all been associated with high levels of unemployment.

Finally, let us think about policy objectives in the area of employment and unemployment. It would be simple to assume that the government's preference would be for everyone who is economically active to be in work—in other words, the unemployment rate would be zero. A nice idea, but impossible in a practical sense. Why? Consider Figure 6.4. This illustrates the dynamism and complexity of the macroeconomic labour market, with unemployment conceptualized as a pool of unemployed labour. The rate of unemployment will reflect the depth of the pool and the force of the flows into and out of it.

Taking inflows first, the pool deepens as new entrants join the labour market from school or college but do not immediately find work. Similarly, re-entrants to the labour market who have been economically inactive but now want to work again will add to the pool if they do not go straight into a job. People who leave employment involuntarily through redundancy or other form of termination, and those who choose to leave their jobs will also cause the pool to deepen. In both cases here we assume that there is a determination to stay in the labour market and find new work.

Now outflows. Unemployed people who find work will cause the pool to become shallower, as will those who decide to end a period of unemployment by ceasing to look for work (they become economically inactive), or permanently retiring.

Stakeholders

Values

Dynamic

Complexity

Figure 6.4 The unemployment pool: inflows and outflows

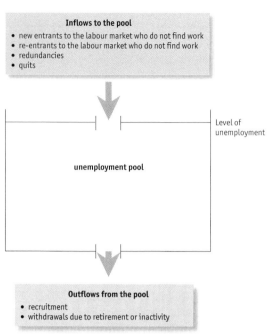

Inflows to the pool
- new entrants to the labour market who do not find work
- re-entrants to the labour market who do not find work
- redundancies
- quits

Level of unemployment

unemployment pool

Outflows from the pool
- recruitment
- withdrawals due to retirement or inactivity

Think for a moment about what will happen to the pool in a period of decelerating economic growth or recession. The forces generating inflows gather momentum. Fewer new entrants and re-entrants to the labour market will immediately find work; more firms are likely to be making workers redundant, and people who voluntarily quit jobs are less likely to quickly find new ones. On the other hand recession minimizes recruitment and stems outflows—overall then, the pool deepens and the unemployment rate climbs.

> ⮑ *Stop and Think*
> What happens to the unemployment pool's inflows and outflows and the unemployment rate when growth is stable and satisfactory?

Your answer to this question may have been that inflows should pretty much dry up and that outflows should increase, perhaps to the point at which the pool is drained completely and unemployment is indeed zero. But in truth, this can never happen. Figure 6.4 suggests that the labour market is a fairly complex entity but there is still a little more to say about it. We can in fact identify two categories of unemployment that in a modern and innovative economy can never be entirely eliminated. These are frictional (or search), and structural (or mismatch) unemployment.

Frictional or search unemployment arises when people find themselves, for any number of reasons, temporarily between jobs without leaving the labour market. There are now some 29 million people in work in the UK. It is surely unreasonable to expect that every single one of these people will either continue in their present job or move seamlessly into another without experiencing a single period of unemployment. At the same time, the fortunes of individual business organizations will vary. Some will lay off staff, others will be recruiting new employees; some organizations will close entirely, while new ones will be created. In this environment of change and displacement some frictional unemployment is naturally to be expected.

Structural or mismatch unemployment is also a consequence of economic evolution. It reflects the fact that over time whole industries decay and disappear, casting the people who have skills and experience attuned to those industries economically adrift. These people are said to be structurally unemployed in as much as the industry in which they worked has disappeared. Not too long ago Britain had large numbers of people employed in the mining of coal. Now there are relatively few miners as we rely more on imported coal and alternative sources of energy. The scrapping of the coal industry was a serious problem for people whose human capital was effectively tied to that industry. Redundant miners cannot overnight become teachers or engineers. Until unemployed people can be retrained there will be a mismatch between their skills and the skills required to fill job vacancies. But as some industries die, new ones are born. A decade ago, mobile phones were relatively rare, now they saturate our societies, creating many new job opportunities, perhaps for retrained ex-miners. Structural unemployment is simply a reflection of this kind of industrial change. It is not pleasant, particularly when it is geographically concentrated in particular places as mining was, but in a market economy it is to some extent inevitable.

Given these complications, what is the employment/unemployment macroeconomic policy objective? In the UK the government defines its intention as follows:

> The Government's long-term goal for the labour market is to achieve employment opportunity for all—the modern definition of full employment. This means that everyone should be given appropriate support and advice to enable them to find and retain a job, with the opportunity to gain skills and experience . . . HM Treasury (2006)

So, reflecting the complexity and dynamism of the labour market, there is no particular target for the unemployment rate. Rather, there is an ambition to ensure that those economically active people looking for work are able to find it. However, interestingly, the UK government has set a long-term target for the employment rate. It intends that this should eventually reach 80%, up from its current level of 74.5%. Implicitly, this suggests that the present level of unemployment may be considered a little too high.

A low and stable rate of inflation

Inflation is a process of continually rising prices. The inflation rate is the average rate of change of the prices of goods and services in the economy over a given period. For example, at the time of writing the inflation rate in the UK is 2.7%. This means that the prices in the UK are on average presently rising at 2.7% per year. Inflation in the UK is measured by the consumer prices index (CPI) which reveals changes in the cost of a representative basket of goods and services—the things that most people buy.

A low and stable rate of inflation is desirable for a number of reasons. For the most part these have to do with the fact that we live in economies that rely heavily on markets to allocate resources. In Chapter 2 we saw how markets are coordinated by price signals. The movements of prices provide incentives to producers and consumers to behave in particular ways. Now, what defines a good signal? One important property is its reliability. Think what would happen to traffic flows were traffic signals to have their timings randomly set. You pull up at a stop light and you're unsure if you're going to be stuck there for one minute, or three, or even ten. The same is true for all other drivers. Our guess is that this would soon result in gridlock and accidents as people jumped traffic lights and made bad driving decisions. Traffic signals do a good job when they're predictable and people feel they can rely on them. In markets, price signals are also better if they're reliable and people feel they can use them to make informed choices—this happens when inflation is low and stable.

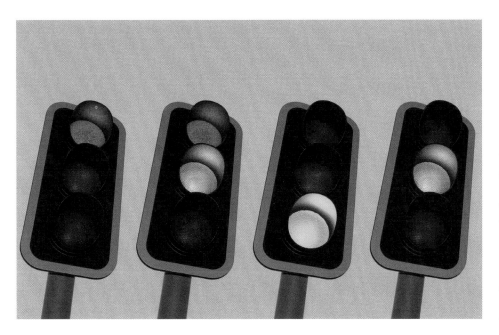

Traffic signals do a good job when they're predictable and people feel they can rely on them. In markets, price signals are also better if they're reliable.

© istockphoto.com/ Philip Ronan

Interaction

We can in fact identify a number of specific costs of inflation. The first of these—in keeping with our example above—has to do with uncertainty. Consumers and producers make decisions in markets by taking account of relative prices, that is the price of one good or service compared to another. When inflation is low and stable, relative prices are easy to read and consumers can make informed choices about whether to buy this or that good, taking price into account. Similarly, producers have good indicators of which markets offer better prospects for investment, and which are best left alone. In the presence of high and, therefore, increasingly variable inflation, such clarity is lost. The general process of inflation across all goods and services masks relative price movements between particular goods and services leading to poorer decision-making. Thus, in a low-inflation environment, if the price of outdoor-wear clothing starts to rise, this is a signal for firms like Timberland to invest more. But in a high-inflation environment poor old Timberland just can't tell if this is a definite signal from the rugged outdoor types populating this market that they want more kit, or just part of the background noise of general inflation. Replicate Timberland's uncertainty across the whole economy and an inflation-induced recipe for some very poorly informed decision-making begins to emerge.

Values

Inflation can also arbitrarily redistribute income and wealth between different groups in society, abstracting from what might be deserved or socially desired. For example, in a low-inflation environment, borrowers find the real values of their debts are maintained and they must pay them off as expected. But in the presence of high inflation the real values of debts are quickly eroded as prices and money wages surge upwards—an unlooked for but hardly merited bonus for borrowers. Savers find themselves in the opposite position. A pensioner may have saved over a working life to provide for his or her retirement but a sudden surge in inflation could rapidly reduce the real value of what has been saved, with no further opportunity to start again. These arbitrary changes are unhelpful in a market economy where it is expected that reward should bear at least some relation to effort or sacrifice.

Finally, the UK authorities identify an important link between inflation control and wider economic prospects. As noted in Mini-Case 6.2, in the mid-1970s inflation in the UK was around 25%. At this rate the pound lost a quarter of its value over just twelve months. In such a climate, annual wage negotiations became the focus for damaging industrial and, indeed, political strife, as workers energetically sought at least inflation-matching pay increases. Moreover, the various steps the authorities took at intervals over many years to bring inflation back under control were themselves damaging to the economy. It is the authorities' view now that low and stable inflation is a necessary condition for sustained economic prosperity.

> Low inflation is . . . an important factor in helping to encourage long-term stability in the economy. Price stability is a precondition for achieving a wider economic goal of sustainable growth and employment. High inflation can be damaging to the functioning of the economy. Low inflation can help to foster sustainable long-term economic growth. Bank of England (2006)

Mini-Case 6.2 Inflation and the international price competitiveness of firms

A further problem with inflation is its potential to erode an economy's international price competitiveness against rival economies. As recently as the mid-1970s inflation in the UK was close to 25% (see Figure 6.7, p. 177). At the same time inflation in Germany—a country with which the UK trades heavily—remained in single figures. What problems and opportunities did this pose for businesses in these two economies? The short answer is that it significantly advantaged German firms—they found it easier to beat off British exports to Germany as these were rising rapidly in price; and their more competitively-priced goods were better able to penetrate UK markets.

❷ Look at Figure 6.7 and compare the inflation rate of the UK to that of the other nations. What do you think the impact of this relative difference might have been on the competitiveness of British exports during most of this period?

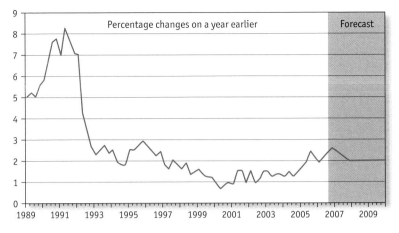

Figure 6.5 UK inflation

Note: Outturns until 2006Q3; forecasts for every second quarter from 2006Q4 to 2009Q4.
Source: HM Treasury (reproduced under the terms of the Click-Use Licence).

With this perspective in mind, the government has established an annual target of 2% for UK inflation. Figure 6.5 depicts recent UK inflation performance, and the evidence is that the target is currently being met. We discuss how this has been achieved later in the chapter.

We have seen in this section that stability is desirable at the macroeconomic level in respect of each of the three areas of concern for policy: economic growth, employment and unemployment and inflation. We have also seen evidence that in each of these respects the UK economy has performed well in recent years. In the next section we introduce the notion of stabilization policy and consider the view that this is something that governments should be prepared to engage in as circumstances dictate. Subsequently, we examine the counter-argument that the role of the government in the macroeconomy should be much more constrained.

The case for stabilizing the economy

One of the big unresolved questions in macroeconomics is whether or not policymakers should try to stabilize the levels of output and employment in the economy. There really is no broad agreement here and Chapter 2 introduced you to the underlying perspectives behind these debates. Some economists—following the tradition established in the 1930s by the famous British economist John Maynard Keynes—suppose that capitalist economies often behave erratically. If they are beset by some unforeseen circumstances, usually known as an economic shock, they can move into devastating recessions from which it may take some time to recover. The implication these economists draw is that, because economies tend not to recover spontaneously or quickly, it is up to governments to help them back into shape using particular macroeconomic tools in fairly expansive ways. In terms of Figure 6.2 this could mean decisive action to counteract a pattern such as the sharp deceleration in growth at the beginning of the 1990s.

However, a second set of economists, broadly in the neoclassical school and including the late American economist Milton Friedman is deeply suspicious of this argument. People like Friedman

Values

argue that capitalist economies, while they can slide into recession, have well-developed and quick-acting powers of recovery. This means that there is no need for governments to excessively meddle in the macroeconomy—it can take care of itself. Moreover, in this view, while government intervention does little or nothing for output and employment, it does have the very dangerous side effect of potentially fuelling inflation. The implication is that if the economy is mostly but not exclusively left to itself, one should expect a GDP growth path similar to that in Figure 6.1, but without any substantial or lengthy deviations away from potential GDP.

To fully understand the basis of the differences between these two groups it is necessary to consider their contrasting views about what can be reasonably done with the two major tools of macroeconomic policy: fiscal policy and monetary policy. We also need to review a little economic history to see how these tools have been used—with mixed results—in the more distant and recent past. We will begin with brief definitions of fiscal and monetary policy.

Fiscal policy involves government expenditure and taxation. As taxation is government income, fiscal policy is the balance between government income and expenditure. For example, expansionary fiscal policy involves governments spending more (through borrowing) than they raise in taxation.

Monetary policy is implemented chiefly through the setting of interest rates, which in the UK, are controlled by the Monetary Policy Committee of the Bank of England.

Spatial levels

The story of modern macroeconomics really begins with the work of Keynes and, in particular, with his 1936 book, *The General Theory of Employment, Interest and Money*. In this volume, and elsewhere, Keynes provided the first comprehensive explanation of how recessions can occur, how they can persist and what governments can do to help economies recover from them. Keynes's work was developed first in the 1920s in response to extremely sluggish British growth throughout this decade; however, it gained a new relevance from 1929 when not just one economy but the whole world slid into a depression of unprecedented proportions. This became known as the Great Depression.

Keynes's explanation of the Great Depression and, indeed, of recessions generally was relatively simple. He argued that the level of activity in an economy was determined by the prevailing level of aggregate demand, that is: the total level of demand for all goods and services. In Keynes's view it was relatively easy for aggregate demand to fall, and once it did there was nothing in the economy which would prompt its early recovery: an economy in recession would very likely stay in recession. Let us think for a moment how this happens. Take an economy that is enjoying steady growth with low unemployment. If, for some reason, businesses become generally pessimistic about the future, they will tend to reduce investment—cutting their own spending until a time when economic prospects have improved. But because many businesses act in this way, the results for the economy and everyone in it are catastrophic. As investment falls, firms are doing two things. First, they are reducing the business that they do with each other—cancelling or not renewing orders for materials and equipment. Second, they are shelving recruitment plans and some will be laying-off employees. You will agree that things do not look good, but potentially this is just the start. The process becomes a reciprocally confirming one. Business confidence was low and businesses reacted as they thought appropriate. But now, as orders dry up and unemployment begins to rise, it's clear they were right—things *are* bad. Demand in the economy now falls even further—firms buy less and less from each other and rising unemployment means that consumer demand is weakening considerably. At some point, this downward spiral will slow but it may be very a long way down before any recovery happens. In the United States during the Great Depression, for example, real GDP fell by 28% and unemployment increased to 25%. In the city of New York alone, there were 1 million Americans unemployed. For a time there, it looked like capitalism itself was collapsing.

Complexity

In Keynes's view, the correct way to understand what was going on in such circumstances was to appreciate the importance of aggregate demand. It is the fall in demand which triggers and feeds economic decline. Eventually the process will come to a halt but, critically, there is no natural recovery mechanism. If aggregate demand eventually falls by say a quarter, firms will have no incentive to produce more output than can be bought by this lower level of demand, and they will

Stakeholders

An encampment in New York during the Great Depression, when real GDP fell by 28% and unemployment increased to 25%. In the city of New York alone, there were 1 million Americans unemployed.

© Bettmann/Corbis

require many fewer workers than before as they are now producing much less. We illustrate the process in Figure 6.6. In panel a) of the figure, the economy is operating at potential GDP (1) and the output of goods and services (2) is bought by consumers and firms (3), meaning that the current level of aggregate demand (4) is sufficient to maintain the economy at potential GDP. However, in panel b) of Figure 6.6, a shock hits the economy and consumers and firms begin to buy less output (1). This means that aggregate demand is falling (2). Accordingly, forms begin to revise their output plans (3), and lay-off workers (4). Output in the economy begins to fall (5). Finally in panel c) it is evident that the process has spiralled down to a sustainable level. Here, firms have fully revised their output decisions (1), and output has stabilized at a lower level (2). We know that this position is stable and sustainable because consumers and firms buy all this output (3), which means that aggregate demand is once again sufficient to maintain GDP (4), but now at a level below its potential. The economy is mired in recession: GDP has fallen and unemployment has risen and, most important, there is nothing on the horizon that will change things anytime soon.

From a Keynesian perspective then, economies are fragile things, prone to crises of confidence. Aggregate demand is the key to improving matters, but how can demand be revived given, in

Figure 6.6 Aggregate demand, output and employment

a) The economy at potential GDP—aggregate demand is sufficient to buy capacity output

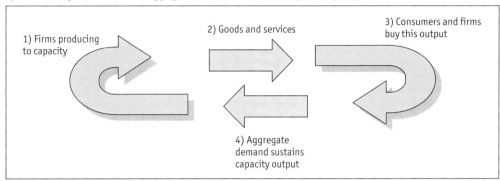

b) Firms have lost confidence—orders are reduced and aggregate demand is falling

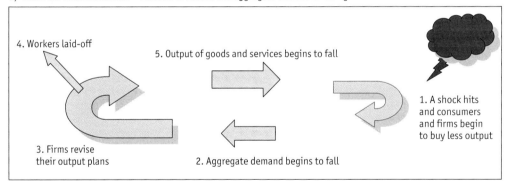

c) The economy in recession—lower aggregate demand sustains lower output, and there is no mechanism that will prompt an improvement in conditions

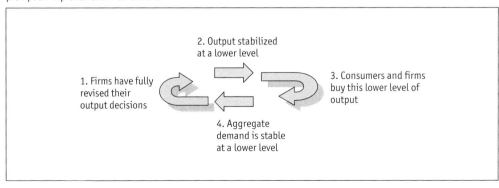

Keynes's phrase, 'the haltering, wavering mood' of business? His solution was again relatively simple. If there was no natural force in the economy capable of generating a recovery in aggregate demand and business confidence, one would have to be created. Keynes proposed that governments should themselves step in and raise aggregate demand using expansionary fiscal and monetary policy. Over time this would rejuvenate business confidence and reverse the depressive processes outlined in Figure 6.6, bringing the economy back close to potential GDP and full employment.

As noted, one form of expansionary fiscal policy involves the government spending more than it receives in taxes; usually this is financed by borrowing. The new spending might be on, for example, new schools, roads or hospitals. In many ways its actual form is less important than the fact of its happening. Once the process has started business takes heart and begins to plan once again for expansion. Of course, some firms benefit quickly and directly—those building the schools, roads and hospitals. But others will also respond as employment and consumer demand begins to revive. In effect the government needs only to initiate economic revival—it is not required to make good the entire aggregate-demand 'gap' on its own. Moreover, as either a supplement or alternative to spending more itself, the government can decide to cut taxes leaving businesses and individual tax payers with more disposable income. This is also a means of prompting an increase in aggregate demand.

Expansionary monetary policy might also be used as a tool of recovery. Were the government to engineer a reduction in interest rates, firms and consumers might respond by investing and spending more freely. However, Keynes was less sure that this approach would work as quickly and directly when compared to fiscal intervention. Lower interest rates would in all likelihood, prompt business and individuals to spend more, but if the government increased its spending there was no possible doubt that aggregate demand would rise.

> ⮑ *Stop and Think*
>
> **Spending and interest rates**
>
> Why might business organizations and individuals choose to increase spending as interest rates come down? The answer is that interest rates indicate the cost of borrowing. With lower interest rates all forms of borrowing become cheaper and therefore economic agents are encouraged to both borrow and spend more.

According to the late Nobel Prize-winning economist Franco Modigliani, what Keynes had outlined in the *General Theory of Employment, Interest and Money* was the following 'need/can/should' case for stabilization policy:

- governments *need* to stabilize the economy—capitalist economies have a tendency to slip easily into recession; they are inherently unstable

- governments *can* stabilize the economy—they have the requisite fiscal and monetary tools

- governments *should* therefore stabilize the economy—there is no case for them not to do so.

Following the end of the Second World War in 1945 Keynesianism came to dominate macro-economic policymaking in the capitalist economies and stabilization policy was widely practised and to apparently good effect. The period from 1945 until the early 1970s became known as the postwar boom in that, in practically all of the western industrial economies, GDP expanded at unprecedented and sustained rates and, as a corollary, employment rates increased and unemployment remained low and stable. Table 6.2 shows average annual growth rates for the so-called G7—the world's leading industrial nations since 1870. The sub-period from 1950–1973 clearly stands in a class by itself in terms of the growth rates collectively achieved by these economies, with particularly strong performances in continental Europe and Japan.

Table 6.2 GDP growth rates for the G7, 1870–1998, per cent

Country	1870–1913	1913–1950	1950–1973	1973–1998
France	1.63	1.15	5.05	2.10
Germany	2.83	0.30	5.68	1.76
Italy	1.94	1.49	5.64	2.28
UK	1.90	1.19	2.93	2.00
USA	3.94	2.84	3.93	2.99
Canada	4.02	2.94	4.98	2.80
Japan	2.44	2.21	9.29	2.97

Source: Snowdon and Vane (2005), adapted from Maddison (2001).

Mini-Case 6.3 Japan: from boom to bust and now recovery?

After the Second World War, against all expectations the Japanese economy enjoyed an 'economic miracle' so much so that by the 1980s it had become the second largest economy in the world and many businesses sought to copy Japanese production techniques.

So when in 1989/90 the Japanese economy plunged into a recession that was to last 15 years there was universal surprise. The years 2004/5 began to see a gradual, if tentative recovery.

The reason for the recession was the end of a speculative 'bubble' that had seen land prices surging and stock market prices booming. When this bubble burst the banks, which had incautiously issued large amounts of loans, were owed vast sums that could not be repaid. The resultant fall in the money supply meant that unemployment began to rise and prices fall. This cut aggregate demand and the falling prices caused even those people in work to stop spending in the knowledge that, if prices are falling, it is better to save now and spend later. The result of this was to cut demand further and deepen the recession.

Faced with these mounting problems the government embarked on a Keynesian expansion programme by hugely increasing government spending (at one point government debt rose to 130% of GDP) and by reducing interest rates to nearly zero per cent.

❓ What was the Japanese government trying to achieve by this combination of expansionary fiscal and monetary policy?

❓ Given the extent of this stabilization programme would you have expected Japan to have recovered from the recession sooner than it did?

Stabilization policy in question

Dynamic

Unfortunately, the postwar boom petered out in the early 1970s and the effectiveness of stabilization policy began to be called into question. This was not just because, as Table 6.2 indicates, growth was much slower in the period 1973–98 for all of the G7, but also because of the appearance of a new macroeconomic problem—inflation. This had never really been much of a cause for concern during the postwar boom when policymakers' minds were quite firmly focused on the need to avoid anything like another Great Depression. However, from the beginning of the 1970s inflation became a worldwide phenomenon. It caused serious difficulties both for economies

Figure 6.7 G5 inflation rates 1964–2002

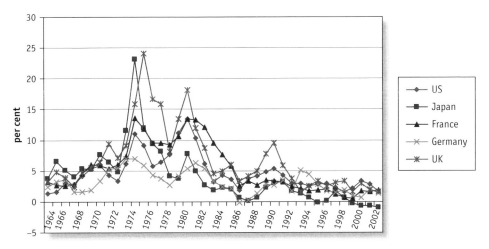

Source: OECD.

generally and for Keynesian economics in particular. Figure 6.7 illustrates the acceleration of inflation in the G5 economies. Particularly noteworthy are rates close to 25% in Japan and the UK in the mid-1970s.

The new inflation was, in the view of monetarist economists, actually caused by over-ambitious employment targets sought by Keynesian stabilization policy. Furthermore, the monetarists also argued that—despite the evidence provided by the postwar boom—stabilization policy was actually pretty ineffective as a means to maintain economies at potential GDP and full employment. The work of Milton Friedman was extremely influential here. Ultimately, his arguments caused economists working in the Keynesian tradition to shift their ground somewhat and, today, monetarists and Keynesians contribute to an eclectic macroeconomics—meaning one that draws on both traditions. But this is to get slightly ahead of ourselves. What we need to do now is get to grips with what became known as the monetarist counter-revolution in macroeconomics.

Keynes's ideas of the 1930s had become highly influential in policy terms because they seemed to provide a policy solution to the devastating problem of depression. Similarly, Friedman's arguments gained currency because they too addressed a burning economic issue, albeit a different one. Friedman revived and restated an old quantity theory of money tradition in economics. Broadly, this held that inflation is 'always and everywhere a monetary phenomenon in the sense that it can be produced only by a more rapid increase in the quantity of money than in output'. In other words, inflation is caused by too much money chasing too few goods. Two things followed from this relationship. First, to reduce the rate of inflation to a desired level, it was necessary to commensurately reduce the rate of growth of the money supply. Second, because government controlled the money supply, the rate of inflation an economy experienced was both its choice and responsibility. Bringing inflation down might not be a costless exercise but governments had it within their gift to maintain a low and stable inflation rate.

To understand Friedman's interpretation of what governments could and could not do in the macroeconomy we need to introduce a concept known as the Phillips curve, named after its originator, A. W. Phillips, whose work was published in 1958. The Phillips curve describes the nature of the statistical relationship between the rate of change of money wages and unemployment in the UK for the period 1861–1957. Remarkably, the relationship appeared to be a stable one. This allowed economists to infer a similar relationship between price inflation and unemployment as

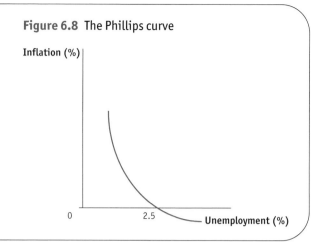

Figure 6.8 The Phillips curve

depicted by the curve in Figure 6.8. Keynesians supposed that the Phillips curve provided a choice for policymakers—they could select from a menu of possible combinations of inflation and unemployment. Most Keynesians at the time viewed inflation as a demand–pull phenomenon, in that inflation is caused by an excess demand for goods and services when the economy is at or above full employment. We can now understand the policymakers' choice as provided by the Phillips curve. Policymakers could—using aggregate demand management—squeeze inflation out of the economy entirely if demand was sufficiently suppressed but at the cost of some higher level of unemployment. In Figure 6.8 this possibility is illustrated by a combination of zero inflation and 2.5% unemployment. On the other hand, lower levels of unemployment are obtainable through expansionary fiscal and monetary policy but at the cost of higher inflation. Thus, in Figure 6.8, as unemployment falls below 2.5% the rate of inflation increases.

For a time it appeared that the Phillips curve fitted snugly into the Keynesian orthodoxy and people like Friedman, with alternative views of how the economy worked, struggled to be heard. However, all that began to change from the early 1970s when two things began to happen. One was the surge in worldwide inflation illustrated in Figure 6.7; the second was the re-emergence of unemployment in many economies, as depicted for the G5 in Figure 6.9. Together these became known as stagflation—a combination of economic stagnation and inflation. Stagflation was a real problem for Keynesian economics and its 'either inflation or unemployment, but not both' Phillips curve view of the world. This is where Friedman was able to seize his opportunity. He actually had to hand an explanation for stagflation and a set of policy measures to deal with it. Both of these centred on an alternative interpretation of the Phillips curve and a different conceptualization of unemployment.

Figure 6.9 G5 unemployment rates 1964–2002

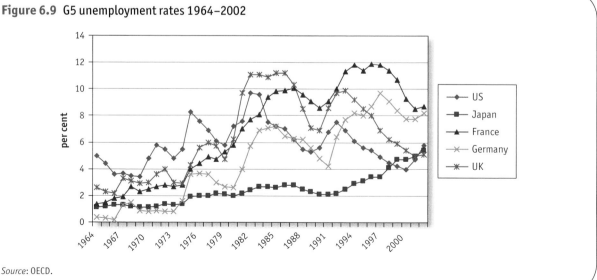

Source: OECD.

From stabilization policy to controlling inflation

Friedman's first innovation was to introduce a role for expectations about inflation into the Phillips curve framework. The way in which this was done is illustrated in Figure 6.10. Here we have a series of Phillips curves (SRPC1, 2 and 3) which all correspond to different expected rates of inflation (shown for simplicity as a series of straight lines). Let us begin at point A in the figure. Here people expect inflation to continue to be zero. The rate of unemployment is given as U_N. Now, let us assume the government follows Keynesian-style aggregate demand management advice to try to reduce unemployment below U_N to a point, U^*. This will entail a movement along SRPC1 from point A to point B—firms, as we would anticipate, expand both output and employment, and there is an increase in inflation from zero to 2%. Remember though that firms and workers had been expecting zero inflation and basing their decisions and negotiations on this figure. These expectations will now change; people adapt to the new rate and therefore expected inflation becomes 2%. Thus the short-run Phillips curve shifts to the right to SRPC2 and the economy moves to point C. Note that unemployment is now back at U_N—the inflation/unemployment policy choice has apparently disappeared. The net result of government intervention has been solely to increase inflation. Were the government to doggedly repeat the exercise and again use expansionary fiscal and monetary policy in another attempt to reduce unemployment, what would happen? Unemployment would once more fall temporarily below U_N (the economy would move along SRPC2 from point C to point D) but once expectations of inflation had been revised, the short-run Phillips curve would again shift right to SRPC3 and the economy would end up at E, with still higher inflation (now 4%) and unchanged unemployment.

The implications of this analysis are quite profound. Friedman concluded that policymakers in fact face a long-run 'expectations-augmented' Phillips curve which is vertical. There is then no policy choice between inflation and unemployment. Given a vertical long-run Phillips curve, the

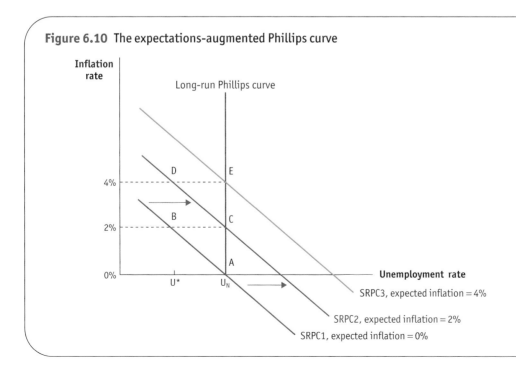

Figure 6.10 The expectations-augmented Phillips curve

Figure 6.11 The expectations-augmented Phillips curve and the natural rate of unemployment

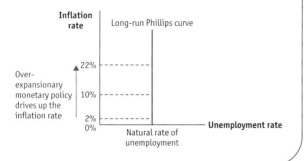

only choice that exists is to have more or less inflation—determined by the rate of monetary growth—at a given unemployment rate. This choice is illustrated in Figure 6.11. If the government persists in indulging in over-expansionary monetary policy it will simply drive up the inflation rate as illustrated; effectively it will be choosing more inflation without any advantage in reduced unemployment. One implication of this analysis is that if governments seek to maintain unemployment below the natural rate accelerating inflation will result.

Recall that Friedman supposed that inflation was simply a reflection of the extent to which the rate of growth of the money supply outstrips the growth of output in an economy, and that to reduce inflation the rate of growth of the money supply had to be reduced. The central point here is that excessive fiscal and monetary expansion clearly contribute to monetary growth and therefore should be avoided. This leads to Friedman's central conclusion that macroeconomic policy should be governed by rules—governments must not be allowed the discretion to indulge in expansionary policy which, in the end, can do nothing except fuel inflation. Recall also that, in Friedman's view, not much is being surrendered when governments agree not to use stabilization policy because economies are inherently stable entities anyway.

What though of the 'given' unemployment rate: are policy makers simply stuck with this—is it effectively fixed? Friedman coined the term the natural rate of unemployment for this given rate of unemployment. It is not fixed or immutable but, he argued, simply a reflection of how smoothly and efficiently the labour market in an economy functions. For example, should trade unions effectively organize segments of the labour market to secure higher wages than would have otherwise been agreed in their absence, the natural rate will be higher as firms employ fewer workers. Similarly, if 'generous' unemployment benefits reduce the incentive for people to take up jobs, the natural rate will also be higher. These possibilities are illustrated in Figure 6.12 by a shift of the long-run Phillips curve to the right. Government action in the labour market to limit the power of trade unions and pay less 'generous' benefits would both serve to reduce the natural rate of unemployment. These cases are illustrated in Figure 6.12 by a leftward shift of the long-run Phillips curve. Note, however, that both forms of government action here are implemented at the microeconomic level and not at the level of the economy as a whole. In Friedman's view, the tools of macroeconomic policy—fiscal and monetary policy—are ineffective in combating unemployment.

It is also worth noting here that a range of other microeconomic policies may be deployed in support of a broader macroeconomic framework. As noted, the macroeconomy is simply the aggregation of all the individual markets of which it is composed. Accordingly, measures such as those in support of competition, or to regulate the activities of the natural monopolies will make contributions to a strong macroeconomic performance. This view is clearly a return to the neoclassical belief in the ability of markets to achieve economic efficiency. If there is a role for the

Figure 6.12 Shifts in the expectations-augmented Phillips curve and the natural rate of unemployment

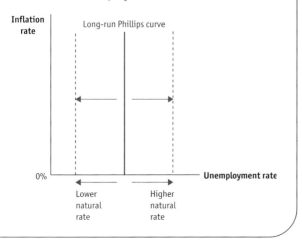

government then it is in the negative sense of ensuring the operation of free market forces so that the economy is able to increase the supply of goods and in so doing return to full employment. This 'supply-side' approach stands in stark contrast to the 'demand-side' focus of Keynesian economic management.

So finally in this section let us return to Modigliani's 'need/can/should' framework for the interpretation of government policy to stabilize the levels of output and employment in the economy. How does Friedman's work fit in here? The Keynesian view suggested that governments need to intervene, they can intervene, and therefore they should. Friedman's conclusion about stabilization policy is precisely the opposite:

- governments *don't need* to stabilize the economy—capitalist economies are inherently stable, unless disturbed by erratic monetary growth
- governments *cannot* stabilize the economy—fiscal and monetary policy are ineffective in tackling unemployment and stimulating output in the long run
- governments *should not* therefore try to stabilize the economy—there is no case for them do so.

Contemporary macroeconomic policy—an eclectic macroeconomics

We now turn to a discussion of the way in which current UK macroeconomic policy has evolved as a result of the debates between Keynesian and monetarist economists, as well as other groups who have followed in their wake. According to the Treasury, UK economic policy employs a framework of 'constrained discretion'. In part, the intention behind this approach is to avoid the temptations of short-term expediency to which governments with complete policy discretion may be drawn. In terms of Figure 6.10, although a move along a short-run Phillips curve from point C to D may look attractive in, say, the run-up to an election because people might be more likely to vote for the incumbent government when unemployment is falling, in the long run it's an economically bad idea. However, nor should macroeconomic policy follow what the Treasury calls 'mechanistically fixed policy rules' that would prevent the authorities responding to even a severe shock. Overall then the UK approach appears to be to prevent frequent, unnecessary and quite possibly damaging bouts of stabilization policy (applause from the followers of Friedman); while retaining the discretion to appropriately respond to major economic shocks (applause from the followers of Keynes).

In practice, 'constrained discretion' has been implemented through the following fiscal and monetary frameworks.

- Fiscal policy is conducted according to two rules: that over the economic cycle any borrowing will be for investment purposes and not to fund current expenditure; and that the government debt-to-GDP ratio will be maintained at the 'sustainable and prudent level' of below 40% over the economic cycle. The general tenor of the approach here is then to accept that fiscal policy should remain a tool of macroeconomic policy in appropriate circumstances but that it should not be used without regard for other macroeconomic objectives such as inflation.
- Monetary policy is no longer under the direct control of politicians or the government. Since 1997 the Bank of England has had operational independence in the setting of interest rates. The Bank is given the noted inflation target by the Chancellor of the Exchequer but its

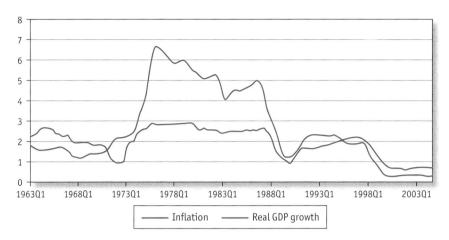

Figure 6.13 Volatility in UK inflation and real GDP growth

Note: Volatility is measured by the standard deviation over rolling seven-year periods. Inflation is measured by the RPI before 1976 and the RPIX thereafter.
Source: HM Treasury (reproduced under the terms of the Click-Use Licence).

Monetary Policy Committee is charged with setting interest rates in such a way as to hit this target (see Case Study below).

Has constrained discretion worked? We have seen that in respect of the three major objectives of macroeconomic policy—economic growth, employment and unemployment, and inflation—the performance of the UK economy in recent years has been very respectable. Figure 6.13 shows that, overall, the economy has been much more stable recently, particularly when compared to the 1970s and 1980s. In fact, both inflation and GDP growth are now more stable than at anytime in the last forty or so years.

There is a widespread recognition that accompanying such an eclectic macroeconomic policy is the need also for governments to ensure that microeconomic policies designed to boost competitiveness are implemented. In this way the supply side of the economy is able to boost economic growth within this stable macroeconomic environment.

◈ *Looking ahead*

There is a broad macroeconomic consensus on inflation control in the advanced capitalist economies—it's best achieved by some form of central bank independence. This happens in the UK, throughout Europe, the United States, and elsewhere. But this does not mean that governments have entirely surrendered the tools of economic management. In an uncertain global environment beset by civil, economic and military conflict, new economic shocks are likely and economics and economic policy will need to evolve further in the light of events yet unknown.

Summary

- There is no doubt that macroeconomic stability is a desirable thing but there has been a lengthy debate in economics about how to best secure it

- The main aims of macroeconomic policy are to produce an environment that promotes stable and satisfactory growth, high employment and low unemployment, and a stable and low rate of inflation

- Whilst advanced economies have experienced prolonged long-term growth this has been subject to periods of short-term instability with economies facing periods of 'boom' and 'bust'

- Economists once urged governments to actively and consistently employ the Keynesian tools of fiscal and monetary policy to keep economic growth and employment on track

- The inflationary experiences of the 1970s and 1980s suggested a different, less hands-on approach was needed. It was argued that government intervention to reduce unemployment could only work in the short run and was the cause of the inflation

- Such an approach emphasized the need to ensure that markets were able to operate freely and that competition should be enhanced

- Now in many of the world's economies we have a much more eclectic approach to the macroeconomy, one that draws on both interventionist and non-interventionist traditions

Case study: what does an independent central bank do?

Interaction

There are four items below on the Bank of England and the macroeconomic policy objective of inflation:

1 a self-description by the Bank of its role in the economy
2 a fan chart of projected inflation
3 a press release covering a decision by the Bank's Monetary Policy Committee to raise interest rates
4 a press release by the Confederation of British Industry (CBI) reacting to the same decision. The CBI is the UK's leading business organization, representing 240,000 firms that together employ around a third of the private sector workforce

After reading these items, answer the questions at the end.

BANK OF ENGLAND—WHAT IT'S FOR

Price stability and monetary policy

The first objective of any central bank is to safeguard the value of the currency in terms of what it will purchase at home and in terms of other currencies. Monetary policy is directed to achieving this objective and to providing a framework for non-inflationary economic growth. As in most other developed countries, monetary policy operates in the UK mainly through influencing the price of money, in other words the interest rate.

The Bank's price stability objective is made explicit in the present monetary policy framework. It has two main elements: an annual inflation target set each year by the government and a commitment to an open and accountable policy-making regime.

Setting monetary policy—deciding on the level of short-term interest rates necessary to meet the government's inflation target—is the responsibility of the Bank. In May 1997 the government gave the Bank operational independence to set monetary policy by deciding the short-term level of interest rates to meet the government's stated inflation target—currently 2%.

Interest rates are set by the Bank's Monetary Policy Committee. The MPC sets an interest rate it judges will enable the inflation target to be met. The Bank's Monetary Policy Committee (MPC) is made up of nine members—the Governor, the two Deputy Governors, the Bank's Chief Economist, the Executive Director for Markets and four external members appointed directly by the Chancellor. The appointment of external members is designed to ensure that the MPC benefits from thinking and expertise in addition to that gained inside the Bank of England.

The monthly MPC meeting itself is a two-day affair. On the first day, the meeting starts with an update on the most recent economic data. A series of issues is then identified for discussion. On the following day, a summary of the previous day's discussion is provided and the MPC members individually explain their views on what policy should be. The Governor then puts to the meeting the policy which he believes will command a majority and members of the MPC vote. Any member in a minority is asked to say what level of interest rates he or she would have preferred, and this is recorded in the minutes of the meeting. The interest rate decision is announced at 12 noon on the second day.

From interest rates to inflation

When the Bank of England changes the official interest rate it is attempting to influence the overall level of expenditure in the economy. When the amount of money spent grows more quickly than the volume of output produced, inflation is the result. In this way, changes in interest rates are used to control inflation.

The Bank's monetary policy objective is to deliver price stability —low inflation—and, subject to that, to support the government's economic objectives including those for growth and employment. Price stability is defined by the government's inflation target of 2%. The remit recognizes the role of price stability in achieving economic stability more generally, and in providing the right conditions for sustainable growth in output and employment. (*Source*: Bank of England)

The inflation 'fan chart' in Figure 6.14 depicts the Bank's estimations of the probability of various inflation outcomes in the future. The bands widen over the time horizon given the increasing uncertainty about more distant inflation rates.

News Release

BANK OF ENGLAND RAISES BANK RATE BY 0.25 PERCENTAGE POINTS TO 5.0%
9 November 2006

The Bank of England's Monetary Policy Committee today voted to raise the official Bank Rate paid on commercial bank reserves by 0.25 percentage points to 5.0%.

The UK economy has recorded its fourth consecutive quarter of firm growth. Household spending has been volatile, but the underlying picture appears to be one of moderate expansion. The recovery in business investment has been maintained. The outlook for growth in the United Kingdom's main export markets remains positive. Credit and broad money growth remain rapid, and asset prices have continued to rise.

Although unemployment has continued to edge up, the margin of spare capacity within businesses appears limited. Oil prices have dropped back, but there are signs that other pricing pressures have picked up. CPI inflation was 2.4% in September. It is likely that inflation will rise further above the target in the near term, but then fall back as energy and import price inflation abate.

Against that background, the Committee judged that an increase in Bank Rate of 0.25 percentage points to 5.0% was necessary to bring CPI inflation back to the target in the medium term. (*Source*: Bank of England)

Consumer appetite for debt is falling. But how does this explain the Bank of England's rise in interest rates?

© Ken Kaminesky/Corbis

Figure 6.14 Current CPI inflation projection based on market interest rate expectations

Percentage increase in prices on a year earlier

2002 03 04 05 06 07 08 09

Source: Bank of England (www.bankofengland.co.uk).

News Release

CBI REACTION TO INTEREST RATE RISE

Commenting on the Bank of England's decision today to increase interest rates, CBI Chief Economic Adviser Ian McCafferty said:

'This move comes as no surprise to businesses, who recognized it would be necessary to deliver longer term economic stability.

Although some commentators are already looking ahead to the next rise, our forecasts suggest that a further increase should not be needed. Consumer appetite for debt is falling rapidly, the economy is showing some signs of a modest slowdown, and the benefits of recent falls in oil prices will help keep inflation under control into the medium term.

The Bank may face some difficult decisions in coming months as shorter term risks to inflation remain. But it must also be mindful of the slower growth that a further rise could create.'

9 November 2006

Now answer the following questions:

❓ What does the Bank see as its core purpose?

❓ Briefly comment on the CPI fan chart—how is the Bank doing on inflation?

❓ Can you explain a recent interest rate decision? Why did the Bank raise the interest rates in November 2006 (see Bank's press release)?

❓ How did the CBI react to the increase in interest rates (see CBI press release)? Why did the CBI broadly support the increase and what would its likely reaction be to further rate rises?

Review and discussion questions

1   What do we mean by economic growth?

2   Why is it desirable that the macroeconomy should be stable?

3   Explain why inflation became viewed as the central macroeconomic problem from the mid-1970s onwards.

4   Why is the Great Depression central to an understanding of the development of macroeconomic thinking and policy?

5   Why do we have independent central banks?

Assignments

1   Take a recent interest rate decision by the Bank of England (summaries available from the Bank of England website). Explain the primary macroeconomic policy concern behind the decision—is it that inflationary pressures in the economy need to be addressed; are these sufficiently low to justify a rate cut; or is the answer somewhere in between? What do the CBI and the Trades Union Congress (the body representing UK trade unions [www.tuc.org.uk]) make of the decision?

2   Compare growth rates, unemployment rates and inflation rates for the United States, Japan, Poland and Germany over the past decade (figures from the OECD—see list of useful websites below). Which countries are doing particularly well and particularly badly? Look at one or two OECD country reports to find out a little about the macroeconomic policies of these economies.

3   Look at the annual reports of some UK-based businesses. What do these reports say about the UK macroeconomic climate and how important is it as an influence on performance?

Further reading

Cleaver, T. (2004) *Economics: the Basics* (London: Routledge). A good and uncomplicated introduction to economics.

Mulhearn, C., Vane, H. R. and Eden, J. (2001) *Economics for Business* (Basingstoke: Palgrave). An introduction to economics for business by the authors of the present chapter.

Online resources

Test your understanding of this chapter with online questions and answers, explore the subject further through web exercises, and use the weblinks to provide a quick resource for further research. Go to the Online Resource Centre at

www.oxfordtextbooks.co.uk/orc/ wetherly_otter/

HM Treasury—www.hm-treasury.gov.uk—This is a key website which contains a wealth of information about the UK economy and its economic policy.

Bank of England—www.bankofengland.co.uk—Useful for researching the UK economy, especially monetary policy.

OECD—www.oecd.org—The Organization for Economic Cooperation and Development consists of the world's leading economies. See in particular its publication 'Going for Growth' (2007).

IMF—www.imf.org—The International Monetary Fund is a vast source of economic information on individual countries.

UNCTAD—www.unctad.org—The United Nations Commission for Trade and Development is primarily interested in the relationship between trade and development but its annual Trade and Development Report's introduction gives a concise overview of current macroeconomic policies.

World Bank—www.worldbank.org—Whilst its primary focus is on developing countries this site also allows you to access economic data and analysis of all countries.

References

Maddison, A. (2001) *The World Economy in Millennial Perspective* (Paris: OECD).

Snowdon, B. and Vane, H. R. (2005) *Modern Macroeconomics* (Cheltenham: Edward Elgar).

Can the marketplace be ethical? Corporate social responsibility

Simon Robinson

Contents

07

Learning objectives

When you have completed this chapter you will be able to:

- Clarify the definitions of corporate social responsibility (CSR), **corporate citizenship** and business ethics
- Examine and assess the free market views of the market and CSR, and how these relate to ethics
- Examine and assess the stakeholder view of business and bring out the implications for CSR practice
- Make a case for CSR in business
- Develop and use a framework for corporate social responsibility that connects to the practicalities of business

Themes

Diversity	**Diversity of business** CSR applies across the wide diversity of business, from small and medium enterprises to global corporations.
Complexity	**Complexity of the environment** The major case study in this chapter shows the complexity of the business environment. This is the context in which CSR has to be worked out. It shows that responses to CSR cannot be simplistic and demands the development of an effective CSR decision-making process. This process is not about asserting or prescribing predetermined views of CSR but about finding appropriate responses through planning.
Spatial levels	**Variety of spatial levels** The business environment operates internally, locally, regionally, nationally and at the global level. The operation of CSR will be examined in this context.
Dynamic	**Dynamic environment** The constantly changing environment leads to new CSR challenges. Effective CSR policy looks to respond to that dynamic environment by ensuring that business managers reflect on their operational practices, including regular reporting on how the business responds to that environment.
Interaction	**Interaction between business and the environment** This chapter shows the rise of corporate citizenship, in which business sees itself as part of a wider community, with mutual and shared responsibilities. In this model, business not only shares responsibilities for the wider social and physical environment but also contributes to the development of ethical meaning in that environment.

Stakeholders	Stakeholders

Awareness of stakeholders, their needs and responsibilities, forms the basis of how corporate social responsibility is determined. This chapter focuses on the need to negotiate responsibility with stakeholders.

Values	Values

Any business embodies values and purpose. These form the basis of any CSR policy. Regular audits reflect on how these values are embodied in practice.

Introduction

Chapter 2 introduced us to the debates about the ability of the free market to produce economic efficiency and this was further explored in Chapter 4 when we considered the ideological divide between left and right. It is clear that attitudes to business depend on where people are located along this ideological spectrum. Put simply, for those on the right, business makes the world go round. It is business (and especially the private sector) that creates the wealth on which all of society depends. For those on the left, businesses (private) are simply out for themselves and will put profits before people ignoring their wider social responsibilities. Any notion of corporate social responsibility (CSR) is a contradiction in terms. Corporations only recognize their economic self interest.

Advocates of the free market argue that in acting out of self interest businesses are able to realize the common good provided that there is competition and freedom. Critics argue that in fact the free market allows business to acquire the power to restrict competition and to exploit consumers and employees. They argue that this will require close government supervision, regulation or direct control and that there is a need for a vibrant 'third sector' of voluntary groups and NGOs.

There has been a growth in social activism from this sector highlighting what is seen as corporate irresponsibility and there have indeed been plenty of examples of this. The explosion of a chemical plant run by the American owned Union Carbide in Bhopal, India in 1984, caused a huge loss of life and a continuing genetic legacy of birth defects and it is argued that the company did not face up to its responsibilities (see www.bhopal.org/whathappened.html for an example of this view and www.bhopal.com for the company's defence of its actions).

The environmental movement has been particularly vocal in its condemnation of what it sees as the cavalier approach taken by corporations to the environment. For example:

- Shell's record, which was first highlighted by the Brent Spar case that we will look at later, is still under intense scrutiny by a range of environmental groups
- Another oil company, Exxon, is demonized as being at the forefront of trying to deny that global warming is a problem by funding 'climate change denial' scientists and using its money to influence politicians not to pass legislation to curb oil consumption
- In 2007, BP, which had managed to brand itself as a Green company, suffered a huge blow to its image when it was accused of ignoring health and safety legislation in the US.

Recent years have seen some spectacular examples of major company malpractice which has resulted in the collapse of companies such as WorldCom and Enron. This chapter explores competing perspectives about the degree to which businesses operate in a socially responsible manner and how CSR can best be promoted.

> ↻ *Stop and Think*
> Before you proceed further with this discussion of CSR, pause to reflect on the purpose of business. Do you agree that it is just to make profit? Or are there other benefits that business should deliver for society?

The emergence of the CSR agenda

Corporate social responsibility is not new. Rowntree of York, now owned by Nestlé, were makers of confectionery and cakes since 1725, and have a long history of care for employees and the wider community.

However, during the 20th century old conceptions of corporate responsibility weakened:

- government took increasing responsibility for the fulfillment of individual and community needs, from education to health to pensions
- there was an increase in cultural and religious diversity within society. This led to many different perspectives about the responsibility of different groups within society
- communities became more fragmented and short-term. There was a breakdown in patterns of behaviour and institutions such as marriage and the family, caused partly by greater wealth and increased mobility
- with the economic boom and practices such as the division of labour Bauman (1985) suggests there was an increasing fragmentation of responsibility. He argued that the division of labour had the effect of creating distance between the individual and the larger group, thus decreasing any sense of overall responsibility, something exacerbated by multinational corporations.

Mini-Case 7.1   Timeline of Rowntree in the 20th century

1904	The company appoint a dentist and a doctor
1904	A model village for the workers is developed
1906	A pension scheme is made available to all employees
1909	Yearsley swimming baths are given by the company to the City of York
1913	Dining facilities for 3,000 employees are built
1916	One of the first Widows Benefits Funds is established
1916–1918	Works Councils are created, developing democracy at work; profit sharing is introduced at about the same time
1921	An unemployment scheme is introduced.

Throughout this time community involvement with schools, the local mental hospital and other local institutions is seen as a key part of the company's role. What marked out the experience of Rowntree was three things:

1 A strong sense of, and pride in, the company's identity as part of the local community. As such they wanted local school children, for instance, to understand the role, purpose and values of the business and how they related to the community.

2 The capacity to reflect on and respond to needs in the workforce and community, such that their view of responsibility was developed over time.

3 Responsibility was played out in relevant practice. There was no division between ethical ideas and the practice.

Part of all this emerged from the Quaker tradition of social activism (www.quaker.org.uk/), exemplified in concern for prison reform and the abolition of slavery. Part was also about a simple and immediate awareness of the local community and the company's part in that community. Any responsibility was not extra to the role of business, but was developed in that context. Hence, they felt no need to justify their concern for the community. This was also a time when:

a) There was limited government social care, leaving many very obvious social needs unmet, and thus a strong sense of shared responsibility.

b) There were strong local communities which stayed together over time and had a practical sense of interdependence.

❓ Why do you think that Rowntree develop such responsible practices?

With such changes the social responsibility of business could no longer be assumed. The idea of corporate responsibility that seemed to occur naturally for companies such as Rowntree now had to be explicitly articulated and justified. Moeller and Erdal note several elements in the experience of business that have led to the increased concern to do just that (2003: 3–4):

● Globalization. Globalization has seen the growth of multinational business such that it is estimated that over half of the largest 'economic units' in the world are corporations. Where such companies could act at one time with little apparent concern for CSR, their effect on the social and physical environment has led to calls for improved accountability. The increase in non-governmental organizations (NGOs), such as Oxfam, Christian Aid and Amnesty International has further encouraged multinational corporations to reflect on their responsibilities at every stage of the production process.

● Information and communications technology (ICT). This has led to increased global transparency, with instant access to immediate information and judgements from many different sources. The result is that companies find it less and less easy to hide what might be controversial aspects of their business.

● Fiscal pressure. Growing fiscal pressure has forced companies to pull out of previous philanthropic ventures. At the same time this has led to greater discussion about the different roles of government and business.

● In the 1960s and '70s business came under increased scrutiny in the areas of equal opportunities and health and safety at work. This led to the establishing of legal standards, which have been a continuing feature of CSR.

● The growing importance of intangible or 'post-material' values. This has involved recognition that in the new economic environment there are an increasing number of values shared by significant parts of society on which depend the continued success of the corporation. This is partly about increased awareness in society of key issues such as the sustainability of the environment.

● As indicated at the start of the chapter, there have been a number of well-documented business disasters, such as Enron, which have brought into question the role and trustworthiness of business.

> **⇒ Stop and Think**
> How far do you agree that social responsibility (e.g. environmental concerns) should be the preserve of government or the state rather than corporations?

Key terms in the discussion of corporate responsibility

In order to understand the debate on the ethical responsibilities of business we need to look more closely at three closely related terms:

Values

Complexity

● corporate social responsibility

● corporate citizenship

● business ethics.

Corporate social responsibility

A simple definition of the term CSR is 'companies integrating social and environmental concerns in their daily business operations and in their interactions with their stakeholders on a daily basis' (European Commission, 2001: 366).

The term CSR was developed in the 1960s and '70s as work practice, especially in the areas of health and safety and equal opportunities, was increasingly questioned, leading to legislation. Since then the exact definition of CSR has developed and continued to develop. The Institute of Public Relations sees CSR as involving philanthropy, enlightened self-interest and straightforward self-interest.

The first of these involves donations of some kind to the local community. The second is about the generation of positive publicity for the company. A good example is of BT sponsoring the Royal Shakespeare Company. Such positive images can be useful also in times of crisis. Prior to the most recent campaigns against Shell it had been involved in a court case about the environment. The court found against the company but the judge implied that he would have fined them more, had Shell's record on environmental work sponsorship not been so excellent. This is why Shell is so keen to promote itself as a socially responsible company (see www.shell.com).

Self-interest refers to investments that would directly benefit the organizaion, such as involvement in economic regeneration projects, or staff training developments.

Gregory and Tafra (2004) have noted that expectations of the business community are increasing all the time. Three themes increasingly stand out:

- the environment
- coporate governance and related business standards
- human rights.

In all these areas mere compliance with codes or standards is seen as no longer adequate. Respect for human rights, for instance, may involve active empowerment of some stakeholders.

Corporate citizenship

Andriof and McIntosh define this as 'understanding and managing a company's wider influences on society for the benefit of the company and society as a whole' (2001). Zadek (2001) uses the useful term 'footprints', the visible effect of the company on the social and physical environment.

Viewing the corporation as a citizen is to set down legal and moral expectations. As citizens we have legal rights and duties, but also a wider role in supporting and enabling the well being of society. Is it possible to see a corporation as having this role?

Views differ on the relationship between CSR and corporate citizenship. Some see the two as synonymous, whilst others see corporate citizenship as focused in community relations. It could be argued that there is a need for a more holistic view of CSR, which seeks to integrate external and internal relations, viewing corporate citizenship as part of that development.

Business ethics

Values

Ethics is the systematic study of how to behave in the right way and how we judge what is right. Business ethics includes exploration of:

- the underlying ethical values of business, including those of any particular professions in business, such as accountants or managers
- how any values might be embodied in the corporation. This includes the development of codes of ethics
- particular ethical policies in areas such as corporate governance or workplace relationships
- underlying ethical theories.

There are two main theories or approaches to ethical reasoning:

- One view of ethics is that they should be based on core general principles. A good example of this is the Ten Commandments, which see actions such as killing or stealing as wrong in themselves. In philosophy this is referred to as the deontological tradition. We have a duty (or *deon* in ancient Greek) to behave in this prescribed manner.

- Another philosophical tradition is utilitarian theory (utility in this sense means happiness or benefit) which questions whether principles are always right and suggests that we discover what is right by looking at consequences. The action that maximizes the best consequences for the most people or groups is seen to be good.

Both these theories have their problems and part of business ethics is about the ongoing debate as to what counts as good or bad. For many companies business ethics and CSR are seen as one and the same. Others lose the term social and simply refer to corporate responsibility, so that ethical concern for all stakeholders inside and outside the company is seen as equal. This chapter works from the view that corporate social responsibility and business ethics are distinct but connected. Business ethics deals with the underlying ethical values of business, and provides a framework of values, expectations and standards of behaviour for CSR.

⮑ *Stop and Think*

Consider the following dilemma that illustrates the two approaches to ethical thinking:

Suppose that there is a promotion round within a business and the best person for the job in accordance with the selection criteria is someone who is not well regarded by colleagues. Is there a duty to appoint this person even though it will cause resentment within the workgroup? Or should this duty be disregarded because it is better to disappoint this one person and keep many others happy?

Justifying CSR

In this section we will examine two alternative perspectives on CSR: free market theory and stakeholder theory. We will reflect on these perspectives with the help of a scenario involving computer games.

In this case there is a fundamental question about whether the computer game company should have any sense of social responsibility beyond signing the contract and ensuring work for the ninety employees. Why should we be concerned for social responsibility?

There are two broad perspectives that seek an answer to this question and we deal with these in the following two sections.

Values

The free market view of CSR

Milton Friedman is often seen as one of the foremost modern advocates of the free market. In relation to the debate about CSR his argument is simple (Friedman, 1983). The role of business is the creation of wealth and thus the prime responsibility of business is to make a profit for its owners, usually the shareholders. In this, the executive director acts as an agent serving the interests of 'his principal', i.e. the owners. The interest of the principal is profit maximization and involvement in any activities in the community outside this sphere would be a violation of trust and thus morally wrong. Friedman does not argue against the social involvement of the company as such, rather simply that the company, and the owners especially, can decide to do what they think is fit. There is no moral or legal obligation on the company to be more socially involved, and the company can follow its own ends, so long as they are legal.

Mini-Case 7.2 Computer games

Following the success of a computer game based upon a scenario set in the frozen north the computer software development company was commissioned by the client company to develop a second game. This time the client wanted increased shock value, and the inclusion of the death of young children. An added incentive would be that if the computer company agreed to this there would be rapid release of monies outstanding from the first game. The manager of the software firm and his engineering staff were uneasy about this request—though initially a little unsure why they felt this unease. They felt there may be wider issues about how such games affect players and about how their firm might be perceived.

As a result of discussions with his staff the manager decided that it was important to clarify the situation. He wrote to his client's legal department and asked if they would confirm in writ-ing that the company wished him to develop a second game and that it was their intention that this should involve increased horror and the death of children. No such confirmation was received—and the money owed to the software development company was rapidly released.

❷ Why do you think the legal department responded in this way?

❷ There were two businesses involved in this case. Does the social responsibility of each of them differ, and if so why?

❷ Who are the important people in this case who might be affected by the decisions of these two companies?

Increasingly violent computer games can raise uncomfortable issues for the manufacturers.

© Estelle Klawitter/zefa/Corbis

If the company executive does decide to get involved in a community project Friedman argues that this is not an obligation but rather a means of achieving the company aims, such as improving the image and reputation of the company and thus contributing to improving profits.

For Friedman, pursuing social responsibility would involve costs that would have to be passed on to the customer, possibly to the shareholder in reduced dividends, and to the employee in reduced wages. Not only is this unfair, it also constitutes a form of taxation without representation and is therefore undemocratic. Moreover, it is both unwise, because it invests too much power in the company executives, and futile, because it is likely that the costs imposed by this approach will lead to a reduction in economic efficiency.

Finally, he argues that the executive is not the best person to be involved in making decisions about social involvement. S/he is neither qualified, nor mandated, to pursue social goals. It is social administrators that understand the needs of the local area and who can determine local priorities. Such a task is better suited to local government and social concern groups, whose roles and accountability are directly related to these tasks. For business to enter this field would lead to a confusion of roles and a raising of false expectations.

According to the free market argument the social responsibility of the computing firm in Mini-Case 7.2 above should have been to take the new contract. To take it would be within the law, and it would fulfil the interests of the owner and the employees. The law would have been responsible for placing an over-18 restriction on any major horror content. In turn it would then be the responsibility of the individual who buys the game to deal with any negative effects, or the responsibility of parents to monitor what their under-18 children are doing. The computer firm could also say that it had no wider responsibility, and that such responsibility to wider society lay with the commissioning company.

> ⊃ *Stop and Think*
>
> Is there one core purpose of business? If so how does that relate to any other role of business?
>
> Is there one purpose generic to all business or do different businesses have different purposes?
>
> Make a list of all the possible purposes of your business or university. How might a public organizaion, such as a university, differ from a business?

There are a number of criticisms of this free market view. Firstly, seeing profit maximization as the exclusive purpose of business is simplistic. Managers may have several different purposes each of equal importance: care for shareholders, clients, the physical environment and so on. Shareholders may want profits but they could be concerned for the environment or for the community in which they live. Our different value worlds are connected. This can only be tested in dialogue with each group of shareholders, and in the light of the nature of the business and its effects on society.

Secondly, there is an assumption that the ethical worlds of social concern and business are quite separate. The initial response of the computer firm employees shows that this is not the case. They were all very concerned about being involved in such a project, and much of that involved their personal sense of responsibility.

Thirdly, it is difficult to predetermine what the responsibility of the business person or the business should be, anymore than it is possible to be precise about the responsibility of, for instance local or national government. In practice there are broad responsibilities but these are continuously being debated and negotiated.

Stakeholder theory and CSR

Diversity

Dynamic

Stakeholders

The computer firm case was, of course, deceptively complex. Firstly, there were two companies involved each of whom was a stakeholder in the other's business. For the commissioning company this was a minor but potentially lucrative relationship. For the computer firm this was a potentially critical deal that would help to keep them alive. Secondly, each company had some very different stakeholders, with different and sometimes conflicting values. The commissioning company, for instance, had a strong line in family entertainment. The game, however, was targeted at late adolescents. This could potentially spoil the company's family image. We do not know precisely why the legal department responded in the way they did, but it can be assumed that they did not want to affect the reputation of the company. In recent times, there was also an increase in customers from different cultures, including the Muslim world, with a strong family ethic. Again, this would seem to be an important argument against involving gratuitous horror.

Up to this point, responsibility to any possible customers would seem to coincide with self-interest. There is little point in trying to sell to one group in a way that would actually affect the company's reputation with other potential customers. It may, of course, be that there are wider responsibilities to children and families. What is the effect of violent games on younger people? Research is inconclusive about this. The precautionary principle might well apply here then. If you are not sure what negative effect your project might have on children or wider society, or how that might reinforce other negative social changes, the precautionary principle suggests that the firm exercise precaution and not become involved in gratuitous horror. Alternatively, it might be possible for such a company to be involved in developing further research around this area. At the very least there are questions about what the social responsibility of the company might be.

For the computer games company these questions are a little different. There are responsibilities to the owner and the employees. However, as computer engineers many employees were part of a wider professional body of engineers. That profession is itself a stakeholder in the sense that any decision made by computer firm might affect the standing of computer engineers in wider society. Recent work on the responsibility of engineers stresses the importance of maintaining the integrity of the profession. The profession itself has a real concern about the effects of any computer games on the wider society.

Reflecting on the different stakeholders reveals the complex and dynamic nature of any situation, and it is often not possible to simplistically divide the interests of the shareholders and the wider stakeholders. Does stakeholder theory then act as the basis for determining CSR?

A stakeholder was initially defined in terms of those groups which were critical to the survival of the business, including employees, customers, lenders, and suppliers (Sternberg, 2000: 49). This has been further developed to 'any individual or group who can affect or is affected by the actions, decisions, policies, practices or goals of the organization' (Carroll and Buchholtz, 2000). This widens stakeholders to government, the community and beyond. For multinational corporations this becomes even more complex.

It is possible to identify different versions of stakeholder theory (SHT), as argued by Heath and Norman (2004). They include:

- strategic SHT: a theory that attention to the needs of stakeholders will lead to better outcomes for the business
- SHT of governance: a theory about how stakeholder groups should be involved in oversight of management, e.g. placing stakeholders on the board
- deontic SHT: a theory that analyses the legitimate rights and needs of the different stakeholders and uses this data to develop company policies.

It is possible, however, to see all these theories as simply aspects of the larger stakeholder view. Sternberg (2000: 49ff) argues against basing CSR on stakeholder theory on the following grounds:

- to be responsible to someone we have to be accountable to them but it is not at all clear to which stakeholders a company is accountable
- it is likely that the interests of stakeholders conflict. How does the firm resolve this?

However, stakeholder theorists argue that it is perfectly possible to be accountable to shareholders and also recognize a shared responsibility for wider stakeholders, including the environment, that has to be worked out in practice. It is not a question of a polarized model of stakeholders versus shareholders but one of identifying shared interests and finding ways of responding to them.

Figure 7.1　Carroll's four-part model of corporate social responsibility

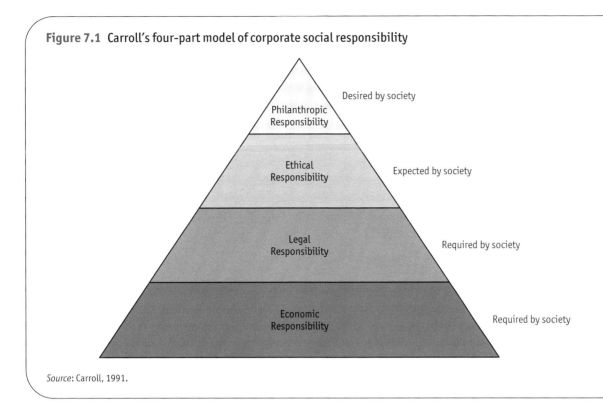

Source: Carroll, 1991.

Carroll suggests a way of getting over that polarized approach involving four areas: economic, ethical, legal and philanthropic (see Figure 7.1). Carroll argues that these different responsibilities are set in consecutive layers within a company, with CSR involving addressing all four layers consecutively.

Corporations have an economic responsibility towards their shareholders to be profitable, and provide reasonable returns on shareholders' investments. Economic and financial gain is the primary objective of a corporation in a business sense and is the foundation upon which all the other responsibilities rest (see Chapter 1).

However, at the same time businesses are expected to comply with the laws and regulations as the ground rules and legal framework under which they must operate. A company's legal responsibilities are seen as coexisting with economic responsibilities as fundamental precepts of the free enterprise system (see Chapters 4 and 13).

Ethical responsibilities within a corporation ensure that the organizaion performs in a manner consistent with expectations of ethics in society. Good corporate citizenship is defined as doing what is expected morally and ethically, and it is important to recognize and respect new or evolving ethical trends adopted by society. It must be noted that the corporate integrity and ethical behaviour of a company go beyond mere compliance with laws and regulations and entail the obligation to do what is right and fair, and to avoid harm.

Finally, Carroll suggests that philanthropic responsibilities include corporate actions that are in response to society's expectation that businesses be good corporate citizens involved in activities or programmes to promote human welfare or goodwill. Philanthropy, 'love of fellow humans' is highly desired by society, however it is not ultimately necessary.

Carroll's view is comprehensive and usefully brings together different views of CSR. However, we are still left with some difficult questions. Firstly, while the primary aim of a business may not be promoting human welfare, if there is evidence that parts of the business are abusing the human rights of its workers, then this is most directly the concern of the business. Secondly if businesses are operating in social and political contexts where corruption or repression exist should the business simply go along with this? It could be argued that businesses should actively promote democracy in, for example areas of economic and political transition.

This takes the complexity of the business environment even further, and leads to further developments in CSR, seeing business as itself a stakeholder in wider society and thus more in terms of corporate citizenship. Feminist ethics, in particular, point to a web of stakeholder relations that stress connectivity, interdependence, power sharing, collective action and conflict resolution. Business is a part of society and its identity is established through how it relates to society, not least in its conduct with those who are affected by, and affect, it. This is further stressed by Heath and Norman (2004). Learning lessons from disasters such as the Enron case, they argue that the real problems emerge from managers who keep their actions secret from the shareholders. Hence, the shareholders are not able to be part of a conversation about values, purposes and ways in which a business is run. They argue that when business is not transparent, responsibility is easily lost at all levels. Responsibility is worked out through dialogue between all stakeholders and shareholders. Only such dialogue can determine a creative and feasible response, and what the possibilities and limits of any CSR might be.

How would this view help the computer games company? It would take them into dialogue, a dialogue that they at least began, by trying to clarify just what the commissioning company meant. If the dialogue had continued it might have led the games company to explore whether the use of horror or the death of children in a computing game was necessarily wrong. It is possible to see these as being used in the context of a game with a moral framework where those who kill the children or allow that to happen can be brought to book. Hence, it might be possible to take the contract and develop a game based in a broader ethical context, thus contributing to a wider social responsibility.

> **⊃ Stop and Think**
>
> In the light of the discussion on CSR, how would you have responded to the request of the commissioning company?
>
> Imagine that you are on the board of the computer games firm. Because of this problem you have been asked to draw up a CSR policy. What would be the main things you would include?

The motivations for pursuing a CSR policy

Values

Diversity

Complexity

Dynamic

From looking at the different argument for CSR we can begin to sum up the main motivations for CSR in terms of:

- self-interest
- mutual interest
- shared responsibility.

Self-interest

In the computer games case it is clear that both companies saw it not to be in their interest to be associated with a request for more violence, etc. It could easily have affected their reputation in other areas of the market. Other arguments that surround self-interest include:

- Business has to be aware of and accommodate itself to social change, and the social values that are a part of that, if it is to survive.
- A long-term view of self-interest demands that business seeks to be involved in society and the solving of society's problems. By so doing, business helps to create a better environment for itself.
- Social responsibility gives business a better image, and thus enables clients to trust them.
- If business can identify and meet the changing expectations and needs of society then government legislation could be avoided.
- Finding solutions to social problems can be a focus for profitable business opportunities.

Mutual interest

Whilst the software firm did not address the worries about the effect of horror games on the players, it is clear that they felt it was in everyone's interest to be aware of this issue. Other arguments for mutual interest include:

- Business has a moral obligation to solve social problems that it has caused or perpetuated.
- Business has great power that it can use to solve problems. It has even greater power if it works in partnership.

Shared responsibility

This involves a shared sense of obligation, such that the good of the whole is of concern for all. In this the business sees itself as part of that whole, and thus has a commitment to work out social responsibility in context. This moves CSR into the perspective of corporate citizenship.

In the computer game case this stage was not reached, largely because there was no full debate or dialogue within the game firm about values or responsibility, and not at all between them and the client. Shared responsibility demands a framework of dialogue and partnership that will lead to the most effective CSR response. CSR then becomes an interactive and learning process, based in core values, working to develop a response in each context, and through partnership and dialogue.

Sethi and Post (1989) characterize these areas as:

- social obligation
- social responsibility
- social responsiveness.

Palazzo and Richter (2005) suggest a parallel view with the headings:

- instrumental
- transactional
- transformational.

It is possible to argue that the business which develops CSR because it has to, or because of self-interest, is not 'genuinely' ethical. The term 'greenwashing' is often used for companies who develop environmental policies just to be seen as trustworthy. However, it is worth noting that many ethical theories involve self-interest, and that few ethical decisions do not contain such self-interest. To deny the interest of the corporation would be to deny the interest of a key part of the local or global community.

An overview of CSR policy and process using Aviva as a case study

A good example of CSR in practice is that of Aviva, the world's fifth largest insurance group. Aviva's approach involves several elements:

Internal/ external

Stakeholders

- A holistic approach that sees CSR as encompassing all stakeholders, internal and external.
- The inclusion of stakeholders, and in particular, customers, in dialogue and planning.
- A transparent framework that includes monitoring and regular reporting.
- Staff development that seeks to communicate core standards across the group. This is particularly important in the light of the multinational nature of the group.
- Finally, a CSR policy that is grounded in reflection on purpose and values and in standards of conduct. The details of these are clearly set out in their policy, and include the concern for staff development, integration, reporting, record keeping and effective monitoring and auditing (see www.aviva.com and click on CSR).

Mini-Case 7.3   Aviva group corporate social responsibility policy

Aviva as a member of the international community recognizes its corporate social responsibility commitments in its various roles, which include insurer, investor, employer and consumer.

We reflect these commitments in a family of eight policies, which relate to:

Standards of business conduct
We are committed to ensuring that our business is conducted in all respects according to rigorous ethical, professional and legal standards

Customers
We seek to provide our customers with a service hallmarked by integrity, quality and care

Human Rights
We respect the Universal Declaration of Human Rights and seek to be guided by its provisions in the conduct of our business

Workforce
We are guided by our aim to be the employer of choice in all countries in which we operate

Health and Safety
We are committed to providing a working environment which is both safe and fit for the intended purpose and ensures that health and safety issues are a priority for all business operations

Suppliers
We regard suppliers as our partners and work with them to help us to achieve our policy aspirations in the delivery of our products and services

Community
We strive to be a good corporate citizen around the world, recognizing our responsibility to work in partnership with the communities in which we operate

Environment
We are committed to a programme of management, continuous improvement and reporting of our direct and indirect impacts, which marks our contribution to the world in which we live.

We recognize that our business activities have direct and indirect impacts on the societies in which we operate. We endeavour to manage these in a responsible manner, believing that sound and demonstrable performance in relation to corporate social responsibility policies and practices is a fundamental part of business success. We are committed to continuous improvement in our corporate social responsibility programme and encourage our business partners to strive for matching performance.

Our business units throughout the world are committed to achievement of our policy objectives. Our performance will be periodically reviewed and externally verified to help us meet our policy goals. At a local level, the heads of our business will revise progress at least annually. We will publish reports regularly.

Approved by the Board of Aviva plc January 2005 (source: www.aviva.com)

❷ How effective a CSR policy do you think this is?

The process and practice of CSR

As noted above CSR is not something that can be determined beforehand and simply applied to any situation. Whatever the appropriate CSR response is can only be worked out in the particular situation. Hence, the company needs to have a process or method for working out CSR in complex and dynamic situations.

Robinson et al. (2007) have suggested a fourfold approach to this involving:

- data gathering
- value clarification and management
- responsibility negotiation and planning
- monitoring and auditing such that profit can be balanced with concern for the social and physical environment.

Complexity

Stakeholders

Values

Data gathering

This involves developing an awareness and appreciation of all issues and stakeholders in any situation. Often this requires more than one group, because any situation might be very complex, and any one group will have a partial perception of the situation. When this is not done, major controversies can be sparked about what the actual data are. The classic example of this is the Brent Spar case, showing how a company can appear to lose the public relations battle through protests that they are acting irresponsibly. How might an effective CSR policy in this instance have avoided what then happened?

Both Greenpeace and Shell had a concern for social responsibility, but Shell did not initially perceive Greenpeace to be a relevant stakeholder, leading to adversarial relations, some very different views of the situation and a corruption of the data.

While Shell's position is that there is no universal solution to the decommissioning of these types of platform, both Shell and Greenpeace argue that what went wrong in this case was that there was not clear and transparent dialogue between all stakeholders.

Many major global industries now have as part of their CSR policy a commitment to dialogue with relevant NGOs. This underlines the importance of identifying and working with stakeholders at the earliest stage. Complex situations can demand an awareness of how the company relates not simply to the immediate situation but to broader aspects such as the supply chain and how subsidiaries do business. A good example is the Nike case.

The very fact of the global controversy surrounding Nike shows the importance of developing a proactive awareness of all aspects of the supply chain. Analysing just what the responsibility of business might be, and developing an effective response that balances all the interests and needs, is another thing, and this will be examined below.

Diversity

Complexity

Dynamic

Interaction

Stakeholders

> ⮕ *Stop and Think*
> Whose responsibility is it to deal with human rights violations?

Value clarification and management

This is the second element in the fourfold approach to CSR in practice. As noted above, the business environment will involve many different values. Any business then has to be clear about its own values, how these inform CSR policy and how it will handle the plurality of values it encounters. In the first of these areas this means developing a statement that makes clear the

Values

Diversity

Mini-Case 7.4 The Brent Spar

In 1995, Greenpeace occupied the Brent Spar oil storage facility owned by Shell, reporting that the Spar was a 'toxic time bomb'. It was only later that the Greenpeace action and the data that they based it on were questioned.

© Greenpeace/Corbis Sygma

The Brent Spar was an offshore oil storage facility owned by Shell and based in the North Sea. In 1992 this huge facility, with six large storage tanks beneath the water, was due to be decommissioned. Because of its size, Shell argued against the usual practice of taking a structure onshore to be broken up. Sinking in deep water, they argued, was in this case the cheapest way of dealing with the problem, but also some claimed the best environmentally. In discussing it with the government, agreement was reached with a date in 1995 established for the sinking of the facility. Shell had not consulted Greenpeace in this process.

On 30 April 1995 Greenpeace occupied the Brent Spar, accompanied by German and UK journalists. Greenpeace reported that they had not been consulted and that the Spar was a 'toxic time bomb', with oil residues and radioactive waste that could seriously damage the marine environment. Dismantling would have to be onshore.

In the subsequent battle, Greenpeace managed the publicity such that when the Spar began to be towed off to the deeper sea it appeared that it was a battle of integrity between a profit-hungry multinational and the NGO who represented the environment.

The result was that Shell backed down under the pressure of intense publicity and the Brent Spar was eventually dismantled onshore and then recycled.

It was only later that the Greenpeace action and the data that they based it on were questioned. Shell argued that there were only 53 tonnes of toxic sludge or oil on the Spar. Greenpeace argued that there was over 14,5000 tonnes of toxic rubbish and over 100 tonnes of toxic sludge. An independent study later noted that there was between 74 and 100 tonnes of oil on board the Spar, and that the greater part of this could be removed easily and this led Greenpeace to make a public apology for this error but not for the general principle that deep sea disposal was damaging.

(For more details, see Entine 2002, or visit www.greenpeace. org)

❷ As CSR director of Shell how would you have handled this case?

(For what Shell sees as the lessons it learned see www.shell.com and search for 'Brent Spar')

Mini-Case 7.5 Nike and labour standards

Much of Nike's footwear is produced in developing countries, and they have been accused of low wages and poor working conditions.

© Getty Images

Nike Inc. is a worldwide producer of sports footwear, clothing and equipment. Most of its products are manufactured by independent contractors. Much of its footwear is produced in developing countries. NGOs noted that 85% of the workforce in Indonesia was female, and that over 30% of the workforce had suffered verbal or physical abuse. More broadly, there were accusations of low wages and poor working conditions. One commentator also accused Nike of abandoning countries who were developing improved conditions and pay in favour of countries such as China, where production costs were lower.

Nike put remedial work into action. This includes attempts to develop increased transparency through working with NGOs. However, the dispute is ongoing.

❓ Go to Nike's website and examine and assess their CSR policy. What criteria would you use to assess it?

---

purpose, attitude and values of the company. A striking example of such a statement is Interface Corp. Interface make, amongst other things, carpet squares and decided that they would develop a strong environmental CSR policy, including encouraging customers to return worn squares for recycling. In the first year of this change their profits increased. The following is the mission statement of Interface:

> Interface will become the first name in commercial and institutional interiors worldwide through its commitment to people, process, product, place and profits. We will strive to create an organization wherein all people are accorded unconditional respect and dignity; one that allows each person to continuously learn and develop. We will focus on product (which includes service) through constant emphasis on process quality and engineering, which we will combine with careful attention to our customers' needs so as always to deliver superior value to our customers, thereby maximizing all stakeholders' satisfaction. We will honor the places where we do business by endeavoring to become the first name in industrial ecology, a corporation that cherishes nature and restores the environment. Interface

will lead by example and validate by results, including profits, leaving the world a better place than when we began, and we will be restorative through the power of our influence in the world. (www.interfaceinc.com)

Such a statement is central to the development of the ethical identity of a corporation. It involves both attitudes and values. It is aspirational, recognizing that CSR cannot be summed up completely in prescriptive codes, involving as it does continued interaction with society. Finally, it embodies the transformative nature of CSR, enabling the customer to become part of the vision. Customer behaviour and values are transformed through involvement in recycling.

The Globally Responsible Leadership Initiative (GRLI) (2005), based in the United Nations Global Compact suggests that the underlying values of CSR include:

- fairness
- freedom
- honesty
- humanity
- responsibility and solidarity
- sustainable development
- tolerance
- transparency.

Managing values, however, involves more than stating the core values of the corporation and enabling others to share and embody them. The business environment includes many different values and raises questions about how they are handled.

- Within the corporation are the values of the staff and the shareholders. We have seen that shareholders may not simply want profits, and there is a need to learn what the values of shareholders and staff actually are. This may involve dialogue about the development of value statements with the internal stakeholders.
- Any business may have a number of conflicting values that have to be held together. The public business of Higher Education is a good example of this, holding together both excellence, in terms of education, and equality, in terms of widening participation.
- There may be occasions where complex and different values lead to conflict and demand that the company or someone within the company make a stand. A classic example of this is the Challenger case.

Even within this one case there is a diversity of business: engineering firms, government organizaions such as NASA, and many different sub-contractors. The diversity meant that there were different values that were fuelling any view of CSR. For the engineers CSR meant proper risk assessment. For NASA and other groups it meant enabling creative partnerships and keeping America ahead in this particular race. The diversity of business and their related values was made even more complex because of the engineering firm's perspective that there seemed to be several different 'clients', companies and different government organizations. The subsequent Presidential Commission noted how, amongst other things, this led to a sense in which responsibility was not fully shared by the different companies.

Ultimately, of course, the explosion adversely affected all the key stakeholders and focused on the ethics of 'whistleblowing' (the practice of an employee within a business informing someone outside of the organizaion about any potential malpractices they have come across). This underlined that an effective whistleblowing system was in the interest of all stakeholders and thus should be a key part of any CSR policy.

↪ *Stop and Think*
What are the problems with whistleblowing?

Mini-Case 7.6 The Challenger 51-L

The Challenger space shuttle exploding on launch. Questions had been asked about the values of safety, responsibility and the awareness of the risks involved.

© Corbis

On 28 January 1986 it took only 73 seconds for the Challenger Space Shuttle to explode in one of the most high profile disasters of the last century. Never before had there been such a programme of space flight, setting out hugely ambitious targets that would have political, social and scientific implications. Many different firms and government agencies worked together. At the same time, there was increasing competition, not least from the European Space Agency. With that came concern about the danger of losing contracts, and attendant financial constraints, raising questions about the purpose of the project.

The engineers employed by Morton-Thiokol Industries identified major structural problems in the Challenger, and struggled between 1985 and 1986 to communicate the implications to the management, to NASA and to other client organizaions. Up to the launch itself, the questions asked by the engineers were about the values of safety, responsibility and the awareness of the risks involved. Such values clashed with managerial values (survival of the firm, keeping the client, keeping a high political profile). The managerial values triumphed.

Responsibility negotiation and planning

Stakeholders

Spatial levels

Interaction

Responsibility negotiation is the third element in deciding what a particular CSR response might be. Firstly, this involves identifying the stakeholders in any situation. Secondly, there is an analysis of the stakeholders in terms of power and responsibility. This enables a full appreciation of constraints and resources in the situation, and leads to an awareness of creative possibilities.

Mini-Case 7.7 Anglo American plc

The mining firm Anglo American have developed an important CSR policy, part of which involves funding the care of employees and their families who have HIV AIDs (Anglo American 2005). However, it could be said that this takes away responsibility for health that properly resides with the local health organizations. It could also be argued that it sets up inequity of care in relation to other HIV AIDs sufferers in the area who do not have good support from under-funded medical resources. It is an open question then as to whether a company should take such responsibility.

Anglo American's response has been to develop a community partnership with local healthcare groups, both in care and in developing public health education around HIV AIDS. This fulfils responsibility to workforce, the wider community, and also enables local healthcare groups to fulfil their responsibility.

❷ Does the company have a responsibility or obligation to act in this way?

Thirdly, responsibility can be negotiated. This does not simply look to the development of goods for all stakeholders, but accepts the need for mutual responsibility and enables its embodiment. Hence, it facilitates a maximization of resources for social responsibility through collaboration.

In this process, several things can be achieved:

- the further development of the ethical identity of the company
- the development of trust and of a sense of shared values with the stakeholders
- reflection on appropriate levels of responsibility
- reflection on how the power of the company can both respond to the effects that they have on the physical and social environment and how they might enable other stakeholders who have little power to fulfil their responsibility.

A good example of the last two points comes from the work of Anglo American.

Similar questions emerge with the issue of human rights. The response of Nike to the questions of labour conditions was to set out a code of practice for all involved in that industry—this to ensure that CSR was not seen as the responsibility of one company. The question remains how a company might respond to a culture that relies on the income from questionable labour or a country that consciously abuses human rights. The answer to the first might be to maintain relations with these groups and to seek to influence the workplace conditions. The answer to the second should involve negotiation with the governments and where necessary, as Anglo American note, reserving the right to stand out against governments who abuse human rights in relation to the company's work.

> **⟳ Stop and Think**
> How does your company or university negotiate responsibility in terms of CSR?

Diversity

Complexity

Interaction

Stakeholders

Audit

If the development of CSR policy and practice is a learning experience then a core part of that has to be reporting. This is the fourth element. Aviva produce an annual report with external independent assurance. This report enables Aviva to see how well policy objectives are being embodied, to manage the direct and indirect effects of the business, and to integrate CSR into products and services.

Anglo American's report (2005) emphasizes responses to environmental challenges. The company base their report in the Global Reporting Initiative. This involves 'triple bottom line' auditing of the financial, environmental and societal dimensions of the corporation, underlining their interconnectedness. It aims to elevate social and economic reporting to the same level as the financial.

The environmental section includes information on:

- total material use
- direct energy use
- indirect energy use
- total water use
- impacts on biodiversity
- greenhouse gas emissions
- ozone-depleting emissions
- total amount of waste
- environmental impact of products.

Anglo American accept that such reporting has been relatively recent for them and that it will develop further. They report fines and legal actions taken against them (73% down from 2004), and environmental incidents (level two incidents up by 5%), alongside reference to awards and effective partnerships. On energy efficiency the 2005 report gives a summary of work across their different companies. This includes an aim of 10% reduction in carbon intensity over ten years. On air quality, sulphur dioxide emissions were decreased by 43% in one company. On water, there is sustained attempt to preserve fresh water and neutralize acidic waste water. The section on biodiversity lists work where companies have been involved in land stewardship and reclamation projects.

Reporting of this nature serves to establish bench marks for performance, but also seeks to engage the imaginations of the different companies. A good example of this is Mini-Case 7.8 noted in the 2005 report in turning waste water from mines into drinking water.

Another approach to auditing is the Business in the Community (BiTC) Corporate Responsibility Index. Companies involved in this, such as Shaftsbury plc., fill in the extensive index questionnaire and the results of this are published in the BiTC index. It provides a way to assess progress and compare progress in other companies.

Perhaps the most famous case study of accusations of corporate irresponsibility concerns Nestlé and its alleged marketing and distribution practices for the selling of infant formula (baby milk powder) in the developing world (see case study p 209). While this is a relatively old case the adverse reaction persists, and for many social activists Nestlé is still one of the faces of corporate malpractice (see e.g. www.babymilkaction.org).

 Mini-Case 7.8   Drinking water for the Emalahleni municipality

Years of mining in the area around Witbank in Mpumalanga, South Africa, have disrupted natural water cycles. Water that would otherwise flow into rivers is leaking into mines, where coal deposits make it acidic. This hampers mining activity and can lead to pollution of local water supplies. At the same time, growing demand from local communities and industry is draining supplies from local reservoirs.

Anglo American and project partner Ingwe began exploratory work in 2002 on the feasibility of a plant that would convert waste water from the mines to drinking water standards. Local communities and water regulators were closely involved in the plans and the project was given the go-ahead in 2005.

The plant and storage dams are being constructed at Anglo Coals Greenside colliery. The water treatment plant will neutralize

The desalination plant at the Emalahleni water reclamation project in South Africa.

© Anglo American plc

acidic water from mines, remove metals and salt and chlorinate the water. Water quality will be monitored regularly.

Waste products from the treatment process will be disposed of alongside other waste from Greenside mine. Ways of recycling—and possibly selling—waste minerals such as limestone, magnesite and sulphur are being explored.

The plant, to be completed by 2007, will provide about 20% of the Emalahleni municipality's daily water requirements. Local communities will also benefit from about 25 permanent positions at the plant and between 100 and 150 temporary jobs during construction.

Neighbouring municipalities are already planning to adopt a similar approach.

(Source: Anglo American Report to Society, 2005: 32)

❓ What is the purpose of incorporating this type of project in company reporting?

◈ *Looking ahead*

The responsibility of business to the physical and social environment will remain contested. Indeed, it is part of the argument from recent CSR writings that if responsibility is to be worked out meaningfully then it has to be worked out with stakeholders and therefore cannot be predetermined. However, there are three areas where CSR seems to be moving into the 21st century. Firstly, there is increased concern for holistic staff development. Holism is whole person learning, engaging feelings and thoughts. This involves enabling staff to develop their part in CSR, and thus own such responsibility themselves.

The GRLI initiative stresses that if the company is developing its CSR policies this also means that stakeholders, and particularly employees, can be enabled to develop their own sense of responsibility, and skills for working out social responsibility together.

Secondly, the global dimension will continue to grow. The work of NGOs and the modern media will force global business to keep reflecting on values and responsibility in practice. This will become evermore complex as business relates to cultures such as China where there is a very different view of the role of business and of social responsibility.

Thirdly, the idea of Global Responsibility will become increasingly owned by groups of which business is only a part, such as cities or regional organizations. This will increase the sense of the business as corporate citizen.

Summary

This chapter has suggested that CSR has moved on from a limited model, largely to do with philanthropy, to one that takes into account the stakeholder network of the business environment. Business still has to make a profit but can see itself as a corporate citizen with responsibilities that it has with other groups in society. These responsibilities have to be carefully negotiated to achieve the best result for stakeholders and the business itself. In all this it is argued that in the global context companies have moved beyond a threshold, 'They have accepted the fact that, beyond profits there is a political, social and environmental dimension to their activities that cannot be ignored. They have moved beyond compliance' (GRLI, 2005: 20). This involves:

- An increasing sense of the company as corporate citizen. Faced by environmental and social issues that are greater than any particular interest there is a position of shared responsibility from which CSR begins

- An awareness and appreciation of the complex and dynamic business environment, including values, issues and stakeholders connected to the company's business

- Business being responsive to an environment that is constantly dynamic. This means the CSR can only be worked out interactively, negotiating responsibility with the different stakeholders. This makes CSR developmental and transformative

- Codes of practice and mission statements will help the core values of CSR to be embedded. However, the ongoing learning process also requires that outcomes be audited

 Case study: Nestlé and infant formula

With the birth rate in the developed countries declining in the 1960s, infant formula companies turned their attention to the developing countries where the birth rate was soaring. In doing this, the companies began to cross the divide between commercial and pharmaceutical industries that existed in the developed world. There, food companies tended to advertise directly to the consumer, while pharmaceutical companies promoted their goods primarily to the health professionals. The formula companies marketing in the developing nations targeted both health professionals and consumers.

In the early 1970s the debate about this practice began. It was argued that advertising implied that infant formula was the best for the baby, and that the use of nurses, employed by the companies, to advise on how to use infant formula was 'endorsement by association' and 'manipulation by assistance'. Promotional techniques ignored three critical factors in the Third World: poverty, hygiene and illiteracy. The mother left hospital with a limited amount of free formula and continued to use it, leading to her milk drying up. The formula was often not mixed correctly, leading to the use of unsterilized water and the baby suffering diarrhoea. The diarrhoea meant that the baby was unable to absorb the nutrients in the formula. The free sample, of course, began to run out and formula was thus thinned out to make it last, often with contaminated water, due to the lack of sanitation. This resulted in the death of the baby from malnutrition and dehydration. Milk banks were not a solution to the problem, as

the poor could not afford even these prices. Based on such arguments it was claimed that the increase in infant morality rate in the Third World and the decrease in breast-feeding were directly connected.

In response to this the United Nations Protein Advisory Group offered guidelines to deal with these problems, but to no effect.

The global debate

In March 1974 the debate became global through Mike Muller's pamphlet *The Baby Killer*. This recast the arguments in a more sensational way and Nestlé's response was to sue. They won the court case but lost the publicity battle, giving the impression of a global giant trying to stamp out the protests of ordinary decent people.

This led to increased collaboration between international health organizations and concerned groups, including the churches and NGOs, culminating in a world-wide boycott of Nestlé goods in June 1977.

Nestlé moved away from a more adversarial approach in favour of dialogue, including:

a) Targeting key professionals, including 300,000 clergy and community leaders, trying to directly refute the allegations.

b) Developing, with the World Health Organization (WHO), UNICEF and the other formula companies, some initial guidelines on practice. These were to develop into the WHO code.

The WHO Code

The WHO code on marketing took until May 1981 to be ratified, partly due to disagreements within the formula industry. The Code directives included that:

- All direct advertising and sampling to consumers should be stopped.
- Labels should carry the advice that breast is best and there should be no text or picture that idealized the formula.
- Marketing should continue but only if it did not undermine breast-feeding.

At this time Nestlé began to widen its non-adversarial approach. It entered into dialogue with the Methodist Task Force, which the American Methodist church had charged to take a detailed look at this issue. Nestlé set up the *Nestlé Coordination Centre for Nutrition* (NCCN), which served as an information centre for key issues in nutrition, and to act as receiver of information that might help Nestlé in meeting new demands and achieving organizational change.

By May 1982 the continuing dialogue led to the development of the *Nestlé Infant Formula Audit Commission*, an independent monitoring agency chaired by Senator Edmund Muskie, former US Secretary of State. Nestlé's practice was seen as increasingly transparent and in line with the code. Hence, support for the boycott of Nestlé products began to wane. The boycott was then officially suspended in October 1984.

The Second Front

On the face of it the issues had been sorted out through the code and the developing dialogue. This led to the gradual scaling down of the NCCN, and eventually of the Muskie Commission. However, opposition still remained in certain quarters. The boycott, backed by the General Synod of the Church of England, had not yet been suspended in the UK.

Some NGOs argued that Nestlé was trying to find ways of getting round the code, and conflict continued over the interpretation of the code in several areas, including the matter of which language should be used for the packaging of formula.

Despite this the Church of England suspended its support of the boycott in 1994, signalling that if they became aware of any attempt to circumvent the code they would support a new boycott.

The early 1990s also saw important moves towards a goal of universal breast-feeding. This led to further pressure on Nestlé especially from UNICEF. In July 1993, UNICEF issued a document *An End to Ambiguities*.

This reflected further frustration with the difficulties in the interpretation of the code. In an attempt to end those ambiguities UNICEF expanded the code, without consulting either WHO or the industry. The first response from Nestlé was to argue that

this went against the code. Hence, far from resolving ambiguities it led to further wrangles.

Subsequent reports from NGOs alleged practices which broke the WHO code, all of which were hotly disputed by Nestlé, both in terms of content and data-gathering methodology.

In May 1995 UNICEF suggested that the only way to end ambiguities was to meet with the formula companies and discuss their sales policy and practice, country by country. For the company lawyers there was the major constraint of US anti-trust laws. To reveal company policy and practice could lead to violation of those laws.

Disputes have continued since then, often in local legal contexts, often discussing minutiae of how to interpret the code. Some groups still continue to argue for a boycott and there is no sign that the different parties could agree on ways forward.

The Nestlé case study is long and complex. It presents a heady mixture of issues: questionable marketing practices, injustice and poverty, as well as matters concerning health and relations between developing and developed nations.

The initial response from Nestlé was divisive and fragmentary, and this could be seen to correspond to the Friedman position, with the market seen as a neutral environment, in which the company should be allowed to do its business. It soon became clear that this could not work and that effective public relations demanded that relations be built up with the different stakeholders. This led to increasing transparency and agreement on values, responsibility and practice—through the WHO code and the Muskie Commission. This was close to a view of CSR which stressed mutual responsibility and collaboration. At one point Nestlé were also moving beyond compliance to a sense of shared responsibility, committing to end all free samples, even though this was not demanded by the code. Thereafter, productive dialogue has collapsed and it is not clear how social responsibility in this area can be effectively worked through (for the views of Nestlé on this issue visit www.babymilk.nestle.com).

❓ How far at any stage in this case study was there real agreement about the data of the case?

❓ Make a list of the different stakeholders in this case. List and compare their values, and their power.

❓ Is there any evidence of effective negotiation of responsibility in this case?

❓ Work with two other students. Imagine that you are the newly appointed CSR team of Nestlé and have been asked to produce a report on this case and to draft a new CSR policy and a statement of values. What would be the main points in the policy and the statement, and how might the reflection on the case inform them?

Review and discussion questions

1 How would you define the nature and limits of CSR?

2 What are the arguments for and against CSR?

3 What part do NGOs play in the development of CSR?

4 How far do the models of CSR noted above apply to small and medium size businesses?

5 Is it possible for an industry that causes harm, such as the tobacco industry, to have a policy of corporate social responsibility?

Assignments

1 If you are in work find out if your employer has a CSR policy. What are the differences and similarities with Aviva's policy?

   OR

   If you are a full-time student, find out what the CSR policy of your Education Institution is and compare it with the Aviva policy.

2 Write a new CSR policy for your Education Institute or place of work, including:

- the vision, ethos and values of the institution
- the different areas within the institution that need policies
- suggestions about how to motivate the staff, and develop ethos, and transparency
- suggestions about how to monitor practice.

3 Imagine that you are starting up a small business. How would you build in concerns about CSR into that process? See BiTC small business page (www.bitc.org.uk/small_businesses/index.html) and the Institute for Enterprise (http://www.leedsmet.ac.uk/enterprise/).

Further reading

To pursue the cross cultural trends in CSR read: Werther, B. and Chandler, D. (2006) *Strategic Corporate Social Responsibility: Stakeholders in a Global Environment* (London: Sage).

To pursue CSR and the Global and developmental agenda read: Crane, A. and Matten, D. (2004) *Business Ethics—a European Perspective: Managing Corporate Citizenship and Sustainability in the Age of Globalisation* (Oxford: Oxford University Press).

Hopkins, M. (2006) *Corporate Social Responsibility and International Development: Is Business the Solution?* (London: Earthscan).

To pursue underlying ethical ideas and cases read: Megone, C. and Robinson, S. (2002) *Case Histories and Business Ethics* (London: Routledge).

Online resources

Test your understanding of this chapter with online questions and answers, explore the subject further through web exercises, and use the weblinks to provide a quick resource for further research. Go to the Online Resource Centre at

**www.oxfordtextbooks.co.uk/orc/
wetherly_otter/**

Business in the Community www.bitc.org.uk

Codes of Ethics for different professions (Centre for Study of Ethics in the Professions, Illinois Institute of Technology) www.iit.edu/departments/csep/PublicWWW/codes

Computing Professionals for Social Responsibility www.cpsr.org

Corporate Responsibility www.corporate-responsibility.org

Corporate Watch www.corporatewatch.org.uk/?lid=2670

Enterprise and CSR
http://ec.europa.eu/enterprise/csr/

Global footprints
www.globalfootprints.org

Green globe 21 (sustainability for travel and tourism)
www.greenglobe21.com

Institute for Global Ethics www.globalethics.org

International Business Ethics Institute (IBEI)
www.business-ethics.org

Scientists for Global Responsibility—Ethical Careers Guide
www.sgr.org.uk/ethics.html

The Institute of Science in Society—Science, Society, Sustainability www.i-sis.org.uk

References

Andriof, J. and McIntosh, M. (eds) (2001) *Perspectives on Corporate Citizenship* (London: Greenleaf Publishing).

Anglo American Report to Society (2005) www.angloamerican.co.uk/

Bauman, Z. (1985) *Modernity and the Holocaust* (London: Polity).

Carroll, A. B. (1991) The pyramid of corporate social responsibility: towards the moral management of organizational stakeholders, *Business Horizons*, July–Aug: 39–48, 40.

Carroll, A. B. and Buchholtz, A. K. (2000) *Business and Society—Ethics and Stakeholder Management* (London: Thompson).

Entine, J. (2002) Shell, Greenpeace and Brent Spar: the politics of dialogue, in *Case Histories In Business Ethics*, ed. C. Megone and S. Robinson (London: Routledge), pp. 59–95.

European Commission, 'Green Paper: Promoting a European Framework for Corporate Social Responsibility', Com (2001) 366 final, Brussels. 18.07.2001.

Friedman, M. (1983) The social responsibility of business is to increase its profits, in *Ethical Issues in Business*, ed. T. Donaldson and P. Werhane (New York: Prentice-Hall), pp. 239–43.

GRLI (2005) *Call for Engagement*.
www.globallyresponsibleleaders.net/

Gregory, A. and Tafra, M. (2004) *Corporate social responsibility: New context, new approaches, new applications: A comparative study of CSR in a Croatian and a UK company*. Paper given at International Public Relations Research Symposium, Bled 2004. www.bledcom.

Heath, J. and Norman, W. (2004) Stakeholder theory, corporate governance and public management: what can the history of state-run enterprises teach us in the post-Enron era? *Journal of Business Ethics*, 53 (3): 247–65.

Moeller, K. and Erdal, T. (2003) *Corporate responsibility towards society: A local perspective*. Brussels: European Foundation for the Improvement of Living and Working Conditions.

Palazzo, G. and Richter, U. (2005) CSR business as usual? The case of the tobacco industry, *Journal of Business Ethics*, 6 (4): 387–401.

Robinson, S. J., Dixon, R. and Moodley, K. (2007) *Engineering, Business and Professional Ethics* (London: Heinemann Butterworth).

Sethi, S. and Post, J. (1989) Public consequences of private actions: the marketing of infant formula in less developed countries, in P. Iannone (ed.) *Contemporary Moral Controversy in Business* (Oxford: Oxford University Press), pp. 474–87.

Sternberg, E. (2000) *Just Business* (Oxford: Oxford University Press).

Zadek, S. (2001) *The Civil Corporation: the New Economy of Corporate Citizenship* (London: Earthscan Publications).

Achieving a better work–life balance

David Chesley and Stephen Taylor

Contents

Learning objectives

When you have completed this chapter you will be able to:

- Explain what is meant by 'work–life balance'
- Identify developments in the business environment which are driving the work–life balance agenda and its increased prominence
- Describe the government's response and its objectives
- Set out the major policies and practices developed by employers in order to permit their staff to better combine working with domestic life
- Examine the dimensions of the 'pensions crisis', and analyse it as a work–life balance issue

Themes

Diversity

Diversity of business

The reasons that increased attention is being given to the achievement of better work–life balance apply to all organizations, but those whose labour markets are tightest have the most to gain from bringing forward initiatives in this area. Public sector organizations with limited budgets are at the forefront of developments, but measures are also increasingly being taken by small and large companies seeking to gain a reputation for being 'employers of choice'.

Internal/external

Internal/external

Responding to the work–life balance agenda requires internal changes within organizations in relation to managing the internal labour market, such as the introduction of more flexible patterns of working.

Complexity

Complexity of the environment

The antecedents of recent interest in work–life balance issues reflect several different developments in the contemporary business environment. Increased competition between organizations has played a part, driven by regulatory changes, by technological innovation and the globalization of economic activity. The tightening of labour markets and the emergence of skills shortages are significant factors, as are the profound social changes that have occurred over the past thirty or forty years. Finally, legal developments have also played an important role, including regulations that emanate from European Union institutions.

Spatial levels

Variety of spatial levels

The significance of the work–life balance agenda varies considerably across the world. The most sophisticated practices are found in the large private corporations that employ highly qualified people in Europe and the USA, but we are increasingly seeing moves in the same direction on the part of public sector organizations and some small employers. There is a good deal less activity in developing countries, but organizations seeking to recruit and retain talented individuals everywhere in the world are increasingly adopting a similar agenda.

Dynamic

Dynamic environment

The widespread use of bundles of employment practices which are designed to improve work–life balance is a relatively recent development and is very much a product of contemporary trends in the business environment. Were these trends to change in the future the issue would become less significant. For example, were labour market conditions to loosen as a result of a deep recession a major reason for adopting such policies would be removed. Moreover, governments would come under pressure to deregulate in this area so as to promote economic growth.

Interaction

Interaction between business and the environment

The rise of the work–life balance agenda is an excellent example of a situation in which organizational practice has been influenced by developments in the business environment. Social, economic, demographic, competitive and regulatory trends have all played a part. The response on the part of employers demonstrates how some organizations have sought to turn the situation to their advantage by developing a positive reputation in key labour markets.

Stakeholders

Stakeholders

The development of the work–life balance agenda by employers primarily relates to the employer–employee relationship and hence to the stake that employees have in organizations. More generally, however, as is reflected in government policy there are advantages to be gained for the wider communities in which organizations are based. Indirectly customers benefit from improved products and services, while shareholders and suppliers benefit from the survival and prosperity of organizations which promote work–life balance.

Values

Values

While most attention focuses on the business case for practices which promote work–life balance, there are major ethical and political issues to be considered too. It can be argued that organizations should not move in this direction purely because of business imperative, but simply because it is right to do so. The same debate is relevant to the regulatory agenda. Irrespective of the role the promotion of work–life balance plays in the meeting of economic objectives, there is a straightforward case for such developments rooted in social justice and the enhancement of the quality of life.

Introduction

Forty or fifty years ago in industrialized countries, and far more recently in most developing countries, the paid workforce was dominated by men to a very considerable degree. The norm was for people to get married in their early twenties and to start a family soon thereafter. Wives, if they had previously had paid jobs gave them up, instead focusing their efforts on bringing up the children and undertaking other domestic duties (see the section on 'A Woman's Place'? in Chapter 5). Husbands, by contrast, were expected to secure full-time employment so as to earn sufficient income to maintain the family. Most jobs were unskilled or semi-skilled and required job holders to work a standard full-time working week of between forty and fifty hours. While plenty of manual workers were employed on shifts, organizations in other sectors tended broadly to restrict working hours to the hours of daylight, opening in the morning and closing in time for employees to return home in the early evening. In this way a form of equilibrium had been established between the working and domestic spheres of our lives.

While it is important not to generalize too much about complex social norms and trends established in different countries, it is generally agreed that this equilibrium has to a great extent broken down in the industrialized countries of the world and is now beginning to do so in developing countries too (Gambles et al., 2006). There have been many, and profound consequences. Some have been positive such as increased affluence and greater equality of opportunity between men and women, but there have also been significant negative consequences. Prominent among these has been a tendency over time for it to become increasingly difficult for employed people to find a satisfactory balance between their domestic and working lives. Materially our lives have improved considerably in recent decades, but in order to achieve this, many of us have had to work harder and longer. Family life is perceived to have suffered as a result, while many more employees claim to be suffering physiologically from stresses and strains associated with their employers' expectations. As a result the quest to find ways of achieving a better work–life balance has moved up our personal agendas, and onwards up to those of many employing organizations and governments. Since the turn of the millennium in particular the issue has become increasingly prominent and widely discussed.

Another aspect of the way work featured in people's lives in the last century that has been disrupted in recent years concerns the balance between working life and retirement. Guaranteeing economic security in retirement through provision of a pension had been established as a key responsibility of postwar (i.e. post 1945) welfare states in Europe, including the UK. Indeed, it can be argued that pensions were one of the cornerstones of the welfare state. In the UK state pensions were based on a contributory principle, with individuals paying in to the system through national insurance contributions (NICs) while working. But in practice the system worked on a pay-as-you-go basis, with pensions financed from tax and NI contributions from the current generation of workers. In effect, despite the contributory principle, state pensions were based on the idea that it was the responsibility of government, and therefore the rest of society, to look after people in retirement. A pension was regarded as a right of citizenship. Men became eligible for a state pension at 65 (and women at 60, though women were less likely than men to have entitlement through the NI system because of their discontinuous working lives), and so these came to be regarded as fixed retirement ages. This was a model of work–life balance in terms of the balance between working life and non-work life (retirement).

However this model has come under strain in recent years leading to a rethink and reform of pension provision, shifting the relationship between the state and the individual and, at the same time, between the state and the market. The high water mark of the old model in the UK was the decision in the 1970s by a Labour government to link the state pension to the rise in average earnings so that pensioners' living standards would keep pace with the rest of society. However in the 1980s this link was broken by a Conservative government, with the state pension being linked instead to the price level. This would mean that pensions would maintain their value in real terms but would fall behind average living standards. The concern driving this change was affordability and the desire of the Conservative government to reduce public spending and taxation. Since the '80s concerns over affordability have been driven largely by ageing of the population. Increased life expectancy raises anew the question of the balance between work life and non-work life: as we live longer should we not expect to work longer too? And, how else can we as a society afford to pay for the incomes of the retired?

In this chapter we will identify the major reasons for the increased interest in the work–life balance that has developed in recent years. We will also argue that it is likely to become very much more significant still in the future, becoming *a* key (if not *the* key) driver of the strategies, policies and practices adopted by organizations in order to interact effectively with their labour markets. In the second part of the chapter we will go on to focus in particular on the responses to date of the UK government and of major employing organizations. The final part of the chapter will turn attention to the pensions 'crisis' and proposals to tackle it.

Mini-Case 8.1 Employee attitudes (CIPD research)

In research by the CIPD, around a quarter of the respondents believed that their hours had contributed to an illness or had a detrimental effect on their mental health.

© istockphoto.com/ Martin Kawalski

In 2003 the Chartered Institute of Personnel and Development (CIPD) carried out a major piece of research into employee attitudes towards their work and their ability to balance it with their home lives. A feature of the survey was the emphasis it placed on people who worked in excess of forty-eight hours a week.

The key findings were as follows:

- 26% of the sample worked more than forty-eight hours a week on a regular basis, 9% worked more than sixty hours a week

- the main reason given for working long hours was the level of the workload

- only 15% of those working long hours had seen any reduction in the previous five years

- 33% of the sample said that when forced to choose between fulfilling a work commitment and fulfilling a home commitment, they would opt for the work commitment. 50% of the long hours workers opted for the work commitment

- the majority said that working long hours had impaired their work performance at some point. Some had made more mistakes, others had taken longer than necessary to complete a task due to weariness

- around a quarter of the respondents believed that their hours had contributed to an illness or had a detrimental effect on their mental health

- half of the respondents working over forty-eight hours a week perceived that they had a good work–life balance

- 45% stated that working long hours had put a strain on their relationships outside work and 11% said that it had contributed towards a divorce

- the long hours workers were found to be conscientious about their work generally, coming in when ill, working on public holidays, refraining from taking the holiday they are entitled to and skipping their lunch breaks

- nearly a third of the respondents said that they found their home lives and work lives equally satisfying, only 7% preferring work life to home life.

❓ Think about your reaction to these findings. Do they surprise you? Do you think that there is a problem of working long hours? What are your own views about working long hours?

(*Source*: CIPD, 2003, *Living to Work?* London: Chartered Institute of Personnel and Development.)

What is work–life balance?

Work–life balance is about changing the way that work is both organized and executed so that everyone, regardless of age, race, gender or ability, can find a way to combine work with their other responsibilities or aspirations. This idea is reinforced by Clutterbuck (2003) who points out that in an individual's pursuit of managing their work–life balance, consideration should be given to an understanding of:

- the differing demands that will be placed on their time and energy
- the ability of the individual to make choices about the allocation of time and energy
- understanding the values that apply to the choices made
- making choices

The outcome, as suggested by Blunsdon et al. (2006) is that a successful work–life balance is one where individuals have integrated both 'life' and 'work' to realize how an individual's quality of life can become 'satisfying', and where the day-to-day juggling of 'conflicting role demands' is less of a strain resulting in less stress.

Why work–life balance is moving up the agenda

Several distinct reasons can be identified for the increased interest in work–life balance issues on the part of employees, employers, trade unions, government and commentators (see Figure 8.1). The reasons vary somewhat from country to country, but one way or another across the world we are seeing a confluence of trends which serve to make employees more interested in securing it and employers more willing to help them achieve it. Here we focus on three sets of developments that have particular relevance in the UK:

- the intensification of work over recent years
- developments in labour markets and the emergence of widespread skills shortages
- major social changes, particularly those relating to the position of women in society.

Figure 8.1 Drivers of work–life balance initiatives

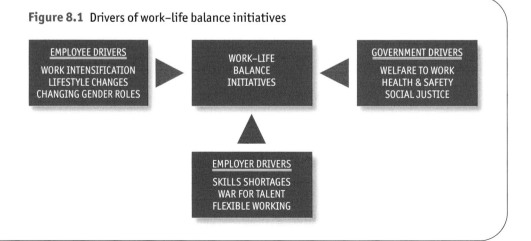

The intensification of work

It is difficult to reach any clear-cut, wholly valid conclusions about trends in the number of hours each week that people spend undertaking paid work. This is partly because the main published statistics (in the UK the Labour Force Survey and the Workplace Employment Relations Survey) are based on self-reporting by employees and are thus not objectively verifiable. Moreover, the average figure for a country's working population is unhelpful because it includes people who work both part-time and full-time. Changes over time are thus as likely to reflect shifts in the proportion of people working on part-time contracts as they are in the actual numbers of hours worked by full-time workers. The result is some disagreement between analysts about the extent to which the numbers of hours worked have increased or decreased in recent years. In the UK, after several decades in which full-time workers worked fewer hours on average each year, the 1980s and 1990s saw little change. If anything, the long term trend was reversed and people started increasing the number of hours they worked (IDS, 2000). Since then official figures show a slight reduction, but this is contrary to the reported experience of many employees. The perception is that we are working more rather than fewer hours each year, the same being true of employees in many other countries (Green, 2006: 45–6).

While we may or may not be working more hours than before as a working population, it is clear that a sizeable minority (at least) are working more hours than they used to. In the UK around 30% of men and 10% of women claim to work in excess of fifty hours a week, while substantially more people than previously report working unpaid overtime on a regular basis. Moreover, as Green (2006: 46) points out, there is no question that the average number of hours worked each week by the adult members of each household *in combination* has risen substantially in recent years. This has occurred as a result of the rapid rise in the number of dual-earner households since the 1970s. Looking at the issue from the perspective of the individual family or couple, therefore, we can safely conclude that very considerably more time is now spent 'at work' (i.e. paid work) than was the case twenty years ago.

Not only do people perceive that they and their partners are putting in more hours of work, there is also an unequivocal perception that they are having to put a great deal more effort into their work. All the major surveys carried out in the UK show that people believe that the speed at which they are required to work and the effort that they are required to expend in order to get their work done has increased a great deal since the 1980s. Moreover, according to successive Workplace Employment Relations Surveys, their managers agree with them. The big increases in the private sector occurred in the 1980s, public sector workers experiencing pressure to work harder in the 1990s (Green, 2006: 50–5). Thereafter the extent of growth appears to have reduced, but it is clear that many people continue to feel highly pressured at work. The 2004 Workplace Employment Relations Survey (see Kersley et al., 2006: 101) found that 76% of employees agreed with the statement 'my job requires that I work very hard', while 40% agreed that 'I never seem to have enough time to get my work done'. In both cases, however, the numbers are highest in the case of managers and professional staff. Here, a good majority state that they feel they have insufficient time to achieve their work. A similar trend towards increased intensification of work is reported by studies undertaken across Europe and in the USA and Australia (Green, 2006: 58–61). The evidence thus strongly points to a situation in which many people are either working a good deal harder and under greater pressure than they used to, or at least perceive that they are.

Importantly the pressures of work intensity and long hours are felt by professional staff and managers. This finding is significant because it is these groups which are growing in size over time as a proportion of the total workforce. In the 1950s and '60s (in the UK as in other industrialized countries) the vast majority of the workforce was employed in manual occupations or in other forms of lower-skilled work. In 1951 only 6.6% of the workforce was classified as 'professional', a further 10.5% being employers and proprietors or managers and administrators. By 1999 21.3% were found to be professionals and 19.1% managers, administrators, employers and proprietors (Labour Force Survey, accessed 2007). Thereafter the way that occupations were officially classified changed, but the trends in the kind of jobs we do continued as before. In 2006 14.7% of the workforce were classed as being 'management and senior officials', 12.7% as professionals, and 14.2% as being employed in associate professional and technical occupations (see also Chapter 5).

We can thus conclude with some confidence that a major reason for the increased interest in work–life balance issues is the perception on the part of employees that they are being over-pressured at work currently. The numbers of hours spent in paid work by members of each household has increased, work has become more intense and demanding in nature and the major growth areas in the job market are in those occupations which require their members to work most intensely.

The reasons behind this intensification of work are rooted in globalization, increased levels of competition between companies, pressure to improve the efficiency and quality of public services and an accelerating pace of technological change, as discussed in relevant chapters of this book. In many countries, including the UK, the decline of trade union membership and, consequently, of the influence of unions in workplaces, has made it harder for employees to resist the trend formally. Perceived insecurity of employment born from the experience of downsizing, restructuring and recession in the recent past also plays an important part in reducing opposition to work intensification at the level of the workplace.

> ⮌ *Stop and Think*
>
> In their study of how work–life balance issues are perceived by different stakeholders in different countries Gambles et al. (2006) found many examples of people who said that they chose to work long hours and that they were not compelled to do so by their employers.
>
> ❓ Why do you think that a large proportion of people actively want to work hard and would resist attempts to force them to work fewer hours?

Labour market trends

If work intensification is the major impulse driving demand for better work–life balance on the part of workers, it is the effects of trends in labour markets which are in large part putting pressure on employers to meet that demand (see IRS, 2002). In the UK, as in some other industrialized counties, the most significant single recent development is the tightening of our labour markets. According to the Chartered Institute of Personnel and Development (2006: 5–7) 82% of organizations report having difficulties filling vacancies, particularly in managerial and professional jobs. A range of factors contribute to these difficulties:

- insufficient numbers of applications made when jobs are advertised
- the applicants who come forward lack the necessary skills or experience
- those who are appointable are seeking more pay than the organizations concerned can offer.

Employers also report having problems retaining their staff. The average staff turnover rate for the UK as a whole in 2006 was 18.3%, a figure which is very high by historical standards (CIPD, 2006: 25). Similar figures have now been reported for ten years, reflecting a long period of stable economic growth and relatively low levels of unemployment.

Demographic trends are also playing an important part. Members of the large postwar baby boom generation are now beginning to reach retirement age. Over a million babies were born at the peak of this boom in 1964, after which fertility in the UK declined sharply (see also Chapter 5). In 1977 there were only 657,000 births, and while the figure has increased somewhat since then, there are still very considerably fewer people available for paid work in their twenties and thirties than there are their forties and fifties. Labour markets are made tighter still by the increased propensity of young people in full-time education until the age of 18 and subsequently to spend three more years studying in colleges and universities.

We are therefore witnessing increased demand for specialist skills, high levels of attrition from the workforce and increasing difficulty finding people with the required skills to fill the vacancies being created. While there remains a fair amount of unemployment (around 1.5 million), this consists principally of people who do not have the qualifications necessary to fill the jobs for which there are skills shortages.

The situation has been ameliorated to a great extent by increased immigration. The expansion of the European Union eastwards since 2004 has provided opportunities for hundreds of thousands of people from Poland, Hungary, Cyprus and the Baltic countries to work in the UK, while levels of immigration from the Middle East and new commonwealth countries has increased substantially over recent years. But there remain significant, if not chronic, skills shortages in many industries, including the public sector.

When faced with skills shortages employers put in place different kinds of strategies, for example:

- reducing demand for people with hard-to-find skills and experience by restructuring their operations
- recruiting people with potential and providing them with the development opportunities necessary to gain the skills that are in short supply
- spending more on increasingly slick recruitment campaigns, and
- simply paying higher wages.

However, increasingly employers are seeking to achieve longer-term solutions by positioning themselves in the labour market as 'employers of choice'. This involves critically assessing not just their terms and conditions of employment, but the whole lived experience of working for them with a view to making themselves more attractive than their chief competitors. The result, they anticipate, is sustained competitive advantage derived from an improved capacity to recruit and retain high quality people.

Providing employees with a better work–life balance is central to any strategy aimed at developing a reputation as an employer-of-choice. It is not enough on its own because employees also seek job security, interesting work and influence over how their jobs are performed, as well as good terms and conditions when they are deciding who to work for (see Taylor, 2001). But for an increasing number of us finding a job which allows us to combine a rewarding career with a full and satisfying home life is a major priority. Employers who can provide such employment are far better placed to compete for scarce staff than those who can not.

A related point is the increasing need, as labour markets tighten, for employers to tap into labour markets that they do not habitually look to when filling vacancies. We refer here to groups within the population who are not looking for traditional full-time employment and may, in fact, not need to work at all for reasons of economic necessity. The major examples are:

- students in full-time education
- women with young children who have chosen to take a break from work in order to concentrate on their upbringing
- people who have taken early retirement
- people over the age of sixty-five
- people with long-term health problems or disabilities who are currently dependent on state benefits.

Many members of these groups would be happy to work on a part-time or casual basis, to undertake a one-off project or to work from home, provided that the job was sufficiently attractive and practical for them to carry out.

Older people, in particular, are increasingly seen as a potential source of experience and expertise that can be tapped by organizations suffering from skills shortages. But to recruit and retain them successfully, employers must provide them with ways of working which enable them to combine the work with other activities. This is also the most effective means of retaining the services of older workers who have a choice about when they are going to retire. Surveys invariably show that a large proportion of older workers have a preference for phased retirement. They will go if the only alternative is to continue working at the same pace, but they will remain for longer if offered the opportunity to work flexibly—especially if they can also begin to draw a pension at the same time. As the population ages and the number of retired people grows in relation to the number of people of working age, employers faced with skills shortages are increasingly likely to offer packages of this kind in order to meet their demand for people.

Social trends

Wider developments in society are also creating greater demand for work–life balance in employment. Of these the one which has had greatest significance over time is increased female participation in the workforce (see Chapter 5). At the start of the chapter we described the prevailing domestic situation in most households during the first two-thirds of the twentieth century. Marriage at a relatively young age was the norm, after which unpaid domestic work was mainly carried out by women, while men were seen as primary breadwinners and went out to work. This state of affairs began to break down after the Second World War, but changed far more rapidly and extensively from the 1960s onwards. By 1971 59% of women were classed as being 'economically active' in the official government statistics. The proportion had risen to 65% by 1981 and to 72% by 1991. It now stands at 74%, compared with a figure of 83% for men. It remains the case that part-time work is predominantly carried out by women, but the majority of women who are employed now work in full-time jobs. Moreover, while progress has been slow, women are now a great deal more likely to be employed in the more demanding managerial and professional jobs than was the case twenty years ago.

Another significant and related social trend is the pronounced tendency for women to have children later in life than they used to. In 1971 the average age of mothers when their first child was born was 23 years and seven months. This has increased steadily since then. In 2004 it was 27 years and one month, and later still (30 years) for women who were married (National Statistics, 2006a: 29–30). The main reason is a wish on the part of many young women to establish themselves in a career before starting a family. As a result, by the time their first child is born, they have a strong incentive to carry on working in their established career. This trend is also reflected in the job tenure statistics for women with children. In 1975 the average amount of time spent in each job by women with children stood at 20 months. It is now 44 months, reflecting the marked increase in the tendency for women to return to work after taking a period of maternity leave and to resume their careers (Gregg and Wadsworth, 1999).

At the same time we have seen a very substantial increase in the number of lone-parent families, the vast majority of which are headed by women. In 1972 only 7% of UK families were headed by a single parent. The figure is now 24%, but there are substantial regional differences. In several London boroughs over half of all children live in lone-parent families, figures of between 40% and 50% being common in the other major cities.

These three social trends have all served to increase the demand for jobs which permit their holders to combine full-time work with domestic responsibilities. Professional women with children are increasingly employed in the most demanding jobs and are having their children once they are well-established in such positions.

For those with spouses and partners there is a knock-on effect because of the need to share childcare and other domestic duties that were overwhelmingly the preserve of women a generation ago. The result is a situation in which men as well as women are likely to be seeking jobs which permit the achievement of a good work–life balance. At the same time many more women are in the position of needing to secure paid employment while at the same time taking sole responsibility for running a home and bringing up a family.

Population ageing (discussed later in this chapter) is also of relevance in this context because of the increased likelihood in the future that employees of working age will have elderly relatives to care for. Already 12% of working population have such responsibilities. As more and more peo-

Many women are in the position of needing to secure paid employment while at the same time taking sole responsibility for running a home and bringing up a family.

© Getty Images/Ariel Skelley

Mini-Case 8.2 Work–life balance in developing countries

In their study Gambles et al. (2006) explored the factors driving interest in work–life balance initiatives in several countries, including some usually classed as developing economies. Here, alongside increased intensification of work, they found other special factors at work:

In *India* the speedy development of the economy in recent years has tended to separate families. The long-established tradition of people living in extended families where domestic duties are pooled to allow several members to go out to work is being put under pressure. Young couples are moving to the cities and form-

ing nuclear family units such as those which predominate in western countries.

In *South Africa* the extensive spread of the AIDS virus plays a major role. It means that many more people, particularly women, find themselves having to take on caring roles while also seeking to develop careers.

❓ Why is work–life balance sometimes seen as an issue of concern only to rich societies, or to their more affluent members? Can the poor afford to care about work–life balance?

ple live into their nineties, this percentage will grow. The result will be further growth in demand for jobs which permit people to combine paid work with important domestic responsibilities.

Government initiatives

Governments and opposition parties have shown an increased interest in legislating to help provide work–life balance for a number of reasons:

- such policies are seen by progressive thinkers as being socially just
- they are popular among voters, media commentators and bodies such as trade unions which provide political funding

- 'family-friendly regulation' can contribute to the achievement of wider economic policy objectives.

In the UK over the past decade all three of these antecedents have played a role in shaping an extensive programme of government action in this field. European directives have also played a significant role (see the Case Study on the EU Working Time Directive in Chapter 13).

Governments, like employers, are right to be concerned about the impact of skills shortages. This is because they pose a threat to the stability of the economy as a whole and to the government's own ability to deliver improvements in the quality of public services. Skills shortages tend to lead to wage inflation, which in turn feeds through into higher prices for goods and services. This leads to higher interest rates and reduces economic confidence as people feel more insecure about the real value of their future incomes. Skills shortages also hinder the ability of companies to meet demand for products and hence tend to reduce the international competitiveness of the economy as a whole. For these reasons some economists have gone as far as to argue that chronic skills shortages are likely to be the trigger for the UK's next recession (see Frogner, 2002).

Government policy in many fields is thus concerned with ameliorating skills shortages. In the UK over recent years we have, for example, seen the relaxation of immigration rules, major investment in primary and secondary education and a steady increase in the number of places being provided in institutions of higher education. Initiatives in the regulation of employment have also played a part, the aim being to encourage as many people as possible to put their skills at the disposal of the economy by undertaking paid work. It is important to remember that there are at any one time millions of people of working age in the UK who are neither working nor claiming jobseekers' allowance. These people are classed by government statisticians as being 'economically inactive'. In 2006 they numbered nearly eight million (National Statistics, 2006b: 80). The major categories were identified above: retired people under the age of 65, parents of young children, full-time students and people with long-term health problems. In order to attract as many as possible into work (and in some cases off welfare at the same time) the government has created legislation that makes it easier for them to combine work with other activities. It also aims to use legislation to make the prospect of working more attractive in general terms. Some policy initiatives have been general in their effect, while others have been targeted at providing assistance to particular groups, such as parents of young children. The major examples are the following.

Working time regulations

The Working Time Regulations 1998 give effect in UK law to the European Working Time Directive. This remains a matter of political controversy because it is so much less rigorously enforced in the UK than in other EU countries and because its imposition was unsuccessfully resisted in the European Court of Justice by the Major government in the 1990s. Nonetheless it is important in that it provides workers with an opportunity to complain to the health and safety authorities or to an Employment Tribunal when they are obliged to work more than forty-eight hours a week against their will on a regular basis. At the time of writing (January 2007) it remains possible for UK employers to require new workers formally to 'opt-out' of the regulations, but this part of the regulations is under sustained attack from other EU countries. Moreover, it must be remembered in any event that staff have the right to opt back in, without suffering any detriment, and 'reclaim' their working time rights if they give their employer three months' notice.

The Working Time Regulations also provide for a minimum of four weeks' paid holiday a year in addition to bank holidays and regulate the number of hours that can be worked overnight. They also seek to ensure that every worker has a break of at least twenty minutes every six hours, a break of eleven hours in any one twenty-four hour period and twenty-four hours rest in any seven day period. Specific additional protection is given under the regulations to young workers under the age of eighteen.

Working Time Regulations provide the number of hours that can be worked over night.

© istockphoto.com

> ⮎ *Stop and Think*
>
> In France in 2000 the government introduced the so-called 'Loi Aubery' (named after the employment minister of the time). This limits all employees, with one or two exceptions, to a maximum working week of thirty-five hours. It was introduced primarily as a means of reducing unemployment by seeking to ensure that what work was available was shared around more evenly. It has proved very controversial, many economists claiming that it has served to slow economic growth and hence has caused unemployment to be higher than it otherwise would be.
>
> ❷ What is your view of laws such as this which require employers to limit the number of hours people work? Would you like to see such a law introduced across Europe?

Part-time workers regulations

A further EU directive seeks to protect part-time workers from unfair treatment by making it unlawful to discriminate against them vis-à-vis equivalent full-time workers. The relevant UK legislation is contained in the Part-Time Workers (Prevention of Less Favourable Treatment) Regulations 2000. The key rights are as follows:

- Part-time workers who believe that they are being treated less favourably than a comparable full-time colleague can write to their employers asking for an explanation. This must be given in writing within 14 days.
- Where the explanation given by the employer is considered unsatisfactory, the part-time worker may ask an Employment Tribunal to require the employer to affirm the right to equal treatment.

- Employers are required under the regulations to review their terms and conditions and to give part-timers pro rata rights with those of comparable full-timers. However, no inspectorate has been created to enforce this.
- There is a right not to be victimized on account of enforcing rights under the part-time workers regulations.

Time off for family emergencies

The right to 'time off for dependents' also has a European origin, the relevant UK legislation being found in the Employment Rights Act 1996 (as amended by the Employment Relations Act 1999). The right is to a reasonable amount of time off during working hours for urgent family reasons. The following are covered:

- to provide assistance when a dependant falls ill, gives birth or is injured
- to make arrangements for the provision of care for a dependant who is ill or injured
- on the death of a dependant
- due to unexpected disruption or termination of the arrangements for the care of a dependant
- to deal with an incident involving a child during the time when an educational establishment has care of that child.

The right is only to unpaid time off and employers must be informed of the intention to take the leave 'as soon as is reasonably practicable'. Dependants are defined for the purposes of the Act as spouses, children, parents or people 'who live in the same household' as the worker. Tenants, lodgers and employees are specifically excluded.

Paternity leave

The right to take two weeks' paid paternity leave has applied in the case of all births occurring after 6 April 2003. This is UK law (the Paternity & Adoption Leave Regulations 2002) which applies to employees who have been employed for twenty-six weeks at the start of the fourteenth week before the expected date of birth of the child. Only fathers who expect to have responsibility for the child's upbringing can take the leave.

Adoption leave

Adoption leave is also available under the same set of regulations to both of an adopted child's new parents. One of them is entitled to take a full year's leave (equivalent to maternity leave), while the other is entitled to take a two-week period of leave (equivalent to paternity leave). Entitlement in either case requires continuous employment for twenty-six weeks at the point at which they are informed that they have been matched with a child/children.

Parental leave

This comprises a right to take thirteen weeks of unpaid leave in addition to any standard contractual holiday entitlement following the birth or adoption of a child. It originates in the EU and was given effect in the UK via the Maternity & Parental Leave etc. Regulations 1999. As matters stand (in January 2007), the leave must be taken within the first six years of a child's life (except in the case of later adoptions). If the child is disabled there is a right to take eighteen weeks leave during the first eighteen years of the child's life. The right currently applies only to employees who have completed a year's service at the time of the birth. In the absence of a relevant collective agreement, it can only be taken in blocks of one week at a time, a maximum of four weeks being taken in any one calendar year.

The right to request flexible working

These regulations go some way to meeting (while falling short of) the demands of campaigners that parents with child-rearing responsibilities should be able to work part-time as a right. The regulations set out quite a complex procedure requiring a parent (or someone with caring responsibilities for a disabled adult) to write formally asking for a one-off change in terms and conditions, together with an explanation as to how his/her request could be accommodated. Any changes made as a result of the request are therefore contractual and permanent. There is no right to demand a year's part-time work followed by a return to full-time working.

The employer can turn the request down if it believes there is a good business reason for doing so. There are eight possible reasons given for legitimately refusing a request:

1 burden of additional costs
2 detrimental effect on ability to meet customer demand
3 inability to reorganize work among existing staff
4 inability to recruit additional staff
5 detrimental impact on quality
6 detrimental impact on performance
7 insufficiency of work during the periods the employee proposes to work
8 planned structural changes.

An appeal mechanism for those who are turned down must be made available by employers, appeals being heard within fourteen days of the request being received. Only one application can be made per person per year.

Complaints can be made to an employment tribunal on the grounds that a request was rejected out of hand without a meeting, that an appeal hearing was denied, or the employer was too slow in dealing with the matter. According to the regulations tribunals are not invited to give consideration as to whether the refusal was itself justified on business grounds or not; however it is sometimes possible for a woman who has her request turned down to bring a claim under sex discrimination law which then requires the employer objectively to justify the decision.

Maternity pay and leave

In the UK female employees who become pregnant have long had a right to take a period of maternity leave and to return to their jobs some months after the baby is born. This right was first established in 1974, and for employees with more than six months' service fifteen weeks before the baby is due, there has always been an additional right to receive statutory maternity pay (SMP) during at least some of the period of leave. The legislation is now found in the Employment Rights Act 1996, amendments having been made several times in this area. In recent years rights in this field have steadily been extended, a new set of regulations being introduced every two or three years—notably via the Employment Act 2002 and the Work and Families Act 2006. Over time it is expected that all employees who have babies will be entitled to take a full year's leave and to receive SMP throughout that period. As matters stand, however (in 2007) the right is to nine months' paid leave followed by a further three months' unpaid leave.

In the UK female employees who become pregnant have long had a right to take a period of maternity leave and to return to their jobs some months after the baby is born. In recent years rights in this field have steadily been extended.

© istockphoto.com/
Knud Nielsen

Stress checks

Since 2003 the Health and Safety Executive (HSE) has added concern about stress-related illnesses to the list of factors their inspectors check when visiting employer premises. To support this initiative the HSE has published detailed guidance on the systematic management of stress at work which indicates clearly that employers are expected to carry out stress-oriented risk assessments alongside their assessments relating to physical injury. They identify six 'key areas of work' that they wish to see 'properly managed'. These are entitled:

- demands
- control
- support
- relationships
- role
- change.

They really serve as a checklist of factors to consider when assessing risk. In principle this means that employers can now face criminal proceedings and be fined if they knowingly allow someone to become ill due to excessive work-related stress. Moreover they could be fined simply for wilfully failing to include stress-related factors in their risk assessments.

Mini-Case 8.3 Persuasion as well as coercion

In March 2000 the then Prime Minister Tony Blair launched a work–life balance campaign with the aim of persuading employers to introduce ways of working which meet the needs of the business and customers while simultaneously improving the work–life balance of their employees and so help them to remain in employment. Whilst the campaign did not set out to be prescriptive, its *raison d'être* has been to encourage employers to implement policies and practices that promote work–life balance over and above the legal requirements, with a view to helping the various stakeholders connected with the business to realize their 'new found balance'. Here we see echoes of a neo-unitarist frame of reference (organizational efficiency and effectiveness benefiting from harmonious working relationships, where the customer remains the final arbiter of the quality and competitive outpourings from the business) twinned with a 'learning culture' in which employee opinion and initiative is encouraged and duly

rewarded! Here we find the organization where employees 'do matter', where 'people mean business', where 'sophisticated and consultative' management styles are brought to the fore.

In order for employers to take advantage of the government's agenda and to allow organizations an opportunity to move into areas of work–life balance initiatives, the government has provided free consultancy advice to employers, with projects set up to assist on bottom-line returns in relation to financial savings, staff absenteeism, staff retention levels and the take-up of work–life balance options by staff. £10.5 million including European Social Fund (ESF) was allocated to this initial programme from 2000–2003, where the take-up by employers resulted in projects representing nearly 426,000 employees.

❷ What are the limits of persuasion? Will businesses be willing to take steps beyond the legal requirements if there is no 'bottom line' pay-off?

Employer initiatives

Employers are obliged, as a minimum, to have in place policies which give effect to the legal rights described above. However, many in practice go a great deal further in helping to provide their employees with the opportunity to achieve a reasonable work–life balance. The following are the most common approaches used:

- The right to move from a full-time to a part-time contract. Often two part-time employees are able to occupy one position on a job-sharing basis.

- Term-time working arrangements allow parents to take unpaid leave during school holidays and to return to their jobs once term starts again. The employer typically replaces them during the holidays with university students who are looking for temporary work during their vacations.

- Compressed hours arrangements permit people a degree of flexibility over the days on which they work. They are employed on full-time contracts but work longer shifts on fewer days. For example, someone might work four ten hour-shifts instead of five eight-hour shifts each week.

- Flexitime schemes allow people to vary their hours on a day to day basis. Fixed hours are typically required between 10 and 12 in the morning and between 2 and 4 in the afternoons, but employees can decide each day how much more they work beyond these core times. Those who work for more than their contracted hours over the course of a month can then ask to take a 'flexi-day' or 'flexi-afternoon' off by way of compensation.

- Homeworking policies permit people to base themselves at home for part or even all the working week.

- Sabbaticals permit people who have completed a defined period of continuous service to take a period of several weeks or months as unpaid leave and to return to the same job or a similar job at the end.
- Crèches are often provided by larger organizations to give parents of children who are below school age access to subsidized childcare facilities. After school clubs and school holiday clubs are sometimes provided for older children to attend while their parents are working.
- Childcare vouchers are often provided as a benefit by organizations which are too small to provide in-house crèche facilities.
- Employee Assistance Programmes (EAPs) have long been provided (or funded) by larger American corporations, as well as some UK organizations. They provide confidential advice to employees about practical matters such as finance and counselling services to people who are feeling over-stressed. Advice about achieving a better work–life balance forms an important part of their work.

Researchers who have examined in detail what happens when employers introduce policies of this kind have reported that their effect tends to be limited in practice. Moreover, this appears to be the case even when a package of measures is introduced and promoted actively by managers as being aimed at improving the work–life balance for employees (see Gambles et al., 2006: 5). This appears to occur because having policies in place does not shift attitudes. The culture of many organizations remains one in which commitment to one's work is seen as a necessity if one's career is to develop, and in which commitment is demonstrated by a willingness to work long hours and to volunteer for additional responsibility. Workplace cultures of this type are very common and are often labelled 'macho'. The ability to cope with pressure is admired, while work–life balance policies are seen as being introduced for political reasons. Taking them up is judged as being the action of a wimp.

For many organizations more is therefore needed than a set of policies. If people are genuinely to attain a better work–life balance, without suffering in career or earnings terms, attitudes need to change. The only way to achieve this is for organizations to promote the benefits of work–life balance relentlessly over a sustained period and to take steps to change their prevalent cultural norms.

Balancing work and retirement —the 'pensions crisis'

The quest to achieve a more satisfactory balance between 'work' and 'life' isn't concerned only with working fewer hours and/or more flexibly, but also the balance between work and non-work (i.e. non-paid work) over an individual's lifetime. Non-work can be involuntary, such as periods of unemployment and sickness, or voluntary, notably years spent in education and retirement. Non-work also includes years spent outside of the labour market as a 'housewife'.

Attitudes to the work–non-work balance can be complicated: it is clearly not the case that individuals always prefer less work and more non-work. For example we have seen that entry of increased numbers of women into the workforce (and a corresponding decline in the proportion of women who are classed as housewives) has been a major process of social transformation during the last century. This entry has been driven in part by economic necessity, but also by a desire to find fulfilment in work. The reluctance of men to take up opportunities for paternity leave may, in part, reflect a preference for work over non-work. Individuals may express a preference to continue working beyond the normal retirement age. Indeed some individuals want never to retire.

On the other hand, a lot of people say they would give up work today if they could (e.g., if they won the lottery). Thus we do not all share the same preferences for work and non-work and how

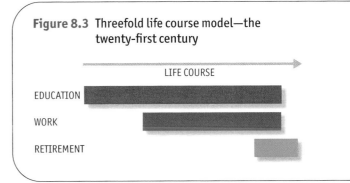

Figure 8.2 Threefold life course model—the twentieth century

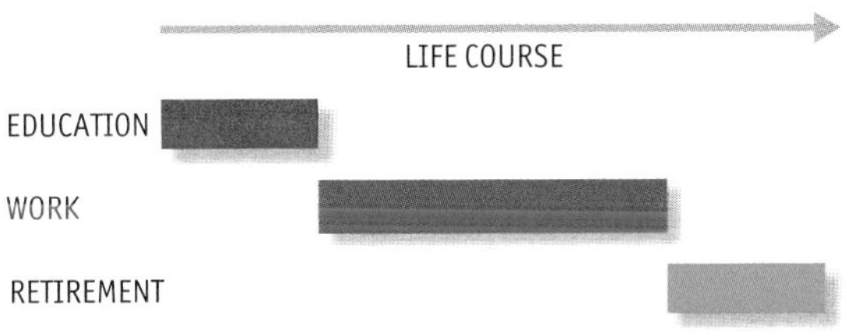

Figure 8.3 Threefold life course model—the twenty-first century

we balance them. However there is a traditional 'model' that can help us to think about this issue—the 'threefold life course model' (Guillemard, 2001: 241) (see Figures 8.2 and 8.3). It involves three successive stages (or 'ages'): education, work and non-work (retirement). This model is actually a fairly modern innovation, associated with the rise of industrial societies. For example, 'retirement' is not a natural part of life but a social convention. It is open to question whether the concept of retirement that we have got used to is the best arrangement for individuals, business or society as a whole. Indeed, Guillemard argues that this model is in fact breaking down and being replaced by a more flexible model in which these ages overlap.

However, the threefold model still has a strong hold in contemporary UK society, and is seen by many as a 'natural' arrangement of the life course. In particular, there is strong attachment to the concept of retirement as a period of economic inactivity at the end of life supported by income in the form of a 'pension'. In recent years the issue of retirement has been dominated by discussion of a 'pensions crisis'. This can be understood as a work–life balance crisis. The way we think about retirement revolves around two questions:

- At what age is it reasonable for individuals to expect to be able to retire?
- How should the incomes of the retired population (pensions) be funded, and who should be responsible for this funding?

Responsibility can be thought of in terms of the balance between the state and the market, or the state and the individual. Should we look to government to ensure an adequate income for people in retirement through a state pension scheme funded by taxation and national insurance contributions (NICs)? In effect this means looking to the current generation of taxpayers, principally those in work. Leaving pensions to be provided through the market might mean individuals contributing to pension schemes on their own account, or contributing alongside employers to occupational schemes. Thus there is a question of how far businesses should be responsible for ensuring decent pensions for their employees.

Stakeholders

At the heart of the pensions crisis are demographic trends, especially the ageing of the population (see Chapter 5). Increased life expectancy (longevity) is producing a shift in the age structure of the population, with a growing number and proportion of people aged over 65. This is accentuated by a falling birth rate which is leading to a fall in the population of working age.

These trends are forcing a rethink in relation to when people should expect to retire and who should be responsible for the funding of pensions. If greater life expectancy is not to result in people being poorer in old age there needs to be:

- a higher level of saving during the years of work to finance the additional years of retirement, and/or
- a rebalancing of work and non-work through later retirement, so that people devote more years to working and saving and fewer years to living off the saving.

Mini-Case 8.4 What is the pension crisis?

'The pension crisis can be looked at from several angles.

- It could relate to the problems that governments around Europe have in funding the state pension schemes that will act as the support to the elderly.

- It could be looking at the problems firms have in meeting the pension obligations they have . . . [taken on through] . . . company pension schemes.

- It could be the problems faced by those who have contributed to company pension schemes but who now find that, as a result of the firms they have been working for . . . going out of business, they do not have access to the pension support they were expecting.

- It could be the fact that fewer young people seem to have pension provision at the head of their priorities and that this could mean that they are storing problems for their future welfare.

- It could be the move by businesses to switch from occupational pension schemes—where employers contribute a sum as well and [through] which workers get fixed pension sums in relation to their final . . . [salaries] to less attractive but cheaper to the firm non-earnings related schemes.'

Underlying these dimensions of the crisis are a number of social, economic and political conditions and trends.
   'These trends are:

- The move to postpone starting families until career aspirations have been established—women having children later in life leading to a fall in the birth rate.

- The move by young people to prioritize things such as house purchase or travel ahead of pension provision.

- The rise in the number of people in the 65+ age bracket as a result of a falling death rate and more successful health care regimes.

- The pressure on governments to reduce the tax burden.

- The increase in the competing demands for government spending.

- A fall in the population of working age—the ones who pay the taxes that can be used to provide pension payments.

- The problems of world economic conditions leading to the fall in the value of stock markets around the world.'

(*Source*: 'The Pensions Crisis—What is it all about and should we be worried?' (3 May 2004), available from the biz/ed website at: www.bized.co.uk/current/mind/2003_4/030504.htm)

The state versus the market

Mini-Case 8.4 brings out some of the benefits and risks of relying on the state or the market to provide retirement pensions. The market encourages individuals to take responsibility for their own security in retirement and enables the exercise of choice. However:

- Some individuals will not be able to afford to save for a pension out of current earnings because of low pay.

- Individuals may not make good choices. This could be because retirement seems a long way off and saving for a pension does not seem to be a priority. Individuals are also at a disadvantage because of the complexity of financial products, and there is a risk of mis-selling.

- Occupational pension schemes do not cover the whole workforce, and employers may opt for schemes that do not guarantee the level of benefit (money purchase schemes). In addition there is a risk of employees losing pension entitlements because of the employer going out of business.

- Pension funds that are invested in shares are vulnerable to the ups and downs of the stock market.

In recent years there has been a significant shift by business away from generous final salary pension schemes that guarantee a pension that is calculated as a proportion of final salary. The rationale for closing such schemes has been on the grounds that they cost too much to run and are too risky. For example, 'The annual National Association of Pension Funds (NAPF) survey found that one in 10 private sector final salary schemes closed to new members in 2006' (news.bbc.co.uk/1/hi/business/6379897.stm). What is more, the same survey also discovered that 67% of final salary schemes in the private sector are now closed to new members. Noteworthy examples of closures in 2007 include Unilever and the Royal Mail, the latter facing a £6.6bn pension deficit. The alternative money purchase schemes involve greater uncertainty and tend to be less generous because they depend on the performance of invested funds. Some see this shift as a dereliction on the part of business of its responsibility to treat employees fairly. On the other hand, it might be argued that final salary schemes imposed unreasonable financial burdens and risks on companies.

The risk to employees of companies going out of business is very real. For example, 'between 1997 and 2005 an estimated 85,000 people lost all or part of their pension when the sponsoring company went bust or the scheme was wound-up' (www.bbc.co.uk). When the market fails there is often pressure for government to step in. In this case the government established the Financial Assistance Scheme to help those whose company pension funds collapsed before April 2005, and the Pension Protection Fund to provide compensation for those whose pension fund collapsed after April 2005.

State provision is not vulnerable to the intrinsic risks associated with the market. In principle governments are able, through the tax and benefit system, to guarantee a generous state pension for all. However:

- there are competing demands on public spending
- governments may be keen to limit or reduce public spending for ideological reasons (as during the years of Thatcherism in the 1980s in the UK)
- governments may face 'tax resistance' from voters, unwilling to pay the higher taxes needed to finance a generous state pension scheme.

Political parties in the UK, especially Labour, have been very wary of 'tax resistance'. Some argue that Labour learned a hard lesson in the 1992 general election (won by the Conservatives) when voters rejected the party's 'tax and spend' approach, including a commitment to raise the state pension and restore the link with average earnings (Driver and Martell, 2006: 92).

The argument about how to solve the pensions crisis is not conducted in terms of the market *versus* the state but the most effective balance and *combination*. This approach was taken by the Pensions Commission in its final report published in 2006 (the Turner Report).

The proposals of the Turner report

The Turner report proposed an integrated set of reforms to both the state and private pensions systems to prevent pensioners getting poorer relative to the rest of society.

The state pension would become more generous and this would be made possible by a combination of higher public spending on pensions and a gradually rising state pension age (SPA)—a higher pension at a later age. Phased increases in the SPA are proposed to track increased life expectancy so that each generation faces the same proportion of adult life contributing to and receiving a state pension. This ensures fairness between generations, and also keeps the necessary increases in public spending within acceptable limits.

To ensure adequate saving through the private system the report proposes automatic enrolment into a National Pensions Saving Scheme (NPSS) for all employees without good existing provision, with contributions from employees (supported by the tax system) and employers. Although individuals can opt out of the NPSS, the idea of automatic enrolment reflects concern that individuals, left to themselves, may fail to make good choices to ensure adequate saving for their retirement (i.e. the problem of inertia). At the same time the national basis of the scheme would enable it to operate on a low-cost basis, thus removing one of the barriers to adequate private saving (i.e. the disincentive of high charges).

Key specific proposals include:

- Contributions to the NPSS would be 8% of earnings (4% from employees' post-tax pay, 1% from tax relief, 3% from matching compulsory employers' contributions). The report estimates that this level of contribution would provide a pension of about 15% of earnings for the median earner.
- The basic state pension would be linked to average earnings, with entitlement based on residency rather than contributions (this would remove the disadvantage faced by individuals with discontinuous working lives, particularly women).
- An indicative gradual rise in the state pension age by one year per decade from 65 in 2020 to 68 in 2050.
- Retention of the current 'two-tier' state system, combining the basic state pension (BSP) with the contributory second state pension (S2P).

> ↪ *Stop and Think*
> What is the pensions crisis?
> Why is it thought that neither the state nor the market can alone ensure an adequate pensions system?

The Turner proposals reaffirm the principle that the state has a responsibility to provide an income for the retired population—individuals cannot be left to rely on their own efforts. However the state cannot deliver adequate pensions on its own, partly because the necessary public spending would require unacceptable increases in taxation. Therefore the state and private systems have to work together. The private system requires individuals to save out of their current income, but employers also have a responsibility to contribute to a savings scheme to benefit their employees.

◈ *Looking ahead*

The moves towards providing people with a better opportunity effectively to combine work and domestic lives are largely a product of long-term trends in the business, demographic and social environments. So long as these remain in place, there is every reason to anticipate a continuation and acceleration of demand for greater work–life balance, its provision by employers and its encouragement by government. Nonetheless much will hinge, at least in the short-term, on prevailing economic conditions. If the economy remains strong and unemployment remains low, employers will continue to be obliged to compete strongly for relatively skilled staff. As work–life balance is something that prospective employees value and seek when looking for an employer, initiatives in this area will be more and more common and will be increasingly well-publicized as employers seek to gain and maintain a positive labour market reputation. Conversely, should economic conditions worsen appreciably and unemployment rise, skills-shortages will rapidly fall down the corporate HR agenda. Employees fearing the possibility of redundancy will be much less well-placed to press for further concessions in this area, while those who are already out of work and looking

for jobs will be happy to accept whatever opportunities to earn are provided, even if it does afford them a poorer work–life balance than they were used to in the past. In such circumstances the maintenance of profitability and hence business survival tends to become the overwhelming imperative for organizations. This is often difficult to reconcile with initiatives such as those we have been describing that are of benefit to employees, but do not add value for the employer except in so far as it makes recruitment and retention easier. In a recession recruitment and retention cease to be such major problems, so were the fortunes of the economy to take a turn for the worst, it could confidently be predicted that interest in work–life balance issues on the part of employers would rapidly decline. Over the longer term, however, the demographic and wider social trends we have indentified in this chapter will continue to drive the work–life balance agenda forward. The population is going to continue to age, women are going to continue having children later in life and will also continue to seek to combine motherhood with a fulfilling career. There will thus remain pressure on government to legislate in this area and we can therefore confidently predict further regulation requiring employers to have in place minimum standards whatever the prevailing economic conditions.

Ageing of the population is a well-established and predictable trend to the middle of the century, although there is uncertainty in relation to birth and death rates in the future. The Turner report has analysed the dimensions of the looming 'pensions crisis' and set the agenda for reform of pensions, embracing both the state and private systems. The pensions crisis is already impacting significantly on business, as can be seen in the closure of final salary or defined benefit pension schemes. Population ageing and the pensions crisis will continue to pose challenges for business in two main areas: labour recruitment and retention, particularly in relation to older workers; and, the funding of state and private pension schemes, particularly through compulsory contributions to a national savings scheme as proposed by Turner.

Summary

- Achieving a better work–life balance is an aspiration that has become more prominent in recent years. Employees and their representatives are keener to demand it, while employers and governments have shown an increased willingness to look for ways of helping them to achieve it

- There are a number of distinct reasons for the increased interest. They include the tendency for working lives to become more intense in recent years, tightening labour market conditions and profound long-term social changes in the realm of family life

- Governments have responded by legislating to force employers to permit a higher degree of flexibility for workers generally and, in particular, for people who have dependent children or other caring responsibilities. The European Union has been a source of many recent legislative developments in this field

- Employers have responded to the demand for greater work–life balance by introducing a range of policies that help employees who wish to do so to alter their work–life balance. However, take-up remains poor in many cases, particularly among men and senior employees. Wider and deeper cultural changes and changes in attitude are going to be necessary if more decisive steps in this direction are to be made

- The ageing of the population is the main contributor to the pensions crisis. The Turner report has analysed the shortcomings of existing state and private provision, and the consequent risk of pensioners becoming poorer in relation to the rest of society. There are major limitations of both the state and the market in relation to pension provision. The solution lies in an integrated package of reform in which the state, individuals and employers share responsibility

Case study: work–life balance in practice: Lloyds TSB and King's Healthcare NHS Trust

Here we describe two of the earliest and most well-established schemes aimed at providing employees of organizations with better opportunities to combine work with domestic and non-work activities.

Since 1999 Lloyds TSB, the fifth biggest banking corporation in Europe, has been running an employment package called 'Work Options' which has received a great deal of positive publicity from trade unions, government bodies and organizations which exist to promote the work–life balance agenda.

Lloyds TSB employs over 75,000 people, the majority of whom are women. The initial trigger for the development of Work Options was a concern about the bank's inability to retain many senior women, but it has since developed into a scheme which is aimed at all employees, male and female, junior and senior alike.

Some of its provisions are aimed specifically at those with caring responsibilities, but for the most part they are available to everyone. Indeed a central feature of the scheme is the way that requests to work flexibly are judged purely on the basis of their potential impact on the business. Personal circumstances are not taken into account.

Another of its features is the way that it goes beyond the statutory minimum requirements that all employers are required to provide, the purpose being to give Lloyds TSB an edge in its main labour markets.

The scheme includes:

- Paid leave for family emergencies or for compassionate reasons.

- Career breaks of up to five years for the purpose of caring for dependants, every effort being made to re-employ at the end.
- An opportunity for employees to reduce hours, increase hours, job share, move to term-time working, to vary their hours, to work from home or to work compressed hours. Requests are only turned down if business would be adversely affected by the change.
- A 'Healthcare Direct' service providing advice and counselling services to employees, including those who are suffering due to work-related stress.

In practice the bank claims that over 85% of requests made under the scheme are approved and that the scheme has had a generally positive impact on the long-hours culture that previously dominated. Overtime costs have been reduced, while surveys carried out among the staff show that the scheme has had a positive motivational impact and has improved employee retention rates. The scheme is regularly reviewed using large-scale surveys of staff who have taken up the opportunities it offers. It has also helped in the process of moving over time from an operation which was open during office hours towards one which serves its customers seven days a week, twenty-four hours a day.

However, interestingly, of the 3,600 members of staff who have applied to work flexibly under the Work Options Scheme, 84% are women and only 18% are managers. There are also parts of the business where take-up has been much lower than others, indicating the persistence of a culture which is unsympathetic to requests to move away from a standard pattern of hours.

A similar philosophy has underpinned the development of work–life balance initiatives at the King's Healthcare NHS Trust in South London, brought together as a package—a scheme called 'Kingsflex'. Here too the major driver for the development of new approaches was a major problem retaining professional women. In the year before the launch of the scheme over a fifth of the Trust's nurses and midwives left voluntarily over and above dozens of retirements, making it increasingly unlikely that the Trust would be in a position to meet government targets for the reduction of waiting lists and waiting times for patients. The scheme was designed by a working party consisting of several managers from across the Trust, a midwife, a clinical scientist and a trade union representative.

The King's Trust employs 4,000 people comprising of managers, administrators and health professionals. Ancilliary services are all outsourced to external providers, so the Kingsflex scheme is only available to relatively highly paid, and in the main, highly-skilled professional workers. As in the Lloyds TSB scheme, all are eligible to apply to take advantage of the scheme but, at the end of the day, decisions about whether to allow a request have to be made by managers in the interests of the organization. For example, it would not be possible, given the nature of the work undertaken by the Trust, for everyone to demand that they only worked daytime shifts on a Monday to Friday basis. But if a request is found to be in the best interests of the service, managers are expected to allow it, even if it might be seen as setting a preced-

ent which other employees will expect to be able to take advantage of too. The scheme is open to anyone, but it is particularly designed to be helpful to nurses and midwives.

The Kingsflex scheme includes the following features:

- A right to request to work on a part-time or job-share basis.
- Reductions in hours of work and alterations in patterns of hours on a temporary basis.
- An annual hours scheme permitting employees to work longer hours at some times of the year (e.g. during term time) and shorter hours—or no hours at all at other times (e.g. during school holidays).
- Career breaks of up to two years, employees returning to the same type of work at the end of their period away. The breaks can be used to undertake caring responsibilities, a course of higher education or in order to travel.
- A flexible holiday entitlement. Employees can 'trade' up to ten days of their annual holiday entitlement for cash, either selling days and taking more money, or buying an additional two weeks' leave in return for a lower salary.
- An opportunity to work from home, where appropriate, for some days of the week or on an occasional basis.

Following the introduction of the scheme there was a slight reduction in staff turnover, but a substantial fall in the number of vacancies. The major impact was thus an ability on the part of managers to fill their vacancies much more quickly. In particular, past employees (mainly women with children) who had left were attracted back to the Trust by the promise of being able to work on a more flexible basis than they had at the time of their resignations.

Interestingly, take-up of the scheme was not huge among existing staff when it was first introduced. Those who did make use of it tended simply to adjust their working hours in quite minor ways, or to buy more holiday entitlement. Requests tended to be approved by managers and there were no appeals made against refusals to grant requests during the first months it was in operation. On the whole it was clinical staff rather than managerial employees who took up the opportunities presented by Kingsflex.

❓ Aside from the retention and motivation of staff, what other advantages do you think these organizations will have gained in business terms from developing their work–life balance schemes?

❓ What other elements could be added to the packages to make them more attractive?

❓ Why do you think so many more women take up the opportunities offered by the schemes than men?

❓ Why do you think they are less attractive to managers, despite the pressure that their jobs inevitably place on them?

❓ How far do you think this kind of scheme could be replicated in other industries and in smaller companies?

(*Sources*: Mahony (2000) and Rana (2002))

Review and discussion questions

1 Studies of differences in attitudes between older and younger people have shown that demand for effective work–life balance is strongest among people who are in their twenties and who are now entering the labour market. Why do you think this is apparently more of a priority for the generations born in the 1980s and 1990s than it was for their parents and grandparents?

2 How far do you agree with the view that workers in western, industrialized countries such as the UK will have no choice but to work harder in the future if living standards are to be maintained in the face of increasing competition from developing economies?

3 To what extent do you agree with the view that employer commitment to work–life balance initiatives is mainly a product of current labour market conditions and that it would disintegrate if there was greater unemployment and fewer skills shortages?

4 Why is it that despite over thirty years of sex discrimination legislation and widespread acceptance of gender equality, work–life balance programmes developed by employers are still so often seen as being 'for women' and are mainly taken up by female staff?

5 What has the pensions crisis got to do with business?

Assignments

1 Critically assess the work–life balance policies and practices developed by your own organization, or one with which you are familiar. List the major factors in the business environment that have determined how extensive or restricted they are? How is this likely to change in the future, and why?

2 Review the measures introduced by governments and by the EU to date which aim to promote the work–life balance agenda. Make a list of points to indicate to what extent you consider these to be sufficient, and what reforms and new initiatives you would like to see brought forward and why?

3 Assume that you have been commissioned as a consultant to advise a company that has staff retention problems and limited funds about how it might nonetheless become a genuine **employer of choice**. What advice would you give in relation to work–life balance initiatives? How would you justify the expenditure required to give them practical effect?

Further reading

Work–Life Balance: a Psychological Perspective is a recent book of articles edited by Fiona Jones, Mina Westman and Ronald J. Burke which looks in detail at the issues discussed in this chapter, including the use of legislation to encourage employers to take steps to improve their employees' work–life balance and examples of some of the approaches taken by employers in practice. The book is particularly strong on the impact of poor work–life balance on people's psychological state. An international perspective is provided in several of the articles.

In 2002 the Chartered Institute of Personnel Development's journal, *People Management* published a supplement covering many aspects of work–life balance practices from the employer perspective. Several feature articles focus on practice in different organizations, including the problems faced in introducing policies. There are also a number of shorter opinion pieces. CIPD also carries out regular surveys looking at employer and employee attitudes. The most recent was published in January 2007.

The Myth of the Work–Life Balance by Richenda Gambles, Suzan Lewis and Rhona Rapoport (2006) sets out in a very accessible way the results of a major international research project looking at a range of work–life balance issues. The book is thought-provoking in that it argues that policies developed by governments and employers are insufficient if a genuine, long-lasting change is to be brought about in the way we balance our work and home lives. Gender issues are dealt with effectively in this context.

Debates about regulatory aspects of work–life balance are explored and summarized effectively by A. C. L. Davies in *Perspectives on Labour Law* (2004). The relevant chapter is number 6 entitled 'Working Time', but the discussion encompasses family-friendly statutes as well as the Working Time Regulations 1998. This is a particularly good source of accessible ideas on the purposes behind the legislation and the economic arguments in favour of laws of this kind.

The reports of the Pensions Commission are indispensable for an understanding of the dimensions of the pensions crisis.

Online resources

Test your understanding of this chapter with online questions and answers, explore the subject further through web exercises, and use the weblinks to provide a quick resource for further research. Go to the Online Resource Centre at

www.oxfordtextbooks.co.uk/orc/wetherly_otter/

www.cipd.co.uk

www.civilservice.gov.uk/diversity/balance/

www.dti.gov.uk/employment/workandfamilies/flexible-working/

www.employersforwork-lifebalance.org.uk

www.eoc.org.uk

www.flexibility.co.uk

www.pcs.org.uk/WorkLifeBalance/

www.tuc.org.uk/work_life/

www.unison.org.uk/worklifebalance/

www.w-lb.org.uk

www.pensionscommission.org.uk

References

Blunsdon, B., Blyton, P., Reed, K. and Dastmalchian, A. (2006) Introduction: work, life and the work–life issue, in P. Blyton, B. Blunsdon, K. Reed and A. Dastamalchian (eds), *Work–Life Integration: International Perspectives on Managing Multiple Roles* (Basingstoke: Palgrave Macmillan), 1–16.

Chartered Institute of Personnel and Development (2006) *Recruitment, Retention and Turnover: Annual Survey Report* (London: CIPD).

Clutterbuck, D. (2003) *Managing Work–Life Balance: a Guide for HR in Achieving Organizational and Individual Change* (London: CIPD).

Davies, A. C. L. (2004) *Perspectives on Labour Law* (Cambridge: Cambridge University Press).

Driver, S. and Martell, L. (2006) *New Labour* (Cambridge: Polity).

Frogner, M. L. (2002) 'Skills shortages', Labour Market Trends, January.

Gambles, R., Lewis, S. and Rapoport, R. (2006) *The Myth of the Work–Life Balance. The Challenge of Our Time for Men, Women and Societies* (Chichester: John Wiley).

Green, F. (2006) *Demanding Work* (New Jersey: Princeton University Press).

Gregg, P. and Wadsworth, J. (1999) Job tenure 1975–1998, in P. Gregg and J. Wadsworth (eds), *The State of Working Britain* (Manchester: Manchester University Press).

Guillemard, A-M. (2001) Work or retirement at career's end?, in A. Giddens (ed.) *The Global Third Way Debate* (Cambridge: Polity).

IDS (2000) 24 hour society, IDS Focus 93, Spring (London: Incomes Data Services).

IRS (2002) Hanging in the balance, Employment Review, 766 (London: Industrial Relations Services).

Jones, F., Westman, M. and Burke, R. (2006) *Work–Life Balance: a Psychological Perspective* (Hove: Psychology Press).

Kersley, B., Alpin, C., Forth, J., Bryson, A., Bewley, H., Dix, G. and Oxenbridge, S. (2006) *Inside the Workplace: Findings from the 2004 Workplace Employment Relations Survey* (Abingdon: Routledge).

Mahony, C. (2000) Ward winners, *People Management*, 28 September: 36–8.

National Statistics (2006a) *Social Trends* (London: HMSO).

National Statistics (2006b) *Labour Market Review* (London: HMSO).

Rana, E. (2002) How does it really work in practice?, *People Management Supplement—Guide to Work–Life Balance*, 26 September 2006.

Taylor, R. (2001) The Future of Employment Relations, ESRC Future of Work Seminar Series.

Europe: an ever-closer union of member states?

Roger Henderson and Stratis Koutsoukos

Contents

09

Learning objectives

When you have completed this chapter you will be able to:

- Understand the institutional and policy-making framework of the European Union (EU) including the European Parliament, Commission, Council and Central Bank and their significance to modern business operations

- Analyse the differing forms of economic integration relevant to EU development and issues arising from successive enlargements

- Explain the recent development of **European Monetary Union** and the impact of the euro on the EU business environment

- Understand the key issues arising from the **EU budget**, including the developing changes to the pattern of contributions and expenditure and explain their significance for selected sectors and regions

- Use case study and scenario approaches to analyse selected key EU industries including the car and airline sectors

Themes

Diversity	**Diversity of business**
	The European Union is host to a variety of public and private organizations in terms of their organizational structure, product-market scope, size, national and corporate culture.
Internal/ external	**Internal/external**
	Diverse European cultures impact on the environment of businesses, for example internally corporate structures need to respond to operating across European boundaries and markets while externally EU policies, for example in regulation or transport, affect their competitive context.
Complexity	**Complexity of the environment**
	The European market is highly competitive and innovative while the policy framework on which the EU operates is in a constant state of flux. For example, regulatory shifts in areas such as competition, agriculture or financial services policy mean businesses have to re-evaluate constantly their strategies within this complex, evolving environment.
Spatial levels	**Variety of spatial levels**
	EU policies at various levels have impacts on business, whether a conflict between national and EU policy over exchange rates and monetary policy, or issues relating to **regional policy** shifts, or local investment decisions.
Dynamic	**Dynamic environment**
	The chapter examines the dynamics of change in the EU, especially in terms of whether the EU is moving towards a deeper or wider integration among its member states.

Interaction	Interaction between business and the environment
	Interaction is an emerging theme following the adoption of the **Lisbon Agenda** to promote innovation, employment and dynamism in the EU.

Stakeholders	Stakeholders
	European businesses face particular stakeholder issues. In addition to the normal range of interested parties linked to ownership, supply chains, finance and consumption of their products and services, interaction within the EU occurs with trade groups, lobbyists, the European Parliament and Commission.

Values	Values
	Businesses operating in Europe must understand and manage ethical and cultural issues arising from the diversity of a union of twenty-seven nations and changes to regional and cohesion policies.

Introduction: the EU and its members

Internal/external

The European Union (EU) is at a critical stage of its development and this chapter seeks to evaluate business and decision-making in this context. There is a significant impact on business strategies and operations of the policies designed, and decisions taken, by European institutions in areas such as competition, the environment, monetary and fiscal affairs, regional development and enlargement.

Within the euro-zone alone, trade and foreign investment have grown significantly in a market of 300 million people sharing a single currency. However, the advent of the euro is just one of several important processes shaping the EU. Others include: enlargement; integration through the single market; standardization of rules and regulations; deregulation of vital sectors such as telecoms, transport, financial services and energy; and globalization. As one of the three major international trading 'blocs', the EU is a vital force on the world stage. It is therefore important that individuals wishing to pursue business careers, wherever they are based, understand how the EU works and the tensions and policy issues it faces.

Members and treaties

Complexity

Stakeholders

The modern history of western Europe covers two contrasting periods of the 20th century. The first half was plagued by the horrors of two World Wars and national fervour; the second half attempts to build the peace through economic and social integration. In attempting the latter there has been a lively debate about how best to achieve this. At the heart of this debate has been the broad ideological divide between those who see the EU as providing a means of expanding the free market and those who see the need for structural economic and political interventions if this is actually to be achieved in practice. Furthermore, key members have sought different outcomes from participation in the European Economic Community (EEC) and later European Union (EU). For example, Germany, for many years the dominant power is seen as favouring a *federalist*, long-term and politically-integrated Europe. A federalist Europe would mean that the institutions of the EU would have a wider range of power to determine policies which would then become binding on the individual countries. France is often perceived as being implicitly protectionist, for example, seeing the EU as a means of giving help to its agricultural sector and with a particular focus on preserving the Common Agricultural Policy. Spain has wanted cohesion and funding

Table 9.1 EU members

1958	1973	1981	1986	1995	2004	2007
Belgium	Denmark	Greece	Portugal	Austria	Cyprus	Bulgaria
France	Ireland		Spain	Finland	Czech Republic	Romania
Germany	UK			Sweden	Estonia	
Italy					Hungary	
Luxembourg					Latvia	
Netherlands					Lithuania	
					Malta	
					Poland	
					Slovakia	
					Slovenia	

support for the southern states while the Italians have desired improved governance. The British sought a loose union; an anti-federalist, free trade, 'cafeteria' approach in which they could choose the policies that suited them. The new eastern accession states see membership as a means to overcome the legacy of centrally-planned Communist rule and embark on sustained development. Thus, although the EU represents a partnership of twenty-seven sovereign nations (Table 9.1), it contains a diverse set of countries with differing aspirations that complicate decision-making and the achievement of consensus.

The modern EU is based on treaties agreed by member governments and ultimately their electorates. Once agreed, the treaties form the 'EU club' rules and the foundation for everything the EU undertakes. In drafting the original Treaty of Rome the European Economic Community (EEC) was charged with:

> Establishing a common market and progressively approximating the economic policies of the Member States, to promote throughout the Community a harmonious development of economic activities, a continuous and balanced expansion, an increase in stability, an accelerated rise in the standard of living and closer relations between the states belonging to it.

The key **European treaties** are:

- 1951   Treaty of Paris—European Coal and Steel Community (ECSC)
- 1958   Treaties of Rome—European Economic Community (EEC) and European Atomic Energy Community (Euratom)
- 1986   Single European Act—Single Market creation
- 1992   Treaty of Maastricht—European Union (EU)
- 1997   Treaty of Amsterdam—amended EEC treaty and paved way for completion of the Single Market
- 2001   Treaty of Nice—amended earlier treaties and streamlined the EU's institutional system
- 2004   Treaty of Rome—the Constitution for Europe
  (The text of these treaties can be found at http://europa.eu)

Under the treaties the EU members delegate some national sovereignty to shared institutions representing their collective interest. The treaties represent 'primary' legislation, from which derive regulations, directives and recommendations. These laws and EU policies generally result from discussions involving the institutional triangle, comprising the Council of the EU, the European Parliament and the European Commission. This institutional triangle only functions effectively with mutual cooperation and trust.

EU expansion and challenges from globalization and terrorism led the member nations to consider revising the EU's rules. The outcome was the 2004 Treaty of Rome establishing a Constitution for Europe. This consolidates and simplifies existing treaties, clarifies the powers of members and sets out to modernize the EU's institutions and streamline its decision-making. It proposes the creation of posts of full-time president of the EU Council and a new EU foreign minister heading a new European Diplomatic Service. The Constitution also enshrines a Charter of Fundamental Rights. National parliaments would check whether proposed new laws could be better implemented at national level and decision-making would be easier via the removal of the national veto in some areas, with more qualified majority voting on asylum, immigration and criminal law issues. However, the EU Constitution will only be implemented if ratified by all member nations, a process that may take several years and amendments, especially as the Dutch and French have rejected it so far.

> ⟴ *Stop and Think*
> Explain what is meant by saying that the EU is a treaty-based framework.

Institutions and decision-making

Council of Ministers of the European Union

The Council of Ministers, 'the Council', consists of ministers from each member state, who vary with the subject under discussion. Hence, transport ministers attend transport-related discussions, etc. It is the champion of national interests with a six-monthly rotating 'presidency' held by each member state in turn. European 'summits' involve heads of state, governments of the member states and the president of the commission and occur twice yearly. The Council has a decisive role in legislation, acting in co-decision making with the parliament. Following the Amsterdam Treaty most legislative decisions are taken by qualified majority voting with unanimity required in a few areas.

European Parliament

Following eastern enlargement the European Parliament (EP) has 785 members, elected for a five year term. It is the champion of the interests of the EU people and its roles are to: approve the member states' choice of president of the EC and endorse the appointment of commissioners; amend and adopt the community budget; amend and approve legislative proposals in co-decision with the Council; and investigate complaints of maladministration in other institutions. With EU decision-making increasingly decided by members of the European Parliament (MEPs), the EP has acquired almost equal legislative powers with the Council, using its position to delay reports or extract concessions from the commission or Council.

The European flag, among others, in front of the Berlaymont building in Brussels, the home of the European Commission.

© istockphoto.com/Franky De Meyer

European Commission

The European Commission is in effect the European civil service and champion of integration. It is responsible for: initiating and drafting legislative proposals; formulating policy; implementing decisions taken by the Council of Ministers and the European Parliament; administering the EU's various funds; and monitoring law implemented by the member states.

Increasingly the EC focuses less on legislation and more on encouraging the member states to align their own policies to common guidelines. The commission comprises 27 members; a president and 26 commissioners, known as the College of Commissioners, nominated by member states. The whole commission must be approved by the EP, an issue in 2004 when President Barroso was forced to reshuffle his proposed team. The main part of the commission comprises 37 departments, or directorates-general (DG) responsible for policy areas.

The Council of Ministers is generally perceived as the most influential decision-making body tasked with approving EU laws. The European Parliament monitors laws and the other bodies and is gradually assuming a higher profile. The European Commission is effectively the civil service or administrative arm which proposes new laws for the Council and parliament to consider. These three institutions work together to formulate policies, the most important of which include:

- enabling businesses and people to trade and work freely (trade, industry policies)
- creating an area of freedom, security and justice across the EU (security policy)
- helping poorer regions (regional policy)
- improving the environment (environmental policy)
- supporting EU agriculture (common agricultural policy)
- giving the EU a stronger global voice (external policy)
- helping nations coordinate their policies to boost growth, stability and employment and the single currency (macroeconomic and euro policies).

> *Stop and Think*
> With reference to the main three EU institutions, where does the balance of power lie and why?

Integration, trade and cultural considerations

Since 1950 world trade has multiplied eighteen times, *foreign direct investment (FDI)* twenty-five times, world production has quadrupled and real GDP doubled. The EU now accounts for 20% of world trade and the EU15 (the 15 members as of 1995) is the source of 40% of global FDI and the host to 21%.

A central feature of the EU is that it operates as a *customs union*. A customs union is where a joint external trade policy exists with the imposition of a common external tariff (CET) on non-member imports. Tariffs are taxes that are levied on goods coming into a country or in this case the EU. The customs union shares revenue from this CET as part of the common budget (see Mini-Case 9.1).

A customs union creates trade among its members but diverts it from those excluded. While EU trade has grown substantially, much of this has been internal, namely intra-EU trade (Figure 9.1). In part this is testimony to the success of the EU and the single market in boosting economic integration among the members.

Restricted free trade: customs union to single market

In terms of economic association the EU is evolving from essentially *negative integration*, featuring the removal of barriers to trade characterized by free trade areas and customs unions, to *positive integration*, implying the building of an institutional framework and policy harmonization, as in monetary union.

Spatial levels

Dynamic

Table 9.2 shows a spectrum of economic linkages encompassing ever closer integration. A *free trade area* such as the European Free Trade Area (EFTA) that covered countries including Austria, Iceland, Sweden, Norway, Finland and Switzerland extends preferential tariff treatment to all members. It is a loose association in which members eliminate trade barriers between themselves but retain their own trade policies with respect to outsiders.

Mini-Case 9.1 High-cost trainers in the UK

Assume UK footwear manufacturers produce trainers for domestic consumption that retail at £60 per pair. In Spain these shoes can be produced and delivered to the UK for £40 but when the UK imposes a £25 tariff on such imports, Spain cannot compete effectively. If, however, the UK and Spain become part of a customs union and abolish all trade barriers between them, UK shoe imports from Spain will increase and to the extent that this replaces expensive UK production it will contribute to *'trade creation'*.

However, suppose China can produce and ship trainers to the UK for £30 per pair. Before the customs union China sold trainers to the UK for £55 (£30 + £25 tariff) but the tariff reduction only applies to Spain. Thus Spanish trainers also replace UK imports from China. Since China is a lower cost producer than Spain, this part of the increased Spanish exports is *'trade diversion'*.

Figure 9.1 Intra- and extra-EU trade

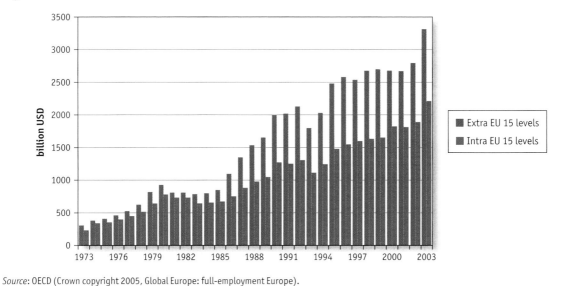

Source: OECD (Crown copyright 2005, Global Europe: full-employment Europe).

Table 9.2 Different types of economic integration

	No internal trade barriers	Common external tariff	Factor and asset mobility	Common currency	Common economic policy
Free trade area	✓				
Customs union	✓	✓			
Single market	✓	✓	✓		
Monetary union	✓	✓	✓	✓	
Economic union	✓	✓	✓	✓	✓

Increasing interdependence can generate common policies as in a customs union. The EU is a customs union but following the introduction of the single market campaign has evolved into a *common or single market*. This abolishes all trade barriers—not just tariffs but non-tariff barriers (NTBs) and mobility restrictions, embracing the free movement of:

- *Goods*—consumers and companies can buy and sell their products anywhere in member states
- *People*—individuals are free to move and work within the EU, however complete abandonment of internal borders has been interpreted differently among member nations
- *Capital*—seen as facilitating the free movement of people, services and goods
- *Services*—encompasses both the freedom to establish a business and the right to offer services in another member state. Some sectors such as banking, transport and insurance which have special regulatory demands have been excluded for separate consideration.

The intention of the EU then is to create a free market across and within the borders of its members but in reality the single market is still 'work-in-progress'. Differences in value added tax

(VAT) rates and regulations remain, cross-border shopping is limited, national governments still prefer to use domestic suppliers for goods and services, labour is far from geographically mobile, and differences in technical standards persist, e.g. for TVs, plugs, modems, faxes, etc.

Moreover, progress is still required in key policy areas to liberalize industries and markets, especially among public interest services. For example, the EU requires a common transport policy to enhance mobility. Hence, rail and air transport need greater harmonization of standards and technical systems whether railway tracks or air traffic controls. A fundamental tenet of the EU model of society is public access to basic, affordable services such as water, electricity, medical provision, gas, etc. Hence the single market programme has shifted focus to promote competition among services previously the preserve of national providers.

> ⮌ *Stop and Think*
> List three examples of how businesses might have benefited from an integrated internal market.

Higher level integration

An even higher order of integration is European Monetary Union and thirteen members of the EU have participated in this since 2000. The monetary systems of participating nations are based upon a common currency, the euro. Euro-zone membership requires policy coordination via a common monetary policy.

Ultimately economic integration may involve *economic (and monetary) union*, implying macroeconomic policy coordination, including both fiscal and monetary policy. Members forego economic independence and a central, federal government dominates macroeconomic policy-making, although some devolution may exist. Currently the EU is some way from full economic union as members retain fiscal sovereignty.

Integration is thus wide in scope and while depicted here in economic terms, political will is also required as progressive interdependence requires the release of ever more sovereignty over domestic decision-making.

EU trade in a global business context

There exists a potential conflict between the expansion of trade in the regional economic blocs, such as the EU, the North American Free Trade Area (NAFTA) and the Asia-Pacific Economic Cooperation Area (APEC) and the expansion of global trade. Regional integration can complement this but should not be at the expense of wider cooperation and trade liberalization. Figure 9.2 illustrates that globalization has become a real challenge for the EU with the arrival of India and China as global trading forces.

China's trade is doubling every three years, while India has shown dramatic growth in services exports. Moreover flows of capital are increasingly global, spurred on by a relaxation of capital controls and financial sector liberalization. Such impacts change the context of European integration; a Europe whose initial goals were internal integration and harmonization, must now adapt to the global economy.

Cultural diversity and business implications

Chapter 5 showed us that culture is the glue that binds a society together; it is about people and their behaviour stemming from their backgrounds, group affiliation, values and practices. Cultural traits derive from various factors, such as: language, social organization, the law, religion, education and political ideology.

Diversity

Figure 9.2 Europe's declining share of global output (in purchasing power parity terms)

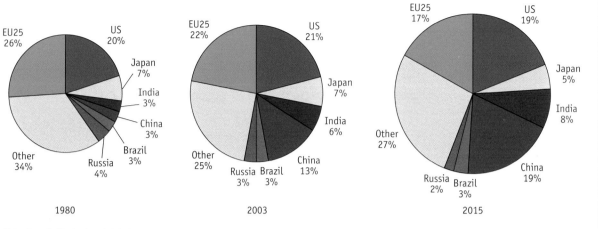

1980   2003   2015

Note: Areas indicate size of global economy.
Source: IMF, Consensus Forecast, HM Treasury (Crown copyright 2005, Global Europe: full-employment Europe).

Europeans share a common heritage but cultural diversity, such that the integration and administration of an enlarged EU comprising 450 million people is an enormous task. At a basic level, there is no single European language and relatively few people can follow a conversation in a language other than their own.

For businesses such cultural aspects impinge on decisions to take a pan-European perspective, treating Europe as a relatively uniform market, or targeting nation-specific or cultural groups. If the latter the diversity of the EU might suggest groupings such as the following:

- Anglo   UK, Ireland
- Baltic   Finland, Sweden, Denmark, Estonia, Lithuania, Latvia
- Mediterranean   France, Spain, Portugal, Italy, Greece, Cyprus, Malta
- Germanic/N. European   Austria, Germany, Benelux
- Central European   Poland, Czech Rep, Hungary, Slovakia, Slovenia, Bulgaria, Romania

> **⊃ Stop and Think**
>
> What other cultural groupings might apply—by history, religion, language, ethnicity?
>
> What are the main cultural and globalization challenges facing companies operating in the new Europe?

The euro and business

Dynamic

Interaction

In this section we will look at macroeconomic aspects of European Monetary Union (EMU) and we will provide a framework to consider the single currency and its strategic and operational implications for businesses.

Exchange rates and the euro

European Monetary Union (EMU) represents a remarkable achievement. Only ten years elapsed between the Treaty of Maastricht which laid the foundations for the single currency and the 2002 introduction of euro notes and coins in twelve nations. The euro has replaced thirteen individual currencies (Slovenia joined in January 2007) that were long-standing instruments, and crucially, symbols of national identities. People now travel and trade across large swathes of Europe using a single currency.

The decision to do away with individual currencies and adopt a common currency is intimately tied to the arguments over whether it is better for the exchange rate of a country to float freely and be determined by market forces (broadly a neoclassical view) or whether it is better for governments to intervene and fix the external value of the currency by having 'fixed' exchange rates (a structuralist view). The adoption of EMU is the extreme version of this. No longer do you need to swap your currency for that of another's if you wish to trade. You simply use the same common currency.

Floating rates offer autonomy to nations (so called economic sovereignty). If, for example the UK was to find that as a result of a decline in competitiveness compared to other countries it was seeing its exports declining it could allow its currency to float downwards in value. This drop in the exchange rate would mean that people abroad could now buy goods valued in the weaker pound more cheaply. The floating exchange rate thus 'disguises' the short-term loss in competitiveness and might allow the government the breathing space to address the underlying competitive weakness.

The problem is that in reality exchange rates are very volatile especially as a result of speculation on the international money markets. This volatility can increase business risk. Mini-Case 9.2 illustrates a potential problem for UK firms of not joining the Euro zone.

To avoid this damaging uncertainty which might deter businesses from 'getting their fingers burned' in this way by trading there is a strong case for fixed rates and ultimately having a common currency. Fixed rates though require cooperation between authorities over the chosen rates and economic policies to sustain them. However, collective action diminishes the individual nation's sovereignty over domestic policy. In practice most systems tried prior to the euro were hybrids, e.g. 'dirty floats' whereby governments manage their currencies between implicit or explicit margins, or semi-fixed systems such as the European Monetary System (EMS), the latter with fixed but adjustable rates.

With the advent of the single market programme, it became clear that transaction costs linked to currency conversion and high risk premia associated with exchange rate fluctuations would hinder realization of the internal market potential. Hence a three stage approach (Mini-Case 9.3) was formulated for the introduction of a single currency, enshrined in the 1992 Maastricht Treaty.

Central to the introduction of the euro was the need to avoid destabilizing inflation that undermines competition, confidence and purchasing power. Accordingly, an independent European Central Bank (ECB) was formed in 1998 tasked with controlling interest rates to effect monetary policy; mainly interpreted as a 'year on year' increase in the Harmonized Index of Consumer Prices (HICP) of less than 2%. During 1997 the European Council adopted three supporting resolutions covering:

- economic growth—to ensure that employment was a key objective
- economic coordination—closer ties between members to embrace financial, budgetary, social and fiscal policies
- Stability and Growth Pact—a commitment to budgetary discipline.

 Mini-Case 9.2   Euro exposure—the case of a northern chemical company

In September 1999 a small, northern chemicals company sold £100,000 of chemicals to a Spanish customer which quoted a euro price of €146,000 at an equivalent rate of £1 = €1.46. The customer subsequently ordered and paid, having been given the *sterling* account details for the chemical company by one of its employees unaware that the company had opened a *euro* account. On completion the exchange rate had moved to £1 = €1.68 so the €146,000 only produced £86,904.76, a 'loss' of £13,095.24 on the expected sum.

Mini-Case 9.3 **The stages of European Monetary Union (EMU)**

EMU Stage 1: 'Convergence'—July 1990–1994

Stage 1 involved measures to progress economic convergence including: consolidation of the single market; the removal of physical, technical and fiscal barriers; and a stronger **competition policy**.

Nominal criteria were specified for the convergence of participant nations' economies:

Price stability—the rate of inflation as measured by the Consumer Price Index was not to exceed that of the best performing three nations by more than 1.5%;
Interest rates—long-term interest rate gaps should not exceed that of the best performing member states by more than 2%;
Budget deficit—planned or actual government deficit was not to exceed 3% of GDP (at market prices) under normal circumstances;
Government debt—not to exceed 60% of GDP (at market prices) unless the ratio is sufficiently falling;
Exchange rates—to have maintained membership of the narrow band of the ERM for at least 2 years without 'severe tensions'

(although it should be noted that the ERM effectively collapsed in 1993).

EMU Stage 2: 'Institutional'—Jan 1994–Dec 1998

Stage 2 was a transitional phase to consolidate convergence. It included the development of the European Monetary Institute (EMI) whose roles were: advisory; to strengthen cooperation between national central banks; and to prepare for the euro. National central banks were to become independent of their governments.

EMU Stage 3: 'Euro'—Jan 1999–Feb 2002

Stage 3 marked the birth of the single currency with payment transfers but not cash transactions. A dual currency situation occurred with 'no compulsion, no prohibition', namely the euro could be used but there was no compulsion to do so. Eventually on 1 Jan 2002 euro bank notes and coins were introduced in 12 nations and national currencies were withdrawn by 28 February.

The Stability and Growth Pact set legally binding ceilings of 3% GDP on euro-zone members' budget deficits, a breach of which would incur fines of up to 0.5% of GDP. However, the pact was widely considered too rigid for countries struggling to grow and in March 2005 the rules were relaxed.

The euro launch achieved a long-standing ambition to cement closer integration. During the 1970s and 1980s many EU nations had experienced lost output and high unemployment through an unstable macroeconomic environment featuring high inflation, high interest rates and unsustainable public finances.

Euro performance

Internally in the euro-zone macroeconomic stability has largely been achieved with convergence reducing inflation from 3.4% in April 2001 to 2% in 2006. However, growth has been disappointing; although real GDP peaked at 3.5% p.a. in 2000, there was a protracted slowdown thereafter to rates below 1%. Low consumer demand and failure to improve productivity have contributed but structural factors are also prevalent. Nevertheless, in complementing the effects of the single market, thereby raising competition and business efficiency, EMU consolidated internal trade and encouraged financial market integration.

In judging its *external* performance as a new international currency, the euro began inauspiciously, falling from €1 = $1.1743 on launch in 1999 to €1 = $0.90 by mid-2001. In part this reflected the dollar's strength, fuelled by high US interest rates as well as doubts associated with the 'euro project', uncertain ECB signals, and fiscal problems among some euro-zone members. However, during the period Jan 2002–2005 the euro rose 33% against the dollar to €1.3276, although again this was partly due to the dollar's performance; weaknesses associated with the Enron and WorldCom scandals, terrorist threats and an expanding trade deficit. On the global stage, the euro was quickly accepted as an international currency; by 2003 it accounted for 33% of outstanding international debt securities and 37% of international loans.

UK and the euro

The UK's stance on the euro was publicized in 1997 by the Chancellor of the Exchequer:

> In principle the Government is in favour of UK membership of the EMU. In practice the economic conditions must be right. The determining factor is UK national economic interest and whether the economic case for joining is clear and unambiguous.

A National Changeover Plan was published first in February 1999 but the euro entry decision is subject to a referendum after agreement by parliament that five economic tests are satisfied:

- *Cyclical Convergence*—'Are business cycles and economic structures compatible so that we and others could live comfortably with euro interest rates on a sustainable basis?' [the key test]
- *Flexibility*—'If problems emerge is there sufficient flexibility to deal with them?'
- *Investment*—'Would joining EMU create better conditions for firms making long-term decisions to invest in Britain?'
- *Financial Services*—'What impact would entry to EMU have on the competitive position of the UK's financial services industry, especially the City's wholesale markets?'
- *Growth, Stability and Jobs*—'Will joining EMU promote higher growth, stability and a lasting increase in jobs?' [the 'catch-all' test that can only be passed if all the others are]

Regular supporting studies have evaluated progress but as yet the government is not convinced that there is sufficient sustainable and durable convergence and flexibility to overcome potential difficulties. If and when an entry decision is made, the changeover in theory could take 24–30 months. In practice the time-scale will probably be shortened as the ECB exists, many businesses already trade in euros, and euro notes and coins are familiar to UK citizens travelling abroad. Meanwhile, the government's stance is that businesses and the public sector should actively prepare for the UK to decide whether or not to adopt the euro. Table 9.3 illustrates the main arguments for and against UK adoption of the euro.

> ➲ *Stop and Think*
>
> How do the advantages and disadvantages of the UK moving to the euro compare with those relating to the arguments in favour of fixed versus floating exchange rates?

Table 9.3 Arguments against and for UK entry into EMU

Arguments against UK entry	Arguments for UK entry
UK growth while 'out'	Reduced exchange rate uncertainty
UK interest rates and economic cycle	Reduced transaction costs
Political and sovereignty issues	Improved competitiveness
Question of whether convergence can be sustained	Greater inward investment and trade
Transition costs and disruption	UK integration into Europe
Potential employment costs	Lower interest rates

Euro business strategy and operations

Internal/ external

Irrespective of UK euro acceptance, UK-based companies must cope with the euro as one of several processes shaping the EU, including globalization, harmonization of standards, technological developments and deregulation. Hence, companies need an overall strategic perspective towards Europe.

Three potential strategies are

- *'Minimalist'*—'wait and see'. A low-cost, reactive, 'late adopter' strategy which might at best involve opening a euro bank account;
- *'Transient'*—'to exploit EU ties'. The company takes advantage of the single market, FDI and the English business language and judges the euro over the medium-term, possibly offering euro pricing in the UK;
- *'Euro-zone Convert'*—'a Euro-zone business'. The company takes an 'early adopter', medium- to long-term view and sees the stimuli from price transparency, the Internet and EU growth potential. It converts to a euro environment, e.g. changes its reporting base to euros and possibly relocates its HQ and operating base to the euro-zone.

Companies must assess their own competitive position and the costs of not being in the euro-zone, as indicated in Mini-Case 9.4.

EU strategy requires businesses to integrate decisions in functional areas such as marketing, production, finance and human resourcing. Since the euro makes prices transparent with exchange rates no longer disguising price differences and competition across borders, pricing is particularly critical. In practice, pricing decisions are complex; varying with a host of factors such as product, brand, specifications, VAT, culture and market access.

Other important strategic decisions stem from whether the EU is regarded as one whole market or discrete national markets and niches. Downward price pressure means that businesses must search for more efficient, flexible and lower-cost sources, product convergence and brand rationalization. Existing relationships with trading partners and agents and logistic arrangements may need reviewing to benefit from scale economies and possibly cheaper eastern European sourcing.

Euro-zone entry may allow UK businesses to borrow more cheaply as income streams in euros may offer cheaper borrowing opportunities than in a high-interest rate UK environment. Companies may also feel it prudent to keep some of their assets in the bank in the form of euros. Dealing with the euro's threats and opportunities requires appropriate staff awareness with human resource management strategy linked to marketing, production and distribution.

Thus UK independence from the euro is not the same as UK business independence. A UK-based business dealing wholly in sterling may still suffer a competitive disadvantage if competitors can source more cheaply in the euro-zone. For UK exporters selling into the euro-zone market quoting in the customer's currency offers a potential marketing advantage (Mini-Case 9.5). The

Mini-Case 9.4   The euro and the UK—Nissan and Toyota

Nissan opted to build the new Micra at Sunderland but the price is that suppliers will be paid in euros. Two-thirds of Micra parts will either come from the euro-zone or be 'competitively priced' in euros. The Sunderland plant offered 30% cost reductions and 24-hour working. (reported in *The Times*, 26 January 2001)

'We are in favour of a single currency because the strength of the pound is unpredictable and has caused us losses . . .' (Scott Browley, Toyota, February 2002)

'Expansion (in the UK) is ruled out due to the euro problem' (Shuhei Toyoda, President, Toyota Europe, May 2003)

'I am not concerned by Britain's not being in the euro: whether or not the UK joins euroland is up to the British people . . .' (Fujio Cho, President, Toyota, March 2004)

[Toyota later suggested that future expansion plans included locations outside of the euro-zone, including Russia]

Mini-Case 9.5   GSM Group and the euro

The UK-based GSM Group is a leading European manufacturer of printed labels and nameplates, fascias and die-cut self adhesive parts. It provides printing and adhesive solutions for the automotive and electronics industries offering a single source for label, nameplate or die-cut needs in most materials tolerant of exposure to heat and petrol. The group also provides customized software and engineering support to customers in what is a very cost conscious environment.

As a proactive organization the Group decided to quote a delivered price in the customer's own or preferred currency. Systems were established to allow quotations quickly in euros (and D-Marks during the legacy period) to German and other customers before the local competition. Within its supply strategy framework GSM decided on euro payments, arguing the car industry is influenced by decisions made in major multinationals such as Nissan to incorporate euro usage into their supply chains.

euro, once an idea owned by politicians and banks, has become an everyday reality for millions of Europeans and their businesses.

> ➲ *Stop and Think*
>
> A Japanese manufacturer has production facilities in the UK, but exports 75% of that production to the euro-zone. Explain the likely currency exposures involved and how the manufacturer can reduce its exposure.

Financing the EU: budget issues and challenges from enlargement

Much of the controversy surrounding closer union between member states revolves around EU financing; notably agreeing revenue streams, determining expenditure on specific policies and coping with accusations of mismanagement and inequality.

Spatial levels

Stakeholders

Values

Budget objectives and composition

An EU budget is needed to: fund common policies, balance the gains and losses from the integration process, promote cohesion and the redistribution of wealth and to provide a 'subscription' for the 'EU club'.

The EU budget differs from the annual March exercise conducted by the UK chancellor. Firstly, it is not a tool of demand management and hence the underlying principle is a balanced budget; expenditure is first determined and thereafter matched by revenue. Secondly, although the EU budget represents a significant sum, approximately €100 billion, this is only 1–1.5% of EU GNP, compared to substantially higher proportions in most western nations, for example, 35% of national GNP in the UK.

Revenue and expenditure

European Community financing has evolved over time. Dependence on member states' contributions existed until 1970 when a system of 'own resources' was established, consisting of customs

Figure 9.3 Percentage contributions to the EU budget

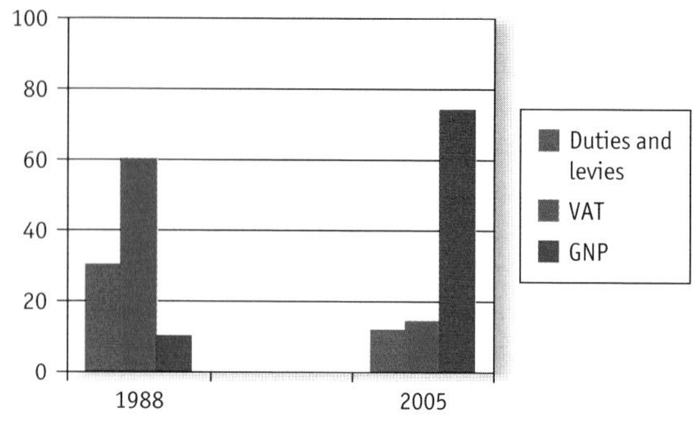

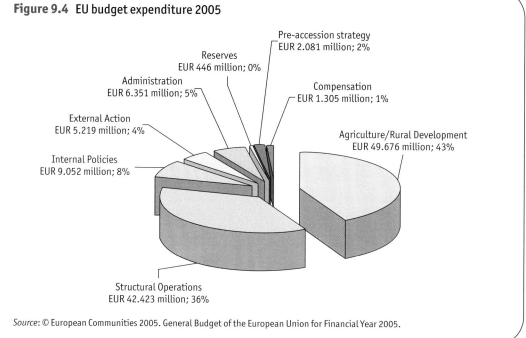

duties on imports into the community based on the Common External Tariff and agricultural levies. Gradually VAT-based elements were introduced based on a notional rate of VAT applied to an identical range of goods in member states. Finally, a fourth resource, or balancing measure, was applied based on the same proportion of GNP in member states (Figure 9.3).

Current revenue derives from four 'own resources', the total amount of which must not exceed 1.24% of gross national product (GNP) of the EU:

- agricultural subsidies/sugar levies (1.5%)
- customs duties (10.1%)
- VAT-based contributions (14.4%)
- GNP-based contributions (74%).

Expenditure dominates the budget and is divided into 'compulsory' and 'non-compulsory' elements: the former refers to obligations under the Treaty of Rome, mainly agricultural expenditure and overseas aid; the latter include the Structural Funds. The breakdown in Figure 9.4 shows that agricultural expenditure (Common Agricultural Policy) still dominates.

Key budget issues and challenges

Not surprisingly there are conflicts over the budget and these can be summarized by four 'I's:

- In-fighting: the politicization of the decision-making process surrounding the budget creates major tensions between the European Parliament and the Council;

Figure 9.4 EU budget expenditure 2005

Pre-accession strategy
EUR 2.081 million; 2%

Reserves
EUR 446 million; 0%

Administration
EUR 6.351 million; 5%

Compensation
EUR 1.305 million; 1%

External Action
EUR 5.219 million; 4%

Agriculture/Rural Development
EUR 49.676 million; 43%

Internal Policies
EUR 9.052 million; 8%

Structural Operations
EUR 42.423 million; 36%

Source: © European Communities 2005. General Budget of the European Union for Financial Year 2005.

Mini-Case 9.6 UK budget rebate

The UK rebate, or abatement, was introduced in 1985. The UK was deemed to contribute disproportionately more than it received from the budget in spite of a poor growth record and low income levels. The imbalance derived from the early EEC when the UK imported large amounts of Commonwealth and non-EEC produce, hence was subject to agricultural levies and import duties. Moreover, since UK citizens spend a high proportion of their income relatively little expenditure went on VAT-exempt goods.

Following hostility over budget contributions and the impending collapse of the CAP, the 1984 Fontainebleau Summit established the principle of corrective adjustment for nations carrying an excessive budgetary burden. The 'Fontainebleau mechanism' involved a rebate of 66% of the difference between the percentage share of the UK's VAT payments and its share of community finance.

By 2005 the UK had become relatively better off and the other largest net contributors (Germany, France and the Netherlands) argued the UK should no longer be subsidized. However, even after the rebate the UK remains a major net contributor. In November 2005, the UK government stated it would only forego part of its €4.6 billion rebate if the budget was 'modernized', implying further CAP reforms.[1]

1 *Financial Times* 17 November 2005, 'Britain plans to compress EU budget talks in effort to secure deal'.

- Inequity: budget contributions, allocations and rebates have caused difficulties between contributor member states;
- Inadequacy: new budget resources have been needed for rapidly increasing expenditure;
- Inefficiency: there have been issues surrounding budgetary controls and fraud.

In-fighting

Setting the budget is a convoluted process involving the joint authority of the European Parliament and the European Council with proposals 'shuttled' between them. The Council has the final say on 'compulsory' expenditure; parliament on other items. Since the 1980s parliament has extended its influence, seeking to increase both the total amount and the share allocated to non-compulsory expenditure. However, tensions have arisen as member states, via the Council, have sought to reduce their contributions and curb what they regard as parliamentary excesses.

Inequity

This refers to nations that are large net contributors relative to their GDP, including the UK (Mini-Case 9.6).

Inadequacy

Budget revenues have struggled to keep pace with expenditure. This is due to: cost escalation in the CAP, accession costs associated with poorer nations such as initially Spain, Portugal, Greece, Ireland and later eastern European nations, the costs of the single market programme, economic downturns and slow growth requiring more support and structural funds, and inefficient and ineffective controls over expenditure and fraud.

Inefficiency

The EU budget has been criticized frequently over the potential for fraud, especially associated with agricultural payments. Although a new independent anti-fraud office exists, difficulties remain with verifying information and legal complexities. Moreover, nation-states are often less diligent than if their own budgets were at stake, thus adding to a culture tolerant of fraud.

The Common Agricultural Policy (CAP)

Since the Treaty of Rome agriculture has been a special case for support, reflecting the need to feed the EU population, the large rural communities and the volatile nature of agricultural product markets the reasons for which we have explored in Chapter 2. The CAP principles are: free movement of agricultural products within the European Union, community preference through the use of protectionism, and cost sharing funded from the EU Budget. Policies have involved both guaranteed minimum price support mechanisms and guidance measures to encourage structural adaptation.

The CAP objectives are to: secure food supplies, raise agricultural productivity, enhance living standards in the agricultural community, stabilize agricultural markets and ensure reasonable prices for consumers. Many of these aims have been achieved, yet the policy has also been criticized for:

- *resource misuse*: market intervention with guaranteed prices creates massive surpluses—butter mountains and wine lakes—with food dumped or sold at heavily subsidized prices on the world market; if farmers are guaranteed prices this encourages them to increase production. The policy successfully increases food supply and farmer incomes but at the cost of unwanted surplus production
- *protectionism*: subsidies to EU farmers and import restrictions keep out competition and create tensions within the World Trade Organization
- *disproportionate cost*: expenses of €40–50 billion per annum
- *inequity*: special support for agriculture is seen as unfair by other EU business sectors
- *environmental harm*: intensive farming led by large agri-businesses is seen as potentially environmentally unsustainable.

Several reforms have been attempted including the 1992 MacSharry Plan which reduced guaranteed prices, restricted the overall CAP budget and favoured direct income support for farmers linked to land 'set-aside' (whereby farmers are paid to take land out of production to reduce surpluses), early retirement and afforestation grants all aimed at reducing agricultural production. Under Agenda 2000 agricultural spending was frozen and emphasis placed on income support, food quality, safety, animal welfare, environmental protection and rural development. In 2002 the Fischler review broke the link between direct subsidies and production. Future payments would be lower and linked to environmental and quality standards with spending focused on broader rural development.

Such reforms are resisted by the large agricultural producers, France and Spain, yet promoted by Germany and the UK. The arrival of new eastern members with substantial agricultural sectors has fuelled debate; hence the CAP is one area where an ever-closer union of EU members is not easily achievable.

> ⊃ *Stop and Think*
> Why does the Common Agricultural Policy (CAP) dominate the budget? What reforms have been and should be made to reduce CAP costs?

Budget reforms

The CAP reforms are part of periodic attempts to amend the EU budget, especially the introduction of medium-term financial perspectives (see Mini-Case 9.7).

The current financial perspective (2007–2013) changes the categories of expenditure (see Table 9.4). Sustainable growth will account for an average expenditure of 46%, broken down 13% on competitiveness and 33% on cohesion. The other major category is preservation and

Mini-Case 9.7 **Financial perspectives 1988–2006**

Delors I—1988–1992

- medium-term approach to provide budgetary discipline
- capped agricultural spending rises to 74% of average GDP growth and doubled the amounts available to the structural funds
- limited the VAT base to 55% of GNP
- introduced a new fourth resource—GNP based contributions.

Delors II—1993–1999

- considered the financial implications of the single market programme
- increased expenditure on structural funds, economic and social cohesion

- raised own resources ceiling to 1.21% GNP (1995)
- uniform VAT rate reduced to 1% and the VAT base lowered from 55–50% in 1999.

Agenda 2000—2000–2006

- to reflect changes in agricultural and structural funds expenditure and enlargement
- budget frozen at 1999 levels (real terms)
- focus shifted from VAT contributions to GNP with ceiling of 1.27% GNP
- agricultural subsidies cut, regional spending reallocated, British rebate retained.

Table 9.4 Overview of the new financial framework 2007–2013

Million € at 2004 prices

COMMITMENT APPROPRIATIONS	2006 (a)	2007	2008	2009	2010	2011	2012	2013	
1. Sustainable growth	47.582	59.675	62.795	65.800	68.235	70.660	73.715	76.785	
1a. Competitiveness for growth and employment	8.791	12.105	14.390	16.680	18.965	21.250	23.540	25.825	
1b. Cohesion for growth and employment (b)	38.791	47.570	48.405	49.120	49.270	49.410	50.175	50.960	
2. Preservation and management of natural resources	56.015	57.180	57.900	58.115	57.980	57.850	57.825	57.805	
of which: Agriculture—Market related expenditure and direct payments	43.735	43.500	43.673	43.354	43.034	42.714	42.506	42.293	
3. Citizenship, freedom, security and justice	1.381	1.630	2.015	2.330	2.645	2.970	3.295	3.620	
4. The EU as a global partner (c)	11.232	11.400	12.175	12.945	13.720	14.495	15.115	15.740	
5. Administration (d)	3.436	3.675	3.815	3.950	4.090	4.225	4.365	4.500	
Compensations	1.041								
Total appropriations for commitments	120.688	133.560	138.700	143.140	146.670	150.200	154.315	158.450	
Total appropriations for payments (b)(c)	114.740	124.600	136.500	127.700	126.000	132.400	138.400	143.100	Average
Appropriations for payments as a percentage of GNI	1.09%	1.15%	1.23%	1.12%	1.08%	1.11%	1.14%	1.15%	1.14%
Margin available	0.15%	0.09%	0.01%	0.12%	0.16%	0.13%	0.10%	0.09%	0.10%
Own resources ceiling as a percentage of GNI	1.24%	1.24%	1.24%	1.24%	1.24%	1.24%	1.24%	1.24%	1.24%

(a) 2006 expenditure under the current financial perspective has been broken down according to the proposed new nomenclature for reference and to facilitate comparisons.
(b) Includes expenditure for the Solidarity Fund (€1 billion in 2004 at current prices) as from 2006. However, corresponding payments are calculated only as from 2007.
(c) The integration of EDF in the EU budget is assumed to take effect in 2008. Commitments for 2006 and 2007 are included only for comparison purposes. Payments on commitments before 2008 are not taken into account in the payment figures.
(d) Includes administrative expenditure for institutions other than the Commission, pensions and European schools. Commission administrative expenditure is integrated in the first four expenditure headings.
Source: European Commission, from *Communication from the Commission to the Council and the European Parliament*: Building our Common Future—Policy challenges and budgetary means of the Enlarged Union 2007–2013.

management of resources amounting to 39.5%. This includes agriculture within a focus on general rural resources.

Regional policy

The funding shift in the 2007–2013 financial perspective reflects greater attention to EU regional policy, notably the structural funds, which now account for around 35% of the EU budget. (See Figure 9.5.) These include the *European Regional Development Fund (ERDF)* used to promote development and encourage industrial diversification in regions that are lagging behind. The convergence regions, previously Objective 1 areas, are those where GDP per capita is below 75% of the EU average. The fund provides basic infrastructure, business and economic activity support for research and innovation, promotion of the information society and sustainable development. Regional competitiveness and employment regions previously referred to as Objective 2 areas require economic and social conversion in industrial, rural, urban or fisheries-dependent areas facing structural difficulties. The *European Social Fund (ESF)* aids the return to the workforce of unemployed and disadvantaged groups.

The UK received €10 billion of structural funds support between 2000–2006 with four areas qualifying for O1 funding (Merseyside, South Yorkshire, Cornwall, West Wales and the Valleys). However, for 2007–2013 regional policy must cope with enlargement which raised the number of O1 eligible regions (with a GDP per capita of less than 75% of the EU average) from 48 to 67. Additionally, 18 regions previously regarded as lagging now suffer from the 'statistical effect' that their GDP per capita rises above the 75% threshold due to the arrival of the accession nations. Moreover, whereas four EU members (Greece, Ireland, Portugal and Spain) were eligible for cohesion fund support (*national* per capita GDP 90% of the EU average), from 2006 all new members became eligible.

To cope with these impacts the commission developed a new structure for EU cohesion policy with three core objectives:

- *Convergence (78% of Structural Funds)*: objective 1 still targets the most deprived regions (under 75% of the EU average GDP), while the 'statistical effect' regions receive transitional financing. The main focus is to support growth and job creation in the least developed member states and regions.

- *Regional Competitiveness and Employment (18%)*: the national component is on employment strategy funded by the ESF with priorities covering: work adaptation, labour supply, and people at a disadvantage. The regional component is funded from the ERDF with priorities for: innovation and the knowledge economy, the environment and risk prevention and accessibility and regional infrastructure.

- *European Territorial Cooperation (4%)*: this covers inter-regional cooperation funded by ERDF aimed at overcoming common problems between neighbouring states including urban, rural and coastal development and the promotion of economic relations and networks.

Enlargement

EU enlargement is not a new concept (see Table 9.1) but in 1993 the European Council set out accession conditions (the 'Copenhagen Criteria'):

- *Political*: stable institutions guaranteeing democracy, the rule of law, respect for and protection of human rights and minorities;

- *Economic*: a functioning market economy and capacity to cope with competitive pressures and market forces within the EU;

Figure 9.5 Regional policy support

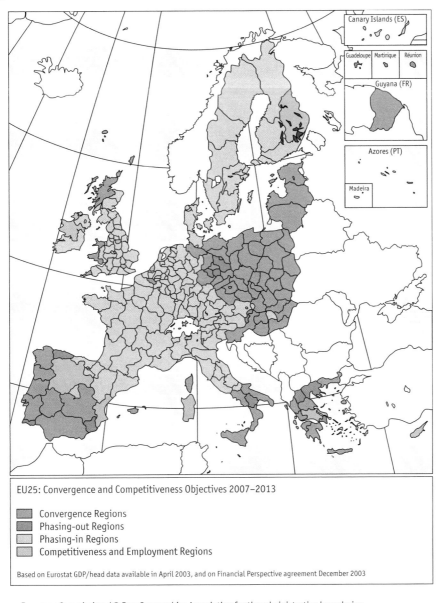

EU25: Convergence and Competitiveness Objectives 2007–2013

- Convergence Regions
- Phasing-out Regions
- Phasing-in Regions
- Competitiveness and Employment Regions

Based on Eurostat GDP/head data available in April 2003, and on Financial Perspective agreement December 2003

Source: European Commission / © EuroGeographics Association for the administrative boundaries.

- *Aquis Communautaire*: the implementation of EU legislation via an appropriate administrative and judicial structure. It implies the ability to assume the obligations of membership, including meeting the aims of political, economic and monetary union.

The precise implications of enlargement remain uncertain (see Table 9.5). General political and social benefits are assumed to flow from the extended zone of peace, stability and prosperity which enhances security, offers political reunification of the EU and links with states to the south and east. Improvements in the quality of life for citizens occur as new members adopt common policies for protection of the environment and the fight against crime, drugs and illegal immigration. New members enrich the EU through increased diversity, the interchange of ideas and better understanding of other peoples.

Table 9.5 Economic advantages and disadvantages of enlargement

Advantages	Disadvantages
Market: enlargement increases the internal market by 20%, raising demand for EU goods	*Budget*: enlargement costs for the financial perspective 2000–2006 were estimated at €40.8 billion
Economic growth: effective 1.5% rise in GDP among new members raises spending power and job growth	*Regional policy*: 'statistical effect' on existing structural fund recipients who lose relative to the new members
Investment: new members offer new FDI opportunities and skilled, but cheaper labour	*Overstated benefits*: many trade and investment effects are due to global forces and restructuring not enlargement
Allocation effects: encourages competition, trade and greater consumer choice and reduces barriers in previously protected markets	*Transition costs*: expense of social, political and economic changes to meet the Copenhagen criteria and balance of payments deficits resulting from 'catch-up' expenditure
Accumulation effects: furthers the process of liberalization in progress since the start of the 1990s	*Uncertain migration*: tensions and costs might arise from widespread migration from the new member states

Enlargement and the UK

For the UK trade links with the 2004 new entrants are minor but growing; having risen by 208% since 1973. The UK is an important market for specific states taking 15–17% of exports from Cyprus, Latvia and Lithuania. While the UK currently invests less than 1% of its total FDI in the new member states, opportunities exist for greenfield investments and privatizations. EU entry reduces the risk premia associated with new entrants and 'locks in' specific attractions, including improved political and macroeconomic stability, a skilled, educated and relatively cheap workforce and opportunities with large infrastructure and regeneration projects.

However, UK firms could lose some markets to manufactures from the new member states where labour costs are lower, although a flood of cheap imports is unlikely because of existing tariff-free access to EU markets. Moreover UK firms compete in tough global markets and not necessarily on labour costs alone. Inward FDI may be lost if new lower-cost entrants become more attractive to aspiring investors and EU growth stalls.

Thus the benefits of enlargement are very dependent on maintaining the momentum for economic reform and liberalization, sound macroeconomic policies and effective use of supporting structural funds to sustain trade and investment.

Doing business in the new Europe

Internal/ external

The Lisbon Summit in 2000 set the following business goals for Europe by 2010 ('the Lisbon Agenda'):

> '. . . that the EU should become the most competitive and dynamic knowledge-based economy in the World, capable of sustained economic growth, with more and better jobs, and greater social cohesion.'

The agenda aims to create an effective internal market with an improved infrastructure and more investment in research and development (R & D) leading to a strong industrial base, characterized by an adaptable workforce, free and fair trade and innovation. To meet these aims the EU requires efficient business-related policies.

Mini-Case 9.8 Car factories drive east

The car industry is the world's largest manufacturing sector, a highly competitive, technologically-advanced assembly industry producing 50 million cars per annum with a vast supply chain. It is vitally important to western Europe where nations such as France and Germany are concerned about 'delocalization' of the industry to eastern Europe.

The Volkswagen Group (VW) led the way in the 1990s buying Skoda and establishing operations in Slovakia and Hungary. Now most new car plants are being built in eastern Europe, such as France's PSA Peugeot-Citroën small car plant in Slovakia and its joint venture with Toyota in the Czech Republic. Hyundai are also building in Slovakia.

The impact on western nations varies. Lower taxes and bureaucracy in the UK have sheltered it from major relocations relative to Germany where union pressures and high wages have influenced domestic giants VW and Opel to look east. The VW group's production facilities in Europe are: UK (Bentley, Cosworth); Belgium; Spain (SEAT); Portugal; Italy (Lamborghini); Poland; Czech Republic (Skoda); Slovakia; Hungary and Bosnia. The Hungarian Gyor plant was originally established to produce a small number of new Audi engines but as the engine became more widely used in the VW group the plant became a major production unit. In this way VW cut its costs without incurring strike action at home.

The car manufacturers deny the eastward shift of production is merely a cost-saving exercise citing labour costs as only one element in a highly automated, technical industry. In reality the market focus of the industry is shifting from saturated western markets to emergent eastern ones. Car registrations in eastern states such as Bulgaria, Czech Republic, Hungary, Poland, Romania, Russia, Slovakia and the Ukraine are expected to grow by 40% to 2010.

❷ Why are most new European car plants now being built in eastern Europe?

A Volkswagen SUV travels by a lift from an assembly line to the test grounds at Slovak Volkswagen plant in Bratislava. The car manufacturers deny the eastward shift of production is merely a cost-saving exercise.

© AFP/Getty Images

Industry policy

EU industrial policy derives from three key treaties: Rome 1958 (article 130); Maastricht 1992 (article 129b); and Amsterdam 1997 (article 157). The intention has been to promote structural adjustment, encourage small- and medium-sized companies, and stimulate innovation. Maastricht also emphasized trans-European network developments in areas of transport, telecommunications and energy.

The main strategies applied are, firstly, the creation of a business environment conducive to developing new technologies and entrepreneurial activity. This includes promoting institutional measures such as venture capital provision, a European patent system and boosting R&D by strengthening links between universities, research organizations and businesses. Secondly, a key

Mini-Case 9.9   The REACH initiative

The 2003 REACH programme stands for the Registration, Evaluation and Authorization of Chemicals and is based on the premise that the growth of chemical substances has been associated with increased allergies and illnesses in the EU. The 2003 policy shifts the onus of testing from governments to the manufacturers involved. Consequently, 30,000 chemicals need to be registered by 2014. The focus will initially fall on the most hazardous items; hence companies must show that the substances they use or manage do not endanger human health or the environment. Extensive testing will be required for some products with broad exemption for low volume, low risk items. The cost is estimated at €5 billion and companies fear a loss of jobs to less-regulated environments in Asia.

Mini-Case 9.10   'What single reform would improve European business?'

In March 2005 the *Financial Times* asked key global business leaders their views on the constraints the EU imposes on their operations. They were asked 'What single reform would improve European business?'

The main responses were: lighter or better regulation; more flexible labour markets; fewer cross-border barriers; a better environment for innovation; liberalization of industries and utilities; speedier execution of decisions; and greater political determination.

Complaints about 'red tape' feature widely; an issue acknowledged by the Barroso Commission struggling to reduce the regulatory burden. The single market aims for free movement of persons yet rigid labour markets exist in countries such as France and there are restrictions of up to 7 years on labour migration from the new member states. At the core of most issues lies political will, especially when it comes to implementing decisions.

B. Groom, 'The Corporate Message to Europe's Leaders', *Financial Times*, 21 March 2005.

focus has been to provide a framework for pan-EU mergers and takeovers via approval of a takeover directive, seen as critical to cementing the single market and enlargement.

Values

However, EU industry policy is a collection of often conflicting programmes. For example, diverse views exist on the benefits of allowing cross-border takeovers, hence debate in the European Parliament has held up the takeover directive. One perspective favours a robust competition policy backed by deregulation to overcome protectionist tendencies that have prevented EU-wide competition. Supporting this approach would be policies to raise productivity in key technologies and clusters involving biotechnology, information technology and creative industries. An alternative view emphasizes restructuring the industrial base with less concern for internal EU competition. This approach takes a more global view, arguing that Europe needs large, efficient businesses competitive with the USA and Far East, such as Airbus Industries in the aviation sector. Such issues are debated at European summits, but there is still reluctance to abandon protectionism as a tool of industrial policy.

For EU business leaders there is often considerable frustration at the policy hurdles faced. They helped to shape the Lisbon Agenda and communicate their views via trade associations, chambers of commerce and the 100,000 plus lobbyists in Brussels, yet struggle to see tangible industrial policy benefits (see Mini-Case 9.10).

Competition policy

EU competition policy follows the neoclassical, free-market philosophy now prevalent in all member states; a liberal-economic vision contrasting with the centrally-planned approach previously experienced by the new eastern members. Competition policy follows articles 81 and 82 of the Treaty of Rome and seeks to ensure the internal market is not distorted. Areas are targeted which hinder efficiency and competitive forces, namely: monopoly, oligopoly, cartels, restrictive practices, subsidies, state procurement and protection. EU competition policy has grown in significance, boosted by the Lisbon 2000 economic reform and competitiveness agenda.

There are broadly five components:

Anti-trust agreements prohibit concerted or restricted practices or agreements among firms that limit competition, unless special circumstances exist to promote technical or economic progress. Enforcement of anti-trust legislation has gathered momentum with actions against cartels covering beer, banking and vitamins, including Hoffman La Roche (vitamins—1979, 2002) and the Austrian banking cartel (2002).

Anti-trust abuse of a dominant position targets monopoly and oligopoly situations where abuse occurs, such as low pricing to eliminate the competition, discriminatory pricing (the charging of different prices for the same commodity) within or between member states, and limits imposed on production, markets or technological development to raise prices and/or profits. The main tests are: a market share of 40% or more; the degree of independence from competitors; the ability to eliminate the competition; or a dominant relationship with suppliers or customers. However, prosecutions are rare, partly because many people feel there is a need for large, globally competitive corporations that are EU and national 'champions'.

Mergers can create or strengthen a dominant position which may lead to abuse. A Merger Regulation was adopted in 1989 (No. 4064/89) which established exclusive commission jurisdiction for mergers between firms with a joint global turnover of €5 billion and within the EU of €250 million each, below which national legislation prevails. During the 1990s the EC became more interventionist and accordingly criticized, for example over prohibition of the GE/Honeywell merger and having decisions overturned by the Court of Justice (Airtours/First Choice; Schneider Electric/Legrand; and Tetra Laval/Sidel). In 2004 a new Merger Regulation (No. 139/2004) placed greater responsibility on firms to assess the impact of any merger or acquisition.

State Aid refers to financial assistance from public funds that distort competition and efficient resource allocation, applying to subsidies, tax breaks, soft loans, preferential procurement and guarantees. Article 87(2,3) of the EC Treaty allows for state aid under circumstances compatible with the internal market, for example, social aid or that given to overcome the effects of natural disasters.

A total ban on state aid is impossible; indeed a fundamental EU tenet is that intervention is necessary for balanced and sustainable economic development. Consequently a history of state aid support exists, notably rescue subsidies for shipping, car, coal and steel industries. These subsidies have been substantially reduced and redirected via regional policy. Despite progress, state aid issues remain, indeed have re-emerged with the accession of former centrally planned economies.

Utilities have been liberalized throughout the EU, boosted by privatization drives and single market reforms. Key sectors are 'network' industries or natural monopolies such as energy, water, postal services, telecommunications, railways and airlines. For years these public interest monopolies were protected but technological developments have exposed operating weaknesses. The commission's liberalization policy based on article 86(3) has created complex packages of directives, restrictive practice and merger case law to open up these areas.

Competition legislation has a special place in EU policy as it defends the collective interest in economic efficiency secured through the single market. Nevertheless, it faces radical challenges.

National competition agencies have grown in stature with often better analytical and legal bases and the European Court of Justice has often expressed concern with DG Competition's interpretations. Moreover, member nations are often reluctant to reduce state support for their companies. The tests will be whether policy can be flexible enough to meet national concerns and link to gains in EU competitiveness and growth required by the Lisbon Agenda.

Mini-Case 9.11   Industry and competition policy and the European airlines

EU economic growth requires an efficient and effective air transport system. There are 280 airports but key hubs are dominated by the large-scale, national 'flag carriers', namely Heathrow (British Airways); Frankfurt (Lufthansa); Paris CDG (Air France/KLM). Overall the European air travel market has grown rapidly—19% between 1998–2001—and in 2002 flag carriers held 72% of the market share (75% in 1998) compared with charters 21% (23%) and low-cost operators 7% (2%). The last-named have expanded since the mid-1990s and now operate out of 120 airports.

Various aspects of industry and competition policy affect this sector: externalities, e.g. environmental costs; protected markets with monopoly and market dominance aspects; state aid supports; factor immobility from structural unemployment in the aviation industry; imperfect information, e.g. pricing and ticket sales; and large-scale merger and acquisition pressures.

Demand is cyclical but more income-elastic for the flag carriers than the low-cost airlines for which relative prices among competing transport modes (e.g. rail) can be influential. The industry's *cost* structure reveals a complex situation with: high fixed costs (planes, facilities); high airport charges (e.g. 20% of Ryannair's operating costs); volatile fuel costs (impact on prices, profits); differing cost structures between flag carriers and low-cost, 'no frills' airlines; and deregulation, liberalization and privatization driving down fares.

The EU airline market has moved from a highly regulated system based on bilateral agreements to a competitive internal market. Prior to 1998 airlines were limited to operating from their national base which restricted mergers. Now any airline holding a valid EU Air Operators Certificate can operate on any market within the EU. Freedom exists to set fares, open new routes and determine capacities. Enlargement nations now belong to the 'Open Skies' Treaty allowing point-to-point service and offering opportunities for the low-cost operators.

Examples of airline companies and competition issues

Alitalia—state aid. The majority state-owned Italian flag carrier was on the verge of bankruptcy in 2005 due to high oil prices, fierce low-cost competition on domestic routes and inefficiencies. In November 2005 complaints were made to the commission about prior state aid to Alitalia and a proposed £400 million bridging loan. To counter these complaints the company sought €1.2 billion in a new equity issue backed by Banca Itesa.

Ryanair—state aid. Founded in 1985 in Ireland, Ryanair grew through heavy marketing and a low-cost, low-price strategy. In 1997 it began flying from Dublin to Charleroi (Belgium) for £79 compared with £179 charged by Aer Lingus (Irish flag carrier). By November 2005 it carried 28 million passengers per annum from 15 bases in 7 countries and had a 23% net profit margin. However, the company has courted controversy with the EU. In 2003, it complained at a rescue package for Belgian airline Sabena, but then Ryanair had to switch from Strasbourg to Baden-Baden when a French court ruled illegal a €1.4 million payment received from Strasbourg Chamber of Commerce for marketing Strasbourg. In 2004 Ryanair denounced the EC when the latter ruled that money given to establish Ryanair's EU base at Charleroi, Belgium constituted illegal aid. The company was forced to repay €4 million to the Walloon regional government.

Air France/KLM—merger. In 2003 these companies announced a merger—one group but two airlines and hubs (Amsterdam, Paris) and three core businesses (passengers 77% revenue; cargo 14%; maintenance 4%). They argued that synergies would arise from: network optimization (226 destinations); asset deployment; and cost savings (maintenance, procurement, sales, distribution, IT and cargo). The merger was approved creating a new operating company, Air France-KLM, conditional upon selling half the French government stake in Air France.

Easyjet/GO—merger. This domestic merger was considered by the UK Office of Fair Trading (OFT) concerned about the over-supply of low-cost routes between the UK and Europe. Subsequent analysis found that leisure and business travellers would still have choice and entry barriers were not high. Consequently the merger was allowed.

❷ Why have low-cost airlines grown in significance within the EU?

❷ Why is state aid a particular problem in the context of the European airline industry?

Europe and the future: ever-closer union or . . . ?

In the future Europe faces major challenges in implementing the Lisbon Agenda and making a success of eastern enlargement. Additional issues relate to deeper integration and smoothing existing relationships, for example, the UK's position on the euro and budget, as well as broader external relations with other trading blocs. In sustaining the 'European model' in a wider context the overall policy issue is how to engage with globalization while mitigating its costs.

The Sapir Report

In 2003 the Sapir Report[2] addressed the wider environment facing the EU and proposed new policy directions consequent upon enlargement. On growth Sapir argued that since the mid-1970s average growth rates had slowed to barely 2% of GDP and 1.7% of GDP per capita, linked to declining productivity growth and diminishing labour utilization. Besides the costs of German reunification, other causes were failures to implement fully the single market programme, reform labour markets and improve labour mobility, and poor responsiveness to global technological change and competition. Stability has been enhanced by low inflation and lower budget deficits but weak growth means several states have not met the 3% deficit ceiling yet need major structural reforms with limited scope for manoeuvre on their macroeconomic policies. Cohesion has occurred at the level of member states; less so on a disaggregated regional basis.

Eastward enlargement adds complexity; large income differentials between the EU-15 and the new entrants require sustained convergence for successful integration. While the new entrants have relatively high levels of human capital, they exhibit a grim legacy of out-dated capital investment, environmental damage and inefficient institutions.

The report recommended a six-point agenda detailing where economic policies could promote sustainable growth and cohesion in the new Europe:

- make the single market more dynamic
- boost investment in knowledge
- improve the macroeconomic framework for EMU
- redesign policies for convergence and restructuring
- achieve greater effectiveness in decision-taking and regulation
- refocus the EU budget.

> **↪ Stop and Think**
> How does globalization challenge the European model of economic development?

Scenarios for 2010

Long-term scenario planning is an important tool for both businesses and nations. In 1997 the European Commission's Forward Studies Unit launched a project *Scenarios Europe 2010*[3] involving scenario planning and brainstorming techniques among experts, civil servants and the commission to generate a set of plausible illustrations of Europe's future.

---

2 A. Sapir et al. (2003).
3 G. Bertrand, A. Michalski and L. Pench (2000).

One such scenario is entitled *Triumphant Markets* in which the early 21st century is seen as a triumph of trade over hostilities, where technology-based productivity fosters market-based, competitive and flexible European economies. Economic indicators such as inflation remain healthy and enterprise flourishes in an open trading environment. Global consensus is reached by the World Trade Organization (WTO), APEC and NAFTA on the market economy model. Europe becomes less reliant on the public sector through implementation of the single market, privatization and reduced state aid and social protection systems. Accordingly the workforce needs to be flexible with adjustable wage costs—low for the non-qualified, very high for top calibre workers. The net result is an emergent poor working class. Budget reforms bring CAP prices into line with world markets and regional policy support is reduced. The focus is on economic integration, enlargement and the euro not political union. In terms of membership the scenario envisages Switzerland, Iceland, Norway, central and eastern Europe, Cyprus and Malta having joined by 2008 with Turkey still negotiating and new candidates emerging in the Ukraine and Belarus. The emergent problems in this scenario are non-military security risks (crime, trafficking, terrorism), concerns with the environment, increasing inequality and exclusion, and changing values as society becomes fragmented, individualistic and the infrastructure suffers from a lack of public investment.

An alternative scenario is deemed *Turbulent Neighbourhoods* in which preoccupation with security requires a European Security Council to combat political instability, regional conflicts,

German border patrol guards search an Afghani national in Neugersdorf, Germany. Under one possible scenario, the eastern borders of Europe could become transit routes for organized crime and illegal immigration.

© Getty Images

terrorism and a 'siege mentality'. The eastern borders are destabilized by turmoil in Russia and the new eastern European members become transit routes for organized crime and illegal immigration. Tensions exist to the south through EU neglect of the Mediterranean neighbours and EU–Turkey relations deteriorate. Such tensions create economic pressures with slow growth, protectionism and a failure to benefit from technological progress, the single market and the euro. The stability pact is circumvented and taxation remains high, while regional inequalities persist.

These are just two among several feasible scenarios and raise issues regarding Europe's future direction, especially in relation to its neighbours and aspiring members.

> **⊙ Stop and Think**
>
> Why are scenarios important for businesses?
>
> What other scenarios are feasible for the EU in addition to those described?

◈ *Looking ahead*

Enlargement is one of the EU's most successful policies and a powerful foreign policy tool. The zone of peace and democracy has been progressively extended and in this 'democratic' sense a closer union of member states exists, stretching from the Atlantic to the eastern Mediterranean, from Lapland to Malta. While geography defines borders, the real Europe is in the mindset of people and businesses, hence enlargement is as much about extending Europe's values and ideals as its boundaries. Nevertheless, an issue is now how large can a sustainable EU become? Bulgaria and Romania followed by Moldova, Ukraine, Turkey, etc.?

The case of Turkey illustrates that further enlargement will widen the geography but also test the core values—liberty, solidarity, tolerance and respect for human rights, democracy and the rule of law.

Fulfilling EU membership goes beyond Treaty requirements to the fundamental philosophy of union. Firstly, there must be a desire for EU membership, something Turkey seems to have whereas Norway and Switzerland do not, even though better placed to meet the accession criteria. Secondly, prospective members must both respect and attain European values—the crucial test for Turkey and former Soviet states. Thirdly, they need to accept and cope with the agreed integration model. Finally, members must share the burden of membership, including the political will to apply EU rules, features the UK has sometimes found difficult.

The 'pick and mix' British perspective is epitomized by the well-worn phrase 'we will join when the time is right' applied to various policies and the EU as a whole. In 1973 the UK joined the EEC, then in 1975 held a referendum on membership. When

Mini-Case 9.12 **Turkey and the EU**

With a relatively young population of 70 million, an export-oriented economy and a developing information society, Turkey's accession has the potential to increase the size and competitiveness of the single market. Elimination of technical and non-technical barriers to trade and adoption by Turkey of EU legislation and standards are gradually increasing competitiveness and product quality. With a services sector constituting 65% of its GDP, a public procurement market of over €30 billion and FDI opportunities, Turkey offers huge potential for European firms.

However, Turkey's standard of living is barely half that of Poland, only 45% of Turkish people of working age have a job, the female employment rate is only 25% and educational standards

are low. The economy has also suffered from high and variable inflation, erratic growth and high levels of public debt.

Economic improvement is a necessary but not sufficient condition for membership. Turkey must prove it can meet the Copenhagen criteria in terms of the rule of law, democracy and respect for human rights. If accepted Turkish entry offers the EU an opportunity to absorb a potentially prosperous, large and overwhelmingly Muslim country which could help to reduce tensions in a divided world.

❓ What are the main the benefits and costs of Turkey joining the EU?

Demonstrators gather in Turkey over joining the EU. There are several economic and political challenges that Turkey needs to overcome before it can fulfil the criteria for EU membership.

© AFP/Getty Images

the EMS was founded in 1979 the UK was not involved, but joined the ERM in 1990 only to leave in 1992. With EMU the UK opted out of stage 3 and is not part of the euro-zone. In 1989 it opted out of the social chapter, which lays down minimum social welfare standards, then under a new government subsequently reversed its position. Not surprisingly, the British are still widely considered 'reluctant Europeans'.

In examining whether or not a closer union of member states exists, the evidence suggests that it has been possible to simultaneously *widen* and *deepen* the EU. Membership has expanded while economic, and to a lesser extent, political integration has strengthened. Sustained peace and prosperity for the general population of Europe contrast starkly with the first half of the 20th century. The success of integration is apparent in that many nations want closer union and increasingly more want to join the European 'club'.

◈ *Summary*

- The EU is a rich, diverse and dynamic environment for businesses. Enlargement of the 'club' from six to twenty-seven members during a fifty year period has added new stakeholders and market opportunities

- Managing this expansion involves complex decision-making based on Treaties and the 'institutional triangle'. Integration has progressed from removing trade barriers to positive progressive building and harmonization of policies, the most significant of which is the experiment with monetary union and the creation of the euro-zone

- The euro is a key building block in the Europeanization process, but challenges national sovereignty at a macroeconomic level and raises strategic questions for firms at the micro-level in terms of markets and pricing, production and financing

- Funding EU development is a key and controversial issue. Gradually, dependence on member states' contributions has been replaced by 'own resources' and a shift from VAT- to GNP-based contributions. Expenditure remains dominated by the CAP in spite of the emerging significance of regional policy

- Doing business in Europe is strongly influenced by the EU policy environment, especially industry and competition policy. These are influenced by the neoclassical, free-market philosophy dominant in member states to enhance the single market and prevent distortion of competitive forces. Key industries such as the utilities, car, telecoms and airlines have all changed radically under such influences

- In attempting to become an ever closer union of member states, Europe faces future challenges in implementing the Lisbon Agenda and making a success of enlargement. Efforts to both deepen and widen integration will create tensions among existing members with differing objectives and require businesses to appreciate different scenarios that may impinge on their operating environment

 Case study: the knowledge economy: Finland and Nokia

During the early 1990s Finland was ill-prepared for EU member-ship, having faced a severe economic recession with unemploy-ment levels of 15% and government debt of 60% GDP. Problems were exacerbated by uncontrolled liberalization of the financial sector and increasing foreign borrowing which over-heated the domestic economy generating high inflation. The collapse of the Soviet Union also destroyed a large portion of an already restricted range of Finnish exports.

A decade later Finland has a strong, diversified economy and is the world's foremost information and communication technology (ICT) specialist country. The transformation is remarkable given that the prior competitiveness of its core forest product industries was maintained by frequent currency devaluations, an option no longer available with transition to the euro. Finland is unique in having refocused its economy so quickly from natural resources to a knowledge-intensive, high value-added industrial base.

At the heart of the transformation lie knowledge and innova-tion. High-technology items now account for 20% of exports compared with 5% in the late 1980s. Research and development (R&D) investment and educational capability have been con-verted into export-led industries aided by a political will to change economic direction. On the supply side the production of new technology-based products and services depends on

Finland has transformed into a strong, diversified economy and is the world's foremost ICT specialist country. Nokia accounted for 25% of Finland's total R&D expenditure and 20% of its exports in 2003.

© istockphoto.com/ Kari Turunen

an educated and trained workforce, while on the demand side innovations require equally sophisticated and participating consumers. Expansion of the Finnish higher education system has complemented economic development; evidenced by the large numbers of researchers relative to other nations. Other factors are strong governance, a social welfare system supporting education, retraining and equality and a national willingness to connect with the outside world.

Since the late 1990s the economic policy focus has shifted towards microeconomic support for innovation, technology facilitation and R&D support. The latter is largely attributable to Nokia which accounted for 25% of Finland's total R&D expenditure and 20% of its exports in 2003. Rarely has one company been responsible for such a fundamental restructuring of an economy.

Nokia was a diversified conglomerate when the early 1990s economic crisis occurred. From a base in forest products, rubber and cables it began developing radio-telephones, electronic voice and data transmission equipment and, from 1976, digital telephony. Nokia's DX 200 digital transfer system became the basis for mobile telephone network developments. During the 1980s the product range was expanded into the telecommunications, consumer electronics and personal computer markets. In 1981 Nordic Mobile Telephony (NMT) was established as the world's first multinational cellular network (1G) and during the decade a common standard (Global System for Mobility-GSM) was developed (2G). By 1991 Nokia had agreements to supply GSM networks in nine countries.

With the onset of recession the company reviewed its strategy divesting non-core activities including paper, rubber, footwear, chemicals, cables, aluminium and television. This left the core focus on telecommunications, aided by the 1991 acquisition of Technophone, then Europe's second largest mobile phone manufacturer. Nokia's series 2100 phone was an instant success; in 1994 target sales were 500,000, actual sales 20 million units. The market for mobiles soared and by 2000 Nokia was the global leader. In 2005 the company had net sales of €34.2 billion and an operating profit of €4.6 billion and of the 58,874 employees, 40% were in Finland and 23% elsewhere in Europe.

The current market is increasingly influenced by data development; convergence of phone, Internet, digital images and computing facilities allowing consumers to perform a variety of communication and entertainment functions. Smaller devices are favoured with complex features and market segmentation is increasingly meeting diverse customer needs. Additionally business users increasingly require connected mobility with e-mail and business applications as standard. To meet these needs Nokia is organized into four business groups: mobile phones; multimedia; enterprise solutions; and networks. These are supported by three horizontal groups; customer and market operations; technology platforms; and research, venturing and business infrastructure. To fund operations its shares are listed on the Helsinki, Stockholm, Frankfurt, Paris and New York stock exchanges.

The company's growth reflects its R&D investment, strategic acquisitions and divestments, as well as astute management. Nokia also benefited from: the availability of educated, skilled manpower left unemployed by the recession; a strong and responsive educational and research environment; and availability of capital to fund ICT developments, including private sector and government venture capital to start new businesses clustered around it. However, success also mirrors the government's foresight to unlock the sector's potential and the responsiveness of the population. This is the sort of flexibility and application that will be needed throughout the EU if the Lisbon growth objectives are to be achieved.

Nokia is now established as the world's largest manufacturer of mobile phones and a leader in mobile and fixed networks. With sales in 130 countries and a leading global brand name, it is one of the European Union's most successful multinational businesses. However, with this status come global pressures. It has R&D centres in eleven countries and production facilities in eight nations, including emerging nations such as India and China.

❷ What characterized the transformation of the Finnish economy?

❷ Why did Nokia change its strategy in the early 1990s?

❷ What lessons does Nokia offer for the future direction of Europe's businesses in a global economy?

❷ What lessons does the Finnish experience offer for other EU nations?

Review and discussion questions

1 Critically assess the argument that the European Union is merely a protectionist trade bloc.

2 Explain how EU firms, or those dealing with the EU, might be able to turn the European Union's cultural diversity into competitive advantage?

3 Examine whether a single currency is necessary for the efficient working of the European single market.

4 Examine why formulating the EU Budget has been such a contentious issue for the EU member states.

5 What are the implications of eastern enlargement for businesses in western Europe?

Assignments

1 Foreign Direct Investment in Europe case study: Select an example of a Japanese company that has entered the European market. Explain the reasons why it chose the country it did and the particular entry strategy. How successful does this appear to have been and what lessons does it offer for indigenous firms?

2 Using a selection of data for a new European member state from www.worldbank.org, prepare a country report for a particular firm considering a foreign market entrance.

3 Select a specific European industrial sector, e.g. cars, telecommunications, etc. and examine restructuring in the industry, e.g. a cross-border merger or acquisition or privatization.

Further reading

De Grauwe, P. (2007) *Economics of Monetary Union*, 7th edn (Oxford: Oxford University Press). A comprehensive evaluation of the costs and benefits of monetary union followed by its present workings covering the ECB, monetary and fiscal policies and the international role of the euro.

Harris, P. and McDonald, F. (2004) *European Business and Marketing*, 2nd edn (London: Sage). An investigation of the

strategic, organizational, marketing and operational features of various companies in the EU.

Jovanovic, M. (2005) *The Economics of European Integration* (Cheltenham: Edward Elgar). The author argues that monetary union and eastern enlargement have amplified existing discrepancies among the member nations. The text looks at the origin, development and potential limits and prospects of the process of European integration by considering the principal EU economic policies and discusses FDI and trans-national corporations.

Tsoukalis, L. (2005) *What Kind of Europe?* (Oxford: Oxford University Press). Argues that European integration is not a politically neutral process and key democratic choices are needed about trade-offs in policy stances for example, between efficiency, stability and equity.

Also:

Creaton, S. (2004) *Ryanair: How a Small Irish Airline Conquered Europe* (London: Aurum Press).

Dahlman, C., Routti, J. and Yla-Anttila, P. (2006) *Finland as a Knowledge Economy* (Washington DC: World Bank).

Department of Trade and Industry (2004) *Trade and Investment Implications of Enlargement*.

EC Com (2005) *Working Together for Growth and Jobs. A New Start for the Lisbon Strategy*.

Wallace, H. and Wallace, W. (2005) *Policy-making in the European Union*. 5th edn (Oxford: Oxford University Press). This is a study of core policy challenges facing the EU and the ways that they are being addressed.

Whittington, R. and Mayer, M. (2002) *The European Corporation* (Oxford: Oxford University Press). This book is based on the Harvard model of strategy and structure of large corporations but with a European focus. It follows the changing strategies and structures of major firms over a forty year period from the 1950s.

EC, *The Community Budget: the Facts in Figures* (Luxembourg) (latest edn).

Henderson, R. (2001) European Central Bank, in *International Encyclopaedia of Business and Management*, ed. M. Warner, 2nd edn, Vol. 3 (Dundee: Thomson), pp. 1821–9.

Rickards, R. (2003) Currency changeover effects on business management in the EU, *European Business Review*, 15(1): 20–4.

Stanek, M. B. (2001) International Monetary Arrangements: the EU and the euro, *European Business Review*, 13(5): 279–91.

 Online resources

Test your understanding of this chapter with online questions and answers, explore the subject further through web exercises, and use the weblinks to provide a quick resource for further research. Go to the Online Resource Centre at

www.oxfordtextbooks.co.uk/orc/ wetherly_otter/

Main EU sites

Europa—EU online http://europa.eu/

Eurostat—EU's Statistical Office http://europa.eu.int/comm/eurostat/

Eur-Lex—EU's portal to Law/Treaties http://europa.eu.int/eur-lex/en/treaties/index.html

European Parliament www.europarl.eu.int

European Sources Online www.europeansources.info

European Central Bank (ECB) www.ecb.int

UK sites

Bank of England www.bankofengland.co.uk

HM Treasury euro issues www.euro.gov.uk

Other

Business Europe www.businesseurope.com

European Voice www.european-voice.com

 References

Bertrand, G., Michalski, A. and Pench, L. (2000) *European Futures: Five Possible Scenarios for 2010* (Cheltenham: Edward Elgar).

Sapir, A. et al. (2003) *An Agenda for a Growing Europe: Making the EU Economic System Deliver*. Report of an Independent High-Level Study Group established by the president of the EC. Mimeo, July, Brussels. Also published as Sapir, A. et al. (2004) *An Agenda for a Growing Europe: The Sapir Report* (Oxford: Oxford University Press).

Business and the changing public sector

Richard Rooke

Contents

Learning objectives

When you have completed this chapter you will be able to:

- Understand the distinctive characteristics of the public sector, and compare it to the private sector of business

- Appreciate that the 'traditional' public sector and welfare state have been challenged by new political and managerial perspectives—often referred to as **new public management**

- Outline the political, economic and social pressures which created challenges for the public sector, opening in the mid 1970s

- Identify the range of competing views about the changing political landscape at the many levels of **governance**

- Explore the political and ethical dilemmas that arise out of public sector reform through case study work

Themes

Diversity	**Diversity of business**
	The 'public sector' is a diverse collection of organizations, changing over time, and meaning different things in different countries. There is a range of delivery mechanisms for public services: public, private and voluntary sectors, and combinations of all of these by means of partnerships.
Internal/ external	**Internal/external**
	This chapter looks at organizational reform within the public sector, driven by changes in the external environment
Complexity	**Complexity of the environment**
	The public sector constitutes an important element of the complex environment of business. Public sector reform is visible both in policy making outcomes and institutional change. The business world now complements public sector services while at the same time being a competitor.
Spatial levels	**Spatial levels**
	Public sector reform at global, national and local level is gathering pace. No longer is the nation-state the only level at which the public sector and the business environment interacts.
Dynamic	**Dynamic environment**
	Change and response to shifting political, social and economic and technological factors will be investigated. We need to differentiate between evolutionary changes, gradual change over time, and the new agendas created by new thinking on public sector management.
Interaction	**Interaction between business and the public sector environment**
	Increasingly the business world interacts with the public sector, often driving change, altering public sector policies and the political environment in which it

works. This is a two-way process and business attitudes also have to be reformulated to fit with the public sector.

Stakeholders

Stakeholders

Stakeholders will be considered as essential drivers of change, in both political and organizational terms.

Values

Values

These reforms have created fears that the old public sector 'ethos' or values are being lost. The use of market techniques and alternative providers raises questions about accountability, equality and justice.

Introduction

This chapter explores a new phenomenon: the creation of what is known as 'new public management', leaving behind what was often assumed to be a well established public sector 'ethos'. What the latter actually meant in quantifiable terms is not clear, but is more akin to a culture that separated the public sector authorities from the private sector. As a brief introduction we can review this change under the following subheadings:

The public and the private sectors

Traditionally, the divide between the public and the private sectors was organizational, ideological and one of different management styles. They performed in response to different political and economic agendas (see also Chapter 1).

Values

Public interest

The public sector saw itself as the bastion of the public interest, responding to social concerns, and driven by ethical considerations. Parliament and town hall were seen as the fulcrum on which society rested. It therefore often defined itself according to a political agenda rather than seeing itself as a managed business-type organization. It set itself apart from the private sector to work for the public—the community—for justice and not for profit. Its stakeholders therefore were described as 'society' in general rather than the more specialized 'owners', or 'consumers' or even shareholders in capitalist business. As such then the private sector was merely a section of society related to business and business alone.

Interaction

Public ownership

Importantly, this was all held together, by 'ownership'. The public sector in all its forms—buildings, services, personnel, finance—was 'owned' by the public, by the state, the government (local or national) and not private-sector individuals or companies. The private sector was owned by individuals, shareholders, finance houses and banks.

Stakeholders

Public services

There were traditional differences regarding how services were to be provided. Public institutions within this welfare state 'ethos' were driven not by a charge or price on their individual services or goods, but by decisions related to social need. As a public concern, it was therefore mainly financed by forms of taxation, and provision was based on need rather than ability to pay.

Values

> **⮑ Stop and Think**
> *The public and the private*
>
> Can you make a distinction between your public side and your private world? How do you define your terms? Is the definition political, or social, or legal? Perhaps it is all three?
>
> In your own lives, does it matter who controls you? Does it matter whether the 'boss' or the 'owner' represents a public sector organization or a private company? In thinking this through you are looking at the present-day debate about how to mix the public and private sectors.

The present era

Dynamic

In the present era, however, both positions—public and private—are increasingly contested. There has been a blurring of distinctions between the two. The public sector now acts under new rules and new thinking. This is something that the business community must learn to appreciate. This is not only important for ethical or workplace concerns, like equal opportunities, or tackling discrimination, but also for the financial rules and controls on contracting and auditing.

Interaction

The public sector in modern developed societies is a major economic player. Successful 'public' projects are seen as a major opportunity for private business, especially in building and services such as consulting, health, transport and managing information services (IT).

At the same time, creating contracts between the private and the public sectors over financing (for example public finance initiatives, public–private partnerships) and creating in-house forms of competition, even new management styles, now mean the public sector needs to adapt to the skills of the private sector. Certainly, public sector managers need to be more aware of how the private sector works. They need to radically improve their own goods and services. This chapter explores how the public sector management environment has changed and why this is significant.

The political environment and public sector management

Spatial levels

No matter the rhetoric about the coming together of the public and private sectors, there remain substantial differences for those who work in the two sectors. This shows itself in differing management approaches and what used to be referred to as a public sector 'ethos'.

Public servants, even those once removed and working in agencies which are almost semi-autonomous, have different 'controllers' than private sector employees. They have to work through a political framework which contains a set of different criteria compared to the private business environment. They are guided by political values and procedures enshrined in the constitutional and democratic framework.

The 'managers' in the public sector not only have to be aware of effectiveness and performance nowadays, they have to be aware of the political agendas that surround them. For many years environment policy and recycling of waste has had a low profile amongst politicians, but now, politically, it is of the utmost importance for the future.

Although there is a relationship between what they provide and the politics, they must be equally sensitive to the electoral systems and the possible shifts in political thinking. These can alter almost overnight the provision and delivery of their services.

Mini-Case 10.1 The balancing act that is public administration

There are many theories to explain how and why public policy is created. One of the more interesting is known as 'Equilibrium theory' borrowed from economics (see Chapter 2). In this view the working of the public administration system is like balancing various interest groups on a fulcrum. The ultimate purpose of good public administration is keeping the system stable, and managing change by changing policies to fit new circumstances. Diagrammatically it looks like Figure 10.1.

In Figure 10.1, business interests are classically weighed against other interests (see Chapter 11). Often it is assumed that business will demand low taxes and the lowest level of regulation to maintain profit and investment, whereas non-governmental organizations (NGOs) and trade unions might be arguing for the opposite. They are therefore situated on either side of the fulcrum. The role of government, and this varies from one country to another, is to manage (governance) the balance (laws, regulation, political leadership) between these interests. Good governance means maintaining an equilibrium between them and as a result helping to create a stable, performing society. Elections and amended policy agendas from new governments ensure an ongoing correction and political response to any new pressures from the interest groups.

Figure 10.1 Equilibrium model

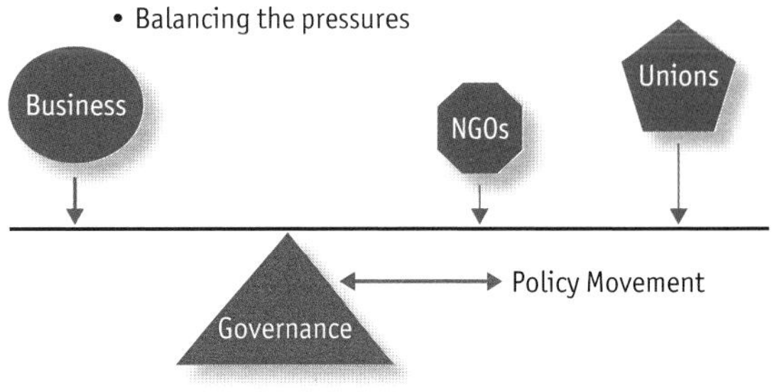

- Balancing the pressures

Business   NGOs   Unions

Governance → Policy Movement

Source: Reprinted from T. R. Dye, *Understanding Public Policy* (11th rev. edn), 2004, based on diagram Figure 2-2 The Group Model, with permission from Elsevier.

❓ Think back to the discussion of the nature of politics in Chapter 4. Is an 'equilibrium' the same thing as a 'messy compromise'? Think about this in relation to reducing and recycling waste (e.g. food packaging).

(*Source*: T. R. Dye (2004) *Understanding Public Policy* (11th rev. edition) New York: Prentice-Hall)

Politics and policy-making

Of course the effectiveness of the services and goods provided by public sector organizations will have an impact on political thinking. If crime rates rise or school examination success rates fall there could be political consequences due to voter dissatisfaction and low approval ratings. For example there may be a change in ministerial responsibilities (a Cabinet 'reshuffle') and/or a shift in policy. Politics is therefore not just about leaders and elections but also about policy-making and these are linked into the political process. So the public sector will always remain a mixture of conflicting pressures—effectiveness (auditing, budgets, costs) *and* politics *and* policy-making.

Complexity

The private sector also has to be aware of the 'politics' and 'policy making', especially economic policy. If private sector businesses are to flourish they too will want to judge the stability and the make-up of the society in which they trade. Yet, compared to the public sector, the private sector will have a narrower political stakeholder base.

Just as different sectors in business act differently, for example service industries are different to manufacturing, public sector managers manage in different environments too. But here again there is a difference. Public sector managers manage at different political levels. In the case above you can see that BT needs to consider the communities it serves but the Department of Health has to be acutely aware of the political power and responsibilities of a host of political 'stakeholders' at different levels. Ultimately BT will answer to its shareholders, and the Department of Health to its ministers and, indirectly, the electorate.

Interaction

Mini-Case 10.2 Stakeholders—public and private

Both public and private sectors refer to their 'stakeholders' and stress the importance of dialogue with them in order to achieve corporate and political success. This does not mean that both private and public sectors prioritize their stakeholders in the same way but there is a convergence nonetheless between the two sides. Key stakeholders for both British Telecoms plc—BT (private) and the UK Department of Health (public) are listed below. Note the differences and the similarities:

Organization	BT plc	Dept of Health (UK)
Examples of stakeholders	Consumers	Patients and public
		Central government and NHS organizations—local and regional
	Shareholders	Local Authorities
	Suppliers	Social Work providers (both public and private)
	Partners (companies)	Charities (legally defined)
	Communities	Voluntary and Community sectors
	Employees	Trade Unions
	Source: BT Stakeholder Dialogue (2005) BT SE report	*Source*: Dept. of Health (2007)

❷ To what extent do private and public sector organizations have to deal with the same range of stakeholder groups?

❷ Can you identify the interests and power of each stakeholder? (For example, do 'consumers' and 'patients' have the same interests and exercise power in the same way?)

Public sector managers will need to understand the different roles of ministers, chief executives, and councillors, otherwise they cannot perform properly. Nowadays too, the private sector must be more aware than before of the complex political environment in which they work, especially when lobbying on their own behalf. In the European Union, for example, policy is made at many levels—the EU institutions, nation-states, regions and even local government agencies.

Central government and local authorities

Spatial levels

Public administration works normally as a relationship between central government and local authorities (or national and local tiers of government). The central government and major departments are located usually in the capital of each country. There may be various layers of sub-national government operating at local or regional levels. These tiers or layers of government all have a relationship to one another.

The nature of this relationship varies between states and through time, especially as regards the division of powers and responsibilities between national and sub-national levels. An important distinction is between unitary and federal constitutions. In a unitary system, such as the UK, power is centralized and the powers of local government are conferred by the centre. Local government is subordinate to national or central government. In federal systems, such as the USA, power is shared.

In the main, the balance of power rests with the central government and its civil service professionals. Management at this level will be different compared to the local, which often constitutes a range of diverse, practical, local needs and concerns.

Political systems

Political systems are not fixed, but can change through a process of constitutional reform. In the UK this has been most obvious because of devolution to Scotland and Wales, on the basis of recognition of their distinct national identities and claims to self-government. Central government, be that at European Union or national level, normally provides a framework through legislation, whereas the detail and implementation of policies is often local or regional (e.g. education policy is set centrally but delivered locally).

Dynamic

There is also a move in the UK to accept some mayoral, city-based political power as represented by the mayor of London and the creation of a GLA (Greater London Assembly). The GLA has power over policies such as fire, sewerage, police and transport.

Managers working within the 'devolved' areas will have diverse agendas, and these will be different again from those of central government and its civil servants. This makes the system complex. There are plans to merge for example the English counties into larger administrative units in the form of regions. There are even regional development agencies (RDAs) across the UK. If full regions are created there will be yet another layer of management-led priorities and tensions.

⮕ Stop and Think

Working at different political levels takes time and knowledge

What if there is an announcement of a new transport policy in your area which affects your business, such as a new railway extension, new parking restrictions, or a tram initiative. To whom do you complain, or lobby for the policy to change?

The planning procedures alone for new initiatives can be lengthy and costly. The impact on the environment, local populations and business can be extensive.

The longest planning enquiry in UK history has been for the Heathrow Terminal 5 project which took 3 years and 10 months to give final government approval for the £4.2bn construction work to begin. Although centrally approved, the project involved up to 13 different local authorities and almost countless interest groups.

Waiting for a plane. The longest planning enquiry in UK history has been the Heathrow Terminal 5 project which took 3 years and 10 months to give final government approval.

© istockphoto.com

Public sector effectiveness

Values

Although the political environment is complex and multifaceted it would be a mistake to assume that it is only of secondary importance for the business world. It is hugely important for economic and political stability. It is a key element of the market and has an enormous impact upon the business community (see Chapter 4).

Interaction

The better the public sector works, the better it is managed, the better it is for the business community, is the general rule. For example, the transport system is an essential concern for moving employees, goods and products. The school and university system is an essential ingredient for creating high value workers.

Interaction

However, there are arguments about public sector effectiveness and debates about which managerial system or style makes it work better. Some argue the 'old' system based on a public-sector 'ethos' was more effective, while others argue for the 'new' management of services based on new leadership techniques, performance management and, perhaps most of all, a new partnership between the private and public sectors.

The public sector is also important in the marketplace because it has great economic 'weight' (as a percentage of GDP) in most modern economies—it is, to put it simply, a 'big spender'. In the UK in 2003/4 total managed expenditure (TME—a measurement of public spending at all levels—central and local) was £460 billion. It had four main priorities in order of economic weight: social protection, National Health Service, education and defence (see Chapter 4 and Figure 10.2).

Figure 10.2 TME: UK

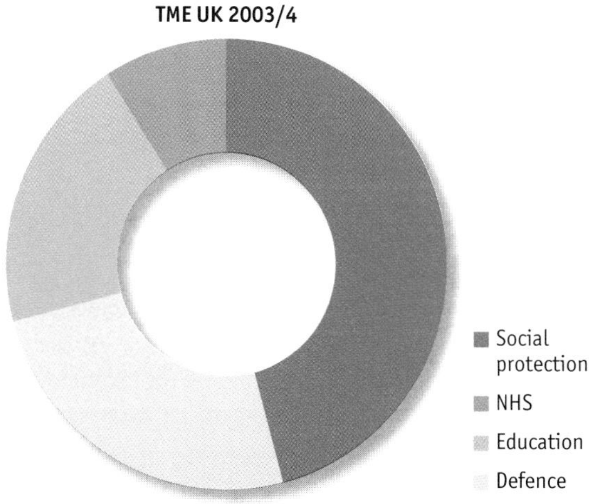

TME UK 2003/4

- ■ Social protection
- ■ NHS
- ▨ Education
- ▢ Defence

Source: P. Cullinane (ed.), *United Kingdom National Accounts: The Blue Book*, National Statistics, 2005.

Mini-Case 10.3 Denmark and France

The development of new public management and the search for 'effectiveness' in public service policy is not restricted to the UK or the Anglo-Saxon world:

Denmark: Over three successive governments since the 1980s Denmark's central and local governments have been both 'modernizing' (new management techniques to include new budget management, decentralization and greater transparency) and creating 'marketization' (setting up competition) which involved contracting-out, consumer choice, privatization and deregulation (Greve, 2006).

France: The debate over French public management continues especially in election years. Their relative decline in overall GDP compared with other similar nations such as the UK has raised questions on the state of the French economy. A fall in GDP per head saw a decline of France from 7th to 17th in the world, and a 'loss of purchasing power' has reinforced the call for new initiatives on downsizing the bureaucracy, reducing taxes, and reforming the state machinery (*The Economist*, October 2006).

❷ To what extent can the movement to effective government value-for-money be seen as a 'global' trend when there are often many different national interpretations of what is meant by being effective? Is it a matter of politics or management competence?

Much of government economic control concerns the TME, getting the balances right. Governments need to build into the economy a working relationship between the public and private sectors which can and will turn to the available capital, finance and tax for its initiatives. Nation states compete to create an environment which encourages business activity and wealth creation, and at the same time preserves social cohesion and political equity.

Interaction

The shift in emphasis since 1979 in Britain and across Europe from the 1980s and 1990s

Since 1979 and through Conservative party dominance up to 1997, but also embracing the new Blair and Brown era of 'New Labour', the basic beliefs of state control and provision have been questioned. The old consensus, and the established bureaucracy that went with it, was reformulated.

Dynamic

Privatization

This led to privatization of public services and the selling-off into the private sector of much of the public housing stock for example. Privatization was the key turning point in creating the future public–private partnerships because it altered the relationship between the two sectors and changed the 'way of thinking' about providing services.

Interaction

It was not just about housing stock, telecommunications and energy supplies but also key elements of welfare provision. The NHS remains as a service free at the point of delivery but new initiatives have moved away from the 'old' model of the state as provider of a health system paid for by tax.

The present era has used new public–private initiatives to build hospitals and manage them. Similarly, new schools have been built by the private sector and to a certain extent even managed by them, breaking the 'old' connections between schools and local authorities. The 'new' Labour

University College London Hospital is the result of a Private Finance Initiative (PFI).

© Reuters/Luke MacGregor

Mini-Case 10.4 Privatization in the UK

The first privatizations in the UK started with the sale of public sector assets, including one million publicly owned houses that were sold in the 'right to buy' scheme. This was followed by a programme of denationalization—e.g. British Telecom—and the setting up of regulatory agencies to monitor the 'new' industries.

Since then, there has been a move toward 'consumer-driven' initiatives, and in-built market mechanisms—or 'quasi markets'—for public sector services.

See: Bishop, Kay and Mayer (eds) (2004) *Privatization and Economic Performance*, OUP.

government from 1997 tried to bridge the gap between the former consensus on welfare provision and the need for 'prudence' in relation to the public finances. At the same time they were still wedded to the need for new ways of creating and effectively providing public services.

New Labour has approved perhaps even more thoroughly than previous administrations the need for correct management of those public services, while encouraging the use of private funding to support the infrastructure of public policy. This has led to many initiatives, often started under the previous Conservative period, new management techniques and public and private finance partnerships (hospital construction, management of vehicles, training establishments).

From the 1970s and especially since the 1980s there have been increased attempts to introduce private business management practice to public policy administration. This has led to privatization, and paradoxically, an increased regulatory control by the state of public policy standards: education, health, police, fire and transport are again notable examples.

New public management

Complexity

What is meant then by 'new public management'? Has the 'old' welfare state and the centralization of governance through the state dwindled? Not quite and not inevitably. The period after the 1970s has seen, across the globe but in Britain especially, the 'old' assumptions challenged and new ways of providing services adopted. The means by which we create and service the 'public good' has altered.

In particular the role of the modern state and its established bureaucracy has been the target of much reform. This reform is targeted at achieving more effective policy-making and a better use of resources. It is this reform that is the 'new' in the 'new public management' ethos as opposed to the 'old'.

Also, and perhaps just as important, the old assumptions about who 'owns' the public sector are being redefined. The state remains legally responsible for providing services based on need (or political pressure defining need) but does not necessarily 'own' the means of provision: the buildings, the people, the 'financing'. These are the two essential elements of the 'new' era.

> ⊃ *Stop and think*
>
> *How do you define the 'new'?*
>
> We tend easily to use the word 'new': a 'new' initiative, a 'new' policy', a 'radically new' way of thinking? Even so, what is meant by 'new' compared to the old? How do we define it so that our analysis of what is going on is helpful to us or our organization or our employers?
>
> In this chapter we have added the concept of a 'new' public management, though it is closer to the truth to talk about a change in emphasis in policy making rather than saying something 'new' has been created. The seeds of change are often implanted in the past. 'New' things evolve over time, and in politics, as in business, this is often the case. Knowing how to define the 'old' helps us define what is 'new' today.

Does that mean that as we have previously known it, the state bureaucracy has decreased in importance? The simple answer is no, but there is some truth in the argument that the state is changing. Its role is leading more toward a position of regulatory power rather than a state-owning, power-centred organization. Or at least in theory.

To understand this argument we have to dip into the process of reform that is not 'new' but based on the past, that is, 'incremental' change. The argument has been made, especially by the British, that the tax burden of the state hinders the inherent dynamic of the economy as a whole. More than this, the public sector often encourages inflexibility and bad management where sectional interests, rather than service to the public, become supreme. In particular, it is argued that public services are 'producer-led' rather than customer focused. As a consequence, the citizen, the customer, the client have all been less than well served. This has been the reasoning behind a whole raft of reforms in the public sector.

Pressure for reform

Although the economy and fiscal policy are important for government, grass-roots social and economic change is also encouraging reform. For example, an ageing population bears on productivity and health policy (see Chapter 5). Part of this problem can be offset by changing immigration or migration rules but this does not solve the essential problem of sustaining economic growth: increasing productivity, balancing public revenues and accelerating the economy. Also the change in technology, and the effects of the so-called new economy, sometimes linked to what is known as the 'information society', are creating their own demands: better trained and skilled students for example.

Dynamic

The effects on nations of all of this are pervasive, often controversial, from demands for greater health improvement for example, but equally a demand for greater flexibility within the workforce: short-term contracting, multiskilling, and greater retraining. This impinges on working practices and the need for retraining and effective educational policies providing even greater 'value-added' goods and services in the economy. Trade and market competition are strikingly more global than before.

All of this has stimulated debate on the future of public governance and the 'reform' of the system. It is accepted that overall the British argument for reform was based on the following though it is to be remembered there are still debates about whether the analysis was correct:

- a need to reverse British economic decline
- improve the efficiency of the economy
- reduce state intervention
- revitalize the private sector
- reduce the role of the trade unions
- strengthen management at all levels.
- increase competitiveness both in the public and private sectors.

Approaches to reform in the context of public service management

One area where reform was to play a part was the use of objective management techniques. The apparent differences between administering public services and managing the private sector were to be reduced (Elcock, 2001). This meant setting up the links between goals and accountabilities, and rational management practices. In many respects this led to the setting up of professional agencies of government. To achieve this, it was argued, would improve the capacity to:

Values

- reduce unit costs and heighten efficiency
- improve speed of transactions and improve quality of service to customers
- use new technology.

These are major claims and much research is now going on to evaluate the new schemes and the thinking behind them.

An outline of the reform strategy and implementation in Great Britain

Dynamic

To think that bureaucratic reform only began in the 1980s would be inaccurate. The reform of the British Civil Service, for example, was recommended in the 1966–1968 period (Fulton Report). One can go back even further, and find that reform of most governments is a norm not an exception. However, it was the Thatcher governments in the 1980s that have been most quoted as starting a fundamental review of British public administration. The evolutionary development of reform occurred as follows:

- 1979   Efficiency Unit created by the Cabinet Office
- 1980   Introduction of Compulsory Competitive Tendering (CCT)
- 1982   Introduction of MINIS Management Information Systems for Ministers
- 1983   Launch of FMI—Financial Management Initiative
- 1988   Efficiency Unit publishes 'Next Steps' with an emphasis on new executive agencies
- 1991   White Paper 'Competing for Quality': introducing market testing
- 1992   Launch PFI (Private Finance Initiative)—the use of public/private partnerships (PPP) for public policy areas
- 1997   The above policies have been backed and widened since the election and the coming to power of new Labour
- 1998   Introduction of Best Value
- 2002   Creating the 'Comprehensive Performance Assessment' (CPA).

Important to the reform is the need for measurement of public policy practice. There is an inbuilt demand to see and to compare performance indicators; a need to regulate and benchmark 'good' and 'best' practice. In central and local government administration this has been driven by specific targeted policies.

First there was the 'compulsory competitive tendering' initiative and then the 'best value' recommendations. The acronyms have sprouted around us. The most recent are the PPP and PFI arrangements and the creation of the comprehensive performance assessment (CPA). A brief survey of these areas is both useful and practical for understanding the 'new' policy environment and its relationship to the business world.

'Compulsory competitive tendering'

Interaction

Introduced in 1980, the compulsory competitive tendering (CCT) initiative was an attempt to ensure that competitive tendering could be applied to a whole range of services normally provided by public sector workers: catering, administration, cleaning, vehicle and grounds maintenance, cleaning and management. The expectation was that competitive pressure would lead to improvements in efficiency.

'Best value'

Interaction

This initiative was launched in 1998 as, in effect, a replacement for CCT. It tries to build on the efficiencies of the CCT but with an even greater emphasis on customer service. This means an increased role for performance improvement; greater emphasis on measurement and definable continual improvement; and strengthened competition structures (Curry, 1999). To achieve this, the following are important:

- greater accountability to customer and citizen alike
- introduce verifiable strategic management for local authorities (i.e. find ways to measure outcomes and link to strategic goals)
- improvement of operational management
- effective financial management
- improvement in performance data.

CCT and 'best value' are important statements of direction. They inform the process both inside government and outside, and especially any relations to the business environment.

At the heart of the present era in political agendas, and their relationship to the business environment are three major factors bringing these various strands together: public–private partnerships, public finance initiatives, and gathering data associated with auditing. These three are important for the public as well as the private sectors.

CPA ('comprehensive performance assessment')

CPA is a new tool (from 2002) which allows local government to review its performance against others. It is one of the primary 'tools' of the Audit Commission that is being used to spearhead local policy improvement.

Interaction

Public–Private partnerships

What is meant by a public–private partnership? On the surface you would think this is easy to define, but in practice it has not been so. In broad terms it could mean any connection or joint venture where the public sector and the private sector work in tandem for a given goal. This has been the reality of the system since the development of states and is not new.

Interaction

Diversity

Some public sector work is always provided in-house of course, but often private firms are asked to tender for public contracts through what is called 'public procurement' (see Chapter 4). This system has strict rules on how contracts are awarded and they are tied to agreed and expressed needs of central and local government.

Even so, the payment for the services and goods under the 'old' system was out of public spending (taxation) in the main and ended up as a part of public debt. This was seen as a problem and an inefficient way to handle modern economies.

The view taken of the UK in the 1970s and beyond was that the overall economy becomes stagnant under the burden of heavy taxation and moreover leads to higher taxes and spirals into further debt, leading finally to rising unemployment and social tension. This is an argument that has spread around the globe, more or less, and is usually tied to the neoliberal agenda and new ways of thinking. Of course, it remains contested and debated. Even so, across the globe and within the EU this remains an important issue for governments:

- This has led to the more defined sense of the PPP (sometimes known as P3) initiative. The purpose of PPP, and how we normally use the 'title', is to involve the private sector and private sector money in the financial risk and development of public services.
- PPP ties together the relationship between the private and public sectors so the private sector in particular is more heavily enmeshed in the responsibility for providing public services. In return the private sector can expect a greater financial leverage (degree of borrowing) within a proposal for improving services, greater management control, and a greater risk.

Mini-Case 10.5 Working with PPPs

Although there is controversy surrounding PPP and later the PFI (see below) on just how effective a method this is in developing services for the public sector, their impact is large. One investment bank, Macquarie, active in the field estimates:

- there were 750 PPPs signed in the UK by 2006 with 500 projects operational
- they were worth in the region of US$90 billion
- 90% were delivered on time with up to 96% satisfaction levels
- PPPs were and are most effective in large complex projects that demand ongoing maintenance
- PPPs are not necessarily suitable for public requirements that change rapidly, e.g. information technology services.

Source: Macquarie (2006), 'Public–Private Partnerships: Lessons learned from the UK', taken from www.markets4poor.org

From another company point of view, Skanska (a company with over 23 PPP deals by 2006) sees the following as benefits for the business:

- secure long-term income streams
- enhance market valuation
- provide for repeat business and referrals if successful
- allow for integrated services.

Source: Skanska (2006) 'PFI in the UK'

❷ Then again you can expect companies such as this to argue this way. So as to balance our approach, can you find a weakness in their arguments, for example from those who would argue from a public sector management point of view and the political control it represents?

- This is carried through by formal negotiations and contracts with the public sector. For fixed terms, sometimes 30 or maybe even 60 years, the private sector takes nominal 'ownership' of the public sector provision though the legal 'ownership' is still debated.

The 'partnership' it is argued becomes more 'real' in that both the public and private sectors are both determined to develop service provision and so the responsibility is shared. The public sector gains, it is said, by new management techniques brought in from the private sector.

Interaction

Also, and often, the financial load is removed from the public account to the private sector. The public sector creates a contract, or some would say takes out a 'mortgage', for the services offered by the private sector. Penalty clauses or some compensatory measures are usually included in case of failure. The private sector gains because it has greater control of its involvement in service provision. It perhaps gains far more financially than under the old rules and practices of normal 'public procurement'.

It can be argued whether PPPs involve a departure from public service. A difficulty is that we do not have agreement on exactly what is a 'public service'. If one argued that a public service is an organization paid for by taxation that would discount selling services by the public sector. For example councils or public authorities who gained income from car parks or car parking, or the renting out of DVDs at the local library, or renting out of property would complicate the scene. This obviously would not be a useful working definition. Others argue that where you have state regulation of price you can define a public service.

Across the globe there have been interpretations of what is meant by PPP both in definition and operation. Much of the debate centres on who 'owns' what, but taken in the round:

- there has been considerable privatization of public service needs, and
- there has been a continuing emphasis on a new agenda to develop the public–private partnership idea
- moreover, in the UK this is a process that is now developed into what is called the 'PFI'.

'Private finance initiative' (PFI)

Interaction

Diversity

Introduced into the UK in 1992 by a Conservative government, and fully embraced after 1997 by the 'third way' politics of the Labour party, there has been a tighter working framework for a PPP known as the 'private finance initiative'. If we are looking for a more prescriptive shape to the PPP idea the PFI is a good format. It relies on a method sometimes known as a DBFO (design, build, finance and operate system), where the private sector offers a total service 'package'.

In general terms this means the private sector designs the public service based on outputs and service needs specified by the public sector. It then sometimes builds it (for example a new hospital) arranges finance, contracts with the public sector on agreed limits and then operates the service. In practice there are different ways that PFI is handled (service provision, free-standing finance, and joint ventures) with different payment mechanisms.

The arguments over creating the PFI continue, mainly over price and effectiveness. In the UK creating a PFI can be an exhausting, long negotiated process and includes a form of comparing what might be the better alternative for providing the service. This is called a public service comparator (PSC), where an attempt is made to compare the overall estimated cost of a non-PFI scheme and the PFI scheme itself.

Data and the auditing

Spatial levels

Diversity

Essential to the whole process is the question of data and the auditing of accounts. Equally important is the degree to which control of the PFI is part of public sector responsibility on one side and the private sector on the other. This has become more relevant and fitting because of the Enron scandal in the USA, although there are plenty more examples around the world. But the extent of Enron's failure showed just how complex and corrupting accounting practices can be in the business environment and has caused worries again in the public sector.

Equally, to say that the public sector has been free of financial mismanagement is also plainly false: witness the problems of ministry IT project failure and mismanagement in the UK although not quite comparable to the Enron case: training, education, health, pensions, immigration, defence have all been touched in one way or another over the last few years.

Mini-Case 10.6 **The pressure for change**

The Parliamentary Public Accounts Committee in the UK produced a critical review of UK Public Services in 2006. As reported by the BBC, 2006, they outlined ten criteria to be used to assess 'public servants' and thereby a public service:

- understanding the needs of its customers
- designing services in the light of this understanding
- consulting with users regularly
- introducing robust and well developed arguments arrangements for delivering services
- employing and motivating capable staff, especially on the frontline

- monitoring service performance and learning lessons so it can innovate
- providing redress when things go wrong
- publicizing services and performance levels to all users
- balancing, not burdening service users with rules and demands for information with the need to safeguard public money
- doing what they say they will, over and over again.

❷ To what extent can these criteria be applied to the private sector of business?

Source: The United Kingdom Parliament: Select Committee on Public Accounts Sixty-third report, 2006: www.parliament.uk/

Even so the argument about the effectiveness of collaboration between two different sectors with two different sets of stakeholders, two differing purposes (profit vs. welfare) and differing managerial approaches remains as a background. However, in an age that demands effective welfare provision and where there is pressure on the 'public purse' (usually the 'borrowing requirement'), many even in the popular press see the PFI initiative as a 'necessary evil'.

The priority remains to make it work, and provide calculable value for money (VFM). Pointedly, there is a need to make sure the partnership (the 'consortium'), the risks, and the financing are all well managed.

Some of the latest research into the workings of PPP/PFI is mixed. Some sectors are working better than others. It may not be surprising to note that where there is understanding and experience across the sectors in working together the results appear to be less contentious. The first Bates (UK government sponsored) review into the process in 1997, followed by a further review in 1999, saw the system improved and recommendations carried out. In particular, the creation of a dedicated PPP management group, the Treasury Task Force (now called 'Partnerships UK'), which coordinates and encourages the development of PPP/PFI. The system usually involves:

1 the private sector assuming a risk within the project
2 the project must manage and offer 'value for money'
3 there should be open competition for the project (normally through the Official Journal of the EC/EU—this is the official document announcing EU projects and the call for tenders).

Also the process demands:

1 the public sector defines its service needs and draws up an 'outline business case'
2 there are detailed outcomes and sharing of risk
3 procurement processes and rules
4 an investment appraisal and a 'full business case'
5 a contract: completion, award and finally implementation.

Mini-Case 10.7 PPP and PFI: findings of research into their effectiveness in the construction industry in the UK

Recent research pinpointed 18 'critical success factors' (CSF) for PPP/PFI projects in the UK construction industry. They illustrate the profound need for competent management at all stages in the development of PPP and PFI schemes. Both the private and the public sector would do well to reflect on the range of skills they need for a successful contract and completion:

1 strong private consortium
2 appropriate risk allocation and risk sharing
3 competitive procurement process
4 commitment/responsibility of public/private sectors
5 thorough and realistic cost/benefit assessment
6 project technical feasibility
7 transparency in the procurement process
8 good governance

9 favourable legal framework
10 available financial market
11 political support
12 multi-benefit objectives
13 government involvement by providing guarantees
14 sound economic policy
15 stable macroeconomic environment
16 well organized public agency
17 shared authority between public and private sectors
18 technology transfer.

Source: Bing Li, A. Akintoye, P. J. Edwards and C. Hardcastle (June 2005), Critical success factors for PPP/PFI projects in the UK Construction Industry, *Construction Management and Economics* 23: 459–71, Routledge.

All of this is in response to the early criticisms of the schemes which illustrated a concern over protracted negotiations, lack of coherence and worries over value for money.

Whatever the difficulties, the system is not an unimportant innovation. It has been estimated that about 7% and rising of UK public debt has been removed and transferred to the private sector. This adds to the already estimated 15% shift following privatization within the UK.

There have been over 750 PPPs in the UK, worth over £50 billion and rising. The following sectors have all used PPPs: health, education, infrastructure (for example transport); government departments (such as Home Office departments and others—prisons, aspects of policing, fire-fighting) as well as other public bodies such as defence all use PPP/PFI in one way or another.

The system has now been used across the globe: partnership appears to be a major trend. What the system demands is a clear and negotiated contract that fulfils the needs both of the public and private sectors. Increasingly evaluations of the schemes are becoming more favourable. Measuring what is happening of course has become a major concern, and is integral to the process.

Data, measurement, statistics, performance indicators

Quantifying data has become a major industry both in the private and public sectors, assisted by new technologies enabling the sharing and collating of data. Even so, data and its measurement have increasingly been seen as essential in policy-making.

Spatial levels

Diversity

The old days of so-called arbitrary political judgements, if they ever existed, have gone. Much decision-making in the modern era demands at least some quantifiable and then qualitative judgement which demands gathering data in forms that are usable and comparative. The degree to which this is now the norm would surprise previous generations of administrators.

Government bodies at every level not only now collate but interpret performance management findings. Measuring performance through indicators has become a major aspect of the public sector environment, not least in detecting the effectiveness and efficiency of a service. Whether a public sector project or a PFI, those who are involved would do well to ensure they embrace the earmarked outcomes, for they will be measured and used in evaluation procedures somewhere and in some form.

> ⮌ *Stop and Think*
>
> '*Lies, damned lies, and statistics*': attributed to Benjamin Disraeli, and Mark Twain and others.
>
> How do we make sure that we are using the statistics and data we collect correctly? Is it really possible to be accurate, objective and effective all at the same time?
>
> Which organizations collecting data can we trust and use? How do we judge them? What criteria do we use to assess the results? Who writes down the criteria?

How exactly performance indicators are used fuels controversy and debate. Eventually the business sector will be judged, rightly or wrongly, by its profitability as much as the effectiveness of the service it provides. In the public sector, by its nature, there will be a demand for more interpretative and qualitative judgement based on the social needs that services are designed to meet.

The political environment always means political opinion and compromise in areas that are often difficult and disputed. Sometimes the social need may outweigh an obvious comparative cost: for example dealing with the fear of terrorism as much as the actual costs incurred by terrorist activity.

The comprehensive performance assessment (CPA) in the UK in 2002 had great influence and is the base for measuring performance and the running of local authorities.

Auditing regimes

Spatial levels

Internal/ external

Diversity

Auditing within the public sector is also of major importance both for the transparency and reliability of the data that is collected. Most countries will have precise forms of auditing following agreed rules and regulations. They will be both internal and external to the public sector organization and once again politically, constitutionally, they will perform at many levels.

The business environment is also audited, for example by company reports and accredited approval of accounts. The public sector is similar and its accounts at central and local level are to be agreed and corroborated by independent accountancy. Equally the public sector is subject to the performance indicators that are created by such bodies as the National Audit Office (NAO) and the Audit Commission in the UK, as well as others.

Auditing organizations

Spatial levels

As with diverse management levels, you will also find different layers of auditing in the public sector. In broad terms there are auditing organizations which cover usually:

1 the central government
2 local government, and nowadays also
3 a European level.

They often work together as much as possible (in the UK there is an appointed Public Auditor Forum) but there will be distinct differences in how they manage.

The National Audit Office (UK)

Spatial levels

In the UK the National Audit Office is the primary auditing organization of central government. It works for, but independently of, parliament, and in particular for the Public Accounts Committee. It publishes reports on the working of central government departments and importantly it also audits non-governmental organizations (NGOs) and executive agencies. The influence of the latter has grown since 1988 following a report from the 'efficiency unit' entitled 'Improving Management in Government: the Next Steps'. Central to the NAO is the question of 'value for money'.

It is to be noted that there are also 'devolved' audit offices, for example for Scotland and Wales, but we shall come back to this later.

 Mini-Case 10.8 Auditing (UK)

At every level of government you will find auditing organizations. They are very useful to the business community because they often provide an early-alert of political debate on business, finance, policy and accounting issues.

Political organization	Auditing organization
EU	European Court of Auditors
Central government	National Audit Office
Local and regional government	Audit Commission

Their reports are usually regular and targeted, and stray between the different layers of political decision-making. For example the National Audit Office in the UK has two main categories of reports: 1) Value for Money (VFM) reports, and 2) Financial accounts and reports on government accounts. Recently they published a new report on '. . . PFI debt refinancing and the PFI equity market' (21.04.2006) detailing new rules in the PFI market for government to make savings. If you were one of the companies building hospitals (a case mentioned in the report) you would do well to read it to judge the impact on the change in rules for refinancing PFI schemes.

The Audit Commission

The Audit Commission is mainly focused on local government in the UK, although its reports and influence go beyond the local. To introduce comprehensive performance assessment (CPA) for local authorities is an important part of the work of the Audit Commission. From it, local authorities are judged and the results made public.

Spatial levels

The underlying purpose is to engage citizens in the process of assessing and improving services by publishing and informing them of performance in their local areas. There are CPAs for single tier and county councils and district councils for example, and interestingly, a separate CPA for the fire and rescue services. The latter is an interesting case study which is reviewed below, because the Audit Commission has taken over direct from central and local levels of inspection to report on the 'modernization' of the fire service.

The European Court of Auditors

Although restricted to how much it may gain in revenue, the EU is a body which has its own finance (part VAT, duties and other funds from member states) and it does play a significant role. For example in regional and social development it provides funds to encourage greater European integration.

Spatial levels

Most countries across the EU benefit directly from EU funding, including the business community, from large to medium and small sized companies. There is a special Court of Auditors which like the local or national auditing systems is used to account for efficiency and effectiveness of EU policy making and its spending.

The political and policy organizations

So far, in looking at the development of the political environment and its impact on business we have concentrated on what are known as statutory bodies. Even so the modern management of the political environment is now more devolved, not only down to local and regional levels but also up to the international scene.

Complexity

More than this, modern politics does not work just through statutory bodies but also through three different kinds of organization:

- statutory
- voluntary
- 'agencies'.

They all operate with different sets of rules. Again, to understand the political and policy spatial scales is to understand how the national governing system relies on the relationship of the so called 'statutory bodies'—those laid down by official statute—and the two other types of organization:

The voluntary sector

In the eyes of many the voluntary sector is the key to 'civil society', even 'citizenship', and within a society a major representation of political and specific interests. Some societies encourage and rely on the voluntary sector as an important element in service provision. The Netherlands and Germany for example have large voluntary sectors.

Complexity

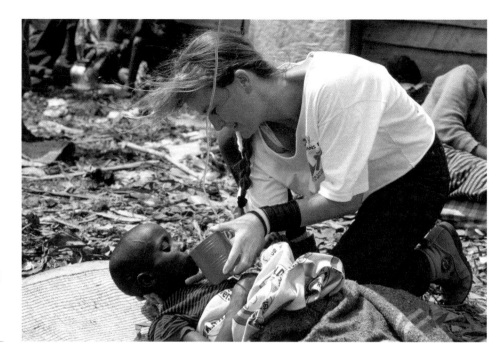

NGOs such as Oxfam and the Red Cross can be highly effective and focused in the best of cases.

© Peter Turnley/CORBIS

Most governments will encourage the voluntary sector, because it is less costly and in some areas more effective than professional organizations or departments. In the UK the 2002 'Cross-Cutting Review' not only called for its modernization but linked it as much as it could into the new public management agenda.

There is of course a potential tension between the 'professional' (sometimes referred to as 'Corporatist Welfare Organizations') and the 'volunteer'. The new political agendas in civil and welfare policies often try to embrace, link and regularize the relationships between the two.

Many 'voluntary' sector organizations are embraced in a wider term—non-governmental organizations (NGOs) such as Oxfam, and Connexions (NACP), the young persons' support group. One definition of an NGO relies on its accountability: NGOs do not refer or account for their actions through formal government procedures. This gives them some independence of action. They can be highly effective and focused in the best of cases.

Agencies, NGPBs

Complexity

Nevertheless to fully recognize the modern political environment is not only to include the voluntary sector but to note the growth of what are known as 'agencies' and 'non-governmental public bodies' (NGPBs—formerly known as 'quasi-autonomous non-governmental organizations' or Quangos).

The creation of 'executive agencies' in the UK originated from the 1998 'Next Steps review'. Of course their history is much longer than this and stretches back into the early twentieth century if not further. But in form, they are organizations which are given specific purposes by government, often reporting direct to a ministry but at the same time removed from direct departmental procedures. Some fall into the category of being created by 'statute', but some operate more like companies, semi-autonomous from government: broadcasters, universities, even libraries, are good examples.

> **➔ *Stop and Think***
> Should all citizens get involved with public service or should we leave it to the 'professionals'? Why not say to citizens it is their right to live in a society but also their responsibility to do something for it? In some countries voluntary or community service is actively encouraged such as in the Netherlands. In some societies citizens are forced to vote (even if they abstain) as in Belgium.
>
> Where we draw the line between professional and 'amateur'—and who decides—is a tricky question.

There are academic debates not only about their effectiveness or even the trend which is building them (sometimes called agentification) and being adopted by countries around the world. It is another form of new public service modelling of governance which is of important interest to citizens and businesses alike.

◈ *Looking ahead*

For some the development of new public management misses the political point and there are battles ahead. The relationship between the public sector and the private sector remains for them one of philosophical distinction, even political action. Even so, it appears the boundaries have now been changed and it is very difficult to see a world that separates the sectors as they were in the past.

Looking ahead means a greater focus on questions of data evaluation, effectiveness, and value for money. Of course, the debates will continue and the political world will shift around the reality of the existing political and social interests within each and every society. Never before though, have we seen so much policy data-analysis being evaluated by so many for so many as in the contemporary era.

The future for the public sector will be one based on statistics and qualitative judgements. The research that goes with this of course will continue hand in hand with the development of the policies. It is and will be a fascinating era for modern, contemporary political societies as they compare themselves with others. The private sector will be involved whether they or others want them to or not. Knowledge of both sectors was, is, and will be the key.

◈ *Summary*

- The public sector of old appears to be on the brink of moving into a new era. Not only is the established order and control through nation-states beginning to alter, but so is the number of dependencies and political levels through which the public sector works. The levels now include local, regional, national, European and international forms

- Privatization has been the spur for an even more thorough, even if evolutionary, process of change with the sharing and moving of the public debt toward the private sector and away from the tax-revenues of the state

- An important part of this movement is the blending, as much as possible, of the private and public sectors into partnerships (PPPs and PFIs for example)

- The most striking aspect of new public sector thinking has been embraced into the terms of 'new public management'. The new management practice tries to shift the management style towards outcomes which are 'consumer' led. In so doing there has also been an increased emphasis on transparency and measurement of performance. This is changing the relationship between the leaders of policy making and those who use the services they promote

- The new era of public administration and management is not yet founded on a fundamental consensus and the details of policy development remain contested. Even so, the process of change appears to be unstoppable taking into consideration present political and economic agendas

Case study: fire safety provision in society from the volunteer to the professional

In the UK, fire policy has been seen as distinctive from other policies even though the language of change has touched its work. Though often popular, its reputation was one of a service needing modernization but belonging to that 'old' public sector resistant to change. It had its severe critics: one member of parliament referred to it as a 'dinosaur' of the old public sector.

Recently though, what has happened to the fire service in the UK is marked and appears to be a part of a 'new' era. This is significant because if such a service founded on such a stable sense of what might be called the 'public good' can change so can most other services.

The process of change has taken both legislation and a change in management thinking. There has been a new piece of central government law on local provision, the Fire and Rescue Services Act 2004, the first major legislative change for over half a century. In it there was a shift of emphasis from fire-fighting to fire prevention and community fire safety.

The internal inspection process, once controlled within the ranks of the fire service at central level by Her Majesty's Fire Inspectorate, is now to be closed from 2007 and its inspection portfolio more or less assumed by the Audit Commission. It is one of the rare cases of the Audit Commission having a specific inspecting brief over a public sector policy. The police service and prison service for example preserve their own inspectorates.

It is a service which is increasingly framed by a 'modernizing' agenda based on performance indicators (sometimes known as best value performance indicators or BVPIs). Underlying the changes have been real difficulties, criticisms and costs. It was a service that had been racked by strikes (1977), which were to be repeated (2002), with continuing sporadic industrial action

The fire service has had a 'modernizing' agenda but underlying the changes have been real difficulties, criticisms and costs, as was highlighted by the national strike in 2002.

© Getty Images

occurring across the country. The fire service was marked for being less than effective as a working environment for 'discrimination' issues such as racism and gender. Even so, the first non-operational female chief executive of a fire and rescue service, Susan Johnson, has now been appointed in County Durham and Darlington. Its central training establishment needed to be audited and checked and was put under parliamentary scrutiny for financial difficulties.

All of this resulted in an enormous pressure for change. It also meant the pressure was at last clarifying areas of fire service practice that could be improved for the sake of the public which the old system seemed not capable of shifting.

Fire and the effects of fire do have a statistical range that can be covered but do the indicators now used help? Coming under the banner of social protection, fire has a small budget for the UK and for most societies. Even so, it has recently been calculated the UK spends over £5 billion (2004) on total fire policy: half on fire prevention measures and half on fire-fighting.

Founded on previous indicators but still encouraged by the Audit Commission they initially published a simple set of fire service performance indicators but there were debates about their relevance (see the commentary in the brackets):

- *Percentage of fire calls where attendance standards were met* (but attending within the specified time did not necessarily show overall effectiveness even if early intervention was essential)

- *Percentage of fire calls where confidence levels have been met* (confidence levels do not always link to outcomes)

- *The average time (in days) between application for fire safety certificates and the issue of notices under section 5(4) of the Fire Precautions Act 1973* (but speed of inspection needs to be equated to outcomes too it has been argued)

- *The average time (in days) between the inspection confirming completion of works and the issue of the fire safety certificate.*

So getting the indicators right was an important element in the argument for change. It will not be surprising that the Audit Commission refined its tools. They have become more precise, more probing. For the Audit Commission this refinement and assessment is the key to performance and the language of assessment is interesting because it draws upon targeted and treatment analysis. The new range of indicators is over 20, and in some cases over 40 in number, whilst still being redrawn for the future. (Source: *Fire and rescue performance framework 2006/07: Guide to service assessment*, Audit Commission, 2006.)

Some argue we can go beyond this and this is where country to country, and not just county to county, comparisons are also of some value. At present the statistics drawn and used by the Audit Commission tend to be national. The next step could be to make them European or even international. If you do this you find some interesting questions if not all the answers. This may seem fanciful to some but it is not from a fire insurance view (which is now increasingly a European not a national market) and touches every person's household spend.

The statistics across Europe, and across the globe, are, of course, dependent on how they are collated but they remain useful pointers. Some recent UN figures, based on the work of Wilmot's world fire statistics, point to an interesting range of percentages of GDP being spent on fire policy—in the following case on fire organizations. Let us look at two (see Table 10.1 and Figure 10.3):

In Table 10.1 overleaf the first column data show how much European countries spend as a percentage of GDP on fire fighting organizations. This is important because it is a part of TME. If the percentage is small, then it allows for governments to spend resources on something else or even allows them to lower taxes.

These figures point to a wide-ranging cost factor in providing fire services and it appears it is dependent on the communities' differing styles of provision. Exploring the lower figures you often find that with countries that rely more on volunteer provision rather than professional, the costs are less.

What these international figures tell us is that the UK is rather expensive compared with like nation-states within the EU. But perhaps we need to explore whether the UK spend is more effective and good value for money? Most societies would see fire deaths as a more relevant figure than GDP spend. To compare another standard figure (the second column—fire deaths per thousand), the indicators point to likenesses but also differences (see Figure 10.4):

The UK in fire deaths per thousand is less favourable than say the Netherlands but it appears to be better than many other European countries. The figures compared with 1992–1993 show a

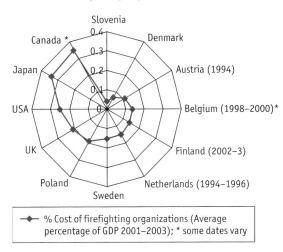

Figure 10.3 Percentage of GDP spent on fire-fighting organizations

→ % Cost of firefighting organizations (Average percentage of GDP 2001–2003); * some dates vary

Source: Created from data taken from World Fire Statistics, Information Bulletin of the World Fire Statistics, 22 October 2006.

Table 10.1 Firefighting organization: comparisons

Country	Column 1 % Cost of firefighting organizations (average percentage of GDP 2001–2003)	Column 2 Population Comparisons for Fire Deaths (2001–03) % Deaths per 100,000 persons
Slovenia	0.04	1.11
Denmark	0.07	1.49
Austria (1994)	0.11	1.31
Belgium (1998–2000)*	0.14	1.35
Finland (2002–3)	0.14	1.83
Netherlands (1994–1996)	0.15	0.68
Sweden	0.15	1.6
Poland	0.19	1.29
UK	0.21	1.04
USA	0.25	1.71
Japan	0.34	1.79
Canada*	0.35	1.25

* Some dates vary.

Figure 10.4 Population comparisons for fire deaths

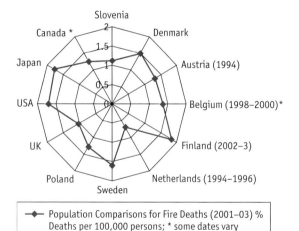

Population Comparisons for Fire Deaths (2001–03) %
Deaths per 100,000 persons; * some dates vary

Source: Created from data taken from World Fire Statistics,
Information Bulletin of the World Fire Statistics, 22 October 2006.

You end up with fundamental questions: why is the UK fire service one of the most expensive in Europe and apparently in fire deaths less effective than at least one of our neighbours? The Netherlands appears to have both low GDP spend and low fire deaths.

A great deal could be developed around these statistics: not least the debate on how national definitions and variations distort the figures. Even so, just these two indicators raise important performance and management questions (see Figure 10.5).

Looking at the 'history' of European fire provision gives us clues. Policies on fire safety and fire-fighting personnel are related to two major forces it appears. First, the growth in general welfare policy since 1945 that included fire provision, and, secondly, the general acceptance that this was to be achieved by state organization of fire services. There was no consensus on how this was to be achieved though and each country followed its own pattern.

In France the military wing of the fire-fighting services, mostly centred on Paris, was upheld. To this was added the municipal, departmental, professional fire-fighters and officers that were then supplemented by a large volunteer sector. In Germany and Austria, the organization of fire-fighting was based on a mix of volunteer and professional personnel. The Dutch managed with a greater emphasis on community fire-fighters and the volunteer was embedded into the heart of the service. In Britain, as with many other public policy areas, the fire service used its volunteers but increasingly turned, both in numbers and in management style, toward a service dominated by the professionals. In the fire safety field, equally, countries developed their own

dramatic drop in the UK from 1.4% to 1.04%. This led to in-depth evaluation from a variety of sources. Two are of note: *World Fire Statistics Information Bulletin of the World Fire Statistics*, 22, October 2006 and *International Fire Statistics and the Potential Benefits of Fire Counter-Measures* (July 2005), the report of a study by a team from the Surrey University Polymer Research Unit.

Figure 10.5 Comparative: is there a relation between spend and fire deaths? Perhaps not!

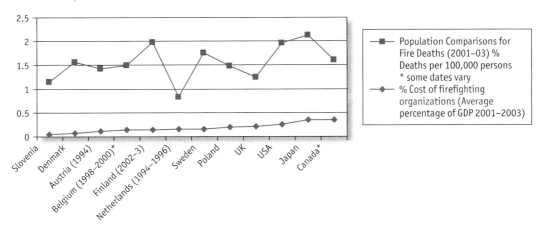

Legend:
- Population Comparisons for Fire Deaths (2001–03) % Deaths per 100,000 persons * some dates vary
- % Cost of firefighting organizations (Average percentage of GDP 2001–2003)

Source: Created from data taken from World Fire Statistics, Information Bulletin of the World Fire Statistics, 22 October 2006.

legislation and patterns of spending through national discussion and fire-related events.

The new public management environment is different from the past. The reforming, evolutionary process of change appears to be unstoppable even in the fire service with its strong work community, politically aware trade union, and an obvious need for its service. In the UK at least the era of new public management has had more effect upon the fire service in the last ten years than the previous fifty it could be argued. Could the fire service, that icon of the old public sector 'ethos' and a prime example of the 'public good', ever be managed by the private sector? Impossible some would say. But in Denmark it is, through the Falck organization, an interesting case-study in itself. Can we preserve differences on the basis of national control or are we now so 'global' we need to think anew? It would appear that the new agendas are not going away whatever your answer may be to this question.

The case above illustrates how one can fine-tune what might be considered normal 'new management' questions:

❷ What are the possible reasons why UK fire safety policy is more expensive than many other nations?

❷ What different factors might contribute to an explanation of why on the surface it appears that the UK is less effective than say our neighbour the Netherlands in dealing with fire deaths?

❷ More important perhaps, can we learn something from the figures and improve fire safety protection policy provision in the UK? What are the arguments for and against 'privatizing' the fire service?

❷ Can we keep community fire safety policy different from one another, relying on 'national' boundaries, or are we now so 'global' we need to think anew?

❷ Does PPP or PFI make a fundamental difference to public sector fire safety?

Review and discussion questions

1. What is a PPP and how does it normally work?

2. What are the advantages and disadvantages of 'new public management'?

3. To what degree are the changes in the public sector brought about by the nation-states themselves or a part of the global nature of present day politics and business development?

4. Are there limits to the partnerships that can be created between the private and public sectors? If so, what are they?

5. What is a CPA, how is it used to improve local government performance, and why is it important to the business community?

6. What are the essential differences in role between the National Audit Office and the Audit Commission?

Assignments

1. Choose a public sector organization or service that would possibly benefit from a PPP or PFI and develop a business case report arguing for its development.

2. Using data available to you from such sources as the OECD, draw up a comparative table of public sector 'variables' (statistics) that illustrate both the differences and the similarities between states in public sector provision in either a European Union setting, or even use a more international comparison.

Further reading

There are two main approaches to reading around the subject; books and noted authors and new research work in academic reviews. Among the many excellent books available to you there are four that might catch your imagination for their depth and clarity. They also contain in themselves excellent bibliographies which will help you spin off into your own search for material and writers:

Ian Budge, Ivor Crewe, David McKay and Ken Newton (2003) *The New British Politics* (Harlow: Pearson Longmann).

T. R. Dye (2004) *Understanding Public Policy*, 11th rev. edition (New York: Prentice-Hall).

Christopher Pollitt and Geert Bouckaert (2004) *Public Management Reform* (Oxford: Oxford University Press).

Stephen P. Savage and R. Atkinson (2003) *Public Policy Under Blair* (Basingstoke: Palgrave Macmillan).

For a thought provoking critique of the 'new' wave see also:

Howard Elcock (2001) *Political Leadership (New Horizons in Public Policy)* (Cheltenham: Edward Elgar). This is available as an e-book using Microsoft Reader.

For reviews, much will depend on the sector you want to examine. There are some fascinating journals to explore. This chapter dipped into many but the following is a list of some of those used to review the latest research:

Accounting, Auditing and Accountability Journal
Business Process Management Journal
Construction Management and Economics
Health and Social Care in the Community
Institute of Economic Affairs
Institute for Fiscal Studies
International Public Management Journal
Journal of Education Policy
Journal of Knowledge Management
Journal of Management Development
Journal of Management History
Journal of Organizational Change
Public Administration
Public Management Review
The International Journal of Public Sector Management
Urban Studies

Online resources

Test your understanding of this chapter with online questions and answers, explore the subject further through web exercises, and use the weblinks to provide a quick resource for further research. Go to the Online Resource Centre at

www.oxfordtextbooks.co.uk/orc/ wetherly_otter/

A good starting point to create your own website list is SOSIG: follow the instructions and the various disciplines and record the sites as you go: www.sosig.ac.uk/

For economic data, including TME, use UK Treasury website: www.hm-treasury.gov.uk/

And for a broader range of UK statistical material use:
www.statistics.gov.uk/

For government and governance, a good starting point is:
www.direct.gov.uk/

For auditing regimes look at:
National Audit Office www.nao.org.uk/
Audit Commission www.audit-commission.gov.uk/
European Court of Auditors www.eca.europa.eu/

References

Bing Li, Akintoye, A., Edwards, P. J. and Hardcastle, C. (2005) Critical success factors for PPP/PFI projects in the UK construction industry, *Construction Management and Economics*, 23: 459–71.

Bishop, M., Kay, J. and Mayer, C. (eds) (2004) *Privatization and Economic Performance* (Oxford: Oxford University Press).

BT (2005) *Stakeholder Dialogue*, BT SE report.

Curry, A. (1999) Innovation in public service management, *Managing Service Quality*, 9(3): 180–90.

Department of Health (2007) website www.dh.gov.uk/

Elcock, H. (2001) *Political Leadership (New Horizons in Public Policy)* (Cheltenham: Edward Elgar).

Greve, C. (2006) Public management reform in Denmark, *Public Management Review*, 8(1): 161–9.

Macquarie (2006) 'Public–Private partnerships: lessons learned from the UK', taken from www.markets4poor.org/

Skanska (2006) *PFI in the UK*, Skanska.

The Economist, October 2006.

The United Kingdom Parliament (2006) *Select Committee on Public Accounts Sixty-third Report*.

Business in the political arena

Paul Wetherly

Contents

11

Learning objectives

When you have completed this chapter you will be able to:

● Understand the reasons for the participation of business as an actor in the political arena

● Understand the political process as a play of interests and power involving interaction between business, government, labour and **civil society organizations**

● Recognize and assess the effectiveness of methods used by business to influence government decisions

● Recognize and assess the effectiveness of methods used by pressure groups to influence business behaviour

● Analyse different perspectives on the influence of business in the political process

● Evaluate evidence from case studies on the political influence of business

Themes

Diversity	**Diversity of business**
	Business participates in the political process through companies representing their own interests and/or through associations representing collective business interests. There may be important differences of political values and interests within the business community.
Complexity	**Complexity of the environment**
	Political influence does not operate just through the formal political process (e.g. elections) but also through public opinion campaigns. Pressure groups may target businesses directly, e.g. through 'consumer activism'.
Spatial levels	**Variety of spatial levels**
	MNCs operate in more than one political arena in different national settings. The political process operates at sub-national, national and supra-national (e.g. EU) levels.
Dynamic	**Dynamic environment**
	Business has to respond to and participate in a changing political environment. Business influence in the political process is not constant but varies over time—it waxes ands wanes.
Interaction	**Interaction between business and the environment**
	Business is involved in a relationship with government. Because it is affected by government decisions business has an interest in influencing these decisions to its own advantage.
Stakeholders	**Stakeholders**
	The range of actors in the political process with which business has to contend can be understood as stakeholders.

Values

Values
The values and interests of business have to compete with those of other groups in society.

Introduction

Interaction

As we have seen in Chapter 4, politics is a feature of all societies and is therefore always part of the external environment of business. Can business stay out of politics? No. Political decisions and actions can have powerful effects in constraining or enabling business activity, and therefore business has a strong interest in participating in the political process. In a democratic political system it is legitimate for business to seek, like other groups in society, to influence government decisions in its own interests. Indeed, democracy can be defined in terms of everyone having a voice in political decision-making, and 'everyone' of course includes business.

Values

It is in the nature of politics that the many voices will often express interests, values and demands that collide or conflict with each other. The interests of business may be opposed by other groups in society, such as trade unions or consumer groups. For example, businesses may press government to relax restrictions on Sunday trading, while government faces demands from trade unions to maintain existing limits and protections. Thus politics can be seen as involving a play of power between groups, each seeking a 'win'. But politics can also allow a process of dialogue, negotiation and compromise, or 'win-win'. Either way, it is clear that business needs to have an effective voice in political debate, and ensure that its needs and interests gain the attention of government. Business is an actor in the political arena. The methods it uses and the amount of power or influence it wields are questions we will consider in this chapter.

The complexity of the political arena

Spatial levels

The idea of a political 'arena' conjures up the image of a physical space in which political battles are fought and compromises worked out. In the modern world politics is still conducted largely at a national level, within the territory of a **nation-state**. However politics is not confined to the national arena. As we saw in Chapter 4, there are multiple levels at which governance is conducted (above and below the nation-state).

Each nation-state, such as the UK, constitutes an independent or sovereign political arena with its own political culture, institutions and rules of the game. In principle each of these national contexts would need to be studied separately to identify differences and similarities—to see how different political systems afford different opportunities for business to influence government decisions. However there are some broad similarities between the advanced capitalist countries, especially democratic government and some shared aspects of political culture such as left–right politics (see Chapter 4).

Within the nation-state the relationship between business and government is not conducted solely at the national level. The status and powers of **sub-national governance** are variable, but in all political systems important interactions between business and government take place at a local or regional level. An important distinction is between federal systems (such as the US) and highly centralized or unitary systems such as the UK. In the UK political power is concentrated at Westminster.

In an era of globalization the political arena in which many UK businesses operate is not confined to the UK political system because multinational corporations (MNCs) operate in more than one country and therefore in multiple political arenas (e.g. imagine a company that operates in the UK, other EU member states, the US, China, Nigeria and Saudi Arabia). Another dimension of globalization is the development of political decision-making beyond or above the nation-state involving inter-governmental organizations (IGOs) and sometimes referred to as supra-national governance. The most important example of supra-national governance in the world today is the European Union.

The ability of business to influence political decisions depends on:

- the level of governance at which decisions are made—sub-national, national, supra-national
- the political culture and values—to what extent these are pro- or anti-business
- the institutions and rules of the game.

The play of interests and power in the political process

In economic life market actors are understood primarily as pursuing private interests—profits of enterprise, consumer satisfaction, higher pay and so on. In contrast politics is often understood primarily in terms of the public interest and the common good. In democracies, in particular, government may be seen as the servant of society whose purpose it is to act for the good of society as a whole.

Values

However, on closer inspection the distinction is not as clear-cut as this suggests. In economic life self-interest is sometimes tempered by public interest motives, as in ethical consumerism and corporate social responsibility. Conversely, private interests may play an important part in the political process. Politicians are motivated, at least in part, by their own self interest to 'climb the greasy pole' and advance their careers. Citizen participation in the political process is often motivated partly by self-interest. For example, individuals may vote for the political party that they feel is most likely to look after their interests. As we have seen, it is legitimate for business to engage in the political process, like other groups, in order to influence decisions to its own advantage. This gives us a different view of politics than the pursuit of the public interest, as the play of interests and power. Rival groups press their interests and values in the political process and bring to bear different degrees of power and influence.

Private sector businesses are run by managers or directors primarily for the benefit of the owners who have invested in them. In the case of public limited companies this means the shareholders, and running the company in their interests means, essentially, pursuing profitability and 'shareholder value'. Thus business will look to government to provide a favourable environment for profit-making through the law and public policy. This might include macroeconomic policies to control inflation, the provision of an efficient transport infrastructure to enable the movement of goods, favourable trade rules and agreements, the reduction of taxation and regulations that are felt to be burdensome, and so on.

Stakeholders

However a range of other interests compete to influence government, and we can think about these using stakeholder theory. Stakeholders in business can be categorized roughly as direct and indirect (or primary and secondary). Direct stakeholders are easy to identify—they are involved in and/or affected by an issue in a direct way, particularly as parties to a decision. Employees and trade unions representing them are direct stakeholders in business. Indirect stakeholders are often less obvious—they are not directly engaged in a decision but are affected by the outcome. Members of the local community and environmental campaigners are indirect stakeholders in business.

Because business decisions can have far-reaching economic and social consequences the number and range of stakeholders can be very large. It can also vary over time according to the ability and willingness of groups to mobilize around particular issues. In other words, stakeholder groups can rise and fall. For example in the 1960s and '70s UK business had to deal with powerful trade unions. Since then union memberships and power have, overall, declined due to legislative and economic changes. At the same time, as we will see, business has had to come to terms with more active indirect stakeholders, such as in the shape of 'consumer activism'. Thus since the 1970s UK business has had to adjust to a shifting stakeholder context. The principal stakeholders in business may be identified as

- shareholders
- managers
- employees
- suppliers
- customers
- competitors
- other economic actors, e.g. firms affected by knock-on or multiplier effects
- local community/wider society (sometimes including future generations)
- government
- the environment (this is an issue rather than a stakeholder—the stakeholder is the local community and wider society).

We can simplify this list by focusing on three categories: business, labour and society. The primary relationship between business and labour (or employers and employees) is a market relationship of contract or exchange—buying and selling. It also involves a relationship of authority or hierarchy within the organization. The focus of these relationships is the 'wage–effort bargain', meaning how much pay employees receive in return for how much effort they have to put in. This bargain is critical for both parties as it determines the livelihoods of employees and the profitability of business. Each party will try to strike the best bargain that it can, and the outcome will depend on their relative bargaining strengths.

However, this economic relationship is governed by law and public policy. For example, labour law determines the individual and collective rights of employees. This means that each party has an interest in trying to shape political decisions so as to alter the economic relationship to its own advantage. For example trade unions will bargain with employers to try to win higher wages for their members, but they might supplement this with a political campaign to secure a statutory minimum wage (or to raise the level of the existing minimum wage). In other words, we can see how the economic interests of business and labour in the market find expression in political action. In all capitalist economies, though to varying degrees, the economic interests of business and labour constitute a core focus of political debate.

'Society' encompasses a wide range of 'civil society organizations' (CSOs) and interests, some of which are connected with business. For example environmental campaigners may see business as contributing to environmental threats such as pollution and climate change, and therefore seek changes in business behaviour or curbs on business activity. Environmental campaigners are usually indirect stakeholders and not involved directly in business decisions. They may put pressure on government to introduce laws or policies that will induce or compel a change in business behaviour. But they may, in addition, target businesses directly through methods such as public relations campaigns or consumer boycotts.

Thus much of what goes on in the political process can be related to interests generated in, or affected by, the operation of markets. Politics can be seen as an expression largely of economic interests and goals, shaping 'who gets what when and where'. Government can be used to alter the distribution of resources and income, and more generally of costs and benefits, that would otherwise result from the operation of the market. Business is an actor in the political arena, and participates in a play of power involving government, trade unions and a range of CSOs. These interactions are shown in Figure 11.1.

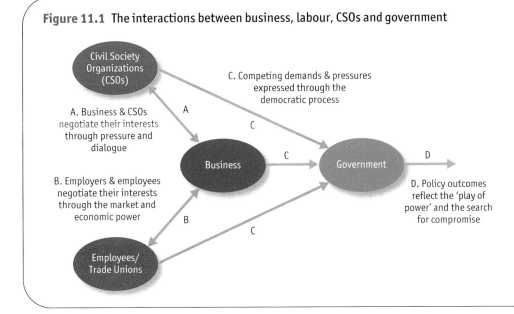

Figure 11.1 The interactions between business, labour, CSOs and government

For each arrow think of an issue and the types of action that might be involved.

> **⊃ Stop and Think**
> To what extent are political debates and conflicts based on economic interests and values?

Mini-Case 11.1 Reducing vehicle emissions in Europe

In February 2007 the European Commission announced plans for legislation requiring European car manufacturers to reduce CO_2 emissions from new cars to 130g per km on average by 2012. In 2005 the industry average was 163g, very far from a voluntary target, set in 1995, of cutting emissions to 140g by 2008. The obvious failure of the voluntarist approach lent force to the argument for legal compulsion.

However the commission's target was the outcome of a political process in which the interests of the car-makers were pitched against the demands of environmental campaigners. The commission had originally proposed a limit of 120g per km, but this had been dropped in the face of opposition from the car industry, represented by associations such as the UK Society of Motor Manufacturers and Traders (SMMT) and the European Automobile Manufacturers Association (ACEA). Opposition came in particular from luxury (i.e. less fuel efficient) car makers. Porsche referred to the proposal as a war waged by makers of smaller cars in Europe against the German car industry. The tougher limit had also been opposed by the German government, and by the

German European commissioner for industry on the grounds that it would decimate the German car industry.

Not surprisingly environmental pressure groups such as Friends of the Earth supported the lower limit and criticized the EU for 'caving in' to pressure from the car industry.

This case highlights a number of points:

- the pros and cons of self-regulation and legal compulsion
- the importance of the EU as a source of business regulation
- the role of business associations in the political process
- the conflict of interests between business and CSOs (environmentalists versus carmakers)
- conflicts of interest within business (makers of small cars versus makers of luxury cars)
- disagreements over policy within government and between different levels of government.

❷ Despite acceptance of the serious threat of climate change, why is it difficult to achieve agreement on political action to reduce CO_2 emissions from cars?

The representation of business interests

Business interests can be represented individually and/or collectively, and relations between business and government can be, accordingly, decentralized or centralized. In other words, individual businesses can choose to represent their own interests through direct dealings with policy-makers, sometimes employing specialist **lobbying** organizations for this purpose. They may also be represented through business associations whose rationale is to speak on behalf of collective business interests. Among the most important of these in the UK are:

Diversity

- Trade associations representing the interests of firms in a particular industry (e.g. the SMMT—Society of Motor Manufacturers and Traders);
- Chambers of Commerce representing business at a local level;
- Confederation of British Industry (CBI) representing the business community at a national level (often referred to as a 'peak' organization).

Spatial levels

Chambers of Commerce also have a national organization which operates at the UK and European levels. Similarly, the CBI maintains offices in Brussels and Washington in order to monitor and influence European and American legislation. Businesses may also join ad hoc coalitions to represent specific shared interests, such as in relation to Sunday trading.

The representation of business interests typically involves a mixture of individual and collective mechanisms, but there is considerable variation between countries in this mix and it is possible to think of a spectrum from highly decentralized to highly centralized systems. In highly decentralized systems the individual corporation is the dominant actor, whereas in highly

 Mini-Case 11.2 The Confederation of British Industry (CBI)

The CBI was created in the 1960s and is recognized as the principal peak association representing business interests in the UK. Its website states:

> The CBI's mission is to help create and sustain the conditions in which businesses in the United Kingdom can compete and prosper for the benefit of all. We are the premier lobbying organization for UK business on national and international issues. We work with the UK government, international legislators and policy-makers to help UK businesses compete effectively.
>
> Working on over 80 policy issues that directly affect business at any given time, the CBI is second-to-none at achieving wins for business. Members can use the CBI to reinforce their own efforts to bring about change in the legislative and regulatory framework within which they must operate. . . .
>
> The CBI is . . . of crucial importance to the entire business community because it can mobilise business opinion and successfully bring influence to bear on government. Such is the strength of the CBI's reputation that government frequently approaches the CBI for advice and opinion.

> No other business organization has such an extensive network of contacts with government ministers, MPs, civil servants, opinion formers and the media. . . .
>
> The CBI enjoys strong support because it gets the results for business at home and abroad.
>
> (www.cbi.org.uk/)

However the balance between companies using the CBI to bring about change in the legislative and regulatory framework and relying on their own efforts is tipped in favour of the latter.

In a survey of British companies in the 1990s 68% of respondents reported direct contact with government, compared to 46% through a trade association and only 24% through the CBI (Mitchell, discussed in Wilson, 2003: 73).

As Wilson comments, 'In Britain as in the United States, authority resides in the individual company and not the trade association or the peak association (CBI)' (2003: 70).

❓ The CBI claims that it works for the 'benefit of all' and achieves 'wins for business'. Are these two compatible?

centralized systems trade associations and **peak organizations** play a more important role. In the UK trade associations and the CBI do enjoy close relations with government (both Labour and Conservative), but on the whole relations between business and government are more towards the decentralized end of the spectrum. In this respect the UK is closer to the USA where:

> business representation . . . is . . . conducted in a manner that is very decentralized and fragmented. It is the individual enterprise, not the trade association or peak organization, that is paramount. (Wilson, 2003: 44)

By contrast a more centralized relationship is characteristic of the 'neocorporatist' systems in European countries such as Sweden.

Understanding the influence of business in the political process

How much power does business exercise in the political process in democracies like the UK? Does business have too much power, or too little? According to Noreena Hertz (2001), business has become more powerful than government and this 'power shift' undermines democracy. Hertz also argues that low voter turnout at elections is based on the (true) perception that governments have lost power so that there seems to be less reason to vote. It is clear that corporations are powerful entities in the modern world and that their decisions have profound impacts on how we live and the future of our societies. But it could be argued against Hertz that political power—that is the capacity to make and enforce laws—still lies in the hands of government and can be used to regulate business behaviour. And that, in democracies this power is ultimately in the hands of the people as a whole. Thus it can be argued that democracy is an effective check on corporate power.

To think about the issues involved in this debate we need to understand the theoretical frameworks that are used. Here we will consider three approaches:

- the pluralist model
- the neocorporatist model
- the business dominance model.

The democratic ideal

As we have seen in Chapter 4, the democratic ideal is 'rule by the people'. This seems to imply that business faces a major problem in making its voice heard in the democratic process and gaining the attention of government. For business leaders and managers, however defined, only make up a small proportion of the population—their voices are easily drowned out!

Of course, it shouldn't be assumed that the interests of business leaders will always be at odds with those of other groups. Indeed pro-business policies to boost competitiveness and economic growth may be widely supported because society as a whole benefits from higher living standards. More generally, business may benefit from a broad consensus in society in support of the market and private enterprise. Such a consensus means that strongly anti-business views are relatively marginal, and the democratic process is unlikely to produce a result that will present a major threat to business interests. It can be argued that there is such a broad consensus in the UK, and that it has tended to strengthen with the decline of socialism as an ideological alternative to capitalism.

Values

However business cannot always rely on such shared interests or a broad pro-business consensus. Even though the old left–right ideological conflict of capitalism versus socialism has lost much of its heat there are still disputes about the balance between the market and the state and political battles over specific policies, and so business must try to ensure that it is not disadvantaged in the democratic process. Democracy involves two broad processes or channels of influence on government:

- the electoral process
- the representation of group interests.

The right of all citizens to vote in regular elections from a choice of candidates is a key component of democracy, allowing the people to choose who will represent them in parliament and govern them. In elections the main players are political parties that compete for votes on the basis of ideologically-based programmes for government.

Values

However voting is not the only form of political participation, and perhaps not the most important form. Being able to vote and stand for office are political rights. But a healthy democracy also depends on a range of civil rights or liberties. These include freedoms of speech, association and assembly. These rights are important because democracy must allow the clash of opinions and beliefs through dialogue, debate and argument.

Civil liberties are also important in allowing the representation of group interests. Individuals are able to join together in associations to pursue shared interests and political aims. Such associations are often referred to as pressure groups or civil society organizations (CSOs). A pressure group is distinguished from a political party by its not putting up candidates for election. In other words pressure groups want to influence the government, not to become the government. Thus pressure groups provide a mechanism for individuals to have an ongoing influence in politics.

The pluralist approach

The *pluralist model* of democracy focuses on the influence of pressure groups. The term 'pluralist' (or pluralism) obviously derives from the word plural, meaning multiple or many. The pluralist model emphasizes that there is a very large number of groups or interests in society competing for the attention of government and trying to influence political decisions (in modern business parlance we can refer to these groups as stakeholders). It suggests that the group process is more like a competitive market than an oligopoly: political power is fragmented and dispersed among groups.

The key roles of groups can be described as:

- interest aggregation, and
- interest articulation.

In other words, groups exist because individuals come together to pursue shared interests (aggregation) and they express these interests in the form of political demands (articulation).

In the pluralist model groups are seen as a vital component of a healthy democracy, together with party competition and elections. This is because the group process provides a vehicle for participation in politics and a barometer of public opinion. Pressure groups therefore help to keep government in touch with and responsive to public opinion. This makes pressure groups a healthy feature of the democratic process.

Diversity

The world of pressure groups is highly diverse. Like businesses, they vary in size from small local groups to large international organizations. There is a continuous process of group formation and dissolution. Groups grow and decline at different rates as issues rise or fall in political prominence, or become more or less fashionable. Like businesses, groups exist in a competitive environment and have to think about how they promote themselves in order to attract members and remain viable. Like business, there are some well-known global 'brands' (e.g. Friends of the Earth, Greenpeace, Oxfam, WWF) and a host of groups that are known only to people involved in that particular issue (unless it suddenly moves up the political agenda). Further, businesses can themselves act as pressure groups. But the key difference is that the purpose of pressure groups is not to produce a good or service or to make a profit but to bring about change in society. This usually involves acting politically to influence government, but can also involve applying pressure to other institutions and organizations, such as business.

Mini-Case 11.3 Sunday trading—group politics in action

John Major's Conservative government introduced the Sunday Trading Act 1994 to liberalize shop opening hours, allowing shops to open on Sundays. This law has helped to transform the nature of Sundays and, with it, the pattern of the whole week and the rhythm of life. Sunday used to be essentially a day of inactivity or 'day of rest'. Now for many people shopping on Sundays has become an unexceptional activity, and Sunday has become more like Saturday in other ways. We have moved towards a '24/7' business model.

Although legal change was necessary to permit Sunday trading, it would be equally valid to say that it is business activity itself that has transformed the nature of Sunday. This illustrates well the way in which market relationships tend to spread into other areas of life, having what some see as a corrosive effect on established ideas, institutions and ways of life. In response to this it may be argued that we need to use the power of government and the law to protect certain aspects of our way of life from invasion by the market—for example to 'keep Sunday special'. On the other hand it can be argued that markets only ever reflect the choices that individuals make—in this case, Sunday trading will only grow if people want to shop on Sundays, and if they want to do so the law should not be used to prevent them. If the law permits shops to open on Sundays it doesn't force anybody to provide them with their custom.

Sunday trading remains a politically controversial issue, and provides a good example of the interaction between business, trade unions and civil society organizations in the political arena. Liberalization in the 1990s was a business-driven agenda reflecting its interests: from a purely commercial point of view no day is different from any other—business has an interest in making sales to anyone at any time. The Sunday Trading Act 1994 was a political victory for the interests of business—particularly big businesses such as supermarkets, DIY stores and high street chains—which campaigned as the Shopping Hours Reform Council. This seems to be a clear example of business being able to use its political clout to win favourable laws from government, against opposition from other groups and interests in society, such as churches and trade unions. This victory was aided by a favourable political context—a business-friendly Conservative government in power and pro-business attitudes in the wider society.

The Sunday Trading Act 1994 did not introduce a free-for-all. Under the Act small shops (under 280 sq m/3,000 sq ft) face no restrictions on opening, while large shops (over 280 sq m/3,000 sq ft) are permitted to open on Sundays only for six hours, between 10am and 6pm. So, under this law, Sunday isn't quite like any other day. However businesses continued to press the case for further liberalization or deregulation, easing these restrictions on Sunday trading so that shops can stay open longer. To pursue this aim a group of large businesses mounted what Mathiason (2006) refers to as a 'vociferous lobby' in response to government consultation on the Sunday trading law in 2006. A campaign under the heading 'My Sunday, My Choice' (initially known as 'Deregulate') was created by Asda, Ikea, B&Q and other large businesses, and the lobbying firm Good Relations was appointed to promote the campaign (Mathiason, 2006).

'My Sunday, My Choice' states on its website that 'The "My Sunday My Choice" campaign has been launched to call for greater choice for both consumers and shop workers—the choice to shop on a Sunday and the choice of whether to work on a Sunday'. The campaign produced a survey claiming that 'Nearly 60 per cent of consumers want to be able to shop when and where they want on a Sunday' (*Observer*, 25 June, 2006).

The website of Good Relations provides an insight into how such lobbying or PR firms may be used by business to support its political aims:

In an age where corporate reputation is increasingly determined by what people see, hear and read about you, it is imperative that an organization's political and media communications go hand in hand. Nowadays it is just as important to communicate your messages with politicians and civil servants or even pressure groups as it is through an interview in the press.

We advise clients on communication issues which involve an understanding of political sensitivities and the public policy agenda. This means that we give them more than the traditional

public affairs offering because we help them to manage their communications issues through the media as well as political channels. (www.goodrelations.co.uk)

However, some big businesses (e.g. Sainsbury and Marks & Spencer) did not join the campaign, and Tesco withdrew after having initially helped to finance the campaign. 'My Sunday, My Choice' also faced opposition from a range of organizations and individuals including:

- members of parliament, especially Labour MPs
- trade unions, especially the Union of Shop, Distributive and Allied Workers (USDAW)
- small businesses, represented by the Association of Convenience Stores
- churches and religious groups
- Keep Sunday Special Campaign

The principal interests that are felt to be threatened by a relaxation of Sunday trading laws are those of

- small shops, particularly convenience stores, for which unrestricted Sunday opening without competition from large stores provides a vital source of business

- shopworkers who may face strong pressure to work more hours on Sundays. Although working more hours on Sundays may be welcome for some, for others it would involve an unwelcome deterioration in work–life balance. 'USDAW found 94% of shop-workers hostile to longer Sunday shopping hours' (Ashley, 2006)
- campaigners who want to 'keep Sunday special', either for specifically religious reasons or from more general considerations of family life.

In July 2006 the Labour government announced that it had decided not to introduce any change to the Sunday trading law. Unlike the early '90s this was a victory for small shops, shopworkers and the 'keep Sunday special' campaigners against the aims of (some) of the UK's major retail businesses (or, at least, a holding of the line).

❷ Do you agree that the Sunday Trading Act is a reasonable compromise between those who want to keep Sunday special and those who want to buy and sell freely?

❷ How do you explain the success of business in winning the Sunday Trading Act, and its failure to secure further liberalization?

The lessons of Sunday trading

The case study highlights a number of points and issues:

- Big business does not win all the political battles it engages in. In other words, the political influence of business varies. By the same token, a coalition of interests can sometimes secure political victories against business.
- The case shows the interaction of business, government and civil society organizations. We can see that each category is quite diverse. 'Government' here refers to the responsible department (Department for Trade and Industry (DTI)) but also refers to MPs. 'Business' includes a range of firms, large and small, and associations. CSOs include trade unions, religious groups and public interest campaigns. The main focus of political influence was government and the law, but we can also see the interaction between business and CSOs. Businesses have to think about the reputational impacts of CSO campaigns. In seeking to persuade the government not to change the law, campaign groups such as 'Keep Sunday Special' were also presenting what they saw as the harmful impact on society of the large retailers' desire to deregulate Sunday trading.
- Business does not always have a common political aim or shared interests. In this example the interests of big business and small business were in conflict, and the large retailers were themselves divided.

A small corner shop in Wigan, Lancashire. For convenience stores, unrestricted Sunday opening without competition from large stores provides a vital source of business.
© John Londei from 'Shutting Up Shop—the decline of the traditional small shop'

- Divisions in the business community tend to weaken its political influence. In this case the withdrawal of Tesco from the 'My Sunday, My Choice' campaign may have been significant.
- The case provides an insight into some of the methods of political influence deployed

by business, especially the ability to create and finance ad hoc associations to campaign on shared interests ('My Sunday, My Choice'), and the employment of specialist public relations consultants.

- The case shows how the political influence of business can vary according to the social and political context. A couple of factors stand out:
  - Although the Labour government was perceived as pro-business it was experiencing political difficulties during its third term in office. Although these difficulties were not related to the Sunday trading issue, it faced opposition from its own backbenchers to any change in the law. A Commons motion opposing any change was supported by nearly 300 MPs, mostly Labour. The government didn't want to risk the embarrassment of a difficult passage through parliament, and possible defeat, for any new law. This would have compounded the difficulties it was already facing.
  - Some of the large retailers were facing a more critical media and public. This was particularly the case for the large supermarkets, facing an investigation by the Competition Commission into the possible abuse of market power by the 'big four', and growing public concerns about the closure of small retailers and the future of the high street. Some commentators suggested that Tesco's withdrawal from the campaign was motivated by a desire to salvage its reputation (Finch, 2006). At the time it was trying to foster an image as a 'good neighbour'. More generally it can be argued that there was a shift away from the consumerist culture that had been prevalent in the 1980s and early '90s. This meant that the 'My Sunday, My Choice' campaign could not generate a groundswell of public support. There was no effective alliance between business and consumers.

Classification of groups

Because the world of interest groups is diverse it is helpful to classify them into a limited number of types. Three distinctions are useful, between:

- ready-made organizations and purpose-built (or associational) groups
- interest groups and cause groups
- insider and outsider groups.

Ready-made or purpose-built

Ready-made organizations exist for other purposes but may also act as pressure groups from time to time in support of their prime organizational goals. Examples of such organizations include businesses, churches, charities and professional associations. The prime purposes of these organizations may be described as follows:

- businesses—to make money
- churches—to worship God
- charities—to help people in need
- professional associations—to safeguard professional knowledge and practice.

These purposes are normally realized through non-political activities (e.g. production of commodities, provision of religious services, raising and distributing funds and other aid, supervising continuing professional development) but participation in the political process may be a useful adjunct. For example lobbying may be used:

- by Asda to try to persuade government to liberalize Sunday trading
- by the Catholic church to encourage a policy of allowing faith schools
- by Oxfam to press for increased aid to Third World countries
- by the Law Society to influence decisions on legal aid.

Associational groups are formed when individuals come together for the prime purpose of pursuing shared goals through participation in the political process. They may develop to become large formal organizations controlling significant resources, operating globally and with some business-like features, such as professionalized staff and management structures. On the other hand they may be small, ad hoc, short-lived, localized, informal, single-issue campaigns. At one end of the scale are organizations such as Greenpeace with the resources and organizational capacity to mount campaigns against giant MNCs such as Shell, involving action in many countries and engaging with several governments and IGOs, and commanding high profile media attention. At the other end are local campaigns to prevent the opening of a new supermarket which may make no impact beyond the local area.

Interest groups and cause groups

The distinction between interest groups and cause groups concerns the type of 'interests' that they promote. In simple terms interest groups exist primarily to defend and advance the interests of their own members, while cause groups exist primarily to promote some wider public interest or good cause. This terminology is not used universally. Heywood (2002) uses the terms 'sectional' and 'promotional' groups, and points out that in the United States the terms 'private interest group' and 'public interest group' are favoured. In the political battle over Sunday trading the 'My Sunday, My Choice' campaign, the Association of Convenience Stores, and the trade union USDAW are all examples of interest groups. Their primary purpose was to secure a legal outcome that would benefit their own members.

- 'My Sunday, My Choice'—to secure the liberalization of Sunday trading to enable large retailers to do more business and make more money
- USDAW—to maintain existing restrictions on Sunday trading to protect its members from pressure to work more unsocial hours
- Association of Convenience Stores—to maintain existing restrictions on Sunday trading to protect its members from competition from large retailers

It is not unusual for 'private interest groups' to use 'public interest' arguments to boost their influence. For example the 'My Sunday, My Choice' campaign chose to highlight the supposed benefit of greater choice for shopworkers and consumers to work and shop on Sundays rather than the benefits to its members of increased sales and profits. When businesses act as pressure groups, either individually or through some form of association, they generally do so for reasons of self-interest. Trade unions and professional associations are other prime examples of economic interest groups. Interest groups can also arise on the basis of other issues, such as community groups campaigning against development to protect their local environment. Although the environment can be seen as a classic 'public interest' issue, local campaigns may reflect the self-interest of the residents in a particular area. For example, people might not want 'unsightly' wind turbines situated in their locality, even if they also think that increased utilization of wind power is important to reduce our reliance on fossil fuels. This type of locally-based opposition is sometimes referred to as NIMBYism (from the 'Not In My BackYard' attitude such groups seem to display).

> ⤷ *Stop and Think*
>
> Do you think it is plausible that Asda campaigned for liberalization of Sunday trading primarily in the interests of shopworkers and shoppers?
>
> Would Asda open on Sundays just because it is so committed to extending choice to shopworkers and consumers even if it made a loss?

Private interest groups can and do sometimes campaign on public interest issues. Professional associations may have public interest objectives, such as the British Medical Association campaigning on public health issues. Trade unions may support campaigns against sweatshops in developing countries, such as Oxfam's 2004 'Play Fair at the Olympics' campaign. Businesses, too, can campaign on public interest issues. Sometimes this reflects the ethos of certain types of businesses, such as Body Shop or Café Direct. But even public limited companies (PLCs) can support public interest goals. For example, the Cooperative Bank promotes ethical investment and consumerism. An example of large companies acting together to promote public interest goals can be seen in lobbying government for tighter restrictions on CO_2 emissions from UK industry. This is partly based on a business case in terms of the opportunities to develop alternative technologies, but it also recognizes that business has a stake in the wider public interest goal of tackling climate change.

Values

Cause (or public interest) groups are based on shared values or principles. They reflect concern for the interests of others, such as those living in poverty in Third World countries, and/or some notion of the wider public interest, such as protecting the environment. Public interest groups do not reflect the direct or immediate interests of their members, although this does not mean that members do not have a stake in the success of the campaigns. The way in which a particular issue will impact upon their own lives can often be a factor motivating individuals to join or support such groups. Members or supporters of environmental pressure groups, such as Greenpeace or Friends of the Earth, recognize that we all have a stake in tackling global threats such as climate change. Campaigners against sport utility vehicles (SUVs) no doubt believe that we would all be better off if everybody were to drive more fuel-efficient cars. So the public interest naturally often involves an element of self-interest.

However some public interest campaigns have apparently more selfless goals. For example campaigns against sweatshops, or for fair trade, appear to be motivated solely by concern for the plight of producers in Third World countries. For example, in 2004 Oxfam ran a campaign, 'Fair Play at the Olympics', to highlight sweatshop conditions endured by workers in Third World countries producing sportswear for western companies such as Nike and Reebok. Consumers who boycotted these products got no personal benefit from doing so (indeed, they are willing to forego what to them might be the great pleasure of wearing the latest Nike trainers). Nevertheless, as we have seen, public interest arguments can sometimes conceal private interests. We might wonder whether trade unions campaigning against conditions in Third World factories are really trying to protect jobs 'at home'. (For information about the campaign go to www.oxfam.org.uk.)

Insiders and outsiders

The distinction between insider and outsider groups concerns the relationships that groups have with government—whether they are in some sense brought inside the policy-making process or left outside. Being on the inside seems to be the best way to exert influence, while being on the outside suggests being ignored by government. Insiders may derive their influence from possession of resources, such as knowledge, that is valuable to policy-makers. They may combine effective influence with a low profile, precisely because their insider methods are often hidden from public view and do not attract media attention. However insiders are obliged to 'play by the rules' if they want to retain a close working relationship with government, and this can limit their activities. For example, they may have to limit their demands to those that are seen as reasonable by policy-makers, and may have to refrain from vociferous public criticism of government since this would undermine the element of trust that characterizes close working relationships. Business maintains a close working relationship with government and constitutes an insider group (e.g. see Mini-Case 11.2 on the CBI).

Outsider groups may combine limited influence with a high profile and this is because, lacking insider status, they are obliged to use more public methods of campaigning. On the other hand, although government might not consult with outsider groups at least they are free to express their demands freely, criticize government, and use public campaigning methods to win support and get their message across. So there are pros and cons to being an insider or an outsider.

The distinction can also be applied to relations between pressure groups and business, and here too there are advantages and disadvantages. Should environmental groups try to work closely with oil companies in order to exert influence on the inside, or will this damage their reputation for independence and their ability to criticize the companies publicly? This has become an issue for environmental groups as large corporations, such as oil companies, have moved more to engage these groups as stakeholders.

> **⊃ *Stop and Think***
> What are the advantages and disadvantages of 'insider' and 'outsider' status?

Pressure group resources

Although 'pressure group' is used as a generic term, we can see that insider groups do not rely so much on exerting pressure to have influence since they work through regular contact, consultation and trust. By contrast outsider groups must rely more on their capacity to exert pressure on government to have influence—their relationship is more adversarial. However it is possible to identify a number of factors that affect the capacity of groups to exert influence, and a range of tactics or methods of influence. Key resources that groups can command include:

- size of membership
- extent of wider public sympathy and support
- finance
- expert knowledge
- capacity to impose sanctions
- personal contacts.

Membership and wider public support are important because they act as barometers of public opinion. Governments are sensitive to shifts in public opinion because they have to retain electoral support. Businesses are also sensitive to these aspects of groups that they deal with because of the potential implications for reputation and customer loyalty.

Expert knowledge can be converted into influence because governments and companies may depend on such knowledge to help them develop public policy or corporate strategy.

On the other hand the capacity to impose sanctions can confer influence because governments and businesses are keen to avoid the damaging consequences of disruption. Sanctions typically involve the withdrawing or withholding of some resource or action, such as of labour by trade unions in a strike or other form of industrial action, of custom by consumers, of funds by ethical investors, or of investment by business. A powerful sanction can simply be the withdrawal of goodwill or approval. For example, business reputation may be enhanced by endorsement of environmental policy by a pressure group with a high level of public support and trust, and consequently damaged by withdrawal of this approval.

Finance is obviously important because it allows groups to mount campaigns and employ other agencies such as professional lobbyists.

Personal contacts and networks can facilitate access to decision makers and provide a context in which shared values and principles can develop. To the extent that senior figures in the business world come from similar backgrounds and participate in similar social networks to those in government this may make policy-makers more receptive to the needs and interests of business.

Pressure group influence

Pressure groups can seek to influence government decisions through the various stages of the policy process, or indirectly through the media and public opinion. Thus the main channels of access can be identified as:

- the executive
- the legislature
- political parties
- the courts
- the media/public opinion.

Pressure groups can seek to influence government decisions through ministers and senior officials at the heart of government. The 'behind closed doors' character of these contacts makes it difficult to have a clear picture of the influence exerted at this level.

© istockphoto.com/ George Cairns

The most direct, insider, channel of access is through the executive, meaning ministers and senior officials at the heart of government. Business is in a strong position to exercise this high-level influence. Contacts at this level can be highly formalized and routinized (as in a corporatist framework), but more often:

> the consultative process is informal yet institutionalized, taking place through meetings and regular contacts that are rarely publicized and are beyond the scope of public scrutiny. (Heywood, 2002: 281)

The 'behind closed doors' character of these contacts obviously makes it difficult to have a clear picture of the influence exerted at this level.

A less direct channel of influence is via the legislative assembly through 'lobbying'. Lobbying involves making representations to legislators in order to try to influence how they vote on specific issues. An increasingly important role is played by professional lobbyists hired by businesses or other pressure groups to help them present their case in the most effective way. Businesses may also employ their own in-house lobbying staff (see the Case Study on the car industry at the end of this chapter).

Groups can exercise political influence through links with political parties. For example, the Conservative Party has been seen as the main representative of business interests in the UK, maintaining strong links with the business community and depending on donations from businesses and wealthy individuals to finance its election campaigns. Conversely, the Labour Party was originally created at the beginning of the last century to represent the interests of working people in parliament and relied on funding from trade unions. In the 1990s New Labour became more successful in attracting increased funding from business as it adopted a more business-friendly approach and moved away from central aspects of 'old' Labour's left-wing or socialist, anti-business, image. Both major parties have become more reliant on donations (and loans) due to falling income through membership subscriptions and the rising costs of election campaigning. Elections are essentially competitions in persuasion, and have become more like marketing campaigns, and the costs have consequently been ratcheted up.

Too close an association with one party can have an obvious disadvantage which is that influence may be negligible when 'your' party is not in office. For this reason it is important for the business community to be able to 'do business' with whichever party is in power. For parties, too close an association with a particular interest can have the disadvantage of limiting the appeal to other voters. This is why 'New Labour' sought to distance itself from the trade unions in the 1990s and be seen as a party of 'middle England' with a positive attitude to business. In a similar way David Cameron tried to widen the appeal of the Conservatives after being elected as leader in 2005 by putting more emphasis on social justice and saying that the party had to 'stand up to' and not just 'stand up for' big business.

Pressure groups can also try to influence government and business through a wide range of campaigning tactics such as petitions and letter-writing campaigns, demonstrations or protests, civil disobedience and forms of direct action. For example, as part of Greenpeace's campaign to protect the Amazon rainforest supporters were urged to write to Kentucky Fried Chicken (KFC) to demand that it stop using soya grown in deforested areas of the Amazon. Greenpeace also employs non-violent direct action to disrupt the operations of whaling fleets. (For more information on these campaigns go to www.greenpeace.org.uk.) Business tends to avoid forms of action outside the formal political process. An exception to this was the involvement of certain types of business, such as farmers and road hauliers, in the fuel protests (against fuel tax) in 2000, including blockading oil depots.

Business is in a strong position to influence public opinion and shape the political consensus within society. It is able to do this through advertising, PR and through a largely pro-business media. It can be argued that successful advertising and branding strategies that build customer loyalty to businesses or products also indirectly create support for the private enterprise system. In addition, business is generally able to rely on a pro-business bias within the media. Media organizations are located largely within the private sector of the economy and so tend to reflect and espouse the interests of business. A large multinational corporation such as News International shares the same interests as other MNCs, and it is not surprising if a pro-business stance is reflected in the editorial policies of the newspapers owned by the company. Business also tends to have good access to media organizations.

Interaction

However this does not mean that the media all speak with one voice in relation to business or are slavishly uncritical. The existence of a 'free press' independent of government is a fundamental component of democracy, allowing scrutiny and criticism of government and business. Editorial and journalistic independence allow for critical views of business to be expressed. Investigative journalism has an important role in exposing corporate scandals or bad practice. Commercial media organizations will respond to market demand for critical views of business among readers and viewers. Finally, public sector media organizations, such as the BBC, operate with a strict editorial policy of political balance. Thus businesses have to manage their relationships with the media.

> **⊃ Stop and Think**
> Do you agree that there is a pro-business bias in the media? What evidence would you use to test this claim? Can you think of examples from your own use of the media? If there is a bias do you think it makes any difference to people's attitudes to business?

Using the court system is not, strictly speaking, a form of political action because of the independence and political neutrality of the judiciary. However it is precisely this independence that sometimes allows a pressure group to challenge a government decision through the courts. The principles of the separation of powers and the rule of law mean that the courts have a role to ensure that the executive acts within its lawful powers. Pressure groups can be successful in forcing a government to reverse a decision through legal action where it can be shown that its actions are not compatible with the law.

Assessing the pluralist model

The main argument of the pluralist model is that, through the group process involving a myriad of groups with diverse capacities and using a range of methods, power is fragmented and dispersed. Of course, if you examine any particular political issue you will find winners and losers—some groups are successful at influencing government and others are not. That is the nature of the competitive group process. But processes of bargaining and interaction at least allow the views and interests of a large range of groups to be taken into account. For example the government engaged in a process of consultation on the Sunday trading laws in 2006 that allowed the views of all interested parties to be heard.

The pluralist model holds that groups promoting one cause or interest tend to be balanced by opposing groups (providing 'countervailing' power), that winners in one battle may lose next time, and that there is no single group or interest that is able to occupy a dominant position overall within the political process. For example, business faces countervailing power from trade unions and a plethora of groups in civil society. Business corporations or association may be successful on one issue but unsuccessful on another.

Diversity

The business community often has a range of interests and these may conflict—business does not speak with one voice. Business has a legitimate voice (or voices) within the political process, but there are many other voices and business does not always get its own way.

The basic pluralist claim that power and influence is fragmented and dispersed has been challenged by a number of alternative models. These all suggest that power is rather more concentrated than pluralists allow and, in particular, that business interests are more prominent.

Neocorporatism—the importance of economic interests

The *corporatist model* (sometimes referred to as neocorporatism) directs attention to the particular influence exercised by economic interests due to their importance within society. More specifically it depicts a 'tri-partite' (or three-way) relationship between government, business and trade unions. The basic rationale of the corporatist approach is that governments need to secure the cooperation and support of business and the trade unions in order to be able to manage the economy effectively. In contrast, government does not require the cooperation of any other group to the same extent. This may lead government to establish formal arrangements for consultation to achieve high-level agreement in relation to economic policy. In effect, business and unions become insider groups. This may be characterized as a movement towards economic planning rather than leaving things to the 'invisible hand' of market forces.

The term neocorporatism is used more narrowly to describe the development of this type of tri-partite arrangement in many of the industrialized capitalist countries in the second half of the last century, especially in Europe. This is often seen as a specific type or *model* of capitalism. According to Wilson:

> Neocorporatism is a form of governance in which organizations representing major economic interests, usually unions and employers' organizations, are given major, privileged opportunities to participate in policy-making in return for accepting responsibilities to assist the state in the governance of society. (2003: 102–3)

In this definition business and the unions have both a representative role and a role in governance. In other words there is an opportunity to influence policy coupled with a responsibility to assist in its implementation. For example, in an effort to tackle inflationary pressures and stimulate growth the trade unions might agree to limit wage demands and business might agree to increase investment. The idea is that this type of agreement would benefit both sides, and government would be able to achieve its macroeconomic objectives.

The neocorporatist phase in the UK

However, neocorporatist tendencies vary in strength from one country to another. The model is a useful tool for understanding some European economies, but is less relevant to the UK, and cannot really be applied to the US. A rather short-lived experiment in neocorporatism was undertaken in the UK in the 1960s and '70s. This was in conjunction with a Keynesian approach to economic policy and was intended to boost UK economic performance by providing an element of 'indicative planning' from the centre that could not be achieved through the arms-length approach of demand management. However the experiment was discarded by the Thatcher governments in the 1980s as part of a move to disengage the state from the economy and rely more on the 'free market'. It has not been resurrected.

Making agreements stick

For neocorporatist arrangements to work government has to have representative organizations for business and labour with which it can reach binding agreements. One of the reasons for the failure of neocorporatism in the UK was that although these 'peak' organizations exist in the form of the CBI (Confederation of British Industry) and the TUC (Trade Union Congress) they were not capable of speaking with one voice on behalf of business or labour and making agreements stick. It was no good having the TUC agree to limit wage increases if member unions and negotiators at local level did not stick to it (a problem referred to as 'wage drift'). And it was no good having the CBI agree to increase investment if individual firms did not carry this out.

> Governments that have made agreements with . . . the CBI have been disappointed to discover that those agreements are not necessarily honoured by individual businesses. In the mid 1960s, for example, after a National Plan was negotiated between business, unions and government to provide for sustained economic expansion, the CBI's commitments on increased investment did not translate into actual increases in investment by individual companies. They continued to base their decisions on anticipated levels of return, not the undertakings of those who represented them. (Wilson, 2003: 71)

In other words, in the UK context both business and labour are too fragmented to enable neocorporatist arrangements to work effectively.

Social partners

Another factor is that neocorporatism relies on a cultural context in which business and labour see themselves as social partners, and this is lacking in the UK. The predominant attitude within business has been rather more sceptical of both the state and trade unions. Neocorporatism involves a compromise with organized labour. It introduces parity between business and the trade unions as 'social partners' sharing policy-making and implementation with government, and involves interference in the right of business to manage its own affairs in response to market signals. Hence the Thatcherite rejection of corporatism went along with legislative reform to weaken the trade unions and restore the 'right to manage'. From the perspective of Thatcherism the problem with neocorporatism is that it gives too much power and recognition to trade unions, and also involves the state in trying to steer the economy when this should be left to the market. But it would appear that the disbandment of neocorporatist arrangements must have involved a loss of political influence by business since it lost its insider status (along with the trade unions).

Values

However another critical view of pluralism suggests that in all capitalist societies business occupies a privileged position in its relations with government. This doesn't mean that neocorporatism makes no difference, but it suggests that the overriding characteristic of the policy process in liberal democratic systems is business dominance.

The privileged position of business

The claim that democratic politics is characterized by business dominance is based on two ideas:

- the advantages that business enjoys in the electoral process and the representation of group interests—business as a political actor
- the crucial importance of business decisions for society as a whole—control without trying.

Control without trying

Lindblom has argued that business occupies a privileged position in policy-making, one that is unmatched by any other group or interest including organized labour. This privileged position arises from the fact that private business makes decisions about the allocation of resources on which the well-being of all individuals in society depends. These decisions constitute the basis of business leadership, or 'corporate power', defined by Luger as:

 Mini-Case 11.4 The privileged position of business in policy-making

According to the American political scientist Charles Lindblom 'the significance of the business leadership role in the market is in a consequent unusual kind and degree of control over governmental policy making given to business' (1980: 72). This means that 'governments award to business managers a privileged position in the play of power in policy making' (1980: 74). Lindlom's argument is set out in the following steps:

1 'many of the functions performed by business managers in the market are essential to society'

2 if these functions are not performed 'widespread discontent and—at an extreme—disorder would follow'

3 'government officials . . . know that widespread failure of business to perform these functions will bring down the government'

4 'consequently, government policy makers show constant concern about business performance'

5 but 'governments . . . cannot positively command business managers to perform their functions'

6 'They will perform only if induced by benefits, gains, or advantages offered them'

7 Therefore governments must 'develop and maintain business profitability through supporting policies'

8 'Policy making consequently comes under a special control by business: government officials must . . . give managers enough of what they need to motivate production, jobs, and growth; and must . . . give them special rights of consultation and actual participation in the actual setting of policies'. (1980: 72–4)

Lindblom also examines the participation of business in the political process through 'interest-group, party, and other electoral activities' and argues, in contrast to the pluralist view, that it is able to exert 'disproportionate influence'.

But the interesting point about the 'privileged position' of business is that it amounts to 'control without trying'. In other words, even if business did not exert influence through the electoral process and other activities it could rely on the bias in policy-making because this results just from the dependence of government on corporate power or business leadership in the market.

❷ Does the fact that 'many of the functions performed by business . . . are essential to society' justify its privileged position in policy-making?

(*Source*: Lindblom, C. E. (1980) *The Policy Making Process*)

the power over what is produced, how these products are distributed, how work is organised, which skills workers need to develop, which advertising images are used to shape consumer consciousness, what kind of technology is developed, and what kinds of pollutants are created. Corporate power shapes the distribution of income, the conditions and location of employment, and thus the future of communities and nations. (Luger, 2000: 3)

Lindblom notes that these decisions 'matter to all members of society . . . [and] loom as momentous as the decisions of most government officials . . . No one can say that . . . [they] . . . are too inconsequential to be labelled public policy' (1980: 72). Similarly Luger likens corporate power to a form of 'private government'. No other group in society makes decisions that matter to everybody in the same way. Lindblom's argument is that government is dependent on these decisions taken by private business to ensure a healthy economy which voters expect government to deliver. This dependence translates into a consistent bias in policy-making in favour of business interests. Governments must pursue policies that maintain business confidence to ensure that business continues to invest, create jobs and generate growth and so to ensure that voters are content.

Business as a political actor

It may be argued that business is able to exercise a 'disproportionate influence' through the electoral process and interest-group (pressure group) activity due to its control of key resources such as organization, knowledge and finance.

The consequences of globalization

Spatial levels

Globalization is a complex phenomenon with many dimensions—political, social and cultural as well as economic. In broad terms it refers to the increasing tendency of economic and other relationships to become 'stretched' across borders so that the nations and regions of the world become more inter-connected and interdependent. Globalization has been facilitated by technological changes—particularly in the fields of transport and communication—that have made, for example, the movement of people between countries both cheaper and quicker (see Chapter 12). Economic globalization itself has a number of dimensions, among the most important of which are:

- the growth and spread of international trade
- the growth of multinational corporations (MNCs) that own or control production facilities in more than one country
- the increasing integration of global financial markets.

It has been argued that one important consequence of economic globalization is to increase the power of corporations in relation to governments. It has done so by increasing the 'exit options' available to business. This means that MNCs can search the world for the most favourable locations for their production activities. To the extent that locational advantage is connected with political decisions, governments are under increased pressure to ensure that decisions are favourable to business in order to attract inward investment by MNCs and prevent production and jobs moving elsewhere. For example MNCs might be expected to favour deregulated (or 'flexible') labour markets where unions are relatively weak, low rates of taxation, and policies to benefit business such as the provision of training and infrastructure. In other words, globalization accentuates what Linblom refers to as the privileged position of business in policy-making. For example:

Automobile manufacturers can switch the production of new models of cars relatively easily between different countries: Ford and GM, for example, have plants in Britain, Germany, France, Spain and Belgium and naturally consider which country will give the highest tax concessions, lowest taxes, least cumbersome regulations and most disciplined workforce in making decisions on car production. The automobiles produced in any one of these countries can be shipped without restriction or tariffs to any other member country; under WTO rules, the automobiles can also be shipped worldwide with only minimal duty being levied. (Wilson, 2003: 17)

It has been argued that globalization will produce a **race to the bottom** as governments reduce taxes on business and avoid or remove regulations that are perceived as onerous for business. For example, governments may feel that making it easier to hire and fire workers will help to attract inward investment. In the UK New Labour's policy of 'flexible' labour markets was intended to make the UK an attractive location for business in a highly competitive global economy.

However in some cases there appears to be very little that government can do in the way of offering effective inducements to business to invest. A case in point is the shift of car production not just, as Wilson discusses, between western European countries but to central and eastern Europe, including the new accession states, and Asia. It appears that governments in the rich countries such as the UK can do little to offset the low-cost advantage gained by car makers from shifting production. 'Labour costs in Poland, the Czech Republic and Slovakia can be less than a fifth of those in countries such as Germany' (Gow, 2006). For example in April 2006 Peugeot Citroën announced plans to close its plant in Coventry putting over 2,000 jobs at risk, blaming, in part, high production and logistical costs (*Guardian*, 18 April 2006). At the same time the company was expanding production in the Czech Republic and Slovakia. Paradoxically the government policy of labour market flexibility that was supposed to attract investment by making it easier to hire labour was also criticized, particularly by the trade unions, for making it easier for firms to shift production by firing workers.

> ⮑ *Stop and Think*
> What is meant by a 'race to the bottom'? Why is this sometimes seen as a consequence of globalization?

The ups and downs of business influence over policy-making

The extent of the 'power shift' from government to business as a result of globalization is disputed. Although MNCs do have increased 'exit options', as shown by the car industry, business is not 'footloose' in the sense of being able to go easily wherever it pleases. The dependence of business on government to provide key inputs such as skills and infrastructure can lock businesses in to particular countries to some extent and give governments some leverage over their activities. More generally, economic globalization is itself not just an outcome of technological drivers but also of government decisions, such as to liberalize trade and capital flows. This means that governments and IGOs remain, to some extent, in control of the process of globalization.

It can be argued that economic globalization has increased the power of business in relation to trade unions and civil society organizations (CSOs) or pressure groups. For example, the trade unions appeared to have little power to force Peugeot Citroën to reverse its decision to close its Coventry plant. Trade unions have been left behind in globalization because they don't operate effectively on an international scale. However globalization has brought with it the rise of effective global pressure groups and protest movements. In particular, the Internet has enabled groups to mobilize international campaigns against business. Well-known examples of successful campaigns are those against Nike (sweatshops) and Shell (pollution), both of which mobilized consumer boycotts.

Business influence—'nothing special' or 'unique'?

Pluralism and the business dominance approaches seem to be at opposite ends of a spectrum—business influence is seen as nothing special in the former and as unique in the latter. However both approaches see business as an actor in the political arena seeking, along with other groups and interests, to ensure that its voice is heard and that policy-makers take account of its interests. In other words, engagement in the political process at some level, either as individual companies and/or through business associations, is a crucial element of business behaviour.

The pluralist approach does not say that business never exercises a decisive influence over government policy. Rather it says that business involvement in political battles is more a case of 'win some, lose some'. The business dominance approach does not say that business wins all political battles. Indeed it recognizes that 'the precise extent of business control appears to wax and wane' (Lindblom, 1980: 82). Public interest groups can win on specific issues (such as Brent Spar) and there can be periods when these groups are ascendant (such as periods when the car industry was on the defensive). But the business dominance approach does argue that business influence is special in that, on the whole, it is unmatched by any other group or interest in society.

> ➲ *Stop and Think*
>
> Do you agree that the political influence of business is 'nothing special', or that it is unique?
>
> Does it matter if there is a bias in favour of business interests in the policy-making process? Does this mean that democracy isn't working properly? Or is it healthy for government to attach so much weight to maintaining business confidence?

Pressure on business from CSOs

Influencing business decisions is unlike political decisions because the former are taken in private whereas the latter are public. In a democracy governments are supposed to engage in consultation and take account of public opinion as registered by pressure groups, whereas business has no such obligation. Government is accountable to the people, business (in the shape of PLCs) is accountable to shareholders. Pressure groups have to penetrate the essentially private world of business. In seeking to do so they are assisted by businesses seeking to operate in a more open way in order to retain their licence to operate. This term refers to the need for business to develop and maintain a level of public trust and sense of legitimacy. This is reflected in the trend towards greater stakeholder engagement. That the public are no longer as willing to take it for granted that business will 'do the right thing' is itself partly the consequence of campaigning by pressure groups.

Pressure group methods in relation to business:

- consultation/stakeholder engagement
- public opinion/media
- ethical consumerism/consumer activism

- disruption through direct action/civil disobedience, e.g. obstruction, protest, damage to property
- legal action.

Ethical consumerism

Ethical consumerism refers to the willingness of consumers to make decisions about how they spend their money based, in part, on their ethical principles or values. The conventional view of the consumer in economic theory assumes that the sole purpose of consumption is self-interest. In this view consumers seek only to maximize their 'utility' or happiness by buying goods or services that satisfy their wants, and by seeking the best quality–price combination that is available. This model of consumer behaviour is undoubtedly insightful—it may characterize fairly how most consumers behave most of the time. However it does not describe how consumers behave all the time, and there is evidence that ethical consumerism is increasing. Ethical consumerism does not mean ignoring self-interest, but trying to balance self-interest with the interests of others. *The Ethical Consumerism Report 2003* defines this as 'personal consumption where a choice of product or service exists which supports a particular ethical issue—be it human rights, the environment or animal welfare'. This might involve being willing to accept products of lower quality or higher price. For example, when people decide to purchase Fairtrade products, such as bananas or coffee, they do so out of regard for the interests of others—in this case the farmers who produce these crops. The whole point of Fairtrade is to improve the incomes of poor farmers in developing countries, and consumers may be prepared to pay a higher price to achieve this. The ethical principle that is involved here is the commitment to do something to combat poverty in the developing world. In choosing Fairtrade products there is an implied criticism of big business for giving farmers a raw deal. In other words consumers may be motivated by a desire to do something *for* the world's poor and, at the same time, to take action *against* big business.

Ethical consumerism is still small-scale, but growing. The *2004 Ethical Consumerism Report*, published by the Cooperative Bank, states that 'ethical consumerism in the UK is soaring and is now worth £24.7 billion a year . . . The overall market share of ethical consumerism has increased by almost 40% in five years.' For example 'Sales of Fairtrade goods, such as tea, coffee and bananas, increased by £29 million to £92 million [in 2003]—growth of 46%'. However, we need to keep ethical consumerism in perspective—the 2003 report notes that 'the total market share for ethical goods and services, as measured by the EPI [Ethical Purchasing Index] is still less than 2 per cent'.

When people decide to purchase Fairtrade products, such as bananas or coffee, they do so out of regard for the interests of others. This is 'consumer activism', an important element of the political arena in which business operates.

© istockphoto.com/John Rodriguez

> **→ *Stop and Think***
>
> Have you ever made decisions about spending based on ethical grounds? Think of examples. What were the ethical considerations that influenced your decisions? Have you ever made decisions about what to buy (or not to buy) as part of an organized campaign, such as a consumer boycott?

Ethical consumerism can be essentially an individual act, but it is often linked to a wider campaign or movement. Campaigning organizations have been important in raising awareness of specific ethical issues or products, and the idea of ethical consumerism more generally. Such campaigns may try to put pressure on government to take action, but they also target businesses directly. Campaigns directed at business might involve encouraging consumer boycotts or publicity campaigns to expose corporate malpractice to public scrutiny. The term 'consumer activism' is sometimes used to refer to these types of campaigns, and they are important elements of the political arena in which business operates. Ethical consumerism can be seen as a conscious attempt to utilize the power that consumers exercise in the form of 'consumer sovereignty' to bring about change. The idea of consumer sovereignty tells us that consumers happen to exercise power through their spending decisions but in an essentially passive way; the idea of ethical consumerism tells us that they exercise this power deliberately and actively. Thus in the *2004 Ethical Consumerism Report* the Director of Corporate Affairs at CFS says 'It is clear that UK consumers are increasingly willing to take action through their wallets to support business that they consider to be ethical and to avoid companies who they consider to be unethical.'

Is business influence in the political process a good thing?

You can see that the answer to the question how much political influence is enjoyed by business is disputed. There is also disagreement over whether business should have a dominant voice in the political process. How you answer this question will depend on whether you think the private interests of business corporations and the business community in general are aligned with the wider public interest, or that there are unavoidable conflicts. It will also depend on whether you believe that business is solely motivated by profit or can be relied on to balance this with concern for the common good.

In the 1950s the president of General Motors claimed that 'what was good for the country was good for General Motors and vice versa', a statement that is often translated as 'What's good for General Motors is good for the country.' In this vein it can be argued that we all have a stake in successful business and therefore business should be the most powerful influence on government. Government needs to manage the economy successfully and to do so needs to take heed of business interests and views.

On the other hand, Luger argues that business does have 'inordinate' influence and that this influence is undesirable. In this view business interests may often conflict with the common good. An example in Luger's analysis is the resistance of the car makers to tighter regulation of vehicle emissions. Therefore business influence in policy-making needs to be checked so that corporate interests can be balanced with, and sometimes subordinated to, those of other groups.

In some cases business may use its political influence to press for policy change in the wider public interest. For example, in 2006 leading UK businesses publicly called on government to introduce tighter restrictions on CO_2 emissions from industry.

◈ *Looking ahead*

As we have seen in this chapter, the power of business in the political arena is open to interpretation within different theoretical frameworks. However we have also seen that the power of business is subject to change. For example Luger argues that although business has maintained a dominant position in policy there have been periods in which its influence has weakened. Looking ahead, it is possible to identify some factors that will affect the relationship between business and government and the influence of business.

New Labour represented a rejection of 'old labour' or socialist policies. In the past socialism had arguably acted as a counterweight to business within politics and society. Thus business dominance has been reinforced by the decline of its socialist challenger. Although left-wing ideas will continue to form part of the political arena it is difficult to see a major revival in the next few years.

It has been argued that economic globalization has resulted in a power shift from government to business in recent decades. As globalization is an ongoing process that is transforming modern societies this will continue to pose challenges for governments in regulating business behaviour and managing their economies.

Business will continue to operate in the context of a more sceptical public, meaning that it has to work hard to retain public trust particularly in relation to ethical issues such as climate change. Business will continue to face demands for greater corporate social responsibility and have to engage with civil society organizations.

Some of the major political challenges in the future will lead to strong pressure for greater regulation of business, shifting power back towards government. This is particularly the case in relation to action to tackle climate change. Effective action will also require greater EU involvement. The proposed EU law to force European car makers to reduce CO_2 emissions is an example of this.

◈ *Summary*

- Political decisions can have powerful effects in enabling or constraining business activity. Therefore business needs to have an effective voice in political debate. Business is a political actor

- Business has to compete with other groups in society for the attention of government. Politics involves a 'play of power' between rival groups and interests, but also makes possible the search for compromise

- Civil Society Organizations (CSOs) may seek to influence government decisions, but they also target business directly to influence decisions and strategy

- Relations between business and government may be conducted in a centralized way through business associations such as the CBI, or in a decentralized fashion in which individual companies are the key actors. In the UK business–government relations tend to be decentralized

- Business influence is exercised through two main channels: the electoral process and party competition, and interest group activity

- There are rival theoretical frameworks for understanding the political influence exercised by business. The pluralist model suggests that power is fragmented and dispersed among a large number of groups. The neocorporatist model emphasizes the key influence of economic interests—business and labour. The business dominance model suggests that business exercises unrivalled political influence

- The effectiveness of business in the political arena matters to business but it also matters to the rest of society. The question here is whether business interests are aligned with the common good. Is what is good for General Motors good for the country?

Case study: the political influence of the car industry

It is difficult to overstate the importance of the car industry in modern societies and economies. Its development in the last century was at the heart of the economic growth of the leading industrial capitalist economies, notably the United States, western Europe and, in the latter part of the century, rapidly developing countries such as Japan. The car industry was seen to exemplify the technological systems characteristic of modern manufacturing. Indeed, the predominant manufacturing system of the twentieth century is sometimes referred to as 'Fordism' because of the pioneering role of the Ford Motor company. Fordism was based on mass production of standardized products on the basis of a highly mechanized assembly line utilizing semi-skilled labour. The high productivity achieved by these methods enabled cheapening of the product and rising living standards (e.g., bringing the cost of car ownership within reach, by the late twentieth century, of virtually the whole population). Thus Fordism is also associated with mass consumption and the rise of 'consumerism'. The car industry was also typified by that other characteristic feature of the twentieth century economic landscape, the giant corporation, and can be seen as a pioneer of globalization. Today Ford, with other car makers, is among the largest multinational corporations. Car use and ownership has also become central to modern societies and the way we live our lives. The car is much more than a mere means of transportation—car ownership has come to be closely associated with ideas about personal identity, status and freedom.

The social and economic importance of the car industry makes it an interesting case study for examining the political influence of business. We might expect that such a key industry, characterized by giant corporations operating on a global scale, will demonstrate a high level of business influence. At the same time, we should remember that other industries and firms may have less capacity to exert influence.

Luger has studied the long-term political influence of the US car industry between 1916 and 1996. The importance of this approach is that, while business influence is likely to vary from time to time and issue to issue, a long-term study reveals the overall pattern. Is business revealed, on the whole, to be a dominant influence on government, or a rather weak one? Luger's study shows that industry influence has varied over time. Up to the late 1980s three periods are identified: the first, up to the late 1960s, is one of business dominance over government policy; the second period, until the late 1970s, involved 'bargaining and compromise' between business and government and resulted in the expansion of regulation; and, the final period to 1988 'was a time of resurgence and triumph of industry over government'

Capitol Hill, Washington DC, reflected in a car mirror. How far does the car industry shape government policy?

© istockphoto.com/Steven Myers

(2000: 14). However, Luger's overall finding is that the US car industry's political influence is evident in each period and, overall, gives it an 'inordinate impact on public policy' (2000: 1). In other words the car industry does not always get its own way in relation to government, and there are periods when government has introduced regulations opposed by the industry. Yet, over the long-term, the industry has been very effective in getting its own way and its power has exceeded that of any other group in society. How has this influence been exerted?

In general terms the answer is that business has control over resources that is unrivalled by any other group, and that it is able to convert this control into political influence. As Luger states, 'the resources available to the large corporation give it leverage over . . . government that is often unmatched' (2000: 3). Put simply: money equals power. This means that individuals and organizations, like businesses, that control large amounts of wealth tend to have more political influence than the rest. As an example of this Luger states that 'in 1997 [it was] estimated that the industry spent over $100 million a year to influence government . . . In contrast, the entire 1996 budget of the main public interest group devoted to auto safety, the Center for Auto Safety, was approximately $600,000' (2000: 184). But this answer is too simple, for in democracies the basic form of political influence is through the vote, and all democracies have rules designed to limit the influence of money in politics. The mechanisms of influence identified by Luger are more complex and subtle, including the following:

- Lobbying—through in-house lobbyists based at the heart of government in Washington, contact between top managers and senior officials in government, and the hiring of specialist lobbyists and PR firms (Luger, 2000: 183).

- As well as acting on their own behalf firms also rely on business groups and associations to represent their (shared) interests. These associations operate at industry level (e.g. trade associations) and in relation to the business community as a whole (e.g. Chambers of Commerce) (Luger, 2000: 183).

- Industry is able to finance technical research to back up its political positions and arguments (Luger, 2000: 183), e.g. through sympathetic foundations and 'think tanks'.

- Businesses make donations to political parties, particularly in the form of election campaign contributions (Luger, 2000: 184). The point is to help to get elected parties and/or candidates that are perceived to be sympathetic to business interests.

- Businesses hire former politicians or government officials to gain inside knowledge of the political process and access to decision makers (Luger, 2000: 184). There is also movement in the other direction—from industry into government.

- In addition to these efforts by business to influence politics, Luger also refers to 'the industry's privileged economic position'. This means that business may not have to do anything to get government to take heed of its interests 'because economic growth and political stability can hinge on a healthy auto industry' (2000: 184–5). (The idea of a 'privileged position' was examined in more detail earlier in this chapter.)

- Large corporations and industries may also derive political influence from activities that are ostensibly non-political and commercial, notably advertising. The marketing of cars in ways that connects with core cultural values—as essential to personal freedom and as expressions of identity and status—has, as well as selling cars, 'provided the auto makers with a reservoir of latent public support' (Luger, 2000: 182).

These mechanisms have afforded to the car industry in America a degree of political influence unrivalled by other groups. This does not mean that other groups can never win political battles with the car industry. As we have seen, Luger identifies the 1970s as a period in which the industry was forced to make compromises over issues such as pollution and fuel economy. Nor does it mean that all industries exercise comparable influence. There may be characteristics of the car industry that boost its political influence—particularly its size and economic importance. Finally, there may be some special features of the US political system that facilitate business influence. In other national contexts there may be a different balance between business and other interests in the political process. However Luger's study of the US car industry provides an interesting and important case of business political influence.

(*Source*: Luger, S. (2000) *Corporate Power, American Democracy, and the Automobile Industry* (Cambridge University Press))

❓ Review your understanding of how the automobile industry is able to exercise political influence

❓ Are there any specific characteristics of the car industry that help to enhance its political influence?

❓ Is the car industry a special case, or do all industries exert comparable influence?

❓ What other groups or interests in society might oppose the car industry and counteract its influence?

Review and discussion questions

1   Explain the main ideas of a pluralist model of the political process.

2   Analyse the claim that business occupies a privileged position in policy-making, and that this has been enhanced as a consequence of globalization.

3   Explain how civil society organizations can bring pressure to bear on business to change its behaviour.

4   Do you believe that business has too much or too little influence in the political process?

Assignments

1   Using newspaper archives and other sources find information on the announcement by Peugeot Citroën in April 2006 of its decision to close its plant in Ryton, Coventry. Answer the following questions:

   ● What were the reasons for the decision?

   ● What was the reaction of the government to the decision? What steps, if any, did government take to prevent the closure?

   ● What was the reaction of the trade unions to the decision? What steps, if any, did the trade unions take to prevent the closure?

   ● What does this example suggest about the balance of power between business, government and trade unions?

2   Compile a brief report on ethical consumerism. Your report should include the following elements:

   ● the meaning of ethical consumerism

   ● an analysis of trends and projections in ethical consumerism

   ● an outline of the methods used to promote ethical consumerism by campaigning organizations

   ● an analysis of the response to ethical consumerism by a large supermarket or retailer.

Useful websites for these assignments

www.fairtrade.org.uk

www.co-operativebank.co.uk (Ethical Consumerism Report)

www.oxfam.co.uk

Further reading

Wilson (2003) is an introduction to business and politics. It uses a comparative approach and considers the implications of globalization for the relationship between business and government. Also see Grant (1993).

For a discussion of pressure groups see Grant (2000). For neocorporatism see Wilson (2003). For business dominance see Lindblom (1980) and Luger (2000). Bakan (2005) and Hertz (2001) provide critical perspectives on the power of the modern corporation.

Online resources

Test your understanding of this chapter with online questions and answers, explore the subject further through web exercises, and use the weblinks to provide a quick resource for further research. Go to the Online Resource Centre at

www.oxfordtextbooks.co.uk/orc/ wetherly_otter/

Find out about the role of business associations by going to the websites for:

Confederation of British Industry www.cbi.org.uk/

Chambers of Commerce www.chamberonline.co.uk/

For campaigning and investigative organizations try out: www.publicintegrity.org/

www.transparency.org/

References

Ashley, J. (2006) A local consumer rebellion that carries a political lesson, *Guardian*, 3 July.

Bakan, J. (2005) *The Corporation: the Pathological Pursuit of Profit and Power* (London: Free Press).

Finch, J. (2006) Tesco plans to be green and a good neighbour, *Guardian*, 11 May.

Gow, D. (2006) Fears for UK car plants as factories shift east, *Guardian*, 2 March.

Grant, W. (1993) *Business and Politics in Britain* (London: Macmillan).

Grant, W. (2000) *Pressure Groups and British Politics* (London: Macmillan).

Hertz, N. (2001) *The Silent Takeover: Global Capitalism and the Death of Democracy* (London: William Heinemann).

Heywood, A. (2002) *Politics* (Basingstoke: Palgrave).

Lindblom, C. E. (1980) *The Policy Making Process* (Harlow: Prentice-Hall).

Luger, S. (2000) *Corporate Power, American Democracy, and the Automobile Industry* (Cambridge: Cambridge University Press).

Mathiason, N. (2006) Retail giants lose Sunday trading fight, *Guardian*, 2 July.

Wilson, G. K. (2003) *Business and Politics* (Basingstoke: Palgrave).

Globalization of business

Dorron Otter

Contents

12

Learning objectives

When you have completed this chapter you will be able to:

- Understand the meaning of globalization
- Outline the sources that are leading to changes in the scope of globalization
- Identify the range of competing views as to the nature of globalization
- Examine the inter-relationship between the external environment and the internal strategic response of business to the challenge of globalization
- Explore the ethical dilemmas that arise out of global business activity

Themes

Diversity — **Diversity of business**

Globalization is often associated with the rise of the major global corporations. It is not just global players that are involved in the business of international trade. Many small companies are involved either in terms of import/export activities or in their own right or as suppliers in increasingly complex supply management chains.

Internal/ external — **Internal/external**

While globalization can be seen as a force that happens 'out there' it is business that both drives this process forward and which in turn has to adopt its internal strategic response to it.

Complexity — **Complexity of the environment**

This chapter will show the complexity of the global external environment and the need for businesses to be fully aware of this when shaping their strategic responses to the challenges of globalization.

However, a primary influence on the process of globalization is the impact of business behaviour in shaping globalization itself and this will need to be examined.

Spatial levels — **Variety of spatial levels**

Globalization adds the supranational level to the focus on business activity and this is the defining characteristic of globalization emphasizing the inter-linkages across the spatial levels from local through to global. What is the nature of the inter-connections between the local through to the global and what is the impact on the spatial levels when different areas are joined together?

Dynamic — **Dynamic environment**

Global business environments change fast and whilst there may be general tendencies that affect all global operations it is also likely that different things will be happening across different parts of the global business. Indeed, one of the reasons for businesses 'going' global is to diversify their risks and take advantage of different market conditions. At the global level however, there is the added risk that problems in one area of the global market can quickly move across all markets.

Interaction

Interaction between business and the environment

The globalization of business activity is having effects on the external business environment and this has necessitated a response from national and global government organizations.

The rapid expansion of business activity and global business activity in general has a particular affect on the environment in the specific context of the global eco-system. There is a widespread belief that business activity is damaging to the eco-system and therefore that businesses should be encouraged to act in a globally responsible way.

Stakeholders

Stakeholders

There are a range of stakeholders involved in shaping and responding to globalization. Globalization intimately links individual decisions to a range of stakeholders culminating in the eco-environment itself. This requires us to enhance our analysis of the shareholder versus stakeholder models looked at elsewhere in this book.

Values

Values

Put simply, 'Is globalization good or bad'? It is important to recognize the range of views that are expressed when seeking to investigate the impact of the transformations brought about by the shift in the spatial level of globalization.

There is an increasing interest in the role of global ethics to address issues associated with globalization. While operating across national boundaries presents business with huge opportunities, what are their responsibilities to the countries in which they operate and to the environmental impact of global business?

Introduction: the impact of globalization on the business environment

Globalization raises a series of questions that need to be explored: What is globalization? When did it start? Is it increasing and in what way? Is globalization good or bad? Who and what does globalization affect? What are the challenges that globalization poses? In relation to business though, we need to consider the strategic response of businesses to the 'challenge of globalization'.

There is one central question that dominates the debate about globalization. While it is clear that globalization can potentially give rise to an increase in prosperity, there are severe doubts as to whether this process will be fair to all both in the present and to those in the future. We will see that there are a variety of perspectives about the impact of globalization and that the role of ethics in relation to globalization needs to be explored. Since globalization occurs across national boundaries this means that we need to consider the global system of rules and regulations that may be needed.

There is no argument that globalization can be seen as an increase in international activity of business but the question is whether this is simply an increase in quantity or that globalization represents a quality change. In other words to what extent does globalization transform the nature of the impact of business activity and behaviour? Some commentators have chosen to argue that the use of the term globalization in relation to business as opposed to internationalization is an acceptance that indeed there has been a transformation in the qualitative nature of business activity across national frontiers.

Mini-Case 12.1   A marriage made in global heaven?

What do Leytonstone in S.E. London, Duracell Batteries, Head and Shoulders Shampoo, Boston, the Far East and Madrid have in common? (*see answer below)

When Proctor and Gamble merged with Gillette in 2005 in a deal costing $57 billion, it was a corporate 'marriage' of two very large global companies. Both Proctor and Gamble and Gillette have operations across many countries and selling an array of products (including Head and Shoulders (a P and G brand) and Duracell batteries (a Gillette brand)). Gillette saw itself as a 'He' company with an emphasis on male products. Its strategy was to develop new products that would create brand loyalty and then subtly upgrade these. This was exemplified by its development of the Mach 3 razor and then its development as a hand held razor but powered by a battery. Gillette owns the Duracell brand as well. The face that was chosen to market the Mach 3 was David Beckham, a local lad made good but a global brand in himself (Real Madrid football club were keen to use him to sell football shirts in the global market, especially the huge new markets in

Southeast Asia). Proctor and Gamble saw itself as a 'she' company with a primary emphasis on female brands. However, it wasn't this gender difference that the companies sought to bring together but what they perceived as their ability to each exploit each other's global advantage especially in new emerging markets.

In Boston, the HQ of Gillette where 92 million razors and 1 billion razor blades were produced in 2004 (containing steel equivalent to twice the weight of the statue of liberty), grave concerns were expressed about the impact on local jobs with up to 6,000 jobs to be lost. The combined company sought to reassure the local community by announcing a $200 million investment in the plant and a rise in corporate donations to local community groups of $4 million in keeping with the company's commitment to being good citizens and neighbours.

❓ What opportunities does the global marketplace offer to the merged company?

Answer: David Beckham

> Implicit in the term 'globalization' rather than the term 'internationalisation' is the idea that we are moving beyond the era of growing ties between nations and are beginning to contemplate something beyond the existing conception of the nation-state. But this change needs to be reflected in all levels of our thought . . . (Singer, 2002: 9)

Singer seeks to argue that globalization raises a new set of ethical questions that need to be considered once business operates across national boundaries. We will explore the degree to which we may also need to re-examine the wider regulations concerning business activity in a globalized world.

One feature of the globalization debate is about the degree to which our knowledge of it is shaped by a euro-centric view. In other words, since much of the literature is written by Europeans or North Americans, we simply get a picture of globalization from a particular point of view. When responding to the challenge of globalization a lot of the literature that exists sees this as an external challenge of 'foreign' firms and the need for firms at the national level to respond by devising an appropriate business strategy.

We must not only be aware that the challenges of globalization to individual firms may differ according to where in the world they are situated but that any analysis of the nature of the relationship between business and globalization must also take a wider view of the challenges that globalization presents than that for individual business behaviour. Not only do we need to look at how other stakeholders are affected but we need to appreciate that it is business activity that is also the primary driver shaping globalization.

Globalization: from local to global?

Stakeholders

While globalization can be seen as primarily the effect of business expansion on a global scale its impact is not confined to the world of business but affects a range of stakeholders. Globalization is not something that takes place 'out there'. Neither is globalization an autonomous or indeed anonymous thing that does things to people. Globalization is a process created by human activities and interactions across national frontiers and we are all involved either as active agents of change or as people affected by change. Chapter 1 highlighted the term 'glocalization' which seeks to stress the relationship between local actions and the global economy. Critics of globalization, especially in relation to the damaging environmental consequences of the trade in global products often implore consumers to 'think global, act local'.

> ⊃ *Stop and Think*
>
> *Globalization and you: the world in your home*
>
> What would you expect to find if you were to construct a consumption diary of everything that you consume in a day and record next to it the country of origin or the headquarters of the companies that produced the things we use every day?

We live in a world of globally organized production where many of the products that we take for granted in our day to day lives have come about through the existence of international trade and the activity of a range of businesses in a global environment. If you did the activity above you could readily understand how the globally organized system of production affects us. The food we eat, the clothes we wear, the kitchen appliances we use, the cars we drive and the computers we use to access the World Wide Web are all here because of global business activity.

However, what about the supply chain of those products themselves? For all of us, use of mobile phones is a modern 'must have'. Globalization is not about large corporate global firms (although this is a major aspect of it), but the supply chain for such global products will often be spread over a range of countries and involving a range of smaller companies.

Charles Hill highlights how Nokia phones which may be designed in Finland and its system of production organized and controlled by the headquarters there, will contain micro-chips from Taiwan but designed by Indian engineers working for a firm in California. The phones may be assembled in Texas and then marketed and sold across a range of markets each using local advertising agencies catering for cultural differences in their campaigns (Hill, 2006).

Now let us take another example. In recent times attention has been given to the concept of 'food miles', in other words the amount of energy consumed by transporting food from farm to factory.

Mini-Case 12.2   **The world in your coffee cup**

Approximately 2.5 billion cups of coffee are consumed in the world per day. Much of this coffee is produced in countries far from where the coffee is eventually consumed. One of the fastest growing sectors in the UK, where 70 million cups are drunk daily, has been the high street coffee shops featuring such global brands as Starbucks and Costa.

A study conducted by the *Guardian* newspaper in 2005, tracked the supply chain of coffee from one such coffee growing area to a local coffee shop in the UK.

The region chosen was that of Choche in Ethiopia, where it is believed coffee was first discovered. Individual farmers grow and harvest the coffee beans and then take their coffee to the nearest village to sell to the trader. The trader is able to check prices of coffee twice a day in the markets in the capital city of Addis Ababa

which is over 250 miles away. Once the trader buys the coffee then it is transported to the capital city where workers are paid less than £1 a day to sort the beans. The beans are then sold at auction to the large multinational roasters. As Ethiopia is a land-locked country, in order to export the beans they must first be transported by road or rail to the Red Sea port of Djibouti and then shipped onwards.

For coffee exports from Ethiopia to the UK this will involve a passage through the Suez Canal and then to Tilbury Docks and to warehouses in Kent. The coffee beans are then roasted and packed off to the consumer outlets.

❷ Who are the stakeholders involved in the coffee market?

One of the first studies to illustrate this is of a yogurt that was marketed as being locally produced in Germany.

In 1993 researchers in Britain and Germany investigated the distances travelled by food, taking into account their ingredients and the materials for their packaging. To produce a small glass jar of strawberry yogurt for sale in Stuttgart, strawberries were being transported from Poland to west Germany and then processed into jam to be sent to southern Germany. Yogurt cultures came from north Germany, corn and wheat flour from the Netherlands, sugar beet from east Germany, and the labels and aluminium covers for the jars were being made over 300 km away. Only the glass jar and the milk were produced locally (Boge, 1993).

Mini-Case 12.2 shows that coffee is truly a global industry and as with the other examples above shows how a range of stakeholders across a range of spatial levels are connected. Truly from local to global.

What is globalization?

Spatial levels

It is the spatial level that is the defining characteristic of globalization. Globalization adds the supranational level to the focus on business activity but emphasizes the inter-linkages across the spatial levels from local through to global. Not only does it impact across a range of businesses but also on individuals, families, communities and at regional, national, international and supra-national levels. What is the nature of the inter-connections between the local through to the global and what is the impact on the spatial levels when different areas are joined together?

We can look at globalization as comprising six main aspects:

- international trade and the creation of the global marketplace
- globally organized production and investment flows
- migration
- communication flows
- cultural flows
- rapid technological change.

International trade and the creation of the global marketplace

Dynamic

Globalization at its simplest can simply be seen as the increase over time of international trade (referred to as *merchandise trade*), and services and often this is how it is described. With trade comes an increase in the amount of markets across national borders.

Trade itself is a vital feature of economic activity within countries or regions, and without trade businesses would not be able to benefit from the ability to specialize and the associated benefits of an efficient division of labour. With international trade we are moving trade to a different spatial level. The central question then is, if by moving trade to the international level, the nature of trade changes. It is clear that earlier civilizations across the globe were involved in widespread trading within regions. However, the foundations of the modern global economy are felt by many to have begun to be laid as a result of the expansion of the western European nations from the 15th century onwards, led first by Spain and Portugal and then followed by Holland, France and pre-eminently with the expansion of the British Empire. What is different about this modern era is that trade was expanding rapidly as **capitalism** was fuelling the industrial revolutions in Europe and North America, and so any understanding of globalization must encompass an understanding of the nature of capitalism on a world scale.

Globally organized production and investment flows

Businesses have recognized the advantages of also organizing production across national boundaries to take advantage of lower costs and specialist advantages in different geographical locations. This can involve the placing of production facilities abroad or the splitting of the stages of production or the functions of the business to take advantage of lower costs or to be nearer to foreign markets.

Allied to this is the increase in the amount and nature of investment that takes place across borders. This can be in the form of foreign direct investment as well as through financial flows of money and portfolio investment.

After 1945, there was widespread talk of a new international division of labour. What was meant was that with the freeing up of financial markets, businesses in the developed nations would begin to set up production in new markets and where resources were cheapest, and in particular this would help the developing world.

Much attention in the literature is paid to the rise of the multinational corporation. Often the term transnational corporation is used to convey the fact that such corporations work across national boundaries.

There has been a big increase in these investment flows, especially in the 1990s. From 1980 to 2002 the world stock of outward investment increased 12 times from $564 billion to $6,867 billion. However, the bulk of this has been between the developed countries themselves (UNCTAD, 2005). In 2002 87% of FDI came from developed countries and they in turn received 65% of all FDI. Again, whilst it is the case that the developing world now receives a higher proportion of FDI than the 1980s half of this goes to China, Brazil, Mexico and Singapore.

As well as flows in FDI the recent explosion in investment flows has come from the rise of stocks and shares flowing across national boundaries. The international financial system has seen unprecedented growth in the last quarter of a century. In particular the role of the IMF has come under intense scrutiny as individual nations have suffered severe financial instability and debt burdens and where the very integration of these financial markets has meant that such crises can spread quickly to other countries.

Migration

A major feature of the development of trade and investment has been the movements of people across both internal national and international borders. Such movements have had profound affects both on the countries and regions from where the migrants leave as well as those to where they go.

Often attention is focused on the problems of immigration without an appreciation of the global forces which shape migration and the enormous contributions that migration makes to the growth of business activity both in the private and public sector. An important aspect of the industrialization process within all countries is that as the towns grow, people will move away from rural areas into the urban ones. Globalization offers people in less developed areas the possibility of moving across national frontiers to developed countries.

Communication flows

Globalization has been greatly influenced by the speed with which communications have improved in the world, both in terms of transport, but also as telecommunications, and the media have come to have a global reach.

Cultural flows

This intermingling of people and the accompanying rise in communication networks have brought into focus the question of how cultures combine. It is clear that globalization has brought together people with different cultural beliefs and the challenge for business is how to deal with this and also to recognize the potential problems that inter-cultural interactions can create.

In order to create global brands and to organize global production and marketing systems businesses have to learn how to operate in cross-cultural contexts.

However, there is a tension here that we will need to explore. To what extent is it possible or desirable for business to adapt their practices across cultural boundaries and what happens if there are conflicts in cultural approaches?

Rapid technological change

There is no doubt that technological change has helped fuel the rapid rise in global economic activity especially in relation to communication and transport, and the end of chapter Case Study in Chapter 3 examines the impact of containerization as one example. Transport costs have fallen and worldwide travel has increased exponentially. This has had a direct impact on the structure of industry with tourism now being the second biggest industry as well, of course, indirectly across a whole range of other business activities.

The rise of the Internet and the global telecommunications revolution in general has created a new environment which encourages global business activity.

The growth of globalization

Dynamic

The World Bank has characterized three waves of globalization.

The first wave was the in the late 19th century with the rapid increase in the industrialization of the main 'western' nations (mainly western Europe, the USA and Canada). There was a big expansion in the growth of world trade as measured by the ratio of merchandise exports (trade in physical goods) to world GDP. This expansion was propelled by the development of what Eric Hobsbawm refers to as 'The Age of Empire'. Colonial powers imported commodities in the form of primary resources from their colonies and then manufactured these into commodities for sale in their home markets as well as for export back into their overseas possessions. Allied to this was an outflow of investment to the poorer countries and there were mass migrations. However, there were tensions between the main industrial powers with domestic firms keen to exploit the opportunities within their own 'empires' but hostile to competition from outside. This competitive rivalry between the countries in western Europe provided the conditions that precipitated the First World War.

The period between the First and Second World Wars was marked by a high degree of instability for the industrial countries with many experiencing severe economic problems. One response to these national problems was for pressure by domestic firms to keep out foreign competition by continuing to erect barriers to prevent international trade. In response to the decision by the USA to erect tariffs, its trading partners followed suit. This represented a 'retreat' from globalization. There was a fall in the proportion of trade to world income from 22% in 1913 to 9% during the 1930s with a marked slowdown in the growth of the world economy.

The third wave of globalization is seen to occur in certain parts of the world after 1945 and then to pick up universal speed from the late 1970s onwards. This was driven by the belief that trade liberalization (the opening of countries' borders to trade and investment by removal of trade barriers), was 'the engine' for the growth of economies.

Perspectives on globalization

Globalization and its effects provokes intense disagreement. The arguments about globalization have been around ever since scholars began to examine the worldwide expansion of markets. We can distinguish three main schools of thought:

Values

- classical and neoclassical thought (globalization is good)
- radical/Marxist writers (globalization is bad)
- structuralist writers (globalization could be good but it depends on getting the national and global structures right).

What unites all three perspectives is that globalization has occurred through the expansion of capitalism on a world scale. What divides them are their views as to the nature of this spatial change and its effects.

Classical and neoclassical views

Chapters 2 and 3 show how Adam Smith highlighted the benefits to an economy of market liberalization and trade and the intimate relationship between trade, development and growth. International trade is important here for two reasons:

1 In providing a source of external funding that boosts the amount of money available to fuel trade internally.

2 It enables further room for the expansion of markets on an international scale.

To give a simple illustration of Smith's argument in favour of trade imagine two countries, A and B, and two goods, wool and wine. For this Smith uses the concept of absolute advantage.

If country A has an absolute advantage in producing wool and country B an absolute advantage in producing wine then it makes sense for country A to specialize in wool and country B in wine. Overall production of both wine and wool will rise as each country is able to benefit from the advantages of specialization and, provided that these gains from trade are shared equitably, both countries will gain.

By the 19th century the sheer success of the first wave of industrialized countries was astonishing and across a whole range of commodities these countries experienced huge rises in productivity. Neither was this confined to industrial goods but the industrialization of agriculture began to see big efficiency gains here. This economic success enabled such countries to both expand and in the process benefit from a huge economic expansion into

Globalization continues to provoke strong feelings today, as this huge march through the streets of Bombay shows.

© AFP/Getty Images

overseas markets both to obtain cheap resources and to find new markets to fully exploit economies of scale. This was of course the Age of Empire referred to in Chapter 2.

This then posed a problem for trade theorists. If, for example, Britain was better than India at producing a whole host of commodities, what benefit would the less productive areas of the world get from opening their borders to trade? Wouldn't trade simply benefit the advanced countries at the expense of the growth and development of the less advanced ones?

Ricardo and comparative advantage

Ricardo refined Smith's theory by arguing that even if country A is better than B at producing both commodities it still makes sense for A to specialize in one and B the other. If A specializes in the commodity in which it has the greater comparative advantage and B in the one in which it has the smallest comparative disadvantage then there will still be overall gains in production. Ricardo still used units of input in relation to output produced as his measure of advantage.

In the world of the 19th century it was easy to argue that the industrialized nations should specialize in manufactures (secondary commodities) and the colonies in raw materials and natural resources (primary commodities). It is still the case today that many countries are heavily reliant for much of their export earnings on only one or two primary commodities.

In the 20th century this theory was refined further by two economists Hecksher and Ohlin, who argued that advantage was related to the cost of a unit of input in relation to output and that the 'factor endowments' of countries could differ. In countries where resources of a certain type were abundant, then the costs of those resources would be low. On a world scale developing countries were abundant in labour, especially in the rural areas, and so it made sense for them to specialize in primary commodities, while in the advanced industrial countries the shortage of labour but abundance of capital meant they should specialize in secondary goods. Thus was born the idea of 'an international division of labour'.

This belief in the combination of free markets and free trade dominates classical thinking and its modern day neoclassical writers. It is important to recognize the strength of their arguments. Given the theory of comparative advantage there is every reason for specialization and trade to occur on a world scale. Trade not only potentially increases the amount of goods that can be produced but also encourages increases in productivity through economies of scale. Trade openness forces domestic companies to become more efficient because of the competitive threat and provides great opportunities to seek new markets. Flows of inward investment bring in much needed technical know-how and can also reduce costs. Outward flows of FDI enable firms to take advantage of market opportunities and cheaper resources and provide invaluable technical improvements to the host countries. There is clear evidence that countries which experience high growth rates are also those which are open to trade and investment.

> ⟳ *Stop and Think*
> What are the benefits of trade and investment to an economy?

However, after 1945 both developed and developing countries chose to intervene in markets and to engage in trade protection policies. The crisis years of the 1970s provided the ideal conditions for the 'rediscovery' of neoclassical thinking. This was given expression in the political system with the coming to power of governments advocating these free market policies, especially in the USA with Ronald Reagan and in the UK with Margaret Thatcher, and the securing of positions by neoclassical policy makers within the two key supranational organizations of the World Bank and the IMF. From the late 1970s there was a discernible shift in the ideas coming out from a range of national and supranational bodies, and perhaps this was encapsulated in 1995 with the World Trade Organization replacing GATT.

> . . . global integration in the flow of goods, services, capital and labor also brings enormous benefits. It promotes competition and efficiency, and it gives poor countries access to basic knowledge in medicine, science and engineering. (World Bank, 1989)

John Williamson sought to encapsulate neoclassical views in what could be seen as a menu for globalization dubbed the Washington Consensus. The World Bank in the report above characterized this approach as 'the market friendly approach'. For many it is these views that embody the term globalization.

Below are grouped together the ingredients that Williamson highlights as being central to the Washington Consensus. In his book *The Lexus and the Olive Tree* Thomas Friedman, a believer in globalization as good school, refers to this as the 'Golden Straightjacket'.

Original Washington Consensus: the menu for the ideal business environment?

- Fiscal discipline—governments should cut the size of their spending and should aim not to run budget deficits
- Reorientation of public expenditures—public spending should be confined to providing 'minimum' social security safety nets and to supporting education and health
- Tax reform—reduce the burden of tax especially on the 'rich' as they will invest more so enabling wealth to 'trickle-down' through the economy
- Interest rate liberalization—governments should not interfere in the financial markets
- Unified and competitive exchange—where possible exchange rates should be arrived at through the free operation of the foreign exchange markets
- Trade liberalization
- Openness to foreign direct investment
- Privatization and deregulation
- Secure property rights—important for private individuals to be free to own property and capital. This will also require a transparent legal system and a fully functioning stock market.

(*Source*: Adapted from D. Rodrik, *Growth Strategies*, 2004)

Radical/Marxist views: globalization is bad—the dependency tradition

The person most associated with radical views of capitalism was Karl Marx. For Marx, 19th-century capitalism posed what he saw as a central 'contradiction'. He was in total agreement with Smith that capitalism led to unprecedented growth but he argued that there was a fatal flaw. The social system of capitalism is very unequal and access to resources and political power is concentrated in the hands of the few. Owners of capital are able to exploit their advantage. The source of this growth was the ability of capitalists to exploit their labourers and as growth and wealth increased the conditions of the workers would deteriorate. This is a central Marxist idea: that growth, rather than being combined and even, can be combined and uneven, providing the conditions for a socialist revolution where the workers would seize control of the economy and run things in the interests of the whole of society and not for the rich elites. However, such a revolution would only occur after a long period of capitalist expansion which would have succeeded in industrializing the economy.

Later on in his life he began to argue that world capitalism might lead to even greater problems for the workers in the less advanced areas because of their even weaker position as subjects of an imperial master. It was this central idea that began to provide the background for later radical writers to argue that capitalism on a world scale works differently in different parts of the global economy. This they referred to as imperialism. A world system had been developed that linked together the spatial levels of the economy and society in such a way as to lead to big divisions in the levels of income and wealth.

Imperial rivalry between nations had moved on from competitive rivalry between firms within the same nations. In order to obtain global competitive advantage, individual nations sought to protect their own large monopoly firms by imposing tariffs in home markets, but aggressively supporting their expansion in existing colonies and in newly acquired colonies with military support as required. It was inevitable then that war between the imperial powers would break out, as happened with the outbreak of the First World War in 1914.

We have seen in Chapter 2 that the inter-war period was a period of unprecedented problems for the world economy, and throughout the world Marxist views about the instability of capitalism and its tendency to increase poverty amongst the many appeared to be true. It is certainly the case that the colonial powers were increasingly finding the strains of controlling their empires difficult.

After the Second World War a period of political decolonization occurred, but for many writers primarily associated with the **dependency** tradition the economic, political and social structures that the postcolonial societies have inherited from the colonial past are so entrenched, that exposure to the world system will lead to their continuing to suffer exploitation.

One line of analysis points to the vastly unequal societies that exist in many Third World contexts. In many of these societies tiny elites control much of the business activities of the country and run these in their own interest often in collusion with foreign multinationals or foreign commercial interests. The legacy of **colonialism** left many economies with an economy that was geared to exporting primary commodities to the world market, and where the huge profits that were gained simply lined the pockets of the rich elites who owned these industries. A lot of this money was then invested abroad so stunting the widening of the industrial base of these countries.

Another strand of the dependency tradition points out that the system of world trade is anything other than free and often the trade rules are clearly discriminatory. The power of the leading countries is such that they dominate the supranational governing bodies and frame the rules in their own favour.

Structuralist writers—globalization could be good if . . .

> The discontent with Globalization arises not just from economics seeming to be pushed over everything else, but because a particular view of economics—market fundamentalism—is pushed over all other views. (Stiglitz, 2002)

After the Second World War a new discipline of 'development economics' was born out of the belief that indeed the situation of the former colonies, or less developed countries (LDCs), as they now came to be called, was different, and that they could not pursue exactly the same path as the developed countries. Amartya Sen, Nobel Prize winner for Economics in 1998, characterized the nature of the task for these countries not as 'industrialization' but as '**late industrialization**'. LDCs faced an already developed capitalist world and so in order to be fully integrated may need time to catch up and a different set of policies to do so. In other words the structure of the world economy meant that there wasn't 'a level playing field' between the developed and developing world, to use a more recent phrase. Furthermore, it was argued that the institutions and structures that are needed for the development of a market system were not yet present in many developing countries. These would need to be constructed before the integration of these economies into the world system. In particular Sen argued for the need for countries to invest heavily in the social and physical infrastructure in such things as education, health, transport, food supply and sanitation provision.

> The overall achievements of the market are deeply contingent on political and social arrangements. (Sen, 1999: 142)

We could look at a number of the structures that might need changing. For countries reliant on primary commodities they suffer from falling commodity prices. In the 1950s the **Prebisch–Singer hypothesis** was developed to explain the problem faced by primary goods exporters. As global

A Filipino anti-WTO (World Trade Organization) protestor. The stated aim of the WTO is to promote free trade and stimulate economic growth, but many argue that free trade only results in the rich becoming richer, and fails to protect the most vulnerable against the inequities wrought by the market.

© Cheryl Ravelo/Reuters/Corbis

incomes increase, whilst the demand for primary products increases, the proportion of income spent on these declines as people spend proportionately more on manufactured goods and services. Paradoxically therefore, the more successful a primary goods exporter is in boosting volumes the lower the price it gets for its goods. Figure 12.1 shows the data (excluding oil), for primary commodity prices expressed as a percentage of the 1977 average price and clearly shows the long-term decline in commodity prices.

Coupled with the high levels of protection on other goods that developing countries can export, the system of world trade seems destined to work against their interests unless reforms are made.

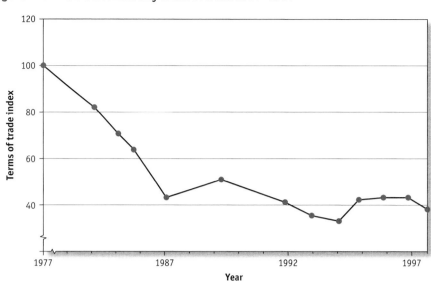

Figure 12.1 Non-oil commodity terms of trade 1977–1997

Source: Michael P. Todaro and Stephen C. Smith, *Economic Development* 9 edn, Pearson Education, © 2005 Addison Wesley.

At the domestic level, many developing countries lack the necessary financial controls and corporate governance rules to stop corruption, and all too often this has been a feature of corporate behaviour. In relation to farmers they may lack the necessary access to credit or information that enable them to take advantage of free markets. Joseph Stiglitz, Nobel Laureate for Economics in 2001, was awarded this prize for his work on market imperfections. People in markets have 'asymmetric' information; they do not each have access to all the information needed to make the best choice for them. In agricultural markets buyers can often control the market price by restricting supply and they have power to drive harder bargains because of their buying power. There may also be 'missing' markets. Farmers might not have access to credit or distribution facilities that would enable them to sell direct to markets but need to use intermediaries (see end of chapter Case Study).

> ➲ *Stop and Think*
> Why might all of the people in developing countries not receive the full benefits for free trade?

For the architects of the 'New International Economic Order' the growth of world capitalism would lead to the convergence in the growth and prosperity of nations, but for radical critics and structural writers this would simply lead to a widening of this gap.

Structuralist writers argue that globalization can be made to work provided that the right economic and political structures are put in place. Here the challenge for policy makers is to build the right type of external environment in which businesses both at the national and international level can grow. For writers such as Stiglitz and Rodrik, there is no doubt that ideally businesses should be free to operate in the world described by the Washington Consensus and that such a list can represent the basic menu for success. However, what such a list does not consider is the speed and order (or sequencing) with which countries should try to achieve these goals, and that the structures that might be needed are not there.

The list below is Rodrik's attempt to argue for 'an augmented Washington Consensus' to consider the types of structural changes that might also be needed to create the right conditions for growth.

Mini-Case 12.3 Cotton

Cotton farmer in Mali, Africa. Large multinational retailers can shop around for the cheapest cotton, whilst high levels of government subsidies given to cotton farmers in the USA means most cotton farmers around the world struggle to make a decent living.

© Fairtrade Media/ David Boucherie

Wool played a hugely significant role in providing the profits that fuelled the British industrial revolution, so couldn't the same be the case for those countries with a competitive advantage in producing cotton, the most common raw material for the world textile industry today?

Three million farmers in Africa are dependent on cotton for their livelihoods. Over time the long run price of cotton has declined on world markets. Cotton producers face fierce competition from across the world. The power of global markets does ensure that only the most competitive cotton farmers will survive and in turn guarantees cheap prices for consumers.

However, is this market fair? Cotton farmers face the collective buying power of very large multinational retailers who can afford to shop around for the cheapest supplies. This situation has been made worse by the high levels of subsidy given by the US government to the 2,000 cotton farmers in the USA.

Cotton farms in the USA are highly mechanized and high tech and produce very large surpluses. In order to find markets for these the US government grants $2 billion of export subsidies which has the effect of reducing the price of world cotton and in eroding the ability of cotton producers in the developing world to compete. Furthermore, high tariff barriers against foreign cotton are erected by the US government.

Whilst the worldwide textile industry continues to provide large profits for the high street retailers, most cotton farmers around the world struggle to make a decent living.

❷ What structures might prevent cotton producers in the developing world from achieving a high profit on their sales?

'Augmented' Washington Consensus

. . . the previous nine items, plus governments need to pay attention to:

- corporate governance
- anti-corruption
- flexible labour markets
- adherence to WTO disciplines

- adherence to international financial codes and standards
- 'prudent' capital-account opening—gradually reduce controls on direct and indirect foreign investment
- exchange rate policy
- independent central banks and inflation targeting
- social safety nets
- targeted poverty reduction

(Adapted from Rodrik, 2004)

> **⊃ Stop and Think**
>
> Compare and contrast the Original Washington Consensus and the Augmented Washington Consensus. What government actions, both nationally and supra-nationally does the latter highlight as being necessary to support the policies outlined in the former?

Rodrik argues forcefully that in the case of the Southeast Asian economies whilst they are open *now* this has only been possible by the government ensuring that careful attention was paid to these issues of speed, sequencing and structures.

Evidence

Stakeholders

In practice it is difficult to resolve these arguments with evidence as all views can select data to 'prove' their case.

Average global income levels are rising across the world. The newly industrializing countries, especially in Southeast Asia are growing at a fantastic rate, and by 2020 China and India will be the largest economies, and Indonesia and Brazil will be challenging.

 Mini-Case 12.4 Roaring tigers and flaming dragons?

In the 1970s, the Southeast Asian economies of South Korea, Thailand, Malaysia, the Phillipines, Hong Kong, Taiwan and others experienced remarkable rates of economic growth. Characterized as the **newly industrialized countries**, (NICs), their success has provoked intense debates as to why they have grown so fast.

For the neoclassical economists the NICs have shown the success of market liberalization and the triumph of their view of the world. Far from turning their backs on the global economy, these countries have embraced extensive opening up to world trade. In these countries trade truly has been the engine of growth.

However, for the structuralists, while it is the case that the NICs have used trade, this was not the only thing that they did, and we need to consider the structural changes that they made *before* they felt able to benefit from trade openness. For Sen, it was important for these countries to have got the social infrastructure in place before external openness. For Stiglitz, the road to the market has to be a gradual one and in particular cannot begin until the state has taken action to reduce poverty. For Rodrik, the role of the state in controlling which industries to build up was crucial as was the order in which market reforms are made. It is also important that the state puts in place the necessary institutions to control the possibility of fraud and corruption. China as the fastest growing economy is the prime example of how its particular road to the market has been carefully managed by the state. The Chinese themselves refer to their system as 'socialism but with Chinese characteristics'.

Dependency writers have found it hard to defend their position in the face of the success of the NICs. However, many of these countries have been characterized as being examples of 'crony capitalism' with small elites dominating businesses and government. Corruption has been rife and there has been a widening in income gaps which have helped fuel ethnic and religious tension. In response to this repressive governments have sought to control their people through denial of human rights. Another major highlight of the development in all these areas has been the environmental damage that has been created.

❓ Why is it difficult to talk about one form of capitalism?

However, across the world the gap between rich and poor is widening both between countries and within them. This is especially the case between Africa and the world, but also there is a perception in the Muslim world that 'western values' and practices are leading to the poverty of the majority of people in these countries economically, politically and spiritually. Amy Chua argues that globalization, in creating rich elites across the world, fuels ethnic and religious tensions which create a threat to internal security across the world and gives rise to global terrorism (Chua, 2003).

Others point to the global problems of the debt crisis, global warming, the global Aids pandemic and other pandemics, and mass migrations. Free trade, it is argued, is not Fair Trade, with primary goods producers vulnerable and with the rigged rules caused by the power of the western-dominated IMF, World Bank, WTO and MNCs. In many parts of the world corruption is rife and serves only to line the pockets of the few.

The global challenge: international business strategy and the global environment

We have seen that globalization impacts across a range of different business types. Businesses which engage with the international economy obviously need to take stock of the global environment as well as the impact of this on the internal environment in which they are operating. Chapter 1 outlined the various techniques that businesses may use when devising appropriate strategic responses. In order to take advantage of the opportunities provided by globalization firms need to match together the competitive environment in which they operate, their particular strategy, operations and organization.

Diversity

The challenges are not the same for all businesses and will depend on the extent to which they are integrated into the global marketplace, either in terms of the competitive marketplace for their products, or their resources. However, no business is isolated from the forces of globalization.

The focus of international business is mostly concentrated on the activities of the multinational companies (MNCs)/transnational corporations (TNCs). International business textbooks view the issue as being the strategic response by MNCs to exploit the opportunities provided by the global marketplace. The scope of international business then is primarily to look at how the internal strategic response to the global challenge is shaped by the global business environment.

Internal/ external

Spatial levels

Critics of globalization emphasize the transnational aspects of this behaviour and the ability of TNCs to exploit natural or human resources and to develop monopoly and political power.

International business strategy

Firms opting to develop a global presence will have a range of possible objectives:

- to aim to increase market sales
- to acquire cheaper resources
- to diversify and spread risk
- to counter the competitive threat of rivals.

Whichever aim the firm has will depend on its analysis of the external environment in which it operates and in particular to the country that it would like to enter.

The global challenge requires firms to take a range of decisions to take account of the different spatial scale that globalization presents. Global businesses need to select the country/ies in which to expand and then the best foreign marketing strategy to adopt. This can range from exports (of

100% finished goods through to exports of components with local assembly and finally to 100% local production), licensing, franchising, joint ventures and more direct forms of foreign investment culminating in total ownership and control.

In any foreign marketing strategy the business needs to be able to coordinate and control its global operations and this is obviously the more so with direct forms of ownership. Obviously the spatial level is crucial here but given the diversity of the businesses involved and the variety of the products involved each business will seek to develop a strategy for coordination and control that best suits its objectives.

The final set of issues that MNCs/TNCs will also need to think about is how to organize and then manage and control the range of functions. Central issues here surround the degree to which the company HQ feels it can allow its local managers to have local autonomy, the prevalence of local marketing needs and the extent to which it is possible to reduce costs by splitting production up across national borders.

We have seen that in order to respond to globalization and gain global competitiveness firms do need to think and act globally. Some authors refer to this as developing 'the global mindset'. In particular the following management challenges for the global organization can be highlighted.

Cross cultural management

Different cultural behaviours at all levels will also need to be considered and this will feed directly into product design and marketing as well as into dealing with customers, suppliers and employees. The issue of 'cross cultural human resource management' is one which is increasingly addressed but there is a widespread feeling, especially, amongst people in the non-western world, that there is a tendency for many western global businesses to assume that the norm to aspire to is a western cultural model and that it is western values of individualism and personal aspiration that are embedded in the supra-national bodies. This is referred to as ethnocentrism.

Global marketing

Successful marketing does depend on designing the most effective global marketing strategy, and crucially in a global context this will depend on the 'cultural distance' between markets. Any successful marketing strategy must be able to mould itself into the prevailing culture of the markets in which it is being implemented.

Global finance

The role of the financial markets is becoming ever more crucial as many countries seek to become integrated into the global economy and financial systems become more open. For the global business whilst this helps dramatically reduce transaction costs it does mean that the following factors need to be considered:

- exchange rate risk needs to be minimized
- the risk of 'financial contagion' is ever present. When one country 'catches a cold' this can rapidly spread to others
- firms need to be able to adapt to different financial procedures

Global ethics for the global business?

Any discussion of the impact of globalization must also encompass an analysis of the way in which global business activity itself impacts on the global environment.

Any consideration of the relationship between globalization and business must involve a discussion of ethics. For many the impact of globalization calls for a new way of thinking about business ethics that requires us to develop a framework to especially look at global ethics.

Singer argues that attitudes to justice are formed in relation to what people feel a fair society would be within their own national boundaries (Singer, 2002). In other words, that if people were to consider how to make the worst off richer it is only the worst off in their own societies that they may consider.

Given the huge inequalities across societies, Singer argues that a just system defined within a national context can simply ignore the reality of injustices across national frontiers.

Global CSR

Given the huge inequalities of wealth, opportunity and income across the world to what extent should businesses which operate directly or indirectly in these environments take more positive action to help? Consider this quotation from the former owner of a British sports clothes and goods retailer:

> When I was a businessman, I had a very myopic view of life . . . I didn't know about the Third World then; I didn't know half the world lives on less than $2 a day. My horizons have broadened. I've begun to find out about this world. (Interview with Sir Tom Hunter, former owner of Sports Division [now owned by JJB] in the *Guardian*, G2, 23/10/05)

Whist it could be argued that it is ignorance of the real situations across the world that prevents companies from developing effective CSR policies, as business spreads across the globe this argument becomes weaker.

The rise of 'ethical consumerism' is pressurizing businesses to respond to the growing awareness of ethical issues, but is this a genuine attempt to develop ethical behaviour or is CSR simply a 'smokescreen'?

Globalization means that different parts of the world are brought together as 'one world' and in so doing what impact might this have for how we view ethics on a global scale?

> [T]he real challenge of globalization is of course that it allows you to consider the transformation of your enterprise, in other words, you can de-aggregate all the core processes of the company, whether it's financial services, manufacturing, R&D, and rebuild them to take full advantage of the massive *arbitrage* that is really the definition of globalization, *arbitrage* in labour cost, in financial cost, but also in pools of skilled employees and in regulatory and administrative hurdles. (Speech by Dr Jean-Pierre Garnier, CEO, GlaxoSmithKline at Advancing Enterprise 2005, 4 February at: www.hm-treasury.gov.uk/media/30C/C2/Dr_JP_Garnier.pdf)

Arbitrage in this context means being able to take advantage of cost differences across boundaries.

> ⮫ *Stop and Think*
>
> If you were a global manager seeking to locate abroad and considering employment conditions:
>
> Should you pay the local wage even if it is very low and workers complain it is barely enough for them and their families to live a decent life?
>
> What if local health and safety standards are below minimum standard in your home market but comply with local laws?
>
> What is your responsibility if you use subcontractors who are employing child labour?

Global citizenship

Adam Smith himself was concerned to highlight the potential of business to exploit the market to their own advantage and he looked to the national government to devise a legal framework and regulations to curb the power of business. However, this assumes that states are the democratic expression of the people and that there is no danger of corruption.

In the case of the global firm many commentators argue that the very fact that the business moves across borders undermines the power of the state and that many global markets are capable of being operated in ways that are not socially responsible. This may be because of the lack of transparent procedures in individual markets or the lack of control at the global level.

The recent financial scandals from the Bank of Credit and Commerce International, Nick Leeson at Barings to WorldCom and Parmalat have all been made possible by people being able to exploit market weaknesses. Whilst it is clear that there are illegal acts, there are also many shades of grey. To what extent is a firm 'taking' advantage of low resource costs or wages in developing countries? If markets result in large profits for the few but poor working conditions for the many is this 'unethical'. What are the global responsibilities that business should adopt, and in the absence of effective global rules should one firm on its own be obliged to act?

For anti-globalizers it is clear that TNCs can abuse their market power to take advantage and boost profits. For dependency writers this is a result of the greater power that TNCs have (when of the largest 100 economies in the world 21 are companies), especially in the less developed world. For structuralist writers, it might not be that firms intentionally set out to abuse their power but that the market structures and social, political structures might encourage a lack of due attention to moral issues.

Employment practices

To what extent is it ethical for global firms to operate different employment practices across national boundaries? There will be differences in labour market conditions across nations but when does 'arbitrage' become 'exploitation'? In many parts of the world there are vast pools of unemployed labour without the social systems to support them. Many of these people have no choice but to scratch a living in the black economy or resort to crime. In Africa we can trace the spread of Aids along the transport routes as lorry drivers and prostitutes combine to spread the virus far and wide.

In Bangladesh as an example, four million children aged from 6–14 work in sweatshop conditions producing anything from shoes to concrete, for twelve hours a day for the sum of 25p a day. It is not just a problem of child labour, but generally wages are very low in many LDCs. Nike is a company which has attracted much adverse criticism for its use of 'sweatshop' labour.

Mini-Case 12.5 Is Dyson cleaning up?

Chapter 1 profiled the well-publicized example of outsourcing of Dyson vacuum cleaners, which moved production of their cleaners to Malaysia while keeping their design, development, marketing, purchasing, logistics and service activities in the UK.

Initially the company attracted adverse publicity as it was seen as sacrificing local UK manufacturing jobs by exploiting cheaper labour conditions in Malaysia. However, the company claims that as a result of this move their costs were significantly reduced, the business is growing and they employ more non-manufacturing people in the UK than before.

Many manufacturing and increasingly service activities are being outsourced to take advantage of lower costs and this has brought accusations of greed and exploitation and yet outsourcing brings jobs and investment to developing countries. It is clear that far from resisting such outsourcing moves, developing countries positively welcome them, not least for providing

the opportunity for local entrepreneurs to innovate and in time develop home-grown enterprises.

Whilst it is the case that wages are lower, compared to local wage rates they are much higher. Not only does this allow the incomes of the workers involved to rise but it provides a much needed boost to local markets through increased purchasing power.

For advocates of 'outsourcing' this is a clear example of the principle of comparative advantage to take advantage of the different skill levels in workforces around the world but which will, in time, lead to a convergence of incomes as higher incomes will help provide the taxes to boost the education systems in the developing world.

❷ What are the arguments for and against this type of 'outsourcing'?

While there are clear international laws forbidding the use of child labour, what if a western buyer purchases such goods from local manufacturers? Is this firm being unethical? If the people were not employed what would they do? What responsibilities should businesses have to try to help these appalling social conditions?

Neither is this simply seen as a problem of the rich world exploiting the Third World. In the former, great disquiet has been expressed about the outsourcing of many activities and the effects on the domestic economy.

Human rights

Many countries do not have full protection of human rights and this presents dilemmas for companies. Is it acceptable for companies to operate in such countries even if they try to treat their employees fairly without trying to pressure the governments for change. What is 'fair' within a national context might not seem so in a global sense. How certain are companies that they are not being able to lower costs by taking advantage of poor human rights or even by their own actions undermining these? Shell's exploration activities in Nigeria have been an example of the problems. Whilst a lot of the oil has been in the Ogoni district of Nigeria, the local people have felt persecuted by the central government and feel that Shell has colluded in this.

Environment

We can here look at two spatial levels. Many countries do not have high levels of environmental legislation and so it is possible for businesses to benefit from not having to worry about costly environmental compliance. There are numerous examples of the effects of global business on local environments. One particularly devastating example was the explosion of the Union Carbide factory in Bhopal, India, where many people were killed and many others subsequently poisoned by a huge gas explosion.

Global business itself is a major contributor to possible climate change through the impact of transport systems. Air travel is now the fastest rising contributor to carbon emissions but shipping also is a major ingredient and all aspects of international trade have severe environmental effects. At the top of all this is the global energy industry which is responsible for the majority of greenhouse gases.

Abuse of market power

What responsibilities do companies have when selling their products in global markets? Tobacco companies have moved sales to the developing world as health concerns and litigation increase in the developed world. Pharmaceutical companies are accused of profiteering from selling drugs at high prices in the developing world and denying desperate people access to the medicines they need by abusive use of copyright.

Attitudes to graft and corruption

Global business will be exposed to environments where corruption and graft might be prevalent. Operating across national legal systems can exacerbate the degree to which corruption and graft are possible and harder to police or detect.

◈ *Looking ahead*

The world economy is poised at a critical phase as we move towards the end of the first decade of the 21st century. For the optimists there is much to look forward to. There is a widespread recognition of the structural weaknesses both at the global level and at the national level in many developing countries.

Trade and investment continue to increase and the lessons of the Southeast Asian crises of 1997 seem to have been learned, with calls for a slower move towards liberalization and a recognition of the need to look at the sequencing and structures to support these reforms. The sheer growth in China and India will continue to absorb much attention. East and South Asia are now the new growth poles in the global economy, but Latin America has grown as well and there have been signs of growth in Africa.

There is a recognition in much of the developed world of the need to help to reduce the debts of many of the poorest countries and to ally this support to gaining a commitment in these countries of the need for greater transparency and democracy. At the supranational level there is a rebalancing of power with many less developed countries joining together to counter the huge bargaining power of the developed world. There is also a pressure from below with citizens in the developing world taking advantage of democratic freedoms,

and consumers in the west exerting their influence through ethical shopping.

However, the history of globalization shows that this cannot be taken for granted and there can be contradictory tendencies. At current rates of growth Africa will not achieve the **millennium development goals** and there are still huge tensions to be resolved especially between the developed and developing world. There is the possibility that the world could fragment into regional trading agreements if agreements on a world scale cannot be achieved.

> The world economy is rapidly fracturing into discriminatory and overlapping trade arrangements, probably revolving around US, EU and China hubs. (Sally, 2004)

It seems unlikely that corporate governance rules could be enforced at the global level, and so attention will need to be focused on how seriously companies accept their global responsibilities. It is consumers and NGOs that will have a great role to play here in pressurizing companies.

In terms of global warming, many businesses are reluctant to accept that they are to blame. There will continue to be expressed commitments to reduce carbon emissions but it remains to be seen how effectively governments will enforce their promises.

◈ *Summary*

- Globalization links together all the spatial levels of business activity. It has grown as a result of the expansion of capitalism on a worldwide scale

- There are competing views as to the effects of this expansion. For neoclassical/neoliberal writers, globalization is good in that it will enable worldwide prosperity to grow and the gap between developed and undeveloped countries to decrease. For radical writers globalization is bad in that it will actually increase inequality both within and between countries and this will lead to instability and conflict. For structuralist writers globalization can be a force for the good

if policy makers put in place the institutions both at national and supranational levels to correct market imperfections and ensure good governance

- The challenges of globalization for business are both operational and strategic and firms must decide on how to expand globally and how to manage and control their global operations

- Linking the strategic response of firms to globalization and its impact are the ethical dimensions of global activity. Analysis of the impact of globalization does involve the application of global ethics across the range of global issues

Case study: coffee

Harvesting coffee beans. The coffee market is failing producers on small family farms for whom coffee used to make money.

© istockphoto.com

We have described the global nature of the coffee market in Mini-Case 12.2. Let us now examine how globalization has shaped this industry and the way in which the stakeholders are affected.

Chapter 2 introduced us to the idea of modern food production as being not agriculture but 'agribusiness', a complex supply and production chain from farm to table. It is interesting to look at how this business is organized.

At the downstream end we have the farmers. One per cent of the world's population are coffee farmers (60 million people) and they are spread all over the world but concentrated in the LDCs. At the upstream end we have the large coffee roasters and upmarket coffee shops. In this market there appears to be a paradox; at the downstream end:

The coffee market is failing. It is failing producers on small family farms for whom coffee used to make money. It is failing local exporters and entrepreneurs who are going to the wall in the face of fierce international competition. And it is failing governments that had encouraged coffee production to increase export earnings.

Ten years ago producer-country exports captured one-third of the value of the coffee market. Today, they capture less than ten per cent. Over the last five years the value of coffee exports has fallen by US$4bn; compare this with total debt repayments by Honduras,

Viet Nam, and Ethiopia in 1999 and 2000 of US$4.7bn. (*Source:* Oxfam report at: www.maketradefair.com)

At the upstream end the coffee market is dominated by four coffee roasters, Kraft, Nestlé, Procter & Gamble, and Sara Lee, each having coffee brands worth US$1bn or more in annual sales. If we add in the German company, Tchibo, they buy almost half the world's coffee beans each year. While profits on the selling of coffee at the upstream end of the process are very high the incomes of many coffee farmers are very low and in many cases are falling.

How has this situation occurred?

For advocates of globalization the market simply rewards those who add the greatest value in the supply chain. The greatest value added is in the activities upstream, which are the roasting, processing, marketing and retailing of the coffee. This is of course the core activity of the coffee companies.

The reason for the very low prices of coffee beans is that there is an oversupply and that many of the beans are of low quality. The logic of the market is that if farmers cannot get a return from their farming then they should seek to produce other things. Attempts to counteract the 'failures' of the market through 'Fair

Trade' are worthy but essentially misguided. They can only ever help a select few farmers and in many ways make life worse for the majority as they do not get to sell their coffee at non-market high prices. Coffee companies counter claims of exploitation by arguing that they are simply trying to maximize shareholder value and that where they can, they seek to assist community development programmes and give financial assistance and encouragement and training to farmers to improve quality. In the long run it is up to governments to retrain those farmers who go out of business.

Structuralists such as Stiglitz point out the reality of free markets. At the downstream end of the value chain the market farmers face structural problems. There may be a lack of basic infrastructure such as roads or transport to local markets, or technical backup. Lack of credit or information about prices leaves farmers open to the possible exploitation by money lenders or the ability of buyers to drive down prices. The logic of the market would be for such farmers to diversify out of coffee into something else, but this may require a long term readjustment which they cannot afford to achieve.

At the global level the coffee-market failure is also a manifestation of the problems of the simple belief in the principle of comparative advantage. Many countries have been persuaded by the international institutions to specialize in such agricultural products, leading to oversupply and the inability of the producers to capture the value that is indeed contained when the product is sold at the upstream end of the market.

In this view the only way for globalized coffee markets to work better is if they are no longer left to be free, but adopt structural reforms. In the case of the coffee market there have been calls for the International Coffee Organization to pressure roaster companies to pay farmers a 'fair' price (above their costs of production) and to work to increase the price to farmers by reducing supply and stocks of coffee on the market. This can partly be achieved through rules that ensure that basic quality standards are proposed by the International Coffee Organization, and that

roasters only buy such coffee. Funds will need to be found to help farmers diversify into other areas of production and these could come either out of a proportion of the profits generated by coffee or through aid from developed countries.

More radical voices accuse the coffee multinationals of abusing their monopoly positions to exploit the market. Since they have such large buying power the companies can drive down prices and force powerless peasants to sell their crops at low prices. Poor farmers do not have the collective strength to resist, neither do they have the information of what prices are being gained at points of sale in markets thousands of miles away. Even if they did it is not the green coffee beans that consumers want. They want to drink their high quality lattes in high quality surroundings and there is no prospect of farmers being able to get higher up the value chain. Recent attempts by Nestlé in the UK and Procter & Gamble in the USA to introduce 'Fair Trade' brands are met by huge amounts of cynicism. These are seen as ways simply of competing with the existing Fair Trade brands and as a PR attempt to portray themselves as ethical when the vast majority of the coffee is still not 'fair'.

(*Sources*: Oxfam www.maketradefair.com)

❷ Why is it argued that the 'free market' in coffee is not fair?

❷ Why do the coffee roasters have different market power than the farmers?

❷ What are the 'structural' weaknesses that affect coffee farmers?

❷ Describe the steps involved in the conversion of coffee from bean to finished product.

❷ What opportunities does this global production chain give to the coffee roasters?

❷ How effective do you think structural reforms as outlined would be in enabling this global market to be fairer to all?

 ## Review and discussion questions

1   What are the strengths, weaknesses, opportunities and threats presented to an individual country by globalization? How might such a SWOT analysis differ between a developed and a developing country?

2   What is 'outsourcing'? Which stakeholders are affected by this and how would we decide if such a tendency is to be welcomed?

3   What are the advantages and disadvantages of international trade?

4   What are the main influences on a firm's decision to 'go global' and how do these determine the way in which it will 'go global'?

5   In what ways can the global marketplace not be 'ethical' and what can be done to make it be so?

Assignments

1 Company case study: Select an example of a company that has engaged in a foreign services marketing strategy and explain the possible reason as to why it chose the country it did and the particular entry strategy. How successful does this appear to be?

2 Using a selection of data for a country from www.worldbank.org, prepare a country report for a particular firm considering a foreign market entrance.

3 You could summarize and comment upon the most recent overviews of the Trade and Development Reports and World Investment Reports published by UNCTAD.

Further reading

Stiglitz, J. (2002) *Globalization and its Discontents* (London: Penguin)—Stiglitz argues from a structuralist perspective. In theory, globalization should improve living standards for all, but the way in which globalization is managed, especially at the global level, needs to be reformed and he is particularly critical of the role of the IMF and World Bank in promoting free markets without putting in place the rules and regulations to ensure fairness.

Stiglitz, J. and Charlton, A. *Fair Trade for All—How Trade Can Promote Development* (Oxford: Oxford University Press)— The authors show what they feel is needed if trade is to be genuinely fair.

Friedman, T. (2000) *The Lexus and the Olive Tree* (London: Harper Collins) and *The World is Flat* (2006) (London: Penguin).

Friedman advocates that the free market is the only way to break down the traditions that hold back economic growth. In the former book he argues that whilst it is the case that many people fear that globalization forces them to alter their behaviour, it is a 'golden straightjacket' to force us to economic success. The latter book reinforces his view that globalization will reduce inequalities.

Isaak, Robert A. (2005) *The Globalization Gap—How the Rich Get Richer and the Poor Get Left Further Behind*—Isaak argues that globalization does cause severe inequality and argues for a better system to shape globalization in the interests of all.

Wolf, Martin (2004), *Why Globalization Works*—An economics journalist working for the FT, Wolf uses data he has collected since the 1980s to show that globalization increases living standards both within countries and across countries.

Online resources

Test your understanding of this chapter with online questions and answers, explore the subject further through web exercises, and use the weblinks to provide a quick resource for further research. Go to the Online Resource Centre at

www.oxfordtextbooks.co.uk/orc/ wetherly_otter/

The following websites contain a host of information presenting the view from the official supranational organizations and a wealth of statistical data:

www.worldbank.org
www.imf.org
www.unctad.org

www.wto.org
www.bitc.org.uk
www.eldis.org An excellent 'gateway' site to access current articles on all aspects of the globalization debate.

The following websites offer a critical view of the challenges of globalization:

www.globalwitness.org
www.globalwatch.org
www.globalethics.org
www.oxfam.org
www.development-ethics.org
www.worldwatch.org

References

Boge, S. (1993) *Road Transport of Goods and the Effects on the Spatial Environment* (Wuppertal: Wuppertal Institute).

Chua, Amy (2003) *World on Fire—How Exporting Free Market Democracy Breeds Ethnic Hatred and Global Instability* (London: Heineman).

Hill, C. W. (2006) *International Business* (London: McGraw-Hill).

Rodrik, D. (2004) Growth strategies, available from: http.www.ksg.home.harvard.edu/drodrik~GrowthStrategies.pdf (accessed 7 March 2007).

Sally, R. (2004) The end of the road for the WTO? *World Economics*, 5(1), Jan–March: 1–14.

Sen, A. (1999) *Development as Freedom* (Oxford: Oxford University Press).

Singer, P. (2002) *One World—the Ethics of Globalisation* (New Haven: Yale University Press).

Stiglitz, J. (2002) *Globalization and its Discontents* (London: Penguin).

Todaro, M. P. and Smith, S. C. (2005) *Economic Development*, 9th edn (London: Pearson Addison Wesley).

UNCTAD (2005) World Investment Report.

World Bank (1989) *Annual Development Report* (Washington DC: World Bank).

Balancing business freedom and the authority of the law

David Amos

Contents

13

Learning objectives

When you have completed this chapter you will be able to:

- Outline the different categories and sources of law

- Understand the relationship between the law of the European Union and that of its member states

- Identify the different legal structures that businesses can adopt and understand how that can have an effect on their development and decision-making

- Identify and appreciate the different competing interests that will influence the law

- Explore the different arguments for and against legal intervention

Themes

Diversity	**Diversity of business**

In this chapter we will look at the different legal structures that a business can adopt. These may vary according to the size and nature of the business and can change as it grows. As we shall see, the legal structure a business adopts can affect its decision-making.

Internal/ external	**Internal/external**

The legal structure of a business also affects its internal and external relationships. For companies in particular there are a number of internal stakeholders. The relationship between these stakeholders is heavily regulated.

That is not to say that a business has a free hand in their external relationships. Again these are regulated in a whole series of ways. The success of a business can be determined by how it manages the legal requirements imposed on it.

Complexity	**Complexity of the environment**

There is a high level of legal intervention into businesses. This is something that businesses clearly need to be aware of, and it will shape their behaviour either directly or indirectly. For many business people this level of regulation inhibits business freedom and unnecessarily complicates their decision-making. As we shall see this view leads organizations that represent business to lobby strongly for deregulation.

Spatial levels	**Spatial levels**

Legal systems operate within geographical boundaries or **jurisdictions**. The law in England and Wales, for example, is different to that in Scotland.

However, the legal environment is an area where the impact of globalization has been felt strongly with law increasingly being made at an international level. Law that is made outside of a national legal system can therefore be central to the law within it. To illustrate this we will look in detail at the impact of European Union law.

Dynamic

Dynamic environment

The legal environment is an extremely dynamic part of the business environment. The law changes on a daily basis. As we have noted above this may be something that adds to the complexity of the environment.

At the same time this simply reflects the different influences that there are on the law. The law isn't simply changed for the sake of it but is altered to reflect and sometimes guide changes in society.

Interaction

Interaction between business and the environment

The law is a balance between different competing interests of which business is just one. As we have seen in Chapters 4 and 11 on the political environment, business has an active role to play in influencing government policy (and therefore the law) so that it is sensitive to their needs. As we shall see, the legal environment determines the parameters within which businesses can operate.

Stakeholders

Stakeholders

Within the legal environment, there are a whole series of different stakeholders, as the law affects us all. In this chapter we will consider how different competing interests can influence what the law is.

More specifically we will look at the different stakeholders within business organizations. Currently the law concentrates on considerations that are internal to the company. However, this is changing as a result of the Companies Act 2006. In particular section 172 of this Act broadens the scope of the parties and issues that company directors should take into account when making decisions.

Values

Values

Given its all-embracing nature, law is inevitably influenced by the prevailing values within society. However, neither values nor the law exist in a vacuum, and they represent the views of important social groups. Those groups tend to espouse ideologies which reflect their interests and therefore in this chapter we look at those interests in conjunction with their values to see how they impact on the law.

Introduction

This chapter will consider the role of the law in society and in particular the way that the law impacts on business activity. It will consider the effect that the law has on businesses in shaping both their internal workings and the external environment in which they operate.[1]

We will start with the basic question of what is the law, and go on to look at various aspects of the superstructure of the law such as the court system and the different sources from which the law is derived. It is clear that the structure of the law has been affected by changes in the political environment and globalization. We will therefore look briefly at the international position, particularly the role of the European Union.

Having sketched out the overall legal framework we will then consider issues that are more specific to businesses. In particular, we will look at the different legal structures that businesses can adopt and how those structures can affect and even determine how businesses operate.

---

1 The law in this chapter is as at 1st April 2007.

It will be apparent from this discussion that the law is not a static entity and its direction may be altered by any one of many competing interests. We have already considered in Chapter 11 the way in which businesses can exert their influence on the law.

We will conclude this chapter by weighing up the arguments for and against legal intervention and indeed regulation in its wider forms, considering the competing interests that need to be balanced and the tension between business freedom and the authority of the law. This discussion will reflect the ideological divides that are dealt with elsewhere in this book (see Chapters 2 and 4).

What is law?

Our starting point has to be to think about what law is. In essence, the law is a series of rules which govern aspects of our behaviour. That is not to say that all rules are necessarily part of the law or indeed that our behaviour is totally governed by the law.

Values

There are a whole series of rules of behaviour which determine how we act on a daily basis. Some of these rules arise from our moral beliefs or accepted standards of behaviour rather than being determined by any law. It is perhaps more accurate to call these norms rather than rules as they prescribe how situations should be and how things should happen.

At a very simple level, it is not illegal to pick your nose and eat what you pull out although it is generally considered socially unacceptable to do so. However, if you were to punch someone else on the nose you would most likely find yourself facing a criminal charge and possibly also having to pay damages to your victim.

The issue of what is legal but generally socially unacceptable is not always so clear cut. It is legal in England to have sex with whoever you wish even if they are married to someone else or are the same gender as you, provided they consent and are old enough. However, this may not always be socially acceptable.

On the other hand, in other countries which have different belief systems sexual behaviour is more regulated. Thus under Islamic law adultery is considered a crime whilst homosexuality is illegal in at least 70 countries. Indeed it is punishable by death in some places.

There is therefore an interaction between laws and norms. Belief systems and therefore social norms can determine what the law is. At the same time changes in the law can help to change attitudes, although it may be difficult to tease out how much impact the law has as against other factors, as we shall see later when we consider the working time directive.

> ⮂ *Stop and Think*
>
> Are there any laws that you would like to change?
>
> If so, explain why this is. For example, do the laws concerned offend your moral beliefs or infringe your personal freedoms?
>
> At the same time are there any laws that you would like to pass? Explain why you would like such laws put into place.

The question then is how do we decide what the law is and when legal action can be taken? In the next section of this chapter we will look at how the law is made. Before we move on though it is worth noting that the law is not just determined by belief systems but also reflects a balance between different and often competing interests.

Mini-Case 13.1 **Northern Metropolitan University**

Stakeholders

Look at the following example and see how many interested parties and legal issues you can identify.

Northern Metropolitan University are seeking to reduce the number of campuses on which the university is based. They therefore want to sell off their Gatlings Field site which is in an affluent suburb on the edge of the city. They will, however, be retaining ownership of three halls of residence which are situated at one end of the site as they bring in a good income for the university. The local people who live around the edge of the site have an active Residents Association and are concerned about what will happen to the land.

The site is bought by Northern Developers Limited (NDL) who want to build a housing estate on it. The university wish to maintain the profitability of their halls and therefore impose various restrictions on the development in the document passing ownership of the land to NDL. They also include a clause ensuring that the university can gain access to Gatling Fields in order to do maintenance work on the drains which run under the land and into the halls of residence.

Through their association the local residents lobby the council over the proposed development. The council take these views into account and impose strict conditions on the planning permission that they grant to NDL. This limits the number and size of the houses that NDL can build and requires them to build extra access roads to the site.

The interested parties here are:	Northern Metropolitan University
	Local residents
	The Residents Association (you can't assume that all the local residents are involved in this or support it)
	Northern Developers Limited
	The students in the halls
	The local council
	The owners of the new houses
The legal issues are:	Ownership of the halls
	Restrictions on the development
	The sale of the land
	Access to the land by the university
	Planning permission

❷ Even in this short and relatively simple example there are therefore a number of different parties and legal issues.

❷ Do you think all the parties got exactly what they wanted out of this situation?

❷ If not, could you have done things differently to ensure that they did?

Categories of the law

There are a number of different categories of the law which help explain the different ways in which the law is formed. In particular, there is private and public law which can either be national or international.

As you might imagine, private law governs the relationship between individuals. This relationship can be determined by the individuals themselves. Contract law is a prime example of private law where it is down to the contracting parties to decide the terms on which their relationship works. Even here though the law may intervene; for example the Sale of Goods Act 1979 implies terms into a contract which give consumers certain rights in relation to items that they have bought.

At the other end of the spectrum is tort law which reflects a sort of social contract. Here the law imposes certain duties on individuals such as a duty to other road users to drive carefully. If that duty is breached to the detriment of another individual he or she can seek compensation.

Individuals therefore can have an influence on the legal relationships between themselves. However, they do also have a relationship with the state which is governed through public law.

Again this can be used to right wrongs which breach public duties through criminal law. On the other hand public bodies themselves can be challenged through the courts by what is known as judicial review.

Public law is concerned with more than wrongs, and indeed may determine the success of a business. As we have seen above an example of this is planning law which clearly can have an impact on the environment within which a business operates.

Sources of the law

In this section we will concentrate on the sources from which the law derives in England and Wales. These are:

- case law/precedent
- legislation.

However, it will become apparent that developments internationally, particularly within the European Union (EU) have had a huge impact on the law within this country and thus a separate section will be devoted to that.

Case law/precedent

England and Wales operates under what is known as a common law system. This means that the law can be developed by the courts through the system of precedent. At its simplest, under this system a court must follow the decision made by an earlier court. On the face of it, this would lend itself to a great deal of certainty, as to find out the law all you have to do is to refer to an earlier similar case. This is not the whole picture, though, for the following reasons:

- Firstly, the decisions that a court must follow are those from what is known as a higher court. We will look at the hierarchy of courts in the following section which will help you understand this point.
- Secondly, in the course of a decision a judge may make a whole series of comments about the case and the issues arising from it. They will also explain how they reached the conclusion that they came to. It is only the latter part of the judgment, the reason behind it, that is binding.

  To illustrate this point, imagine a case where a company is being sued by one of its employees who has contracted asthma as a result of working with a particular chemical. The judge finds in the employee's favour as he had not been issued with a face mask, in breach of the relevant regulations. This decision can be used as authority for the argument that any other employer who does not issue face masks when using such a chemical will be found liable.

  However, if the judge goes on to make some general points about which face mask is the best to use when handling the chemical concerned the guidance given is not binding on other judges. That being said the comments the judge made can be referred to in later cases if they are relevant.
- Lastly, if the facts of the case are not entirely the same it is open to the court to 'distinguish' it from the matter at hand. Thus if in our example the person working with the chemical in a later case was not exposed to it in as concentrated a form as the employee in the first case the judge would not need to follow the first decision.

The system of precedent is therefore not entirely satisfactory as it leaves many grey areas.

It should be noted that most of continental Europe and indeed Central and South America operate under a completely different system known as codified or civil law. Here the basic law is contained in a series of detailed codes which judges must simply apply to the situation that faces them. There is therefore no system of binding precedent. The law of the EU borrows heavily from such systems.

Legislation

This is now the primary source of law in the UK and is divided between Acts of Parliament and what is known as delegated legislation. Acts of Parliament go through a detailed system of scrutiny within parliament before they are passed. Once they are approved, however, they are the highest form of law except where they are over ridden by EU law.

No less important is delegated legislation, so called as the power to make the law is often delegated to the relevant ministers or authority. This is usually published in the form of what are known as statutory instruments.

This legislation is also subject to scrutiny, but such monitoring is limited. A lot of legislation is therefore passed with little comment. Despite this lack of monitoring, important areas of the law are passed in this way, as for example with the Companies (Tables A–F) Regulations 1985 which set out a standard format called Table A for a company's Articles of Association (effectively its internal rule book).

It is the case that there is a vestige of judicial control over legislation insofar as a court can issue what is known as a declaration of incompatibility if the legislation does not comply with the Human Rights Act 1998. The courts can also interpret legislation if there are ambiguities within it. However, technically parliament is sovereign and thus the courts simply have to apply the legislation that they have enacted.

One by-product of the primacy of legislation is that parliament is subject to influence that can be exerted on government and MPs by pressure groups and lobbyists. There is therefore a much greater interrelationship between this branch of law making and the political environment that businesses operate in.

That being said it would be naïve to suggest that judges are not subject to political pressures or do not have their own political views. Indeed, it has been argued that in England at least the judiciary are overwhelmingly from a narrow social stratum and might reflect the views of that stratum (see for example Griffith, 1997). This, however, may change as a new and more open system of appointment has been adopted.

Importantly though, judges are subject to minimal control and are therefore largely unaccountable for their actions. Whilst this does allow them to be independent it does also give them a great deal of power.

⊃ Stop and Think

In this section we have talked about the primacy of legislation.

What is meant by this?

Why do you think that this is an important principle?

Structure of the courts

We mentioned earlier how the system of binding precedent was one of the two main sources of domestic law in England and Wales. In order to fully understand how this operates we need to look at the structure of the courts. To help you understand this section you should look at Figure 13.1 overleaf.

To some extent the court that a case is heard in is determined by the type of issue that is being dealt with. The primary split in this regard is between civil and criminal courts. However, there has been the advent recently of more specialist courts such as those dealing with technology and

Figure 13.1 Simple outline of the structure of the courts in England and Wales

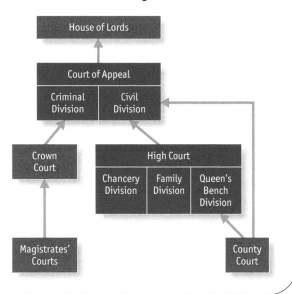

construction cases and commercial disputes. The structure is also due to change shortly with the creation of a Supreme Court which will replace the House of Lords.

Criminal cases

The majority of cases will, however, go down one of two routes. Criminal cases will always start in the Magistrates Court. Less serious matters, such as most driving offences will stay in that court with more serious cases being referred to the Crown Court.

If a party is unhappy with the decision made by the Magistrates Court they can appeal and have the matter reconsidered in the Crown Court. In certain cases there is the possibility of appeal to the High Court although this would be less common.

In turn, if a party is dissatisfied with the decision in the Crown Court they would generally appeal to the Criminal Division of Court of Appeal.

Any appeal from the Court of Appeal would be to the House of Lords. For the purposes of considering precedent the House of Lords is the highest authority. Any decision made there would therefore bind the Court of Appeal, and so on down the line.

Civil claims

As for civil disputes, such as an argument over a contract or a personal injury compensation claim, where the case starts can vary according to the value and complexity of the claim. Traditionally the lower value and less complex claims would start in the County Court.

Recent changes to the way that civil cases run now mean that the procedures across both the County Court and the High Court are essentially the same. However, a matter still has to be worth over £15,000 to be started in the High Court or £50,000 if it is a personal injury matter.

The High Court has three main divisions which deal with different types of case. These are Family, Chancery and Queens Bench. For businesses the latter two are the most important as they contain within them separate Companies and Commercial Courts. Outside of the divisional structure there is also the Technology and Construction Court which deals with disputes in building, engineering and computing.

As with criminal matters, parties can appeal to the Court of Appeal—in this case the Civil Division. Again from there the final recourse domestically is to the House of Lords with this being the highest authority for the purposes of precedent.

The European Court of Justice

In line with developments in the political and economic sphere, the EU now has an overarching role to play in the structure of the courts in England and Wales. Thus the European Court of Justice is the highest court when there is a European dimension to a case. Cases can be referred to this court from any of the courts that we have mentioned above. In addition, national courts have a responsibility to protect and apply EU law.

Tribunals

Aside from the system outlined above there are less formal fora for resolving disputes. An example of these which is important for businesses is the Employment Tribunal (ET) which can be used to deal with breakdowns in the employment relationship. Thus for example if you feel you have been unfairly dismissed or have been discriminated against as a result of your race, sex, disability or trade union activities you can take a claim to the ET.

Alternative dispute resolution

One feature of the system in the UK and other countries is the high costs parties can incur in resolving disputes through the courts. The adversarial nature of the system where one party has to beat the other to win their case means that business relationships can be soured. Success in a court action can therefore be a pyrrhic victory as existing clients are lost.

There has therefore been a rise in what is known as alternative dispute resolution (ADR). This takes different forms but the basic principle is that parties to a dispute should try to resolve it in their own way without the formalities, costs and delays inherent within the court system. Indeed such an approach is suggested in the rules governing the Civil Courts which have been reinforced by a number of important court decisions.

In a business context there may be standard industry contracts which have clauses in them setting out a mechanism by which disputes can be dealt with without having to go to court. A good example of this is the NEC Engineering and Construction Contract. This contract was first prepared by the Institute of Civil Engineers in 1993. It has since been amended twice, most importantly following the government commissioned Latham report which called for a team working approach within the construction industry.

> ↩ *Stop and Think*
>
> In this section we have looked at the different courts that cases can be heard in. Why do you think that there are so many courts that parties can appeal to?

The European Union

So far we have concentrated on the legal system in England and Wales, but as we have seen elsewhere in this book the phenomenon of globalization has had an impact in all aspects of the business environment. In the legal environment there are a number of worldwide bodies and agreements which have an influence on international business, such as the United Nations, World Trade Organization, International Monetary Fund (IMF) and World Bank. The most important example of a 'supra-national' legal order can be seen in the development of the European Union (EU) (see Chapters 4 and 9).

Spatial levels

The first thing to appreciate about the EU is that as soon as a country becomes a member of it, European law becomes an integral part of that country's domestic law. It is therefore essential to have some knowledge of EU law particularly as it has a tremendous impact on how and where businesses can operate within the EU.

Sources of European law

Primary sources

The primary sources of European Law are the European Community Treaty signed in 1957 and the Treaty on European Union 1992 and their amending Treaties. The clauses in these treaties are called articles and as we shall see these can confer rights on individuals as well as institutions.

Secondary sources

Article 249 of the EC Treaty sets out the five types of secondary EC law:

- regulations
- directives
- decisions
- recommendations and opinions.

Regulations have general application and therefore bind all of the member states. They do not need to be put in force by national legislation and are intended to achieve uniformity of law across the union. Examples of these include regulation 1612/68 on the free movement of workers and regulation 2679/98 on the functioning of the internal market.

Directives are addressed to specific member states and are not directly applicable. Instead they will direct that members enact appropriate national legislation to achieve a set aim by a set date. They are therefore aimed at achieving harmonization rather than uniformity of the law. Prominent directives include directive 2003/88 on the regulation of working time (which we shall consider at the end of the chapter) and directive 93/98 on the protection of copyright.

Decisions represent a sort of hybrid of the above two. Like directives these are addressed to specific bodies although these can be institutions and individuals as well as member states. However, like regulations they are directly applicable and therefore do not require legislation at a national level. They are frequently used by the Commission to grant companies import or export licences and to notify member states of their Common Agricultural Policy and Structural Funds allocations.

Recommendations and opinions are not legally binding but should be taken into account by national courts. These are sometimes known as soft law—a term which covers other items such as codes of conduct issued by Community institutions. It is still necessary to be aware of these as whilst they may not have direct legal force they still constitute part of the regulatory regime that companies operate under.

As in the UK, legislation is supplemented by the work of the courts, in this instance the European Court of Justice. This court is made up of one judge per member state.

In terms of secondary sources the influence of the court has been twofold. Firstly, it has set out a number of general principles of Community law to assist in considering Community legislation. The principles are necessarily widely drawn and include equality, fundamental human rights and legal certainty.

More specifically, the case law of the court has helped develop understanding of European law. Probably the most striking example of this came with the development of the principles of 'direct effect' and supremacy which we will consider later.

Who makes European law?

Having seen what the different sources of the law are in the EU it is instructive to briefly consider who makes the law in the EU, particularly as the system is different to that which operates in the UK and is therefore subject to influence in a different way. Essentially there are three separate entities which have an input into the legislative process:

1 the European Parliament, the representative body of the peoples of Europe

2 the Commission, the representative organ of the general interests of the Community and

3 the Council of the European Union (or the Council of Ministers as it is popularly known), the representative institution of the member state governments.

As with the UK parliament, the European parliament consists of directly elected representatives. The council meanwhile is made up of one representative from each member state who is authorized to bind the government of that state. The personnel of the council will change depending on the subject being discussed, so for example if the issue at hand is farming then the agriculture minister will attend.

Lastly, there is the commission. There is one commissioner from each member state who is nominated by their own government. The current British commissioner is former Labour MP Peter Mandelson who has special responsibility for trade.

Once appointed a commissioner's responsibility is to the EU as a whole. They therefore have to be approved by the European Parliament and take an oath to act in the interests of the EU rather than their national government. It is beyond the scope of this chapter to consider exactly how EU legislation is made. It is enough to say that there are three separate procedures:

● consultation

● cooperation

● co-decision.

The type of procedure used depends on the legislation but within each procedure there is an opportunity for the parliament, council and commission to have an input.

Generally, the commission has the exclusive power of legislative initiative and the parliament and the council act jointly to adopt the measures that it puts forward.

Who enforces European law?

Here again there are differences between the UK and the EU. The most important of these concerns the role of the commission. Essentially this is twofold. Firstly, it can bring before the European Court of Justice a member state which is not fulfilling its obligations. Secondly, it ensures that the community rules on competition, which are of direct relevance to businesses, are adhered to.

It is also important to note that EC laws do allow rights for individual citizens which can be enforced through their own national courts. It does this through the concept of 'direct effect'. This principle was first elucidated by the European Court of Justice in the Van Gend En Loos case 26/62 (1963) E.C.R. 1.

EU law is therefore a central component of the legal environment. Indeed, the EU plays a fundamental role in determining the parameters within which a company can operate. In particular, in order to achieve its aim of a single market the EU has established rights for the free movement of:

● goods (established in Article 28 and the Cassis de Dijon (120/78) case)

● persons (found in Article 39) and

● services (laid down in Article 49).

Allied to these is the right to freedom of establishment (Article 43) which allows individuals and companies to set up businesses in other member states under the same conditions as citizens/companies of the host state. These positive rights are supplemented by measures to control anti-competitive practices such as agreements between companies to share markets or price fixing (see Articles 81 and 82).

In September 1960 Van Gend En Loos imported a chemical product called unreformaldehyde from Germany into the Netherlands. They were charged a duty of 8%. This was 5% higher than the duty which operated when the 1957 EC Treaty came into force.

Van Gend En Loos sought to recover the difference between the two rates. They therefore took the matter to the Tariefcommisie; the administrative tribunal having jurisdiction over customs duties in the Netherlands. In turn, the Tariefcommisie referred the matter to the European Court.

The case was based on Article 12 of the Treaty of Rome which dealt with fiscal barriers to trade. (This is now Article 25.) The imposition of the additional tariff was argued to be in breach of this article.

In order to be successful in their case Van Gend En Loos had to show first of all that Article 12 had 'direct effect'. This means that it gave them individual rights that they could rely on in the court in the Netherlands.

In considering this issue the court argued that the Treaty didn't only create obligations between nations but covered individuals as well. Indeed they pointed out that the preamble to the treaty 'refers not only to governments but to peoples'.

As a result the court concluded '. . . the Community constitutes a new legal order of international law for the benefit of which the states have limited their sovereign rights . . . and the subjects of which comprise not only Member States but also their nationals . . . Community law, therefore, not only imposes obligations on individuals but is also intended to confer upon them rights . . . '

The rights and obligations of EC law could therefore be enforced by individual parties in national courts. This, along with the concept of the supremacy of EC law established in the Costa (6/64) case, has worked to ensure the uniform application of EC law across all of the member states. It has therefore been central to ensuring the effectiveness of the European legal system and the attainment of the aims of European integration.

There are certain criteria to be fulfilled for direct effect to apply and therefore it does not cover all EU legislation. There have also been various refinements to the general principle. However, it does show the importance that the EU has now assumed in the legal environment.

❷ In this Mini-Case study, we have looked at how, under the principle of direct effect, individuals have been given rights to enforce certain elements of EU law in their own national courts. Why do you think that this principle is important?

Business organizations

Diversity

Internal/ external

So far we have looked purely at the external legal environment. Businesses clearly have to be aware of this as it can have a huge impact on the decisions they make. However, in order to understand fully how businesses operate and make decisions we have to look internally, particularly at the different legal structures that businesses can adopt:

- sole traders
- partnership
- limited liability partnerships
- companies.

Sole traders

Here an individual is the sole proprietor of the business. They therefore have sole control over the business and can take all the profit from it. However, at law they also have unlimited personal liability. What this means is that they are responsible for any debts and losses.

In terms of setting up the business, as the sole owner they have to finance it themselves, although of course they can take out a loan to do so. Legally there are virtually no formalities involved in

Mini-Case 13.3 Cadbury Schweppes—A timeline

Before looking at the legal issues surrounding the different business forms it may help to briefly consider the history of a major British company to see how its legal structure evolved over time in response to the growth of the company and the challenges it faced.

Schweppes

1783   Jacob Schweppe invents system to manufacture carbonated water

1790   Schweppe forms partnership in order to help him expand the business

1792   Partnership dissolves as a result of events in Europe. His partners return to Europe and Schweppe continues the business in London

1834   Firm is bought out by John Kemp-Welch and William Evill who extend the product range

1886   Schweppes formed as limited company following death of John Kemp Welch

1897   Schweppes floated as public company

1923   Wholly owned subsidiary formed to promote overseas development

1969   Merger with Cadburys

Cadburys

1824   John Cadbury opens shop in Birmingham

1831   John Cadbury rents a small factory to make drinking chocolate and cocoa

1847   John Cadbury goes into partnership with his brother Benjamin. The partnership rents a larger factory in the centre of Birmingham

1879   The company's Bournville factory is opened

1899   Cadbury Brothers incorporated as limited company

1969   Merger with Schweppes

1969   Cadbury Schweppes listed on London Stock Exchange

1969—date the company engages in a whole series of international acquisitions which help it to increase its market share so that by 2003 it is the world leader in sugar and functional confectionery, number two in gum and number three in soft drinks.

We can see from the above that the companies which went on to form Cadbury Schweppes took a similar route in the legal structures that they adopted. Both went from sole trader to partnership and then to company as they expanded their operations. We consider the reasons for this below when we look at the different legal forms that a company can take.

Before we do so you should note that legally it is not necessary to take the same route as Cadbury and Schweppes and if you wish you can simply set up as a company right from the start.

Before looking at the next section on the different types of business organizations, explain why you think that Cadbury Schweppes adopted different legal structures over time.

(Source: www.cadburyschweppes.com/EN/AboutUs/Heritage/ This site gives more details of the history of the two companies.)

starting such a business, although they do have to keep the necessary financial records for tax purposes. There are certain requirements in terms of the name of such a business but that aside such enterprises are largely free of regulation.

This freedom from constraint may be an incentive for an individual to set up such a business although becoming a sole trader may not always be a positive choice. In some industries, such as the building trade, it may benefit larger companies to classify people who are in effect employees as self employed. This is because it may allow them to avoid certain elements of the legislation governing employment.

Partnership

Partnerships are also characterized by a relatively light regulatory touch. They are governed by the Partnership Act 1890 which defines the relationship as one 'which subsists between persons carrying on business in common with a view to profit' (section 1(1)). Usually, when a partnership is formed the partners will draw up a document called a deed, which is in effect a constitution for the partnership. This will deal with issues such as who provides the capital for the organization, the management structure and the allocation of the profits.

However, it is not essential to have such a document as the Partnership Act will govern the relationship in the absence of the necessary provisions. Under the Act there is an assumption of

In a partnership, any partner can bind the firm, meaning they can enter into contracts on behalf of the firm, sign cheques, employ people, and other such matters.

© istockphoto.com/
Nuno Silva

equality between the partners. Thus, in the absence of any agreement to the contrary, partners are deemed to have equal rights to manage the business. In addition, they will be entitled to an equal share of the profits but will contribute in equal share to any losses.

As with sole traders most partnerships have unlimited liability. However, as there is more than one person involved the liability is joint and several. This means that whilst each partner is jointly responsible for all of the debts a debtor can choose to recover the money from only one partner. If that did happen, the partner who paid the debt could recover the money they had paid out from the other partners.

The necessary corollary of this is that any partner can bind the firm. They can therefore enter into contracts on behalf of the firm, sign cheques, hire employees and other such matters. That being said, a partnership can remove this power but has to notify people outside the partnership that it has done so. The partnership relationship does therefore involve an element of trust as the individual's business identity is not separate but bound up in their membership of the partnership.

The most common and largest partnerships are formed by professionals. There are two main reasons for this. Firstly, the law restricts unlimited partnerships to 20 members although solicitors and accountants are exempt from this. Secondly, the finance for partnerships comes from the partners themselves. Whilst they can take out loans this means that there is a limit to the amount of capital they will have access to and therefore the size of undertakings that they can pursue.

The other factor which can inhibit the size of partnerships is the problems associated with unlimited liability. The bigger the partnership, the greater the risk is for the individual partners. This problem has recently been addressed with the advent of limited liability partnerships.

Limited liability partnerships

As a form of business organization limited liability partnerships (LLPs) are a relatively new innovation being allowed for under the Limited Liability Partnerships Act 2000. They are something of a hybrid. Whilst they are still technically partnerships they share many of the central features of companies, so for example the owners are called members rather than partners.

As their name suggests the main advantage of such an organization is that a member's liability will be limited. This means that their responsibility for any debts of the LLP would be restricted to the amount that they invested. At the same time, they have a separate legal personality. We shall discuss this in more detail in relation to companies but essentially this means that any legal action will be taken against the organization rather than the individual partners.

On the downside, LLPs are regulated more closely than a traditional partnership as they have to abide by many of the rules which cover companies.

Companies

Despite its merits the limited liability partnership does not solve the other issue that tends to inhibit the size of undertaking that a partnership can contemplate: access to large amounts of capital. Companies, of whatever type, have managed to resolve this problem by allowing unlimited numbers of people to invest capital in the business. The number and size of the investments are controlled by the company itself which can issue what are known as shares to the value of the capital that they require.

Internal/ external

Having large numbers of investors does pose problems over who runs the company. Clearly it would cause difficulties if thousands of investors wanted to have a say on every minute aspect of the company's operation. This issue has been resolved by separating the people who own the business (shareholders) from those who run it on a day to day basis (directors and company secretary).

The reality for many small companies is that this separation may be illusory as the shareholders will also be directors. For larger and thus economically more important companies this separation is central to their existence. To understand how this works in practice we need to look at the different individuals involved in the organization and what their roles are. See Figure 13.2 showing the structure of a company, to help you grasp the interrelationship between the different bodies and individuals concerned.

Separate legal personality

The starting point for considering a company's structure is the idea that the company itself has a separate legal personality, as this provides the context within which to place the various elements of a company's organization.

Complexity

The notion that a company should be a separate legal entity was first established in the case of *Salomon* vs. *Salomon* (1897) AC 22. The effects that this can have can be seen if we look at the facts of this case (see Mini-Case 13.4).

Figure 13.2 Company structure

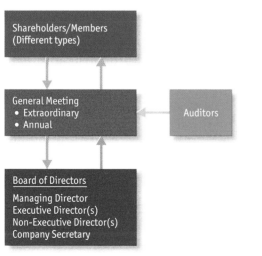

Effect of separate legal personality

We have already seen in relation to LLPs that separate legal personality means that individuals within a company are largely protected from legal action which has to be taken against the company rather than individuals within it. The concept does also mean that a company can enter into contractual relationships with its shareholders/members. Most obviously, a shareholder can be an employee of the company and can take action against it if the contract of employment is breached.

Stakeholders

The designation of the company as a separate legal entity also has an impact on the nature and role of the different individuals within it.

Internal/ external

Mini-Case 13.4 *Salomon* vs. *Salomon* and separate legal personality

For many years Aron Salomon had successfully traded on his own as a leather merchant and boot maker. It was a family business and four of his sons worked with him. His sons pressed him to give them a share of his business and in 1892 Mr Salomon set up a company to carry their wishes into effect.

The shareholders of the company were Mr Salomon, his wife and his four sons. The company bought the business from Mr Salomon for £40,000, £10,000 of which was financed by a loan given by Mr Salomon to the company which was secured on the company's assets (this is known as a debenture). Despite the sale, Mr Salomon retained a majority interest in the company and was one of its directors—the other two directors being his sons.

Unfortunately, the company hit hard times as a result of both a down turn in the footwear trade and a series of strikes. Mr Salomon obtained a loan for the company from a Mr Broderip by using his debenture as a security. However, the interest payments on this loan were not met and Mr Broderip wound up the company. The company's assets were sold which paid off Mr Broderip and left some money available for other creditors.

Mr Salomon sought to recover this money to pay off the debenture/loan that he had secured over the company's assets. The other (unsecured) creditors objected to this on various grounds but argued in particular that the company never in reality had an independent existence. It was in effect Mr Salomon under another name and he could not owe money to himself.

The House of Lords roundly rejected this argument. The company had complied with the necessary legal formalities to be properly incorporated. It therefore had an entirely separate legal identity and so could be in debt to Mr Salomon. As his loan was secured he therefore took precedence over the creditors.

❷ When you look at the facts of this case can it really be said that the company was separate from Mr Salomon?

❷ Do you think the court's decision was a fair one for the unsecured creditors?

❷ Assume your answer was no to one or both of these questions, how do you think you could justify this decision?

Shareholders/members

These are the people who provide one of the two sources of finance for the company, the other being loans. They are essentially people who make an investment in the company in the hope of making some gain on the money they have put into it. They are generally a mix of large institutions such as pension funds and individuals although this does depend on the size and type of the company.

Although technically they are known as members they are commonly referred to as shareholders. This is because the capital of the company is divided into shares with those who have invested in the company being given certificates recording the amount of capital that they have. The liability that a member will have for any debts of the company is limited to the extent of the shareholding that they possess.

The shares provide the potential profit that a member can make on their investment. Firstly, the share itself is a form of property and can thus be bought or sold as with any other form of property. For many larger companies the price of their shares is quoted on the stock exchange. Secondly, if the company is doing well it can give its shareholders a sum of money called a dividend. This will be calculated according to the size of holding that a member possesses. It should be noted that there are different types of share, some of which may give preference to a member in receiving a dividend.

The shareholders are the owners of the company and although they don't run it on a day to day basis they do have some control over what happens within it. This can be exercised internally at either an Annual or Extraordinary General Meeting or externally through court action.

Directors

The people who do have hands-on control of the company are the directors. They are collectively known as the board and are given the opportunity to discuss the operation of the company at board meetings. Their role has been subject to much scrutiny in recent years with a series of reports including Cadbury, Greenbury, Hampel, Higgs and Smith being prepared.

These reports have looked at various aspects of the running of companies. In particular, they have considered the roles that different types of directors play, issues surrounding directors' pay, the auditing of companies and accountability to shareholders. The reports have built on each other's findings and have evolved a code of best practice known as the Combined Code on Corporate Governance.

Amongst other things the Combined Code covers the make up and operation of the board, directors' pay, accountability and auditing and relationships with shareholders. Under the listing rules for the London Stock Exchange companies have to outline in their annual financial report how they have complied with the Combined Code and if they haven't why they have departed from it.

Whilst it is only the larger companies that are listed the Institute of Directors have commented that 'the Code has had a noticeable wider impact on governance' (Institute of Directors Fact Sheet on Corporate Governance in the UK).

One of the areas that are covered by the combined code is the different types of directors. These will have more or less involvement with the running of the company and indeed some directors may not be members of the board. We need to look in particular at:

- the managing director
- executive director
- non executive directors.

The managing director (otherwise known as the chair of the board) is central to the running of the company, providing a link between the board and the senior executives within the company who will implement the board's decisions. The combined code clearly sets out that there should be a division between the running of the board and the running of the company. This is to avoid any one individual becoming too powerful and not subject to sufficient checks on their actions.

Executive directors are working directors who are employees of the company. They will generally have responsibility for a particular function within the company such as production or marketing.

Non executive directors are less engaged with the running of the company on an ongoing basis but are no less important. They may well be part-time and will often be appointed for their expertise outside of the company. The reason for this is bound up with the role that they play. Firstly, they can act as monitors of the performance of the company. Secondly, on a more long term basis they can have an input into the strategic direction of the company.

Non executive directors therefore have an important supervisory role to play which is recognized in the combined code. It suggests that there should be 'a strong presence' (Combined Code on Corporate Governance 2006 p. 5) on the board of non executive directors and places store on their independence from the firm. Independence here is defined largely in financial terms—although of course non executive directors will still be paid by the firm.

Directors' legal duties

As can be seen from the above the directors hold a powerful position within the company. It is they who act as on its behalf, concluding contracts, taking out loans and other such matters. Given that they are in effect dealing with other people's money there are some protections built into the system.

Specifically Part X of the Companies Act 1985 deals with the enforcement of 'fair dealing' by directors. This covers issues such as restrictions on directors taking financial advantage of their position in the company, share dealings by directors and their families and restrictions on the company's powers to make loans to directors and people connected with them.

Overall a director has a duty to manage the company with reasonable diligence, care and skill. They also owe a duty of good faith towards the company. This means, for example, that they must not make any secret profits from their position. Finally they must exercise their powers for the benefit of the company and not for their own purposes.

If they do not meet these standards then legal action can be taken against them.

Company secretary/auditor

The other two main elements within the organization are the company secretary and the auditors. The company secretary can be a director but their role is largely administrative and will involve issues such as convening meetings, keeping company records and accounts.

The auditors have a more important role in monitoring the company's activities in relation to financial matters. The Companies Act 1985 requires the company to appoint professionally qualified and independent auditors who will review and approve the company's accounts (s384). They will then report to the members on the accounts.

In theory therefore the auditors can act as an important check on any financial abuses. However, recent high profile cases in America have exposed weaknesses in the system with auditors, Arthur Andersen, being implicated in the scandals surrounding Enron and WorldCom.

In both of these cases the companies concerned grossly misrepresented their financial position. In the case of WorldCom they recorded expenses as investment and inflated their income. This misreporting of their financial position amounted to over three billion dollars and inevitably the company crashed. As for Enron, they used a series of partnerships to disguise their debts and overstated their profits by 600 million dollars. Again the company collapsed shortly after the true figures were revealed.

Arthur Andersen's close involvement with the Enron affair lead to their demise as a firm. They surrendered their license to practise in the United States and lost nearly all of their clients worldwide.

There was widespread concern after these scandals broke that they represented a deeper systemic problem with the auditing of companies (see for example the documentary *Bigger than Enron* at www.pbs.org/wgbh/pages/frontline/shows/regulation/view). As a result the Sarbanes-Oxley Act 2002 was passed to tighten up the whole system in America by imposing external oversight and regulation on auditors.

> ⤵ *Stop and Think*
>
> In this section we have looked at the different parties involved in the structure of a company and have highlighted the role played by non executive directors and auditors.
>
> Why do you think it is important to have independent scrutiny of what a company is doing?

Annual General Meetings and Extraordinary General Meetings

Stakeholders

Internal/ external

Having looked at the different entities and the roles that they play we now need to consider the arena where the different entities come together and the owners of the company (the shareholders) can exercise some vestige of control.

The primary internal mechanism for doing this is the annual general meeting. This meeting appoints the directors and auditors and decides how to distribute the dividend if there is one. By law, the first AGM has to be held within 18 months of the formation of the company and thereafter it must be held at least once a year.

There may be issues that need to be decided between the AGMs and the device for doing this is the extraordinary general meeting. These are held at the discretion of the directors but they must call an EGM if a request to hold such a meeting has been submitted by at least a tenth of the paid up shareholders. The shareholders could do this, for example, to exercise their right under section 303 of the Companies Act 1985 to pass a resolution removing one or all of the directors.

Auditors can also requisition an EGM if they are tendering their resignation. This power is only rarely used and would only really arise if the auditor felt they were not getting the necessary cooperation from the directors to allow them to properly comment on the accounts.

Complexity

Internal/ external

Legal action by shareholders

The internal control which can be exercised by shareholders is supplemented to some extent by the legal action they can take. This power is limited by what is known as the rule in *Foss* vs. *Harbottle*. This means that any action against directors has to be taken by the company and not the shareholders themselves as it is the company (the separate legal personality) that has been wronged rather than the shareholders. This does of course give most power to those with the biggest shareholding.

There are, however, certain circumstances in which individual shareholders can take action themselves. Under s459 Companies Act 1985 they can take court action where they have been or are being treated in an unfair or prejudicial manner. This might happen for example with activities designed to increase the power of majority shareholders or to illegally enrich the directors at the company's expense. Action can also be taken at common law if there has been a fraud on the minority of shareholders.

➲ Stop and Think

So far in this section we have looked at the different types of business organizations and the law surrounding them. Imagine you were starting up a new business with a group of friends which involved making high quality chocolates.

Which form of business organization would you adopt?

Explain the reasons for your decision.

Would your answer differ, if at all, if you were merely seeking to open a small shop with your spouse to sell such chocolates?

In answering these questions you can, if you wish, refer back to your answer to the question posed about Cadbury Schweppes.

What is the company for?

Having considered the company's structure we need now to consider the purpose of a company and in whose interests it is run. The answer to this question is fundamental to our understanding of the way that a company might act in any given situation (see also Chapter 1).

There are a whole series of individuals and organizations who might have an influence on the decisions that a company makes, referred to as stakeholders (see Chapter 4). It may therefore seem that the company has to balance all of those interests before deciding what to do.

Stakeholders

At law however, the position is less complex. In England and Wales, the current position is outlined in s309 of the Companies Act 1985. It is worth reproducing the relevant subsections in full.

> (1) The matters to which the directors of a company are to have regard in the performance of their functions include the interests of the company's employees in general, as well as the interests of its members.

At first sight, it might therefore seem that employees are at the centre of the decision-making process. However, there are no reported cases of this section having been enforced. In any event, the section goes on to qualify this requirement.

> (2) Accordingly, the duty imposed by this section on the directors is owed by them to the company (and the company alone) and is enforceable in the same way as any other fiduciary duty owed to a company by its directors.

The nature of a director's duties in this context will change under s172 of the Companies Act 2006. However, the company will still be central as the duty under the new s172 is to promote the success of the company.

Despite its separate legal personality the company is really the collective identity of the members who are the shareholders. Although the powers of the shareholders may be subject to certain limitations their interests are nevertheless the primary factor in any decision-making.

As we have seen, shareholders are investors and so their main motivation is in a suitable return on their investment. This may particularly be the case for institutional investors who at law may have to have this as their central aim. Thus in *Cowan* vs. *Scargill and Others*, Megarry VC made it clear that in a pension fund 'a power of investment . . . must be exercised so as to yield the best return for the beneficiaries' and that trustees (the people who run pension funds) 'must put to one side their own personal interest and views' (1985 Ch. 270 at p. 287). If we consider that in 2001 occupational pension funds accounted for £800 billion of assets we can see how important this decision was (HM Treasury, 2001: 5).

In order to satisfy the shareholders a company must therefore have the maximization of profit at the core of its activities. However the profit motive does not necessarily mean that it is in the best interests of a company to act unethically or not be alive to social issues.

As we have pointed out in other chapters, such behaviour can result in damaging consumer boycotts, as for example with the campaigns against companies who traded in South Africa during the apartheid era. Indeed some campaigning bodies seek to persuade investors to sell their holdings in companies who they believe are guilty of unethical behaviour. The Campaign Against the Arms Trade, for example, has a Clean Investment Campaign geared towards bodies such as local authorities and universities which may be susceptible to public pressure on such issues. In view of such pressures social responsibility may have a commercial rationale.

However, given the core purpose of companies is to maximize the return for investors there is a limit on the level of social responsibility that a company can exercise. Indeed some have argued that the law governing companies, in placing primacy on shareholder's interests, acts to prohibit ethical behaviour.

Thus in his critique of the corporation, Bakan points to the 'best interests of the corporation' principle. This determines that 'managers and directors have a legal duty to put shareholders' interests above all others and no legal authority to serve any other interests' (Bakan, 2005: 36). According to Bakan this means that corporate social responsibility is illegal unless in some way it benefits the company.

If this is the case then is the answer simply to change the legal structure of companies and to regulate them in a way that forces them to pursue social rather than economic goals? Posing such a question necessarily leads us to consider our understanding of the role of law in society in a more contextual sense. What are the values and ideas that inform how the law is made? How do we balance the different competing interests in society when making the law?

> ⊃ *Stop and Think*
>
> In this section we have considered the legal structure of a company and how that might impact on its behaviour.
>
> What issues and personalities do you think a company should take into account when making decisions?

Values and the law

Values

In considering the questions posed at the end of the last section we need to remember that the law does not exist in a vacuum and is not a static entity. It reflects the values of the society in which it is made and changes with them. If a law does not do this it can fall into disrepute and be overturned.

In the United States in the 1920s, the era of 'prohibition', the Volstead Act prohibited the sale of alcohol. This was an enormously unpopular measure which was breached by large sections of American society. It also helped to cement the position of organized crime which controlled the production and distribution of alcohol. It was thus repealed within 15 years.

This is not to suggest that unpopular laws are always repealed. What is the law is often determined by those who have wealth, power and influence within a society. The state and therefore the law will largely reflect their interests and preoccupations (see Chapter 11).

The influence of values and culture should not be discounted however. As we have seen in Chapter 4 the law is bound up with politics, and the nature and extent of legal intervention in social and economic life is the subject of ideological dispute (also see Chapter 2). Those on the left favour regulation as a way of controlling business behaviour and to counter the undesirable effects of the market. Those on the right favour less regulation (deregulation) to allow businesses to manage their own affairs. In this view regulation is supported when it is necessary to allow markets to operate.

> ↪ *Stop and Think*
>
> Before looking at the debate over levels of regulation consider again the chapters which have looked at the different belief systems which might potentially have an impact on law making.
>
> What influence do you think that these belief systems, both religious and ideological, should have on the law?

How far should the law intervene—regulation vs. deregulation

Deregulation?

Deregulation involves reducing or removing the 'burden' that regulation places on business. It is based on the idea that businesses should have more freedom to run their own affairs and to compete freely in the market.

Values

Interaction

Freer competition can encourage efficiency. A negative example of this comes with the EU's Common Agricultural Policy. Under this policy, the EU effectively pays subsidies to farmers by guaranteeing them a minimum price for their products. This is backed up by tariffs which help block imports of goods from outside the EU. As a result not only is there no incentive for farmers to increase their productivity but prices for consumers are set at an artificially high level.

It is also argued that deregulation, particularly of labour laws, encourages flexibility and therefore can act to reduce costs. These costs can be substantial. Thus in May 2005 the UK government measured the administrative burden on business at £13.7 billion annually (Cabinet Office, 2006: 8). The government has set targets to reduce this despite recognizing 'Many of the administrative burdens of regulation originate at EU level' (Cabinet Office, 2006: 3).

A system of Regulatory Impact Assessments which have to be undergone before any legislation is passed has also been put in place. These assessments are a sort of cost–benefit analysis which largely focus on the economic consequences of any new legislation.

Despite these measures, the British Chamber of Commerce has estimated that the cumulative cost of regulation since 1998 comes to £55.6 billion (British Chamber of Commerce, 2007). The government therefore clearly has a long way to go to achieve its target.

This issue is central to any argument in favour of a lighter regulatory touch as reducing costs means increased competitiveness. This does not only mean competitiveness for individual companies, but nation-states as well, who can encourage inward investment by promoting the business friendly environment that they offer.

The World Bank in its annual *Doing Business* reports provides indices of these sorts of policies (see www.doingbusiness.org/EconomyRankings/). Countries are ranked according to such measures as ease of hiring and firing workers. Clearly in a globalized and increasingly competitive world economy this imposes pressures on countries to offer the most 'competitive' and business-friendly conditions.

The benefits of deregulation can arise in a more indirect fashion. In their Annual Report for 2006 the Better Regulation Commission argue 'Tying people up in red tape makes innovative thinking all but impossible' (p. 10). However, they do not use that as a justification for complete deregulation but rather regulating in a different way.[2]

---

2 The commission is an independent advisory body set up the government after the 2005 Budget. Its job is 'to help foster a continually improving regulatory framework for the UK's public, private and voluntary sectors' (Annual Report for 2006, The Better Regulation Commission, p. 5).

The arguments for relaxing the burdens of regulation are therefore primarily economic. Those in favour of regulation are more multifaceted although they still have an economic dimension.

Regulation?

The case for regulation was summed up rather neatly by Brendan Barber (General Secretary of the British Trade Union Congress) who pointed out 'everyone is protected by regulations every day. At work we are protected from exploitation. When shopping we are protected from shoddy deals. And as citizens we are protected from toxic pollution, fire-trap buildings and dangerous vehicles. Law, including regulation, is the difference between anarchy and civilisation' (TUC, 2006).

There are therefore different strands to the arguments advanced by those in favour of regulation. Primarily these are defensive, being largely concerned with protection of employees, consumers and the environment. However they are underpinned by a positive ideological argument that emphasizes the social benefits of regulation.

The argument in favour of protecting employees can take various different forms. From a strictly economic point of view a workforce that feels vulnerable is likely to plan its spending

Mini-Case 13.5 Asbestos

Asbestos is a mineral which was used widely in Britain until the 1980s because of its heat resistant qualities. There are three main types of asbestos: blue, brown and white.

As a result of the potentially fatal consequences of exposure to asbestos the use of blue and brown asbestos in Britain was banned in 1985. A similar ban was placed on the use of white asbestos in 1999. Despite the ban in Britain asbestos is still used in many countries throughout the world.

Inhalation of asbestos fibres can cause a number of diseases, particularly lung cancer, asbestosis, mesothelioma or pleural plaques. In 2004 there were 1,969 work related deaths from mesothelioma and 100 from asbestosis in the UK alone. It is estimated that in the UK the number of deaths from mesothelioma will rise to a peak of 2,450 some time between 2011 and 2015 (Health and Safety Commission, 2006: 8).

The reasons why the figures are growing despite the ban are twofold. Firstly, there is a time lag between exposure to asbestos and the onset of symptoms. This can be anything between 10 and 45 years. Secondly, there is still a vast amount of asbestos that was fitted in buildings that has yet to be removed.

Given the long period of time between exposure and health impacts it might be thought that businesses were unaware of the dangers of working with asbestos. However, as long ago as 1930 Dr E. R. A. Merewether and the then Engineering Inspector of Factories C. W. Price published the 'Report on effects of asbestos dust and dust suppression in the asbestos industry'. This showed the links between exposure to asbestos and industrial diseases. The report did lead to legislation concerning use of the substance but asbestos continued to be used for many years.

Not everyone who is exposed to asbestos will contract a fatal disease and even if they are affected it may result in a lesser condition such as pleural plaques. This is a scarring of the lung tissue which does not normally cause health problems. The presence of such a condition can, however, cause anxiety in the individual victim as to whether they may contract a more serious condition.

There is an ongoing court case in England on this issue which is now going to the House of Lords. The Law Lords decision will have broad consequences as can be seen when we look at the cost of asbestos litigation. We noted above the likely increase in the number of asbestos-related deaths. It was estimated in 2004 that the rise in claims that could result would see an increase in costs to British insurers and the state of up to £20 billion (Dyer and Jones, 2005).

However, as has already been suggested, the economic argument may not be the most fundamental in deciding when and how far the law should intervene. In the case concerning pleural plaques the victims obtained judgement in their favour in the High Court. After this decision one of their lawyers, Ian McFall commented 'This is good law, which puts people before profits' (Dyer and Jones, 2005) suggesting a deeper moral and philosophical argument for intervention.

❷ Do you agree that law which puts people before profits is good law?

❷ Assume that you do agree; should this be the criterion for deciding what the law is in every situation?

accordingly. Workers who feel that they could lose their jobs tomorrow are less likely to make long term or expensive purchases such as houses, cars or holidays.

The strictly economic argument can intersect with those of a more social nature as can be seen if we look at the issue of health and safety at work. The Health and Safety Executive has estimated that workplace accidents and work related ill health costs the British economy as much as £22.2 billion a year (HSE Economic Advisors Unit, 2004: 6). Coupled with that economic cost is the social cost in terms of pain, grief and suffering. A stark example of this comes when we look at the effect of exposure to asbestos (see Mini-Case 13.5).

Alongside the economic and social arguments there may be political reasons for intervention. In recent years awareness of the need to protect the environment has increased resulting in legislation such as the Environmental Protection Act 1990. This imposes legal sanctions for those who might be responsible for pollution in a variety of situations, including those where land is contaminated, or fumes and gases are emitted from a building.

In taking such measures this legislation puts into practice the idea that the party who creates the pollution should pay the cost of it. Whilst such legislation could be said to inhibit business freedom it does fit neatly with the ideas of democracy and social solidarity which underpin the case in favour of regulation. This is that if a company's behaviour is detrimental to the lives of a country's citizens and communities the electorate should have the power, through their representatives, to control that company. This case is made strongly by Bakan (2005).

Those who advance such arguments would point to incidents such as the Bhopal disaster which took place in India in 1984. In this case, there was a chemical leak from the factory of American corporation Union Carbide. The leak resulted in the death of several thousands of people and the injury of many thousands more. After several years the company reached a multi-million dollar settlement of the law suit that arose out of the disaster, although the matter still provokes controversy. For those in favour of regulation, cases such as this show the need for control over the conduct of companies.

There are therefore a number of political and economic arguments in favour of intervention. Indeed greater regulation is not necessarily inimical to business success. As we have seen, the political and moral argument that economic gains should be enjoyed by all potentially has the economic benefit of greater consumption.

In fact, the argument that there should be some level of regulation is not as controversial as it may seem. The EU regulates how companies compete with each other and even the World Trade Organization, which has free trade philosophy at its core, supervises the Agreement on Trade Related Aspects of Intellectual Property (TRIPS).

The agreement was entered into as manufacturers, particularly from developed countries, were increasingly concerned by the billion dollar trade in pirated products which was affecting their profitability. The regulations oblige WTO members to grant and enforce rights to property which is the product of intellectual activity, such as new inventions.

There is therefore not a completely free market. The state has to intervene in order to correct the distortions that can arise from the market and create the conditions in which businesses can flourish. As the Better Regulation Commission say 'We would all be rather disappointed if basic protections such as a clean environment . . . and a good education for our children were not fulfilled' (Annual Report, 2006: 12). The issue therefore is not regulation vs. deregulation but rather what level and what type of regulation is acceptable?

Self-regulation?

However, it is important to recognize that the process of regulation is not simply carried out by the state through legislation. Businesses may therefore sometimes judge it better to regulate themselves through their own codes of conduct and trade associations as a way of fending off more stringent regulation by government. The newspaper industry has just such a body in the form of

Children outside the Union Carbide factory a month after the chemical leak, which resulted in the death of several thousands of people.
© Bettmann/Corbis

the Press Complaints Commission (PCC). (See the PCC's website at www.pcc.org.uk/about/whatispcc.html.)

Self-regulation may not always be possible and desirable and therefore the law will intervene. The process of law making is a balancing act between different competing interests and value systems. The level and type of legal intervention is therefore very much a result of the political process.

Interaction

Businesses do have a role to play in this as whilst they do not have votes they can still influence legislators both directly and indirectly (see Chapter 11). This influence can be used in both a positive and a negative way. Businesses may therefore press for laws to be removed as well as passed in order to protect their position.

One area where businesses clearly would like their influence to be felt given its direct effect on their operation is employment law. This is also an area where views informed by differing ideologies have a practical impact. It is therefore instructive for us to consider as our Case Study one particular aspect of this area which has excited some controversy: the working time directive.

◈ *Looking ahead*

As a result of the Companies Act 2006 there will be a major change in the legal environment for businesses in England and Wales in the very near future.[3] Although it is not possible to summarize such a wide ranging piece of legislation here, we can identify parts of the Act which have an impact on our analysis of the interaction between the legal environment and decision-making in businesses.

In particular, Chapter 2 of Part 10 of the Act sets out in clear terms the duties imposed on directors. Specifically section 172(1) sets out a series of matters which a director must consider when taking any action. It is worth setting out in full the list contained in the section:

(a) the likely consequences of any decision in the long term,
(b) the interests of the company's employees,
(c) the need to foster the company's business relationships with suppliers, customers and others,
(d) the impact of the company's operations on the community and environment,
(e) the desirability of the company maintaining a reputation for high standards of business conduct,
(f) the need to act fairly as between members of the company.

Arguably a well-run company would take all such factors into account anyway. However, it is interesting to note that a company now has a statutory duty to consider the position of external parties such as customers and the community.

As we have already seen, the existing requirement under s309 of the Companies Act 1985 to have regard to the interests of the company's employees has proved to be something of a dead letter. It therefore remains to be seen exactly what effect section 172(1) will have.

It should be said though, that the overriding duty under s172(1) is to promote the success of the company. Section 170 also makes it clear that the duties enshrined in the Act are owed by a director to the company (and therefore apparently not to anyone outside the company).

That aside the Act does also extend the situations in which shareholders can take legal action for breach of duty. They will therefore have a general right to bring a claim rather than the limited instances under the current law.

Lastly, some of the internal controls imposed on private companies will be relaxed. Amongst other things therefore, the requirements to have AGMs and a company secretary will be abolished. That being said it will be open to companies to have both if they so wish.

On a broader level there will also be a change to the structure of the court system. Specifically, the judicial arm of the House of Lords will be replaced by a Supreme Court. At one level this is a huge change as it severs any link that the judiciary has with parliament. However, there will simply be a straight transfer of the judges from the House of Lords to the new court. In practical terms this is therefore unlikely to have any effect on the decisions made in Britain's highest court.

◈ *Summary*

- The law is not a monolithic entity. It is therefore formed in different ways and has a number of different categories. This is not surprising given the range of activities that are covered by the law

- The law can not be seen in isolation and in particular is closely linked to the political environment. The law has therefore been influenced by the process of globalization which is considered elsewhere in this book. Law is therefore increasingly made at an international level rather than within the nation-state. A good example of this is the European Union whose actions and decisions are a central part of the legal environment of business

- The law also determines the different structures a business can adopt. For companies in particular their structure does much to determine their decision-making process. Some commentators argue that as a result a company's underlying dynamic is the mere pursuit of profit to the exclusion of social responsibility

- The law does not exist in a vacuum and therefore is strongly influenced by the prevailing values within society. These values reflect different competing interests. This diversity of views and interests is partly played out in arguments over how much legal intervention there should be, particularly in areas which affect business activity. However, there is always a level of regulation and on occasions that may be helpful to business

3 It was announced in late February 2007 that major elements of the Act including the governance of directors would come into force on 1 October 2007.

Case study: the working time directive

The working time directive was adopted by the member states within the European Union in 1993. As its name suggests it sought to protect workers by limiting hours of work and pre-scribing minimum rest and holiday periods.

The United Kingdom did not put in place the necessary regulations enacting the directive until 1998 and only did so after losing a court case on the issue (*United Kingdom of Great Britain and Northern Ireland* vs. *Council of the European Union* (1996) ECR I-05755). Even when it did put the necessary regulations in place it kept an opt-out so that individuals could agree not to be subject to the 48 hours maximum working week allowed for under the directive.

Whilst there are exceptions to the regulations such as the provisions on unmeasured working time (regulation 20(1)), it is the opt-out which has probably excited most controversy. The EU have sought to end the UK's use of the opt-out and in May 2005 the European Parliament voted to remove it by 2010. How-ever, the UK is still in favour of the exemption and the issue is still subject to negotiation.

The central core of the business argument over this issue is one of flexibility. Thus John Cridland, deputy director-general of the CBI (a representative group for employers) argued 'Those who have argued for the ending of the opt out simply do not understand the realities of the modern workplace. The ability for individuals to opt out . . . is a vital part of the UK's flexible labour market' (Laitner and Taylor, 2006).

Specifically the CBI feel that the opt-out provides 'the most economic and efficient means for tackling upturns in labour demand' (House of Lords European Committee, 2004: 13). Thus the opt-out could help deal with skills and labour shortages. In addition there are certain areas where work that was started would have to be finished (ironically one of these areas is safety maintenance). The CBI go on to argue 'that labour market flex-ibility made the UK an attractive place to do business' (House of Lords European Committee, 2004: 13).

Not surprisingly the TUC advances quite a different view which is strongly in favour of ending the opt-out. There are several strands to their argument. In general, they are critical of what they call the UK's long hours culture. Specifically they feel that working long hours is bad for people's health. In particular, they point to increased risk of 'heart disease, chronic headache, irritable bowel syndrome, diabetes, stress and accidents at work' for those who work longer hours (TUC, 2004). At the same time they argue that long hours are actually indicative of economic inefficiency being a symptom of poor productivity and bad management (House of Lords European Committee, 2004: 14 and TUC, 2004).

In addition the TUC point to abuse by employers of the opt-out clause. Under the regulations workers have to agree to work over

48 hours a week. However, the TUC argue that employers are forc-ing workers into such agreements by a variety of methods such as making this part of their contract or handbook or just by straight bullying.

Whilst there is research to suggest that in fact many workers do long hours of their own volition (see the Chartered Institute of Personnel and Development, 2003: 11; see Chapter 8), the Labour Force Survey suggests that most full-time employees wanted to work fewer hours. That being said, for many this is subject to there being no resulting cut in pay (Department of Trade and Industry, 2004: 16).

However, finance is not the only reason for working long hours, with the amount of work that people have to do and the expectation of employers also being important factors (Depart-ment of Trade and Industry, 2004: 16). Not surprisingly there-fore there is evidence to suggest that the vast majority of employers support the opt-out and feel their efficiency would suffer if it were removed (House of Lords European Committee, 2004: 13).

Despite this, the figures seem to suggest that the propor-tion of the population working more than 48 hours a week has gradually declined since the regulations were introduced in 1998. In evidence to the House of Lords European Committee in 2004 the DTI suggested that the proportion had fallen from 23.3% of full-time employees in spring 1998 to 20.4% in spring 2003 (p. 15). The regulations would therefore seem to have had some effect although it would be too simplistic to attribute all of this reduction to them.

As we saw at the very start of the chapter, our behaviour is influenced by many other factors than the laws that we live under. For many companies therefore the effect of legislation may be determined by broader factors such as the competitive conditions that they operate under (Edwards, Ram and Black, 2004).

The working time directive may therefore be completely irrel-evant in most workplaces where the norm is to work much less than 48 hours a week. As we have seen this is the case for nearly 80% of full-time employees. According to the ONS, in 2006 the average full-time worker did 39.5 hours a week (Office for National Statistics, 2006).

The relationships within firms may also have an impact on how individuals react. Thus in a firm with a recognized trade union there is more likely to be consultation with the workforce over pay and conditions, although this is done in a collective sense with the relationship being mediated through trade union representat-ives (Kersley et al., 2005). Union organization is much weaker in smaller firms (Kersley et al., 2005: 13 and 14) where the rela-tionship between employee and employer may be more direct.

The relevance of this for the working time directive is that there is evidence that 'Employees tended to work more than 48 hours a week with greater frequency . . . in workplaces without a recognised union' (Kersley et al., 2005: 28).

It is important therefore to consider the law and its impact in a broader sense. It is clearly an important factor in determining how businesses operate, but cannot be seen in isolation. The competing interests and influences that help to create the law also determine how it is implemented. Consideration of the law is therefore not simply a technical issue but something that brings together many of the themes that run throughout this book.

❷ Explain whether you think people's working hours should be regulated.

❷ Should employers and employees not be free to agree between themselves the terms and conditions of their relationship?

Review and discussion questions

1. Outline the different sources of the law in the UK. In what areas can business have an influence on what the law is?

2. How does the law of the European Union affect businesses? Do you think its impact has been positive or negative?

3. Describe the different legal structures that a business can adopt. What are the advantages and disadvantages of the different structures?

4. How far should decisions made about legislation be influenced by ideological considerations?

5. Summarize the arguments for and against legal intervention. Could the different viewpoints be reconciled through greater degrees of self-regulation?

Assignments

1. Research and comment on the process of carrying out a Regulatory Impact Assessment by visiting www.cabinetoffice.gov.uk/regulation/ria. In particular, are there any issues or parties that are not currently considered in this process which should be included? Are there any of the current issues or parties that are included that might be taken out of the process?

2. Consider and compare section 309 of the Companies Act 1985 with section 172(1) of the Companies Act 2006. In the light of these two sections what factors should a company consider when making any decisions?

3. 'Newspapers breach the PCC Code for commercial gain. The more flagrant the breach, the more substantial is the likely commercial gain' (Jonathan Coad (2003) The Press Complaints Commission—some myths about self-regulation, *Entertainment Law Review*, 14(8): 211–14). Outline the arguments for and against self-regulation of the press via the PCC.

Further reading

As has already been pointed out, the law is forever changing and therefore care should be taken when reading any book on the law, as its contents may be out of date. It is also the case that law books can prove to be something of a struggle even for lawyers as they are necessarily very technical.

With this in mind, the books recommended below are geared towards those who are not experts in the law and give you an overview of the relevant areas.

Oxford Dictionary of the Law (2003) 5th edition (Oxford: Oxford University Press). Law, like many other subjects, has its own language. You may well find in your reading that you come across a term you are unfamiliar with. If so, this is the book for you.

James Holland and Julian Webb (2006) *Learning Legal Rules,* 6th edition (Oxford: Oxford University Press). This book provides a good starting point for studying and applying the law. If nothing else you should read chapter 1 which gives a good overview of the basic structure and sources of the law.

Karen Davies (2006) *Understanding European Union Law* (London: Routledge). European law can be very difficult to grasp. This book provides a simple and helpful overview of the main issues.

Andrew McGee, Christina Williams and Gary Scanlan (2005) *The Law of Business Organisations* (Exeter: Law Matters). This book largely focuses on companies, but is well structured, and therefore you can use it to give you more detail on some of the legal points discussed in the Business Organizations section of this chapter. This book will have to be revised before the end of 2007 to take account of the new Companies Act.

Denis Keenan (2006) *Smith and Keenan's Law for Business,* 13th edition (Harlow: Pearson Education). This is a more all-embracing text than *The Law of Business Organisations.* It does cover the central elements of company law but also looks at broader legal issues affecting businesses such as employment and contract law. Again this will have to be revised shortly.

J. A. G. Griffith (1997) *The Politics of the Judiciary,* 5th edition (London: Fontana). A seminal text on the role of the judiciary. Whilst not specifically related to business it does give an insight into a central element of the legal system.

Joel Bakan (2005) *The Corporation* (London: Constable). (See also the film of the same name.) A critique of the company as an institution, written by a Canadian law professor. As we have discussed above, Bakan argues that the legal structure of a company makes it act in a way that puts profit before social considerations.

Online resources

Test your understanding of this chapter with online questions and answers, explore the subject further through web exercises, and use the weblinks to provide a quick resource for further research. Go to the Online Resource Centre at

www.oxfordtextbooks.co.uk/orc/ wetherly_otter/

www.companieshouse.gov.uk—Companies House incorporates companies and collects in, and stores, all the information they are expected to file on incorporation and annually.

www.dti.gov.uk—the Department of Trade and Industry site contains a wealth of information that is helpful to businesses.

www.opsi.gov.uk—has the full text of all UK legislation since 1987.

www.europa.eu—the European Union website.

www.cbi.org.uk—Confederation of British Industry.

www.chamberonline.co.uk—the website for the British Chambers of Commerce. As mentioned above, it contains the Burdens Barometer—an annual survey of the cost to British business of government regulation.

www.brc.gov.uk—the website for the Better Regulation Commission.

www.tuc.org.uk—the website for the main employee organization in the UK, it has a wealth of material relating to all aspects of employment and regulation.

References

Bakan, J. (2005) *The Corporation* (London: Constable).

Better Regulation Commission (2006) *Annual Report for 2006* (accessed 12 April 2007) www.brc.gov.uk

British Chamber of Commerce (2007) *Burdens Barometer 2007* (accessed 12 April 2007) www.chamberonline.co.uk

Cabinet Office (2006) *Simplification Plans—a Summary* (accessed 12 April 2007) www.cabinetoffice.gov.uk

Chartered Institute of Personnel and Development (2003) *Living to Work?* (accessed 12 April 2007) www.cipd.co.uk

Combined Code on Corporate Governance (2006) (accessed 12 April 2007) www.frc.org.uk

Department of Trade and Industry (2004) Working time—widening the debate: a preliminary consultation on long hours working in the UK and the application and operation of the working time opt out (accessed 12 April 2007) www.dti.gov.uk

Dyer, C. and Jones, R. (2005) Workers win test case in asbestos claim, *Guardian*, 16 February 2005 (accessed 12 April 2007) http://business.guardian.co.uk

Edwards, P., Ram, M. and Black, J. (2004) Why does employment legislation not damage small firms? *Journal of Law and Society*, 31(2): 245–65.

Griffith, J. A. G. (1997) *The Politics of the Judiciary*, 5th edition (London: Fontana).

Health and Safety Commission (2006) *Health and Safety Statistics 2005/06* (accessed 12 April 2007) www.hse.gov.uk

HM Treasury (2001) *Institutional Investment in the UK: a Review* (accessed 12 April 2007) www.hm-treasury.gov.uk

House of Lords European Committee (2004) The Working Time Directive: a response to the European Commissions review HL paper 67 (accessed 12 April 2007) www.publications.parliament.uk

HSE Economic Advisors Unit (2004) *Interim Update of the 'Costs to Britain of Workplace Accidents and Work-Related Ill Health'* (accessed 12 April 2007) www.hse.gov.uk

Institute of Dirctors, *Fact Sheet on Corporate Governance in the UK* (accessed 12 April 2007) www.iod.com

Kersley, B., Alpin. C., Forth, J., Bryson, A., Bewley, H., Dix, G. and Oxenbridge, S. (2005) *Inside the workplace. First findings from the 2004 Workplace Employment Relations Survey* (accessed 12 April 2007) www.dti.gov.uk

Laitner, S. and Taylor, A. (2006) Move to scrap work hours opt-out foiled, *The Financial Times*, 8 November 2006.

Office for National Statistics (2006) *2006 Annual Survey of Hours and Earnings: first release* (accessed 12 April 2007) www.statisticsdownload.gov.uk

Press Complaints Commission (accessed 12 April 2007) www.pcc.org.uk

TUC (2004) *Press release: Time to end long hours working*, 30 March 2004 (accessed 12 April 2007) www.tuc.org.uk

TUC (2006) *Press release: TUC comment on red tape review*, 11 December 2006 (accessed 12 April 2007) www.tuc.org.uk

Case law

Cowan vs. *Scargill and Others* (1985) Ch. 270

NV Algemene Transporten Expeditie Onderneming van Gend en Loos vs. *Nederlandse Administratie der Belastingen*, Case 26/62 [1963] ECR 1

Salomon vs. *Salomon* (1897) AC 22

Entrepreneurship and enterprise

Alison Price and Martyn Robertson

Contents

14

Learning objectives

When you have completed this chapter you will be able to:

- Define and appreciate the role of **enterprise and entrepreneurship** in all its forms
- Examine how entrepreneurship and **enterprise** inter-relate
- Explore the important role played by micro businesses and small and medium enterprises (SMEs)
- Analyse the strategic response of **entrepreneurs** in different market environments
- Outline why entrepreneurship in the UK is encouraged within disadvantaged communities and with under-represented groups

Themes

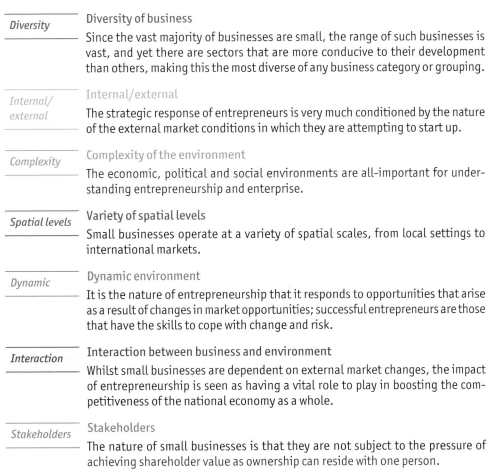

Diversity
Diversity of business
Since the vast majority of businesses are small, the range of such businesses is vast, and yet there are sectors that are more conducive to their development than others, making this the most diverse of any business category or grouping.

Internal/ external
Internal/external
The strategic response of entrepreneurs is very much conditioned by the nature of the external market conditions in which they are attempting to start up.

Complexity
Complexity of the environment
The economic, political and social environments are all-important for understanding entrepreneurship and enterprise.

Spatial levels
Variety of spatial levels
Small businesses operate at a variety of spatial scales, from local settings to international markets.

Dynamic
Dynamic environment
It is the nature of entrepreneurship that it responds to opportunities that arise as a result of changes in market opportunities; successful entrepreneurs are those that have the skills to cope with change and risk.

Interaction
Interaction between business and environment
Whilst small businesses are dependent on external market changes, the impact of entrepreneurship is seen as having a vital role to play in boosting the competitiveness of the national economy as a whole.

Stakeholders
Stakeholders
The nature of small businesses is that they are not subject to the pressure of achieving shareholder value as ownership can reside with one person.

Values
Values
The values of the entrepreneur impact directly on the way in which the business is conducted.

Introduction

Diversity

'Enterprise' and 'entrepreneurshipare' key terms within business, both within the UK and for economic development and wealth across the rest of the world. Determining and achieving 'competitive advantage' is the core of successful entrepreneurship as appreciating the source of this advantage provides small businesses with the route to creating a sustainable competitive strategy of growth and development.

The purpose of this chapter is to provide an understanding of what enterprise means, what it means to be an entrepreneur, or intrapreneur, and to explore their role within society. This chapter will explain what is meant by key terms—enterprise; entrepreneurship; small–medium sized enterprise (SME); entrepreneurial skills and intrapreneurship. This is particularly important as the usage of these terms can vary in different forms of literature (particularly popular media like newspapers but also within business articles or academic journals). It will also explore the forms of entrepreneur that exist within the UK, appreciating the values that drive entrepreneurs to start different forms of organizations. It will examine how sometimes clear articulation of an entrepreneur's values can be used to form competitive advantage for businesses, using examples such as the origins of 'The Body Shop' and 'The Co-operative Bank'.

Interaction

From this initial understanding of enterprise, the chapter will then focus upon the importance of starting new businesses, or ventures, for the UK economy or 'UK plc'. This section will explain how SMEs impact upon the development of the UK economy, and explore 'gaps' in potential —between what could be achieved and what is actually being achieved. Identifying the gaps shows that not all members of society have the same opportunities to start their own business: there is untapped potential for enterprise in the UK. This gap between potential and activity will then be explored for specific groups—females, deprived areas, Black and Minority Ethnic communities (BME).

Understanding enterprise and entrepreneurship

As Peter Drucker remarked in 1985, 'innovation' and 'enterprise' have become 'buzz words' widely used in the media, and it is therefore necessary to be very precise about the differences between them. Enterprise is a word that creates positive associations of a) 'creating' and b) 'activity' when we hear it used in the media and on the television, but it has specific meanings when used in business literature. This can cause confusion as both the terms 'enterprise' and 'entrepreneurship' can mean different things to different people. For example, within the business environment, the term 'enterprise' is often used as a noun, as another word for a firm (e.g., a 'small–medium sized enterprise'—SME), but it can be used as an adjective to describe an individual as being 'enterprising' (industrious) or innovative (as in creative). Such a person may then be called an 'entrepreneur', but it is important to recognize that not all small business owners are true entrepreneurs! This is because to be an 'entrepreneur' has specific implications of 'creating' a business, rather than just owning or running it (that is, adding value by creating and developing a business opportunity, rather than simply being the owner or manager).

These overlaps and distinctions of meaning can cause confusion if not clearly appreciated. Therefore this chapter will firstly outline these important terms and use them to understand the role that entrepreneurs, their small businesses and their creativity can play within the business environment and the growth of the UK economy—but be careful and remember that you may need to recognize that other sources (books, newspapers, etc.) may use them to mean other things!

What is enterprise?

Enterprise can be broadly understood as 'making things happen, having ideas and doing something about them, taking advantage of the opportunities to bring about change' (SGE, 1999). This suggests enterprise in its widest sense involves the ability to use personal *entrepreneurial capacity* (attitudes, skills and competences) for innovation and small business development (Davies, 2002). However the term enterprise stems from economic theory and has been described as the opportunity created by any 'disequilibrium in supply and demand' (Casson, 1982). This means that recognizing a customer need (demand) that is not currently being met (supply) creates an opportunity to be enterprising and for a business to meet this demand.

Dynamic

But the term enterprise suggests much more than just meeting an untapped market, as it implies creative solutions and innovation. Schumpeter (1936) introduced the notion of 'creative destruction' (see Chapter 2) within economic theory as entrepreneurs became recognized for their potential to create change (be 'creative') and see new opportunities within the existing environment (even by 'destroying' the existing to create the new). This then becomes one of the hallmarks of capitalism—the relentless pursuit of innovation by entrepreneurs and the inevitable consequence of destroying previous commodities and ways of doing things.

However, this association of the term enterprise with change and activity should also be recognized as having resource implications. Peter Drucker described true enterprise not as just starting-up a business, but as achieving an 'upgrade in yield from resources' (1985: 25) whilst Timmons called it the 'pursuit of opportunity without regard to the resources currently under one's control or influence' (1989: 16–17). Both of these definitions recognize the need for access to resources (including those not yet currently available) to create a new venture, but Drucker places the emphasis upon the talent of the entrepreneur to add significant value to existing resources, whilst Timmons highlights an entrepreneur's vision operating beyond existing resources.

Within these broad understandings of what enterprise is, two ends of a continuum emerge—one end is the business definition of enterprise as a new venture or business (a start-up), with the other being a broader concept of enterprise which suggests change and can equally be applied to social objectives (see social entrepreneur). 'An *enterprising person* is one who comes across a pile of scrap metal and sees the making of wonderful sculpture. An enterprising person is one who drives through an old decrepit part of town and sees a new housing development. An enterprising person is one who sees opportunity in all areas of life' (Rohn, 2005).

However, the traditional outcome of enterprise is a small business or venture and therefore enterprise, as used within the business literature, can be defined in the following way: '*enterprise* is a set of qualities and competencies that can be employed in different settings, whilst *entrepreneurship* involves the process of creating and developing new ventures' (Enterprise Insight, 2005: 23).

What is 'an enterprise' or SME?

The word *enterprise* suggests a large or small business, but it can also be a social business, like a charity or not-for-profit venture, or even used to described a project, or hobby. To clarify the term, business text books tend to refer to SMEs when they specifically mean a small or medium sized business rather than ventures, activities or charity, because an *SME* is a short-hand expression for a small–medium sized business.

Internal/ external

To determine whether a business is large, small or very small (a 'micro' business) it is important to know the number of people working in the company (the employees) and the economic activity of the company (turnover or balance sheet).

Table 14.1 shows a way of classifying businesses according to size. These guidelines provide boundaries to the classification of the size of a business. It must also be appreciated that different sectors require different organizational structures and sizes to deliver their business

Table 14.1 European definition of a SME and micro business (2005)

	No. of employees (headcount)	Either/or (less than or equal to in euros)	
		Turnover	Balance sheet total
Micro business	0–9	2m euros	2m
Small business	10–49	10m	10m
Medium sized business	50–250	50m	43m

Source: http://europa.eu

effectively—i.e. a web design company can be very effective as a micro business with only one expert, the entrepreneur and business owner, working alone.

Who is the small-business manager?

The *small-business owner or manager* is responsible for the day-to-day operation and organization of the business. This can either be the person who set up the business or might be a manager that the entrepreneur employs to run the business. Some SMEs are 'family businesses' and have been run by generations of owner-managers from within the same family, with the true entrepreneur having been the visionary who started the business.

Who is an entrepreneur?

An *entrepreneur* is defined by the DTi (the UK Department of Trade and Industry) as 'anyone who attempts a new business or new venture creation, such as self employment, a new business organization or social enterprise' (2004) and can be described as someone who is enterprising (having ideas and making them happen). However the popular media tends to suggest that all small business owners are 'entrepreneurs' and it is important to understand that these terms do not mean exactly the same thing in business. Firstly because, as Drucker (1985) suggested, an entrepreneur does not need a profit motive and therefore need not be running a small business (as it is possible to be a *social entrepreneur*, creating a not-for-profit organization or a charity) and secondly because some business owners do not display the true characteristics of an entrepreneur.

Drucker believes that 'the entrepreneur always searches for change, responds to it and exploits it as an opportunity' (Drucker, 1985: 25) rather than manages a business. This broader definition accepts that an entrepreneur is more than a manager and allows us to include people that are driven to be creative and entrepreneurial in all areas—this helps define different kinds of entrepreneur, who all act to create change whilst within a large company, or working for the benefit of society.

Defining the entrepreneur as social, serial or an intrapreneur

Values

A *social entrepreneur* is a specific term for someone who employs business principles and business start-up techniques for societal good and social benefit (see Chapter 1). This 'third' sector (voluntary/not-for-profit/social enterprise) of the economy has grown significantly over the last

Jamie Oliver's restaurant 'Fifteen' is a social enterprise: all profits from Fifteen go to provide disadvantaged young people with a working environment in which they can start a career in the restaurant business.

© Getty Images

twenty years. The government defines social enterprises as 'business with primary social object-ives whose surpluses are principally reinvested for that purpose in the business or in the com-munity, rather than being driven by the need to maximize profit for shareholders and owners' (Social Enterprise Action Plan, 2006). It is estimated that at least 55,000 businesses, with employ-ees, fit this definition of social enterprise (Small Business Service, 2006). This forms about 5% of all businesses with employees, with a combined turnover of £27 million, providing a contribution to the GDP of £8.4 billion (Social Enterprise Action Plan, Cabinet Office, 2006).

A 'serial' entrepreneur

Entrepreneurs that start many businesses may be referred to as *serial entrepreneurs*. This can be because their original businesses fail (30% of SMEs fail within the first three years) and also because they learn from each business and take that learning into the next one. This behaviour can also be seen in successful entrepreneurs, such as Richard Branson, who has taken his innovative vision of business to a range of new markets, including train travel, the soft drinks market, membership gyms and even bridal fashion.

Dynamic

Mini-Case 14.1 Social entrepreneurs creating entrepreneurs!

Train 2000 was established in 1996, as a non-profit distributing social enterprise, in order to promote a range of high quality business support services for women. Our founder members, drawn from the voluntary, private and education sectors, recognized that the existing business support provision failed to recognize the specific needs of women seeking self employment as it was mainly inaccessible and inappropriate. Their vision of an integrated business support service laid the foundations for the way in which we now deliver our services, and has enabled it to be recognized as one of the leading women's enterprise development organizations in the UK.

Mission and Objectives: Train 2000 seeks to be an innovative organization that provides quality enterprise and employment services for women and influences policy in order to improve the economic position of all women. We achieve this mission in three key ways:

1 Through providing a range of quality, client sensitive enterprise and employment services for women in Merseyside.

2 By influencing local, regional, national and international policy and practices in the area of women's economic development.

3 By developing and maintaining Train 2000 as a sustainable organization able to achieve its mission. www.train2000.org.uk

❷ What are the motivations for social entrepreneurs?

Values

Some of these businesses have been more successful than others, but they all have reflected the Virgin business style and ethos and the learning from one business sector is applied to another.

Diversity

What is an 'intrapreneur'?

Internal/external

An *intrapreneur* has been defined as 'a person within a large corporation who takes direct responsibility for turning an idea into a profitable finished product through assertive risk-taking and innovation' (*American Heritage Directory*, 1992). This is a relatively new term which builds upon our understanding of an entrepreneur as a person who has ideas and makes things happen, but

Successful entrepreneur Richard Branson launching another branch of the Virgin brand, Virgin Mobile.

© Corbis

within the context of a larger business, or corporation. This brings together the words 'intra' (corporate) and (entre) 'preneur' to help our appreciation of how large companies may innovate and grow through the 'intrapreneurship' of their staff.

Intrapreneurs are recognized as being those staff within large businesses who display the entrepreneurial traits more normally associated with starting a business and may see opportunities that the corporation may have initially overlooked. This can mean encouraging a business to introduce a new product or service that it was not actively seeking to develop at that time.

What makes an entrepreneur?

There are many authors who have sought to create a list of the most important *traits* or characteristics that entrepreneurs have and they tend to include some, or all of the qualities identified by Gibb (1996; 1999) and Enterprise Insight (2005) that are listed below:

- innovator
- catalysing change
- seizing opportunity
- resourceful
- opportunity seeking
- creative
- having an ability for problem solving
- able to coping with uncertainty
- opportunistic
- risk takers.

However *trait theory*—that is the theory of identifying and understanding the specific human characteristics of an entrepreneur—is complex and remains controversial (Steiner, 1979; Chrisman, Bauerschmidt and Hofer, 1998). Counter-theories suggest that the situation or environment (Kuratko and Hodgetts, 2001) are equally important factors to consider as a natural ability or personality traits.

These two theories address a central question that may be asked in relation to how leaders in general are created—the question as to whether they can be 'made' through environment and education, or whether someone is just 'born' with the attributes, skills and the capability (the 'traits') to become enterprising (Jack and Anderson, 1999). These two different schools of thought are

Interaction

 Mini-Case 14.2 Post-it notes

The most commonly recognized example of intrapreneurship is the story of Art Fry who developed 'Post-it notes'. This development, now essential for any office, was actually once a 'failed' product, a non-sticking glue, being an innovation with no obvious use!

Art Fry used the non-sticking glue on small strips of paper to mark pages in a hymn book at church, after it had failed to provide the new product that 3M were seeking. This innovation showed him the potential of this product and Post-its have now become an essential item, with a range of further innovations

(brand extensions) from this original concept, securing a major long term income stream for the 3M.
www.3m.com

❷ In the light of this example, can you explain the meaning of the maxim 'Innovators learn that it's better to ask for forgiveness than for permission'?

❷ Can you think of other examples of successful intrapreneurship where new product/service developments have been initiated by employees within the business?

ACCOUNTING
FINALIZE PRESENTATION
DRY CLEANERS
CALL HUMAN RESOURCES
PRESENTATION AT 3PM!
BASE RENT AMOUNT
RENT PER SQ. FT.
PAY BILLS
ORDER LUNCH
MEETING
VACATION
CHECK EMAIL
CALL

actually very important to consider, as they have different implications for the way governments may support start-up businesses and create the most conducive environment for them. The UK government accepts a role in supporting entrepreneurs, having stated their commitment to 'making the UK the best place in the world to start and grow a business' (SBS Action Plan, 2004 and 2004a). But many feel that although the governments can only create the right environment for enterprise to flourish, they cannot make people into entrepreneurs.

> **⮑ *Stop and Think***
> Do you understand the precise business meaning of enterprise and entrepreneur? Can you identify the different types of entrepreneur? Can you name any famous entrepreneurs?

Key dimensions in the development of small business

The business environment can contribute to some of the reasons why many small businesses are not successful. We have seen that survival rates for new businesses in the UK average at approximately 70% within their first three years (SBS 2006 (www.sbs.gov.uk/survival)). However the government is still encouraging more start-ups, with the Union of Industrial and Employers' Confederations of Europe (UNICE)—the voice of business in Europe—calling upon 'entrepreneurs to create the new sources of wealth' within Europe (UNICE, 1999).

There are three key dimensions we can identify in the development of small business:

1 stage of business growth

2 sector

3 values.

1 Stage of growth

Businesses can be said to have several stages to start-up, as listed below.

Stages of Business Start Up:[1]
A. Idea
B. Proven Idea
C. Planning & Development
D. Ready to Start-Up
E. Business Growth
F. Maturity
G. Exit Strategy

These stages show the business development from the original idea (A), to researching and proving the idea (B) and then the planning and development (C) which leads to the final 'start' of the

---

Post-it notes are an example of 'intrapreneurship', and transformed a failed product into an office essential.

© Corbis

1 Business Start Up @ Leeds Met Model of Business Start Up developed by Roberston, M. (2000) from Churchill N. C. & Lewis V. L. (1983), The five stages of Small Business Growth, *Harvard Business Review*, 63(3): May–June, and Stevenson, H. H. Six dimensions of entrepreneurship, in Birley, S. and Muzyka, D. F. (1997) *Mastering Enterprise*, FT Pitman.

Figure 14.1 Stages of business growth

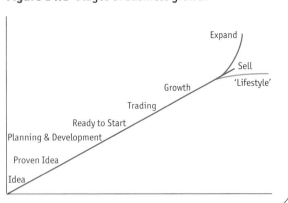

business (D). From this position of actually trading, the business then hopefully enters a phase of expansion ('business growth' (E)) until a point when the business stays relatively static as a small business (possibly as a 'lifestyle' business (F)) or continues to grow (E) until it reaches a major shift in organizational structure and the development of the business—such as being bought up by a larger company, or becoming a franchise. These major changes in a business can be called 'exit strategies' (G) as they can be the way that the entrepreneur that started the business exits the business, having taken it as far as they want to. These stages can be depicted in a linear diagram of growth.

Figure 14.1 suggests that business growth is a 'linear' activity, that is, that it is always moving forward and has specific separate stages. However, although this methodical approach is possible, most entrepreneurs experience these stages as more random and are often less able to plan to move towards these stages. Recent research (NCGE, 2006) suggests that graduates tend to start businesses in response to interest or a contract from a client (a 'first sale') and this first opportunity is often not planned for, but responded to. From this first bold move, a business often develops and formalizes and the stages of development then unfold. This more complex, less distinct approach to business start-up is likely to be the experience of most start-ups, not just graduates, as these phases of start-up can be inter-linked.

It is however helpful when thinking about a new venture or business to think about these stages as each makes different demands on the business and its staff. This means that the skills of the entrepreneur may need to be developed over time as the needs of the business change.

In order to start any new business or venture effectively, it is important to know what 'resources' are available—just as in the same way, when trying to create a specific meal, all the ingredients must be available, or substitute ones need to be found that will work just as well.

> **⊃ Stop and Think**
>
> Could you start a new business? What would you need to do it? Can you write a list of the resources you require? Do you remember the 'traits' that describe an entrepreneur—do you feel that they describe you?
>
> What about your capabilities—are you able to start a new business? What do you know about business? What areas might you need to develop new skills in?
>
> What skills do you have that would be good for selling, purchasing, negotiating, managing, working with colleagues or employing staff?
>
> Write a list of things you might need to learn, develop or buy in from someone else (such as an accountant or a lawyer).

Many 'would-be' entrepreneurs feel that they lack knowledge or skills to start-up (SBS, 2002) and any new venture is heavily dependent upon the skills and knowledge of those who are starting it up. There are many checklists or models to help with the assessment of the resources available to start-up a business but few consider both personal and physical resources. The 'MAIR' model below draws together six elements providing an appreciation of the personal capacity and business development required to start-up any new venture or project.

1 motivation and commitment

2 abilities and skill

3 idea in relation to the market

4 resources

5 plan and strategy

6 organization and administration.

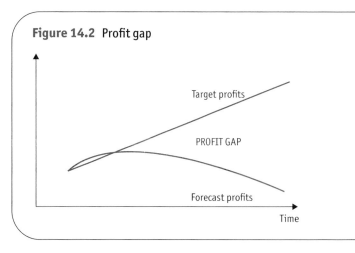

Figure 14.2 Profit gap

The 'MAIR model' presents the personal capacity required to start up—the knowledge, support, skills and confidence. From its origins, 'MAIR' (Gibb and Ritchie, 1982) has been adapted and developed (Hartshorn and Richardson, 1993) and is now more relevant for all new start-ups (including those from disadvantaged or underrepresented areas or groups such as university graduates or women) as it includes some additional elements, such as confidence to start up. Assessing each of these areas within the start-up process allows for planned *capacity building*. This is defined as 'helping organizations to develop their resources (people, buildings, etc.) so that they are better able to meet their aims. A term commonly used when an initiative or training programme is likely to increase the ability of the individuals or organisations to improve their performance, or take the lead, in specific economic or business development activities' (DTi, 2004).

The growth paths of small firms

It is important to determine how firms can achieve growth. One way is to undertake a *gap analysis*. This analysis involves establishing:

- the targets for achievement or the desired position
- the expected achievements if it did nothing to develop new strategies.

There will probably be a gap between what the organization would achieve without new effort and what it wishes to achieve. New strategies will have to be developed in order to close the gap. The gap can be broken down into more focused areas (e.g. a profit gap (see Figure 14.2), a sales gap (see Figure 14.3)).

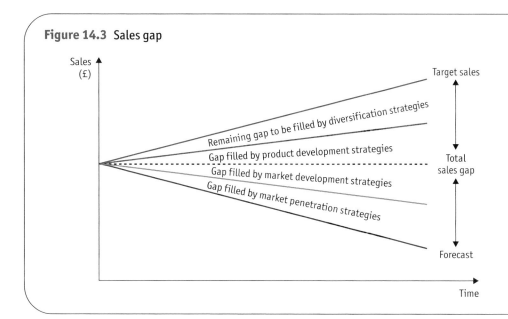

Figure 14.3 Sales gap

The sales gap can be filled by an appropriate combination of the following product market growth strategies:

- market penetration (increased sales to existing markets, through quality improvement or cost efficiencies)
- market development (increasing the number and scope of markets)
- product development (improving or expanding the range of products sold)
- diversification (new areas of activity to bring in additional profits).

For SMEs the gap filling strategies are through internal or joint development. Internal development or organic growth is generally slower and less disruptive, but enables the firm to acquire skills and knowledge and to spread the cost. It may mean that the business never catches up with established companies. Joint development (licensing, joint ventures or selling through agents), shares risk, costs and expertise with others but can present difficulties when the various parties work together and the weaker partner dictates the pace of development.

2 Sector

Having recognized that the stage or phase of a business can have an impact upon the skill requirements and activities of a small business, the second aspect to consider is the sector in which the business operates. Within the business environment, specific business sectors can be determined (see Table 14.2).

Diversity

Interaction

Each sector makes specific demands on the businesses that operate within them, and it is also clear that some sectors are more likely to be conducive to SMEs than others. Let us explore aspects of the business environment for some of these sectors and their implications for the future of the business.

Table 14.2 Classification of industries and sectors

Aerospace and defence	Healthcare
Agriculture	Horticulture
Automotive and parts	Household
Biotechnology	Information security
Broadcasting and media	Leisure
Building and construction	Marine industries
Chemicals	Medical
Computing and electronics	Materials/metals/minerals
Distribution	Oil and gas
Education	Property services
Energy	Radio
Engineering	Retail
Environmental	Software services
Financial	Telecoms
Fisheries	Utilities
Food and drink	

Source: derived from the *Financial Times* classification of stock market companies.

General building contractors

Construction, a highly fragmented sector, is an easy sector to enter and leave because of the nature of the work (defined as churning). It is characterized as being labour intensive with a relatively low level of entry capital required to set up in business. No one firm has a significant share of the market. Entry is also helped by the prevalence of contracting and sub contracting, alliances and the range of specialist trades in the industry. Sixty-nine of the businesses are either sole traders or partnerships. This reflects the large number of small and medium sized jobs uniformly spread across the UK, the ability of firms to operate in local markets and their flexibility to respond to customers' requirements. These factors provide little scope for economies of scale. Cash flow is particularly important for small construction firms because of the costs associated with stock and work in progress.

Restaurants and cafés

This sector is one of the most volatile sectors of the economy. It is characterized by the relative ease of setting up a restaurant business, frequent closures and changes of ownership and its responsiveness in providing catering services readily where demand arises. It relies heavily on personal service and, as such, its workforce is a key element in its success.

The rise of supermarkets

Chapter 3 showed that the expansion of market share by supermarkets has been at the expense of small firms. The survival of small food retailing firms is likely to be dependent upon meeting local needs through a combination of long or anti-social opening hours and satisfying the attitudes and tastes of their customers (e.g. ethnic, healthy, concerns for the environment, etc.). see also the Sunday trading Mini-Case in Chapter 11). The petrol filling station sector used to be dominated by small firms but due to environmental and safety issues and intense price competition, large chains and supermarkets are now dominant. Similarly, other small businesses such as confectioners, tobacconists and newsagents (CTN) and off-licences have been severely affected by supermarkets as consumers have adopted a one-stop shopping attitude.

Market position

There are four market positions that frame the behaviour of small firms. Burns (2001) described them as

- market trader (low price/low differentiation in a focused market)
- commodity supplier (low price/broad market)
- niche player (focused market/high differentiation, high price)
- outstanding success (high price in a broad market).

The *commodity supplier* quadrant is dominated by large firms, as they have set high barriers to entry and the significance of economies of scale is critical. SMEs find it very difficult to compete so should avoid this market position at all costs.

The *market trader* quadrant allows consultants' to work from home, metal fabricators to operate from low cost workshops, or market traders to sell their range of highly competitive products to the general public, as it is possible to compete with a minimum of overheads at the smallest stage. Even though SMEs can compete on price in this quadrant it is difficult to grow the firm beyond a certain size without incurring significant costs.

The *niche player* quadrant allows firms to differentiate their offering so that it is highly valued by customers and has a developed unique selling proposition. This situation enables it to charge a premium price. Being a niche player involves four things: establishing what makes the product or service unique; specializing in customers and/or products to meet their precise needs rather than focusing on the process; stressing the strengths of the firm and its USPs (innovation, flexibility, personalized service); and finally emphasizing the non price elements of the marketing mix. Even though there is a need to be aware of changing market conditions this quadrant offers the best opportunities for small firms to develop, succeed and to grow as larger firms find it difficult to compete in small focused markets.

For example, Karan Bilimoria of Cobra Beer identified a niche market for smoother, less gassy Indian beer that would perfectly complement Indian cuisine. This company now has one of the fastest growing beer brands in the UK with a current turnover at retail value of £80 million (Enterprise Insight, 2005).

The *outstanding success* quadrant occurs when firms who initially differentiated their product, offering in a niche market, discover that it has broad market appeal and experience rapid and considerable growth. However large firms can feel threatened by a large number of extremely effective niche companies. This was the case in the computing industry and for IBM in particular.

IBM launched the personal computer in 1981, altered the way that business was done, sparked a revolution in home computing and set the global standard. The machine had an open architecture which meant that other firms could produce compatible machines. IBM anticipated charging a licence for the use of its software but niche companies reverse-engineered the software and were able to produce clones of the machine without charge (Twenty Five Years of the IBM PC, BBC News 2006).

In the computer sector it is possible for small firms to establish a niche in the software services sector. Success here is increasingly dependent upon competitive pricing and quality of service provision. Small firms have to reduce costs in order to stay competitive in an industry which is increasingly dominated by the larger companies.

3 Values of enterprise

Values

Whilst the stage of the business and the sector will have a major impact upon the business and its staff, it is the values of the entrepreneur that will impact upon the way business is conducted. This is the third dimension. Every person has a value system or set of values that guide and direct the way that they conduct their activities. While some businesses make their business ethics explicit as a form of competitive advantage (such as fair trade or recycled products) the values that under-pin all the decision-making in a business indicate the values of the entrepreneur.

Chapter 7 discussed in detail the contemporary arguments about ethics in large complex companies, but how do values affect those businesses starting out? Enterprise can be thought of as 'value neutral'. This is because the skills or approach to starting a new venture are in themselves neither good nor bad. However, a national survey shows that there is a strong perception that those who are successful in business have low morals or ethics (SBS, 2002). Obviously the outcomes of all business activity and decision-making can be judged as positive or negative, but this is because of the values of the people who are engaging in the enterprise, not the act of starting a new venture. Values are therefore an important part of enterprise and have an impact upon small business start-up.

> **⏎ Stop and Think**
>
> Imagine shopping early one morning, so early that the street is empty, and on the floor, you find either:
>
> **a)** 50p
> **b)** £5
> **c)** £50
> **d)** £500
> **e)** £5000
>
> Do you keep it? (and would the amount make a difference?)
>
> If you had found the money in a wallet or purse, with a name and address, would that make a difference?
>
> Explain any changes in your thinking and try to express the values that you have that would cause you to act (Price, 1997).
>
> Now reflect on your learning and thinking in this task. If you were an entrepreneur, how might your values be seen in action in your small business? Would you tell a large customer that they had overpaid you? Would you pay your bills on time?

Some well-known entrepreneurs started their businesses because their values do not match existing business practice and they seek to follow a more responsible approach to business. This can create competitive advantage, when communicated effectively to customers who also appreciate a more ethical stance.

Values

Recognition of appalling working conditions across the world has resulted in a consumer interest in 'fair trade'. This has resulted in new entrants using their values to enter existing markets,

Mini-Case 14.3   The Co-operative Bank: 'customer-led, ethically guided'

The Co-operative Bank, which was founded under cooperative principles in 1844, launched an ethical policy in May 1992, under the following philosophy 'At the Co-operative Bank, we always remember that it's your money in your account. Our role is simply to take good care of it for you—and not do things with it that you wouldn't do yourself.'

This resulted from a major ethics survey of 30,000 customers in which the majority (84%) of customers who responded be-lieved that it was a good idea for the Co-operative Bank to have a clear ethical policy. Their new policy statement was endorsed by 78% of customers and a further survey in 2001 has shown that this support had increased to 97% of customers. (www.co-operativebank.co.uk)

❷ Does it matter to you as a customer whether your bank makes loans to companies that might be considered unethical, such as arms manufacturers?

such as Cafédirect successfully entering an apparently saturated market with an ethical new coffee. Penny Newman, the owner who blazed a trail for Cafédirect, took it from a niche market position and placed it into the mainstream, with the fair trade hot drinks brand now sold through most of the major supermarkets (Enterprise Insight, 2005). Green and Blacks also entered the confectionary market by making a unique selling point of their ethical stance to sourcing cocoa beans, and have since been sold to Cadburys (see discussion of ethical consumerism in Chapter 11).

As with the Body Shop (now sold by entrepreneur Anita Roddick to large corporate L'Oreal), the values of the entrepreneur can be seen within the activity of the business venture, the way it operates and the products it sells.

> ➲ *Stop and Think*
>
> Imagine that you are the owner of a business that has an ethical policy and fair trading practices and uses these in marketing campaigns as part of its competitive advantage.
>
> Do you still:
>
> a) *bluff* when negotiating the purchase of raw ingredients in order to get a good price for yourselves, and therefore offer the best price to your customers?
>
> b) *exaggerate* the demand for your product when trying to establish your brand with new retailers?
>
> Is this normal business practice, or unethical practice? Where do you draw the line?
>
> What are your ethics? (Price, 1997).

Chapter 7 showed that defining the values of a business can be complex, but customer awareness of business impacts means that it is increasingly becoming an issue. Some customers now include the impact of the business upon the environment, or their treatment of their suppliers (i.e. whether they employ children to work in factories abroad or have different standards of health and safety internationally) within their decision to purchase a product.

Stakeholders

As this trend develops, it could be argued that positive ethical values are no longer offering a competitive advantage but are becoming the expected industry practice, as businesses move towards a strategic and long term approach to their social responsibilities. This growing recognition that all business decision-making is built upon values shows the link with enterprise.

> ➲ *Stop and Think*
>
> Are businesses like Cafédirect the exception rather than the rule? Do the pressures that small businesses are under make it difficult for them to prioritize ethical issues?

Mini-Case 14.4 Train 2000: a social enterprise with clear organizational values

All of Train 2000's activities are underpinned by our organizational values, which are:

To be inclusive, recognizing the needs of individual women and particularly ensuring that we reach and respect the needs of disadvantaged and underrepresented women.

To be innovative, continually improving the way we work and provide services by incorporating new ideas, information and methods.

To work in partnership, adding value to what we do by working with others to build trust, develop mutual understanding and through reciprocal actions develop social capital.

To strive for quality, committing the organization to improvement and high standards in all aspects of its activities and working environment.

www.train2000.org.uk

❷ Is it only social enterprises that need to consider their underpinning values?

The importance of new businesses and SMEs

The impact of one individual small company could be easily overlooked as not making much contribution to the economy, but as 99% of all businesses within the EU are defined as micro, small and medium-sized businesses their impact is huge, providing 65 million jobs within Europe (see Figure 14.4) (http://europa.eu/).

There are approximately 4.3 million businesses in the UK and 3.7 million of those are run by the self employed. Small and medium-sized enterprises (SMEs) are significant and important,

Figure 14.4 Share of enterprises, employment and turnover by size of enterprise, UK, start 2002

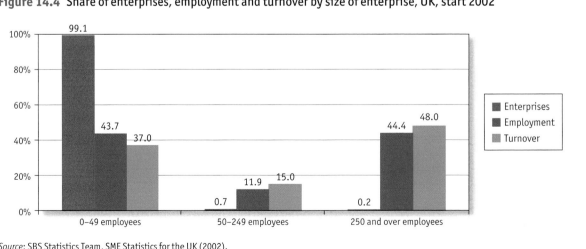

Source: SBS Statistics Team, SME Statistics for the UK (2002).

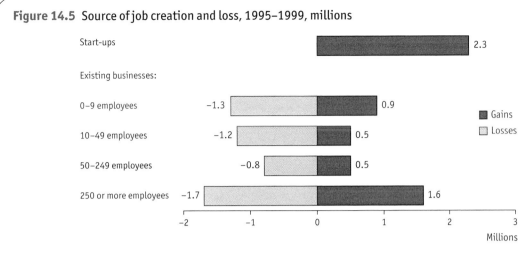

Figure 14.5 Source of job creation and loss, 1995–1999, millions

Source: Dale and Morgan (2001) (SBS/TBR job creation study).

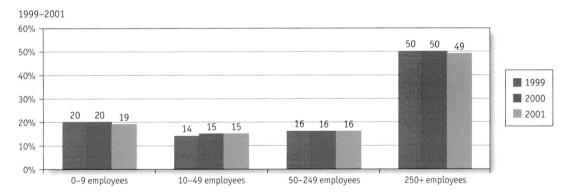

Figure 14.6 Share of gross value added (GVA) by business size, per cent, UK, 1999–2001

Source: ONS Annual Business Inquiry (special analysis). Excludes some industries where data are not comparable.

accounting for 52% of the national turnover and 56% of employment (SBS, 2004). Their contribution to job creation is also substantial (see Figure 14.5). In the period 1995 to 1999 85% of all jobs created were in small firms. The contribution of small businesses to output is similar to that of large businesses, and productivity outstrips large business in some sectors (agriculture, construction, wholesaling and business services) (see Figures 14.6 and 14.7).

The DTi's 'Strategy for prosperity for all' (DTi, 2003), showed that the UK still faced a persistent productivity gap of at least 20% with its major competitors—France, Germany and the USA—and that it was still a middle ranking country in terms of GDP per head despite its recent growth.

A number of studies (Reynolds et al., 2001; 2002) have been undertaken which show the importance of small firms and entrepreneurship. The Global Entrepreneurship Monitor (GEM, 2001 to date) has repeatedly stated that small firms are the real driving force behind economic growth.

Figure 14.7 Productivity (GVA per employee) by sector and size of business, UK, 2001 (£000s)

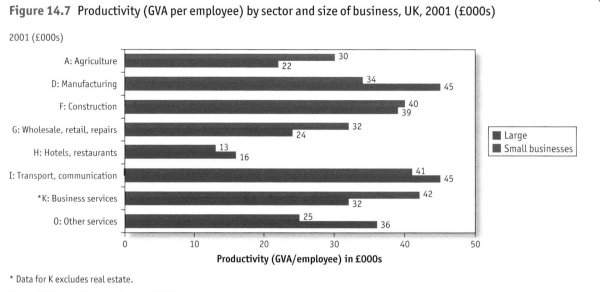

2001 (£000s)

* Data for K excludes real estate.

Source: ONS Annual Business Inquiry (2001).

Figure 14.8 The GEM conceptual model 2001

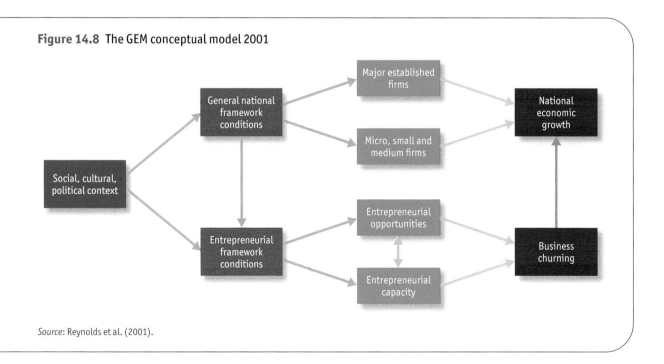

Source: Reynolds et al. (2001).

The GEM Conceptual Model (Figure 14.8) shows that it is crucial to have an entrepreneurial framework which provides both the capacity and opportunity to encourage innovation, creativity and enterprise. The introduction of new entrants to the market increases competitive pressures and forces existing firms to increase efficiency in order to stay in the market.

This model shows how social and cultural forces impact on the economy and the entrepreneurial conditions that either encourage or dissuade individuals from being enterprising. If the conditions

Figure 14.9 GEM 2004, total entrepreneurial activity

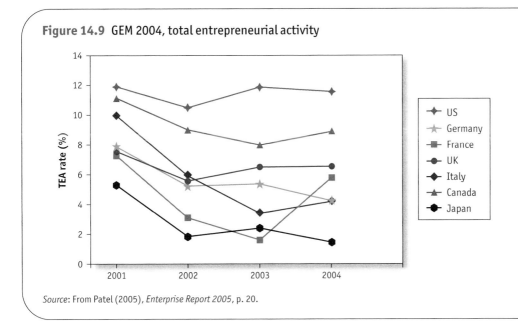

Source: From Patel (2005), *Enterprise Report 2005*, p. 20.

are positive then a greater number of opportunities will exist and hence improve economic performance. If there is not a climate for assisting new businesses to start and grow, and there is a lack of new ideas or innovations, then minimal change in the economy will take place and performance will be poor. Entrepreneurial capacity and opportunities affect 'businesses churn' (the difference between businesses starting and ceasing to trade), and results in the business population constantly changing. This significantly impacts on SMEs where over a third of the stock of businesses has started in the last three years.

The UK is still lagging behind the USA and other nations in terms of entrepreneurial activity and remains only moderate by international standards (Harding, 2002; 2004). The UK has an average level of entrepreneurial activity both globally (Reynolds et al., 2001) and within the European Union (Cowling, 2003).

TEA (total entrepreneurial activity) is the percentage of the population for each country engaged in some form of entrepreneurial activity (see Figure 14.9).

Small businesses can therefore stimulate competition within a market economy and rejuvenate existing and established markets with a new approach. Virgin, although now a large company, has continued to apply the 'entrepreneurial spirit' that started the company, to develop new products and services which range from airlines and soft drinks to railway services.

Strengths and weaknesses of small businesses

Competitive advantage is a vital concept within business, and the conditions that it is argued are necessary both at the national and business level are explored in Chapter 3. Competitive advantage is the essence of what makes each business different to another business and should form the basis upon which business operates. This could be the reason why customers use one business, or call upon its services, rather than another. One reason might be that a new business offers something that you cannot get anywhere else (think about new products when they are launched—such

Diversity

as the Apple 'iPod', Xbox or Sony Playstation); or it might just be that they are the nearest place that sells that product.

> **⮩ Stop and Think**
> Think about your own shopping behaviour. When do you choose something from a particular location, even though you could buy it cheaper elsewhere?

Whatever the cause, it is important to identify what this advantage is to ensure that it can provide a long term or 'strategic approach to outperforming other business' (Porter, 1980). In some cases this can be achieved by small firms operating in a niche market.

The competitive edge of small firms is achieved in an innovative and imaginative manner with the best possessing significant foresight and vision. Paul Smith, fashion designer, said that, 'the key has been to explore alternative routes that no one else has thought of'.

Interaction

SMEs experience positives and negatives, due to their size and capacity, as to how they operate in the business environment.

Strengths of small businesses may include the following:

- flexibility in their structure and approach enables small businesses to respond to changes in the business environment and adapt quickly in the marketplace. For example, employees might be asked to undertake a variety of tasks. Flexibility is aided by utilization of technology that has become accessible, affordable and adaptable

- responsiveness to large firms who sub-contract to them. Use of advanced technology and flexible systems ensures a fast turn round

- lean organization structure, lack of bureaucracy and low overheads means that they deliver on quality and price

- capability to identify new market opportunities and bring ideas, products and services to market quicker than their larger competitors

- geographical dispersion together with closeness to the customer and understanding of local culture ensures the cooperation of their community to support their enterprise.

Weaknesses of small businesses may include the following:

- difficulty with cash flow
- lack of ability to influence the business environment

Mini-Case 14.5 eBay entrepreneurs

Nearly 70,000 people in the UK are making a living by selling goods on eBay (eBay Survey 2005). Launched in 1995, eBay is a well-known website that brings together buyers and sellers across the world to buy the things they want and sell the things they don't, as they trade directly with each other supported through the eBay site. It was originally started by Pierre Omidyar in September 1995 to help his wife find more items for her collection (hobby). The site now has over 114 million customers worldwide, with 7.4 million in the UK. Up to 2.7 million British items are on sale every day and items worth more than £2bn have been sold on eBay's UK website in 2005.

eBay has also become a low cost route to business start-up and is providing new opportunities for those who traditionally find many barriers to starting a business (such as those with caring responsibilities for the elderly or children) as they can use the site as a way to run a business from their home or outside core work hours. However eBay entrepreneurs can also be existing small businesses selling through auctions to boost sales. The recent survey shows that the average eBay shop employs nine staff, and almost half earn more than three-quarters of their income through the site.

www.startups.co.uk

❷ What is the competitive advantage of eBay?

- lack of appropriate managerial experience and depth in certain specialisms; inability to create functional departments
- difficulty in providing staff development, training and career paths
- generally under-capitalized and do not have sufficient resources to keep abreast of changes in market conditions
- difficulty competing with large firms, e.g. as larger firms are able to benefit from 'economies of scale'
- legal changes and requirements are proportionally more costly and difficult to implement
- often have to work within short timescales and planning horizons
- the relationship with large firms is not balanced: large firms possess power and exercise significant control, may be late with payments, and generally only use SMEs for small and intermittent purchases and express no loyalty as price, quality and delivery are more important.

Widening participation in enterprise

We have seen in Chapter 5 that it is important to consider the world of business in terms of equal opportunities and the participation of different groups in the economic life of the country. For example, women are underrepresented in management positions—a problem that is sometimes referred to using the metaphor of the 'glass ceiling'. Here we will look at the representation of women, ethnic minorities and the baby boom generation in small businesses and enterprise.

Female entrepreneurs

In the UK roughly 620,000 majority-women-owned businesses generate around £130 billion turnover (Rt. Hon. Jacqui Smith, Minister for Women and Equality speaking at 2nd Prowess Conference, 2004). However, if the same levels of female entrepreneurship as in the US were achieved, Britain would gain three-quarters of a million more businesses (Chancellor of the Exchequer Gordon Brown, Advancing Enterprise Conference, 04.02.05). Furthermore women starting up in business will tend to provide a more immediate contribution to the economy because three times as many women come into self employment from unemployment than men (SBS Promoting Female Entrepreneurship, March 2005).

There are some distinctive features of female entrepreneurs. Forty-eight per cent of women entrepreneurs own a business in the service sector, compared with 36% of male entrepreneurs. Their competitive edge is achieved by offering a product or service unfamiliar to the market, and which has fewer competitors. They are more likely than male businesses to be offering a product or service to the market that has been developed in the last year and to use technology in their products or services (British Chambers of Commerce, July 2004, *Achieving the Vision, Female Entrepreneurship*). Tracey Powell, who founded Tiger Bay Beverages in 2001, spent two years developing a range of smoothies and juices. 'We needed a unique selling point, and set upon extending the shelf life, to avoid wastage without adding preservatives' (Enterprise Insight, 2005). It has also been found that women starting to run a business are likely to be more professional and responsible than males, as 70% of women-owned businesses seek advice at the start-up phase compared with 64% of all businesses (SBS Promoting Female Entrepreneurship, March 2005). They are more likely to use an accountant and external advice than majority male-owned businesses (Dr Stuart Fraser, Finance for Small and Medium-Sized Enterprises, 2005) and 33% of them compared to 20% of male businesses had used government programmes to fund their business start-up (British Chambers of Commerce, July 2004, *Achieving the Vision, Female Entrepreneurship*).

Females are under represented in the self employed population (only 26% of the self employed population) even though women account for 44% of all economically active people. Furthermore they are half as likely to be involved in start-up activity as men (Global Entrepreneurship Monitor 2004). In the USA the Women's Business Act 1988 put in place a long-term infrastucture to support women's enterprise development. (Since then women's business ownership has increased significantly.) Women face significant barriers to starting a business, which include access to finance, fear of debt, perceived high risk of running a business, significant time commitments competing with caring responsibilities of parents and children, and finally a lack of self confidence that the business will be successful. Once in business women's experience and treatment on financial matters shows that they can pay significantly higher margins on term loans than male-owned businesses (2.9 versus 1.9 percentage points over Base). Females can experience difficulty in obtaining funds as they have no financial track record and cannot relate to advisors operating in a male dominated business environment which lacks appropriate female role models. In recognition of this, pressure has been put on the banks to provide more sensitive staff. Business support agencies are seeking to overcome discrimination and preparing females more appropriately for business.

Black and minority ethnic (BME) entrepreneurs

BME businesses can appear to be generally dependent upon their local market and this apparent inability to trade beyond the local area places significant constraints upon their businesses growth. This target group is perceived as being hard to reach, socially excluded, and living in areas of multiple deprivation where language and culture are either misrepresented or misunderstood. The traditional links into business through the Small Business Service, Business Links and the Chamber of Commerce are not normally accessed. Self employment rates are among the highest in Pakistani, Bangladeshi and Chinese groups and lowest in the Black group (Caribbean and African) (see Figure 14.10).

Successful black minority enterprise development has been achieved through specialization available in expanding niche markets. Even though writers have claimed BMEs have advantages

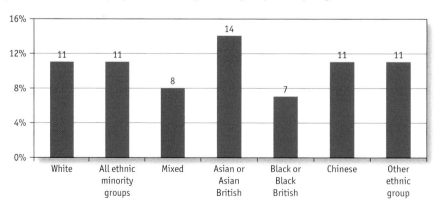

Figure 14.10 Self employment[1] rates by ethnic group, UK, Spring 2003

[1] Self employment as a rate of all economically active people of working age.

Source: SBS Statistics Team, from ONS Labour Force Survey (Spring 2003).

Figure 14.11 Self employment[1] rates by age group, UK, Spring 2003

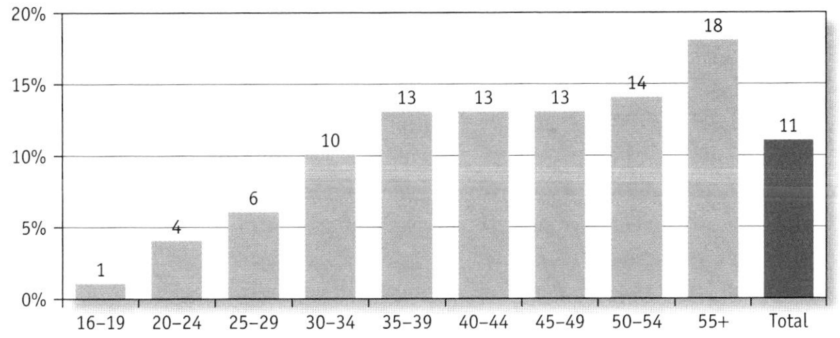

[1] Self employment as a rate of all economically active people of working age.

Source: SBS Statistics Team, from ONS Labour Force Survey (Spring 2003).

of informal networks to access informal sources of finance and family labour (Deakins and Freel, 2003), there is a need to develop an infrastructure to support them and their communities, by promoting and supporting work with young people to build their confidence, and encourage the development of their enterprise and personal leadership skills. The formal support currently available for all business starts and existing businesses (business planning, assistance and skills, marketing advice, access to funding, legal advice) has to be sensitively delivered to meet the needs of this group. The potential contribution of ethnic minority entrepreneurs to the regeneration of inner cities, confirmed by national data, is significant (Deakins and Freel, 2003).

Entrepreneurs from the 'baby boom' generation

The 'baby boomers' are the generation born after the end of the Second World War who are now in their 50s and entering their 60s. Over-55 year olds represent 20% of businesses, which is significantly greater than their representation within the population as a whole. In some cases these individuals have increasingly found that they cannot get jobs because of 'ageism' and are therefore required to operate as self employed free agents with a portfolio of contracts and contacts. They work flexibly, have a wealth of experience and are generally adequately funded and resourced (see Figure 14.11).

◈ *Looking ahead*

What then are the initiatives that the UK government can take to encourage enterprise?

There is considerable debate about the type of businesses to be supported. Some commentators wish to see economic impact, whilst others link performance to social, environmental, intellectual, political and economic factors. Those seeking economic returns support high impact, high growth and high technology organizations, whilst community

voices support a broad spread ranging from social and low level service operations to larger economic concerns. The government's role is one of intervening where market failure might exist and the private sector might not invest.

The UK government recognizes the importance of the SME sector and has sought to embrace it within its macroeconomic policy. The government and regional development agencies (RDAs) have therefore been charged with a number of goals.

There is a need to build an enterprise culture, encourage a more dynamic start-up market and build the capability for small business growth. There is a recognition that access to finance needs to be improved and, as we have seen, that more enterprises in disadvantaged communities need to be encouraged. Exchange between small firms, the business environment and their various stakeholder groups needs to be developed and all of this must be nurtured with better regulation and policy.

In the belief that such activity needs to take place on the ground, the Small Business Service of the DTi (SBS) was set the challenge of increasing the proportion of adults considering going into business or becoming self employed from 12% in 2001 to 14% in 2005. Further discussion of these trends on entrepreneurial activity can be obtained from either the SBS or Global Entrepreneurship Monitor websites.

The government delivers help, support and assistance to the SMEs to boost economic activity. Policy is now determined by the Treasury, because of the economic impact and the Small Business Service. Delivery of policy to SMEs is by the regional development agencies. The government seeks to intervene where it thinks it is appropriate and when it can achieve maximum electoral, political and economic impact. This does not necessarily mean that all parties in the economy are treated equally by the state. The 'New Labour' government sought to maximize gap filling by targeting certain groups, (clusters, deprivation areas, uncompetive regions) and implementing policy initiatives that supported disadvantaged and under represented groups and those which addressed social inequality. For example, the regional economic strategy of Yorkshire Forward (the regional development agency for Yorkshire and Humber) is designed to help improve the economic climate in the region. Objective 2 of this strategy was a business birth rate strategy: 'business birth rates are a key performance indicator. The Yorkshire and Humber region cannot rely on inward investment. It just won't happen in the current climate' (Yorkshire Forward, 2002). The strategy aims, by the year 2010, to double the number of new, sustainable businesses and to increase the survival rate of new firms in existence for at least three years from 59.7% to 70%.

In the past the EU has supplied financial support to under-performing regions to stimulate economic and social activities; however this is currently under review as a result of budget constraints. Key business clusters have been targeted for support so that the region's sustainable growth objectives would be met. These included advanced engineering and metals, biosciences, chemicals, the digital industries, food and drink, financial and legal services and the creative industries.

Each RDA supports disadvantaged sectors, people and areas to grow and supports the individual regions of the UK. Government intervention of this nature is designed to support business start-up. Alongside this is a growing appreciation by workers of the life-styles that could be possible through developing entrepreneurial skills. Increased options of part-time, short-term and contract working have seen more people taking hobbies on to the Internet as businesses or starting-up themselves. Looking ahead, it is clear that enterprising opportunities are becoming more important, not only to the government in its attempt to boost the UK economy, but to the people within the UK.

Summary

- The term enterprise is used in many ways and can refer to:
  - profit making or a mission to change society
  - an activity or a set of skills
  - a venture or project
  - a small business or SME
- An *entrepreneur* is an individual who has ideas and makes them happen
- Enterprise activity (innovation and creativity) when displayed in a large corporation, is described as 'intrapreneurial'
- *A small business* can be described as 'a business with fewer than 50 employees' (Small Business Service DTi, 2004)
- '*Enterprise* is a set of qualities and competencies that can be employed in different settings, whilst *entrepreneurship* involves the process of creating and developing new ventures' (Enterprise Insight, 2005: 23)
- Values can provide a business with competitive advantage, if clear and promoted to the customer, but all business activity can be seen as the result of values
- The government supports the idea that innovation, creativity and enterprise can be encouraged and runs social programmes to support under-represented groups to start businesses or social ventures
- An SME can be thought of as undergoing several stages of development, but they may not be recognized as separate phases by the entrepreneur
- Each of these stages calls upon different skills within the entrepreneur and it is important that this is recognized to ensure that the business can grow

Case study: the female entrepreneur (interview)

Background

The company, a digital data and network provider, distributes digital data online, anywhere in the world, with total security and management, and 24×7 support and resilience. It provides leading software and advanced network management solutions that substantially increase efficiency and reduce cost. The female managing director is married and 35 years old.

Her background

'I've got an engineering father and an artist of a mother. My inspiration has been my grandfather, who used to be managing director of Ford Motor Company. I chose a business studies degree, sponsored by the De La Rue Group, security printers. They expected me to work for them six months every year during my placement periods. After graduation I joined Crossfield Electronics, one of their companies in the printing/publishing division. I went round the world with them and came into contact with everyone in the company. I changed jobs every year and after ten years became a director. One of my strengths is marketing. I ran my own business unit and obtained experience of running my own team, sourcing and developing products and meeting sales and profit targets. All of this was supported by the plc.

I left them and worked as a director for Fuji responsible for technology product management and distributors worldwide. Opportunities to develop a distributive managed network for the printing industry culminated in a strategic alliance and joint venture with British Telecom and Cytex. With their financial backing I was offered a directorship and the opportunity to set up the business. It was exactly what I was looking for. They asked me to write a business plan, decide space, equipment and financial requirements, how many staff, the business objectives and determine the strategy. I'm used to managing my own domain, taking decisions and seeing the way that I'd like my company to go. I see myself as a leader—an inspirationalist.

Product/market interface

It's never easy to identify gaps in the marketplace. The hardest thing is being the leader because you spend substantial sums of money developing the marketplace only to find competitors entering the market and eroding your share and profitability. For three years we spent substantial sums building the marketplace. My experience is in the digital printing process market, from computer to plate—taking digital data and writing it immediately onto the printing plate. The technology has been around for 15 years. It took ten years for the market to understand the benefits. In order to get ahead and stay ahead of the market you need to be a big company with deep pockets to get a huge return. If you are a small business with minimal backing it's a big risk. We were

too advanced for the market and ran out of money before the market was ready to adopt the product. Customers were not ready for the new technology or concept. Sometimes it's better to be a follower rather than a leader. Perhaps it's better to go into an informed market so that you can differentiate what makes your product offering special. It's a huge effort to create, define and establish market need.

Change of direction: triggers for change: management buy out

At this point the major investors decided not to invest any more money and withdrew all support. I decided to review my position and consider a management buy out using venture capital finance.

Standards within and education of the market is crucial

Standards and quality are essential within this environment. We have built our product into an industry standard called job definition format—an open interface that can interchange with 72 other vendor products. I chair one of the industry standards committees.

We have customized our software to enable our customers to put their own branding on it. With customized fields we can manage their processes effectively and independently, process more data from all of our customers and allow the customer to track and effect changes to design and content of their material. The printing and publishing industry is focused on speed, costs out and quality. Removing manual processes and errors is crucial. That's what we do.

Our entry into the market was four years later than our major competitor. We ran a system with central managed servers rather than putting distributed servers on every customer's site. This reduced costs. Central databases are at the heart of our processes. We are now quicker on upgrades, managing our customer solutions and open to new ideas. Our speed of response gives us competitive edge.

Barriers to success

As a woman, you are going to hit a lot of walls. You just have to work around them and prove that you are good. It's very challenging in a technology world. They think you are a secretary and you don't know a lot. That kind of attitude makes me so driven that I almost over-prove nearly everything I do. You just carry on doing your job, you do it well and you don't make a big thing of being a woman. You just say I'm a business-person, and I'm good. Macho doesn't work. Show vulnerability. Play to your strengths —women's skills, use charm. I've had endless help throughout my career and I still get it. Women aren't scared to ask for help so they get people to help them. I've built up a huge support network.

Running the business

Really believe in what you do. You have to have a passion to do it because it's hard work. You will hit lots of highs and lows. There's a lot of unpredictability in setting up your business. You should surround yourself with good people. Get a good core team in place. People are crucial. It's all to do with reputation and net-working. All the staff have a passion for the business and an understanding of the market. They have contacts which enable us to recruit new staff and reach new customers.

When you are running a small business everyone has to be pre-pared to do everything. We were looking for staff that has core skills. The operations team require technical competence. Our development team is based in Israel and we have sales teams in the USA, Paris and London. We are looking for people who'll get on in the team and who believe in what they are doing and are hard working. We often have to ask people to go home because we all work round the clock. For the first three years I worked 20-hour days, six days a week. You can't walk out on it—its part of you. The management team set the standards, build the culture and set the field for the business. New people either fit in or they don't. If they don't they go.

A successful business is one where you have the right product in the right market delivered at the right time. It has to have unique selling points. There has to be a significant potential market opportunity. The quality of the staff is important. This company only develops because of the people in it. Ensure you have the right people, the right quality of service and the right product.

Monitoring and control

We always track the following week by week. Our sales forecast, the costs within the business and cash flow. We are always on tar-get with our costs. Because customers are unpredictable sales are more difficult—we have a hard and soft sales forecast pipeline. Hard forecasts are customers who have actual proposals where we are 50+% certain of closure. We have a weighted forecast to account for unpredictability. We always assume that some cus-tomers will have a 40% chance of closure in this month whereas others might be a 100% chance. The weighted average reflects this and revenue is made up from hard and soft forecasts. From this we set revenue and cost targets. Keep an eye on your cash! Look after it. Get a good accountant or accounting system. If you are not collecting your money in, you're likely to get bad debts.

Venture capitalist's expectations

A venture capitalist is the majority shareholder, but they have left the management team with a sizeable stake of the business so that we are motivated to run it. Don't ever expect money for nothing. You have to put your life on the line; you have to indem-nify the business. You have to put your own money in, whether that's mortgaging your house or your car. They expect a commit-ment that proves you believe in that business as much as you say you do.

Venture capitalists always discuss their exit. Before they put their money in they want to know how they will get their money back. They will ask you for the names of your competitors. Would they be interested in buying you out? Are there any other indus-try players that would be interested in buying your type of tech-nology to complement their own solutions? They are always looking for potential buyers who might have an interest in your type of business. They look at the return on their investment because if they can get a good return going forward they'll keep investing, particularly if they can see significant growth poten-tial. Our venture capitalist was very interested that our techno-logy is transferable—possible to get a quicker return on their money if the core investment was transferable to other sectors.

The future

In five years time we will be in more countries and moving into other sectors. There's always that sense of adventure and the challenge of making it happen.'

❷ What kind of entrepreneur is talking and what qualities does she have?

❷ What skill development has taken place during the growth of the business?

❷ How has the business chosen to compete and what is its competitive edge?

Bibliography

Bolton, B. and Thompson, J. (2000) *Entrepreneurs Talent, Temperament, Technique* (Oxford: Butterworth-Heinemann).

Gibb, A. (1984) Developing the role and capacity of the small business advisor, *Leadership and Organisational Development Journal*, 5(2).

Review and discussion questions

1 What do you understand by the term 'enterprise'—how do you define it?

2 Explain the difference between being a serial entrepreneur and a small-business owner-manager.

3 What is the difference between a micro business and a medium sized business?

4 What stages of growth might an entrepreneur experience in developing a business?

5 Illustrate with examples, how an entrepreneur's values can provide competitive advantage to a small business.

6 Are entrepreneurs 'born' with the necessary skills or can they be 'created'? If the latter, then what are the conditions that need to exist to develop an entrepreneurial environment?

Assignments

1 *Skills*: You are thinking about becoming an entrepreneur but need to understand whether you have the skills to start up a business on your own, or whether you should create a team with broader skills. Undertake a self-analysis of your current skills and either devise a personal development plan to gain the additional skills you might need to start a new venture, or indicate the skills you need in additional team member(s).

2 *Supporting new and under-represented groups to start a business*: Conduct some research on your local area, using the Internet to look at your RDA (regional development agency) or local government site to find out where areas of need or deprivation are within your region. Suggest some activities that could help people in these areas start their own businesses if they wanted to.

3 *Understanding entrepreneurs*: Find a local entrepreneur to interview, or choose a famous one from the list below and use the Internet to try to understand the following:

What type of entrepreneur are they?
What sector do they work in?
How many businesses or business ideas have they had?
What stage of growth is their business in now?
How have their values impacted upon their business?

Suggestions of entrepreneurs to study include:
Stelios Haji-Ioannou; Jamie Oliver; Bill Gates; Alan Sugar; James Dyson; Anita Roddick and Richard Branson.

Further reading

These books encourage and develop entrepreneurship skills. There are chapters on family and international businesses and on social entrepreneurship. They also have additional mini and long case studies.

Burns, P. (2006) *Entrepreneurship and Small Business* (Basingstoke: Palgrave Macmillan).

Southon, M. and West, C. (2002) *The Beermat Entrepreneur* (Harlow: Pearson).

Burke, R. (2006) *Small Business Entrepreneur—guide to running a business* (Burke Publishing).

Online resources

Test your understanding of this chapter with online questions and answers, explore the subject further through web exercises, and use the weblinks to provide a quick resource for further research. Go to the Online Resource Centre at

www.oxfordtextbooks.co.uk/orc/ wetherly_otter/

British Chambers of Commerce: www.chamberonline.co.uk/
The British Chambers of Commerce comprise nationally a network of quality-accredited Chambers of Commerce, all uniquely positioned at the heart of every business community in the UK.

Confederation of British Industry: www.cbi.org.uk/
The CBI is a vital source of expert advice and information, and a forum for the generation of ideas, best practice exchange and high-powered networking.

Federation of Small Businesses: www.fsb.org.uk/
The FSB is the largest campaigning pressure group promoting and protecting the interests of the self-employed and owners of small firms.

Forum of Private Business: www.fpb.co.uk
The FPB helps its members cope with day-to-day problems by influencing laws and policies affecting businesses and supporting their profitability.

Institute of Directors: www.iod.com/
As a worldwide association of members, the Institute of Directors (IoD) provides a network that reaches into every corner of the business community.

National Federation of Enterprise Agencies: www.nfea.com
The NFEA is a network of independent, but not for profit, Local Enterprise Agencies committed to responding to the needs of small and growing businesses by providing an appropriate range of quality services, particularly, but not exclusively, targeting pre-start, start-up and micro businesses and assisting in building their ability to survive, to sustain themselves and to grow.

Small Business Bureau: www.smallbusinessbureau.org.uk
The Small Business Bureau works closely with Opinion Formers in the UK and Europe in pressing for change where change is necessary.

Business Link: www.businesslink.org/
Business Link is the national business advice service.

Chambers of Commerce: www.chamberonline.co.uk/
Chambers of Commerce is a useful contact to provide information on conferences, exhibitions, registers, publications, training and legal advice.

Companies House: www.companieshouse.com/
Companies House is the government agency responsible for company registration in Great Britain.

Department of Trade and Industry: dti.gov.uk
The Department of Trade and Industry works with a wide range of individuals, groups and organizations, to increase UK productivity and competitiveness.

Department for Work and Pensions: www.dwp.gov.uk/
This site offers help for unemployed people including support for self-employment.

References

American Heritage Directory (1992) 3rd edition (Boston: Houghton Mifflin).

Bolton, B. and Thompson, J. (2000) *Entrepreneurs Talent, Temperament, Technique* (Oxford: Butterworth-Heinemann).

Burns, P. (2001) *Entrepreneurship and Small Business* (Basingstoke: Palgrave).

Casson, M. (1982) *The Entrepreneur: an Economic Theory* (Oxford: Oxford University Press).

Cabinet Office (2006) *Social Enterprise Action Plan 2006*. www.cabinetoffice.gov.uk

Chrisman, J. J., Bauerschmidt, A. and Hofer, C. W. (1998) The determinants of new venture performance: an extended model, *Entrepreneurship Theory and Practice*, Fall: 5–30.

Cowling, M. (2003) *The Contribution of the Self-Employed to Employment in the EU*, SBS.

Davies, H. (2002) *The Howard Davies Review of Enterprise and the Economy in Education* (Norwich: HMSO).

Deakins, D. and Freel, M. (2003) *Entrepreneurship and Small Firms* (Maidenhead: McGraw-Hill Education).

Drucker, P. (1985) *Innovation and Entrepreneurship—Practice and Principles* (Oxford: Butterworth-Heinemann).

DTi (2003) *A Government Action Plan for Small Business: the Evidence Base* (London: DTi).

DTi (2004) *The Case for Women's Enterprise* (London: DTi/Prowess).

Enterprise Insight (2005) *The Enterprise Report 2005— Making Ideas Happen* (Oxford: www.starttalkingideas.org/policy).

Gibb, A. (1984) Developing the role and capacity of the small business advisor, *Leadership and Organizational Development Journal*, 5(2).

Gibb, A. (1996) Entrepreneurship and small business management: can we afford to neglect them in the twenty-first century business school? *British Journal of Management*, 7(4): 309–21.

Gibb, A. (1999) Creating an entrepreneurial culture in support of SMEs, *Journal of Small Enterprise Development*, 10(4): 27–38.

Gibb, A. and Ritchie, J. (1982) Understanding the processes of starting small businesses, *International Small Business Journal*, 6: 70–80.

Global Entrepreneurship Monitor Focus on Social Entrepreneurs (2004) GEM, www.gemconsortium.org/

Harding, R. (2002) *Global Entrepreneurship Monitor 2002* (London: London Business School).

Harding, R. (2004) *Global Entrepreneurship Monitor 2004*, (London: London Business School).

Hartshorn, C. and Richardson, P. (1993) Business start up training: the gender dimension, in Allen, S. and Truman C. (eds.) *Women in Business: Perspectives on Women Entrepreneurs* (Routledge).

Jack, S. and Anderson, A. (1999) Enterprise education within the enterprise culture, *International Journal of Entrepreneurial Behaviour and Research*, 5(3): 110–25.

Kuratko, D. F. and Hodgetts, R. M. (2001) *Entrepreneurship—a Contemporary Approach*, 5th edition (New York: Harcourt College).

Leeds Initiative (2005) *Enterprising Leeds*, Leeds initiative, Leeds.

NCGE (2006) *Career-Making: Graduating into Self-Employment*, Leeds Met Human Resource Development Team.

Patel, R. (2005) *Enterprise Report 2005: Making Ideas Happen* (London: Enterprise Insight).

Porter, M. (1980) *Competitive Strategy: Techniques for Analyzing Industries and Competitors* (New York: Free Press).

Price, A. (1997) Corporate social responsibility, in Boddy, D. and Paton, R. (1998) *Management* (Harlow: Prentice Hall).

Prowess (2004) Rt. Hon. Jacqui Smith, Minister for Women and Equality, speaking at 2nd Prowess Conference, www.prowess.org.uk

Reynolds, P. et al. (2001) *Global Entrepreneurship Monitor Report 2001* (London: London Business School).

Reynolds, P. et al. (2002) *Global Entrepreneurship Monitor, 2002 Executive Report* (London: London Business School).

Robertson, M. (2000) Business Start Up @ Leeds Met Model of Business Start-up, from Churchill N. C. and Lewis V. L. (1983) The five stages of small business growth, *Harvard Business Review*, 63(3): May–June.

Rohn, J. (2005) Business philosopher quoted in *The Enterprise Report 2005—Making Ideas Happen*, www.starttalkingideas.org/policy

SBS (2002) *Household Survey of Entrepreneurship*, Sheffield Small Business Service.

SBS (2004) *A Government Action Plan for Small Business*, Small Business Service, 03/1592 London.

SBS (2004a) *A Government Action Plan for Small Business: the Evidence Base*, Small Business Service, 04/517 London.

Schumpeter, J. A. (1936) *The Theory of Economic Development*, 2nd edition (Cambridge MA: Harvard University Press).

Scottish Get into Enterprise (SGE) programme (1999), www.scottish-enterprise.com

Small Business Service (2006) *Annual Small Business Survey 2005*, DTI.

Small Business Service Analytical Unit (2006) *Survival Rates of VAT Registered Businesses—1994–2003 Key Results*, www.sbs.gov.uk/survival

Steiner, G. A. (1979) *Strategic Planning* (New York: Free Press).

Stevenson, H. H. (1997) Six dimensions of entrepreneurship in Birley and Muzyka *Mastering Enterprise* (Harlow: FT Pitman).

Timmons, J. A. (1989) *The Entrepreneurial Mind* (Andover, Mass: Brick House Publishing).

Twenty Five Years of the IBM PC, BBC News 2006.

UNICE (1999) *Fostering Entrepreneurship in Europe: the UNICE Benchmarking Report* (Brussels: UNICE).

Yorkshire Forward (2002) Regional Economic Strategy: www.yorkshire-forward.com

Business and sustainable development

Eamonn Judge

Contents

15

Learning objectives

When you have completed this chapter you will be able to:

- Understand the meaning of **sustainable development** in relation to business
- Outline the influences leading to changes in the significance of sustainable development
- Identify alternative views about sustainable development as it relates to business
- Examine links between the external environment of a business in relation to sustainable development and the internal strategic response of business

Themes

Diversity

Diversity of business

Concern with sustainable development arises from environmental and resource issues which are typically analysed globally, but which emanate from activities occurring at a local level, and which can be responded to locally. Thus, all types of business organizations contribute to the problems which the concept of sustainable development relates to, from MNCs to SMEs, from universities to schools, and from local governments to charity organizations. And they can all contribute to reducing the problems.

Internal/ external

Internal/external

It is clear that business activity imposes external costs on the environment. Already businesses are being urged to reduce their 'carbon footprints' and this will require firms to change their internal production processes.

Complexity

Complexity of the environment

The relationship of business to its overall environment—political, economic, social, and technological—is highly complex, but the natural environment is as complex as any of these. Businesses are asked to take responsibility for their activities which are allegedly having a serious effect on the global natural environment. Yet our knowledge of these effects is the outcome of very complex research, and not all observers are equally agreed about their causes.

Spatial levels

Variety of spatial levels

Different spatial levels, from global to local, are crucial to our understanding of issues associated with sustainable development, and the way in which they can be responded to at different spatial levels, from the global right down to the individual firm.

Dynamic

Dynamic environment

The key aspect is that the main contributors to the problems of environment and resources are not necessarily those who suffer from them. A problem created in one country produces effects on the other side of the globe. But equally, global business processes like international trade produce global environmental threats. So an appreciation of the dynamic environment is a key aspect of sustainable development issues.

Interaction

Interaction between business and its environment

This chapter is centrally involved with this key theme of the book. Business in its myriad activities has a major impact on the natural environment, but changes in the natural environment impact back, or strike back, at business.

Stakeholders

Stakeholders

A wide range of stakeholders can be directly and indirectly affected by a firm's impact on the environment. These may be local sufferers, or they may be sufferers in another country. Firms are not islands, but parts of complex supply chains, and other firms forwards or backwards in the supply chain may be part of an environmental problem with which a firm is directly, if often unknowingly, involved.

Values

Values

Sustainable development raises complex ethical issues, because most often those who suffer from environmental problems are not those who create them. Environmental damage today can store up problems for the future and so firms are forced to consider directly their ethical stance in relation to present day equity issues as well as the future impact on equity of decisions taken today.

Introduction: the impact of sustainable development issues on the business environment

Historical context

In antiquity cities were sometimes abandoned, and whole civilizations disappeared. This happened perhaps because resources supporting such societies were exhausted, or there were environmental changes which the city or civilization could not cope with, such as climate change, or natural disaster. Their populations disappeared, leaving archaeologists to ponder how sophisticated civilizations flourished in what is now desert or jungle. But up to about 1800 the human influence on the global environment was limited: the globe was sparsely populated and still largely in its natural state, no matter what happened in particular local areas.

Complexity

Chapter 3 showed us that from about 1800 changes occurred in the UK associated with the Industrial Revolution. Rapid population growth, urbanization, and industrialization, along with other trends like colonization and empire building created in the nineteenth century spectacular wealth and poverty. Despite the consequent accelerating change, with a growing world economy interrupted by world wars and depressions up to 1945, there was still a perception until the 1970s that the undesirable 'side effects' of such rapid economic development were 'local'. Since then, the global environmental impact of business (and other actors) has been a major concern.

Spatial levels

This growing awareness of the environmental impact of business activity was highlighted by environmental disasters in the 1980s. In 1982 at Chernobyl, Ukraine, a nuclear accident polluted eastern Europe. In 1984, at the Union Carbide plant at Bhopal, India, the atmospheric release of methyl-isocyanate killed and injured thousands. Larger oil tankers caused maritime disasters which polluted marine environments, such as the EXXON Valdez oil spill off Alaska in 1989. One could regard these disasters' effects as localized, yet they were generated by globalized processes of economic development. However, a more pervasive phenomenon from the 1980s onwards was the melting of the polar ice caps, with effects on sea levels and climatic patterns. Hurricanes became more frequent; Hurricane Katrina which inundated New Orleans in 2005 being a major example.

But awareness of global environmental problems arose much earlier than these disasters. From the early 1970s, several studies drew attention to them. One report (Meadows et al., 1972) created a sensation with computer projections of future trends in global population, agricultural production, natural resource use, industrial production and pollution. It highlighted approaching conflicts between population growth and industrial growth, alongside the probable incapacity of the world to grow enough food, and produce enough resources such as oil and other basic materials, as well as cope with the consequent pollution. Oil in particular would run out in less than 30 years. But despite the 1970s oil crises, technological development, more efficient resource use, and extensive and successful oil exploration reduced concerns about resource scarcity: the problem receded.

Moving from history to the present day

But the problem was not banished, only postponed. Underlying trends in population and resource use were still upwards (see Table 15.1), and the availability of data and capacity to analyse it increased rapidly. Studies in the 1980s by the United Nations culminated in the Brundtland Report (WCED, 1987). This advocated long-term strategies to counter the threat posed by these trends. It brought to public notice, but did not invent, the term 'sustainable development' (this was coined by the World Conservation Union in 1980, but it did not define it). It advocated the exploration of the complex relationships between people, resources, environment and development as being essential to the development of sound strategies of cooperation and mutual trust within the world community.

The Brundtland Report was a notable advance. By trying to show how we could continue to develop without destroying ourselves or our children, it projected the most well known definition of sustainable development:

> development which meets the needs of the present without compromising the ability of future generations to meet their own needs.

This definition was highly meaningful, but what did it mean in practice? It was in many ways a 'lowest common denominator' definition which everyone could agree with. More concrete steps were needed to make it a reality, and this happened with the UN Conference on Environment and Development at Rio de Janeiro in 1992, the so-called Rio Summit or 'Earth Summit'. But before we consider this, let us outline the nature of the problems in more detail, to see how business helps generate them, but also suffers from them.

Table 15.1 How global indicators of relevance to the environment have been changing

	1970	2000	% change
Population	3.6 bn	6.1 bn	+69
Auto production	22.5 mn	40.9 mn	+82
Oil consumption	2,189 MTOE	3,332 MTOE	+52
Natural gas consumption	1,022 MTOE	2,277 MTOE	+23
Coal consumption	1,635 MTOE	2,034 MTOE	+24
GDP ($-1999)	$16.3 trillion	$43.2 trillion	+165
GDP ($-1999/cap)	$4,407	$7,102	+61

Note: MTOE = million tons of oil equivalent.
Source: Charles Kibert, University of Florida, 2006 at: web.dcp.ufl.edu/ckibert/Poland/index.htm.

Figure 15.1 The composition of global greenhouse gas emissions in 2000

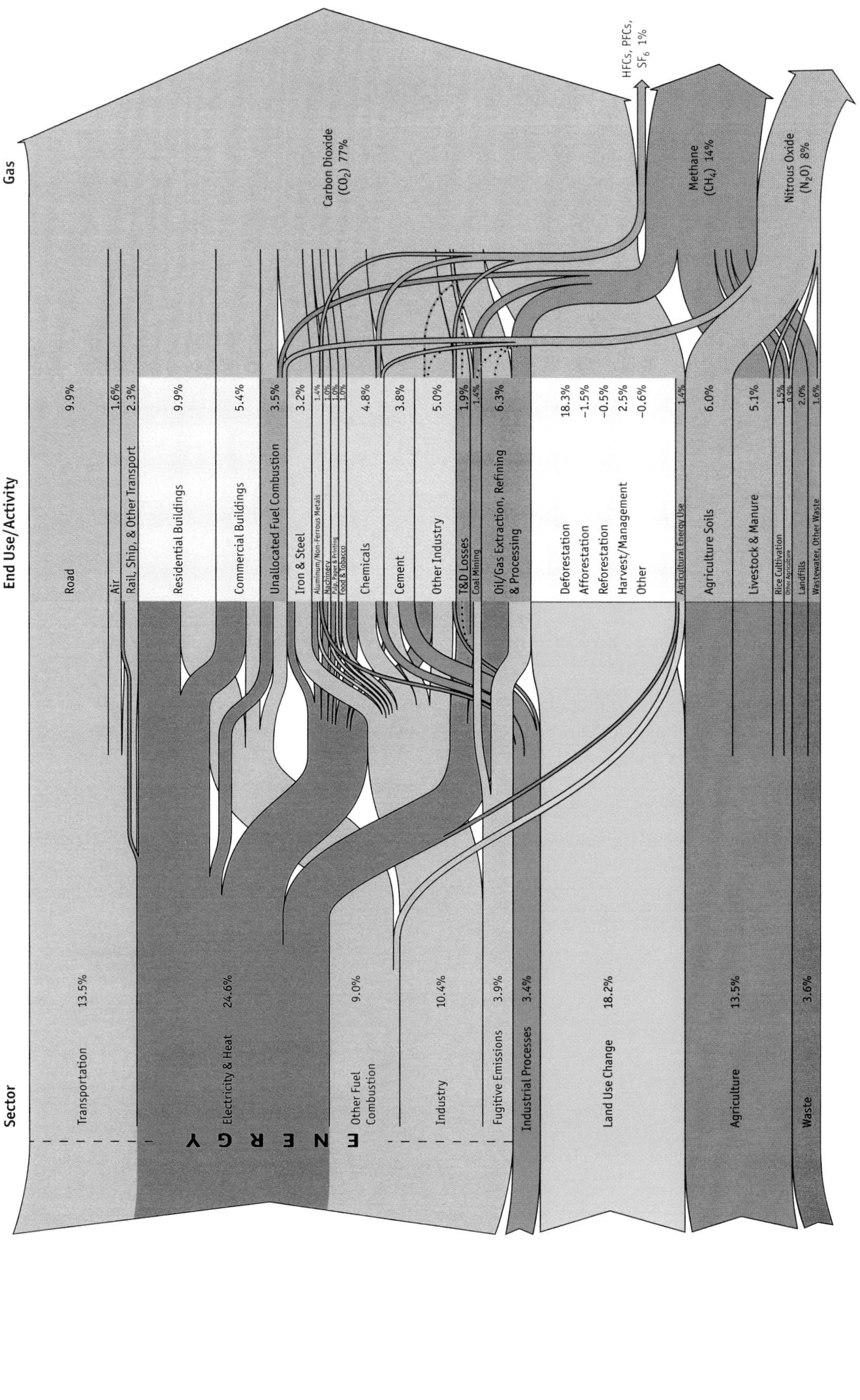

Sector	End Use/Activity	Gas
Transportation 13.5%	Road 9.9%	
	Air 1.6%	
	Rail, Ship, & Other Transport 2.3%	
Electricity & Heat 24.6%	Residential Buildings 9.9%	Carbon Dioxide (CO₂) 77%
	Commercial Buildings 5.4%	
Other Fuel Combustion 9.0%	Unallocated Fuel Combustion 3.5%	
	Iron & Steel 3.2%	
	Aluminium/Non-Ferrous Metals 1.4%	
	Machinery 1.0%	
	Pulp, Paper & Printing 1.0%	
	Food & Tobacco 1.0%	
Industry 10.4%	Chemicals 4.8%	
	Cement 3.8%	
	Other Industry 5.0%	
Fugitive Emissions 3.9%	T&D Losses 1.9%	
	Coal Mining 1.4%	
	Oil/Gas Extraction, Refining & Processing 6.3%	
Industrial Processes 3.4%		
Land Use Change 18.2%	Deforestation 18.3%	
	Afforestation -1.5%	
	Reforestation -0.5%	
	Harvest/Management 2.5%	
	Other -0.6%	
	Agricultural Energy Use 1.4%	Methane (CH₄) 14%
Agriculture 13.5%	Agriculture Soils 6.0%	
	Livestock & Manure 5.1%	
	Rice Cultivation 1.5%	Nitrous Oxide (N₂O) 8%
	Other Agriculture 0.0%	
Waste 3.6%	Landfills 2.0%	
	Wastewater, Other Waste 1.6%	

HFCs, PFCs, SF₆ 1%

ENERGY

Source: World Resources Institute at www.wri.org

The current global environmental problem and business, and the international response

The current global environmental problem

Global warming

Global warming is not the only issue, but possibly the best known one. Global warming describes the phenomenon associated with the release of 'greenhouse gases' (GHGs) into the atmosphere. These gases (mainly carbon dioxide (CO_2), but also methane, and other gases) are generated by the burning of fossil fuels (coal, oil, natural gas, etc.) for space heating, electricity, industrial processes, and, increasingly, transport. But natural processes also generate GHGs. Thus the waste from farm animals produces much methane. This is evident in Figure 15.1, which illustrates the sources and outputs of GHGs. Figure 15.2 illustrates the rapid growth of CO_2 emissions since 1900.

They are called GHGs because of their action. They collect in the upper atmosphere and prevent solar heat being reflected back into space. This heat collects, so it is like a greenhouse. The immediate effect, over many years (see Figure 15.3) but only recently noticeable, is to melt the polar ice caps. This will cause rising sea levels to flood low lying coastal regions, e.g. Bangladesh. Some island states will disappear. Cities like London are at risk. The possible consequences for business and the economy are obvious.

Complexity

But rising sea levels are not the only problem. Also serious, and happening already, is climate change: warm areas get cold, wet areas become dry, and agriculture suffers, especially in poorer countries. Unpredictable and disastrous weather phenomena emerge, e.g. Hurricane Katrina.

These changes produce enormous economic costs. Disasters are costly, but the threat of disaster increases insurance costs, a major business expense. Thus Katrina damaged oil rigs in the Gulf of Mexico which increased insurance rates, and also increased oil prices because of production uncertainties. Threats to business are paralleled by political instability. As climate changes, water

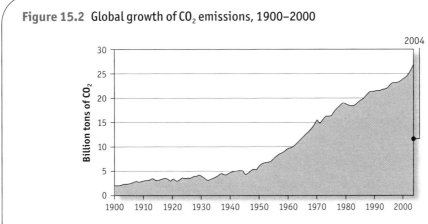

Figure 15.2 Global growth of CO_2 emissions, 1900–2000

Source: World Resources Institute, www.wri.org

Figure 15.3 Increase in the surface temperature of the Earth from AD 1000 to AD 2100

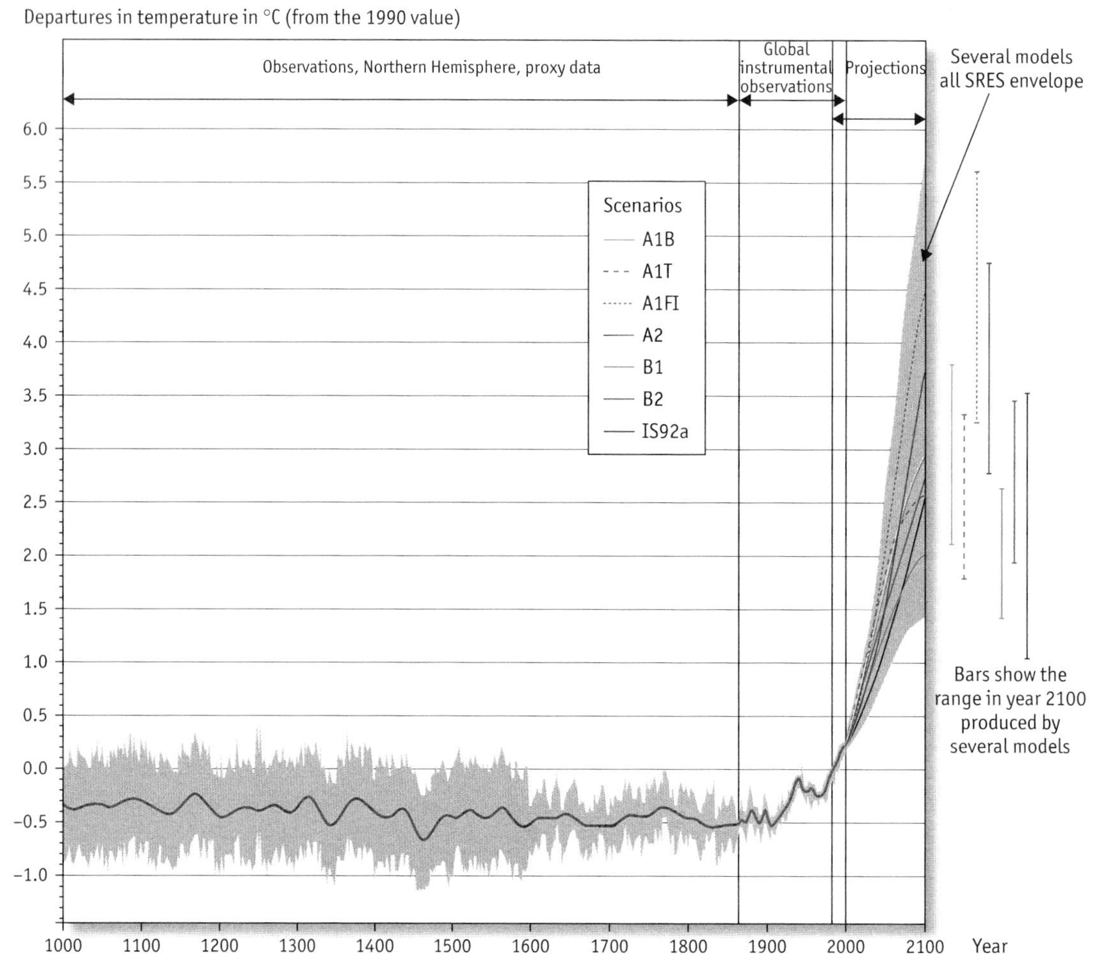

Departures in temperature in °C (from the 1990 value)

Source: Intergovernmental Panel on Climate Change (IPCC), at: www.ipcc.ch

resources can become scarce, and the possibility of conflict between countries which share river systems increases. Though we talk of sea levels rising, in fact, useable water is scarce, and various types of business activities accentuate the problem. How is this? (See Mini-Case 15.1, p. 423.)

Pollution and resource depletion

Apart from GHGs, we can refer to a range of other important global environmental problems under this general heading.

Interaction

Burning fossil fuels also produces acid rain. Sulphur dioxide in the smoke from coal burning power stations combines with atmospheric moisture, making sulphuric acid. This falls as rain, maybe far away, and destroys forest and agricultural areas because the soil is too acidic. This damages both food production and tourism (previously beautiful forests die and tourists stay away). Equally, motor exhausts cause photochemical smog which is a health hazard. People die of respiratory failure, and in cities such as Los Angeles, industrial plants close down if pollution rises too high. Also, certain gases produced by industrial processes (especially CFCs) accumulate up high some 15–50km. This destroys the ozone layer in the upper atmosphere, and allows in ultraviolet radiation from outer space. The ozone layer above the polar ice caps is already much depleted.

Mini-Case 15.1 Water, water everywhere, and not a drop to drink?

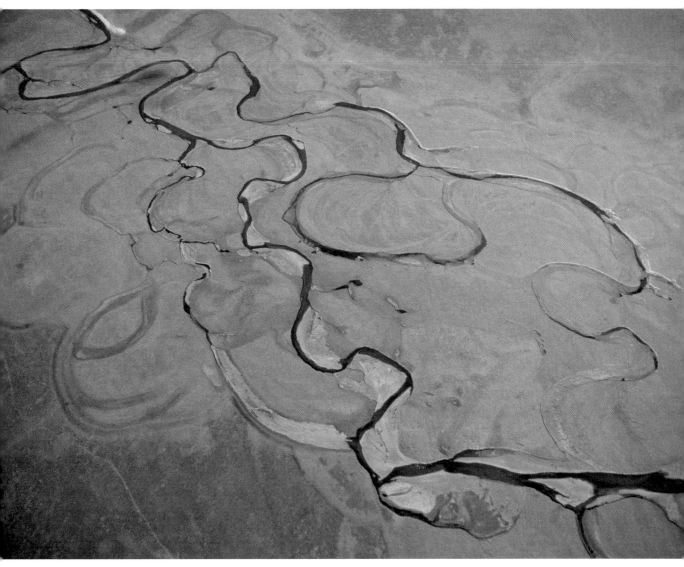

Aerial view of the Rio Grande. Between the USA and Mexico this major river has declined over 25 years to almost a dribble.

© Yann Arthus-Bertrand/Corbis

Values

Most water is sea (95%), and is not useful. Of the rest, 3% is in the polar ice caps, and only the final 2% is useable in rivers, lakes, underground water, etc. This is unequally available. The minimum daily personal requirement for consumption and sanitary needs is 50 litres. Where water is scarce only 30 litres is available. Consumption in the European Union is 200 litres, and in the USA 500 litres. The real problem, however, is not personal consumption, but the water to grow products. This can be enormous. The water to grow a kilogramme of potatoes is 1,000 litres. A kilogramme of beef requires 42,500 litres. And it takes 25 bathtubs to produce 250 grammes of cotton for a shirt. This might not seem problematic until one appreciates where some products are grown. Thus, for example, American farmers are subsidized to grow cotton in areas requiring irrigation. This cotton is sold on world markets below production cost. Cotton producers in developing countries are bankrupted, and many such as in India sell their kidneys to survive, or worse, commit suicide.

Many major rivers are declining, not just because climate change reduces rainfall, but because of water abstraction for irrigation. The Rio Grande between the USA and Mexico has declined over 20–25 years to almost a dribble, and the gushing river of cowboy films is just a memory. Where this occurs in politically dangerous areas in Africa, the Middle East and Asia, there is a war risk. As population and production increases the problem gets worse. And countries like the USA are in fact exporting water (embodied in products as 'virtual water') from areas where it is scarce, while common sense suggests that products should be grown where the natural conditions are optimal without needing scarce water.

Even a bunch of flowers from your local supermarket is problematic. Flower companies in areas like Kenya which export to UK are accused of stealing water illegally at night from rivers, and hence endangering the livelihoods of local farmers who have inadequate water for their crops. How these flowers end up in the supermarket near you is discussed in Mini-Case 15.5.

❓ Why does the relative scarcity of water mean we need to carefully consider the equity issues surrounding its distribution?

Excessive exposure to ultraviolet radiation leads to increased blindness and skin cancer. In addition it aggravates the global warming process.

Growing crops which require excessive fertilizers and irrigation degrades soil quality and exhausts water supplies. And industrial production generates waste products which pollute air, water and land, and ultimately degrade the agricultural resource base. Rivers run to the sea, and liquid run off from land fertilizers and other chemicals concentrates pollutants in the food chain, as they are absorbed by marine life and then eaten by humans, with consequent health problems. Equally, fish stocks decline not only through over-fishing but because the sea is polluted. This problem is aggravated by direct waste dumping at sea.

Values

The ecology of regions is delicately balanced. Human activities may eliminate species by habitat destruction (for instance, logging in rain forests of Amazonia or Southeast Asia which feeds raw materials to the furniture industries) which may have unpredictable effects. Equally, the long-term migration of species as climate changes, brings new flora and fauna which can destroy native species. Even more difficult, and more unpredictable in its effects on genetic diversity, is the introduction of genetically modified organisms (GMOs) and plants. These are often associated not just with attempts to design disease-free and improved plant varieties, but represent attempts by multinational companies to take patents on seed varieties on which they have a monopoly.

Apart from water, oil is a major problem, but emerging nations, like China and India, exacerbate the problem. These most populous countries have rapidly increasing car ownership levels. It is predicted that by 2030 China alone will consume 99 million barrels of oil daily, but current world production is only 75 million barrels, and declining.

Thus, while global warming captures most attention, there are a range of other effects which are related to it. We may now consider the international responses to these linked threats.

International responses: the 'Earth Summit' and after

This conference changed the international legal framework for environmental issues. It created an 'Earth Charter', or an environmental bill of rights which set out the principles for economic and environmental behaviour of peoples and nations. Several agreements emanated from the conference, in particular:

- the Rio Declaration
- Agenda 21
- UN Framework Convention on Climate Change.

The Rio Declaration

This covered many issues relating to the mutual environmental behaviour of nations. Overall, it aimed to establish: 'a new and equitable global partnership through the creation of new levels of cooperation among States, key sectors of society, and people' (Ison et al., 2002: 109). However, the declaration could be described as 'soft law', that is, it lacked an enforcement or compliance system.

Agenda 21—Global Programme of Action on Sustainable Development

Agenda 21 is: 'a comprehensive plan of action to be taken globally, nationally and locally by organizations of the United Nations System, Governments and Major Groups in every area in which humans impact on the environment' (www.un.org/esa/sustdev/agenda21.htm). Again, it had no legal sanctions, but lots of commitment: 'Perhaps the most important impact of Agenda 21 has been at the local level where Agenda 21 officers have been able to try out practical ideas which seek to implement sustainable development on the ground' (Ison et al., 2002: 111).

UN Framework Convention on Climate Change

This was directly concerned with the problem of global warming, and led to the 1997 Kyoto Protocol. Here the developed countries committed to reducing 1990 emission levels of six GHGs by 5% by 2012. It introduced emissions trading, whereby countries which were having difficulty meeting their emissions reduction targets could buy emissions allowances from other countries with spare capacity. The Kyoto Protocol was a significant initiative. But the USA, producing 25% of global GHGs, refused to sign the protocol, and still refuses. Thus, global warming is generated by few countries, but many countries, mainly the poorest, suffer from it (see Figure 15. 4). This is an enormous injustice.

Complexity

Values

A related issue is the lack of universal agreement on global warming. While most scientific opinion suggests global warming is fact, evidenced in tornadoes, glaciers melting, etc., others say that this comes within the natural variation observed over millennia, and responses to counter something that is not due to human activity will simply impose unnecessary costs on the world economy. And it is true that the research underpinning conclusions about global warming are at the frontiers of science. Of course, if you are a major GHG generator, like the USA, reduction costs will be high, so cynics feel that arguments against global warming have an ulterior motive.

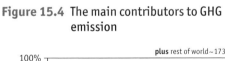

Figure 15.4 The main contributors to GHG emission

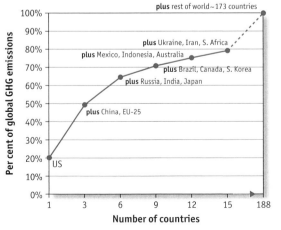

Source: World Resources Institute at www.wri.org

After Rio

Spatial levels

Ten years after Rio, a conference was held in Johannesburg in 2002 to review progress. The World Summit on Sustainable Development (WSSD) sought to address sustainable development in its entirety: economic, developmental, environmental and social dimensions. Together with the Doha Development Agenda, 2001 (on trade) and the Monterrey conference on Financing for Development (2002), the WSSD was reckoned to have shaped a global partnership for sustainable development. The partnership included 'commitments to increased development assistance and market access for developing countries, and better protection of the environment. The follow-up of the WSSD is being monitored by the UN Commission for Sustainable Development (CSD). For 2004/2005, the focus was on water,

Mini-Case 15.2 Globalization and sustainable development

The reference to WSSD in conjunction with the other above mentioned conferences underlines the relationship of sustainable development issues to general processes of globalization, and the organization of world trade. This general area was discussed in Chapter 12. Making progress on sustainable development is complicated by globalization/trade issues. World trade has expanded enormously since 1945. In 1970 one-eighth of production was traded internationally, and now it is a fifth. This is due to reductions in international trade barriers, either tariffs or other restraints on trade. This was initiated by a series of international agreements from 1947 under the General Agreement on Trade and Tariffs (GATT), and implemented from 1995 by the World Trade Organization (WTO). This progressed on to other factors which affected trade, such as product standards imposed for health and safety reasons, and environmental quality.

This has led to problems. The benefits of increased trade come within a context where the WTO and its trade agreements is more powerful than institutions responsible for environmental protection, health, human rights, etc. This has led, it is argued, to an unbalanced world economy 'where the interests of exporters and big companies usually seem to be given a higher priority than environmental protection, for example, or the concerns of local communities' (Bracken, 2005: 3). Developed countries are in a

better position to exploit reductions in trade barriers than many developing countries, so that the latter lose out relatively, while also suffering from adverse environmental consequences of increased world trade, which itself encourages unsustainable use of transport (of which more later). Making the current trade rules support better environmental and developmental objectives is being actively discussed in the continuing Doha discussions, but progress is slow.

At a more local level, the 'Single Market' in the European Union, with much reduced border controls, means that, for instance, stringent and costly German environmental controls on waste disposal encourage sharp operators to profit by trucking waste into the Czech Republic, where it is hidden in, for instance, abandoned Soviet aircraft hangars, to be discovered later. The trucks cannot be checked easily at the borders because of the requirement for free movement of goods. Political negotiations to truck the waste back will take several years. We refer to such phenomena again later in Mini-Case 15.4 on land fill taxes for waste.

❷ How has globalization increased the pressure on the environment and what are the implications in terms of spatial levels for how these problems might be addressed?

sanitation and human settlements, and for 2006/2007 it was on energy, industrial development, air pollution and climate change (see Mini-Case 15.2).

The application of sustainable development frameworks to environmental issues

Conventional frameworks for dealing with environmental issues

Values

Before the idea of sustainable development evolved, conventional, or classical, economics saw pollution and environmental problems as 'side effects' of the production/consumption process. Western Christian cultures within which such economic philosophies developed, believed the environment was something to service and benefit humanity, to be exploited. This is traceable almost to biblical ideas from Genesis about God's creation of the Garden of Eden for Man to live in and enjoy. Many cultures, on the other hand, see the environment as a living thing, of which humanity is a part. This idea has much in common with modern notions of sustainable development. One could say however that the conventional economic approach was not that extreme. In 1930s Communist Russia, the environment was something to be subdued and transformed for the greater good of socialism. In fact, Soviet dictator Stalin was called 'transformer of nature'. This led to unwise decisions which devastated large regions of the former Soviet Union (the Aral Sea in Kazakhstan, which lost 50% of its area, was in 1960 the world's fourth largest lake). Less well known, but similar, was the contemporaneous drive of Nazi Germany to transform nature by conquering 'lebensraum', or 'living space', in the 'East' (that is, eastern Europe and Russia). It was defeated in 1944/45, but not before the Jews perished in the Holocaust as scapegoats for the debacle.

The approach of conventional economics was not to ignore environmental costs, but to keep them in balance with the general costs and benefits of economic activity from an overall societal viewpoint. Hence, such 'side effects' were called 'externalities', and were considered to be 'divergences between private and social costs'. The latter can be positive or negative, but in the cases we are considering they are usually negative externalities. That is, social costs are greater than private costs, and social costs can be reduced to acceptable levels by instituting taxes to equate social marginal cost with social marginal benefit. A classical example of this, introduced in Chapter 2, is the use of road pricing to reduce traffic congestion to a level where the road tax paid by the marginal driver added to his private costs is just equal to the benefit to him of the trip he is making. Economists refer to this as 'internalizing the externality' and is popularly referred to as 'making the polluter pay'. Such ideas existed for many years, and have been implemented on a small scale in cities like Cambridge and Durham, and on a larger scale abroad in cities like Singapore. The successful application to London in February 2003 is probably the largest example to date. There have been many government reports on road pricing since the 1960s, but actually implementing anything nationally has been a political 'hot potato' to successive governments afraid of electoral unpopularity. The Eddington Report (HM Treasury/DfT, 2006) recommends charging all transport users (not just road users) for the CO_2 emissions they generate, and this appears to have a wide measure of cross-party support. It will not happen quickly, and possibly not during the lifetime of this book.

Internal/ external

Road congestion is an easy example of the use of the conventional economic approach to controlling an environmental problem. Despite the practical implementation, the situation is simpler in that most of the problem consists of road users imposing costs on other road users. But other types of environmental goods can be more difficult. Unlike road traffic, perpetrators (those causing the problem) are most often not sufferers. It may also be difficult to identify who actually are the perpetrators and sufferers. Also, you can only impose charges if it is possible to establish ownership of, or property rights in, the thing that is being charged for (such as road space). The problem is that many environmental goods have badly defined property rights. Who owns the atmosphere? Who owns the oceans? But even if we can establish ownership, it may still be hard to quantify the environmental costs that have to be charged for, and then establish practical charging systems. Nevertheless, as we have indicated already, it is not impossible, and the Kyoto Protocol has already instituted the idea of 'emissions trading' (see Mini-Case 15.3 below).

The concept of sustainable development (SD)

Definitions of sustainable development

We have the Brundtland definition already outlined:

> development which meets the needs of the present without compromising the ability of future generations to meet their own needs.

In fact there are over seventy definitions. The above definition is intuitively graspable, though it would be useful to point to some key characteristics which get us to the essence of what sustainable development is about. We can point to two key ideas:

Mini-Case 15.3 Carbon trading or 'funny money'

Cooling towers at a coal fired power station with a wind farm nearby. Climate change may cost us 20% of world GDP if it is not checked.

© istockphoto.com/ Hans F. Meier

The principle of 'emissions trading' is simple. It keeps the level of a pollutant (in this case CO_2) at a target level by putting a price on it. Producers get permits which allow them to emit a certain amount of carbon, and they use these permits to cover their own emissions, or else invest in clean technologies which allow them to sell some of the permits to another company which has exceeded its permit quota (in 2005 the Scottish and Southern energy company spent 9% of its pre-tax profits on buying carbon credits from its rivals). This creates a market in the permits. The problem is that once you set the overall total and allocated permits, you are merely keeping within that total and shifting the total around between those who are buying and those who are selling permits. Thus, the total does not decrease by definition, though it could be in principle organized to do so over a period, and this would be the intention of Kyoto.

After the establishment of the Kyoto Protocol, the European Union instituted an Emissions Trading Scheme (ETS). Each member state set a cap on the carbon emissions that would be allowed and issued permits accordingly. The first round of the scheme from 2005–2007 had mixed results. It seems the caps were set too high in some countries (but not high enough in Britain), and several countries produced much lower emissions than they estimated. Hence, prices collapsed. But there is inevitably a learning process, and the 2008–2012 round can be run with tighter limits.

The effect of ETS on companies is remarkable. Their possible liabilities for purchase of permits has to be indicated on their balance sheets, and investors are very keen to know what a company's emissions position is. The possibility following the Stern Report is that emissions may be taxed in the UK and this could have a very significant effect on the stock market. The Stern Report is a major government report about the threats facing us from climate change (HM Treasury, 2006). Climate change may cost us 20% of world GDP if it is not checked, and the point just made about taxing emissions is just one specific aspect of the general message of the Stern Report: the polluter must pay.

❓ What are the problems of attempting to levy taxes on polluters?

- inter-generational equity (IRGE): that is, fairness between generations, or, being as fair to our grandchildren as we are to ourselves

and

- intra-generational equity (IAGE): that is, fairness between different interest groups in the same generation.

It is common to talk about the two ideas from the point of view of what is called 'weak' and 'strong' sustainability:

- Weak sustainability (WS): to achieve IRGE we should aim to pass on to future generations a constant 'aggregate capital stock' (AGS), though its composition may change; to achieve IAGE we should aim to compensate the poor and disadvantaged by support programmes.

- Strong sustainability (SS): to achieve IRGE, the idea of AGS does not apply: losses of environmental capital must be replaced; to achieve IAGE, we still compensate, but we also emphasize the *collective* value of ecosystems and environment.

But whether we go for strong or weak definitions we need to consider how we measure them.

Development of sustainable development initiatives

The key issue here is how to value environmental goods. There are problems which are well known in using conventional GDP measures with environmental goods. An increase in GDP can be consistent with an increase in environmental degradation. And expenditures to reduce degradation are regarded in economic accounting terms as an increase in welfare because they increase GDP, rather than being a cost which actually reduces welfare. Hence, alternative measures which reflect this have been devised, for instance, the Index of Sustainable Economic Welfare (ISEW) devised by the Stockholm Environmental Institute in 1994. Thus:

Values

ISEW = Personal consumption + non-defensive public expenditure − defensive private expenditures + capital formation − costs of environmental degradation + services from domestic labour − depreciation of natural capital

In a conventional GDP measure, the first two negative quantities would be positive, while the last two items, one negative and one positive, would not appear in the equation at all. Thus, in the UK since the 1970s GDP has increased annually, but ISEW has declined.

> ⮑ *Stop and Think*
> Think of two concrete examples each for (a) and (b) which probably:
>
> (a) increase GDP but reduce ISEW
>
> (b) reduce GDP but increase ISEW

From here the development of environmental indicators is a key step. The UK government published its first set of indicators of sustainable development in 1996, and these have been updated since, and form the basis for evaluating the progress being made towards both national and international sustainability targets. The current version is from July 2006 (DEFRA, 2006). Many indicators are defined at national, regional and local level. A subset of twenty key indicators apply to the whole of the UK in relation to the four priority areas outlined in the 2005 UK Government Sustainable Development Strategy (DEFRA, 2005a), namely, sustainable consumption and production, climate change and energy, protection of natural resources and environmental enhancement, and the creation of sustainable communities and a fairer world. The indicators include such as GHG emissions, resource use, waste generation, bird populations, fish stocks, ecological impacts of air pollution, and river quality. Very few items get a 'tick' in the latest summary assessment, and resource use gets a big black cross against it.

Once we can quantify the main things that need to be influenced, the next step is to consider how we influence them.

Types of approaches for dealing with environmental problems

As suggested already, while we talk about the global dimension of environmental problems, many of the responses to them are implemented at a local level. So we often hear the phrase: 'Think globally, act locally'. It is common to classify policy responses into either 'market based' and 'non-market based'.

'Market based' policy measures

Values

A first approach is by processes of bargaining and negotiation. If property rights in the environmental goods—air, water or whatever—can be assigned to some party, this is possible. The question of course is, who will they be assigned to? Equity and ethics suggest that 'the polluter pays'. But if there are too many polluters or sufferers, bargaining is difficult, and it may be impossible to set up any scheme. In this case, the alternative may be a tax.

With environmental taxes, the polluter pays a tax related to the environmental damage. This creates an incentive to reduce the damage, for instance as in the case of a carbon tax. The problem here is that it may be hard to estimate the correct tax level, so that if it is set too high, society loses out because the polluter cuts back production too much, whereas if it is set too low, there is insufficient reduction in the environmental damage.

'Non-market based' policy measures

Here government establishes standards for things like air quality, water quality, chemical processes, waste incineration, etc. The polluter then decides how to meet standards, adopting the least costly approach. A regulatory body may be appointed to monitor compliance and to take action for breaches of standards. Regulatory systems can be rather blunt instruments. Different firms may be more easily placed to achieve the targets, and might be encouraged to overachieve if some form of trading solution were possible, whereas if the target is easy to achieve, the company can sit back and do little. Equally, if the targets are set too stringently, firms may incur unnecessary costs to meet them.

We may also include, under non-market based measures, the use of public exhortation, persuasion and education in environmental matters. There is a lot to do in informing both the public and business about the nature of environmental problems, to facilitate the introduction of appropriate policy measures.

Policy frameworks

Spatial levels

The previous paragraphs described the broad principles underlying policy, and this section considers what has actually been done in policy terms for the UK and the European Union. Up to the 1970s environmental regulation in the UK was piecemeal, with several inspectorates working independently in relation to land, air, water and nuclear power. From the 1970s there were attempts to unify the various areas of environmental regulation, and, from the 1980s, in the light of developments outlined at the start of the chapter, environmental policy ceased being a national concern, and took on progressively a European, and then global dimension. The attempts to unify or integrate the various areas of environmental regulation led in 1990 to the Environmental Protection Act which gave legislative backing to the idea of Integrated Pollution Control (IPC), looking to control pollution across media (land, water, air, etc.). This embodied the principle in environmental regulation, of whatever process, of requiring the implementation of the Best Available Technique Not Entailing Excessive Cost (BATNEEC). This gave explicit recognition to the economic dimension in what had, up to then, been the principle of the Best Practicable Means (BPM). Following the Environment Act 1996, all the functions of the different environmental agencies were incorporated for the first time into the Environment Agency.

Alongside legislation on pollution control, there are two other areas of legislation which have significant environmental dimensions. Firstly, land use control under the various Town and Country Planning Acts determines where industry and any land use/structure with environmental impacts may be located in relation to other land uses. Secondly, there is legislation on the conservation and protection of wildlife and the natural environment. This is controversial as there is often conflict between the desire of business to exploit natural resources, and the desire for conservation.

From the 1970s, changes at UK level took place in parallel to Europe-wide and subsequently international initiatives, as the cross-boundary dimensions of environmental processes expanded with growth in the European and global economy. At European Union level, the need to create a 'level playing field' for the operation of the Single Market meant that environmental regulation across the union had to be integrated, so that member states could not compete unfairly by operating laxer environmental regimes. Equally, from the 1980s the global dimension became important. Early initiatives from the EU were the European Directives on Air Pollution of 1984, and later in

Mini-Case 15.4 Paying for waste: the spy in the wheelie bin?

Local authorities have instituted recycling schemes for household waste, with different bins for different waste. Chips installed in the bins ('the spy in the wheelie bin') will charge households for waste which cannot be recycled.

© istockphoto.com/
Sava Miokovic

In 1996 the government introduced land fill taxes. The burying of waste cannot go on ad infinitum: there are not enough holes. The land fill tax was designed to reduce the need for holes by increasing the recycling of waste by taxing every tonne of 'active' waste (which includes household and commercial waste) deposited at landfill sites. When first introduced the tax was £7 per tonne, but by 2005/06 it was £18 and this will increase by at least £3 per annum up to £35 in the longer term. The tax can be substantial for a large company or large local authority. While it can lead to fly tipping by crooked operators, the natural reaction of companies is to look at ways of recycling to avoid the tax. (Of course, if you are not an island state, as the UK is, avoiding land fill taxes may be possible by exporting the waste surreptitiously across the nearest border, as we mentioned in Mini-Case 15.2.)

The bill to a large local authority for land fill tax for household waste can be several million pounds per annum (Liverpool City Council paid £3.6 million in 2005/06), and local authorities have instituted recycling schemes for household waste, with different bins for different waste. But the move now is to install chips in the bins (called the 'spy in the wheelie bin') to weigh waste and to charge households for waste which cannot be recycled. This will of course bring the price mechanism to bear at the point at which the waste is generated, encourage less waste, and also apply the principle of 'the polluter pays'.

❓ Would you try to produce less household waste if you were charged for it?

1995 there was the Integrated Pollution Prevention and Control Directive which aimed at IPC in the same way as the UK 1990 Act, but more comprehensively. The overall body of EU environmental legislation is vast and encompasses over 500 items, and derives ultimately from the various European Community Treaties. In general the principle of subsidiarity applies, whereby the principles of environmental directives are embodied in the legislation of individual member states, and only issues which cannot be dealt with at this level will be decided at EU level.

The UK/EU interface also goes forward to global issues which we have discussed, and one area of regulation worth mentioning with a global dimension already discussed is carbon trading. This is just one of several examples in the UK and EU where there have been attempts in the last fifteen years or so to use the price mechanism in environmental regulation. We have also discussed road pricing. Other areas where we see the use of the price mechanism being introduced in the policy framework are, for instance, in waste management (see Mini-Case 15.4, p. 431).

Though we have said much so far about the links between sustainable development and business, we move on now for the rest of the chapter to talk about this per se.

Sustainable development and business

Values

Business is one of the significant contributors to environmental problems, yet at the same time it provides us with our livelihoods. The need to focus environmental measures so as not to impose excessive economic costs on society as compared with the reduction in environmental costs has also emerged in discussion. Overall we need to maintain high/stable economic growth within acceptable environmental limits. Thus this section, after the previous ones which set business in a broad relationship to issues of sustainable development, considers sustainable development issues within the context of the internal operations of a business. It will become quickly apparent that this presents not only challenges to a business in terms of how it can reduce its environmental impact, but also opportunities, in terms of the way in which these challenges collectively also present business opportunities in helping businesses to meet the challenges facing them. It also raises the issue of the responsibilities of businesses in terms of considering their activities in ethical terms. As the whole issue of business ethics was considered in Chapter 7, this latter aspect will only be referred to in passing here.

Defining sustainability in relation to business

The following definition of sustainable business conveniently places it in parallel with the Brundtland definition:

> Sustainable business . . . means taking the goal of sustainability, living and working in such a way that human society will be possible for generations to come, and translating that into the changes required of an individual organization—changes which maintain the organizations capacity for producing human benefits, including the profitability needed for survival, while optimising the environmental balance of its operations. (Crosbie and Knight, 1995: 15)

Spatial levels

We then pose the same question: what does it mean in practice? How do the notions of sustainable development work their way into the individual business? There is almost no aspect of the operations of the average business which does not in some way relate. We can usefully employ here the format of Hutchinson and Hutchinson (1997) in terms of looking at four aspects of a business: its site history; the production processes it employs; its product and the communications processes surrounding it; and the external environment of the business. These fit into the well established framework of what is generally called 'environmental and ecological auditing', and the processes developed from about the mid-1980s in the USA. This was given a further boost after the 1992 'Earth Summit', and not long after in 1995 the European Union devised an Environmental Management and Auditing System (EMAS). In the same year the International Standardization Organization (ISO) set up a committee to develop an environmental management system for global application. It established ISO 14001. While EMAS applies to the EU, and is especially prevalent in German-speaking countries, ISO 14001 is applied worldwide. The EU has adapted its system so that those firms which have ISO 14001 can achieve EMAS by a series of modifications to ISO 14001.

The audit is a broad way of looking at the operations of a company or organization to sketch out how sustainability issues reach into every part of its operations. Each of the four aspects mentioned above can be broken down into several sub-aspects, and many of them are whole areas of research by themselves. One aspect of the fourth area (external environment) will be taken to provide the main case study of the chapter, namely on sustainable transport for a large business. But once we have considered each of the four aspects, we shall look at a difficult issue. What do these issues actually mean to a business and government in practice?

Site history

All sorts of dangers may lie hidden in a site, and once a company buys it, it buys all the risks attached to it. Insurance companies may refuse to insure if they suspect hidden risks. There may, perhaps, be concealed noxious substances which could be disturbed and released into the atmosphere during construction or production. An 'Environmental Impact Assessment' (EIA) would be necessary, which is one aspect of an eco-audit. An EIA involves gathering all the information that exists on the site, and developing an assessment of the environmental issues and risks pertaining to past activity on the site, and the relationship of this to any proposed expansion of existing activities, or initiation of completely new activities.

The production process

This concerns the actual production process, particularly energy use and waste generation, plus the product life cycle. Companies waste about 30% of their energy (mainly in buildings). Thus:

> Electricity and gas metering in business appears to be chaotic. Many businesses have estimated metering, and most are unable to be really sure what energy they actually use, unless they have an energy saving programme in place. This situation is untenable. (Sustainable Development Commission, 2005: 31)

It has been calculated that a 20% reduction in energy costs is equivalent to a 5% increase in sales. So helping the environment can be good business.

Reducing total energy use is only one aspect. The sources of energy can also be examined to encourage recycling of energy and the use of renewable energy (e.g. wind and solar power). This can also represent business opportunities in terms of developing new ideas and techniques. The whole area of micro power generation has started to mushroom as new designs of small wind-powered turbines which can be attached to buildings come on the market (B&Q started selling them in September 2006).

Apart from wasting energy, firms may produce substantial waste in the production process. Dealing with waste after generation to minimize impact (for instance, ensuring that companies hired to take waste away do not dump it illegally) is an obvious first requirement, but even more useful are efforts at minimizing the waste generated in the first place. (The land fill tax in Mini-Case 15.4 above looked at this.)

→ *Stop and Think*

How do you think companies might try legally or illegally to avoid land fill tax?

What precautions might be instituted to counter instances of illegal waste disposal?

*Internal/
external*

Looking at energy use and waste generation leads to the whole product in terms of a life cycle assessment (LCA). An LCA examines all environmental impacts associated with the life of a product from raw material extraction, to pre-production processes, to actual production, and through to distribution and final disposal of the used product. This is easily said, but for many products each of these stages involves quite significant environmental impacts, apart from the production process itself. For instance, furniture industries need to ensure that scarce timbers illegally gathered from threatened tropical forests are not being used by them. Equally, so many harmless looking products wear out and have to be disposed of, and they often contain poisonous components which leak into the atmosphere, the earth or water systems: fridge mountains, PC mountains, old cars and so on. So there are regular calls to put a tax on such items to pay for their eventual disposal.

Product and communications

The environmental features of a company's production activities can be exploited for its own wider advantage. This may be in terms of protecting itself from the wider public consequences of unforeseen environmental crises, promoting its products, or promoting the image of the company in terms of not only its financial reporting, but also its environmental reporting.

Stakeholders

In terms of crisis management and risk assessment, we have already referred to environmental disasters, but these can also be public relations disasters which damage the wider image of the company by affecting adversely its product brands and stock market standing. Environmental disasters are nearly always unexpected, yet require immediate company responses to restore confidence and minimize damage to its reputation. When disasters occur there may be attempts to conceal information. However, openness and transparency is the best policy, and companies should prepare for unlikely but possible eventualities, by carrying out risk assessments of what could happen, and making reaction plans ready in case something does go wrong.

Stakeholders

Values

Disasters apart, the daily operations of the company may be an asset to be exploited. Companies which have ensured that they source their inputs from other companies which have employed environmentally desirable methods, have produced their products to the highest environmental standards, and have ensured that waste products can be disposed of in the most environmentally efficient way, have a story to tell, or sell, in their marketing activities. This is called 'green marketing', and it is a story to tell not only to consumers and customers, but also to staff, shareholders, investors, the media and regulatory authorities. However, it has to be a believable and honest story. Consumers and the media soon spot exaggerated or false claims which are intended to boost sales or public image. Such claims are often called 'greenwash'.

Product design, packaging and eco-labelling also present opportunities for environmental gains. Materials can be saved in production and packaging. Packaging can be used not only to provide useful environmental guidance on the product, but also information on safe disposal of the used product and packaging (eco-labelling). Clearly, some of these features will have an obvious benefit to the company, in terms of saving raw materials and the use of energy. But others will have benefits further down the line reducing transport costs, and landfill or incineration costs. Moreover, the opportunity exists by doing this to portray the company additionally in the best possible light. For example, next time you go to your supermarket, check out the product lines for the brand 'Duchy Originals'. The stated commitment on the packaging to sustainable farming methods, and the avoidance of pesticides and GMOs, is no doubt genuine, but it is also an excellent sales promotion tool.

Finally, there is environmental reporting. Companies are required to produce annual reports setting out their accounts and financial position. While there is not the same legal requirement for a corporate environmental report (CER), the environmental threats which companies now face both at home and abroad mean that a CER can be almost as important to judging the health of a company, and whether it is a safe investment prospect, as its annual financial statement. Hence a transparent annual CER is produced by major companies. These set out the environmental policies and targets of the company, the systems in place to achieve them, and progress towards achievement.

The external environment

Here we consider two aspects of the external environment of the company which are important to the theme of this chapter, but which seem to get little coverage in the many textbooks which now exist on 'corporate environmental management'. The external environment will here refer to the links which a company maintains with other firms, customers and organizations to produce its goods and services. The first aspect of these links we call the supply chain, and the second aspect will be the environmental management of the transport demands generated by the activities of the firm or organization.

And yes, you, the reader, are closely implicated here. As a student using this book at an educational institution, you are involved in the activity of an organization which may be one of the largest employers and generators of income in the region you live in. You may be one of up to 50,000 or more students moving back and forth from home to institution, and between parts of it, and generating your own part of the massive environmental footprint of your institution. Hence, in contrast to many texts on the theme of this chapter, we mark out transport as a key aspect (with a Case Study).

The supply chain and its environmental management: Any company or organization is only one link in the long process which leads to someone somewhere getting a product or service they need. A tree felled in a forest in Scandinavia leads by a long intervening set of operations—raw materials processing, transport, warehousing and storage, further intermediate manufacturing, further transport and storage, final processing, transfer to retail distributors—to a box of matches purchased from a corner shop. This sequence of operations is referred to as the supply chain. A company examining its environmental profile will need to look at not only its own internal operations and processes, but at the supply chain as a whole, to see where changes can be made which will improve the overall environmental performance of the chain.

Environmental transport strategies: Transport is one of the most important factors in the whole global environmental problem, yet it is one of the most intractable, and getting worse. It is forecast that by 2020, 'transport is likely to account for more than half of global oil demand and roughly one fourth of global energy-related CO_2 emissions' (International Energy Agency, 2001). The reason it is intractable is that the demand for cars and commercial vehicles is growing much faster than technological improvements in engines can reduce CO_2 emissions, especially in central and eastern Europe, and developing countries like China and India. The demand for air transport is growing rapidly too. Also, it is not just a growth in numbers: road transport (and air transport to a lesser extent) is a very flexible form of transport which reduces the constraints on location, and leads to not only more journeys but longer journeys.

Dynamic

Reducing the environmental footprint of the transport activities of a business raises conflicts to the extent that critics argue it may raise costs and reduce economic growth. It is often argued that investment in transport infrastructure boosts the rate of economic growth generally, and that it is crucial for improving the economic prospects of declining or peripheral regions. However, if the forecasts of the effects of unrestricted growth in GHGs are borne out, and to which transport is a major contributor, it can be argued that the effects on economic growth of global warming will be much more disastrous than the effects of cutting back transport growth in the first place. This was the basic message of the Stern Review (HM Treasury, 2006).

Thus, a company or organization seeking to reduce the demands it places on transport systems and energy related requirements will need to consider the following factors; its choice of mode for moving goods or people; the storage/packaging facilties it uses for transport; where it gets its inputs from, and the destinations of its products; the travel patterns of its employees; the problems of accessing its site; health and safety issues associated with transport; possible alternatives to travel; and the noise and related environmental intrusion associated with the company's travel and transport activities. Companies and organizations devote considerable effort to developing 'company travel plans', or 'green transport strategies', which look at several or all of these factors, and much government advice is published (DfT, 2002).

Choice of mode: In many cases the choices available in the mode of transport a company uses to receive and forward goods may be restricted by site characteristics, the type and value of the goods, and the urgency of receipt and despatch. But it is clear that different modes have different environmental characteristics regarding energy use and emissions, and companies may be able to adjust their practices accordingly.

Storage and packaging for transport: For large companies the demand for warehousing and storage facilities, and for facilities to pack up and dispatch goods, can be massive. Inventories are dead money, and companies try to minimize them. One way is to have 'just in time' production methods, so that component suppliers are organized in the supply chain to bring in deliveries just before they are needed. Thus, transport substitutes for storage. This is accentuated in the activities of companies like large supermarket chains, such as Tesco and ASDA. These companies need to keep their stores supplied around the clock. Cash tills connect directly to the computerized inventory systems to indicate instantly the demand around the country for a full profile of products. Economies of scale combined with an efficient motorway system encourage the concentration of warehousing and distribution systems into large logistics centres serving the whole country from a few major bases. This substitution of transport for storage facilities generates energy use. And it also leads to situations where goods which could be obtained locally are shipped from the other end of the country.

Input sources and product destinations: This means that companies seeking to minimize their environmental footprint in transport terms need to consider where they get their inputs from, and where they send them to. As just indicated, it is surprising how much resources are spent shifting goods around the country to places where they already are, and generating GHGs in the process. This is illustrated in Mini-Case 15.5 below.

Employee travel patterns and alternatives to travel: Journeys to work, school or college constitute a major proportion of daily travel. Growing car use and declining public transport are key features of this phenomenon. The drive to reverse the use of the car and to encourage us to use more environmentally friendly modes like public transport, cycling or walking has been going on for many years as a way of reducing the peak hour problem. But growing recognition of the GHG problem has sharpened this drive.

Companies also need to ask if travel is necessary in the first place. This applies especially to travel on company business. Is it always necessary to drive? Can public transport be used? Can an

Mini-Case 15.5   Food miles and powered flowers

To see how transport and sustainability enter into seemingly ordinary business operations, we may consider the implications of a visit to a supermarket to buy a bunch of flowers, or just to shop for food. Consider flowers first.

You think that the flowers came from greenhouses in the UK, or maybe from Holland. In fact, they are likely to have come from Kenya, or some similar location. Weekly, 600 tonnes of cut flowers are jetted into the UK, 250 tonnes from Kenya. 17,000 tonnes came from Kenya in 2004, worth £46.1 million, but producing 33,000 tonnes of CO_2 emissions annually. Each flower imported creates far more than its own weight in CO_2.

The concept of **food miles** was introduced in Chapter 2 and refers to the distance travelled by food from where it is grown to the mouth that eats it. And one may ask why our local supermarkets ship food from the other end of the country when it could be bought off local farmers. There can be explanations for this related to supply contracts, and where major warehouses are located. But it does not cancel the fact that if all our food

came from within 20 km (12.4 miles) of where we live, we could save £2.1bn annually in environmental and congestion costs. Moreover, transporting food around the country is actually a bigger issue than air freight. About 30% of road freight is agricultural produce, and the tonnage has increased by about a quarter in 20 years, and is being transported about two-thirds further. But air transport of food is still important: transport of food consumed in the UK produced 19 million tons of CO_2 in 2002, but though air transport accounted for only 1% of food tonne miles, it produced 11% of the corresponding CO_2 emissions. It is suggested that supermarkets should label food with the distance it has travelled so that we can buy accordingly. In fact, one study (DEFRA, 2005b) argues that by itself food miles would not be an adequate indicator of sustainability, but nevertheless it encapsulates the importance of the issue.

❷ Would your decision to purchase a product be affected by the amount of miles it had travelled?

Flower farming in Kenya. Each flower imported into the UK creates far more than its own weight in CO_2.

© AFP/Getty Images

employee work at home and not travel to work? Can telephone/video conferencing be used to avoid travel?

Other factors: site access, health and safety, noise, etc.: Increased car ownership means more workers drive to work. Insufficient parking space may be available. Larger delivery vehicles may have difficulty approaching and manoeuvring around within the site. Problems of noise, inhalation of toxic fumes, visual intrusion, etc. become an on-site as well as off-site problem. Dealing with these problems can be considered an internal issue, not related to sustainability issues, but they do relate back. Take parking. If employees drive to work and you have the land, why not pave it over? But land is expensive, and there may be more productive uses for it. Moreover, paving land has a significant impact on water resource problems. People pave over their gardens for parking. Firms provide car parks to satisfy employees (what more emotive issue can there be in any organization than parking?). But paving over reduces the area into which water can soak to build up ground water reserves, and the rain runs into drains and to the sea.

Internal/ external

Stakeholders

Company travel plans: Unlike the local transport plans which UK local authorities produce, these plans (also called 'green transport plans') are for a company or organization. But they do relate to local transport plans, and are usually developed in close consultation with the local authority and public transport operators, and also with other employers facing the same issues. Studies show that even limited travel plans can achieve 3–5% reductions in the number of employees travelling to work alone by car, and more ambitious plans which include such measures as public transport discounts and parking restrictions on site can achieve 15–30% reductions, or even more, within two to four years. Environmental sense is good economic sense. Research shows that it typically costs a firm £300–£500 per year to maintain a car parking space, but to operate a travel plan costs only £47 a year per full-time employee. It will be useful to take one example of a company travel plan as the main case study as it illustrates so much. But before we do this, we need to consider for this whole section: what does sustainable development actually mean to business (and government)?

The significance of sustainable development for business

Values

The previous sections have indicated how a business may review its operations and interpret them in a sustainable development context. But would they all want to? Would it not reduce their profits?

Critics accuse some companies of being against sustainable development measures. The oil company EXXON has been accused of funding pressure groups that cast doubt on the scientific basis of predictions of global warming. Other companies are accused of using their sustainable development or 'green' initiatives as a way of advertising but without any serious basis to them, while others are accused of using them to cover up other undesirable aspects of their business ('greenwash'). For instance, as Chapter 2 showed, Tesco has been accused of doing this to cover up the hold it has developed on the food and convenience goods business, driving many small operators out who might have sourced goods from the local market area, and been actually much more sustainable than Tesco in their operations.

Equally, the suggestion is made that many companies may see sustainable development initiatives as expensive frills which interfere with making profits, and they only engage in them to the extent that it generates good publicity and promotes the image of their products generally. No doubt this may be so in some cases. But there is mounting evidence that companies are taking more and more notice of sustainable development issues, both because of straight issues of survival, and because they realize it makes good business sense, and also presents business opportunities.

Spatial levels

Companies with global operations, such as the banks HSBC and Standard Chartered, will be highly conscious of the risks that global warming presents. Apart from increased insurance premiums, they face the risk that many of their global operations may simply be submerged by rising sea levels. Equally, looking at current operations from a sustainability point of view actually starts to indicate that there may be a lot of money to save. And the business opportunities which are possible by responding to global warming have been estimated to be about £500 billion, so there is much for the enterprising company to go for.

Many companies have already determined to become carbon neutral in their operations. BSkyB was the first company in the FTSE100 to become carbon neutral in 2006. Having said that, remember that only four of the world's ten largest companies have targets for reducing CO_2, and many would think that these are the companies that should be leading the way (Uren, 2006).

We may also look dispassionately at what government is doing. One would get the impression from the foregoing discussion that government at all levels is working hard to promote sustainable development. The UK government and the European Union have numerous measures to promote it, and there are many international agreements. However, we should consider many aspects of the discussion in a wider perspective that merges into considerations addressed in other chapters of this book. Indeed, we have already hinted at this in our earlier discussion of links to world trade agreements. Many environmental objectives and measures conflict with measures and objectives in other parts of the economy. It is said that politics is the art of the possible, and governments try to stay in power by seeming to satisfy as many as possible of the conflicting objectives of as many pressure groups and stakeholders in society as possible. Thus, the best possible gloss will be put on every aspect of government activity. A sharp observer needs to watch out for 'greenwash' not only from companies, but from government too.

Looking ahead

Sustainable development is headline news. The global environmental crisis makes progress with sustainable development policies an immediate priority, but yet progress seems to be slow, and voices raised against doing anything at all still strident. Where will we be in another five or ten years? Much depends on a variety of imponderable factors. Clearly, if we carry on as we are the future looks gloomy. Climate change, along with environmental degradation and exhaustion of key resources, especially oil, promise us extended periods of global instability, if not widespread war, within the next 5–15 years. It does not seem sensible in this situation to talk about environmental protection measures leading to a slowdown in economic growth, as economic growth will have collapsed as a result of not doing anything.

On the other hand, some not very improbable events could radically change the prospects for achieving sustainable development. One such might be a change of policy direction in the USA, which at present produces about a quarter of global warming emissions. A commitment to sign up to the Kyoto Treaty could have a distinct knock-on effect. The portents in this direction seem quite favourable, and once it had happened the energizing impetus of the 'can do' effect of American governmental support for sustainable development policies could lead to fast change in many related areas. Equally, we seem to be on the threshhold of both technical change which may produce rapid change in many areas, such as the evolution of cheaper non-polluting power sources, and of political change, where public attitudes are changing cumulatively, making many environmental measures more publicly acceptable. We have of course to hope that this is the scenario which actually occurs.

Summary

- Until the last two hundred years man made very little impact on this planet. But since about 1800 cumulative processes have led to a situation where in the last 30–40 years we see ourselves faced with a variety of disasters induced by climate change, and threats to economic, social and political stability, through to resources shortages and environmental pollution
- The idea and strategy of sustainable development is put forward as a way of ensuring that we collectively live within the constraints of our resources, and the capacity of the environment to absorb the effects of our presence on the planet
- Sustainable development involves cooperative action at global, national and local level. Governments at all levels may set frameworks of laws and regulations involving a variety of market and non-market tools to keep the impact of our activities on the environment within acceptable limits
- Business in all its forms is a central part of this process, being both a major source of the problems in the first place, but also a major contributor to solving them, and also a major beneficiary in many ways from having them solved.

In conclusion:

- Business activity is a major contributor to global environmental problems (though not everyone agrees with this)
- And global environmental problems are a major threat to business activity
- But global environmental problems are also a potential opportunity for business
- Concepts of sustainable development provide a framework for global thinking and local action
- Most areas of business activity can be reframed in the light of these concepts to make a contribution to sustainable development, while at the same time in most cases actually improving its economic efficiency

Case study: sustainable transport for a large business: the case of Leeds Metropolitan University

There were 2,287,540 students in UK higher education in 2004/2005. A high percentage live away from home, or come from abroad (some 318,395) and they are heavy consumers of transport. There were 109,625 full-time academic staff, and 51,030 part-time staff, plus many administrative and support staff. Higher education is a large foreign currency earner. It is big business. But some universities are massive, and equate with very large corporations both in their financial turnover, and in the environmental footprint generated by their transport activities. Thus, you, the reader, and every student in the UK is directly and intimately connected with this chapter's theme, and you have your part to play.

Leeds Metropolitan University is a good example. It is one of the largest universities in the country, with 52,000 students and 3,500 staff. Its turnover is about £135 millions per annum. Of course, its economic impact is far larger than this, as the student body is a not insignificant proportion of the total population of the city, and they are all consumers and spenders. The university has three major campuses. One of the campuses is on the edge of the city centre, on a restricted site. A second campus is five miles north from the city centre, on an outstanding but inaccessible parkland site (see photo below), while a third campus is fifteen miles away in Harrogate. Figure 15.5 illustrates the distribution

of the various facilities in Leeds itself, and you can see the potential transport problems as a result.

The central campus has always had restricted parking facilities, and staff pay for spaces. The suburban campus has more parking space, and free parking has been an attraction for students with cars. The central and suburban campuses lie on one of the most congested traffic arteries in the city (leading out to affluent commuter suburbs and dormitory towns in the Yorkshire Dales). (Adjacent to the city campus is Leeds University campus with a further 33,000 students.) Some faculties are split between sites, and students and staff move daily between the two campuses creating further traffic. The area between the Leeds campuses is densely populated with Victorian houses subdivided into student flats. The relationship of the university in the city to the overall problems of daily urban traffic congestion and long term sustainability are obvious. (The sites described above can be viewed via Google Earth—download to your PC from Google. Find Leeds, then look for Otley Road north out of the city. Compare the photograph of the suburban campus reproduced below with the Google Earth view. What do you notice?)

Stakeholders

The university works closely with the City Council, and with transport operators, in order to progress its various planned developments.

Headingley Campus of Leeds Metropolitan University in late 2000

Source: Estates Department, Leeds Metropolitan University

Figure 15.5 Location of main university facilities in Leeds

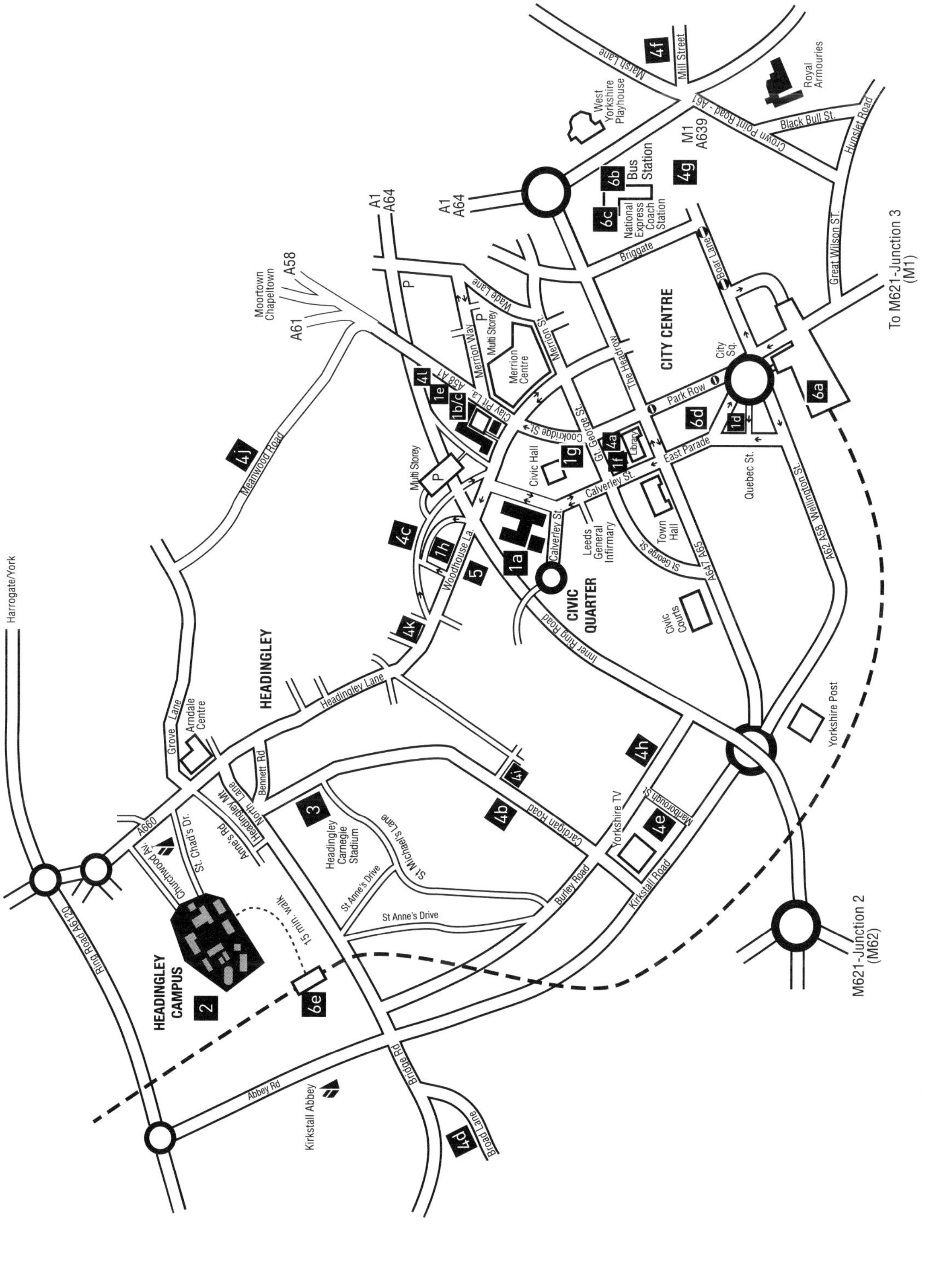

Note: Central area 'Civic Quarter' sites are 1a to 1h; suburban site or Headingley campus is 2; and student residences are 3a to 3j.

Source: www.leedsmet.ac.uk

It is required to develop a 'green transport plan', to show that its plans are within a sustainable development framework. It would do this anyway as it has its own sustainability policy and environmental objectives (in fact, in 2007, the university won the accolade of 'greenest university' in the UK). The university has been developing its environmental transport strategy since 1999, and it published its first 10-year plan in 2002 (these are available on its website at www.leedsmet.ac.uk), but such plans are never once and for all things, as the university grows continuously (4% student growth per annum), and plans are constantly reviewed and updated. The 2002 plan had targets, inter alia, relating to increasing the level of walking, cycling and public transport use, and reducing single occupant car use from 45.5% to 30% for staff, and 25% to 12% for students. Halfway into the plan there has been significant progress on some targets due to improvements in rail services, public transport discount schemes, and increased university presence in the Leeds central area. But single occupant car use has reduced only slightly, and attention is moving to traffic management measures focusing on the suburban campus. In 2002 46% of staff travelled to this campus by car, but only 21% did so to the central area sites. The problem is difficult. The suburban site is relatively inaccessible, and only two access roads lead into the very large campus through residential areas. Improving site access so that public transport and delivery vehicles can access the campus easily, even before the introduc-

tion of more stringent traffic management, necessitated the removal of much on-street parking within the campus (did you look at Google Earth to see what the difference was compared to 2000?). But parking was still largely unrestricted: whether staff or student you could drive around until you found a space. From August 2007 parking has been charged for, and annual passes for staff allocated according to a transparent eligibility procedure with annual charges related to income. No passes are available for students.

❷ Compare the situation at Leedsmet with your own university or college. Has your institution got a green transport plan? If not, do you think it should have one?

❷ Ask your classmates how they get to the campus, and whether they would consider changing their travel behaviour if they currently drive. If not, why not?

❷ Do you agree with the view that it is wrong to charge employees for parking on a business property? Surely this is an expense which should be absorbed by the business or organization?

❷ How would you assess a proposal to allocate passes by a balloting process, with everyone, staff and students, having an equal chance of getting one?

Review and discussion questions

1   It is sometimes argued that climate change has positive aspects for business, e.g. melting polar ice caps reduces transport distances for some sea voyages. Consider what other positive aspects of climate change there might be for business, and how they compare to the costs of climate change.

2   How would you respond to someone who argued that business had no real interest in becoming more environmentally responsible, and only compulsion by government would bring about change in business practices?

3   There are still groups who argue that the changes associated with what is described as 'global warming' fall within the range of natural variation, and policies to

change business practices to counter its effects will impose needless costs on the economy and yet not make any difference to what is happening. What would you say in response to such arguments?

4   'Market' approaches to environmental regulation are increasingly preferred to 'non-market' approaches, and are gaining more public acceptability in areas like paying for road use. But do you feel that the public will accept the idea of paying for the amount of rubbish each household produces? What problems do you foresee in implementing such a policy?

5   What would you say if you heard someone express the view that global environmental problems are too complex and too far away for individuals and businesses to have any influence on them?

Assignments

1 Look at the environmental policies of your own university or college, or one near you. Does the institution you have chosen seem to be addressing the issues raised in this chapter?

2 Use the Climate Analysis Indicator Tool (CAIT) available at www.wri.org (register first) and compare the GHG emissions of the UK with the USA and with two other countries with lower emission levels. You can easily navigate and pick from the list of countries. Print the

screen results so that you can compare them more easily. What do you conclude?

3 Visit the website of a FTSE100 company of your choice and study critically its environmental profile. (See the list of FTSE100 companies at uk.finance.yahoo.com/. Click on FTSE100 and the list appears. Choose a company and type its name in the Google, Yahoo or other search engine.) Each company has a lot of environment-related information on its site. Does it convince you?

Further reading

Blair, A. and Hitchcock, D. (2001) *Environment and Business* (London: Routledge). Provides a useful contextualization of environmental issues into business, and will allow many aspects of this chapter to be explored in greater depth.

Hutchinson, A. and Hutchinson, F. (1997) *Environmental Business Management: Sustainable Development in the New Millennium* (London: McGraw-Hill). A good text on the practical implementation of environmental strategies in business organizations.

Ison, S., Peake, S. and Wall, S. (2002) *Environmental Issues and Policies* (London: Prentice Hall). A rigorous but readable background to many of the technical, theoretical and policy issues discussed in this chapter.

Starkey, R. and Welford, R. (eds) (2001) *The Earthscan Reader in Business and Sustainable Development* (London: Earthscan). A collection of readings that looks critically at the real involvement of business with sustainable development, but also its capacity to do more.

Online resources

Test your understanding of this chapter with online questions and answers, explore the subject further through web exercises, and use the weblinks to provide a quick resource for further research. Go to the Online Resource Centre at

www.oxfordtextbooks.co.uk/orc/ wetherly_otter/

The following suggestions are a tiny proportion of even the most useful sites. Generally, surf with care, and consider whether promoters of a site have an axe to grind.

The quality daily newspapers:
www.guardian.co.uk

www.times.co.uk

www.telegraph.co.uk

www.independent.co.uk

Government departments and related organizations:
www.defra.gov.uk: DEFRA (Department of Environment, Food and Rural Affairs) provides UK sustainability reports and much more.

www.dft.gov.uk: The Department for Transport provides material on environment/transport related issues, including the company travel plans.

www.parliament.uk/commons/: House of Commons Environment, Transport and Regional Affairs Committee.

UK local authority sites all have the same address format, e.g. Leeds City Council is www.leeds.gov.uk

European sites:
www.europa.eu: European Union general site

www.eea.dk/: European Environment Agency

http://ue.eu.intcomm/dg11/index_en.htm: European Union Environment Directorate

Various United Nations sites:
www.oneworld.org/uned-uk: UN Commission for Environment and Development

www.un.org/esa/sustdev/csd.htm: UN Commission for Sustainable Development

http://unep.frw.uva.nl: UN Environment Programme (UNEP)

Environmental pressure groups, e.g.:
www.foe.org.uk: Friends of the Earth

www.greenpeace.org.uk: Greenpeace

Other environmental websites:
www.wri.org: The World Resources Institute. Especially useful for issues related to global warming. You can register to use the Climate Change Analysis Tool which allows you to create your own analyses, looking at particular variables and countries. Figure 15.3 was created using this tool.

www.ieep.org.uk: Institute for European Environmental Policy

Websites of complete courses on sustainable development: watch out for reputable sources. The following from which Table 15.1 was adapted, is a good example:
web.dcp.ufl.edu/ckibert/Poland/index.htm

References

Bracken, D. (2005) *The World Trade Organization and Sustainable Development: a Guide to the Debate* (Chatham House, www.chathamhouse.org.uk)

Crosbie, L. and Knight, K. (1995) *Strategy for Sustainable Business: Environmental Opportunity and Strategic Choice* (London: McGraw-Hill).

DEFRA (2005a) *Securing the Future: UK Government Sustainable Development Strategy*, www.sustainable-development.gov.uk

DEFRA (2005b) *The Validity of Food Miles as an Indicator of Sustainable Development*, Department of Environment, Food and Rural Affairs.

DEFRA (2006) *Sustainable Development Indicators in your Pocket 2006*, www.sustainable-development.gov.uk

DfT (2002) *Making Travel Plans Work: Lessons from UK Case Studies*, Department for Transport, at: www.dft.gov.uk

HM Treasury/DfT (2006) *The Eddington Transport Study: The Case for Action: Sir Rod Eddington's Advice to Government*, HM Treasury/Department for Transport, www.hm-treasury.gov.uk

HM Treasury (2006) *The Economics of Climate Change: the Stern Review*, www.hm-treasury.gov.uk

Hutchinson, A. and Hutchinson, F. (1997) *Environmental Business Management: Sustainable Development in the New Millennium* (London: McGraw-Hill).

International Energy Agency (2001) *Towards a Sustainable Energy Future* (Paris: OECD).

Ison, S., Peake, S. and Wall, S. (2002) *Environmental Issues and Policies* (London: Prentice Hall).

Meadows, D. H., Meadows, D. L., Randers, J. and Behrens, W. (1972) *Limits to Growth* (Washington, DC: Potomac Associates).

Sustainable Development Commission (2005) *Climate Change Programme Review: the Submission of the Sustainable Development Commission to HM Government*.

Uren, S. (2006) Only four of the world's 10 largest companies have targets for reducing carbon dioxide, *Guardian*, 6 November 2006, also: www.forumforthefuture.org.uk

WCED (1987) *Our Common Future*, UN World Commission on Environment and Development/Oxford University Press.

Conclusion: themes and issues—looking ahead

Dorron Otter and Paul Wetherly

Contents

16

Learning objectives

- Give a broad overview of the likely future trends in the business environment
- Integrate the main predictions from the 'Looking ahead' sections of the previous chapters
- Develop your own views as to the changing nature of the business environment

Themes

Diversity	**Diversity of business**
	While we have explored the diversity of the business world, one common problem all businesses share is that the future is uncertain. It is important that all businesses are able to try to minimize this uncertainty by looking ahead.
Internal/ external	**Internal/external**
	Inevitably the future will bring external changes to the business environment and it is how businesses react to these changes that is important.
Complexity	**Complexity of the environment**
	We have explored the complexity of the business environment and how difficult it is to predict change. However, we have also seen that there are a range of techniques we can use to try and make sense of this future uncertainty, and this chapter will make use of the PEST framework to map out the general possible shape of the future business environment.
Spatial levels	**Variety of spatial levels**
	Globalization and technology are dramatically altering the distance between the spatial levels. One major area of interest is the degree to which inequality between people and regions will close or widen in the future.
Dynamic	**Dynamic environment**
	The one certain thing that can be said about the future is that it will be uncertain and that change is a dynamic process.
Interaction	**Interaction between business and the environment**
	How will businesses both manage future changes and in turn what will be their impact on the future of the business environment? Business activity has an enormous impact on our future lives.
Stakeholders	**Stakeholders**
	The recognition of the influence that business will play on the future of humanity means that we will have to consider the full range of stakeholders involved in and affected by business decisions.
Values	**Values**
	How we make sense of the impact of changes depends on our ethical values. There is the hope as we move on into the 21st century that these values will become a central concern to business decision-makers.

Introduction

Looking back to Chapter 1, we saw the contradictory nature of our claims to be able to use fore-casting techniques to analyse the future. Whilst we argued that there are a range of techniques that can enable businesses to gain a sense of where they are at present and that may then act as a guide to determining their strategic response, we need to be aware that they operate in a world of risk and uncertainty and that present predictions can in the future turn out to be wrong.

Complexity

However, the main thrust of this book has been to show that by a careful examination of under-lying political, economic, social and technological factors we can identify important themes and features of the business environment which can help us to better understand business behaviour in the present as well as having a tentative stab at predicting future changes.

This chapter will bring together the main outlines of what is likely to happen within the business environment in the next few years. The structure of the book was intended to allow you first to develop the broad PEST framework developed in Chapter 1 and which was then first applied to the context of the UK. We then sought to outline the main trends in the business environment by examining each aspect of the PEST framework and then focusing on what we see as the key issues shaping it.

Each chapter ended with a short 'Looking ahead' section where we explored the things that are most likely to develop in the future in each of the key issue areas. This chapter seeks to knit together the common threads in these predictions using the PEST framework and so look ahead to the future trends in the business environment. Having worked through the rest of the book you should be in a position to develop your own views as to the shape of the business environment in general and how this may impact and be affected by individual areas of business activity. Please feel free to disagree with this particular overview!

The nature of changes in the business environment is itself often contradictory and uncertain. Change can be achingly slow and sometimes extraordinarily rapid. It is difficult to appreciate the changes that are taking place over a long time when we are most often concentrating on the 'noise' of the here and now. There are contradictions in the evidence that we see and as Chapter 2 showed not all people see the same evidence and draw the same conclusions.

Complexity

> **⮂ Stop and Think**
>
> Ultimately business behaviour is shaped by human beings in their particular business environments. To what extent do we always behave rationally? Are you as an individual always rational in your beliefs and behaviours or has chance played a significant role in your life?

There is a search in academic life for rational explanations in how change occurs and many of us hope that in the end no matter how 'messy' the environmental influences might be, we will be able to explain why things have occurred and therefore attempt to predict on this basis why things might occur. Equally there are analysts who argue that we have to accept that we are all living in an uncertain world where the information we have is imperfect and that change will not be rational and predictable. In this view it is chance events and the way in which we respond to these that is the driver of change. We have also stressed in the book that while we can separate out the indi-vidual changes in the PEST framework, in reality many of these operate at the same time and interrelate in complex ways.

In order to get a better idea of the possible future developments in the business environment it is vital to look back into the past. While the past is not a reliable guide to the future, history does enable us to learn a lot about ourselves. Indeed the future business environment will be dominated by attempts to try and secure the stable path of peace and prosperity that was so difficult to achieve in the 20th century. In order to look ahead to the future we need to look back! This is the focus of the next section.

When looking ahead we can take varying positions ranging from outright optimism as to what is likely to happen to dire pessimism. It will be interesting to see where you feel you lie on this continuum!

Mini-Case 16.1 What do young people think of the future?

In January 2007 The Future Leaders Survey 2006–2007 conducted by the sustainable-development charity Forum for the Future and the Universities and Colleges Admissions Service (UCAS), was published. This survey received responses from 54,240 young people aged 17–21 who had applied to universities and colleges for the academic year 2006–2007, and asked them about their hopes and fears for the future in 25 years time. A narrow majority expected the quality of life in the UK to have improved but 91 per cent thought climate change would have a serious impact and 80 per cent thought that inequality between rich and poor countries would have grown. Most people believed that global oil reserves would run out and that many more wild animals would be extinct. While most were optimistic that human civilization would survive into the next century 76 per cent believed that lifestyles would need to change radically.

The majority felt that they were more affected by crime, less healthy, more worried about the future and more materialistic than their parents and yet also felt that in the future they would look for happiness more than money. This they felt would be found in such things as having an interesting job and spending time with family and friends.

There were differences between men and women in their responses. In general women were more pessimistic about the future quality of life and more likely to do something about this now by taking positive action to change their lifestyles.

When asked who was responsible for the changes needed to make the world a better place it was thought that this was the role of governments, individuals and businesses (in that order) with education and the media also having a role.

❷ What are the main implications that can be drawn from how young people in this survey are viewing the business environment?

❷ What are the opportunities and threats that these findings might present for businesses if they accept them as being likely to occur?

❷ How far are your own views in accord with the findings in this survey?

(*Source*: www.forumforthefuture.org.uk)

> ➲ *Stop and Think*
> What are your hopes and fears as to the nature of the future business environment in which you will live and work?

Looking back to the future

The aim of this section is to briefly review the key features of the 20th century that will shape the 21st century. There are lessons that policy makers seek to learn from this experience, and of course irrespective of what those lessons are, we cannot escape from the specific ways in which, from local to global, the business environment was shaped by decisions taken during this century. There remain fundamental disagreements as to the exact nature of the lessons that people feel should be learned and the particular strengths/weaknesses in the environment that have been developed.

Dynamic

The history of the 20th century can be seen as the gradual and, in some cases, painful development of modern capitalist political and economic systems with each country working out its own specific ways of combining the state and the market economy. In the first half of the 20th century the deep problems that faced the continued growth in the industrial world were seen to be primarily the failure to appreciate the importance of the role of governments in ensuring economic efficiency at the national level, and in promoting effective economic and political relations between countries. Economic relations between countries were hindered by the absence of adequate rules to regulate trade, and the inability to develop political mechanisms to resolve the rivalry between countries resulted in the catastrophic conflicts of two world wars.

The global business environment post-1945

Three worlds

The global order after 1945 could be characterized as consisting of three different worlds. The 'first' world was composed of the 'western' leading industrial nations led by the USA, and the 'second world' was the communist countries of the USSR, the countries of eastern Europe with which it was allied after the Second World War as well as the new People's Republic of China. We discussed the broad shape of the business environment that these countries tried to develop, in Chapter 2.

    In the post war period many of the former colonies of the western European powers, e.g. India and many countries in Africa and the Far East, fought for and gained independence, and now their policy makers had a choice to make: to pursue the first world capitalist economic model or the second world of communism. In the optimism of the birth of new nations anything seemed possible and many countries argued for a 'third world' model. The use of the term 'third world' did not mean to imply inferiority. Far from it. It was the belief that by studying how industrialized countries had developed, the new developing countries could copy their successes, avoid their failures and recognize that in trying to develop now, the circumstances they faced were very different and therefore required different approaches. Crucially there was a belief amongst many of these countries that, if they were to develop rapidly, they would need to protect themselves in terms of world trade, whilst seeking to exploit their huge advantages in terms of cheap labour and primary resources. It was also felt that in order to grow quickly such countries would need more direct forms of government intervention.

    While there were clear differences in the ways in which countries in these worlds sought to organize their business environments, at the time each group of countries was optimistic that their systems would work in their individual contexts.

The first world order

Given the instability of the inter-war period, there was a desire amongst national policy makers in the 'first world' to devise a system of international rules which would prevent protectionist trading policies and so help build national and world economic trade, development and growth whilst avoiding political conflict. As the USA was the strongest country after the Second World War, its policy makers were determined to create a future world where international trade could take place to secure markets for its output. However, there were strong economic arguments, (coming especially from the economist J. M. Keynes), that there needed to be a recognition that countries, especially the war ravaged countries of western Europe, needed help in building up their national economies so that they could compete on a world scale. In order for them to do so they might need the help of trade protection in the short term. The vision was that over time and through a progressive series of trade negotiations (or rounds of trade talks) trade barriers would eventually be removed and trade would be free of restrictions. At the heart of this was the General Agreement on Tariffs and Trade (from 1947) which became the World Trade Organization in 1995 (now with 150 members). It was felt that, by allowing countries time to build up their competitive strengths and by getting them to sign up to targets for tariff reduction, eventually all countries would be able to trade freely. International agreements and promises would prevent individual countries trying to 'go it alone' and a return to the protectionist policies of the inter-war period.

    In 1944 the negotiations for the future of the world political and economic system took place in the USA in the small New Hampshire town of Bretton Woods. At the political level there was a desire amongst the western nations to rebuild their economies as quickly as possible and to seek to integrate these into both an economic and political block to resist the rise of the 'second' world of communism in the Soviet Union and its satellite countries in eastern Europe. These countries

Diversity

Spatial levels

Diversity

were not involved in the Bretton Woods talks and sought or were forced to stay within their own communist bloc. In the East there was a determination to prevent Japan from ever again becoming a dominant military power. Here too there was the need to secure an economic environment where friendly countries could develop along capitalist lines and avoid falling under the influence of the USSR and the newly emerging communist China.

Spatial levels

At the global level it was hoped that the formation of the United Nations would help nations come together to resolve differences without recourse to war and this was established in 1945. To bind together the capitalist countries in a military alliance, NATO (the North Atlantic Treaty Organization) was established in 1947. Within western Europe the process of integration began with the formation of the European Economic Community (in 1959).

In 1945, in order to develop a stable global financial system to support the development of this world economic system, the International Monetary Fund was established. Its aim was to help countries who experience balance of payments problems borrow money to help them finance their debts whilst adopting policies to improve their international competitiveness. Just as it was accepted that Europe would need inflows of capital, (especially from the USA), either as foreign direct investment or in the form of official aid (the Marshall plan), so it was accepted that many of the poorer countries of the world would need development assistance if they too were going to be in a position to compete in the new world economic order. At the same time the International Bank for Re-construction and Development or as it is most often called, the World Bank, was established for this purpose.

At the global level, trade expanded rapidly both in terms of the amount and its importance to the world economy, as measured by ratio of world merchandise exports to world GDP. However, the pattern of trade was highly influenced by this division within the world economy. Developing countries exported mainly primary products, agricultural goods and minerals, while Europe and North America exported manufactured goods and increasingly a range of services and high technology goods. The system of trade rules, whilst allowing for the gradual reduction of tariffs across a wide range of manufactured goods and services, also allowed persistently high tariffs to protect the agricultural goods produced by European and North American farmers. Communist countries stayed out of this system and formed their own trading alliances.

Domestic business environment in the first world

Political, economic and technological environment

At the domestic level, developed capitalist economies began to develop a different approach to managing their economies. As we have seen, this involved a much greater role for the state in providing welfare systems, supporting industry and overseeing the macroeconomic environment (see Chapter 6). In Britain this has been called the 'Keynesian welfare consensus' and in western Europe, the 'social market'. There was a widespread acceptance of the need for governments to intervene both at the macro and microeconomic levels as well as in directly taking responsibility for social transformation in the fields of education, health and social security.

For many commentators, the period 1945–mid 1970s in the first world was 'the golden era', with an unprecedented period of economic growth. In 1957 the Conservative Prime Minister, Harold Macmillan was attributed with the phrase 'You have never had it so good', and in the 1960s the Labour Prime Minister, Harold Wilson, talked of the future being 'forged by the white heat of technology'.

There was a general rise in prosperity, and the big gains in productivity brought about by the increase in mass production techniques and constant technological improvement meant that people could also become mass consumers. House ownership soared and the reductions in the prices of household goods coupled with rising wages meant that people could fill their houses with a range of consumer goods. Car ownership rose as well, and the expansion of air travel fuelled by the growing charter companies, brought foreign travel within the reach of the average household.

Social environment

The rapid rise in living standards was remarkable, and brought about profound changes in the social and cultural lives of people. Some went as far as to argue that there was indeed a social revolution and the term the 'swinging sixties' was coined to try to capture the mood. A particular focus was on young people bringing to the fore the importance of the music industry, especially pop and rock, and the arts in general. The development of television was another major factor. Great improvements were made in health and education. A change in attitudes towards sex and marriage ushered in, what was called, in the UK, 'the permissive society' and a much more liberal atmosphere regarding individual behaviour. However, for many these changes did not go far enough.

It was not just this perceived slowness to achieve social change that caused people to protest. Against the background of rising prosperity the tension between the superpowers of the USA and the USSR, and their respective allies, meant that there was a real fear of a nuclear war. There were also protests on a range of issues from the American war in Vietnam, the apartheid regime in South Africa, campaigns against nuclear arms and a growing awareness of the environment. As Higher Education expanded this social activism was particularly marked amongst students.

Gender relations were altered by this change in attitudes and the rise of feminism and the development of a more reliable range of contraceptives, including the pill, together with the greater need for labour helped to create the conditions where women were able to challenge for equal opportunities with men.

Another major change in many developed countries was large scale immigration as people from former colonies arrived to fill the vacancies that economic growth was providing. Whilst the impetus for this came from the need for businesses to attract new sources of labour as the economy grew, the social environment for immigrants could be hostile. Fears were raised about the possible damage that immigration could create and there was a rise in racist activity. A particular pattern of immigration was established with concentrations of people from particular regions of the world choosing to settle in particular local areas. For policy makers this posed a challenge. How should this new found diversity be handled?

Lessons to be learned?

The optimism of the 1950s and 1960s was knocked by the severe economic crisis that many countries across the world experienced in the 1970s. In the developed countries the type of balances that had been struck between the role of the state in intervening in the economy and the market appeared now not to be working and the oil price rises of the 1970s posed great strains on these economies. This sudden and unexpected rise in oil prices was a result of willingness of the oil producers, especially in the Middle East, to exert their political and economic power. This brought into stark view the degree to which oil underpins the technologies that create the economic prosperity of the developed world.

Across the range of developed economies government budgets were under severe strain. In the Communist world, especially of the Soviet Union and eastern Europe, it was increasingly recognized that the systems were suffering from economic stagnation and that a policy change was needed. In the developing countries, against a back drop of spiralling debt problems, (especially in Latin America), and falls in living standards in Africa it appeared that their attempts to adopt a different model of development had failed.

However, it was clear many of the countries in Southeast Asia were industrializing very rapidly. These so called 'Asian Tigers' (e.g. Hong-Kong, Taiwan, Singapore, South Korea and Thailand) were experiencing very rapid growth, and at the same time were exporting a range of manufactured and high technology goods. The lessons appeared obvious from these regions that the path to growth lay down the route of globalization and that this meant rapid trade liberalization. A recent convert to this economic policy was also China with a move to 'an open door' policy in the late 1970s.

This period at the end of the 1970s and into the 1980s saw a change in the nature of the ideas about the policies that it was felt were now needed to be adopted across the world at national level and the thinking that took place at the supranational level. On the right wing of the political spectrum and the neoclassical school of economic thought came the belief that the lesson that needed to be learned is that there is no substitute for the free market at both the national and global level. In this analysis the best way to create an ideal business environment was to go back to basic economic principles as embodied in what came to be called the 'Washington Consensus' (see Chapter 12). It is enterprise, competition, free trade and technological change that are key.

This could be seen to be a step change in the process of globalization. The adoption of new economic policies based on the liberalization of markets in the developed world spread to the developing world, especially in Latin America and India. In the late 1980s the collapse of the Soviet Union and the rapid changes in eastern Europe saw these countries eager to effect a transition from state planning to market liberalization. Chapter 12 highlighted the optimism embodied in the 'Washington Consensus' that implied that there was essentially one road for all in the development of capitalism.

However, as we saw this experiment in the restoration of free market policies itself was to come under attack from structuralist economists and political commentators from the left (even if not very far to the left). The actual experience of implementing these policies appeared not to be so simple and created short term economic and social instability. It is argued that the lessons from the 20th century need to be reappraised and it to these views that we will now turn.

Looking ahead: the political environment

A new approach to combining the state and the market?

Internal/ external

The key feature of the political environment of business is the relationship between the market and the state. We have seen that, in relation to business, the political process is important in that it can potentially provide the essential support mechanisms for the operation of the market, or equally it can hinder the development of business growth.

There is also general agreement that it is economies which operate within a stable capitalist system that are the most successful, and that for capitalism to exist as an economic system it must be supported by appropriate political institutions and processes as well as rules to ensure fairness.

This section seeks to explore the future relationship between the political and economic environment of business. As we saw in Chapter 2, there are fierce disagreements about the precise nature of capitalism.

Is there a new consensus?

Chapter 4 showed that there is still a distinction to be drawn between the left and right. For the right the emphasis is on creating a free and open market within which there is a limited role for the government. For the left there is more scope for government intervention in response to widespread market failures and the need to address deep rooted and persistent inequalities. Green critics argue that there is a problem with the narrow pursuit of economic growth inherent in many economies and there is urgent need for political action to curb pollution.

Diversity

The dominant view about the best political system is that there is a need for open, accountable and transparent governments. It is argued that it is democratic systems that are the best way of promoting these features. Within such systems there tends to be political stability with clear property rights and the rule of law to protect people in the pursuit of their economic goals. However, in many places of the world democracy is fragile and internal conflicts between ethnic and religious groupings make its development very difficult and indeed dangerous. There are many examples where business can flourish even in the absence of 'western' style democratic systems and capitalism is capable of developing within different political systems. The success of the newly industrialized countries is evidence of this. In China, the communist party maintains its grip on political power and has blocked democratic reform. It asserts its right to develop a capitalist economy albeit 'with Chinese characteristics' (the development of a market economic system within a communist political system).

In the developed world, the primary role for the political system, as regards business, lies in enabling macroeconomic stability and then allowing relative freedom at the microeconomic level so that businesses can be free to succeed (or indeed not succeed) according to their own endeavours. Where intervention is justified, it is in relation to areas in which there are market abuses, such as with monopoly power or the breaking of laws, or market failures in areas such as the provision of merit or public goods. Increasingly, attention is also now in the areas of environmental protection.

Businesses themselves have a great deal of political power both in terms of their economic strength and in terms of their ability to influence the political process. Across the world there is disquiet that governments can become too 'pro-business' and that they will fail to control abuses of monopoly power. One clear problem for the political process in democratic countries is that political parties rely on funding from the private sector. It is likely that the issue of party funding will be highlighted in the future with calls for state funding to free parties from the possibility of undue influence.

Interaction

From the perspective of the present, there appears to be general agreement as to the broad features of the nature of the most conducive domestic and global business environment and we explored this in Chapters 2, 3 and 12. The only game in town seems to be the capitalist one, which recognizes that for markets to work efficiently they need to be supported by a range of structures that entail political interventions at both the national and supranational levels. Within the richest countries of the world there is a tendency to see this agreement as a cause of the relative lack of interest that electorates have in the political process. It is difficult to get excited about political battles if they take place only in the centre ground, and in the affluent countries most political systems are dominated by two parties with very little in the way of policy difference between them. However, in many ways this relative lack of sharp disagreement shows the success that the developed countries have had in developing stable political systems.

However, even small differences in approach can still result in changes in policy that can have significant impacts on businesses and it is still the case that there are broad left–right perspectives. A stable political system does not mean that political decisions cease. In reality government policies are constantly changing and affect businesses both directly and indirectly. Businesses cannot afford to take a position of disinterest in political decisions.

As the 20th century ended we saw the development of the view that markets need supporting structures and that exactly how policies were to be implemented required careful thought, both in terms of the precise sequence of steps that might need to be taken, and the speed at which they might need to occur. It is also increasingly acknowledged that different countries might need to do things differently even when pursuing the same goals. This was discussed at the global level in Chapter 12, and the domestic economic policy changes were outlined in Chapter 6. The political and legal debates were outlined in Chapter 4 and Chapters 10 and 13.

Challenges for the future political environment

The future will be concerned with five main issues:

Global governance

Firstly, at developing the institutions and rules that will enable all countries to feel that they are able to share in the benefits of a globalized world. It is still the case that the global order is

Diversity

characterized by sharp income inequality, and that in so many parts of the world there is war, conflict and political instability. Thus looking ahead a major focus will be on our ability to develop the supra-national political and economic institutions to deal with these problems. In the poorest parts of the world the necessary prerequisite for economic growth is political change from within and political and economic support from without. Internally, many governments are far from perfect with abuses of human rights and widespread corruption. Externally it is acknowledged that if these internal reforms are carried out then external advice and direct financial support are needed if the Millennium Goals (see Chapter 12) are in any way to be achieved.

Spatial levels

However, attempts to develop supra-national governing institutions create the fear that national sovereignty is being undermined, and take place in an era when people increasingly want to have more local control over their affairs. At the very time that attention is focused on the development of global political organizations, we see a tendency for people to want to have more local and regional power.

Global power of big business

Values

Stakeholders

Secondly, people are also fearful that the increasing private power of global businesses allows them to circumvent the traditional national safeguards for employees, consumers and the wider stakeholders provided by national governments. Chapter 13 predicted that changes in UK company law do reflect this move to encouraging firms to consider the wider interests of stakeholders (while still laying down that the ultimate interests in the business lie with the owners). The issue of how best to ensure that businesses do not abuse their global market positions and operate in a globally responsible way will be very important (see Chapters 7 and 12).

Global climate change

Interaction

The third challenge is that posed by global warming. Global problems will require global cooperation but will we be able to develop the cooperative instruments that will enable the reductions of carbon emissions to take place? There is a considerable groundswell of pressure from the environmental pressure groups and green issues are widely discussed. However, there need to be changes in our consumption and production patterns and there is a political reluctance to force these changes through and difficulties in getting the international cooperation required.

This partly lies in our own seemingly irrational responses to the prospect of climate change. On the one hand we urge our politicians to take action but when that action appears to conflict with our individual desire to consume we cry foul. In 2007 the British government attempted to test the readiness of the public to accept the wider application of the congestion charge that has been successful in London by asking people to say whether they would accept road pricing generally. To do this a special website was set up by the prime minister's office. The resultant huge and overwhelmingly negative responses to the prospect of road pricing led to the hasty withdrawal of the website!

In the same year the Stern report tried to map out the likely future and show that urgent action was needed. There is a clear message in this report that tries to appeal to the enlightened self interest that we explored in Chapter 7. For Stern, doing nothing in the short term would lead to huge costs caused in the future by global warming. By taking action now the costs (estimated at around 1% of gross domestic product) will be easily recouped by the benefits of the slowdown in our carbon emissions.

There is room for hope, not least because some of the indications of the potential problems are already with us, and there is now widespread acceptance that global warming is a reality. Individuals are showing their willingness to change their shopping habits fuelled partly because of health concerns. Legislation regarding packaging is now much stricter and there is an increase in the amount of energy from renewables. By 2010, 6% of the UKs energy will be supplied by wind power. Supermarkets are improving their labelling so that the environmental cost of the food can be measured. In homes and business there is increasing awareness of the need to conserve energy and there is a commitment to ensure that all new buildings will be carbon neutral by 2010.

However, for many environmental critics this is too little too late. The vast mass of homes, factories and offices emit large amounts of carbon, car ownership and use continue to rise, and the public has an insatiable appetite for air travel which is now the fastest growing source of carbon. There will continue to be pressure from green groups for governments to impose tighter restrictions, taxes and fines on carbon emitters, but the business community will continue to argue for such restraints to be voluntary. Many businesses have already begun to develop environmental audits but always in the hope that cutting such costs will also make good business sense in terms of improving image as well as any real money savings. The real problems will occur when, and if, the need to make deeper cuts to our carbon footprints begins to raise costs in the short and medium term. There is the risk that current attention to environmental and ethical concerns turns out to be about short term fashion choices rather then a long term change in market behaviour.

> ⟳ *Stop and Think*
> What changes in your lifestyle do you think might be needed if you were to lessen your 'carbon footprint'?

Global inequality

The fourth issue concerns the problems of poverty, hunger and conflict that will continue to be a major concern for many of the people in the developing world. Here is the global contradiction. In the developed world, and for some in the developing world, incomes rise and for radical and green critics the laws of economics need to be fundamentally altered. It is not scarcity that is the basis of the economic problems in the economically and politically powerful communities but abundance that is the real economic problem. In contrast many people do not appear to share in this growth and the gap between income groups causes the potential for great unrest.

Spatial levels

Global political instability

Finally, it is not only the threat of global climate change that threatens our future security. Political instability continues to affect many parts of the developing world and this makes it difficult for businesses. Nowhere is this more evident than in the uncertainty over the security of energy supplies as they are to be found in many of these areas. The world has had to cope with this for a long time now but the dramatic and immediate effect of '9/11' brought this instability directly into individual lives. This has continued with subsequent bombings on trains in Madrid and London and in many other places across the world. The war in Iraq and subsequent occupation by the USA and its allies and the war in Afghanistan continue to dominate the international political agenda, in particular highlighting the ethical issues of the limits to national sovereignty and the difficulties of ensuring global cooperation. However, the 'war on terror' brings these issues into our personal lives. The threat of terrorist acts affects all of us in a direct and personal way and is likely to be an ever present danger to personal and business activity.

Interaction

Looking ahead: the economic environment

What is marked about the present economic environment is the relative lack of polarized views as to how economic success can be achieved. This is in contrast to the debates and indeed vastly different economic approaches that were developed in the 20th century. It would be easy to view the future optimistically.

Economic stability and growth

With the exception of Africa and some parts of the Middle East, most countries in the world have experienced steady and indeed in some cases rapid economic growth. There have been threats to this stability but these have largely been resolved by a combination of the global economic institutions managing to steady the international economy, and by internal economic reforms, and so the world economic outlook remains very positive. Compared to the economic recessions and 'boom and bust' of the 20th century the new century has dawned with an era of low inflation, high employment and growth in many parts of the world. Even in the case of Africa there is at least agreement on the main priorities for action, even if there are different views as to how this can be achieved, and frustration that promises have not been translated into action. It is to be hoped that in the future such policy advice will be enacted and help provide stability and growth to some of the poorest people on the planet.

There is now a rich source of advice on how to manage modern economic systems. The work of strategists such as Porter in examining how both national and international competitiveness can be established was examined in Chapter 3. We have seen how the development of the structuralist critique of the Washington Consensus has resulted in the acceptance that, whilst different countries may develop different ways of implementing market reforms and do things in a different order, essentially it is through states supporting the market mechanism and only directly intervening in cases of market failure that economic success lies. Of course, as we have seen, this does not mean that we agree as to how we get there.

Complexity

Diversity

We saw in Chapter 2 how difficult it is to forecast economic changes, and even stability can mask short term turbulence. The fact that, on average, growth is rising is no comfort to the individual business. In reality the economic environment facing a particular business is always in flux and the key to maintaining competitive advantage lies in maintaining or boosting productivity. Developed countries have a much better understanding of the main drivers here, and clearly it is the knowledge economy and globalization that will in future drive economic change. We explored how this might occur in Chapter 3, and in Chapter 14 we looked at the possible ways in which enterprises either in the SME sector or in business in general might develop. It was clear that for an entrepreneurial culture to emerge there is a need for government support in terms of advice and skills training.

We have seen that the UK's recent economic record has been remarkable, and that there is broad agreement about the need for governments to adopt a pro-business stance. Chapter 10 showed how the focus of public sector management is geared towards providing the services that will support the private sector.

We will explore the future of technology more fully below, but clearly the recent long term growth rates in the world economy and the rise in general living standards have been fuelled by the revolutions in the new technologies coupled with the remarkable growth of Southeast Asia and especially India and China.

The China effect

This 'China' effect is the cause of much speculation. For many commentators, a major ingredient in the growth of the developed world has been the ability to import low cost goods from the newly industrializing countries, which has kept inflation low and led to a consumer-led boom. Dangers are seen on the horizon. There are fears that the time is coming when the rapid growth of the free market in China will come up against the restrictions imposed by the lack of a democratic structure. The ensuing political instability might cause a decrease in China's growth rate to the detriment of the rest of the world. The Chinese government itself is well aware of what it sees as the threats to the 'harmony' of its economic and political structure. The rising gap between the urban rich and the rural poor in China is very large. Internal migration in China is leading to one of the biggest movements of people in history, and this puts real pressure on the public services in the urban areas. Unskilled rural migrants work in the very low paid construction and services industries and this fuels resentment between the rich and poor. The rapid pursuit of economic growth in China poses a real threat to the natural environment. There is no doubt that the future of the Chinese economy will have a major impact across the world.

> ⤷ *Stop and Think*
> To what extent has the recent economic growth across the world been 'made in China'?

Threats to economic stability and growth

The one certain thing that we can say about the economic environment is to prepare for the unexpected! Despite this outward calm there are many problems facing the world economy and individual national economies.

Environmental protection—threats and opportunities

We have seen that the Stern report points to a future of huge economic costs if we do not take action now, and shows that for this to occur there needs to be international cooperation. Despite recent supportive noises in the USA there is still great uncertainty that there can be a concerted attempt to reduce carbon emissions. There is a cry of double standards from the less developed countries, in that they see requests for them to agree to carbon cuts as being hypercritical when the developed world was able to ignore environmental costs for much of its history, and when they are still the main polluters. Even where countries are at relatively equal levels of development and are locked into cooperating in many other areas such as the EU, the attempts at reducing carbon emissions through the European emissions trading scheme have not been particularly successful. However, as was argued in Chapter 15, perhaps this issue above all will indeed come to assume significant importance as the potential impact is appreciated by governments and business as well as citizens and consumers. Perhaps we are on the verge of the genuine rise of the global citizen and the globally responsible business, and if so, will we see significant changes in the economic environment as sustainability moves to the centre of our concerns?

Spatial levels

There is increasing recognition within the business community about the real pressure on the natural resources of water, food and energy and their implications in terms of future costs of production. Coupled with the need to reduce carbon emissions there are, therefore, real incentives for businesses to try and develop technologies of production that do not rely on carbon burning fuels. It is highly likely that businesses will have to adjust to a world of green taxes, cuts in carbon emissions, green technology and the need to become more energy efficient.

However, this in turn allows businesses to exploit new market opportunities created by the challenge of global warming. There is already evidence that retailers are changing their product ranges in response to changes in demand, and many businesses are targeting ethical and sustainable ways of producing. More directly there is scope for a range of businesses to develop new green technologies.

World trade

There is continued uncertainty about the future of world trade. The success of the Chinese economy has caused balance of payments problems in its trading partners, particularly the US and EU. There are mutual accusations of not playing fair and there remains the possibility of trade wars. Another major fault line lies in the inability of the developing countries to gain what they see as a fair system of rules that will enable them to share in the growth of globalization. The inability to agree has stalled the world trade talks and in the meantime we see the development of strong regional trade groups revolving around North America, Europe and Southeast Asia which can cause potential rivalry.

Role of Europe

Chapter 9 focused on the impact of the European environment and showed how the Sapir report viewed the future. This was largely positive with the central concern being how to ensure that the structures can support the widening of the EU membership whilst trying to raise the steady but generally low economic growth of most member countries. The one problematic issue concerns the view of many of the European politicians that if this is to be achieved then greater cooperation will be needed and a constitution for Europe agreed. The problem for them is that there is widespread reluctance within countries from the electorates to allow this to happen. For the UK, the key possible change will continue to be the question as to whether it should adopt the euro as its currency.

Looking ahead: the social environment

We explored the nature of the social environment in Chapters 5, 7 and 8. One major area highlighted was the rise in affluence in general, and the widening income gap between people, and this will continue to be a focus of attention. The other major concern is that the rise in consumerism has distracted attention from our role within our families and local communities, and our responsibilities as national and indeed global citizens.

Affluent societies

Values

Interaction

As affluence increases in much of the developed world, this has enabled businesses to target a range of high value activities. A brief look at the television schedules or the weekend newspaper supplements shows the industries that are booming; fashion and beauty, health, well being and food, home improvements, travel, sports and leisure and the arts and culture are all prominent. Of course we also see the range of high value (and high tech) consumer goods from cars, computers and washing machines. Shopping has now become the number one social activity in many households and is often referred to as the 'new religion'. Another focus of social commentators is the rise of a 'celebrity culture'. There is a fascination with the lives of the rich and famous whether it is royalty, fashion icons, footballers, performers or indeed business people.

Businesses are keen to use the status of celebrities to market their products and sell an image of the desirable lifestyles that can be had by using the same products as the rich and famous. The widening of the income gap between this section of society and the rest merely adds to the allure of the celebrity status. They lead lives which are unattainable for the rest of society, and yet that makes people more interested in them and keener to try to follow, even if only in a small way.

For some this 'cult of celebrity' is simply an inevitable outcome of the pattern of demand in society, with those supplying the needs of the marketplace simply reaping their just rewards. If people further want to introduce a touch of glamour into their ordinary lives then there is no harm in this.

Social problems

Affluenza

For others, there are dangers both to the individual and to the wider global society. The problem is that their example creates a feeling of continual dissatisfaction amongst the rest of society and

Mini-Case 16.2 Have you caught the 'affluenza' bug?

As we entered the 21st century there was a rise in interest as to what constituted happiness. The conventional wisdom was that if individuals and, therefore, society were to be richer then what was required was for them to become more affluent.

This view has come to be questioned both by social psychologists and by a revival of what is known as 'happiness economics'. It has been argued by some psychologists that as societies become richer there is a rise in the range and level of mental problems reported by people and that people seem to become more insecure and suffer higher stress levels. The term 'affluenza' has been developed to try and describe this tendency. It is argued that the symptoms of this 'virus' are seen in people being obsessed with money, wanting to look good in the eyes of others and wanting to be famous. It causes depression, anxiety and the need to take comfort in substance abuse.

There has been a recent surge in economic research into what people say about what makes them happy. The findings are clear.

While on average people with higher incomes are happier than those on lower ones, as people get richer they do not in fact get any happier. What seems more important to people is their relative status. We are not happy if we feel poorer than other groups in society. It is also clear that it is not just income that makes us happy but a range of other factors such as levels of education, stable relationships and friends, security in the home and at work, leisure and fitness. This has led to calls for the development of new ways of measuring well being to incorporate these more subjective factors.

❷ If the findings above are accurate, what does this say about the nature of the society that will develop in the future?

❷ If the findings are true, what might individuals, government and businesses do to improve well being?

encourages a constant emphasis on consumption as the only route to happiness. This is highly damaging psychologically for many people. They feel constant pressure to work harder and for longer to increase their spending power. There is the added danger that, for some people, their inability to improve their standards of living in an environment of the allure of celebrity can spill over into resentment that fuels violence or a feeling of hopelessness. Furthermore, the lifestyles of the rich are seen as being unsustainable, if we were all to adopt these and bring with them the threats of environmental degradation.

So the general rise of affluence seems to have a contradictory affect on people's well being. It is argued that as we get richer, paradoxically people become more insecure and less happy, and this is the attention of much research across the disciplines of economics, marketing, psychology, health, criminology and sociology. The term affluenza has been developed to give expression to this.

Social inequality

We have seen that this affluence is not spread equally in business. The distribution of income and rewards is skewed in a very particular way. There is a very small group of very rich people, and particular concern is expressed about the gap between executive pay and the rest of the working population. The British newspapers are full of the stories of how the large annual bonuses earned by city brokers are spent. In 2007 the whimsical phrase of the 'have nots and have yachts' was coined. It was no coincidence that the Annual Yacht show was held in London just after the Christmas period when the bonuses were paid out.

Quality of life issues

It is clear that increasingly people are much more concerned about quality of life issues. The affluent seek to maintain healthy lifestyles through eating organically and joining expensive and exclusive leisure clubs. Vast sums are spent on beauty products or even cosmetic surgery. Some worry so much about their appearances that this can itself lead to eating disorders and substance abuse, which needs to be corrected by lengthy spells in rehabilitation clinics.

The rest of the economically active society seeks to try and aspire to these lifestyles but, with the lack of cash, find they are unable to do so. They face a constant struggle to make ends meet, and in trying to boost income find themselves working longer hours, and in so doing needing to seek more flexible ways of working. To cope with such pressures some turn to alcohol or recreational drugs.

Family life—children and the elderly

Across all groups there is a focus on the role of children, parents and family life and the elderly. There are grave concerns expressed about the lives children are leading. The consumer generation is seen as being particularly problematic for its effects on children, and businesses need to tread carefully in this area. Children do represent an enormous market opportunity for businesses, but there are concerns that they exploit this potential to the detriment of children. It is argued that the food and computer games industries are particularly at fault, encouraging a sedentary lifestyle and the eating of foods high in fats and sugars. It will be interesting in the future to see how this affects the market for products targeted at children and young people.

The pressure to earn higher incomes mean that parents and guardians of children find it difficult to combine work and family life, and so in the future there will be increasing calls for family friendly working policies. All too often in the past it is mothers who were seen as being the ones that needed to demand the right to work flexibly. Increasingly though there are many fathers who would like the chance to look after their children and business practices have to change to reflect this. It is also clear that the wider issues of gender differences in the labour market will have to be addressed.

The longevity of people's lives will place increasing strains on families and welfare services and it is clear that the levels of state support will not be sufficient to cope. The greying of the population is not all bad news as this group does provide a huge potential market for new business products, especially in the leisure and recreation industries, and we should all be able to look forward to living healthier and longer lives providing we are able to plan our pensions and keep healthy.

Migration

The onward march of globalization will also increase migration. This will mean that it is important for countries to develop appropriate ways of handling the diversity of communities. Immigration brings clear economic benefits to countries, as migrant workers are often very skilled or else are prepared to work more flexibly than indigenous workers. However, unregulated immigration can impose unexpected increases in appropriate welfare provision and fuels ethnic suspicions. The inability to resolve cultural and ethnic differences can lead to tensions, and may provide the ideal environment for this to result in extreme political protests in the form of racist behaviour and actions. It is important in the future that diversity is handled effectively.

The business response

Internal/ external

How then will the world of business be shaped by these changes? Obviously these social changes combine to alter the nature of the demand for many products. Technological change and globalization have resulted in the lowering of costs of a wide range of basic necessities from food to electronics, and it is difficult for businesses to make money in these low value areas. We have seen how business in general will ideally seek to move up the value chain by producing high quality manufactured goods and that there is a sectoral shift to services and high tech manufactured goods. The rise in incomes in much of the developed world means that to all intents and purposes it is not scarcity that is the main problem for many people but abundance. Increasingly the spotlight is on our over-consumption of everything from food to fuel, and there is an ever increasing problem of the waste that we are creating.

It is argued by many social commentators that consumers will increasingly seek to identify themselves with the products they buy, and the message for businesses is to try and build a brand that will appeal to this desire. We saw in Chapter 3 how supermarkets are trying to go 'up-market' by developing new quality food products and tapping into the new health and ethically conscious market. An example of this desire for consumers to identify with the products they buy and through their purchases make statements as to who they are could be seen in 2007 with the selling of a re-usable cotton shopping bag by Sainsbury's. This bag was designed by Anya Hindmarch and displayed the logo 'I am not a plastic bag'. Such was the interest in the bag (which sold at £5) that people queued outside stores on the day they were introduced. They sold out immediately and within hours were being auctioned off by eBay for up to £160.

Businesses will continue to concentrate on the need to constantly improve product design, and the public relations and marketing functions will remain key to many businesses. While the real prize could be seen in the ability to build and develop truly global brands, this desire of consumers for choice also does allow specialist businesses to operate in niche markets. The food and drinks industries are good examples of this, where global brands coexist along with specialist food suppliers and small independent brewers and wine producers and merchants.

However, it is clear that the issue which will dominate the social agenda as we look ahead is the social responsibility we have as consumers, citizens and within the businesses in which we work. Here the clash between our desire to increase the amount of resources we need to satisfy our consumption patterns and the impact that this may have on the quality of our lives (or indeed that of future generations) is thrown into stark contrast. Recent research shows that we are confused. There is now a widespread recognition of the reality of global warming and the need for changes in individual and business behaviour but a lack of knowledge about how to go about this. Looking ahead it will be interesting to see the extent to which businesses and consumers do indeed alter their behaviour in relation to what they see are their social responsibilities.

Mini-Case 16.3 Is the sky the limit?

For many environmental groups, whilst air travel currently only contributes 5.5% to all global carbon emissions, it is the fastest growing source of new carbon emissions. As such it is seen as a test case for how serious we are about reducing carbon emissions and therefore the prospect of global warming. The problem is that on current forecasts there is going to be a continued growth in demand for air travel. The combination of a rise in incomes, and the fall in the price of air travel as a result of technological improvements to aircraft, and government legislation in ensuring greater competition had encouraged the growth of air travel in the past. In the future low cost short haul operators and now the prospect of the low cost business model being applied to long haul will mean that on current projections air travel will increase 300% in the next 20 years.

It is not only green groups who are uncomfortable with this prospect. Mark Ellingham, the founder 25 years ago of the travel guide company the Rough Guides, the bibles for the growing numbers of backpacking globe trotters, has likened the ill effects of the tourism industry to that of the tobacco industry. He argues that, despite the availability of so called 'eco-tourism', there is no such thing as an ethically responsible holiday despite the undoubted benefits that tourism can bring. Richard Branson has made a commitment to use the profits from his Virgin airline to offset carbon emissions in the short run, and to invest into research and development into bio-fuels and more fuel efficient aircraft.

Green groups argue that whilst the development of the carbon offsetting industry is welcome in the short run (allowing for the fact that many of the schemes are as yet unproved), the only course of action is for the levying of large green taxes, and for individuals to drastically cut the number of flights that they take and restrict airport expansion.

❓ Will you be willing to cut the amount of journeys you take by air in the future?

❓ How realistic is it to expect people to take individual responsibility?

❓ What are the actions that could be taken by the airline companies and government to reduce the carbon emissions from air travel?

Looking ahead: the technological environment

Dynamic

It is in the technological environment that imaginations are always likely to run away with people. There is the tendency to intermingle hard edged scientific development and prediction with science fiction, and here we see clearly the gap between optimists and pessimists. However, the rate of technological change is very fast and our newspapers are keen to report any possibility of a technological breakthrough, no matter how fanciful.

Internal/ external

We saw in Chapter 3 that technology is very important in boosting productivity and competitiveness, and we also saw that in order for businesses to take advantage of the potential of technology there needs to be both a supportive external and internal environment in which it can be developed.

Creating the knowledge economy— opportunities

Technology and the creation of competitive advantage

Complexity

Externally there needs to be the creation and maintenance of a knowledge economy and governments appreciate the need for the development of both knowledge and skills. This will require continued investment in education, and the creation of an entrepreneurial culture as discussed in Chapter 14. Governments can encourage the growth of technology clusters and provide vital support services. Internally it is how the knowledge is used and how the necessary organizational changes are made that will enable technological change to translate into productivity growth. Businesses clearly need to use technology to innovate, but the climate for innovation depends crucially on the appropriate business models in terms of internal organization, relationships with suppliers and partners and development of human resources.

New technologies

The new technologies of IT, nano-technology and bio-technology will continue to grab attention but as we have seen, technological change can often involve very simple changes. There is scope for technological change across the range of the value chains of businesses. It is clear that the spectacular advance of the Internet and e-business has contributed to the recent rise in growth rates in many parts of the world. The growth in the use of mobile phones will continue apace, and on current projections there will be 4 billion mobile phone owners by the end of this decade. The revolution in communications does indeed have major implications for the strategy and structure of business.

The technological revolution based on the new technologies has also combined with the increase in globalization to create what, for many commentators, is a new paradigm of the 'network age'. In the old industrial age of the 20th century production needed to be vertically integrated (all stages of the production process kept together geographically) because of the high costs of transport and communications. In this new age it is argued we will see an increasing horizontal organization of business activity. It is now possible for organizations to organize their activity in functional areas located in different parts of the globe, e.g. research, marketing, education and training, distribution and production split into separate processes outsourced across the world.

What is likely to be the impact of the new technologies? Quite clearly the spread of information and communications technology will bring about great benefits in terms of enabling people to gain access to knowledge. This will greatly help in terms of a wide range of activities, from participation in the political process and, therefore, greater transparency, through to access to research and market information. We are already well down the line of enabling every home in the developed world to have high speed Internet access, the ability of computer games consoles to be integrated to the Internet and the bringing together of mobile phone telephony and Internet access in one hand-held device. On the horizon is the development of natural language input and output for computers, and wearable computers.

However, a closer analysis of these growth rates does call for caution over technological flights of fancy. Growth rates in the US and Europe have been steady rather than spectacular and where growth rates have been high such as in Southeast Asia there have been a host of other factors that have created the environment for growth. India perhaps remains an exception to this. By targeting the IT sector India has managed to establish a strong competitive advantage.

What technology has done though, is to change the way in which businesses are organized, especially as a result of the speed with which information, goods and people can be moved around. Bio-technology and nano-technology mean that businesses can undertake rapid new product development and seek to build new markets, particularly in the areas of food production and health.

Interaction

Threats of technology

Slaves to the machine?

We have seen that there are challenges posed by these new technologies. The public on the one hand has much to gain by new revolutionary products and by the lowering in costs that can occur, and yet on the other remain sceptical about the motivations of companies and the possible future impact of untried technology, especially in relation to bio- and nano-technology. There is also concern that the impact of IT serves also to increase the intensity of work, with people being expected to be available '24/7'.

Stakeholders

Private gain or public good?

There will always remain a tension between the private motivations of businesses to harness technology to boost productivity and therefore profit, and the public desire to see technology improving the human condition. While it is public investment that is vital in providing the educational infrastructure for the knowledge economy it is the private sector that is primarily responsible for translating this knowledge into product development. Across the developed countries, typically 50–60% of research and development is in private companies, with universities responsible for around 15–20%, and public research institutions between 15–20%. Private research is even higher in the developing world. This means that there is a potential conflict between the desire of the private sector to use technology to establish competitive advantage, and the desire of the public to be both protected from unsafe technologies and to fully be able to benefit from those that will improve the quality of our lives. The activity of pharmaceutical companies is one source of great scrutiny, as is the digital revolution. The prospect of a 'wired' world causes frustration when people see the control of the technology in the hands of large organizations such as Microsoft and Google. There is building pressure for the need to develop open-source operating systems, and governments have to guard against the creation of monopoly power and bridge the digital divide between developed and developing countries and high and low income groups.

Ethics

There will continue to be improvements in the prevention of illness and healthcare, leading to a better quality of life and longevity of lives for many of us. However, the rapid advances in bio-technology cause unease as often the ethical implications of these developments require the need for a slow and considered approach which lags far behind the pace of change. The need for businesses to carefully consider the ethical implications of the technologies that they use will become a crucial aspect of developing globally responsible leadership. In order to supervise and monitor this, governments too will have to be careful to put in place the necessary safeguards that do not

Values

prohibit innovation and yet provide the democratic safeguards and necessary health and safety considerations.

Complexity

The world of technology by its very nature is futuristic. Technology is constantly changing and has the potential to be world changing. However, as we have emphasized in our discussions, the actual impact of technology depends itself on a whole range of factors contained within the business environment.

This chapter has attempted to both look back, and then look forward, and spot the main factors that will affect the future business environment. Inevitably this has taken place at a general level, but by using the PEST framework we have been able to identify some key future developments. In the Case Study that follows we will show how the past impact of PEST factors has impacted on one business in particular, and what may happen as we look ahead.

◈ *Summary*

- Analysis of the underlying political, economic, social and technological factors helps us to map out the important themes and features of the business environment which can act as guide for the future

- The nature of the business environment is complex and we need to be aware that events may not turn out as we expected. Even where our predictions are carefully rooted in rigorous analysis unexpected changes that we did not anticipate can occur

- Nevertheless by a careful examination of the business environment we can identify key future trends and businesses need to attempt this type of analysis when planning their strategies

- Despite the relative calm in the business environment in the last 20 years, there have been major changes in how we live and work. It is clear that globalization and technological change will continue to be significant factors in shaping change but as important can be slowly developing changes which over the long period can have major impacts

- There are real challenges that face us all in the future and increasing attention will fall on the global responsibilities of us all as individuals, citizens and in our roles in business

- The one certain thing we can say about the future is that it will change. We will all differ as to the nature of our optimism or pessimism about this uncertain future. How things turn out will fundamentally depend on the degree to which we can successfully analyse the changing nature of the business environment and respond to the unexpected changes

Case study: the football business. From pork pies to prawn sandwiches?

In 2005, Roy Keane, the then captain of Manchester United, bemoaned the lack of atmosphere generated by his team's supporters at their home ground of Old Trafford. He felt that too many people in the crowd were there simply as a result of corporate hospitality and were more interested in the food and drink provided than the football itself. Keane seemed to yearn for the days when football crowds were mainly vociferous working class men whose only distraction would be the half time pork pie and cup of tea (or Bovril!).

The football business demonstrates clearly how the changing nature of the external environment can alter business strategy and structure. Traditionally, football was seen as a working man's sport with football teams firmly rooted in their local communities.

Whilst the players were indeed local, and in some cases, national heroes, they still lived alongside their supporters and their wages, whilst higher than those of many of their fans, were not significantly so and reflected the short playing span that they could have.

Ownership of football clubs was mainly by local entrepreneurs attracted by the opportunity for local status as well as, in some cases, a philanthropic desire to put something back into the community. The revenues from football came almost wholly from gate receipts. Whilst attendances at some games could be large, generally most clubs did not make significant profits.

During the last 20 years the environment of football, particularly in the UK but also in Europe, has radically changed. The rise in affluence of its core support has presented clubs with the potential to market a range of products associated with the club, especially football shirts. The main source of revenue is now television income, and this has been made possible by the satellite and digital revolution, with the new TV providers such as BSkyB eager to use the appeal of football to draw in subscribers for their wider TV packages. This has meant that the audiences for a football match are not constrained by the capacity of the ground but can now truly be national and indeed global ones. However, this potential income is not equally shared.

In the process the footballers and football clubs at the top levels in their respective countries, have been transformed into celebrities and businesses have been quick to harness their marketing potential. Sponsorship for the football shirts is eagerly fought over and all businesses compete to have their brands linked to football and football stars.

This global reach of football has not spread evenly. The impact of the social and technological changes has been such as to create a very large gap between the top football clubs in the premier divisions and the clubs in the lower leagues. It is very difficult for teams outside of these elites to now compete with the level of resources that the elite teams now have at their disposal. In Europe the main aim of these clubs is not simply to try and win their respective national league (which is still important for national prestige) but to finish high enough in the league to guarantee entry into the European Champions League where the TV rights and global recognition are much higher.

There are criticisms that football has deserted its traditional support as ticket prices soar and matches are scheduled for the TV rather than at times to suit the fans. The disproportionate rewards of the top clubs are seen by some as starving the lower divisions of resources, so restricting the ability of these clubs to nurture the local talent of the future. On top of this there have been accusations of corruption in many areas of football, and calls for governments to take action rather than leaving this to the relevant football authorities. Others complain that essentially, while the quality at the top level has improved, all too often it is the same few teams who win the trophies with the majority of teams simply coming and being second best.

In the UK, local entrepreneurs can no longer afford to buy such potentially lucrative clubs and slowly we are witnessing the premier league clubs being taken over by very rich global entrepreneurs. In order to succeed, these clubs have to attract the best managers and players, and vast sums are paid out in wages and salaries. The more successful the club is on the pitch, then the greater the likelihood that they can be the global brands, and so cash in on the TV rights and the merchandising of club-related products.

Of course, not many clubs can make this global breakthrough, and for those that fail on the pitch or fail to raise the necessary investment to break through there is the prospect of rapid relative decline.

The football authorities are keen to broaden this mass appeal of football and are keen to transform the experience of watching football into a pleasurable one. To this end facilities at grounds have been much improved with many clubs moving or wanting to move to brand-new stadia. Part of the impetus for this has come from government in response to the dual problems of hooliganism and poor safety in many of the older football grounds. Great efforts have been made to remove the elements of hooliganism that blighted the game in the 1970s, and the insistence on all-seater stadia has improved the safety and comfort of many spectators. Indeed some clubs are now keen to develop new state-of-the-art grounds in the knowledge that with the appetite for football being so high they can recoup the capital outlay with ever higher ticket prices and the prospect of rising TV revenues.

There have been a host of measures to develop diversity into football from the grass roots level up. Many clubs are active in the local community and there is an attempt to make the game more appealing to women and children, both in terms of participation as well as in terms of their being active supporters. However, it is the global appeal of football that has been the primary driving force in the game, with national leagues eager to exploit this potential. It is no surprise that in order to govern this international sport there has been the need to develop global football governance. In Europe it is UEFA and at the international level FIFA that are the ultimate guardians of the regulatory framework.

What is likely to happen in the future? It is clear that this process of moving from a club rooted in its local market to trying to target the global market will continue. Most of the top clubs now have clear global marketing strategies. To succeed in the business a major requirement is access to large sums of money, and the risks associated with losing out on this investment because of losing out on the pitch means that it is only private entrepreneurs with vast fortunes who will be prepared to assume ownership.

Changes in the social structure, coupled with the development of satellite and digital technology in an environment of increasing globalization, will mean that football will increasingly become a global commodity, as important for the associated products it sells as for the football itself. A brief glimpse into the nature of the professional sports market in the USA reveals a future where increasingly it is television and product placement that determine the environment of the sport, and where the salaries of the top stars rise ever higher.

❓ Has the quality of football improved?

❓ What possible disadvantages will there be for football in the future if present trends continue?

❓ What have been the main changes in the business environment of football that have caused the developments referred to above?

❓ Looking ahead to the future what are the prospects for the football business?

Review and discussion questions

1   Out of all the possible things highlighted in the chapter what do you feel most optimistic about?

2   What fears do you have for the future of the business environment?

3   Are there any other things that you feel should be considered as we look ahead to the future of the business environment?

4   Which businesses do you feel will be best able to take advantage of the future business environment?

Assignments

1   Most company annual reports will offer their views as to the nature of the business environment in which they are operating. Write a press release that captures the main highlights of one such report.

2   Write a report which analyses how you see the business environment affecting a business or business sector that you want to profile for a business magazine.

3   You have recently joined your local chamber of commerce/regional development agency as a business analyst. You have been asked to give a presentation about the general business environment and the implications for the SME sector in your region. Your job is to research the main local, national and global factors that are most likely to impact in your region and prepare a presentation to report your findings.

Online resources

Test your understanding of this chapter with online questions and answers, explore the subject further through web exercises, and use the weblinks to provide a quick resource for further research. Go to the Online Resource Centre at

www.oxfordtextbooks.co.uk/orc/ wetherly_otter/

www.bbc.co.uk: The BBC website is a good source of information both in written archives and in terms of its 'listen again' archives. The best programmes to listen again to are the *In Business* and *Analysis* series which always contain views about the future. In 2007 the annual 'Reith' lectures were given by Jeffrey Sachs, an economist and business strategist on the subject of the future of the business environment.

www.unctad.org
www.worldbank.org: See in particular the annual World Economic Outlook that can be downloaded from this site.
www.bankofengland.org
www.hm-treasury.gov

All these sites contain annual reports profiling the economic and business environment and giving predictions as to the future.

www.forumforthefuture.org.uk: This site profiles and champions the case for sustainable development.

www.technologyreview.com: This site is run by MIT in the USA, one of the leading technology universities in the world.

www.foresight.gov.uk: This is the UK government's science and technology programme to research into the future.

For local business information look up the web addresses of your local Chambers of Commerce or Regional Development Agency if operating in your area.

Glossary

absolute advantage if two countries produce the same range of goods one has an absolute advantage over the other if it can produce greater quantities of the goods using the same amount of resources. Adam Smith showed that where this is the case it is better for each country to specialize in the goods in which it has an absolute advantage so increasing total production. Trade could then occur so that each country would be able to increase the amount of all goods available to it (see also **comparative advantage**).

acid rain burning fossil fuels releases gases such as sulphur dioxide and nitrogen dioxide into the atmosphere. These gases are transported by prevailing winds, and combine with moisture to produce 'acid rain', devastating natural vegetation and ecological systems.

affluenza the term used to refer to the alleged tendency of people to suffer a range of mental illnesses as a result of striving to increase their incomes so that, paradoxically, higher incomes lower the quality of life.

age structure structure of the population in terms of the proportions in each age band.

ageing population falling death rates (increased longevity) result in a growing number and share of elderly in the population, and increasing average age.

Agenda 21 a document about sustainable development formulated at the Rio conference in 1992.

agentification the increasing use of 'professional' agencies rather than civil service based ministries is known as 'agentification'.

aggregate demand the total level of demand for all goods and services in an economy.

allocative efficiency (see **efficiency**).

alternative scenarios a form of environmental analysis in which alternative possible futures are identified.

apropriate technology the use of technology best suited to the external environment in which business is operating. Most often used to highlight the need for developing countries to adopt 'low-tech' solutions.

basic economic problem scarcity, requiring the allocation of resources between competing wants or needs, the need to minimize resource use and the need to ensure equitable distribution.

best value a term used both legally and managerially to quantify and qualify the 'best value' services available to the public from service providers: this was building on previous recommendations in relation to **value for money** (see below).

biodiversity the totality of species and life forms on earth.

birth rate the number of births per 1,000 of the population.

bureaucracy the paid (normally) civil servants or officials and their system of public administration.

business often defined narrowly in terms of the private sector, but a broad definition includes the public and 'third' sectors. Business involves the transformation of inputs into outputs to produce goods and services for customers or users.

business class (**capitalist class**) social group defined by ownership and control of business.

business dominance refers to the claim that business exercises unrivalled influence in politics.

capitalism an economic system in which the means of production are overwhelmingly privately owned and operated for profit; decisions regarding investment of capital are made privately; and where production, distribution, and the prices of goods, services, and labour are affected by the forces of supply and demand in a largely free market.

capitalist class (see **business class**).

caretaker state refers to the main role of government being the provision of goods and services, rather than the classical role of exercising authority.

central government and local authorities most developed countries have developed public administration systems that often embrace central control and local delivery.

circular flow of income in a simple model of a market system money (or income) flows between firms and households in the form of payments for labour and commodities.

civil disobedience a tactic used by some campaigning organizations involving a willingness to break the law in order to protest a law or business action.

civil society organization (CSO) usually used as another term for pressure group—a voluntary association formed to campaign on specific issues, e.g. Greenpeace.

class social group defined by common characteristics or social position, especially occupation.

class structure a way of classifying the population according to class positions, e.g. working class and middle class.

colonialism the term is most often used in the context of the expansion of European powers across the globe from the Spanish and Portuguese conquests of South America and then the dominance of countries such as Britain, France and Holland in North America, the Far East and Africa. There is a fierce debate as to the effects of colonialism. Refer also to **imperialism**.

common good what is good for society as a whole, as opposed to purely private interests.

comparative advantage even if one country is better at producing all ranges of commodities compared with another, trade will still lead to overall gains in production. Here the more efficient country should specialize in the goods in which it has the greater comparative advantage and the less efficient country should specialize in the goods in which it has the smallest comparative disadvantage. In this way total production of the two countries would increase and trade will enable both countries to benefit.

competition the existence of competition is seen as being vital if businesses are to behave in an efficient manner. In reality competition may be prevented by monopoly power and in some cases can be 'destructive'.

competition policy a major policy impacting on the EU business environment which aims to ensure that competition in the single market is not distorted by anti-competitive forces such as monopoly, oligopoly, restrictive practices, or state interference.

compulsory competitive tendering introduced as an administrative mechanism to determine effective competition procedures for public services.

complements these are commodities that we buy as a result of buying another commodity, e.g. if the demand for car transport increases so will the demand for petrol.

comprehensive performance assessment (CPA) a means by which to determine the effectiveness of public service provision.

constitution the highest form of law and a device for limiting the power of the state; sets out the rules about making rules.

consumer sovereignty the claim that consumers, not firms, are ultimately in charge of the economic system through their spending decisions. In a free market system it should be the consumer who has the power to decide what should be produced. If there are anxieties that this is not the case and that producers have the power then there needs to be consumer protection.

consumerism an attitude in which consumption is seen as a prime source of personal well being (see also **materialism**).

corporate citizenship this term views corporations as members of society with similar rights and responsibilities to citizens.

corporate social responsibility (CSR) the idea that private sector businesses should be judged according to criteria of social benefit, not just profit. This also refers to the responsibility that corporations have to society. The extent of that responsibility is a matter for debate.

cosmopolitan society a society that is open to a wide range of cultural influences (see also **multiculturalism**).

culture refers to the set of values, beliefs and lifestyles that characterize a group or society.

death rate the number of deaths per thousand of the population.

declaration of incompatibility the courts have the power to declare any piece of legislation incompatible with the provisions of the Human Rights Act 1998. This Act brought the European Convention on Human Rights into UK law. The power of the courts is limited as a declaration of incompatibility does not affect the ongoing operation of the law. There is, however, a procedure by which the government can remove the incompatibility following such a declaration.

demand–pull inflation inflation associated with an excess demand for goods and services when the economy is at or above full employment.

democracy (see also **liberal democracy**) a political system in which political power is in the hands of the people: 'rule by the people'.

deontological ethics this theory argues that there are certain core ethical principles that apply in any situation, such as 'It is wrong to kill another person'.

dependency often used to describe the inequality of power and forms of economic domination that characterizes the relations between rich and poor countries. Dependency theory emerged from the work of André Gunder Frank and the United Nations Economic Commission on Latin America under Raul Prebisch. Reacting against theories of development and modernization that contended that poor countries would inevitably follow the stages of western economic development, dependency theorists argued that these countries faced systematic 'underdevelopment' within the world economy.

dependency culture the argument that state benefits can foster dependency on the part of recipients and undermine independence.

design, build, finance and operate system (DBFO) a working system for developing PPP and PFI developments.

destructive competition there are areas of business activity in which unregulated competition could be harmful.

Cutting costs could mean endangering health and safety to workers and consumers and so regulation is needed. There are also whole areas of business where it would be better to have only one firm (see **natural monopoly** below).

devolution the sharing or giving up of power from central to local level, e.g. the establishment of a Scottish parliament.

disposable income the amount of income that people can actually spend after all taxes, etc. have been deducted.

distributive efficiency (see **efficiency**).

divisional structure a type of organization structure based on semi-independent operational units or divisions.

economic growth the process of increasing the output of goods and services produced by the economy or, more strictly, the process of increasing productive capacity.

ecosystem a community of interdependent living organisms, plants and animals, set in the non-living components of their surroundings.

efficiency refers to the way in which the three parts of the economic problem are resolved.

For a business to be efficient in an economic sense it must produce so that: customers get 'value for money' and this will happen if prices equal marginal costs (allocative efficiency); the average cost of each unit of output is minimized so that resources are being used as efficiently as possible (productive efficiency); the distribution of the output is 'fair' and creates equity (distributive efficiency). Deciding on what is equitable is very contentious. In the neoclassical perspective the free market is the best way of achieving this. Structuralist and Marxist critics argue that unregulated markets can lead to exploitation of consumers and employees and create a divided world where there is gross inequity. The Green movement argues that it is the planetary system that is being exploited and that our present prosperity endangers that of future generations.

elasticity of demand price elasticity of demand refers to the responsiveness of demand to changes in price. It determines the effect on a firm's revenue of price changes. Income elasticity of demand is the responsiveness of demand to changes in income.

emissions trading creating a market in carbon dioxide emissions whereby countries and companies receive licences to emit carbon dioxide. If the companies exceed their emission limits they must buy permits from other companies which have reduced their emissions. This creates an incentive to reduce emissions on the part of an individual company.

empirical research the gathering and use of evidence to try and prove the validity of theories.

employer of choice an employing organization which has gained a reputation for being a good employer in the employment market. Employers of choice are characterized by competitive terms and conditions, the provision of developmental opportunities for staff, fair dealing, involving employees in decision-making, interesting work, and an interest in work–life balance.

enlargement the EU has grown via several waves of new entrants, although enlargement commonly refers to the 2004 accession of ten new members, largely from eastern Europe.

enterprise 'making things happen, having ideas and doing something about them, taking advantage of the opportunities to bring about change' (SGE programme 1999: see Chapter 14 References).
   'Any attempt at new business or new venture creation, such as self employment, a new business organization, or the expansion of existing business, by an individual, teams of individuals or established businesses' (Irwin and Wilkinson, 2001).

enterprise and entrepreneurship 'enterprise is a set of qualities and competencies that can be employed in different settings, whilst entrepreneurship involves the process of creating and developing new ventures' (Enterprise Insight 2005: 23: see Chapter 14 References).

entrepreneur anyone who attempts a new business or new venture creation, such as self employment, a new business organization, social enterprise or the expansion of an existing business by an individual, teams of individuals, to established business (DTi, 2003: see Chapter 14 References).

environmental analysis the more or less systematic analysis of the business environment to assist business strategy and performance.

environmental footprint in relation to an individual company or organization, its total environmental impact, referring to direct and indirect resource use, generation of waste and effluent, plus any other changes it imposes on the natural environment. For a whole economy, it is the land and sea area needed to provide all the energy, water, transport, food and materials it consumes. Thus, if the population of the whole world lived at the same level as the UK, it would require three worlds to sustain it.

environmental uniqueness the recognition that each business operates in an environment that is, in some ways, unique to it.

equal opportunity the idea that people from all backgrounds should enjoy the same chances to benefit from valued opportunities, e.g. in education and employment.

equality of outcome equality between people measured in terms of outcomes such as income and wealth.

equilibrium analysis the use of demand and supply diagrams to predict the effects of changes in markets. An essential part of microeconomics.

equity (see **efficiency** above).

ethical consumerism bringing ethical considerations into spending decisions, e.g. fair trade.

ethnocentrism belief in the superiority of one's own culture over other cultures. In business, this can mean a tendency for many western global businesses to assume that the norm to aspire to is a western cultural model, and that it is western values of individualism and personal aspiration that are embedded in the supra-national bodies.

EU budget the means to fund common policies, balance the gains and losses from integration, promote cohesion and redistribute wealth. Expenditure dominates with substantial sums allocated traditionally to the Common Agricultural Policy (CAP) and increasingly regional policy. Contributions have increased progressively necessitating new resources such as VAT and later GNP-based measures.

euro-centric view focusing on European culture or history to the exclusion of a wider view of the world; implicitly regarding European culture as pre-eminent.

European integration a process of economic association in which progressive integration requires policy harmonization and institutional changes rather than merely the removal of trade barriers.

European Monetary Union a three-stage process involving convergence of participants' economies, the establishment of a common monetary policy run by the European Central Bank, and ultimately the introduction of the single currency, the euro.

European treaties agreed by member states' governments and ratified in their parliaments, these are the legal basis for the EU and its operations, e.g. Treaty of Rome that founded the EEC, Treaty of Maastricht that formed the EU.

executive the branch of government that is concerned with implementing public policy and law.

executive dominance refers to the dominance of parliament by the executive (government) through control of a parliamentary majority coupled with party discipline.

expert opinion a form of environmental analysis relying on expert views, often using external consultants.

external environment environmental forces that operate in the world outside the organization.

federal state a state in which power is shared constitutionally between the centre and localities (as opposed to a unitary state).

final or finished goods and services goods and services purchased by their ultimate users.

final salary pension a form of employer-sponsored occupational pension arrangement. It is the most common type of 'defined benefit pension schemes'. It pays former employees a pension calculated as a percentage of the salary that was being received at the date of retirement or in the final years of work prior to retirement.

fiscal policy measures that alter the level and composition of government expenditure and taxation.

first past the post (FPTP) electoral system used for parliamentary elections in the UK, in which the winning candidate in each constituency needs just to obtain more votes than any other candidate (not necessarily a majority). Criticized by supporters of proportional representation (PR).

five forces Porter's (1980) framework for analysing competitive forces in a market.

flat structure a type of organization structure or principle based on delayering, i.e. stripping out management layers.

food miles the distance food travels between producer and consumer, commonly used to highlight the impact on the environment caused by production of carbon dioxide emissions during transport.

Fordism describes the mass production assembly line techniques pioneered in the automobile industry but then adopted across manufacturing industry in the early to mid 20th century.

foreign direct investment investment of capital by a government, company, or other organization in production and marketing operations that are located in a foreign country.

free market in a strict sense refers to a market that is free of government regulation or intervention. In practice supporters of the free market advocate minimum government.

freedom (see **liberty**) a key political principle referring to the ability of individuals to decide for themselves how to live their own lives, often linked with arguments in favour of the 'free market'.

frictional or search unemployment arises when people find themselves, for any number of reasons, temporarily between jobs without leaving the labour market.

functional structure a type of organization structure based on functional departments, e.g. finance, marketing, HR.

generalization to make a statement that is intended to be of general application.

generation gap because of cultural change people of different ages exhibit different values and lifestyles.

genetically modified organism (GMO) creation of plants, animals and micro-organisms by unnatural manipulation of genes, perhaps taking DNA from one species and inserting it into another unrelated one. GMOs can spread and cross with naturally-occurring organisms. Proliferation in an unpredictable way may produce unknown consequences. GMOs are a form of genetic pollution.

glass ceiling a metaphor to refer to the under-representation of women in senior positions, especially management, above a certain level of advancement.

global warming the heating up of the earth's atmosphere mainly due to burning fossil fuels, leading to global climate change.

globalization the processes by which it is argued that the world economy has become more integrated. Globalization can be seen as an increase in flows across national boundaries. These include not only economic flows of trade and investment in the form of multinational companies and international finance but also the transmission and mixing of cultural influences, migration and increased communication. The benefits and drawbacks of these processes, and the extent to which they may be controlled or influenced, are the subject of much controversy.

governance the means by which a government governs in all its forms and all its levels.

government can refer to the process of governing (see also **governance**), or to those who are in government, the government of the day.

Health and Safety Executive (HSE) the government body charged with enforcing health and safety regulations in the UK. Together with local authorities, HSE inspectors regularly examine premises to check that regulations are being fully complied with.

hierarchical structure a type of organization structure based on layers of authority with power concentrated at the top.

ideology a set of political belief and values, e.g. liberalism, socialism.

immediate environment refers to those aspects of the business environment that are relevant to day-to-day decision-making and operations, e.g. the behaviour of competitors.

imperialism imperialism is a policy of extending control or authority over foreign entities as a means of acquisition and/or maintenance of empires, either through direct territorial conquest or through indirect methods of exerting control on the politics and/or economy of other countries. The essential feature of the Marxist theories of imperialism, or related theories such as dependency theory, is their focus on the economic relation between countries, rather than the formal political relationship. Imperialism thus consists not necessarily in the direct control of one country by another, but in the economic exploitation of one region by another or of a group by another.

individualism no single meaning, but can refer to the idea that as individuals we make our own choices, as well as to the idea that people tend to behave in a self-interested way.

inflation the process of continually rising prices.

institutional triangle the three decision-making bodies that implement EU laws and policies: the Council of the EU; the European Parliament; and the European Commission.

integration refers to the extent to which people from different ethnic and religious backgrounds participate as members of a common society rather than living separately.

intensification of work the process by which employers place increased pressure on employees to work longer hours and/or to expend greater effort so as to increase productivity.

inter-governmental organization (IGO) (also intergovernmentalism) an association of sovereign nation-states usually for the purpose of treaty or common action, e.g. World Trade Organization (WTO).

internal environment this phrase reminds us that managers have to operate within an environment that is constituted by the organization itself, e.g. relations with other colleagues and departments.

intrapreneur an intrapreneur has been defined as 'a person within a large corporation who takes direct responsibility for turning an idea into a profitable finished product through assertive risk-taking and innovation' (*American Heritage Directory*, 3rd edition, 1992: see Chapter 14 References).

ISO 14001 an international standard of best practice for carrying out environmental management systems audits, policies, etc. It sets out a range of criteria which companies must satisfy to achieve the standard.

joint ventures a commercial undertaking entered into by two or more parties, usually in the short term. Joint ventures are generally governed by the Partnership Act (1890) but they differ from partnerships in that they are limited by time or by activity.

jurisdiction essentially this is the geographical scope within which a court or parliament can exercise its power. The nature of jurisdiction has changed with the rise of globalization particularly in the member states of the European Union.

Keynesian welfare consensus broad agreement (consensus) between the main political parties and within society (in the 1950s and 1960s) that government should be responsible for managing the economy, especially to secure full employment (Keynesian), and provide a range of welfare services such as health and education (welfare).

late industrialization after the end of the Second World War, many former colonies (see **colonialism**) gained their political independence. Amartya Sen argues that in order for these countries to develop they would need to industrialize using a different set of economic policies than that followed by the western capitalist countries.

left wing has no single meaning, but generally refers to an ideological viewpoint that supports greater state involvement in business and society, and greater equality.

liberal democracy (see **democracy**).

liberty (see **freedom**).

licence to operate the idea that corporations need to retain a level of public trust and legitimacy.

Lisbon Agenda the Lisbon Summit in 2000 set the goals for the future economic development of the EU to 2010, notably that the EU should become the most competitive and dynamic, knowledge-based economy in the world, capable of sustained economic growth, with more and better jobs, and greater social cohesion.

lobbying   a method of political influence through advocacy and persuasion of policy makers.

locational advantage   companies, especially MNCs, have the option to locate their operations in response to potential business advantages, such as cheap labour.

macroeconomics/microeconomics   macroeconomics is the study of the economy in terms of the broad aggregates of employment, inflation, economic growth, trade, and the balance of payments as well as levels of inequality. Microeconomics is the study of individual product and resource markets.

macroeconomic policy   is action by policymakers to improve aspects of the performance of the whole economy.

majority-minority city   the phenomenon of ethnic or religious groups that are minorities in a national context coming to form a majority in a particular city.

marginality   whenever we make a decision we do so 'at the margin', in other words we weigh up the advantages of the next decision to be taken against the disadvantages of not doing it. By studying these marginal costs and benefits we should not only be able to make better decisions but should be able to predict how economic actors are likely to behave.

market   a system of voluntary exchange, created by the relationship between buyers and sellers.

market failure   whilst markets do mostly work efficiently there are large areas in which they fail to work or else will need government support or control to enable them to do so.

market structure   refers to the number and size of sellers in a market, e.g. oligopoly.

materialism   an emphasis on material living standards and possessions as a prime source of well being, e.g. that a good life means having more money (see also **consumerism**).

matrix structure   introduces a horizontal principle cutting across departments, e.g. on the basis of project teams.

millennium development goals   eight goals that all 191 United Nations member states have agreed to try to achieve by the year 2015. The United Nations Millennium Declaration, signed in September 2000, commits the states to:

- eradicate extreme poverty and hunger
- achieve universal primary education
- promote gender equality and empower women
- reduce child mortality
- improve maternal health
- combat HIV/AIDS, malaria and other diseases
- ensure environmental sustainability
- develop a global partnership for development.

minimum wage   the national minimum wage (NMW) in the UK imposes a statutory duty on all employers to not pay below a defined minimum.

mixed economy   a mix of private and public sectors, e.g. a predominantly capitalist economy with some element of public ownership of industry (nationalization).

money GDP   GDP unadjusted for inflation.

monetary policy   measures that alter interest rates or the money supply.

money purchase pension   a form of employer-sponsored occupational pension scheme, also sometimes called a 'defined contribution scheme'. Employee and employer contributions are made into separate individual pension accounts and then invested. At retirement the money in the account is used to purchase an annuity from an insurance company which pays a weekly or monthly pension for the rest of the retiree's life.

multicultural society   a society in which many ethnic and religious communities co-exist, as opposed to a society with a homogeneous culture.

multi-level governance   governance takes place on a number of spatial scales—national, sub-national, supra-national.

multinational corporation (MNC)   a company that has production facilities in more than one country (i.e. undertakes foreign direct investment) including securing supplies of raw materials, utilizing cheap labour sources, servicing local markets, and bypassing protectionist barriers. Multinationals may be seen as an efficient form of organization, making effective use of the world's resources and transferring technology between countries. On the other hand, some have excessive power, are beyond the control of governments (especially weak governments), and are able to exploit host countries, especially in the Third World, where they are able to operate with low safety levels and inadequate control of pollution.

nation-state   refers to the conjunction of a system of political rule (a state) and a population comprising a national community (nation).

National Pensions Saving Scheme (NPSS)   a government-sponsored pension fund proposed by the Turner Committee as a means of increasing pension savings in the UK. From 2012 all employers who do not operate an occupational pension scheme will have to contribute a sum equivalent to 3% of their pay-bill into NPSS accounts set up for their staff. A further 4% of pay will be contributed by employees and 1% as a result of tax relief. Membership will be voluntary, but new employees will be automatically enrolled.

national sovereignty   the capacity of a nation to govern its own affairs: national self-determination.

natural monopoly   in industries where the capital costs are very large it is often sensible to only have one firm operating so that as output expands the capital costs are spread across the output, thus lowering average costs.

natural rate of unemployment the rate of unemployment which reflects the prevailing level of competitiveness of the labour market.

neocorporatism a system of political representation in which privileged status is accorded to business and labour, which may be seen as partners with government in formulating and implementing economic policy.

neoliberalism a label given to the revival of classical liberal ideas in the 1980s, often referred to as a free market ideology.

new international division of labour after the end of the Second World War there was the hope that, with the emergence of developing countries, investment would flow from the developed to the developing world because labour resources would be cheaper there.

New Labour a term coined by Tony Blair to distinguish the modernization of Labour party politics under his leadership, as opposed to 'old Labour'.

new public management (NPM) a general term for new management practices introduced in the public sector since the 1970s.

New Right a label given to the character of right-wing politics in the 1980s especially in the UK and the USA. No single meaning but usually refers to a combination of neoliberal and conservative ideas.

newly industrialized countries countries which have recently increased the proportion of industrial production in their national income and of industrial exports in their trade. The NICs have been the most rapidly growing part of the world economy in the last quarter of the twentieth century. There is no standard list of NICs: they include the 'East Asian tigers', Hong Kong, South Korea, Singapore and Taiwan, and various other countries including Brazil, China, India, Malaysia, Mexico, South Africa, and Thailand, and their number is growing.

occupational segregation a measure of the extent to which males and females are found in different occupational groups.

old Labour a reference to traditional Labour party values and policies such as public ownership and redistribution of income, often used pejoratively by supporters of New Labour.

opportunity cost scarcity means that choices have to be made about what to produce. If you choose one thing then something else is given up and the opportunity cost is the cost of the next most desirable alternative.

organization culture the values and beliefs of an organization.

organization structure refers to the internal layout of an organization, e.g. in terms of departments and lines of accountability.

organizational design all organizations are subject to processes of conscious design intended to enhance performance, e.g. by changing the organization structure.

outsourcing the buying in of components, sub-assemblies, finished products, and services from outside suppliers rather than by supplying them internally. A firm may decide to buy in rather than supply internally because it lacks the expertise, investment capital, or physical space required to do so. It may also be able to buy in more cheaply or more quickly than manufacturing in-house.

peak organization usually in reference to the CBI and TUC, as organizations which represent the interests of business and labour as a whole.

PEST analysis a form of environmental analysis in which environmental forces are classified as political, economic, social and technological.

pluralism a model or theory which emphasizes the dispersal and fragmentation of political influence among a large number of groups and interests in society.

politics no single definition, but may be seen as the activity that is concerned with determining the rules under which we live in society.

popular sovereignty the idea of popular rule (see also **democracy**).

portfolio investment the list of holdings in securities owned by an investor or institution. In building up an investment portfolio an institution will have its own investment analysts, while an individual may make use of the services of a merchant bank that offers portfolio management.

positive action measures to recruit from under-represented groups, e.g. through targeted advertising of job opportunities or training.

potential GDP the real GDP associated with the full employment of all an economy's resources.

poverty contested term referring to those who are poor according to some absolute or relative measure. An absolute measure has no regard to average living standards whereas a relative measure defines poverty in relation to the general living standards within the society.

Prebisch–Singer hypothesis the theory predicts that the terms of trade between primary products and manufactured goods tend to deteriorate over time. Developed independently by economists Raul Prebisch and Hans Singer in 1950, the thesis suggests that countries that export primary commodities (such as most developing countries) would be able to import less and less for a given level of exports. Prebisch went on to argue that, for this reason, developing countries should strive to diversify their economies and lessen dependence on primary commodity exports by developing their manufacturing industry. This may initially mean that such countries need to protect their domestic industries from open trade.

precautionary principle the presumption that no new technology should be introduced if there is a potential risk that the costs might outweigh the benefits even if there is no hard evidence that this may be the case.

precedent the system by which a court will follow an earlier decision from another court on the same point. The lower courts such as the High Court or County Court are generally bound to follow the decisions of more senior courts such as the Court of Appeal or House of Lords.

price elasticity of demand measures the 'responsiveness' of demand to changes in price. It is the percentage change in the quantity demanded as a result of a small percentage change in price.

private finance initiatives (PFIs) a fully developed set of rules and regulations governing the relationship between private and public sectors with targeted advice on financing.

private sector consists of all businesses in some form of private ownership.

privatization mainly refers to the transfer of assets from the public sector to the private sector (e.g. the privatization of nationalized industries and the sale of council houses) but can include opening tax-funded services up to competition from private sector businesses, and contracting out.

The fear of monopoly power persuaded many people in the 20th century that many key industries should be directly run by the government. In the UK many such industries were nationalized post-1945. This was reversed by the Conservative governments from 1979 with a wave of privatization which encouraged their private ownership and tried to extend market mechanisms even into areas of the welfare state such as education and health.

process innovation the introduction of new methods in the production process through application of knowledge.

producer-led sometimes put forward as a criticism of public services, i.e. that they are run in the interests of the producers rather than the consumers or users.

product innovation the development of new or improved products through application of knowledge.

production possibility frontier this illustrates the potential combinations of output that a country can attain if it uses its given resources efficiently.

productive efficiency (see **efficiency**).

productivity measures the rate at which inputs are converted into outputs. Productivity is rising if, for any given level of resource input, output rises. Productivity is also defined as the quantity of goods and services that people produce in a given time period.

profit the excess of total revenue over total costs. Profit is the primary motivation of private sector business.

public interest (see **common good**).

public–private partnerships (PPPs) a fully developed set of rules and regulations governing the relationship between private and public sectors.

public sector the part of the economy that is owned and controlled by the state, including public services.

public service comparator (PSC) an administrative device to ensure that a comparison is made between public and private service costs and effectiveness when considering PPPs and PFIs.

race to the bottom the claim that nation-states are obliged to reduce the 'burden' of regulation and taxation on business in order to attract inward investment.

real GDP GDP adjusted to strip out the effects of inflation.

recession a decline in real GDP that lasts for at least two consecutive quarters of a year.

regional development agencies (RDAs) organizations created by government to aid and focus on regional development.

regional policy a key policy area involving transfers to regions performing below the EU average and facing structural difficulties. It has increased in significance following enlargement.

relative prices the price of one good or service compared to another.

resource depletion the using up once and for all of natural resources which cannot be renewed, e.g. oil.

right wing has no single meaning, but generally refers to an ideological viewpoint that opposes greater state involvement in business and society, and accepts or supports inequality.

Rio conference or **Rio summit** a global environmental conference held in Rio de Janeiro from 3–14 June 1992.

secularism a secular society is one in which religion is a weak source of values and beliefs, and has been displaced by science and reason.

separate legal personality this is the legal device by which those who own a company are distinguished from it. Once a company is accepted as being properly formed it has an independent legal identity which gives it separate rights and responsibilities.

separation of powers a constitutional principle referring to the separation of the three main branches of government: legislative, executive, and judicial.

single market the single, common or internal market of the EU involves the abolition of obstacles to trade among members. It embraces the four freedoms covering the movement of goods, people, capital and services.

social cohesion refers to the extent to which society is held together, e.g. by shared values rather than some people feeling marginalized or excluded.

social enterprises 'businesses with primary social objectives whose surpluses are principally reinvested for that purpose in the business or in the community, rather than being driven by the need to maximize profit for shareholders and owners' ('Social Enterprise: a strategy for success' www.dti.gov.uk/socialenterprise).

social justice a political principle that is concerned with the fairness of society, particularly in respect of the distribution of income.

social mobility a measure of the chances of people from different backgrounds to attain positions of high status and/or income, e.g. for working-class children to 'move up' into middle-class occupations.

social partners usually in reference to business and labour, as partners in a shared endeavour to secure the health of business and the economy.

socialism a left-wing political ideology, involving a critique of capitalism and support for state regulation and/or control of business.

sovereignty a term referring to the highest form or source of authority, e.g. parliamentary sovereignty.

spatial level the territorial or geographical scale at which business or other activity takes place, e.g. local, national, global.

Stability and Growth Pact a commitment to budgetary discipline among euro-zone members. It sets a ceiling of 3% GDP on government borrowing, a breach of which could invoke substantial fines (up to 0.5% GDP). Considered too rigid and politically unpopular, its rules were relaxed in March 2005.

stagflation a combination of economic stagnation and inflation.

stakeholder any individual or group that is affected by (and thus has a stake in) business decisions.

stakeholder analysis a form of environmental analysis based on identifying key stakeholders and assessing their interests and potential influence.

stakeholder theory the view that business has many stakeholders. These are groups who have an interest in or are affected by business. Hence, it is argued that business should take these groups into account.

state a narrow definition refers to the capacity to make and enforce rules within a defined territory backed up by coercion. In a broader sense refers to the public sector (see also **caretaker state**).

statutory maternity pay (SMP) the minimum amount of money that employers are obliged to pay employees while they are taking periods of maternity leave during and following the birth of a baby.

structural or mismatch unemployment arises when labour is released from declining industries without the skills to be readily absorbed into new or existing industries.

sub-national governance a level of political authority below or within the nation-state e.g. local government.

supply chain the chain of organizations involved in transforming raw materials into goods and services for the end-user.

supra-national governance a level of political authority above the nation-state e.g. the EU.

sustainable development an approach to economic and social development that seeks to strike a balance between the need for economic growth, and equity between social groups and between generations, especially in terms of issues of global resource depletion and global environmental degradation.

SWOT analysis a form of internal–external environmental analysis to identify strengths, weaknesses (internal), opportunities and threats (external).

Thatcherism a label given to the ideology of the Thatcher governments in Britain in the 1980s. At one level the term simply recognizes Thatcher's dominance of British politics during this period, but the ideological content is usually referred to as neoliberalism or the new right.

transnational corporation a firm which has global presence, range of markets, production and/or subsidiaries (see also **multinational corporation**).

treaty an international agreement between two or more nation-states which becomes binding in law. The most obvious example of this is the Treaty of Rome which founded the European Economic Community, the forerunner of the European Union.

trend extrapolation a form of environmental analysis based on identifying and projecting trends, e.g. sales figures.

trickle down the idea that inequality may benefit the poorest members of society because the high rewards at the top motivate improved economic performance from which all benefit.

two-party system Britain is often characterized as a two-party system because the two main parties—Conservative and Labour—have dominated national politics for the last century.

unitary state a state, like the UK, in which power is concentrated at the centre, as opposed to a federal state in which power is shared between different levels of government.

utilitarian ethics this theory argues that something is right when it maximizes the greatest good for the greatest number.

value chain Porter sees the firm as comprising a set of horizontal functions (e.g. procurement, IT, human resources) and vertical operations, both upstream towards the market and downstream towards the sources of the resources, across which it is possible to add value by changing the way things are done (see Porter, 1985, Chapter 3).

value for money (VFM) a legal and managerial term introduced to encourage local and central government to evaluate the provision of public services.

Washington Consensus a set of policies promulgated by many neoliberal economists as a formula for promoting economic growth in many parts of Latin America by introducing various market-oriented economic reforms which are designed to make the target economy more like that of first world countries such as the United States. It was first presented in 1989 by John Williamson, an economist from the Institute for International Economics, an international economic think tank based in Washington, DC. It is so-called because it attempts to summarize the commonly shared themes among policy advice by Washington-based institutions at the time, such as the International Monetary Fund, the World Bank and the US Treasury Department, which were believed to be necessary for the recovery of Latin America from the financial crises of the 1980s.

welfare state refers to the growth of state expenditure on a range of public services such as education, health, housing, social services and income support.

Index